MW00780326

THE ADMINISTRATION OF JUSTICE FROM HOMER TO ARISTOTLE

BY

ROBERT J. BONNER, Ph.D.

Hon. Litt.D., Toronto; Hon. Litt.D., Dublin
Corresponding Member of the Academy of Athens

AND

GERTRUDE SMITH, Ph.D.

Professor of Greek, University of Chicago

VOLUME II

δίκας τε δοῦναι καὶ λαβεῖν ηὗρον Ἀθηναῖοι πρῶτοι.
—Aelian

THE LAWBOOK EXCHANGE, LTD.
Clark, New Jersey

ISBN 978-1-58477-117-3 (Set)
ISBN 978-1-61619-367-6 (Vol. I)
ISBN 978-1-61619-368-3 (Vol. II)

Lawbook Exchange edition 2001, 2014

The quality of this reprint is equivalent to the quality of the original work.

THE LAWBOOK EXCHANGE, LTD.
33 Terminal Avenue
Clark, New Jersey 07066-1321

*Please see our website for a selection of our other publications
and fine facsimile reprints of classic works of legal history:*
www.lawbookexchange.com

Library of Congress Cataloging-in-Publication Data

Bonner, Robert Johnson, 1868-1946.
   The administration of justice from Homer to Aristotle/ by Robert J.
Bonner and Gertrude Smith.
      p. cm.
   Originally published: Chicago : University of Chicago Press, c1930-1938.
   Includes bibliographical references and index.
   ISBN 1-58477-117-8 (cloth : alk. paper)
   1. Justice, Administration of (Greek law)--History. I. Smith, Gertrude,
Ph.D. II. Title.

KL4345.B66 2000
347.38--dc21   00-050693

Printed in the United States of America on acid-free paper

THE ADMINISTRATION OF JUSTICE
FROM HOMER TO ARISTOTLE

THE UNIVERSITY OF CHICAGO PRESS
CHICAGO, ILLINOIS

—

THE BAKER & TAYLOR COMPANY
NEW YORK

THE CAMBRIDGE UNIVERSITY PRESS
LONDON

THE MARUZEN-KABUSHIKI-KAISHA
TOKYO, OSAKA, KYOTO, FUKUOKA, SENDAI

THE COMMERCIAL PRESS, LIMITED
SHANGHAI

THE ADMINISTRATION OF
JUSTICE FROM HOMER
TO ARISTOTLE

BY

ROBERT J. BONNER, Ph.D.

Hon. Litt.D., Toronto; Hon. Litt.D., Dublin
Corresponding Member of the Academy of Athens

AND

GERTRUDE SMITH, Ph.D.

Professor of Greek, University of Chicago

VOLUME II

δίκας τε δοῦναι καὶ λαβεῖν ηὗρον ᾿Αθηναῖοι πρῶτοι.
—AELIAN

THE UNIVERSITY OF CHICAGO PRESS
CHICAGO ⋅ ILLINOIS

PREFACE

The main theme of the first volume of the *Administration of Justice from Homer to Aristotle* is the growth and development of the judiciary. The present volume is devoted to matters of practice and procedure. We have, however, not attempted to describe all the suits civil and criminal and their distribution among the various magistrates, judicial officers, and boards and the process of litigation from the initiation of a suit to the verdict. These topics have been treated amply by Lipsius in *Das Attische Recht und Rechtsverfahren*, pages 53 ff. But since this work was begun with the publication of the first part in 1905 and completed in 1915 many of Lipsius' conclusions and opinions have been questioned and refuted.

In the following pages a number of aspects of Athenian litigation have been treated in considerable detail, the choice of topics being more or less arbitrary. Our purpose has generally been to bring conveniently together in one volume the results of various articles, monographs, and books, in which the work of Lipsius and other scholars working in this field has been either criticized or amplified. A certain amount of this material was included in Volume I, where it seemed advisable to combine it with the discussion of the judiciary, e.g., the treatment of the ἀνάκρισις, a discussion of the date of the introduction of written evidence, and certain features of homicide trials. The chapter on "Litigants" is necessarily in a large measure descriptive and expository, but even here matters at issue have been discussed in full detail. Of a different character is the chapter on "Oaths." In order to give a complete picture of the importance of the oath in Athenian public life, we have gone beyond its use in litigation. It has been suggested that in this volume we discuss the merits and demerits of the Athenian judicial system. This we have with some misgiving attempted to do in the last chapter.

v

vi PREFACE

In the matter of translations we have used Kennedy's version of Demosthenes. For other authors we have in general used the translations which are available in the Loeb Classical Library.

We wish to thank the American Council of Learned Societies and the University of Chicago for grants which have made the preparation and publication of this work possible. Thanks also are due to Dr. Lloyd Stow, now assistant professor of Greek in the University of Oklahoma, for the invaluable assistance he rendered us at every stage of the work. We wish to thank also Miss Julia Henderson for her competent assistance in proofreading and in the preparation of the Index.

It is hoped eventually to add a third volume devoted to various aspects of other Greek legal systems.

Robert J. Bonner
Gertrude Smith

University of Chicago
January 1938

TABLE OF CONTENTS

CHAPTER I

INTRODUCTION

The names of a multiplicity of both private and public suits are known and recognized for the fifth and fourth centuries in Athens.[1] But an investigation into their origin and the date of their institution proves rather disappointing.[2] It is often impossible to determine even approximately when the actual suit was created. Therefore any attempt to discuss the origin of Athenian suits must be attended with a great deal of conjecture, which in turn calls for caution and hesitation in making statements of a very definite character. However, such an investigation, even though it affords little that is conclusive in the way of settling the exact period at which different suits arose, may yet yield some points of interest in indicating how one suit grew out of another and hence how the great variety of suits arose.

The Athenians had great respect for the antiquity of law, and hence it was their custom to attribute laws to their famous and more ancient lawgivers, Draco and Solon. Some of these attributions there is no reason to doubt. Others, however, must be treated with extreme caution. We possess no evidence for the period between the Heroic Age when the administration of justice was largely an informal thing and the codification of the laws by Draco. Yet this was a formative period when many of the suits which are so well known in later times must have been instituted in some form. In

[1] Cf. the Index to Lipsius, *Das Attische Recht und Rechtsverfahren*, pp. 994 f., *s.v.* γραφή and δίκη.

[2] Ancient writers were interested in classifying the offenses which were the basis for suits. In his description of Hippodamus, Aristotle says that among other tripartite divisions he recognized three offenses for which lawsuits (δίκαι) could be brought, namely, ὕβρις, βλάβη, θάνατος (*Politics* 1267B; cf. Newman, *ad loc.*). Hermann-Thalheim (*Griech. Rechtsalt.*, pp. 38 ff.) traces in Attic law a threefold classification of offenses, ὕβρις, κακουργία, and φόνος. Demos. xxiv. 192 classifies the subject matter of laws from a different point of view, by distinguishing those which have to do with individuals and those which have to do with the state.

some cases the laws of Solon were doubtless restatements of
the laws of Draco. Furthermore, in making his code Draco
did not initiate entirely new laws, but to a large extent, like
the early lawgivers generally, he reduced to writing a mass
of customary law which his codification put in an orderly
and usable form, thus removing the administration of justice
farther from the whim of the magistrate and making it more
equitable. There is frequently disagreement among ancient
writers about the attribution of particular laws to particular
lawgivers. There was a law to the effect that a citizen who
had no occupation was to be punished and that any citizen
might bring suit against him. The procedure was the γραφὴ
ἀργίας. Plutarch attributes this law to Solon, but says that
Theophrastus believed that it was the work of Peisistratus.[1]
Diogenes Laertius[2] attributes it to Solon, but quotes Lysias
as attributing it to Draco. The truth of the matter is probably that there was an old tribal law which prohibited idleness. This Draco included in his code, and it was later adopted by Solon.[3]

The origin of many suits may thus be pushed back into
very early times. A man was always quick to avenge any
injury to himself or to his property. It cannot be determined
when the state offered him assistance by establishing suits
for dealing with his wrongs. But the earliest codes always
dealt with such offenses. Maine[4] sees in the codes a means
of protection against the degeneration and corruption of
customary usages. This is undoubtedly true, to some extent
at least. The early codes contained provisions regarding
assault, housebreaking, arson, all sorts of family matters,
debt, slavery, transfer and distribution of property, business
relations, perjury, religious matters, homicide, sumptuary
legislation.[5] Many of the suits which would be used to deal
with infractions of these laws must go back as far as Draco at

---

[1] *Solon* xxii.   [2] i. 55.

[3] Cf. Freeman, *The Work and Life of Solon*, p. 137.

[4] *Ancient Law*, p. 16; cf. p. 25.

[5] Cf. Bonner and Smith, *Administration of Justice from Homer to Aristotle*, I,
67 ff. (hereafter referred to as *supra*, I).

least. For example, various laws regarding theft are attributed by Demosthenes to Solon.[1] But Draco must have had some regulations concerning theft and the procedure against it in his code.

Solon is regarded as having established several different types of action for theft: summary arrest of the alleged wrongdoer, a complaint to the archon who took over the suit, a public suit, or a private suit before an arbitrator.[2] This is an illustration of a wrong which could be handled by either a public or a private suit, γραφὴ κλοπῆς or δίκη κλοπῆς. ὕβρις furnishes another example, for both γραφὴ ὕβρεως and δίκη ὕβρεως are known. Perhaps the explanation is that in some crimes which would naturally be handled by private suits it was necessary if the victim were incapacitated to give opportunity τῷ βουλομένῳ to prosecute.[3] It may be suggested that in each case the private suit is earlier.

If one studies the lists of suits known in Athens, it becomes apparent that many suits overlap others. This is due to the fact that the original suit was very general in its terms. Then many specific suits were instituted which covered parts of the general charge. The charge of ἀδικία in the decree of Cannonus is extremely general. There soon arose γραφὴ ἀπάτης τοῦ δήμου and δίκη καταλύσεως τοῦ δήμου, which would certainly be covered by the decree. Likewise δίκη ἀφορμῆς, the suit to recover capital, is only a specific form of the δίκη χρέως. In this way many suits grew out of others.

In some cases the time at which a suit originated can be determined with at least some degree of accuracy. It is clear that some suits belong to the period of the fully developed democracy. For example, the various actions against sycophants could not have been instituted until sycophants became a feature of Athenian life under the fully developed democracy. And the process known as προβολή could have

---

[1] xxiv. 105, 113, 114; xxii. 26.

[2] Demos. xxii. 26; cf. Freeman, *op. cit.*, p. 125.

[3] In English common law, in a number of cases both a civil and a criminal suit are permitted. The reason for this is that the action complained of might give rise to a breach of the peace.

developed only after the ecclesia became strong. Some inferences may be drawn about the antiquity of certain suits
from the bodies and magistrates who had charge of them. In
general, in the case of the Areopagus it is to be expected that
cases handled by that body are of considerable antiquity
because the tendency was to deprive this court of its privileges and duties and it is extremely unlikely that it acquired
jurisdiction over any new cases after the time of Solon. From
the earliest time of which we have record the Areopagus had
jurisdiction over homicide cases, a jurisdiction which it
never entirely lost. The δίκη φόνου is undoubtedly older
than the code of Draco, since in the main Draco merely reduced to writing practices which were already in existence.
For the δίκη φόνου we have a comparative wealth of evidence.[1]
Although we do not know when the state took charge in
homicide, yet it is clear that it preserved in the δίκη φόνου
most of the features which appear in the attitude toward
homicide in the Heroic Age. And by piecing together the
information in Homer, the fragments of Draco's code, and
the various pieces of evidence from the fifth and fourth centuries we have a fairly complete picture both of the family
attitude which started action for homicide and of the various
stages in the development of homicide procedure. This is
far more information than the evidence usually affords.
For example, the Areopagus continued through the fifth
and fourth centuries to try some cases of ἀσέβεια, although
in general the dicasteries had charge of these cases. It may
plausibly be argued that since the Areopagus had general
surveillance in all matters of religion, all such cases originally came before the Areopagus. This indicates the great
antiquity of the *graphé asebeias*. Homer and Hesiod furnish
an excellent description of the public attitude toward impiety which was to result in the *graphé asebeias*, but it is
impossible to say when such an action was instituted. The
earliest recorded case is that brought against Aeschylus for
divulging the Mysteries in his plays.[2]

[1] Cf. *supra*, I, 111 ff.
[2] Schol. on Arist. *Nic. Ethics* 1111a; Aelian *V.H.* v. 19; Clem. Alex. *Strom.* ii. 387.

The creation of new magistrates was doubtless occasioned by excess of new business, too great for the existing magistrates to handle. Some of this new business may have been in the form of new types of suits. Lipsius[1] suggests that the *eisagogeis* may have been created to handle monthly suits. At any rate they handled such suits. Lipsius further suggests that the date of the institution of the office may be the middle of the fifth century, when the press of business necessitated new boards for handling it, and although it cannot be proved, this is a plausible suggestion. The development of the monthly suits themselves must have been due to commercial reasons. They, like δίκαι ἀπὸ συμβόλων, could have been of consequence only after Athens had become an important trading center.

On the other hand, sometimes the duties of an official changed fundamentally and his old duties were assumed by a new board. So when the polemarch ceased to be a military officer, military offenses were tried by his successors, the generals.

Constitutional changes occasioned new laws which gave rise to some new suits. For example, Solon's laws on adoption and bequests may have given rise to the various suits regarding inheritance. Solon is credited by Aeschines[2] with a law against outrage which protected a child, or a man, or a woman, free or slave, from any injury or assault. Doubtless this law explains the origin of the δίκη ὕβρεως and the γραφὴ ὕβρεως. Again Aeschines[3] attributes to Solon a law providing for punishment by ἀτιμία of men who had not gone on all of the campaigns to which they were assigned or who had been guilty of cowardice. The suit used against such offenders was the γραφὴ δειλίας.[4] In the work of Cleisthenes may be included the decree of Cannonus, which provided for trial by the ecclesia of those who were charged with doing wrong

---

[1] *Op. cit.*, p. 84; for an opposing view cf. Wilamowitz-Moellendorff, *Aristoteles und Athen*, I, 223.

[2] i. 15.   [3] i. 29.

[4] Aeschin. iii. 175 f. For a convenient summary of the laws of Solon cf. Freeman, *op. cit.*, pp. 112 ff.

to the people (ἐάν τις τὸν τῶν ᾽Αθηναίων δῆμον ἀδικῇ).¹ ἀδικία is a very general charge, and in fact no γραφὴ ἀδικίας is known.² Miltiades was charged with ἀπάτη ᾽Αθηναίων, a more specific offense, but certainly included in ἀδικία.³ To Cleisthenes the institution of ostracism is also attributed.⁴

This survey shows that it is futile to attempt to discover the origin of all the Athenian suits the names of which are known.

¹ Cf. *supra*, I, 205 ff.

² The γραφὴ ἀδικίου was a charge used against officials for misuse of authority.

³ Herod. vi. 136.   ⁴ *Supra*, I, 193.

CHAPTER II

LITIGANTS[1]

Before the time of Draco only injured parties could institute legal prosecutions, either personally before the magistrates who had full authority to give final decisions in all cases that came before them or indirectly through the agency of an Areopagite in the Areopagus. Draco extended the privileges of litigants in two ways. In the last section of the socalled constitution of Draco, the only genuine portion of the document, the injured party was permitted to lay information (εἰσαγγέλλειν) before the Areopagus. This means that he had the right to appear in person before the council and no longer had to depend on enlisting the interest of a member of the council in order to get justice.[2] Secondly, in his code Draco made it lawful for any citizen to slay out of hand any homicide who returned illegally from exile, or to arrest him and take him before the proper magistrates.[3] In the resulting inquiry the alleged criminal would be prosecuted by the citizen who arrested him. The permission given by this provision to any citizen to prosecute in this particular type of case is the precedent for Solon's famous prescription τὸ ἐξεῖναι τῷ βουλομένῳ τιμωρεῖν ὑπὲρ τῶν ἀδικουμένων.[4]

Litigants were obliged to handle their cases before a magistrate themselves. The hearing was doubtless more or less informal, as may be gathered from the fifth-century ἀνά-κρισις, which was a survival of the pre-Solonian magisterial trial.[5] As the name indicates, the proceedings consisted chief-

---

[1] Lipsius (*Das Attische Recht*, pp. 789–803) has sufficiently answered the question as to who could be a litigant.

[2] Arist. *Ath. Pol.* iv. 4; cf. *supra*, I, 95.

[3] Cf. *supra*, I, 119 ff.

[4] Arist. *Ath. Pol.* ix. 1; cf. *supra*, I, 168.

[5] Cf. προανακρίνειν in Arist. *Ath. Pol.* iii. 5; cf. *supra*, I, 283.

ly of questions addressed by the magistrates to the litigants.
That the litigants also questioned each other is indicated by
the later practice when either litigant was allowed to call up
his opponent in court and address questions to him. Examples are found in the earlier orators and in the *Apology*
of Plato.[1] Under these circumstances it was no great hardship to require litigants to take their own cases. But when
they had to face the big juries of the fifth and fourth centuries
and deliver set speeches to an unusually critical audience it
was quite a different matter. Their predicament was comparable to that of litigants under the Solonian system when
the decision of the magistrate was appealed and the litigants
had to appear before the Heliaea, which was a numerous
body.[2]

A litigant could always, with the permission of the jury,
have the assistance of others in presenting his case in court.
This assistance was of two kinds. A man might refrain from
speaking himself and secure another to speak in his stead, or
he might have others speak for him at the conclusion of his
speech. Strictly speaking, the first type of advocate should
be called ὁ ὑπεραπολογούμενος and the second type ὁ συναπο-
λογούμενος.[3] But both are denominated indifferently συνήγορος or σύνδικος. Συνήγορος etymologically means "one who
speaks with another"; σύνδικος, "one who aids another in
litigation." "Advocates" in the sense of οἱ συναπολογούμενοι
are constant features in fourth-century litigation, but οἱ
ὑπεραπολογούμενοι are comparatively rare. Only in exceptional circumstances could a litigant be excused altogether from
speaking.

The first appearance of "advocates" of this class (οἱ
ὑπεραπολογούμενοι) was at the trial of Miltiades in the assembly in 489 B.C.[4] for deceiving the people. Owing to a severe wound, from which he eventually died, he was unable
to speak in his own behalf, but was defended by his friends

[1] Lysias xii. 25; xxii. 5; Plato *Apol.* 24C ff.

[2] For the composition of the Heliaea cf. *supra*, I, 162 f.

[3] Lycurg. i. 138.

[4] Herod. vi. 136; cf. *supra*, I, 197, 299.

(προκειμένου δὲ αὐτοῦ ἐν κλίνῃ ὑπεραπελογέοντο οἱ φίλοι). As Miltiades was present in the assembly, lying on a couch, he may very well have informally requested the ecclesia to listen to his friends speaking in his behalf since he was obviously in no position to defend himself. But his friends may have come to his assistance without either his request or the permission of the assembly, for any member could address the assembly. At the trial of the generals before the assembly in 406 B.C., Euryptolemus, the relative of one of the generals and a friend of another, arose and proposed to speak in their defense (ὑπεραπολογησόμενος).[1] In the course of the proceedings at this meeting of the assembly the generals were not heard at all. They had already spoken at the previous meeting.[2] In one other case the whole burden of the defense was assumed by another. Isocrates was drawn into a lawsuit in connection with a trierarchy in 355 B.C., but, owing to illness, was unable to handle the case in court. In his stead his adopted son Aphareus appeared. Here Aphareus was a real advocate (ὑπεραπολογούμενος).[3] A somewhat similar case occurred in the practice of Demosthenes in 350 B.C. It was a special plea in *Apollodorus* v. *Phormio*,[4] in which the defendant spoke first. He was represented by counsel:

> Phormio's inexperience in speaking and utter incapacity you see your-selves, men of Athens. It is necessary for us his friends to state and ex-plain to you those particulars which, from having so often heard him re-late them, have become known to us; that when we have rightly informed you and put you in possession of the case you may give a just and con-scientious verdict.

Phormio was originally a slave and never learned Greek well enough to appear before the sensitive and critical Athenians.[5] It would appear that he had given utterance to a few halting sentences asking to have others speak for him.

Permission of the jury to call upon advocates was re-

---

[1] Xen. *Hell.* i. 7. 16.   [2] *Ibid.* i. 7, 9.

[3] Isoc. xv; cf. Jebb, *Attic Orators*, II, 132; Bonner, "The Legal Setting of Isoc-rates' *Antidosis*," *CP*, XV, 193 ff.

[4] Demos. xxxvi. 1.   [5] *Ibid.* xlv. 30, 81.

quired[1] but never refused. Requests are often informal and perfunctory, and the acquiescence of the jurors is assumed. A lengthy and elaborate appeal to the jurors to hear an advocate is found in Hyperides.[2] At first advocates were generally drawn from the litigant's friends, relatives, clubfellows, and fellow-demesmen.[3] These were the men who knew him and his affairs best. But in course of time advocates tended to become professional in private as well as in public suits and the practice of paying advocates arose. Demosthenes cites a law which forbade the paying of advocates in private suits:

> If anyone enter into a combination[4] or join in bribing the Heliaea or any of the courts at Athens or the senate, giving or receiving money for corrupt purposes, or organize a club for the subversion of the democracy, or, in the capacity of advocate, receive money in private or public cases, for any such act an indictment shall lie before the thesmothetes.[5]

This law is regarded as undoubtedly genuine by Drerup[6] and by Staeker.[7]

The law has some indications that may help to fix an approximate date. The occurrence of the word ἡλιαία points to an early date, but the occurrence of δικαστήριον also shows that the Heliaea may be the court of the thesmothetai.[8] Both ἡλιαία and δικαστήριον are mentioned for the sake of precision and accuracy. The reference to bribery points to the late fifth century, when jury bribery was so successfully

---

[1] *Ibid.* xxxiv. 52.

[2] iv. 11.

[3] Demos. xxxii. 31; Isoc. xxi. 1; Andoc. i. 150.

[4] συνιστῆται really means "entering into a conspiracy to defeat the ends of justice" as is shown in xlvi. 25: ἐξαπατῶν δὲ τοὺς δικαστάς, συνιστάμενος δ'ἐπὶ ταῖς δίκαις.

[5] 'Εάν τις συνιστῆται, ἢ συνδεκάζῃ τὴν ἡλιαίαν ἢ τῶν δικαστηρίων τι τῶν 'Αθήνησιν ἢ τὴν βουλὴν ἐπὶ δωροδοκίᾳ χρήματα διδοὺς ἢ δεχόμενος, ἢ ἑταιρείαν συνιστῇ ἐπὶ καταλύσει τοῦ δήμου, ἢ συνήγορος ὢν λαμβάνῃ χρήματα ἐπὶ ταῖς δίκαις ταῖς ἰδίαις ἢ δημοσίαις, τούτων εἶναι τὰς γραφὰς πρὸς τοὺς θεσμοθέτας (xlvi. 26 [trans. Kennedy]); the date of the speech is 351–350 B.C.; cf. also xx. 152.

[6] "Über die bei den Attischen Rednern eingelegten Urkunden," *Jb. f. cl. Phil.*, Supplbd. XXIV (1898), 304–5.

[7] *De litis instrumentis*, pp. 28 ff.

[8] Cf. *supra*, I, 156 f.

practiced on a large scale by Anytus in 409 B.C.[1] One might
expect this exploit of Anytus to be followed by legislation.
The archonship of Euclides in 403–402 B.C. is a likely date for
a law that would affect mainly the rich. No poor man could
bribe a jury. Similarly, the provision against organizing clubs
points to the same date, for clubs played a very prominent
part in the revolutions of 411 and 404 B.C. There were at least
two motives for legislation against the payment of advocates.
The rich had a great advantage over the poor in that they
had the means to retain advocates.[2] In the second place, although it was quite in accordance with the democratic spirit
that mutual helpfulness should be encouraged among the
citizens,[3] when these services were rendered for a fee and
tended to become professional public opinion became hostile.
The records of fifth-century litigation are not sufficient to
enable us to trace the progress of advocacy.[4] But the fact
that Thucydides emphasizes the activities of the clubs in litigation as a prominent feature of their work in 411 B.C. shows
that advocacy was a common practice in the fifth century.[5]
Here again the facts point to the democratic restoration as
the most likely date for the law regarding advocacy.

   The law forbidding the payment of advocates could not be
enforced,[6] but it nevertheless embarrassed the advocate who
could not claim relationship or close association with the litigant. He would at once be suspected of appearing for financial
reasons. In *Theomnestus* v. *Neaera* the plaintiff made a brief introductory statement without evidence[7] and then introduced
his brother-in-law, the litigious Apollodorus, who made the
real speech. Theomnestus does not rely upon the relationship, but upon the wrongs done to Apollodorus by Stephanus,
the *kurios* of Neaera, as a ground for calling Apollodorus as

---

[1] For the whole question of bribery of courts see the excellent discussion of
Calhoun, *Athenian Clubs in Politics and Litigation*, pp. 66 ff.

[2] Demos. xxi. 112; xlvi. 26.   [3] Hyper. i. 19–20.

[4] Cf. Blass, *Attische Beredsamkeit*, I, 40 ff.

[5] Calhoun, *op. cit.*, pp. 85 ff.

[6] Lycurg. i. 138.   [7] Demos. lix. 1–15.

advocate. The hostility of Apollodorus toward Stephanus is the main reason why the former was willing to appear as an advocate, but when Theomnestus comes to put the matter to the jury, his own need of help is also emphasized:

> I have to ask a favor of you, men of the jury, which it becomes me to ask, being a young man and having no experience in public speaking; that you will allow me to call Apollodorus to be my advocate upon this trial. For he is older than myself, and has more knowledge of the laws, and he has been injured by my opponent Stephanus, and he has given close attention to these matters; so that there can be no prejudice against him for retaliating on the party who first attacked him.

In another speech in the Demosthenic corpus the plaintiff Epichares, a young and inexperienced speaker, tells the jury that he has been

> betrayed by persons who, after being trusted by me on account of their enmity toward Theocrines, after hearing the facts and promising to cooperate with me in this cause, have now left me in the lurch and settled with my adversary, so that I shall not even have an advocate to plead for me unless some of my relations should be kind enough to assist me.[1]

Epichares pays lip service to the fiction that advocates are normally a man's relatives, friends, and associates. But both Theomnestus and Epichares make it clear that advocates or their principals were ready to explain the appearance of a particular advocate on the ground of his hostility to the other side in the case.

An advocate, however, who was not closely related to, or associated with, a litigant was more or less on the defensive. Handbooks on rhetoric regularly suggest reasons that may be given by an advocate for his appearance in a case:

> Ἐὰν δὲ ὑπὲρ ἄλλου λέγῃς, ῥητέον ὡς διὰ φιλίαν συνηγορεῖς, ἢ δι' ἔχθραν τοῦ ἀντιδίκου, ἢ διὰ τὸ τοῖς πράγμασι παραγενέσθαι, ἢ διὰ τὸ τῷ κοινῷ συμφέρον, ἢ διὰ τὸ ἔρημον εἶναι καὶ ἀδικεῖσθαι ᾧ συνηγορεῖς.[2]

After the middle of the fourth century the advocate is a well-established factor in litigation. The pretense that the advocate is a relative or an associate is abandoned. He is the one who is most able to help the litigant. Plaintiffs and pros-

---

[1] *Ibid.* lviii. 4.

[2] Anaximenes 36, in Spengel-Hammer, *Rhetores Graeci*, I, 87, ll. 18 ff.

ecutors were quick to realize how helpful advocates were to their clients and took every means to neutralize their influence by attacking both their motives and their character.[1] Demosthenes, in his speech against Midias, protests against the advocate in the name of democracy: μὴ γὰρ ἔστω μηδεὶς ἐν δημοκρατίᾳ τηλικοῦτος, ὥστε συνειπὼν τὸν μὲν ὑβρίσθαι τὸν δὲ μὴ δοῦναι δίκην ποιῆσαι.[2] The most bitter attack on advocates is found in Lycurgus in his speech against Leocrates.[3] He goes so far as to say that those who plead the cause of the defendant should themselves be put on trial. In contrast with Lycurgus, Hyperides, in reply to an attack on advocates, says:

> Of the many excellent features of democracy which one is more in keeping with the democratic spirit than the custom of allowing anyone who wishes [τὸν βουλόμενον] to go to the aid of an inexperienced man who is involved in dangers and is unable to defend himself adequately?[4]

The words τὸν βουλόμενον inevitably recall the same words in the Solonian law which permitted anyone who wished to prosecute a wrongdoer in the place of the injured party who was incapable for any reason of seeking justice for himself. Thus interpreted advocacy becomes a praiseworthy exhibition of the spirit of mutual helpfulness so characteristic of the Greek ideal democracy.

Comparatively few speeches of advocates have been preserved. Where the advocate substitutes for the principal, his speech is in content not distinguishable from the speech of a litigant. Typical examples are Apollodorus' speech as an advocate in the case of *Theomnestus* v. *Neaera*[5] and the speech for Phormio in *Apollodorus* v. *Phormio*.[6] Some believe that Demosthenes delivered the speech, but there is scarcely enough evidence to warrant this conclusion.[7]

---

[1] Demos. xlviii. 36: ἵνα μὴ αὐτίκ' ἐξαπατήσωσιν ὑμᾶς οἱ ῥήτορες, οὓς οὑτοσὶ παρεσκεύασται ἐπ' ἐμέ; cf. lviii. 53.

[2] xxi. 207.

[3] i. 135.

[4] iv. 11; cf. i. 10.

[5] Demos. lix. 16 ff.

[6] *Ibid.* xxxvi.

[7] Cf. Sandys and Paley, *Demosthenes' Select Private Orations*, II, xxvii, n. 1; Blass, *op. cit.*, III, 1, 461 ff.

Quite a different type of speech is the fourth oration of
Isaeus, delivered in behalf of Hagnon and Hagnotheus,
claimants for the estate of Nicostratus, a mercenary soldier
who died abroad. It is a careful and shrewd commentary on
the case as developed by the main speaker, and forms the
nearest approach we have to an address by a modern lawyer
to a jury after the evidence has been produced. The writer of
the argument to the speech says that Isaeus himself delivered it, which statement, however, is improbable.[1] It was
inevitable that in many of these συνηγορίαι there should be
much virtual evidence. In the fifth oration of Lysias, the advocate really testifies to the public services of Callias. Isocrates' *Nicias* v. *Euthynus* is an advocate's speech which the
advocate delivers in place of the plaintiff. Much of the matter in the speech is hearsay, but some of the statements are
made on the speaker's own knowledge without corroboration.
In all probability this speech is a mere rhetorical exercise.
But this need not make it less useful for the examination of
the technique of an advocate's speech.[2]

Sometimes the advocate asked for a favorable verdict as a
recognition of his own services to the state: ἀλλὰ καὶ τῶν
ξυνερούντων αὐτοῖς ἄξιον θαυμάζειν, πότερον ὡς καλοὶ κἀγαθοὶ
αἰτήσονται, τὴν αὑτῶν ἀρετὴν πλείονος ἀξίαν ἀποφαίνοντες τῆς
τούτων πονηρίας.[3] There were doubtless many advocates, however, who merely made emotional appeals to the juries which
are on the same plane as the tears and gestures of female relatives and children who were brought into court.[4] None of
these appeals has been preserved. The advocate who, like
Apollodorus,[5] was more skilled in the laws than his principal
might often give technical aid and advise as to the conduct
of the case as well as speak in court.[6]

Helpful as advocates undoubtedly were, nothing could
serve the interest of a litigant so well as a speech delivered by

[1] Forster, *Isaeus*, p. 128.

[2] Isoc. xxi; cf. Jebb, *op. cit.*, II, 221 ff.; Bonner in *CP*, XV, 384 ff.

[3] Lysias xii. 86.

[4] Cf. Socrates' condemnation of the practice, Plato *Apol.* 34C ff.

[5] Demos. lix. 15.　　　　[6] Lycurg. i. 59.

himself. But there were many litigants unequal to this task. To meet this situation there appeared a new profession, the writing of forensic speeches to be recited, as their own, by litigants in court. The origin of the profession of speech writer or logograph could not be anterior to the development of the art of rhetoric by Corax and his pupil Tisias in Syracuse during the establishment of democracy after the fall of tyranny in 466 B.C. Tisias is said among his other services to rhetoric to have composed the most effective speech of his day for a Syracusan woman in a claim for money owed: καίτοι ἄλλα τε Τισίας ἐς λόγους ἐσηνέγκατο καὶ πιθανώτατα τῶν καθ᾽ αὑτὸν γυναικὶ Συρακουσίᾳ χρημάτων ἔγραψεν ἀμφισβήτησιν.[1] This is the first instance of a written forensic speech.

There is good evidence for believing that Pericles was the first Athenian to reduce a speech to writing, while others were still extemporizing with the help of memorized commonplaces.[2] One may suppose that this practice refers to forensic speeches such as his speech as prosecutor of Cimon, or as representative of Aspasia, or in his own defense. A passage in Plutarch's *Life of Pericles*[3] seems to indicate that in debate he trusted to his own oratorical ability and the inspiration of the moment rather than to set speeches. This is what would be expected. A man may make an exceedingly effective set speech in a deliberative body, but in debate no one can anticipate the turns a discussion will take. The best preparation, as the Xenophontic Socrates pointed out, was a sound knowledge of the needs of public policy.[4]

The speech-writer, or logograph, as he was called, was primarily a rhetorician. Often he was a teacher,[5] as Isaeus was the teacher of Demosthenes. But he was much more than a writer of a speech to be recited by his client. There is plenty of evidence that he advised his client very much as

---

[1] Paus. vi. 17. 8; Blass warns us to take the statement with caution (*op. cit.*, I, 21).

[2] Cf. Suidas, *s.v.* Περικλῆς: πρῶτος γραπτὸν λόγον ἐν δικαστηρίῳ εἶπεν, τῶν πρὸ αὑτοῦ σχεδιαζόντων. Cf. Blass, *op. cit.*, I, 35, n. 5.

[3] viii. 4: περὶ τὸν λόγον εὐλαβὴς ἦν, ὥστε ἀεὶ πρὸς τὸ βῆμα βαδίζων εὔχετο τοῖς θεοῖς μηδὲ ῥῆμα μηδὲν ἐκπεσεῖν ἄκοντος αὑτοῦ πρὸς τὴν προκειμένην χρείαν ἀνάρμοστον.

[4] Xen. *Mem.* iii. 6; iv. 2. [5] Cf. Isoc. xiii. 9 ff.

does an English solicitor.[1] There was no man who could do more for a client than Antiphon,[2] whether his business lay in the courts or in the assembly. And in the *Clouds*[3] the chorus promises Strepsiades that on the completion of his legal education many clients will come to consult him on "claims and counterclaims."

It is not easy to determine the kind of services which a logograph might perform for a client beyond preparing the speech for him to recite in court with the evidence properly distributed. Where different remedies were available, the logograph doubtless suggested the best procedure.[4] This was important as an opponent was ever ready to take advantage of any false step. "It is the practice," says Demosthenes, "with defendants who have done wrong, in order to defeat the proceedings against them, to suggest that some other proceedings which are not practicable should have been adopted."[5] It was *de jure* the business of a magistrate to reject a case which did not lie within his jurisdiction. But the magistrates were chary of rejecting a case if a litigant insisted. In the matter of citation, interpretation, and application of laws, the services of an experienced logograph would be invaluable. Especially was this true in cases of unconstitutional legislation (γραφὴ παρανόμων), or the devolution of estates as seen in the speeches of Isaeus. No one could be deceived by the naïve statement of a litigant that he got the laws he cited from the official copies[6] or that his technical knowledge of litigation was the result of study and investigation forced upon him by his present predicament.[7] The advice of a logo-

---

[1] Demos. xlvi. 1: οἱ γράφοντες καὶ οἱ συμβουλεύοντες ὑπὲρ Φορμίωνος πολλοί.

[2] Thuc. viii. 68.

[3] Aristoph. *Clouds* 471.

[4] Cf. Demos. xxii. 25; liv. 1.

[5] xxi. 27. The abuse of impeachment as a process in trivial matters, which was so roundly condemned by Hyperides (iv. 1-4; cf. *supra*, I, 296), was in all probability due to the influence of logographs upon their clients.

[6] Lysias i. 30.

[7] Demos. liv. 17: ἀνάγκη γάρ μοι ταῦτα καὶ ζητεῖν καὶ πυνθάνεσθαι διὰ τοῦτον (defendant) γέγονεν.

graph could be useful in instituting cross-actions and counter-suits which were so constantly used in litigation.

There are no definite proofs as to the help given by a logo-graph to his client in what may be called the strategy of litigation. But Xenophon has recorded in his memoirs of Soc-rates how Socrates advised his friend Crito to retain the services of one Archedemus, a man of affairs and an excellent speaker, to look after his legal business. Archedemus per-formed his task so well that others also employed his services. Nowadays such a man would be a solicitor or an attorney. One may imagine that Crito could very well take care of his own forensic speeches and that Archedemus confined his activities to securing evidence on which to base countersuits and to negotiating with those who were willing to compromise or surrender at discretion. But the statement that he was a very competent speaker[1] would seem to indicate that if cases came to court he may very well have aided his patron either in the preparation of his speech or as συνήγορος.

A prosecutor must to the best of his ability anticipate the arguments of the defendant. In arbitration cases, where practically all the evidence was filed, the logograph had at his disposal documents which betrayed the line of defense fairly well;[2] but in other cases very little that was helpful to a liti-gant was necessarily disclosed at the *anakrisis*.[3] But there were other sources of information open to litigants regarding the intentions of their opponents. Litigants frequently refer to the help they have received from friends,[4] and indeed there were not a few services which friends could successfully un-dertake. It was not an uncommon practice in Athens for per-sons involved in a dispute to talk over the matter with each other and with their friends. If the dispute finally came be-fore a court, the information gathered in these informal talks

[1] Xen. *Mem.* ii. 9. 4: πάνυ μὲν ἱκανὸν εἰπεῖν.

[2] Demos. xxvii. 53; xxxix. 22.

[3] Cf. *supra*, I, 283 ff.; Dorjahn ("Anticipation of Arguments in Athenian Courts," *TAPA*, LVI, 274 ff.) has additional reasons in support of this view.

[4] Demos. liv. 1.

might often prove very valuable. A client of Hyperides says
in substance:

> When I learned the extent of my calamities, then I called my friends and
> relatives and we read the copy of the contract. After we had discussed the
> case, it was decided to go to Athenogenes [the defendant in the subsequent
> suit] and talk over the matter with him.[1]

The discussion revealed the fact that Athenogenes intended
to rely on the contract. Consequently, Hyperides had to emphasize in his speech for his client the equity of his side in the
dispute. Similarly in the Dionysodorus case in the Demosthenic corpus,[2] before the suit was filed there were some
charges and recriminations between the parties which may
well have been helpful to both sides. For Athenians were
neither taciturn nor discreet; a wary defendant or his friends
could pick up useful hints as to the intentions of the prosecutor both from the conversation of the prosecutor and from
that of his friends in the various haunts where citizens were
wont to spend much of their leisure time.[3] Hence the frequent appearance of such statements as "I hear that my
opponent proposes to say thus and so" or any similar expression. But it is not always safe to assume that every time a
litigant uses such language he has actually discovered anything about his opponent's intentions. Anticipation of possible arguments of an opponent was commonly taught in the
schools of rhetoric. The practice gave the speaker the advantage of getting the ears of the jury first. If the opponent did
not in fact use the anticipated argument, nothing was lost.
It might very well be that the refutation was so effective that
the argument was abandoned.

A man's enemies were quite ready to help his opponent in
litigation by imparting any useful information. For example,
Demosthenes received considerable information and encouragement from the enemies of Midias.[4] And there are
even cases in which intimate friends of a litigant are said to

---

[1] iii. 10–12; cf. Dorjahn, *op. cit.*, pp. 278 f.

[2] lvi. 11–14, 21–22.

[3] Lysias xxiv. 19–20; Isoc. xviii. 9.

[4] xxi. 23; cf. Aeschin. ii. 155; Demos. xix. 332; xx. 105.

have divulged to the other side matters which were damaging. Thus Apollodorus accuses his *quondam* friend Nicostratus of betraying him to his opponents in a suit:

Accordingly, he first conspires against me with my opponents in a lawsuit, and binds himself by oath to support them; after the proceedings had commenced, he discloses to them my case, with which he was acquainted [τούς τε λόγους ἐκφέρει μου εἰδώς].[1]

In *Epichares* v. *Theocrines*[2] the plaintiff refers to the desertion to the defendant of men who knew the details of his case. It is also possible that a logograph might betray his client. It was charged by Aeschines that Apollodorus profited by seeing in advance of delivery the speech written by Demosthenes for the defendant in *Apollodorus* v. *Phormio:* "You," said Aeschines to Demosthenes, "wrote a speech for the banker Phormio and were paid for it; this speech you communicated to Apollodorus, who was bringing a capital charge against Phormio."[3] Plutarch[4] not only supports the charge of Aeschines against Demosthenes but says that Demosthenes wrote speeches both for Phormio and for Apollodorus in their litigation with each other. But the speech for Apollodorus in his suit for false testimony against Stephanus, who was a witness for the defendant in *Apollodorus* v. *Phormio*, is not now regarded as the work of Demosthenes.[5]

Another source of aid to litigants was the clubs to which most citizens of standing belonged. Thucydides, in recounting the activities of the oligarchs in the revolution in 411 B.C., says that Peisander achieved co-operation among "the clubs which already existed in the state for mutual support in politics and litigation."[6] Thucydides uses the term ξυνωμο-

---

[1] Demos. liii. 14.   [3] Aeschin. ii. 165.

[2] *Ibid.* lviii. 4, 42.   [4] *Demosthenes* xv.

[5] Schaefer, *Demosthenes und seine Zeit* (1st ed.), III, 2, 184–93. A very convenient and brief discussion of the subject is found in Sandys and Paley, *op. cit.*, II, xxxix ff.

[6] Thuc. viii. 54. 4; this translation closely follows that of Dale. Jowett's "for the management of trials and elections" or Smith's "for the control of courts and officials" carry implications which are not to be found in the Greek: τάς τε ξυνωμοσίας, αἵπερ ἐτύγχανον πρότερον ἐν τῇ πόλει οὖσαι ἐπὶ δίκαις καὶ ἀρχαῖς. Grote (*History of Greece*, VIII, 16) described the clubs as "associations, bound together by oath,

σίαι ("sworn associations"), but the older designation is
ἑταιρεία. A member of such an association is ἑταῖρος ("companion"). "As early as Homer, ἑταῖροι is used in certain passages of men who are united by a peculiar relationship, distinct from ordinary friendship or ordinary companionship in
arms."[1] The activities of the clubs in anti-democratic move-
ments, especially in the revolution of the Four Hundred,
naturally lead us to expect that their activities in litigation
would be largely unlawful. To some extent this is true, but
it is quite clear from Calhoun's investigations that there were
plenty of legitimate services an organization of a litigant's
friends could render. It is to be noted that references to activities of a club in court are in the very nature of litigation
almost certain to concern only those which are unfair or
illegal.[2] For example, a client of Isaeus claims that his opponent has brought an action against him, "trusting to his
associates and tricky speeches."[3] It is evident that the speaker has in view activities that are not commendable.

One type of service which any member of a club could
render would be the service referred to above—the collection
of information regarding the manner in which the opponent
intended to conduct his case. The club affiliations of a citizen
increased materially the number of friends who were on the
lookout for hints that would help a litigant to frame his case
so as to meet his opponent's attack.

As advocates the club members would be particularly
effective because they for the most part belonged to the better classes, and were accustomed to taking part in public
business. According to Grote:

Among these clubs were distributed most of the best citizens, the good
and honorable men, the elegant men, the well-known, the temperate, the

---

among the wealthy citizens, partly for purposes of amusement, but chiefly pledging
the members to stand by each other in objects of political ambition, in judicial
trials, in accusation or defense of official men after the period of office had expired,
in carrying points through the public assembly, etc."

[1] Calhoun, *op. cit.*, p. 5.

[2] *Ibid.*, p. 40.

[3] Isaeus, *Frag.* xxiii. 2 (Thalheim): πιστεύων δ'ἑταιρείαις καὶ λόγων παρασκευαῖς.

honest, and moderate men etc. to employ that complimentary phraseology by which wealthy and anti-popular politicians have chosen to designate each other, in ancient as well as in modern times.[1]

This view of the membership of the clubs is doubtless partially justified by the decisive part they played in the revolutions of 411 and 404–403 B.C. But Calhoun[2] has shown that the clubs extended beyond the ranks of the oligarchs. Many distinguished democratic leaders from Cleisthenes down were club members. Socrates is represented as saying that men who engaged in public affairs must belong to clubs if they wished to be influential.[3] The fact remains, however, that in any club which concerned itself with politics and litigation there would be a considerable number of men whose services as advocates would be useful and desirable.

Demosthenes, in his speech against Midias, has emphasized the disadvantage under which the poor labor in litigation with the rich:

οὐ μέτεστι τῶν ἴσων οὐδὲ τῶν ὁμοίων, ὦ ἄνδρες Ἀθηναῖοι, πρὸς τοὺς πλουσίους τοῖς λοιποῖς ἡμῖν, οὐ μέτεστιν, οὔ. . . . . καὶ μάρτυρές εἰσιν ἕτοιμοι τούτοις καὶ συνήγοροι πάντες καθ' ἡμῶν εὐτρεπεῖς· ἐμοὶ δ' οὐδὲ τἀληθῆ μαρτυρεῖν ἐθέλοντας ὁρᾶτ' ἐνίους.[4]

Contributions of money would be welcome to most litigants. In spite of the law forbidding advocates to accept fees, advocates could always be hired either directly or indirectly.[5] Money could always be contributed by relatives, friends, and associates. Andocides charges that Callias, wishing to be rid of him for business reasons, gave Cephisius one thousand drachmas to prosecute him for impiety.[6]

The subornation of witnesses would often cost money. Though perjurers ran little risk even if their falsehoods were detected, the public disgrace and partial *atimia* that might follow discovery would enable them to demand money for

[1] *Op. cit.*, p. 16.

[2] *Op. cit.*, pp. 18 f.

[3] Plato *Apol.* 36B–C.

[4] xxi. 112.

[5] For indirect remuneration see the relations of Crito and Archedemus in Xen. *Mem.* ii. 9. 4; cf. Demos. li. 16.

[6] i. 121; cf. 132 for references to other funds collected by the enemies of Andocides.

their services. Thus the notorious witnesses who testified to the death of a woman who was forthwith produced alive and well in court must have received compensation for their testimony.[1]

The poor also suffered if they lost their cases, for litigants who were compelled to pay large sums of money in fines or damages were often in need of ready money to save themselves from ultimate *atimia* if they could not pay by the ninth prytany. It was the acid test of friendship, second only to ransoming a prisoner of war[2] or contributing to the dower of the daughter of an indigent friend, not to fail in such circumstances.[3]

There are indications that in the fifth century efforts were made to influence jurors in a pending suit. In the *Wasps*, Philocleon rejoices in the personal appeals of litigants for his aid as he stands waiting for the court to open:

> Is there any creature on earth more blest,
>   more feared and petted from day to day,
> Or that leads a happier, pleasanter life,
>   than a Justice of Athens, though old and grey?
> For first when rising from bed in the morn,
>   to the criminal court betimes I trudge,
> Great six-foot fellows are there at the rails,
>   in anxious haste to salute their Judge.
> And the delicate hand, which has dipped so deep
>   in the public purse, he claps into mine,
> And he bows before me, and makes his prayer,
>   and softens his voice to a pitiful whine;
> "O pity me, pity me, Sire," he cries,
>   "if you ever indulged your longing for pelf,
> When you managed the mess on a far campaign,
>   or served some office of state yourself."[4]

---

[1] Isoc. xviii. 51 ff.; cf. Demos. xxix. 28 for alleged bribery of witnesses. Isaeus v. 8 says of members of a club: τὰ ψευδῆ ἀλλήλοις μαρτυρεῖν. Cf. also references to the orators cited by Calhoun, *op. cit.*, p. 81, n. 1; also references in the comic fragments: Menander, *Frag.* 537 (Kock): τί βούλει; πάντα σοι γενήσεται, ... φίλοι, δικασταί, μάρτυρες, and Eubulos, *Frag.* 74 (Kock), and Philemon, *Frag.* 65 (Kock).

[2] Antiph. v. 63.

[3] Cf. Demos. liii. 6 ff.

[4] Aristoph. *Wasps* 550 ff. (trans. Rogers).

There are in the sources no examples of this practice of personal appeals made by litigants to jurors before the trial began, but there is an apposite passage in Pseudo-Xenophon showing that suitors from the allied states approached jurors when their cases were about to come before court:

νῦν δ' ἠνάγκασται τὸν δῆμον κολακεύειν τὸν Ἀθηναίων εἷς ἕκαστος τῶν συμμάχων γιγνώσκων ὅτι δεῖ μὲν ἀφικόμενον Ἀθήναζε δίκην δοῦναι καὶ λαβεῖν οὐκ ἐν ἄλλοις τισὶν ἀλλ' ἐν τῷ δήμῳ, ὅς ἐστι δὴ νόμος Ἀθήνησι· καὶ ἀντιβολῆσαι ἀναγκάζεται ἐν τοῖς δικαστηρίοις καὶ εἰσιόντος του ἐπιλαμβάνεσθαι τῆς χειρός.[1]

There is in Antiphon[2] a story of a most irregular procedure to prejudice a jury against a prosecutor on the eve of the trial. A chorus boy in training had been given some medicine for a throat affliction. He died shortly afterward. At first the relatives took no action and imputed no blame to the choregus who was responsible for the care and training of the boys. But it so happened that the choregus had impeached some officials for peculation. The day before the case was to come up for trial in the court of the thesmothetai, Diodotus, the brother of the deceased, was "induced" by the defendants and their friends to charge the choregus with homicide. Time was pressing, so Diodotus, before laying a charge of homicide, went before the jury in the court of the thesmothetai at the end of a session and denounced the choregus as a homicide. The next day he tried to enter the case with the king archon for trial, but the king archon refused to accept the case because there was not sufficient time left of his year of office for completing the preliminary hearings required by law. Thus the plot failed because the choregus could not be excluded from court as a polluted person.[3] It was hoped, however, that the jurors, having heard the story of Diodotus, might be

---

[1] *Ath. Pol.* i. 18; the *Wasps* was presented in 422 B.C. and the treatise on the constitution appeared about 425 B.C. The similarity of phraseology has been noted by editors of Aristophanes; cf. *Wasps*, 553–55:

.... κἄπειτ' εὐθὺς προσιόντι
ἐμβάλλει μοι τὴν χεῖρ' ἀπαλήν, τῶν δημοσίων κεκλοφυῖαν·
ἱκετεύουσίν θ' ὑποκύπτοντες, τὴν φωνὴν οἰκτροχοοῦντες.

[2] vi. 10–21.   [3] Cf. *infra*, pp. 199 f.

strongly prejudiced against the choregus, who escaped a charge of homicide on a technicality. That this was not the actual result is shown by the conviction of the officials.[1] It would seem that Diodotus made his announcement in an interval between cases or at the end of the court session before the jurors dispersed. In this way interested persons apparently could announce the cases to be tried at the next session of the court.[2]

In the fifth century, when the personnel of a court was fixed for a year, such appeals to jurymen were easy; but in the elaborate system of jury selection in the fourth century, appeals either to individuals or to panels would be difficult if not impossible.[3] Other means were devised to influence public opinion. When Demosthenes was engaged in litigation with the redoubtable Midias, a charge of desertion of military post was brought against Demosthenes by Euctemon. Demosthenes claims that the reason for the suit was that all might see the official notice: "Euctemon of Lusia has indicted Demosthenes of Paeonia for desertion of post."[4] At any rate, the case was never brought to trial. Military offenses were well calculated to arouse hostile public sentiment in which any jury would share. But it was dangerous to bring a groundless or ill-founded criminal charge. In the present case, Euctemon, the prosecutor, was disfranchised for failure to go on with the case. Cases like this are to be distinguished from prosecutions undertaken with the purpose of eliminating an opponent by means of an adverse verdict.[5]

Another means of arousing public sentiment against a man was by means of προβολή (presentment in the ecclesia). In the case of crimes which affected the public interest a prospective prosecutor might bring the matter before the ecclesia

[1] Antiph. vi. 28.

[2] Cf. Aristoph. *Wasps* 242 ff., 687 ff.; *supra*, I, 249. Socrates is represented as talking informally to the jurors on the conclusion of his case (Plato *Apol.* 38C).

[3] Cf. *supra*, I, 367 ff.

[4] xxi. 103.

[5] Calhoun (*op. cit.*, pp. 48 ff.) has a full discussion of all such countersuits.

in the manner provided by law.[1] Both prosecutor and defendant as well as their supporters spoke. The vote was by a show of hands and had no legal effect. It was like a modern resolution of Congress, a mere expression of opinion. But if the vote was against the prosecutor, it was useless to pursue the matter further. He would almost certainly fail to win a verdict in court, and he might even incur a fine for failure to obtain a fifth part of the votes. On the other hand, a favorable action by the ecclesia did not oblige him to take any further action. But if he decided to go on with the case, he had made a public demonstration of the strength of his charge and had public sentiment with him. The jurors, drawn from the membership of the ecclesia, could not fail to be affected by the result of the *probolé*, and the prosecutor might well hope for a favorable verdict in court. It so happens that Demosthenes, though successful with his *probolé* against Midias, did not prosecute him before a heliastic court. Political considerations and a sum of money dissuaded him. However, he prepared a speech for delivery and published it. It is to this speech that we owe our chief knowledge of *probolé*.

No judicial system can function properly without adequate provision for the prosecution of public offenders. Athenians were quite aware of the importance of criminal prosecutors. Lycurgus, himself perhaps the most conscientious and severe prosecutor in Athenian legal history, says:

The three most important provisions for guarding and preserving democracy and the welfare of the state are the established laws, the legal processes, and the verdicts of the courts. For it is the function of the law to proclaim what ought not to be done, of the accuser to denounce those who are liable to the penalties prescribed by law, and of the judge to punish those who are thus brought to justice. Consequently neither the law nor the verdict of the judge is of any avail without someone to bring offenders to justice.[2]

Solon provided for freedom of prosecution to insure the enforcement of his own laws in the interest of the masses. Any-

---

[1] Lipsius (*op. cit.*, pp. 211 ff.) has a full and satisfactory discussion of all phases of προβολή as a process. He makes no comment on its use in the strategy of litigation.

[2] i. 3–4.

one who wished (ὁ βουλόμενος) might intervene and prosecute a wrongdoer whether he had himself suffered from the wrongdoing or not. It is commonly said that in Athens there were no public prosecutors, only volunteers. In theory this is true, for in the normal administration of criminal justice Athens relied wholly upon volunteer accusers. But where the public interest was particularly involved, chosen advocates were employed. Solon himself had been chosen to represent the state in an arbitration with Megara regarding the ownership of Salamis.[1]

The best-known case in which public advocates were employed in the fifth century was the trial of Cimon. In 463 B.C., Cimon was charged with accepting bribes from King Alexander of Macedon. The accusation was made at his audit, according to Aristotle,[2] and Pericles κατηγόρησε τὰς εὐθύνας Κίμωνος στρατηγοῦντος νέος ὤν. Plutarch[3] says that the matter came up before a court (πρὸς τοὺς δικαστάς). But Plutarch's statements indicate that it was first broached in the assembly by his "enemies who formed a coalition against him" (τῶν ἐχθρῶν συστάντων ἐπ' αὐτόν). In his life of Pericles,[4] Plutarch says that Pericles was chosen by the people as one of Cimon's accusers: ἦν μὲν γὰρ εἷς τῶν κατηγόρων ὁ Περικλῆς ὑπὸ τοῦ δήμου προβεβλημένος. Elpinice, sister of Cimon, is said to have approached Pericles as the most aggressive (σφοδρό-τατος) prosecutor of her brother with a plea on his behalf. Dismissing her with a smile and a jest, Pericles "at the trial was very gentle with Cimon and performed his task in a perfunctory manner."[5] According to the account of Plutarch, the charge against Cimon came up in the assembly by way of an εἰσαγγελία where Pericles pressed the matter vigorously. The case was referred to a court with elected prosecutors. In the interval between the proceedings in the assembly and those in the court Elpinice interceded with Pericles, the most

---

[1] Plut. *Solon* x. It was on this occasion that Solon is said to have quoted two lines interpolated into the Catalogue of Ships to support the Athenian claims.

[2] *Ath. Pol.* xxvii. 1.   [3] *Cimon* xiv. 3.   [4] x. 5.

[5] Plut. *Cimon* xiv: πλὴν ἕν γε τῇ δίκῃ πραότατον γενέσθαι τῷ Κίμωνι καὶ πρὸς τὴν κατηγορίαν ἅπαξ ἀναστῆναι μόνον, ὥσπερ ἀφοσιούμενον.

dangerous of the prosecutors. Technically Aristotle is in error in calling the case εὔθυνα. The audits of generals were different from those of other officials. Their official acts could be dealt with not only in the regular audit but also by εἰσαγγελία or ἐπιχειροτονία.[1] It need occasion no surprise that Aristotle in a mere reference to the trial should use εὔθυνα in a broad sense in referring to a trial involving the official conduct of a general. Isocrates is guilty of the same confusion regarding the εἰσαγγελία of Timotheus which he calls εὔθυνα.[2]

Another well-known criminal case in which public prosecutors participated is that of Antiphon and Archeptolemus, who were tried for treason (προδοσία) in 411 B.C. The matter came before the boulé by way of information from the generals. The decree of the senate providing for the trial is quoted from Caecilius by Pseudo-Plutarch.[3] This was really an εἰσαγγελία which the boulé disposed of without reference to the ecclesia. The generals were instructed to arrest and produce the alleged traitors in court for trial and to prosecute them with the aid of any ten members of the boulé they chose (οὕστινας ἂν δοκῇ τοῖς στρατηγοῖς προσελομένοις μέχρι δέκα). The selection was authorized by the decree of the boulé but the method of selection was left to the generals. As usual, volunteers were invited to share in the prosecution (κατηγορεῖν [δὲ] τοὺς ᾑρημένους συνηγόρους καὶ τοὺς στρατηγοὺς καὶ ἄλλος ἄν τις βούληται).

The frequent mention of public advocates in the literature and their evident unpopularity point to their widespread use. In some cases the kind of trial in which they were employed can with reasonable certainty be recognized. It has been inferred from a passage in Aristophanes' *Wasps* that advocates were employed in γραφὴ καταλύσεως τοῦ δήμου.[4] Bdelycleon is arguing with the chorus, who wish him to permit his father

[1] Cf. Wilamowitz, *Aristoteles und Athen*, II, 243 ff.; Lipsius, *op. cit.*, pp. 294 ff.

[2] Isoc. xv. 129; cf. Wilamowitz, *op. cit.*, II, 251.

[3] *Vita Antiphontis* xxiii.

[4] 482–83; Gilbert, *Beiträge zur innern Geschichte Athens*, p. 88; cf. Starkie, *ad loc.* and Excursus VII.

to join them and proceed to the court where they are to sit. He proposes a conference which they scornfully reject, calling him an enemy of democracy (μισόδημος), a lover of tyranny (μοναρχίας ἐραστής), a pro-Spartan, and a sympathizer with Brasidas.[1] They warn him that soon he will be brought to trial on these charges and be denounced as a conspirator (ξυνωμότης) by an advocate (συνήγορος). Aristophanes chooses here to represent the advocate as being the real prosecutor, as indeed was frequently the case.

There is also in Aristophanes[2] a reference to a trial of Laches which is the first on the docket in the court in which Philocleon and his fellow-dicasts in the chorus were to sit that day.[3] Cleon was to be the prosecutor and the son of Chaereus the advocate who notified the dicasts to be on hand betimes.[4] There is no immediate indication of the nature of the case. The words "everybody says he has a hive of money"[5] point to embezzlement of public moneys. Wilamowitz[6] regards the Trial of the Dog[7] as a burlesque of the trial of Laches scheduled for the day. It is a clever conceit to contrive that the first case tried in the domestic court by the fireside should reflect more or less accurately the recent εὔθυνα of the general Laches. The defendant is a dog named Labes of Aexone. The name Labes thinly veils the name of Laches, who was also an Aexonean. At the same time the name involves a pun on λαμβάνω which is quite appropriate in a trial for peculation. The audience is left in no doubt as to the identity of the prosecutor, an unnamed dog, Κύων from Cydathene, Cleon's own deme.[8] That the trial had to do with an audit seems clear from the words ἐγὼ δ' ἐβουλόμην ἂν οὐδὲ γράμματα, ἵνα μὴ κακουργῶν ἐνέγραφ' ἡμῖν τὸν λόγον, "I wish that he had never learned to write that he might not have

---

[1] *Wasps* 474–76.   [2] *Ibid.* 240 ff.

[3] Dracontides was also to be tried (*ibid.* 157).

[4] *Ibid.* 686 ff.; cf. 242–43.   [6] *Op. cit.*, II, 244.

[5] *Ibid.* 241.   [7] *Wasps* 890 ff.

[8] Cf. Starkie, note on *ibid.* 895; in the *Knights* 1023 Cleon calls himself κύων (public watchdog).

sent in falsified accounts to our hurt."[1] Cleon, the prosecutor in the guise of a dog, merely opens the case. The real prosecutor is Xanthias the advocate.[2]

In the *Acharnians* there is a bitter and moving complaint of the older men who are haled into court and convicted by youthful advocates skilled in the artifices of the new rhetoric:

οἱ γέροντες οἱ παλαιοὶ μεμφόμεσθα τῇ πόλει.
οὐ γὰρ ἀξίως ἐκείνων ὧν ἐναυμαχήσαμεν
γηροβοσκούμεσθ' ὑφ ὑμῶν, ἀλλὰ δεινὰ πάσχομεν,
οἵτινες γέροντας ἄνδρας ἐμβαλόντες ἐς γραφὰς
ὑπὸ νεανίσκων ἐᾶτε καταγελᾶσθαι ῥητόρων

. . . .

ὁ δὲ νεανίας ἑαυτῷ σπουδάσας ξυνηγορεῖν
ἐς τάχος παίει ξυνάπτων στρογγύλοις τοῖς ῥήμασι·
κᾆτ' ἀνελκύσας ἐρωτᾷ, σκανδάληθρ' ἱστὰς ἐπῶν,
ἄνδρα Τιθωνὸν σπαράττων καὶ ταράττων καὶ κυκῶν.[3]

The affected style of the youthful advocates is freely criticized by Aristophanes.[4] In the *Knights*, when old man Demus repents of his former mistakes (ἁμαρτίαις), the sausage-seller reassures him as follows:

> You're not to blame; pray don't imagine that.
> 'Twas they who tricked you so. But answer this;
> If any scurvy advocate should say,
> "Now please remember, justices, ye'll have
> No barley, if the prisoner gets off free,"
> How would you treat that scurvy advocate?
>
> DEMUS: I'd tie Hyperbolus about his neck,
> And hurl him down into the Deadman's Pit.[5]

Philemon the Younger says bitterly that physicians and advocates alone can slay with impunity: μόνῳ δ'ἰατρῷ τοῦτο καὶ συνηγόρῳ ἔξεστι, ἀποκτείνειν μὲν ἀποθνῄσκειν δὲ μή.[6]

[1] *Wasps* 960–61; the error of the scholiast in interpreting these lines has long misled commentators; ὡς γραπτὸν δεδωκότος λόγον τοῦ ἀπολογουμένου κυνός; cf. Wilamowitz, *op. cit.*, II, 244–45, and Starkie's elaborate note on the passage.

[2] *Wasps* 903 ff.

[3] Aristoph. *Acharnians* 676–80, 685–88.

[4] *Frag.* 198 (Kock); for words ending in -ικος which were affected by students of the new rhetoric cf. *Knights* 1375 ff.; *Wasps* 1209; *Clouds* 747, 1172–73; Peppler, *AJP*, XXXI, 428–44.

[5] 1356–63 (trans. Rogers).   [6] *Frag.* 3 (Kock).

In modern communities the embezzlement and misappropriation of public funds by officials do not normally attract more public attention than do murders, kidnappings, divorces, and dishonest financial operations by which the investing public is robbed. In Athens, however, the financial dishonesty of officials was the type of crime that attracted by far the most attention. In the *Wasps*,[1] Philocleon expatiates upon the joy of listening to the piteous and tearful pleas of the defendant's children to the dicasts to pass their father's accounts (τῆς εὐθύνης ἀπολῦσαι). In an earlier passage Philocleon tells what delight he takes in his importance when prominent persons (μεγάλοι καὶ τετραπήχεις) try to win his sympathy as he waits for the opening of the court.[2] In still another passage Philocleon imagines that some ὑπεύθυνος has bribed the cock that woke him for his daily duty in court:

> The cock which crew from eventide, he said,
> Was tampered with, he knew, to call him late,
> Bribed by officials whose accounts were due.[3]

In view of the importance of prosecution of dishonest officials one might well expect that steps would be taken to safeguard the public interest by appointing public advocates in trials of this kind. It has been suggested that the old men in the *Acharnians*[4] who were haled into court and fined by a youthful advocate were prosecuted for financial dishonesty.[5] These "treasury prosecutions" originated with officials chosen by lot. Thus there was no continuity of authority in the same hands. Consequently the real work of the treasurers was handled by subordinate officials, viz., secretaries and undersecretaries.[6] In one instance two men engaged in the

---

[1] Aristoph. *Wasps* 570 ff.

[2] *Ibid.* 554–57; cf. *supra*, pp. 22, 23, n. 1, where the passage has been quoted for another purpose.

[3] *Ibid.* 100–102; for other references to ὑπεύθυνοι see *Knights* 258–60, 823–27; *Peace* 1185–88; *Acharnians* 983.

[4] Aristoph. *Acharnians* 676 ff.

[5] Müller-Strübing, *Aristophanes und die historische Kritik*, p. 323.

[6] To these Müller-Strübing adds sycophants such as Ctesias in *Acharnians* 839. Just why sycophants should be classed with secretaries he does not make clear.

prosecution are mentioned, Cephisodemus[1] and Euathlus. Cephisodemus is denominated "advocate." Euathlus is not so denominated in the present passage but elsewhere he appears as an advocate:

ἔστι τις πονηρὸς ἡμῖν τοξότης συνήγορος
ὥσπερ Εὔαθλος . . . . παρ' ὑμῖν τοῖς νέοις.[2]

With the case of Thucydides in the *Acharnians*,[3] Müller-Strübing associates a passage in the *Wasps*[4] in which Bdelycleon maintains that the dicasts are really the dupes of the prosecutors. While they think they are themselves deciding the case, the prosecutors, bribed by the defendant, contrive to get him off. No matter if the "advocate" comes late for court he gets his fee just the same.

And if one of the defendants give him a bribe he shares it with someone in office associated with him in the case [καὶ κοινωνῶν τῶν ἀρχόντων ἑτέρῳ τινὶ τῶν μεθ' ἑαυτοῦ] and the two of them concert the matter and make a show of zeal, while like a couple of sawyers they play into each other's hands [ξυνθέντε τὸ πρᾶγμα δύ' ὄντε ἐσπουδάκατον, κᾆθ' ὡς πρίονες ὁ μὲν ἕλκει, ὁ δ' ἀντενέδωκε]. But you gape at the paymaster and don't see what is going on.

According to Müller-Strübing, the official associated with the advocate is a secretary or undersecretary who is the technical prosecutor in the case. Starkie says: "The scribes formed a separate class at Athens. They had enormous power, since, being permanent officials, they had a thorough knowledge of the working of the constitution, and the various lot-appointed Boards had to depend on them for information."[5] Starkie is wrong in thinking that there was a class of professional secretaries who passed from board to board. Ferguson says:

There was no possibility of there existing at Athens such a thing as a professional class of secretaries; for no individual could hold the office more

[1] Aristoph. *Acharnians* 705: τῷδε τῷ Κηφισοδήμῳ τῷ λάλῳ ξυνηγόρῳ.

[2] Aristoph. *Frag.* 411 (Kock).

[3] 703 ff.   [4] 686 ff.

[5] *Op. cit.*, Excursus VII; Starkie is following Müller-Strübing, *op. cit.*, and Caillemer in Daremberg-Saglio, *s.v.* "Grammateis."

than twice in a period of twenty years, and, as a matter of fact, in the whole period of Athenian history, there is not a single instance of the same person holding the office a second time.[1]

This statement of Ferguson definitely rules out the secretaries as civil servants with a more or less permanent tenure of office. But without officials with more familiarity with finance and government than could be acquired by boards and secretaries selected by lot for one term only, it is difficult to see how so-called treasury prosecutions could be effectively handled. These actions had to be based upon the records of boards and treasurers. Naturally some official had to furnish the information and take the initiative. It is to such an official that Aristophanes refers in the *Wasps*.[2] The loose use of the word ἀρχόντων need occasion no concern, as Müller-Strübing points out.[3] It may be suggested here that the requisite professional knowledge and continuity in office may be found in the undersecretaries who could advise their superiors in technical matters connected with their office.[4] It may very well be that for this reason the ὑπογραμματεῖς were very unpopular, as Starkie remarks. ἡ πόλις ἡμῶν ὑπο-γραμματέων ἀνεμεστώθη, καὶ βωμολόχων δημοπιθήκων, ἐξαπατώντων τὸν δῆμον ἀεί.[5] Both Lysias and Demosthenes mention the office with scorn.

And yet from a slave he has become a citizen, and has exchanged beggary for wealth and the position of underclerk for that of lawgiver! And here one might even make it an accusation against you that, whereas your ancestors chose as lawgivers Solon, Themistocles, and Pericles, in the belief that the laws would accord with the character of their makers, you have chosen Teisamenus, son of Mechanion, and Nicomachus, and other persons who were underclerks [ὑπογραμματέας]; and although you feel that the magistracy is depraved by people of this sort, it is just these men who have your confidence. Most extraordinary of all, though it is not permissible for the same man to act twice as underclerk to the same magistracy [ὑπογραμματεῦσαι μὲν οὐκ ἔξεστι δὶς τὸν αὐτὸν τῇ ἀρχῇ τῇ αὐτῇ], you author-

---

[1] *Athenian Secretaries*, "Cornell Studies in Classical Philology," VII, 36.

[2] 692.   [3] *Op. cit.*, p. 338.

[4] Cf. Vinogradoff, *Outlines of Historical Jurisprudence*, II, 82 ff.

[5] Aristoph. *Frogs* 1083 ff.

ize the same persons to have control over the most important affairs for a long period.[1]

It is true that there was a restriction upon the employment of the same man as ὑπογραμματεύς twice by the same board, but this did not prevent their passing from board to board and in this way becoming professional. This dislike and jealousy of the ὑπογραμματεῖς is due no doubt to the fact that while they may not have appeared officially, it was well known that they furnished the ammunition for the prosecution.

The simile of the sawyers[2] has caused the commentators some difficulty. Two men at either end of a crosscut or ripsaw achieve their purpose by giving and taking the saw in turn and so their task is accomplished. There is no need to suppose that the sawyers represent the prosecution and the defense.[3] All that is meant is that the prosecutor and his advocate, bribed by the defense, co-operate to secure an acquittal instead of a condemnation.[4] Bribery both of officials and of prosecutors is mentioned in the fourth century also.[5]

The relation of the paid advocate to undersecretaries and other minor officials is a matter of interest. It is obvious that in many cases the success of a prosecution could not be left to the doubtful forensic ability of an underofficial, or to the chance appearance of volunteer prosecutors. A simple solution was to secure the services of a paid advocate. Pericles was appointed by the ecclesia as one of the prosecutors of Cimon. This is what is to be expected in cases of high crimes and misdemeanors which involve the public interest. And in the *Acharnians*, where is pictured the fate of the old man

---

[1] Lysias xxx. 27–28; cf. Demos. xix. 200, 237, 249; Antiph. vi. 49.

[2] Aristoph. *Wasps* 693–94.

[3] Müller-Strübing, *op. cit.*, p. 337.

[4] In the prosecution of Cimon, Pericles was an elected public advocate and played into the hands of the defense by handling the case in a perfunctory manner. Here there is no question of bribery by the defense; Pericles was influenced by the pleas of Elpinice, the sister of Cimon (Plut. *Pericles* x. 5; cf. *supra*, pp. 26 f).

[5] Cf. Lysias xx. 10; Aeschin. i. 107: λογιστὴς γὰρ γενόμενος πλεῖστα μὲν τὴν πόλιν ἔβλαψε δῶρα λαμβάνων παρὰ τῶν οὐ δικαίως ἀρξάντων.

baited and harried in court by a youthful advocate skilled in
rhetoric, the remedy proposed is that the ecclesia shall take
action:

> ψηφίσασθε χωρὶς εἶναι τὰς γραφάς, ὅπως ἂν ᾖ
> τῷ γέροντι μὲν γέρων καὶ νωδὸς ὁ ξυνήγορος,
> τοῖς νέοισι δ᾽ εὐρύπρωκτος καὶ λάλος χὠ Κλεινίου.[1]

Just what did the proposed action contemplate? It might
mean a plea that on each occasion when an advocate was to
be appointed care should be taken to see that "the youngster
sue the youngster and the old man sue the old."[2] But since
this is comedy it may be a suggested bit of legislation governing the choice of advocates elsewhere than in the ecclesia. It
will be recalled that in the trial of Antiphon the boulé authorized the generals to choose any ten members of the boulé
as advocates. In the passage in the *Acharnians*[3] the young
man is said to have secured his appointment by intrigue
(σπουδάσας). This may very well refer to an appointment by
the ecclesia, determined by politicians or engineered by the
clubs which were interested in politics and litigation.[4] It is
not impossible that boards might appoint their own advocates for treasury prosecutions. Some color is given to this
conjecture by the fourth-century practice of appointing by
lot ten advocates to assist the *logistai* in auditing the accounts
of retiring officials. It may be that in the thoroughly democ-
ratized constitution of the fourth century some of the appointed advocates of the fifth century are now chosen by lot.

There are two kinds of accounting. The cripple in Lysias[5]
reminds the council that he is not before them accounting for
public moneys (λόγον δίδωμι) officially expended, nor under-
going an inquiry (εὐθύνας ὑπέχω) into other official acts while
in office. The first kind of accounting (λόγον διδόναι) was
required only of those officials who expended public funds.[6]

---

[1] Aristoph. *Acharnians* 714–16.   [2] *Ibid.* 718.   [3] 685.

[4] Thuc. viii. 54; cf. *supra*, pp. 19 ff. In the *Wasps* 687 ff., Chaereus, a henchman
of Cleon, is the advocate who notifies the dicasts to be on hand next day betimes.

[5] xxiv. 26.

[6] Officials who did not handle public funds were required to file a statement to
that effect; cf. Aeschin. iii. 22: ᾿Αλλ᾽ ἔστι τις ἄνθρωπος ὃς οὔτ᾽ εἴληφεν οὐδὲν τῶν

The officers in charge of the financial audit and all charges connected with it were the ten *logistai* and ten *synegoroi* chosen by lot. It is the functions of the *synegoroi* that are of immediate concern. On receiving the accounts these two groups of officers checked them with the appropriate official records. This investigation which the ὑπεύθυνοι attended was in the nature of an *anakrisis*. In fact, an ancient source says:

'Αριστοτέλης ἐν τῇ 'Αθηναίων πολιτείᾳ οὕτω λέγει· λογιστὰς δὲ αἱροῦνται δέκα παρ' οἷς διαλογίζονται πᾶσαι αἱ ἀρχαὶ τά τε λήμματα καὶ τὰς γεγενημένας δαπάνας καὶ ἄλλους δέκα συνηγόρους, οἵτινες συνανακρίνουσι τούτοις· καὶ οἱ τὰς εὐθύνας διδόντες παρὰ τούτοις ἀνακρίνονται πρῶτον, εἶτα ἐφίενται εἰς τὸ δικαστήριον εἰς ἕνα καὶ πεντακοσίους.[1]

Besides the financial accounts these officers investigated all indictments of offenses which were punishable by a fine, such as embezzlement (κλωπῆς), accepting bribes (δώρων), and maladministration (ἀδικίου). Whether the *logistai*, advised by the *synegoroi*, found any shortcomings in the audit or not, they had to bring the ὑπεύθυνος into a court of 501 dicasts presided over by themselves for a final discharge or a trial as the case might be. In a trial the *synegoroi* acted as official prosecutors.[2] If the court confirmed the discharge it was sealed with the state seal.[3] In the trial volunteer accusers were invited to participate.[4]

It is strange to find in the Athenian system provision made for allotted public prosecutors even in one class of cases. The lot was surely a poor way to select a competent lawyer. But

---

δημοσίων οὔτ' ἀνήλωκε, προσῆλθε δὲ πρός τι τῶν κοινῶν . . . . αὐτὸς ὑποβάλλει καὶ διδάσκει ὁ νόμος ἃ χρὴ γράφειν· κελεύει γὰρ αὐτὸ τοῦτο ἐγγράφειν, ὅτι οὔτ' ἔλαβον οὐδὲν τῶν τῆς πόλεως οὔτ' ἀνήλωσα.

[1] *Lex. Cant.*, p. 20, *s.v.* λογισταὶ καὶ συνήγοροι. This note cannot have been drawn entirely from the corresponding treatment of λογισταί in Arist. *Ath. Pol.* liv. 2. Lipsius (*op. cit.*, p. 104, n. 201) observes: "Der letztere Zusatz stammt aus anderer Quelle, verdient aber darum nicht minder Glauben."

[2] Lipsius, *op. cit.*, p. 104; Wilamowitz, *op. cit.*, II, 232; Gilbert, *Const. Antiqu.*, p. 227.

[3] Demos. xviii. 250; cf. Bonner, "The Use and Effect of Attic Seals," *CP*, III, 401–2.

[4] Aeschin. iii. 23.

the situation in regard to the audit was unusual. Only a careful scrutiny of accounts could disclose irregularities. If irregularities were discovered, how was the official to be punished? Obviously the power of determining the matter could not be left to the *logistai* or any other board. It must come before a court. It was the rule that magistrates and boards presided in trials that concerned matters which fell within their own jurisdiction. Consequently they could not both preside and prosecute. No citizen could be expected to prosecute such cases without a knowledge of the details of the examination made by the *logistai* unless they were published. To this there are obvious objections. The difficulty was met by associating with the *logistai* a similar group called *synegoroi* to assist and advise the *logistai* in reaching a decision. In case of a public trial the *synegoroi* were in an excellent position to prosecute the alleged offender. In fact, no one else could deal effectively with the case. There was little risk in intrusting a prosecution to an inexperienced citizen. He need only introduce the case and trust to volunteer assistants to push the case effectively. Moreover, it must not be forgotten that citizens had the right to present themselves for allotment to office,[1] and that men suitable for the task of handling cases in court might very well have sought the office of συνήγορος. In any event we may be sure that no serious practical difficulties developed, for the system worked for many years.

In the fourth-century literature there is no mention of elected public advocates in the types of cases in which they served in the fifth century.[2] This situation is probably to be explained partly by the existence of allotted advocates for the prosecution of dishonest officials and partly by the general dislike of paid public advocates reflected in the comedies. The new democracy refused to employ special counsel as undemocratic. There were exceptions, however. Hyperides twice represented Athenian interests abroad. In a dispute be-

[1] Isoc. xv. 150; Lysias vi. 4; xxxi. 33.

[2] Lipsius, *op. cit.*, p. 206, n. 97.

tween Delos and Athens regarding the management of the
temple of Apollo in Delos, Hyperides was chosen by the
Areopagus to present the Athenian case before the Amphictyonic Council.[1] He was also chosen by the city to defend an
Athenian athlete who was charged with a foul at the Olympic
games.[2] In the Harpalus affair he appears with nine other
public advocates. When Harpalus, the absconding treasurer
of Alexander, escaped from Athens it was said that prominent
Athenians had received substantial bribes from him. A commission of Areopagites was appointed to investigate the matter. The report of the commission (ἀπόφασις) charged nine
public men with receiving bribes. The name of Demosthenes
headed the list. Prosecutions were launched by action of the
ecclesia and ten advocates were appointed to prosecute.
Demosthenes was convicted. The speech of one of the public
advocates, Hyperides, against Demosthenes is extant, as also
are speeches of Dinarchus against Demosthenes, Philocles,
and Aristogiton.[3]

In the matter of repealing or revising laws the court of
revision consisted of five hundred citizens drawn from the
dicasts under the presidency of the thesmothetai. Any citizen
could appear for or against the proposed legislation but the
ecclesia always selected five advocates to defend the old laws.[4]
Men whose names were stricken from the citizen rolls of the
demes for any reason had a right of appeal to the ecclesia. In
these cases the deme was represented by the demarch and
five chosen prosecutors.[5] A tribe might also choose advocates
in the tribe assembly to support one of its members. Thus

[1] Hyper. *Frag.* xix (Kenyon); Demos. xviii. 134; cf. *supra*, I, 364.

[2] Paus. v. 21. 5 ff.

[3] For the procedure in such cases see *supra*, I, 364. For the accounts of the
Harpalus affair cf. Plut. *Moralia* 846B–C; 848F; *CAH*, VI, 450 ff.

[4] Cf. Plato *Crito* 50B; the law cited in Demos. xxiv. 23 provides for the selection
of five advocates, but in Demos. xx. 146 only four advocates are named. Kahrstedt,
in Pauly-Wissowa, *s.v.* Σύνδικος, suggests that Leptines himself was the fifth.

[5] Arist. *Ath. Pol.* xlii. In other litigation also in which the deme interests were involved advocates acted; cf. Gilbert, *op. cit.*, p. 207; Chapot, in Daremberg-Saglio,
s.v. "Syndicus."

the tribe sent advocates to assist Andocides when tried for impiety in 399 B.C.[1]

These instances show that the state, as represented by the boulé or the ecclesia or possibly financial boards, employed counsel in important cases as did also the deme, and the tribal, assemblies. But in spite of the law forbidding the same man to serve on more than one case,[2] Hyperides is known to have served on three occasions. It is significant that even where special prosecutors were employed the right of volunteers to appear was always acknowledged.

The practice of using elected advocates in public cases is reflected in private practice. A volunteer prosecutor was often aided by others. The chief prosecutor laid the indictment but all spoke. Thus Meletus indicted Socrates,[3] but Anytus and Lycon also delivered speeches. Similarly, Andocides was accused by Cephisius, assisted by four others among whom was Meletus. Andocides was supported by Cephalus and Anytus. The latter may be the same Anytus who helped to prosecute Socrates.[4] Both of these cases were tried in 399 B.C.

[1] Quite a different type of σύνδικοι were those elected by vote for a number of years after the restoration of democracy in 403 B.C. to handle cases arising out of claims to confiscated property or other property cases where the state was the interested party. A good example of the kind of suit in which these σύνδικοι acted is Lysias xvii; cf. xviii. 26; xix. 32. Lipsius (*op. cit.*, p. 115) properly classifies them as *ausserordentliche Behörden*.

[2] Demos. xx. 152.

[3] Plato *Euthyphro* 2B.

[4] Judeich, in Pauly-Wissowa, *s.v.* "Anytos" 3.

CHAPTER III

SYCOPHANTS

Solon permitted any qualified citizen to prosecute wrong-doers to enable the members of the lower classes to protect themselves in their newly granted rights and privileges.[1] He intended by this momentous measure "to accustom citizens like members of the same body to be sensible of and to resent one another's injuries." Solon believed that the best-governed state[2] was that in which those who had suffered no wrong were as diligent in prosecuting and punishing the wrongdoers as those who had suffered wrong. In a large measure Solon's hopes were justified. Athens developed high ideals of citizenship. There was apparently no lack of prosecutors, for several were often associated in the same case. Socrates, for example, and Andocides were both prosecuted for impiety in 399 B.C., and in each case there were three prosecutors. Public opinion approved of those who served the city zealously and criticized those who failed to take their share of public responsibility. "We alone," says Pericles, "regard the man who takes no part in public affairs not as one who minds his own business, but as good for nothing."[3] Demosthenes makes a strong point of the persistent failure of two politicians to do their duty as prosecutors of men who had wronged the city:

How comes it then, Timocrates and Androtion, when it is more than thirty years since one of you commenced his political career, and in that period many generals have wronged the republic, and many orators too, who have been tried before your countrymen, and some of whom have suffered death for their crimes, while others withdrew into exile, which was an act of self-condemnation—how comes it that neither of you ever ap-

[1] Arist. *Ath. Pol.* ix.

[2] ἥτις οἰκεῖται κάλλιστα τῶν πόλεων (Plut. *Solon* xviii. 5).

[3] Thuc. ii. 40. 2.

39

peared as the accuser of any of them, or ever was seen to express indignation at the wrongs of the state?[1]

Certain types of wrongdoing affected the public only in the person of an individual. Common examples are slander, robbery, assault, and battery. In these and other such cases the aggrieved parties could usually be counted upon to bring the offender to justice. This would particularly be the case after the development of rhetoric, when injured persons could use the services of professional speech-writers to assist them in the prosecution.

Prosecutors are sometimes at pains to stress their patriotism and public service. "I consider it the duty of a good citizen to undergo dangers for the democracy and not to keep quiet about public matters for fear of incurring personal enmity," says Andocides.[2] Aeschines observes:

When I saw that the city was being seriously injured by the defendant, Timarchus, who, though disqualified by law, was speaking in your assemblies, and when I myself was made a victim of his blackmailing attack .... I decided that it would be a most shameful thing if I failed to come to the defence of the whole city and its laws, and to your defence and my own.[3]

It will be observed that the speaker admits his own personal interest in having the defendant punished because he had personally suffered at his hands. But the best-recorded expression of a citizen's duty to prosecute wrongdoers is found in Lycurgus, that uncompromising enemy of all public wrongdoers. "In aid of my native land and the temples and the laws I have brought this case [ἀποδέδωκα τὸν ἀγῶνα] as I should, justly and honestly."[4] The significance of the prefix ἀπο in the phrase ἀποδέδωκα τὸν ἀγῶνα marks his action as a debt or a duty which he owed the city, as Lofberg points out.[5]

More substantial encouragement was offered volunteers by granting them a liberal share of fines, confiscations, and moneys recovered for the treasury by prosecutors in certain

[1] Demos. xxiv. 173 (trans. Kennedy).

[2] iv. 1.   [3] i. 1–2.   [4] i. 149.

[5] *Sycophancy in Athens*, p. 2.

types of action, namely, "denunciation" (φάσις), "inventory" (ἀπογραφή), and prosecutions for usurpation of citizen rights (γραφαὶ ξενίας). Φάσις was used against those who contravened laws and regulations regarding commerce, customs, and mining, and against guardians who mismanaged the property of their wards. Anyone who cut down more than the number of olive trees permitted by law could also be prosecuted by φάσις. The successful prosecutor received one-half of the value of the property confiscated or of the fine levied. No forensic speech deals with a case of φάσις.[1]

The most common use of ἀπογραφή was to recover state property that was unlawfully in the possession of individuals, e.g., the relatives of a man whose property was confiscated, or a state debtor. The successful prosecutor received three-fourths of the property recovered.[2]

Athenians were extremely jealous of the rights of citizenship. The notorious case of *Theomnestus* v. *Neaera* is a γραφὴ ξενίας. The laws protecting Athenian citizenship from usurpation are cited in full in this speech:

ἐὰν δὲ ξένος ἀστῇ συνοικῇ τέχνῃ ἢ μηχανῇ ἡτινιοῦν, γραφέσθω πρὸς τοὺς θεσμοθέτας Ἀθηναίων ὁ βουλόμενος, οἷς ἔξεστιν. ἐὰν δὲ ἁλῷ, πεπράσθω καὶ αὐτὸς καὶ ἡ οὐσία αὐτοῦ, καὶ τὸ τρίτον μέρος ἔστω τοῦ ἑλόντος. ἔστω δὲ καὶ ἐὰν ἡ ξένη τῷ ἀστῷ συνοικῇ, κατὰ ταὐτά, καὶ ὁ συνοικῶν τῇ ξένῃ τῇ ἁλούσῃ ὀφειλέτω χιλίας δραχμάς.[3]

The prosecutor, if successful, obtained one-third of the fine inflicted, or of the proceeds of the sale of the person or property of the alien defendant.

Such motives on the part of volunteer prosecutors as public spirit and the expectation of legitimate financial gain are highly praiseworthy. But, strangely enough, Athenian public opinion not only tolerated but approved political and personal motives as well. Prosecution in the courts was a

---

[1] For a discussion of the problems involved cf. Lipsius, *Das Attische Recht*, pp. 309 ff. Lofberg (*op. cit.*, pp. 26 ff.) has fully discussed this form of action as employed by sycophants. For the statement of Pollux that φάσις could be used against sycophants cf. *infra*, p. 71.

[2] Cf. Lipsius, *op. cit.*, pp. 299 ff.; Lofberg, *op. cit.*, pp. 28 ff. A modern parallel to this type of case would be the action against a bankrupt for concealment of assets.

[3] Demos. lix. 16; cf. Lofberg, *op. cit.*, pp. 31 f.; Lipsius, *op. cit.*, pp. 416 ff.

well-recognized means of vengeance on one's enemies. Prosecutors readily avowed in court their personal hostility to the
defendant.[1] It was only when men made a profession of prosecution for financial gain that public opinion was hostile.
Such persons were known as "sycophants." The English
word is a mere transliteration of the Greek συκοφάντης. The
original significance of the word has been a matter of dispute
since the time of Plutarch.[2] The words συκοφάντης and συκο-
φαντέω occur commonly enough in the orators, but it is very
difficult to extract a satisfactory legal definition from the
ancient sources. A client of Demosthenes says: "A sycophant is one who brings all kinds of charges and proves
none."[3] This suggests the false accuser. A client of Lysias
adds the notion of blackmail: "It is their practice to bring
charges even against those who have done no wrong. For
from these they would gain most profit."[4] In the same vein is
a statement of Isocrates: "They advertise their powers in
their attacks upon men who are entirely innocent and so get
more money from those who are clearly guilty."[5] Lysias[6] refers to the Thirty as sycophants, though their first measure
was to execute a number of sycophants. Here συκοφάνται is
equivalent to πονηροί. The sycophant is the πολυπράγμων. For
English readers Kennedy, himself a lawyer, has brought out
the various implications of συκοφάντης: Such a man, he says,
was "a happy compound of the common barretor, informer,
pettifogger, busybody, rogue, liar and slanderer."[7] "It included calumny and conspiracy, false accusation, malicious
prosecution, threats of legal proceedings to extort money, and

[1] Lysias xiii. 1; xiv. 1–2; Demos. xxiv. 7–8.

[2] For the various suggestions cf. Lofberg, *op. cit.*, pp. vii–viii; Murley, *CP*, XVI, 199; Cook, *Class. Rev.*, XXI, 133; Hommel, *Berl. Phil. Woch.*, XLVIII, 1127 f. .

[3] Demos. lvii. 34.

[4] Lysias xxv. 3.

[5] Isoc. xv. 24; cf. xxi. 5: οἶμαι δὴ πάντας εἰδέναι ὅτι μάλιστα συκοφαντεῖν ἐπιχειροῦσιν οἱ λέγειν μὲν δεινοί, ἔχοντες δὲ μηδέν, τοὺς ἀδυνάτους μὲν εἰπεῖν, ἱκανοὺς δὲ χρήματα τελεῖν.

[6] xii. 5.

[7] In Smith, *Dictionary of Greek and Roman Antiquities*, s.v. "Sycophantes."

generally, all abuse of legal process for mischievous or fraudulent purposes."[1] If to this all-embracing definition we add any kind of scoundrel (πονηρός) on the authority of Aeschines,[2] we have a wider definition than any Greek writer or scholiast or lexicographer has recorded; but it would afford the drawer of an indictment little assistance. The meaning which συκοφάντης has in a particular passage depends much upon the circumstances. But it is at best an ugly word and the litigant who applied it to his opponent wished to get the full benefit of all its implications.

Litigation was the handmaiden of politics in Athens.[3] Young men with political ambitions sought to advance their fortunes by prosecuting officials at their audits, and politicians for bribery, corruption, misappropriation of public funds, illegal legislation, and other high crimes and misdemeanors. Pericles, for example, first came into public notice by his prosecution of Cimon for accepting bribes during his military command: πρὸς τὸ δημαγωγεῖν ἐλθόντος Περικλέους, καὶ πρῶτον εὐδοκιμήσαντος ὅτε κατηγόρησε τὰς εὐθύνας Κίμωνος στρατηγοῦντος νέος ὤν.[4] Aristophanes tells us Hyperbolus the demagogue acquired a legal education before he entered politics:

> How can *he* learn evasion of a suit,
> Timely citation, damaging replies?
> Hyperbolus, though, learnt them for a talent.[5]

Naturally there was no objection to the prosecution of dishonest officials and public men. Indeed, the administration of justice would have broken down if competent men had refused to participate, even if they expected to profit politi-

---

[1] *Orations of Demos.* (trans.), III, 345; cf. also Navarre's definition in Darem.-Saglio, *s.v.* "Sycophanta": "Délation, escroquerie et chantage, ces trois termes résument assez exactement, comme on le voit, l'industrie complexe du sycophante."

[2] ii. 99.

[3] Cf. Thuc. viii. 54. 4: τάς τε ξυνωμοσίας, αἵπερ ἐτύγχανον πρότερον ἐν τῇ πόλει οὖσαι ἐπὶ δίκαις καὶ ἀρχαῖς.

[4] Arist. *Ath. Pol.* xxvii; cf. *supra*, pp. 26 f., 33, n. 4.

[5] *Clouds* 874–76: πῶς ἂν μάθοι ποθ' οὗτος ἀπόφυξιν δίκης
ἢ κλῆσιν ἢ χαύνωσιν ἀναπειστηρίαν;
καίτοι ταλάντου τοῦτ' ἔμαθεν Ὑπέρβολος.

cally from their activities. But abuses appeared. In the *Knights* of Aristophanes,[1] Cleon is accused of squeezing men subject to audit (πιέζων τοὺς ὑπευθύνους) and of prosecuting inoffensive citizens, men of means who shrink from litigation (πλούσιος καὶ μὴ πονηρὸς καὶ τρέμων τὰ πράγματα). The choregus in Antiphon says that his accuser Philocrates made a practice of accusing ὑπεύθυνοι and playing the sycophant: Φιλοκράτης γὰρ οὑτοσὶ ἑτέρους τῶν ὑπευθύνων ἔσειε καὶ ἐσυκοφάντει.[2]

It must at all times have been a difficult matter to distinguish between a public-spirited prosecutor and an unscrupulous sycophant who posed as a public benefactor.[3] In the *Plutus*, Aristophanes pictures a sycophant, who had been deprived of his livelihood by the reforms instituted by Plutus, as claiming to be an indispensable public benefactor:

SYCOPHANT: Alas! What a shame that I, good and patriotic citizen that I am, should be so abused.

NEIGHBOR: You a good and patriotic citizen?

SYCOPHANT: As never man was.

NEIGHBOR: How do you make a living?

SYCOPHANT: I superintend all public and private affairs.

NEIGHBOR: You do? Why?

SYCOPHANT: I want to. Is it not my duty to help the city to enforce the laws and hinder men from doing wrong?

NEIGHBOR: But does not the state appoint judges for just that purpose?

SYCOPHANT: But who accuses?

"Anyone who wants to" (ὁ βουλόμενος), replies the neighbor in the language of Solon's law which permitted anyone who pleased (ὁ βουλόμενος) to prosecute. "Well, I am the one who wants to," responds the sycophant.[4]

There is plenty of evidence that sycophancy at its worst was quite prevalent in Athens in the late fifth century. Aristophanes in the *Acharnians*,[5] presented in 425 B.C., rep-

---

[1] 259 ff.; cf. 824–25.

[2] Antiph. vi. 43. The word σείω is used generally of legal processes or threats to secure money; cf. Aristoph. *Knights* 840; *Peace* 639.

[3] Cf. "the watchdog of the people" (κύων τοῦ δήμου), Demos. xxv. 40.

[4] *Plutus* 899–918; cf. Lofberg's translation of the passage, *op. cit.*, pp. 2 f.

[5] 902 ff.

resents Dicaeopolis as making a deal with the Boeotian for some of his wares. "What price do you ask?" says Dicaeopolis. "Or will you take some goods from here in exchange?" "Indeed I will, something that Athens has but we have not," replies the Boeotian. After suggesting sardines or crockery of which the Boeotian will have none, Dicaeopolis exclaims, "I have it. Take a sycophant."[1] When Dicaeopolis sets up his market-place under the separate peace he had made with the Lacedaemonians, he proclaimed, "Let no sycophant come within these bounds."[2] Rogers quite properly renders συκοφάντης by "informer," for it is in the capacity of informers that sycophants appear in the play. As Dicaeopolis concludes his bargain with the Megarian for the sale of his daughters disguised as pigs, a sycophant appears to denounce them as contraband of war subject to seizure and immediate sale. "Ah, here it is again, the source of all our woes," exclaims the Megarian.[3] The reference is to the activities of Athenian sycophants in enforcing the customs laws against the Megarians some time before the passage of the final law excluding the Megarians from the harbors of the empire and the market of Attica.[4] These officious and troublesome informers are guilty of no wrongdoing; they are πολυπράγμονες, as the search of the clothing of Megarians for contraband articles shows.[5] Public opinion was the sole check upon this activity of sycophants.

Aristophanes is said to have won distinction by attacking the sycophants: φασὶ δὲ αὐτὸν εὐδοκιμῆσαι συκοφάντας καταλύσαντα· οὓς ὠνόμασεν ἠπιάλους ἐν Σφηξίν, ἐν οἷς φησιν Οἳ τοὺς πατέρας (αὐτῶν) ἦγχον νύκτωρ, καὶ τοὺς πάππους ἀπέπνιγον.[6]

---

[1] Aristophanes is quick to pun on words that suggest in sense or sound either of the parts of συκο-φάντης. Puns on φάσις, a process much favored by sycophants, and the river Φᾶσις are obvious and apt (*Acharnians* 725–26, 908; *Birds* 68; *Knights* 1256). More common are references, some quite far-fetched, to σῦκα (*Wasps* 145, 897; *Knights* 529; *Plutus* 946).

[2] *Acharnians* 725.   [3] *Ibid.* 820–21.

[4] Bonner, "The Megarian Degrees," *CP*, XVI, 238 ff.

[5] For the correct interpretation of ἐσυκοφάντει Μεγαρέων τὰ χλανίσκια cf. Van Leeuwen, note on *Acharnians* 519.

[6] *Vita Aristoph.* xii. 7 (Bergk).

One would like to believe that the reference is to a comedy against sycophants, perhaps the Γεωργοί as Zielinski suggests,[1] rather than to his various strictures on them in his different plays.[2] For the sum total of these passages could hardly have produced a κατάλυσις συκοφαντῶν.

Isocrates' choice of the sycophant motif in the *Antidosis* is significant. His *apologia pro vita sua* in imitation of Plato's *Apology of Socrates* takes the form of a forensic speech. He imagines his prosecutor to be a sycophant who brought an indictment against him and made use of some of the slanderous or unfavorable statements about his teaching that were made in the real *antidosis*.[3] There was a twofold advantage in this device. The public was accustomed to hearing and reading orations, and would be inclined to read a disquisition in the form of a forensic speech. Furthermore, the case against Isocrates is at once discredited by the fact that the prosecutor as a sycophant belonged to a well-known and highly obnoxious class of citizens.

In the orators litigants bandy back and forth charges of sycophancy in the hope of embarrassing their opponents. This practice shows that the speech-writers, who doubtless knew the temper of the courts, believed these charges would help their clients.[4] In anticipation of such charges litigants assure the dicasts that, like Trygaeus in the *Peace*, they are not sycophants or lovers of lawsuits.[5]

Sycophancy could not have flourished before the establishment of the heliastic courts under Cleisthenes[6] even though the freedom of prosecution was granted by Solon. The early success of the sycophants was due mainly to their skill in the new rhetoric which was introduced about the middle of the fifth century. It gave them a distinct advantage over their

[1] *Die Gliederung der altattischen Komoedie*, pp. 42, 106.

[2] *Wasps* 1037; *Ecclesiazusae* 562–63; cf. the notes of Starkie and Rogers.

[3] Jebb (*Attic Orators*, II, 131–32) has not put the case clearly; cf. Bonner, "The Legal Setting of Isocrates' *Antidosis*," *CP*, XV, 193 ff.; Norlin, *Isocrates*, II, 181–82.

[4] Lysias vii. 1; Aeschin. i. 1; cf. Antiph. v. 59, 79; Demos. xxii. 4; xl. 32.

[5] Aristoph. *Peace* 191; cf. Lysias xxxii. 1–2; Aeschin. i. 1; Demos. xxxix. 1; liii. 1.

[6] Cf. *supra*, I, 196.

older opponents.¹ A passage in the *Wasps*² refers to sycophants as an ancient evil, describing them as "chills" and
"fevers" which plagued "your fathers and grandfathers."
Allowing for the comic exaggeration in the matter of time,
this passage indicates that sycophants were regarded as a
serious menace to the proper administration of criminal
justice as early as the middle of the fifth century. In the last
years of the century it is clear that sycophancy had become a
pernicious profession. The revolution of 411 B.C. aroused the
democrats to take stern, not to say harsh, measures against
all those who were in any way identified with the oligarchic
revolution. One instance was the law depriving the soldiers
who had remained in Athens during the rule of the Four
Hundred of the right to sit in the assembly or to be members
of the council.³ There was also the decree of Demophantus.⁴
This was not an ordinary decree but the adopted report of a
legislative commissioner, as the words τάδε Δημόφαντος συν-
έγραψεν indicate.⁵ Anyone who in the future should participate in any way in the overthrow of the democratic constitution was declared a public enemy whom each and every
citizen bound himself by oath to slay: καὶ λόγῳ καὶ ἔργῳ καὶ
ψήφῳ καὶ τῇ ἐμαυτοῦ χειρί.⁶

In such an atmosphere sycophancy flourished. A regular
reign of terror resulted, as the following quotation from a
speech of Lysias shows, even when one has made due allowance for forensic exaggeration:

> You know that Epigenes, Demophanes and Cleisthenes, while reaping
> their personal gains from the city's misfortunes, have inflicted the heaviest
> losses on the public weal. For they prevailed on you to condemn several
> men to death without a trial, to confiscate unjustly the property of many
> more, and to banish and disfranchise other citizens; since they were capable
> of taking money for the release of offenders, and of appearing before you
> to effect the ruin of the innocent. They did not stop until they had involved

---

¹ Cf. Aristoph. *Acharnians* 676 ff., and *supra*, p. 29.

² 1037–42.   ³ Andoc. i. 75.   ⁴ *Ibid.* 96 ff.

⁵ Cf. F. D. Smith, *Athenian Political Commissions*, pp. 71 ff.

⁶ Andoc. i. 97.

the city in seditions and the gravest disasters, while raising themselves from poverty to wealth.[1]

In the *Frogs*,[2] Aristophanes urged the citizens "to end the reign of terror" (κἀφελεῖν τὰ δείματα). Within a few months the unexpected disaster at Aegospotami left no option in the matter and a general amnesty was declared by the decree of Patroclides.[3] When, after the surrender of Athens, the Thirty were installed, their first measure was against the sycophants. Nothing so well shows the general detestation in which sycophants were held as the popular approval of this measure with regard to τοὺς ὁμολογουμένους συκοφάντας. They were brought to trial before the boulé and condemned to death:

ἔπειτα πρῶτον μὲν οὓς πάντες ᾔδεσαν ἐν τῇ δημοκρατίᾳ ἀπὸ συκοφαντίας ζῶντας καὶ τοῖς καλοῖς κἀγαθοῖς βαρεῖς ὄντας, συλλαμβάνοντες ὑπῆγον θανάτου· καὶ ἥ τε βουλὴ ἡδέως αὐτῶν κατεψηφίζετο οἵ τε ἄλλοι ὅσοι συνῄδεσαν ἑαυτοῖς μὴ ὄντες τοιοῦτοι οὐδὲν ἤχθοντο.[4]

Another measure of the Thirty was aimed indirectly at sycophants. They removed some of the obscurities and restrictions in the laws, ὅπως μὴ ᾖ τοῖς συκοφάνταις ἔφοδος.[5]

The best examples of the activities of the kind of sycophant "who brings all sorts of charges but proves none"[6] are afforded by Demosthenes' own experience as related in *De corona*:

Afterwards when those who were bent on doing me mischief conspired and brought indictments, audits, impeachments, and the rest of it against me, not at first in their own persons, but in such names as they imagined would most effectually screen themselves (for you surely know and re-

---

[1] Lysias xxv. 25–26 (trans. Lamb). Thalheim, in his edition, dates the speech *ca.* 400 B.C.

[2] 688. The play was produced in 405 B.C.

[3] Andoc. i. 77 ff.

[4] Xen. *Hell.* ii. 3. 12; cf. Arist. *Ath. Pol.* xxxv. 3, who says with regard to these executions: ἐφ' οἷς ἔχαιρεν ἡ πόλις γιγνομένοις, ἡγούμενοι τοῦ βελτίστου χάριν ποιεῖν αὐτούς. Cf. Diod. Sic. xiv. 4; Lysias xxv. 27; *supra*, I, 332.

[5] Arist. *Ath. Pol.* xxxv. 2; for the law forbidding the teaching of rhetoric cf. *supra*, I, 328; Xen. *Mem.* i. 2. 31; Grote, *History of Greece*, VIII, 47 ff. If enforced for any length of time the law would have materially reduced the activities of sycophants.

[6] Demos. lvii. 34.

member that every day of that first period I was arraigned, and that
neither the desperation of Sosicles, nor the malignity of Philocrates, nor
the madness of Diondas and Melantes, nor anything else was left untried
by them against me), on all those occasions chiefly through the gods, secondly through you I was preserved. . . . . On the impeachments when you
acquitted me and did not give the prosecutors a fifth part of the votes you
pronounced that my policy was best; by my acquittal on the indictments
my motions and counsels were shown to be legal, by your passage of my
accounts you acknowledged my whole conduct to have been honest and
incorruptible.[1]

It is altogether likely that Sosicles, Diondas, and Melantes
were, like Philocrates, sycophants acting as agents for others
(συστάντων οἷς ἦν ἐπιμελὲς κακῶς ἐμὲ ποιεῖν).[2] Aristogiton, who
was at least once convicted of sycophancy, brought seven
indictments against Demosthenes.[3] The suits are called simply γραφαί, without qualification, but they undoubtedly mean
prosecutions for illegal legislation, just as in the passage
quoted from De corona. The words ἐν οἷς δὲ τὰς γραφὰς ἀπέφευ-
γον, ἔννομα καὶ γράφειν καὶ λέγειν ἀπεδεικνύμην[4] leave us in
no doubt. Aristogiton prosecuted Demosthenes twice on his
audit. Like Sosicles and the others, Aristogiton failed to win
any of these cases. Aristophon, a politician of the early fourth
century, was acquitted seventy-five times on indictments for
illegal legislation.[5] These prosecutions were more largely political in the age of Demosthenes, as compared with the earlier period of the history of the γραφὴ παρανόμων. Verdicts were
determined to a considerable extent by the political views of
the dicasts, but the fact remains that a very considerable
number of these prosecutions were based upon inadequate
grounds, as is shown by the verdicts of acquittal. It is also
true that many of them were instituted by sycophants.

Hyperides cites a number of cases of a different class where
sycophants failed to obtain a verdict:

You, Polyeuctus, and those who are of your opinion seem to me to fail
entirely to recognize the fact that no democracy in the world, no monarch,

[1] Ibid. xviii. 249–50.   [2] Cf. infra, pp. 55 f.

[3] Demos. xxv. 19: τί γὰρ ἂν γένοιτο συκοφαντίας καὶ παρανομίας δεινότερον, ἐφ᾽
οἷς ἀμφοτέροις οὗτος ὤφληκεν. Cf. ibid. 37.

[4] Ibid. xviii. 250.   [5] Aeschin. iii. 194.

no nation is more magnanimous than the people of Athens; they allow no individual citizen or group of citizens to be persecuted in the courts but afford them protection. Teisis of Agraulae first listed as public property the estate of Euthycrates which amounted to more than sixty talents. Next he promised that he would enter suit to sequester the property of Philip and Nausicles, alleging that their wealth came from unpaid mining royalties. But the dicasts were so far from heeding any such language or coveting the property of others that the man who attempted to play the sycophant failed to receive a fifth part of the votes and was in consequence fined and disfranchised. And is not this action of a jury only last month deserving of great praise, may I ask? Lysander charged Epicrates of Pallene, who had worked a mine for three years, with encroaching on public property. With him were associated about the wealthiest men in the city. Lysander promised to recover for the state three hundred talents which he claimed these men had realized by their operations. Nevertheless the jury, having regard not for the promises of the prosecutor but for justice, decided that there was no encroachment.[1]

Here we have two types of cases favored by sycophants because they involved a substantial financial reward for the successful prosecutor. Teisis filed an ἀπογραφή claiming that the estate of Euthycrates was liable to confiscation. His share would have amounted to forty talents. He lost the case and being disfranchised was unable to prosecute similar cases against two other citizens as he had promised. The other type of case is φάσις, used in mining cases where the defendant is charged with encroaching on state property. In this case a number of men were in the deal, and it was claimed that the sum involved was three hundred talents, of which the prosecutor would have received one-half. The effect of the verdict in this one case restored confidence in the mining industry to the profit of the state in increased royalties.[2] Here again the charges were ill-founded, but the stakes were large. If the sycophant could bribe the dicasts with the prospect of rich confiscations and fines he might win his case.

The words of Hyperides deserve credence. They were uttered before men who had every opportunity to know whether they were true or false. The last case was less than two months old.

Probably the most dangerous type of sycophant was the

[1] iv. 33–36.   [2] Hyper. iv. 36.

blackmailer, who threatened or started criminal proceedings against a citizen of means and then proposed to drop them for a consideration. Isocrates has left a brief description of the *modus operandi* of the blackmailing sycophant.[1] A certain Callimachus had entered suit for damages and took care to let it be known in the lounging places of the town that he had been badly treated by the defendant. In due time some of the intimates of Callimachus approached the defendant and pointed out the unpleasantness and risks of litigation involving a huge sum of money. In litigation, they said, many things turn out contrary to expectation, and chance rather than justice determines the verdicts. And so it was to the advantage of the defendant to be free from such weighty charges by the expenditure of a small sum of money. The speaker makes it clear that the suggestions of the intimates of Callimachus were the usual method of handling these things (τῶν εἰθισμένων περὶ τῶν τοιούτων λέγεσθαι). The upshot was that the speaker gave Callimachus the comparatively small sum of money, two hundred drachmas, 2 per cent of the amount claimed. As this was a civil case, the "holdup" took the form of a settlement by way of an agreed arbitration (δίαιταν ἐπὶ ῥητοῖς). The decision of the arbitrator made the agreement a binding transaction reduced to a form which could be pleaded in bar of any action at law involving the same matter.

It is quite apparent that the mere threat of prosecution was sufficient to frighten a peaceable man who had the means to pay the small sum required to free him from the annoyance and danger of litigation even if he had a higher opinion of Athenian justice than the intimates of Callimachus had.[2]

Undoubtedly litigation was feared. Antiphon in the first Tetralogy puts forward the fear of prosecution as a motive for murder. This was a mere rhetorical exercise, but it is significant that it was a *topos* in the schools. One meets it in actual litigation. A client of Lysias, who was charged with the murder of his wife's paramour caught *in flagrante delicto*, relied in his defense on the Athenian law which permitted the

---

[1] xviii. 9–10.   [2] Cf. Demos. lviii. 34.

outraged husband to punish the wrongdoer even with death if he wished. The relatives of Eratosthenes, the alleged adulterer, argued that he was guiltless of adultery but was caught and slain by means of a plot. In answer the speaker denies that there was any hostility on his part toward Eratosthenes and lists the likely reasons for so deadly an enmity:

> For he had neither subjected me to slanderous impeachment, nor attempted to expel me from the city, nor brought any private suit against me, nor was he privy to any wrongdoing which I was so afraid of being divulged that I was intent on his destruction.[1]

In the definitions of sycophancy given by the orators blackmail is mentioned more than once.[2] Specific examples are not wanting. Reference has been made to the cases of Epigenes, Demophanes, and Cleisthenes.[3] Other blackmailers are freely mentioned, such as Theocrines,[4] Aristogiton,[5] Timarchus,[6] and Ariston. The defendant in *Ariston* v. *Lycophron* has this to say of Ariston's activities as sycophant-blackmailer: "He goes around, summoning all men to court and whoever of them refuses to pay money to him he brings into court and prosecutes, but he takes no proceedings against those who are willing to pay."[7]

The extreme triviality of the charges made by sycophants is well illustrated by this fragment of Teleclides. Speaking of a sycophant, he says:

> Charicles gave the man a pound the matter not to name,
> That from inside a money bag into the world he came;
> And Nicias, also, paid him four; I know the reason well,
> But Nicias is a worthy man and so I will not tell.[8]

But here and there in the literature of the period we get stories which show how dangerous sycophants were. For ex-

[1] Lysias i. 44 (trans. Lamb).

[2] Isoc. xv. 24–25; Lysias xxv. 3.

[3] Lysias xxv. 25–26; cf. *supra*, pp. 47 f.

[4] Demos. lviii. 43; cf. Lofberg, *op. cit.*, pp. 83 ff.

[5] Demos. xxv. 47; cf. Lofberg, *op. cit.*, pp. 78–83.

[6] Aeschin. i. 107.   [7] Hyper. i. 2.

[8] Plut. *Nicias* iv. 4 (trans. Clough).

ample, Diognetus, a brother of Nicias, was so hounded by the sycophants that he went into voluntary exile.[1] Charmides in the *Symposium* of Xenophon[2] says that freedom from sycophants is one of the things that reconcile him to his poverty. When he was rich he had to pay court to them. Undoubtedly he was speaking of blackmail, as the words τοὺς συκοφάντας ἐθεράπευον clearly indicate. Another man who suffered much from the exactions of sycophants was Nicias. Plutarch tells us that "he gave to those who could work him harm no less than to those who deserved his favors."[3] So terrified was he of sycophants and blackmailers that he avoided all public appearances and social engagements as far as possible. "Since he was disposed to be thus cautious of public informers, he would neither dine with a fellow-citizen, nor indulge in general interchange of views or familiar social intercourse."[4] Crito, the friend of Socrates, was also much annoyed by sycophants, as we learn from the *Memorabilia* of Xenophon:

> I remember that Socrates once heard Crito say that life in Athens was difficult for a man who wanted to mind his own business. "At this moment," added Crito, "actions are pending against me, not because I have done the plaintiffs any wrong but because they think I would sooner pay than have trouble."[5]

When Crito proposed to smuggle Socrates out of prison he anticipated trouble from the sycophants who might seek to prosecute or blackmail the friends of Socrates but reassured Socrates that they were easily bought (εὐτελεῖς). Crito also expressed concern lest the friends of Socrates might be criticized for allowing the case to come to trial at all when it could have been prevented (καὶ ἡ εἴσοδος τῆς δίκης εἰς τὸ δικαστήριον ὡς εἰσῆλθεν ἐξὸν μὴ εἰσελθεῖν).[6] It has been reasonably suggested that Crito may have had in mind a settlement with the accusers of Socrates.[7] It need hardly be said that, just as Socrates rejected the idea of jail delivery, so he would not have agreed to any such financial settlement. It may be objected that Meletus, who laid the charge, was some-

---

[1] Lysias xviii. 9.

[2] iv. 29 ff.

[3] *Nicias* iv. 3.

[4] *Ibid.* v. 1.

[5] ii. 9. 1.

[6] Plato *Crito* 45A–E.

[7] Lofberg, *op. cit.*, p. 40.

thing of a fanatic and not the sort of person to be bought off.
This is doubtless true, but the concern of Crito regarding
public opinion in the matter indicates a pretty general idea
that most prosecutors could be bought off.

Neither Lofberg nor anyone else has, it would seem, discussed the question of the victim's security after he had paid
blackmail. Perhaps he had no assurance that threats would
not be renewed by the same or other sycophants and more
money demanded. In the only case where we know the details of a "settlement" out of court in a civil suit, viz., by an
arbitration (ἐπὶ ῥητοῖς), Callimachus revived the suit. The
result is not known. In the cases of Patrocles and Lysimachus, who paid him altogether twelve minas in the same matter, Callimachus remained satisfied.[1]

There are indications that sycophants with common interests tended to form associations. On two occasions[2] we hear
of ἐργαστήρια συκοφαντῶν. Whether these were real clubs of
sycophants or mere temporary organizations of rascals for a
specific case is quite immaterial. It does seem possible that
in these groups there might have been some understanding
that when one sycophant made a satisfactory settlement with
a victim the others would leave him alone. Only in some such
fashion as this could a victim be assured of immunity when
he had once paid.[3]

As it was a punishable offense to drop a prosecution once it
was started, a settlement out of court by means of an arbitration (ἐπὶ ῥητοῖς) could not be used. But one suspects that
formal reconciliations between forensic enemies which are so
common in the orators may sometimes have been occasioned
by the payment of money. But this is a mere suspicion without foundation in the sources.

[1] Isoc. xviii. 6–7; cf. supra, p. 51.

[2] Demos. xxxix. 2; xl. 9.

[3] For clubs of sycophants see De Vos, De sycophantis, pp. 40–45; Leisi, Der
Zeuge im Attischen Recht, p. 119; Calhoun, Athenian Clubs, pp. 79–81, 95–96;
Lofberg, op. cit., p. 60; Lipsius (op. cit., p. 909, n. 33) roundly rejects the view that
there were clubs of sycophants, but Hommel (op. cit., p. 1131) agrees with Calhoun
and Lofberg as against Lipsius.

The sycophant was always ready to put his services at the disposal of others for hire. As an agent, his knowledge of law and rhetoric could be put to various uses. He might act as an advocate on occasion, if we are to class as sycophants those who took money for their services as pleaders in court contrary to law.[1] Perhaps the most useful service a sycophant-agent could perform was to bring countersuits against an accuser of his client. A good illustration is the suit brought against the choregus in Antiphon[2] by Philocrates, a professional sycophant. The purpose of the charge of homicide was to disqualify the choregus for prosecuting a group of officials for misappropriation of public funds.[3] Midias[4] attempted by a similar maneuver to discredit Demosthenes. He hired a sycophant, Euctemon, to charge Demosthenes with a military offense. It made no difference that the case never came to trial; it was enough that all men should see a notice to the following effect: Εὐκτήμων Λουσιεὺς ἐγράψατο Δημοσθένην Παιανιέα λιποταξίου. Aristogiton, another notorious sycophant, was the paid agent of the pro-Macedonian party and prosecuted Demosthenes seven times.[5]

There is no indication of the amounts paid to the sycophant-agent. In desperate cases where he risked a fine of one thousand drachmas and the loss of the right to bring a similar prosecution in the future the compensation must have been considerable. The one thousand drachmas given by Callias to Cephisius to indict Andocides for impiety may very well have been intended to cover a possible fine. If he escaped the fine, he had his fee. Such an arrangement would put the sycophant on his mettle. It was a great convenience for politicians, particularly during the struggle with Macedonia, to attack their opponents through the medium of an agent who could be disavowed if need be. The disadvantage lay in the

---

[1] Cf. Demos. xxi. 113; xlvi. 26; Lycurg. i. 138; *supra*, pp. 10 ff.

[2] vi. 21.

[3] For a full account of the case see Calhoun, *op. cit.*, pp. 49–51; cf. Lofberg, *op. cit.*, pp. 49 ff.

[4] Demos. xxi. 103.

[5] *Ibid.* xxv. 37; for other attacks on Demosthenes cf. *supra*, pp. 48 f.

fact that an agent must sometimes be protected and defended in court. Agents could also be intrusted with proposing and carrying decrees and laws which benefited their employers.[1]

If one accepts the statement of Aeschines that any rogue might be called a sycophant, those who were professional witnesses, such as Polyeuctus, Timocrates, and Euctemon, may be included among the sycophants,[2] as well as the bribers of dicasts, ecclesiasts, and officials.[3] Perhaps the best example of the rascal-sycophant-agent is Pythodorus, the expert forger of seals and documents.[4] But in estimating the effect of sycophancy on the administration of justice in Athens it would be better to take no account of these lesser breeds of so-called sycophants.

In modern systems, though there are no counterparts of the Athenian sycophant, there is nevertheless the possibility of much unnecessary and unjustifiable litigation. Certain checks are provided. In civil cases the prospect of paying the entire cost of the litigation acts as a strong deterrent upon a prospective plaintiff. In criminal cases, while the decision as to whether the evidence available is sufficient to warrant a trial lies with the official prosecutor, he must first present enough evidence to the grand jury to obtain a true bill against the accused. Sufficient evidence must be offered at the hearing to establish a prima facie case.

In Athens, however, the costs of litigation were comparatively slight. The payment of them would not have frightened anyone who was anxious to proceed with a doubtful case. So a different kind of deterrent was devised. Any prosecutor in practically all public suits[5] who failed to obtain one-fifth of the votes was liable to pay a fine of one thousand drachmas.[6] Neither the law as cited by Demosthenes among the documents in the Midias case nor the part quoted in

[1] *Ibid.* xxiv. 3, 66, 203.
[2] *Ibid.* xix. 216; xxi. 139; xxix. 28.
[3] Lofberg, *op. cit.*, pp. 54 ff.
[4] Isoc. xvii. 33–34.
[5] For exceptions see Lofberg, *op. cit.*, p. 88.
[6] For the law see Demos. xxi. 47; cf. lviii. 6; Plato *Apol.* 36A–B; Andoc. iv. 18.

Epichares v. *Theocrines* (ὥσπερ ἠκούσατ᾽ ἐξ αὐτοῦ τοῦ νόμου, ἐὰν
ἐπεξιών τις μὴ μεταλάβῃ τὸ πέμπτον μέρος τῶν ψήφων, χιλίας ἀποτίνειν)[1] makes any reference to any other punishment beyond
the fine. The same is true of the many casual references to the
πέμπτον μέρος in the orators. But in other sources it is very
definitely said that there was an additional penalty of partial
ἀτιμία: ᾿Αθήνησιν οὖν ἐν τοῖς δημοσίοις ἀγῶσιν ἐὰν μὴ μεταλάβῃ
τις τὸ πέμπτον μέρος, χιλίας ἀποτίνει καὶ ἔτι πρόσεστί τις ἀτιμία
οἷον (μὴ) ἐξεῖναι μήτε γράψασθαι παρανόμων μήτε φαίνειν μήτε
ἐφηγεῖσθαι.[2] It is also implied very definitely in others: ἐὰν
γὰρ μὴ μεταλάβῃ τὸ πέμπτον μέρος τῶν ψήφων καὶ ἀτιμωθῇ ὁ
ἐνδείξας ἐμὲ Κηφίσιος οὑτοσί, οὐκ ἔξεστιν αὐτῷ εἰς τὸ ἱερὸν τοῖν
θεοῖν εἰσιέναι, ἢ ἀποθανεῖται.[3] The nature of the ἀτιμία is not
set forth clearly in the sources. A passage in Andocides
(ἑτέροις οὐκ ἦν γράψασθαι, τοῖς δὲ ἐνδεῖξαι)[4] shows that the penalty concerned only the particular kind of process that was
employed in the case in question. For example, one might
be prevented from using any kind of γραφή and still could
use φάσις, ἀπογραφή, or ἔνδειξις. If one failed to pay the fine,
in process of time he automatically became a state debtor
and as such was ἄτιμος.

In theory perhaps the magistrate who accepted a criminal
case and conducted the *anakrisis* might refuse to bring it up
for trial if he deemed the evidence of wrongdoing unsatis-
factory; but such a rejection might very well have had un-
pleasant consequences for the magistrate at his audit. Moreover, he had little or no evidence before him at the *anakrisis*.[5]
There was apparently an exception in the case of the *euthynoi*
who received complaints against a retiring magistrate. They
had the right to reject a case on their own authority:

ὁ δὲ λαβὼν τοῦτο (τὸ ἀδίκημα) καὶ ἀνακρίνας, ἐὰν μὲν καταγνῷ, παραδίδωσιν τὰ μὲν ἴδια τοῖς δικασταῖς τοῖς κατὰ δήμους, τοῖς τὴν φυλὴν ταύτην

[1] Demos. lviii. 6.

[2] Theophrastus in Schol. Demos. xxii, cited by Lipsius, *op. cit.*, p. 449, n. 110.
Cf. Pollux viii. 53.

[3] Andoc. i. 33; cf. Demos. xxvi. 9.   [4] i. 76.

[5] Cf. *supra*, I, 289 ff.; Calhoun, *CP*, XIV, 338 ff.

εἰσάγουσιν, τὰ δὲ δημόσια τοῖς θεσμοθέταις ἐπιγράφει. οἱ δὲ θεσμοθέται, ἐὰν παραλάβωσιν, πάλιν εἰσάγουσιν ταύτην τὴν εὔθυναν εἰς τὸ δικαστήριον.[1]

This specific statement regarding the *euthynoi* would seem to indicate that other officials were not expected at the *anakrisis* to accept or reject the case on its merits.

In the cases that came before the Forty (the bulk of the δίκαι) the arbitrators sifted the evidence and exhibited any weakness in it. They could not, however, prevent the suitor who lost in their court from appealing. There was a further check on unwarranted private suits. If the plaintiff failed to secure at least one-fifth of the votes, he was obliged to pay the defendant an obol for every drachma of his claim. This was the ἐπωβελία. It was not applied to all δίκαι.[2] It may be assumed that the fine was imposed automatically by the verdict of more than four-fifths of the jury and was collected in the usual way.

As long as the sycophant confined himself to mere threats of prosecution there was little or nothing to be done about it. But if the suit was once filed and proceedings begun, the prosecutor who dropped it was liable to a fine of one thousand drachmas and the loss of the right to bring similar suits in the future. He was in the same case as if he had carried the suit to trial and got less than one-fifth of the votes. In fact, the two matters are dealt with in the same law, as cited in Demosthenes: ἐάν τις μὴ ἐπεξέλθῃ ἢ ἐπεξιὼν μὴ μεταλάβῃ τὸ πέμπτον μέρος τῶν ψήφων, ἀποτισάτω χιλίας δραχμὰς τῷ δημοσίῳ.[3] If Lipsius is correct in assuming this law to be genuine, it means that in a general criminal statute there was always this provision, just as there was the provision that ὁ βουλόμενος might prosecute.[4] According to law, legal proceedings were started when the case was posted on the public notice board.

---

[1] Arist. *Ath. Pol.* xlviii. 5; cf. *infra*, p. 259, n. 2, for discussion of ἀνακρίνας reading.

[2] Cf. Lipsius, *op. cit.*, pp. 937 ff.

[3] xxi. 47.

[4] Cf. *supra*, I, 166 ff. It need scarcely be remarked that the rule did not apply to civil suits; cf. Demos. lviii. 20: ἀλλὰ προσήκει τοὺς ἀντιδίκους ὑπὲρ μὲν τῶν ἰδίων, ὅπως ἂν αὐτοὺς πείθωσι, διοικεῖσθαι πρὸς ἀλλήλους, ὑπὲρ δὲ τῶν πρὸς τὸ δημόσιον, ὅπως ἂν οἱ νόμοι κελεύωσιν.

If a prosecutor failed to proceed with the *anakrisis* he was liable to the fine.[1]

There are plenty of indications that this law intended to check the blackmailer-sycophant was not always enforced. It is known that for the purpose of encouraging prosecutors in certain types of suits no penalty was attached to failure to obtain at least one-fifth of the votes. Consequently, it is not unreasonable to assume that the same was true of the penalty for dropping these suits after they had been instituted.

Some evidence for this conclusion is available. The prosecutor of a guardian for κάκωσις ὀρφάνου was not liable to a fine if he failed to obtain one-fifth of the votes or even a single vote.[2] The reason for this is plain: orphans must be protected in their rights at all costs. Prosecutors must on no account be discouraged in their efforts to bring wicked guardians to justice. It is not surprising to find instances in which such cases were dropped before they came to trial. In *Epichares* v. *Theocrines* the defendant summoned Polyeuctus before the archon λαβὼν δὲ τὰς τριακοσίας δραχμὰς παρὰ τοῦ Πολυεύκτου, καὶ τὰ δεινὰ ταῦτ' ἀποδόμενος μικροῦ λήμματος ἐφ' οἷς τῷ πατρὶ ἐτιμήσατο δέκα ταλάντων, ἀπηλλάγη καὶ τὴν γραφὴν ἀνείλετο προδοὺς τὸν ὀρφανόν.[3] This is not a savory case, but it is clear that Epichares finds fault with the bribery rather than with the dropping of the case, which was doubtless permitted by law. One can well imagine that the threat from an honest prosecutor of legal proceedings, carried even to a summons, might frighten a guardian into doing justice to his ward. If this were true, it would be useless to proceed with the prosecution. Another example of exemption from penalties is a γραφὴ ξενίας. In the case against Neaera, Apollodorus proposed to drop the case against Neaera if he were convinced by conclusive evidence of the maternity of certain children whom he mentioned.[4] This offer would not have been made in open court if it would have rendered Apollodorus liable to a fine and partial disfranchisement.

---

[1] Demos. lviii. 10.   [2] Isaeus iii. 46–47.   [3] Demos. lviii. 32.

[4] *Ibid.* lix. 121; cf. *ibid.* 53, where Phrastor dropped a suit against Stephanus.

The exception in this case is easily understood, for the Athenians were very jealous of their citizenship, especially when it came to have a financial value in the way of indemnities and doles. There is no evidence that a failure to obtain at least one-fifth of the votes in a γραφὴ ξενίας carried no penalty, but it seems from this incident to be wholly unlikely that it did.

There was still another case which was ἀκίνδυνος. It was the indictment of one for injuring the sacred olive trees.[1] Here again it may plausibly be assumed in the absence of evidence that there was no penalty for dropping such a case.

It is evident that the motive which determined the dropping of a suit was of extreme importance. If the prosecutor accepted money he was, in modern terms, guilty of compounding a crime. But there were many good and sufficient reasons why an honest prosecutor might drop a case. The choregus in Antiphon[2] was forced to drop a prosecution of some officials when he was finally brought to trial for the death of a chorus boy in training under his charge. This is an extreme case. But others equally effective might be conceived, such as the serious illness of a prosecutor or the death of an indispensable witness. Many a modern prosecutor has been obliged to nolle prosequi a case because of the disappearance of witnesses.

Demosthenes himself dropped his suit against Midias, though in the published speech he reproaches Euctemon for dropping the suit started against himself. It is impossible to determine what, if any, difference there was between these two cases. Evidently exceptions were permitted and evasions tolerated. Calhoun[3] has pointed out that the law could be evaded with impunity. A case in point is mentioned in *Epichares* v. *Theocrines*[4] where the defendant is charged with having dropped a case against Demosthenes by the following device. When the case was called, an affidavit was produced that Demosthenes was ill and unable to attend. Though this was not true, the result was that the trial was postponed,

[1] Lysias vii. 37.   [3] *Op. cit.*, p. 58, n. 6.
[2] vi. 38.   [4] Demos. lviii. 43.

sine die as it turned out, for the plaintiff neither contested the affidavit nor resumed the case (καὶ οὔτε τότε ἀνθυπωμόσατο οὔθ' ὕστερον ἐπήγγελκεν). Epichares claimed that this was no new device but one frequently employed by men of the stamp of Theocrines.

In those instances in which prosecutions were dropped for good and sufficient reasons, one is compelled to inquire whether the prosecutor himself accepted the responsibility or whether he was officially authorized to drop the prosecution. Lipsius, influenced by the fact that where a prosecutor failed to obtain the requisite number of votes the fine was *ipso facto* registered against him as part of the verdict of the court, believed that the magistrate was empowered either to permit a case to be dropped if the reasons seemed adequate or to register the fine on his own authority.[1] A passage in Demosthenes[2] would seem at first sight to show that the penalty was automatic. After referring to a charge of λιπο-ταξίου which Euctemon had been hired to bring against him, Demosthenes adds: ἐφ' ᾗ γὰρ ἐκεῖνος ἠτίμωκεν αὐτὸν οὐκ ἐπεξελθών, οὐδεμιᾶς ἔγωγ' ἔτι προσδέομαι δίκης, ἀλλ' ἱκανὴν ἔχω. The words may refer to Euctemon's failure to pay the one thousand drachmas assessed against him by the magistrate before whom the case was filed. Persistent failure to pay would incur ἀτιμία. But the words may equally well refer to the partial ἀτιμία incurred for dropping a prosecution. This penalty, however it was inflicted, could be enforced only by the watchful vigilance of volunteer prosecutors. Any person prosecuted by one who had been deprived of the right to file such an indictment could be confidently relied upon to see that the prosecutor desisted. To all intents and purposes it could be said of such a person ἠτίμωκεν αὐτόν. Furthermore,

---

[1] Meier-Schömann-Lipsius, *Der Attische Process*, pp. 912 ff.; Lipsius, *op. cit.*, pp. 448–50. Platner (*Process und Klagen*, I, 127), takes the contrary view, as do Calhoun (*op. cit.*, p. 58, n. 6) and Lofberg (*op. cit.*, pp. 86 ff.). Caillemer, in Darem.-Saglio, *s.v.* "Graphé", believes that the legitimacy of the reasons for which the case was dropped could not be determined by a magistrate. The Athenians were too jealous of magisterial authority to delegate to a magistrate the decision of matters which lay within the province of a court of law.

[2] xxi. 103.

the words οὐδεμιᾶς ἔγωγ' ἔτι προσδέομαι δίκης, ἀλλ' ἱκανὴν ἔχω seem to indicate that Demosthenes might have taken further action, viz., the collection of the fine by the appropriate legal action, such as that taken in *Epichares* v. *Theocrines*. The defendant Theocrines was prosecuted on at least four charges, one of which was that, having dropped a suit against one Micion, he was liable to a fine of one thousand drachmas. Now if it is true that when a prosecutor dropped a case the magistrate made a notation of the fine of one thousand drachmas and passed it on to the proper authorities for collection, it would seem that this notation would have been sufficient to establish the guilt of Theocrines. But Epichares says nothing of any such record. First he has Theocrines' denunciation (φάσις) of Micion read, next the evidence of witnesses who saw it exposed (ἐκκειμένην). Then he called the Overseers of the Port (ἐπιμεληταὶ τοῦ ἐμπορίου) and their secretary before whom the case came.[1] The purport of this testimony was "that Theocrines gave in a denunciation against the vessel of Micion and that the denunciation was exposed in public for a long time, and being called to the *anakrisis*, he did not attend or proceed with the case." It is obvious not only that there was no penalty registered but that nothing whatever had been done officially that could be accepted as evidence. It is equally obvious, moreover, that without the intervention of Epichares or another volunteer prosecutor Theocrines would never have been obliged to pay the fine. That the acceptance of a bribe to drop a case was the real offense may be suspected from the fact that Epichares alleges that Theocrines made a business of taking bribes under these circumstances, and proposed to call as witnesses the bribers or victims, among whom are Hyperides and Demosthenes.[2] The latter refused to testify[3] because, according to Epichares, he had settled his difference with Theocrines by inducing him to drop a γραφὴ παρανόμων by a safe device already discussed.[4] But this does not explain how Demos-

[1] Demos. lviii. 6–10, 26.

[2] *Ibid.* 34–35.

[3] *Ibid.* 42.

[4] Cf. *supra*, pp. 60 f.

thenes for political reasons and the sum of thirty minas dropped his case against Midias for assault and had the assurance to salvage what he could of the attack on Midias by publishing the speech he had prepared for the court.[1]

On the whole the law could not have been an effective check on sycophants. In one fashion or another it was possible to evade it. In the first place there were types of cases that were excepted from the provisions of the law in the public interest. Where there was collusion between the parties the case could be continued until it was officially forgotten. Lipsius[2] supposes that permission to withdraw a case could be secured. In this way he would explain the case of *Demosthenes* v. *Midias*. This view, however, is open to grave doubts.

Besides this indirect means of restraining and punishing sycophants there were legal processes that could be used against the sycophant directly. Isocrates mentions three:

> They applied to the sycophant more stringent laws than to other criminals; for, while they placed the trial of the greatest crimes in the hands of a single one of the courts, against the sycophants they instituted γραφαί before the thesmothetai, εἰσαγγελίαι before the senate, and προβολαί before the general assembly.[3]

There is no information regarding the form of the indictment. It is difficult to see how one could draft or prove a general charge of sycophancy such as is freely made by litigants against their opponents. Even Aeschines' definition is vague.[4] So far as is known, the only law under which a sycophant could be held liable was the ancient law cited by Demosthenes: ἔστι δὲ δήπου νόμος ὑμῖν, ἐάν τις ὑποσχόμενός τι τὸν δῆμον ἢ βουλὴν ἢ δικαστήριον ἐξαπατήσῃ, τὰ ἔσχατα πάσχειν.[5] The law was enforced by εἰσαγγελία,[6] and the death penalty could be inflicted.[7] The law resembles closely the curse pronounced by the herald at the opening of the ecclesia: διόπερ καταρᾶται καθ᾽ ἑκάστην ἐκκλησίαν ὁ κῆρυξ οὐκ εἴ τινες ἐξη-

[1] Schaefer, *Demosthenes und seine Zeit*, II, 108–9.

[2] *Op. cit.*, p. 450, n. 113. [4] ii. 145. [6] xlix. 67.

[3] xv. 314 (trans. Norlin). [5] xx. 100. [7] xx. 135.

πατήθησαν, ἀλλ᾽ εἴ τις ἐξαπατᾷ λέγων ἢ βουλὴν ἢ δῆμον ἢ τὴν
ἡλιαίαν.[1] It will be noted that instead of λέγων in the curse
the law has ὑποσχόμενος, which is not a very suitable word to
apply to a prosecutor in court, although, as it happens, it is
precisely the word used by Hyperides of sycophants.[2] But at
the time of the drafting of the law the sycophant was not as
yet a problem.[3]

There is an interesting record of proceedings taken against
the men popularly regarded as responsible for the condemnation of the generals after the battle of Arginusae. The procedure began by a προβολή and the charge was τὸν δῆμον
ἐξαπατῆσαι:

And not long afterwards the Athenians repented, and they voted that
complaints [προβολάς] be brought against any who had deceived the
people, that they furnish bondsmen until such time as they should be
brought to trial, and that Callixenus be included among them. Complaints
were brought against four others also [προυβλήθησαν] and they were put into
confinement by their bondsmen. But when there broke out afterwards a
factional disturbance, in the course of which Cleophon was put to death,
these men escaped, before being brought to trial; Callixenus indeed returned, at the time when the Piraeus party returned to the city, but he
was hated by everybody and died of starvation.[4]

The exact steps in the process are not at all clear. Normally
the *probolé* was brought by any citizen who wished to
strengthen his case against a notorious wrongdoer. The
known examples of *probolai* include charges of disturbing
religious festivals, sycophancy, and deceiving the people by
false promises.[5] These are all cases that would naturally
arouse wide popular interest and concern. The vote of the
assembly was a mere resolution without legal effect. The
prosecutor was free to drop the matter or to indict the alleged

[1] xxiii. 97.

[2] iv. 35–36, quoted *supra*, pp. 49 f.

[3] Cf. *supra*, I, 208–9.

[4] Xen. *Hell.* i. 7. 35 (trans. Brownson). For another reference to the authorization of *probolai* by the ecclesia as a regular proceeding cf. Pollux viii. 46: προβολαὶ
δ᾽ ἐγίγνοντο τοῦ δήμου ψηφισαμένου. Cf. Lipsius, *op. cit.*, p. 214, for a discussion of
probolé and the definition of Pollux.

[5] Demos. xxi. 10; cf. Lipsius, *op. cit.*, p. 212, n. 118, and pp. 213 ff.

wrongdoer. In this case it would seem that the ecclesia ordered by decree that Callixenus and any others responsible for the miscarriage of justice be brought to trial. Five were brought before the ecclesia and committed to trial.

Probolai were normally brought into the ecclesia by the thesmothetai at the instance of a prosecutor. Whatever irregularities there were in the case of the generals are not important; for some individual must in any case have taken the initiative by introducing the original decree. The action of the assembly in committing the accused for trial instead of limiting itself to expressing an unfavorable opinion regarding them is of little consequence. In the last resort the ecclesia could do as it liked in its judicial capacity.[1]

Xenophon does not say that Callixenus and the others were sycophants, but in effect they were. Indeed, Suidas actually calls Callixenus a sycophant:

ἐναύειν· Καλλίξενος ὁ Ἀθηναῖος διὰ συκοφαντίαν ἆθλα ἀπηνέγκατο τῆς ἀναισχυντίας καὶ ἀσεβείας, ἐν ἄστει μισούμενος καὶ πενόμενος καὶ ἀποκλειόμενος λιμῷ ἀποθανεῖν· ἐπεὶ μήτε ὕδατος ἐκοινώνουν αὐτῷ μήτε πυρὸς ἐναύειν ἐβούλοντο, ὥσπερ οὖν κοινωνεῖν τοῖς βουλομένοις καὶ δεομένοις.

Diogenes Laertius[2] says that not long after the death of Socrates the Athenians felt such remorse that they put Meletus to death and banished the other accusers. If there is any truth in this statement, the charge must have been the same as in the proceedings against the prosecutors of the generals, ἀπάτη τοῦ δήμου. The story was apparently unknown to Xenophon, who has something to say of the fate of Anytus and his son who fell into evil ways: "So Anytus, even though dead, still enjoys an evil repute for his son's mischievous education and for his own hard-heartedness."[3] It seems that if Anytus had been banished Xenophon could hardly have failed to mention it in this connection. There is no place in the plan of Plato's *Apology, Crito, Euthyphro,* or *Phaedo* for any reference to the fate of Socrates' accusers.

---

[1] It is not impossible that we have here a contamination of *probolé* and *eisangelia,* which, if approved, regularly terminated in an indictment.

[2] ii. 43.   [3] *Apol.* 30–31 (trans. Todd).

Isocrates and Aristotle agree that against sycophants there were both *probolai* and *graphai*. Aeschines also mentions *probolé*: τῶν δὲ συκοφαντῶν ὡς κακούργων δημοσίᾳ προβολὰς ποιούμεθα.[1] There was, according to Aristotle, regular provision for *probolé* of sycophants in the sixth prytany: καὶ συκοφαντῶν προβολὰς τῶν Ἀθηναίων καὶ τῶν μετοίκων μέχρι τριῶν ἑκατέρων, κἄν τις ὑποσχόμενός τι μὴ ποιήσῃ τῷ δήμῳ.[2] Among the *graphai* before the thesmothetai Aristotle mentions γραφαὶ συκοφαντίας.[3] It has been observed that Pollux identifies the two procedures: προβολαὶ δὲ ἦσαν καὶ αἱ τῆς συκοφαντίας γραφαί.[4] This loose and inexact expression[5] finds a measure of justification in the close relationship between *probolé* and *graphé* in practice. *Demosthenes* v. *Midias* is the leading case. Demosthenes first "presented" Midias to the assembly on a charge of assault and battery. The vote was against Midias. Demosthenes, with this prejudgment of the case in his favor, indicted Midias in the regular way. Had the people voted otherwise it is not at all likely that Demosthenes would have pushed the case. Similarly in the case of Callixenus *et al.*, the *probolé* was followed by the filing of an indictment, presumably a γραφὴ ἀπάτης τοῦ δήμου.[6] Perhaps a better case is that of Agoratus. He was charged with sycophancy in δίκαι, γραφαί, and ἀπογραφαί: περὶ δὲ συκοφαντίας, ὅσας οὗτος ἢ δίκας ἰδίας συκοφαντῶν ἐδικάζετο ἢ γραφὰς ὅσας ἐγράφετο ἢ ἀπογραφὰς ἀπέγραφεν, οὐδέν με δεῖ καθ᾽ ἕκαστον λέγειν.[7] He was convicted and fined ten thousand drachmas. The procedure here described could be either *probolé* or *eisangelia* followed by a γραφὴ συκοφαντίας. Lofberg regards it as a *probolé*.[8]

Aristotle does not define sycophancy except in so far as he very clearly differentiates sycophants from those who make promises to the people which they do not fulfil. The fact that

---

[1] ii. 145.   [3] *Ibid*. lix. 3.

[2] *Ath. Pol.* xliii. 5.   [4] viii. 46.

[5] Cf. Latte, in Pauly-Wissowa, *s.v.* Συκοφαντίας Γραφή.

[6] Cf. Lipsius, *op. cit.*, pp. 214, 382.

[7] Lysias xiii. 65; ἀπογραφή was a favorite suit with prosecutors and sycophants.

[8] *Op. cit.*, p. 92. Latte (*op. cit.*) approves.

Aristotle paired the two types of offense shows that he realized how closely they were related. One is reminded of the
definition of Aeschines: "It is συκοφαντία when one person,
insinuating an accusation [αἰτίαν ἐμβαλών] into the minds of
the people, calumniates a man in all the meetings of the assembly and before the senate."[1] Lipsius[2] thinks that "gegen
Sykophantie nur dann Probole zulässig war, wenn durch sie
das Volk selbst irregeleitet und zu unglücklichen Massnah-
men verführt worden war." He cites the proceedings against
Callixenus *et al.* as a case in point. This is undoubtedly true.
There was a provision that six *probolai* against sycophants
could be introduced in the "sovereign" (κυρία) assembly of
the sixth prytany. Why the restriction to six? Could *probolai*
be introduced at other meetings? Gilbert thinks they could.[3]
Aristotle gives a list of the matters that must be provided for
in the *agenda* of the ἐκκλησία κυρία in each prytany. He then
proceeds:

> In the sixth prytany, in addition to the business already stated, the
> question is also put to the vote whether it is desirable to hold a vote of
> ostracism or not; and complaints against professional accusers [συκοφαντῶν
> προβολάς], whether Athenians or aliens domiciled in Athens [τῶν μετοίκων]
> are received, to the number of not more than three of either class, together
> with cases in which an individual has made some promise to the people
> and has not performed it.[4]

One is puzzled to understand how citizens and metics
could alike be sycophants. It is clear that a metic could carry
on private litigation under the aegis of his *prostatés*, but it is
strange that he could be ὁ βουλόμενος and prosecute citizens.
Even citizens could do so only if they were in full possession
of their citizen rights. This difficulty has not escaped notice.
Clerc[5] advances the theory that a metic could prosecute a
public offender only when he himself was personally wronged.
As a case in point, he cites the prosecution of Stephanus for
false imprisonment as an adulterer by Epainetus of Andros.[6]

[1] ii. 145.

[2] *Op. cit.*, pp. 213 f.

[3] *Const. Antiqu.*, p. 303.

[4] *Ath. Pol.* xliii. 5 (trans. Kenyon).

[5] *Les Métèques athéniens*, pp. 113 f.

[6] Demos. lix. 64 ff.; cf. Hommel, in Pauly-Wissowa, *s.v.* "Metoikoi."

Perhaps Lysias, who prosecuted Eratosthenes on his audit, may be classed here because of the judicial murder of his brother by the Thirty.[1] But it is quite unlikely that there could be a sufficient number of such metics to warrant a charge of sycophancy against three each year.

It may be suggested that in the informal procedure of a *probolé* a metic might be "presented" as a sycophant, even though he was not actually engaged in litigation. A metic like Melas the Egyptian, as head of a group of sycophants,[2] might fall within the definition of a sycophant-agent and be liable for "presentation" without actually participating in a prosecution.

Sandys, in his note on the passage in Aristotle,[3] is of the opinion that a foreigner who desired to accuse anyone of an offense against the people was required to obtain special permission for that purpose from the proper authorities. But, as Lofberg points out,[4] the passages in Andocides upon which Sandys relies deal with immunity (ἄδεια). Such persons were really μηνυταί. A good example is Teucrus,[5] who turned state's evidence against those implicated with himself in the profanation of the Mysteries. In any event such cases could not have been frequent enough to produce sycophants of sufficient importance to rank with citizens. There were other ways of dealing more effectively with false informers.[6]

In a passage in Aristophanes there is a reference to prosecutors of some kind in the words:

---

[1] Lysias xii. Kahrstedt(*Studien zum Öff. Recht Athens*, I, 302) has some discussion of the metics and other aliens as prosecutors. The twelfth oration of Lysias does not fit into his theories, so he disposes of it as follows (p. 304, n. 1): The speech against Eratosthenes was written by Lysias for his *prostatés*. Afterward he published it as a "Broschüre" with such changes as were necessary to make it appear to be a speech of Lysias himself. This is a heroic measure for disposing of an inconvenient matter. Kahrstedt, moreover, offers no explanation of the importance of the metic as sycophant, unless he assumes that Aristotle (*Ath. Pol.* xliii. 5) is speaking of the time when in practice the *prostatés* had disappeared.

[2] Isaeus v. 19.   [3] *Ath. Pol.* xliii. 5.   [4] *Op. cit.*, p. 90.

[5] Andoc. i. 15: δευτέρα τοίνυν μήνυσις ἐγένετο. Τεῦκρος ἦν ἐνθάδε μέτοικος, ὃς ᾤχετο Μέγαράδε ὑπεξελθών, ἐκεῖθεν δὲ ἐπαγγέλλεται τῇ βουλῇ, εἴ οἱ ἄδειαν δοῖεν, μηνύσειν περὶ τῶν μυστηρίων, συνεργὸς ὤν.

[6] Dioclides was put to death (Andoc. i. 65–66).

ἐπὶ τοῖσιν ἀπράγμοσιν ὑμῶν
ἀντωμοσίας καὶ προσκλήσεις καὶ μαρτυρίας συνεκόλλων,
ὥστ' ἀναπηδᾶν δειμαίνοντας πολλοὺς ὡς τὸν πολέμαρχον.[1]

It is not easy to understand why citizens involved in litigation should rush to the polemarch for help,[2] and it is vain to
speculate on the kind of aid they sought. It seems best to let
the question rest. Lipsius[3] believes that in actual practice the
metic was permitted to prosecute wrongdoers without the
interference of a *prostatés*. Hommel goes even farther and
says that metics became so closely associated with the citizen
body "dass sich sogar die Sycophanten vielfach aus ihren
Reihen rekrutierten."[4] This seems to be the correct view. It
is quite natural, especially in the fourth century, that democracy should welcome aid from men who, though not citizens,
had long been resident in Athens. They fought the enemies
of Athens in the field: Why should they not be encouraged to
attack public wrongdoers in the courts?

It can be assumed that sycophants were "presented" only
once a year. If sycophants were such a curse as the reader of
the orators and Aristophanes is led to believe, why such restraint? Two reasons may be suggested. The principal one is
that a resolution regarding the alleged sycophancy of an individual was easy to put forward. No proof was needed, only
denunciations. There must have been many οὓς πάντες

---

[1] *Wasps* 1040–42.

[2] The commentators afford little or no aid. Blaydes is satisfied with quoting the
scholiast who adds nothing to Arist. *op. cit.* Van Leeuwen cites Aristotle and supposes that the harassed citizens are seeking aid against *peregrinos istos sophistas*,
without suggesting what sort of aid they sought. Whether they are called sophists
or sycophants is of little consequence. Without sophists there would have been few
sycophants. Rogers refuses to offer any explanation. Starkie, too, is at a loss, but
he conveniently cites several explanations offered which need not be repeated. He
is right in saying: "We must suppose that the ἀπράγμονες sought his help against
the alien sycophants." Lipsius (*op. cit.*, p. 64, n. 1) gives it up, but on p. 620, n. 1,
he says in reference to *Wasps* 1042: "Bei dem es doch am nächsten liegt, mit Römer
Studien zu Aristophanes S. 108 f. an eine γραφὴ ξενίας zu denken, mit der der
bedrängte Bürger sich gegen Sycophanten wehrt." In the time of Aristotle (*Ath.
Pol.* lix. 3) the thesmothetai introduced γραφαὶ ξενίας, but it may well have been
different in the fifth century. Cf. Lipsius, *op. cit.*, p. 86, who uses Aristophanes' evidence in assigning the suit to the *nautodikai*.

[3] *Op. cit.*, pp. 791 f.   [4] *Op. cit.*

ἤδεσαν ἐν τῇ δημοκρατίᾳ ἀπὸ συκοφαντίας ζῶντας, to quote the words of Xenophon in describing the sycophants executed by the Thirty.[1] The public approval with which these measures met[2] shows that if a general charge of sycophancy as distinguished from an indictment based upon a specific law could be made at will by interested persons in the assembly even once a prytany, there was grave danger that the public service would suffer. If a man received an adverse vote in the ecclesia, his usefulness as a prosecutor would be impaired if not ruined. If the resolution failed, the mover was free from any kind of punishment. Freedom of prosecution in Athens, like the freedom of the press in modern communities, could not be endangered.

The use of *eisangelia* against sycophants is attested by Isocrates only. The process was available in any "sovereign" assembly. No certain instances of its use against sycophants are known. Aristotle does not mention it as a proceeding to be used against sycophants. The Thirty, it is true, had sycophants tried by the boulé. The process was *eisangelia*, but the administration of justice at that time was far from normal.[3]

There are no certain instances of γραφὴ συκοφαντίας except in connection with *probolé* in the cases of Callixenus *et al.* and Agoratus.[4] It is known that Aristogiton was once condemned for sycophancy: τί γὰρ ἂν γένοιτο συκοφαντίας καὶ παρανομίας δεινότερον, ἐφ' οἷς ἀμφοτέροις οὗτος ὤφληκεν;[5] There is no mention of the kind of process used, but the word ὤφληκεν affords a slight clue. It clearly implies a court action, viz., a γραφὴ συκοφαντίας. The close relationship between *probolai* and *graphai* perhaps explains the remark of Pollux: προβολαὶ δὲ ἦσαν καὶ αἱ τῆς συκοφαντίας γραφαί.[6] The *probolé* was a test of public sentiment. If it was unfavorable to the accused, an indictment and regular trial followed at the option of the pros-

---

[1] *Hell.* ii. 3. 12.

[2] *Ibid.* and Arist. *Ath. Pol.* xxxv. 2–3.

[3] Xen. *Hell.* ii. 3. 12: καὶ ἥ τε βουλὴ ἡδέως αὐτῶν κατεψηφίζετο. Cf. *supra*, I, 332.

[4] Xen. *Hell.* i. 7. 35; Lysias xiii. 65.

[5] Demos. xxv. 19.   [6] viii. 46.

ecutor. In exceptional cases a ψήφισμα might be introduced providing for a trial.

Pollux mentions "denunciation" (φάσις) as a process used against sycophants.[1] It at once arouses suspicion. Lofberg[2] suggests that "it was probably employed against those who made a business of attacking merchants and traders by bringing φάσεις against them." This is in agreement with the view of Lipsius.[3] The explanation may lie in the desire to protect commerce and mining by allowing the use of a process that brought some profit to the successful prosecutor of this type of sycophant, the half of the fine levied. But it is a matter for suspicion that Isocrates[4] did not add it in his list of processes against sycophants. It would have strengthened his argument. That special care was taken to protect merchants and shipowners from sycophants is shown by the laws cited in *Epichares* v. *Theocrines*.[5] The text of the law is not preserved, but the speaker discusses it at some length. It was aimed at those who "presented" merchants and shipowners. The law absolutely forbade one to "present" (φαίνειν) a merchant or shipowner: εἰ μὴ πιστεύει τις αὐτῷ δείξειν ἐν ὑμῖν γεγενημένα περὶ ὧν ποιεῖται τὴν φάσιν· ἐὰν δέ τις παρὰ ταῦτα ποιῇ τῶν συκοφαντούντων, ἔνδειξιν αὐτῶν εἶναι καὶ ἀπαγωγήν. The only proof of sycophancy in this type of case would be the failure to persuade at least one-fifth of the jury. If a prosecutor took action immediately after the counting of the votes, the alleged culprit could be arrested summarily (ἀπαγωγή) as one caught in the act. If there was any delay, the prosecutor must then proceed by ἔνδειξις.[6] The penalty would in all probability be determined by the jury in addition to the penalty of one thousand drachmas:

ὅτι δ'οὐ ταῖς χιλίαις μόνον ἔνοχός ἐστιν ἀλλὰ καὶ ἀπαγωγῇ καὶ τοῖς ἄλλοις, ὅσα κελεύει πάσχειν ὁ νόμος οὑτοσὶ τὸν συκοφαντοῦντα τοὺς ἐμπόρους καὶ τοὺς ναυκλήρους, ῥᾳδίως ἐξ αὐτοῦ τοῦ νόμου γνώσεσθε.[7]

[1] viii. 47.

[2] *Op. cit.*, p. 92.

[3] *Op. cit.*, p. 314.

[4] xv. 314.

[5] Demos. lviii. 10–11.

[6] Pollux viii. 49; cf. Lipsius, *op. cit.*, p. 329.

[7] Demos. lviii. 10.

In the nature of the case sycophants could rarely avail themselves of δίκαι. But there are some examples, such as the case of Callimachus in Isocrates.[1] He brought a charge of homicide against an opponent. The case failed utterly when the woman alleged to have been slain was produced alive in court. Another suit for manslaughter prosecuted by an alleged sycophant was that of the choregus in Antiphon.[2] A client of Lysias[3] was charged before the Areopagus with wounding with intent to kill on what were claimed to be very trivial grounds. A similar case is dealt with in the third oration of Lysias. But neither of these cases is conclusive. In *Theomnestus* v. *Stephanus* the plaintiff recalls that the defendant brought a charge of homicide against the notorious Apollodorus. His account of it is as follows:

> He wished to drive Apollodorus into exile from his country. He brought a false charge against him, that he had once gone to Aphidna in search of a runaway slave that belonged to him, and that he had there given a blow to a woman, and that she had died of it; and he suborned some slaves and got them to represent that they were Cyrenaeans, and gave notice to Apollodorus to appear on a charge of murder in the court of Palladium. And Stephanus conducted the prosecution, and affirmed on oath that Apollodorus had killed the woman with his own hand, imprecating destruction upon himself and his race and his house, affirming facts which never took place, and which he never saw nor heard from any human being.[4]

In Isaeus the claimant to an estate is said to have "acted at the instigation of Melas, the Egyptian whose advice he followed in everything."[5] Presumably Melas was to receive a share of the estate for his services. This may be inferred from the speaker's statement that some friends never received from Dicaeogenes "money they had lent him, others were deceived by him and did not receive what he had promised to give them if he should have the estate adjudicated to

---

[1] xviii. 52.   [2] vi.   [3] iv.

[4] Demos. lix. 9 ff. (trans. Kennedy).

[5] v. 7-9, 40. Melas was probably a resident alien; cf. Wyse, *The Speeches of Isaeus*, p. 415.

him." Perhaps the wrongdoing of Melas and other friends of the claimant consisted in perjury only.[1]

The encouragement of strife and litigation is injurious to the public interests. One count in the indictment of the sycophant is that he was responsible for unnecessary litigation. In the *Son of Tisias* v. *Callicles* the plaintiff claims that his opponent is a sycophant.[2] In all probability Callicles had merely shown himself resourceful in finding various causes of action against the son of Tisias for the purpose of ruining him and getting possession of his farm. He was assisted by claims put forward by Callicrates and a cousin. Such a man was doubtless, in the words of the speaker, "a bad and grasping neighbor,"[3] but scarcely a sycophant in any reasonable legal sense of the word.

The laws against sycophants had to be set in motion by volunteer prosecutors. Naturally, the victims of sycophants would be the first to avail themselves of these laws for their own protection unless they happened to be peaceable (ἀπράγμονες) men who shrank from litigation and preferred to pay for protection. In the *Memorabilia*,[4] Xenophon has preserved an instructive account of how Crito, upon the advice of Socrates, availed himself of the services of Archedemus, who, like a modern lawyer, proceeded to attack the sycophants with their own weapons to the great advantage of Crito and those of his friends who employed Archedemus.

> I remember that he once heard Crito say that life at Athens was difficult for a man who wanted to mind his own business. "At this moment," Crito added, "actions are pending against me not because I have done the plaintiffs an injury, but because they think that I would sooner pay than have trouble."

---

[1] One is inevitably reminded of the common-law crimes of champerty and maintenance. "Maintenance is the officious intermeddling in a suit that in no way belongs to one by maintaining or assisting either party with money or otherwise to prosecute or defend it"; "Champerty is a bargain with a plaintiff or a defendant to divide the land or other matter sued for between them if they prevail at law, whereupon the champertor is to carry on the party's suit at his own expense" (Clark, *Criminal Law*, p. 322).

[2] Demos. lv. 1–2.

[3] In § 31 he is said to have forged a document.   [4] ii. 9.

"Tell me, Crito," said Socrates, "do you keep dogs to fend the wolves from your sheep?"

"Certainly," replied Crito, "because it pays me better to keep them."

"Then why not keep a man who may be able and willing to fend off the attempts to injure you?"

"I would gladly do so were I not afraid that he might turn on me."

"What? don't you see that it is much pleasanter to profit by humoring a man like you than by quarrelling with him? I assure you there are men in this city who would take pride in your friendship."

Thereupon they sought out Archedemus, an excellent speaker and man of affairs, but poor. For he was not one of those who make money unscrupulously, but an honest man, and he would say that it was easy to take forfeit from false accusers. . . . . He soon found out that Crito's false accusers [τῶν συκοφαντούντων τὸν Κρίτωνα] had much to answer for and many enemies. He brought one of them to trial on a charge involving damages or imprisonment. The defendant, conscious that he was guilty on many counts, did all he could to get quit of Archedemus. But Archedemus refused to let him off until he withdraw the action against Crito and compensated him. Archedemus carried through several other enterprises of a similar kind; and now many of Crito's friends begged him to make Archedemus their protector, just as when a shepherd has a good dog the other shepherds want to pen their flocks near his, in order to get use of his dog. Archedemus was glad to humor Crito, and so there was peace not only for Crito but for his friends as well.[1]

[1] *Ibid.* (trans. Marchant).

CHAPTER IV

SPECIAL PLEAS

When a defendant appeared before the magistrate, judicial official, or board and joined issue with the plaintiff on the merits of the case, the proceeding was known as εὐθυδικία.[1] If, however, the defendant claimed that in law the issue was not actionable (μὴ εἰσαγώγιμον εἶναι τὴν δίκην), he was privileged to enter a special plea which, in fourth-century practice at least, was tried separately.[2] Special pleas and de-

---

[1] Isaeus vi. 3; vii. 3; Demos. xxxiv. 4.

[2] Doubtless the judicial official or board before whom the case was brought had the right to refuse to take the case to court if for good and sufficient reasons it was not deemed εἰσαγώγιμος; cf. Lipsius, *Das Attische Recht*, pp. 819, 845; *supra*, I, 289. The basis upon which a magistrate could summarily reject a plaint has been well stated by Calhoun, *CP*, XIV, 343-44: "The magistrate knows the laws governing the admissibility of actions, for he is in possession of official copies. That is to say, he knows what several actions fall within his jurisdiction, the times at which they may properly be instituted, and the persons in whom the right of action is reposed as well as the issues of fact that may properly be raised by the plaintiff's declaration in each several action. These laws he applies to facts of which he takes judicial notice, or those which appear on the face of the complaint, or are conclusively established by admissions of the plaintiff, or by the plaintiff's refusal to plead. If any of these facts, so established, constitutes a bar to the admissibility of the action, he has no choice but to dismiss the suit at whatever point in the proceedings its inadmissibility is established. But if its inadmissibility is not so established, and an issue of fact is properly tendered by the plaintiff, the magistrate cannot dismiss the action." There is no good ground for supposing, as Calhoun does (p. 340, n. 1) that a magistrate would reject a complaint because it was barred by the "statute of limitations." The claim of Apollodorus against Phormio was outlawed, yet it came to trial even in the face of the opposition of Phormio (Demos. xxxvi, 26-27).

There is one recorded case in which the king archon rejected a charge of murder, not because it did not come within his jurisdiction but because it was so late in the year that there was not time enough to hold the three προδικασίαι which, according to law, must be held a month apart (Antiph. vi. 38, 42). The plaintiff complained but took no action: καὶ ὅτι οὐκ ἠδίκει αὐτούς, μέγιστον σημεῖον· Φιλοκράτης γὰρ οὑτοσὶ ἑτέρους τῶν ὑπευθύνων ἔσειε καὶ ἐσυκοφάντει, τούτου δὲ τοῦ βασιλέως, ὅν φασι δεινὰ καὶ σχέτλια εἰργάσθαι, οὐκ ἦλθε κατηγορήσων εἰς τὰς εὐθύνας (*ibid*. 43).

It would also seem that if a complaint or indictment was not properly drawn, the magistrate could require it to be amended. In *Dionysius* v. *Agoratus*, an ἀπαγωγή before the Eleven, the plaintiff was required to insert the words ἐπ' αὐτοφώρῳ in the indictment. If he had refused, it is manifest that the Eleven would not have

murrers of English law and *exceptio fori* of Roman law were in Attic law variously denominated as ἀντιγραφή, παραγραφή, and διαμαρτυρία. Early in the fourth century ἀντιγραφή disappeared from Athenian practice, and the διαμαρτυρία was used only in inheritance cases, while παραγραφή was used for all other cases. In the following pages an attempt is made to trace the earlier history of these pleas and describe their working in practice.

In the scanty records of fifth-century litigation there are no certain references to special pleas of any kind. In a speech of Isocrates which Blass puts in the year 399 B.C.,[1] the διαμαρτυρία is mentioned as a procedure quite familiar to the dicasts.[2]

The procedure in a *diamartyria* was as follows.[3] If the defendant pleaded that the case was not actionable, the prosecutor had the right to put forward a witness to support his claim that the case was actionable. The defendant must now prosecute the witness for perjury. If he succeeded, the plaintiff might be totally debarred or compelled to change his procedure or his plaint. If the witness was acquitted, the original case as filed went to trial. This type of procedure is well illustrated in *Aristodicus* v. *Pancleon*.[4] Aristodicus brought action against Pancleon before the polemarch. The nature of the case is unknown. In his rejoinder the defendant pleaded that since he was a Plataean and consequently in

---

accepted the indictment (Lysias xiii. 85–87; Lipsius, *op. cit.*, p. 819; Calhoun, *op. cit.*, pp. 342–43). In a claim for an estate the speaker was obliged in the *anakrisis* to add to his pleading that his mother was the sister of the testator. Otherwise it seems his claim would have been rejected. In this way he claimed the estate not as the grandson of Aristarchus I, the testator, but as the nephew of Aristarchus II, who was in possession (Isaeus x. 2; cf. Wyse, *The Speeches of Isaeus*, p. 651; Lipsius, *op. cit.*, p. 819, n. 55; Calhoun, *op. cit.*, p. 343).

[1] Isoc. xviii; it has been variously dated from 403 to 397 B.C.: cf. Blass, *Attische Beredsamkeit*, II, 214; Jebb, *Attic Orators*, II, 235.

[2] For the moment the date of the διαμαρτυρία is postponed.

[3] The fullest account is found in Harpocration, *s.v.* διαμαρτυρία; cf. Wyse, *op. cit.*, pp. 233 ff.

[4] The unknown speaker of Lysias xxiii, entitled κατὰ Παγκλέωνος ὅτι οὐκ ἦν Πλαταιεύς, gives an account in §§ 13–14 of a previous suit brought by Aristodicus against Pancleon and tells the result.

possession of Athenian citizen rights the case should not come before the polemarch. Aristodicus thereupon produced a witness who testified that Pancleon was not a Plataean. Pancleon denounced the witness (ἐπισκηψάμενος) but did not prosecute him. Consequently the case was tried before the polemarch. The plaintiff won the suit.

An example of the opposite type of proceeding where the defendant supported his plea by a witness is found in Isocrates.[1] Callimachus brought action against the speaker as being responsible for the confiscation of a sum of money by the Ten who succeeded the Thirty. The speaker agreed to settle the case by the payment of two minas. The agreement was sanctioned in a δίαιτα ἐπὶ ῥητοῖς. Such an arbitration was as binding as any other and rendered the matter *res judicata*. Callimachus, disregarding this legal settlement, again sued the speaker, who pleaded the arbitration in bar of action and supported his rejoinder by a witness. Callimachus did not denounce or prosecute the witness. The case was in consequence dismissed but in some to us unknown fashion he re-entered the same suit (πείσας δὲ τὴν ἀρχὴν πάλιν τὴν αὐτὴν δίκην ἐγράψατο).[2] The defendant met the new action by pleading that it was contrary to the amnesty, and entered a *paragraphé* according to the recent law of Archinus: ἄν τις δικάζηται παρὰ τοὺς ὅρκους, ἐξεῖναι τῷ φεύγοντι παραγράψασθαι, τοὺς δὲ ἄρχοντας περὶ τούτου πρῶτον εἰσάγειν, λέγειν δὲ πρότερον τὸν παραγραψάμενον.[3] The *paragraphé* was tried separately and the defendant spoke first.

This is one of the earliest if not the first case that came under the law of Archinus, as is indicated by the opening words of the speaker:

εἰ μὲν καὶ ἄλλοι τινὲς ἦσαν ἠγωνισμένοι τοιαύτην παραγραφήν, ἀπ' αὐτοῦ τοῦ πράγματος ἠρχόμην ἂν τοὺς λόγους ποιεῖσθαι· νῦν δὲ ἀνάγκη περὶ τοῦ νόμου πρῶτον εἰπεῖν καθ' ὃν εἰσεληλύθαμεν, ἵν' ἐπιστάμενοι περὶ ὧν ἀμφισβητοῦμεν τὴν ψῆφον φέρητε, καὶ μηδεὶς ὑμῶν θαυμάσῃ, διότι φεύγων τὴν δίκην πρότερος λέγω τοῦ διώκοντος.[4]

[1] xviii. 11.   [3] Isoc. xviii. 2.
[2] *Ibid.* 12; cf. Lipsius, *op. cit.*, p. 857, n. 41.   [4] *Ibid.* 1.

The law belongs to the archonship of Euclides, 403/2 B.C.[1]
It has been pointed out that the words τοιαύτην παραγραφήν
(this kind of *paragraphé*), as used by Isocrates, indicate that
a *paragraphé* is not a novelty to the dicasts.[2] The novelties
are the reversal of the order of the speeches and the application of a *paragraphé* to cases brought contrary to the amnesty
in the opinion of the defendant. There is no reference to a
paragraphé before Isocrates' speech against Callimachus, but
this does not prove that it did not occur. In the Herodes
murder case in Antiphon, about 416 B.C., the defendant argues that he should not be tried as a κακοῦργος before the
Eleven but as a homicide in the Palladium.[3] Although the
technical argument is treated separately in the speech from
the proof of his innocence, this does not amount to a special
plea argued before the main issue was tried. But the resem-
blance struck the author of the Hypothesis, who says the
defendant τὸ μὲν τῆς κακουργίας ἔγκλημα ἀπολύεται παραγρα-
φικῶς. This case does not prove that *paragraphé* did not exist
at this time. It merely indicates that it would not be used in
endeixis.[4]

Some time in the early part of the fourth century the
paragraphé used in amnesty cases was extended to practically
all civil suits, with the exception of cases involving the
devolution of estates in which a special plea was still managed
by *diamartyria*. All special pleas in the speeches in the Demosthenic corpus, with the exception of an inheritance case,
are *paragraphai*. A different type of special plea called
ἀντιγραφή is found in the Pancleon case of Lysias.[5] The speaker summoned Pancleon as Aristodicus had previously done[6]
before the polemarch. Pancleon entered a demurrer, an *ex-*

---

[1] Cf. Lipsius, *op. cit.*, p. 846.

[2] Calhoun, *CP*, XIII, 170.

[3] Antiph. v. 8 ff., 16, 95–96.

[4] Calhoun, *op. cit.*, pp. 170 ff.

[5] Lysias xxiii. The speech is of uncertain date, but must belong to the fourth
century. It in all probability antedates the extension of *paragraphé* to other than
amnesty cases. Wilamowitz (*Aristoteles und Athen*, II, 368 ff.) has shown that this
speech is genuine and has analyzed it in a very satisfactory manner.

[6] *Ibid.* 13–14.

ceptio fori, called ἀντιγραφή.[1] The plaintiff spoke first and devoted his speech entirely to proving that Pancleon was not a Plataean. Not a word is said about the main issue, which is quite distinct as the words τῆς τε ἀντιγραφῆς ἕνεκα ταυτησὶ καὶ αὐτῆς τῆς δίκης show. It has been noted that in this speech alone in Lysias the speaker when introducing a witness always says καί μοι ἐπίλαβε τὸ ὕδωρ. This would seem to indicate that the time allowed for the speech was quite brief.[2]

Aside from *Aristodicus* v. *Pancleon*[3] and the *diamartyria* referred to in the Callimachus case of Isocrates,[4] there are no examples of *diamartyria* except in inheritance cases. The *paragraphé* of Archinus was apparently extended to all civil cases except devolution of estates, ἐπιδικασίαι or διαδικασίαι κλήρου. For such cases a *diamartyria* (oath by a witness) to the effect that μὴ ἐπίδικον εἶναι τὸν κλῆρον ὄντων παίδων γνησίων[5] was particularly effective. If the witness was acquitted of perjury, the claimants of necessity abandoned their pretentions and the child or children remained in possession.[6] This applied not only to the present claimants but to future claimants. This was a simple and convenient process in a *diadikasia* where several claimants who based their claims on different grounds might appear. Under these circumstances it seems likely that the convenience and practical advantages to be derived from *diamartyria* rather than any legal requirement determined its use in inheritance cases.[7] So far as the *paragraphé* is concerned, no one with any familiarity with litigation would have used it to protect himself in the possession of an estate against several claimants. In a *diadikasia* there are, strictly speaking, neither plaintiffs nor defendants. Consequently even if the law permitted a *paragraphé* the pro-

---

[1] *Ibid.* 10; cf. 5: ἐπειδὴ δέ μοι αὐτὴν ἀντεγράψατο μὴ εἰσαγώγιμον εἶναι.

[2] Cf. Wilamowitz, *op. cit.*

[3] Lysias xxiii. 13–14; cf. *supra*, pp. 76 f.

[4] xviii. 11; cf. *supra*, p. 77. [5] Demos. xliv. 46.

[6] Cf. Calhoun, *op. cit.*, pp. 176–77.

[7] *Ibid.*, p. 178, n. 1, as against Leisi, *Der Zeuge*, p. 29, and Beauchet, *Histoire du droit privé de la République athénienne*, III, 596, n. 2.

cedure would be tedious and the result might be inconclusive.[1]

It would seem reasonable to suppose that special pleas argued separately would be as desirable in criminal as in civil cases. Such was the view expressed by Meier-Schömann-Lipsius in *Der Attische Process*.[2] The only evidence cited for this view is the reference to a *graphé* in Harpocration, *s.v.* διαμαρτυρία: οἱ νόμοι κελεύουσι διαμαρτυρεῖν ἐπὶ ταῖς γραφαῖς ταῖς τοῦ ἀπροστασίου τὸν βουλόμενον ὁμοίως τῶν ξένων καὶ τῶν ἐπιχωρίων. Glotz accepts this view without discussion.[3] Lipsius was the first to doubt the occurrence of either *diamartyria* or *paragraphé* in public cases.[4] But he merely gives the reasons for his doubts without attempting to settle the question. But Calhoun[5] has made it quite clear that the law of Archinus did not apply to criminal cases. Much weight is given to the fact that the terminology of the law of Archinus is applicable only to civil suits. In the section of this law cited by Isocrates,[6] which seems to be a genuine quotation,[7] two words occur which in a law could refer only to a civil process. They are δικάζηται[8] and ἐπωβελία. If either party lost a *paragraphé* he forfeited to his opponent one-sixth of the amount at issue. In a public suit this *poena temere ligantium* took the form of a fine of one thousand drachmas and denial of the right to bring a similar *graphé*, *endeixis*, *apagogé*, etc., in the future if the prosecutor failed to obtain at least one-fifth of the votes.[9]

---

[1] Cf. Calhoun, *op. cit.*, pp. 176 f., for the difficulty if not the impossibility of using a *paragraphé* in an inheritance case. There is, however, a possibility that if, at a subsequent time, a claimant appeared and sued for an estate settled by a *diamartyria*, a *paragraphé* might be the simplest way of handling the case. It would be a choice between another *diamartyria* with the attendant risks and a *paragraphé* pleading the previous acquittal of the witness in bar of action; cf. *ibid.*, p. 173, n. 10.

[2] P. 841.

[3] Darem.-Saglio, *s.v.* "Paragraphé."   [5] *Op. cit.*, pp. 179 ff.

[4] *Op. cit.*, p. 858.   [6] xviii. 2, quoted *supra*, p. 77.

[7] Cf. Calhoun, *op. cit.*, p. 170; Hommel, *Berl. Phil. Woch.*, XLIV, 541.

[8] Calhoun, *op. cit.*, p. 183, n. 4; Hommel, *op. cit.*, p. 543.

[9] Lipsius, *op. cit.*, p. 940.

It is significant that in the records of litigation there is no instance of *paragraphé* in a public suit.[1] Andocides does not resort to a *paragraphé* though he appeals to the spirit of the amnesty. After praising the moderation of the citizens in the amnesty which both friends and foes recognized, he asks not as a right but as a favor that they deal with his case in the same spirit: μὴ μεταγνῶτε, μηδὲ βούλεσθε τὴν πόλιν ἀποστερῆσαι ταύτης τῆς δόξης.[2] Agoratus[3] without doubt appeals to the amnesty in his defense against an *apagogé* for homicide. "I understand," says the prosecutor, "that he intends to refer to the oaths and agreements, and will tell us that his prosecution is a violation of the oaths and agreements that we of the Piraeus contracted with the party of the town." The fact that the prosecutor speaks first, however, shows that Agoratus did not resort to the *paragraphé* provided by the law of Archinus. In spite of the sophistical arguments of the prosecutor[4] to the contrary, Agoratus should have been protected by the amnesty.[5] In the *dokimasia* cases in Lysias[6] there is only one direct reference to the amnesty. The accuser of Evandros[7] says that he hears that Evandros καὶ τὰς συνθήκας ὑμᾶς ὑπομνήσειν. In Lysias xxxi there is no direct mention of the amnesty but merely the vaguest reference to the spirit of reconciliation.

The case of Philo of Coele shows how criminal cases, brought into court contrary to the amnesty, were handled: ἐνδειχθέντα παραπρεσβεύεσθαι, καὶ περὶ μὲν τοῦ πράγματος οὐδὲν ἔχοντα ἀπολογήσασθαι, τὰς δὲ συνθήκας παρεχόμενον, ἔδοξεν ὑμῖν ἀφεῖναι καὶ μηδὲ κρίσιν περὶ αὐτοῦ ποιήσασθαι.[8] Philo did not deny the facts but merely claimed the protection of the

---

[1] For the moment the discussion of *diamartyria* in public suits is deferred.

[2] Andoc. i. 140. [3] Lysias xiii. 88. [4] *Ibid.* 88–89.

[5] Cf. Frohberger-Thalheim (*Lysias Reden*, I, 73–74), who admits the applicability of the amnesty but believes that he might have entered a *paragraphé*.

[6] xvi, xxv, xxvi, xxxi; cf. Cloché, *REG*, XXIX, 24–25. [7] xxvi. 16.

[8] Isoc. xviii. 22. ἔνδειξις here is used in a general sense of "indictment" (Lipsius, *op. cit.*, p. 335, n. 65). Normally a case of παραπρεσβεία would come to the thesmothetai from the *euthynai*, if the system of *euthyna* described by Aristotle (*Ath. Pol.* xlviii. 3–5) was in force at the time (Lipsius, *op. cit.*, p. 398, n. 88).

amnesty and was discharged without trial. It is hard to see just why the case ever came to court. The magistrates before whom such cases were filed had the power to refuse to accept them.[1] According to Andocides,[2] ἀγράφῳ δὲ νόμῳ τὰς ἀρχὰς μὴ χρῆσθαι μηδὲ περὶ ἑνός. As it did come to court, the probable procedure was as follows. The prosecutor made his charge and Philo replied that the charge was correct and claimed the protection of the amnesty which was granted by the court in some fashion that justified Isocrates in saying that there was no trial. In any event there was no *paragraphé* in which the accused spoke first.

It is not wise to pay too much attention to Andocides' discussion of the amnesty law. For example, he is manifestly wrong when he says that Meletus, who assisted in the arrest of Leon of Salamis, was safe from a charge of homicide or βούλευσις at the hands of the sons of Leon ὅτι τοῖς νόμοις δεῖ χρῆσθαι ἀπ᾿ Εὐκλείδου ἄρχοντος.[3] His immunity depended upon the fact that only those who murdered αὐτοχειρίᾳ could be tried for murder. It is also doubtful whether this law, as interpreted by Andocides, provided complete immunity for all offenses which antedated the restoration of democracy after the overthrow of the Thirty.[4] The case of Philo and the considerations drawn from the terminology of the law of Archinus are amply sufficient proof that *paragraphé* did not apply to public cases.[5]

The date of the introduction of *diamartyria* is undetermined. It was a well-known process at the time of the delivery of Isocrates' eighteenth speech and was undoubtedly older than the *paragraphé* of Archinus. In Isocrates xviii, where the *paragraphé* of Archinus is spoken of as a novelty to the dicasts, the procedure of *diamartyria* is quite familiar to them. This would seem to indicate that it was in use before the archonship of Euclides. Glotz,[6] speaking of the relative

---

[1] Cf. *supra*, p. 75, n. 2.   [2] i. 89.   [3] i. 94.

[4] Calhoun, *op. cit.*, pp. 181 f.; cf. Schreiner, *De corpore iuris Atheniensium*, pp. 92 ff.; Hommel, *op. cit.*, pp. 543 f.; Platner, *Process und Klagen*, I, 157.

[5] Cf. Hommel, *op. cit.*   [6] *Op. cit.*

antiquity of *paragraphé* and *diamartyria*, says: "Des deux procédures, la plus ancienne est celle de la διαμαρτυρία, qui semble une vague survivance de l'antique cojuration." This is a most attractive suggestion. We have in *diamartyria* one of the most striking survivals of compurgation to be found in Athenian law. It has some affinities with the evidentiary oath out of which it grew.[1] The evidentiary oath began as an exculpatory oath allowed to the defendant alone; soon it was allowed to the plaintiff as well. This feature appears in *diamartyria* also.[2] In *Aristodicus v. Pancleon*,[3] the plaintiff resorts to a *diamartyria;* in the Callimachus case[4] the defendant presents a witness. When *paragraphé* displaced *diamartyria* in all private suits except inheritance cases, in practice it is always the direct heirs who resort to a *diamartyria*. In theory there is no reason why the claimants might not each have a witness testify to the contrary—that the estate is subject to claim at law (ἐπίδικος) because there are no heirs. But such a proceeding would be cumbersome and would entail dangers for the witnesses and the claimants. We may be sure that it is not a matter of accident that in the records of inheritance cases there are no references to a *diamartyria* of claimants.

In addition to its use in inheritance cases, *diamartyria* continued to be used in public suits. Harpocration[5] speaks of *diamartyria* in connection with γραφαὶ ἀπροστασίου. This process was intended to punish a resident alien who had not registered his *prostatés* as the law required. Here ὁ διαμαρτυρῶν of the plaintiff might tesify that there had been no registration and the metic would have to prove his case by prosecuting the witness for perjury. The procedure puts the burden of proof upon the defendant, who now becomes the plaintiff. Presumably the defendant also had the right to put forward a witness to testify, for example, that he was not in

[1] On the analogy of διωμοσία, an oath taken by both parties at the *anakrisis*, διαμαρτυρία means a deposition that could be offered by both sides. It is nowhere said explicitly that the witness to a *diamartyria* was sworn, but it seems wholly improbable that such an important witness would not be sworn.

[2] Cf. *infra*, p. 190.   [3] Lysias xxiii. 13–14.   [4] Isoc. xviii. 11.

[5] *S.v.* διαμαρτυρία; cf. Wyse, *op. cit.*, pp. 233 ff.

fact a resident alien and consequently had done no wrong in
not registering a *prostatés*. We have a speech of Lysias entitled πρὸς τὴν ᾿Αριστοδήμου γραφὴν διαμαρτυρία.[1] Here obviously the *diamartyria* is that of the defendant to meet the
charge of Aristodemus.

More than one hundred types of suits, public and private,
are mentioned in the sources. These were distributed among
a dozen or more magistrates, judicial officials, and boards.
The distribution of suits has been worked out pretty satisfactorily in modern handbooks, but there are still difficulties.
The average Athenian citizen who as dicast, litigant, presiding officer, or spectator became more or less familiar with
procedure could easily, with the aid of friends and legal advisers,[2] select the right procedure. Mistakes in seeking the
proper court could be corrected by the officials who entered
cases for trial, but prosecutors might successfully insist, as in
the two cases against Pancleon,[3] and have the case filed as
they wished. In some cases the Athenian code offered a
choice of remedies for a grievance.

> Solon provided not one but many ways of proceeding against wrong-
> doers. . . . . Take theft for example. Are you able-bodied and confident
> in yourself? Take a thief to prison: but you risk the penalty of a thousand
> drachmas. Are you not strong? Take the magistrates with you; they will
> do it. Are you afraid of this too? Indict him. Do you distrust yourself
> and are you too poor to pay a thousand drachmas? Sue him for larceny
> before the arbitrator, and you will run no risk. None of these courses is
> the same. For impiety in like manner you may take to prison, indict, sue
> before the Eumolpids, or lay information before the king. And in all other
> cases the situation is much the same."[4]

A resourceful opponent was always ready to make capital
out of any false or unwise step on the part of a plaintiff or
prosecutor. "It is the practice with defendants," says Demosthenes,[5] "who have done wrong, in order to defeat
the proceedings against them, to suggest that some other
proceedings which are not practicable should have been
adopted." But he adds that sensible dicasts should pay no

---

[1] *Frag.* xv (Baiter and Sauppe).   [3] Cf. *infra*, pp. 110 f.

[2] Cf. *supra*, pp. 15 ff.   [4] Demos. xxii. 25 ff.   [5] xxi. 27.

attention to them. The extent to which defendants were willing to go in order to prejudice the dicasts against those who resorted to special pleas is well exemplified in two cases in the Demosthenic corpus. Lacritus, a merchant of Phaselis, demurred to a claim made by an Athenian moneylender that he was not liable for the money because there was no contractual relationship between himself and the plaintiff. The speech of the plaintiff who has become the defendant in a *paragraphé* opens as follows:

> The Phaselites are doing nothing new, men of Athens, only what they are in the habit of doing. They are famous people for borrowing money on your exchange, but when they have got it and have drawn up a maritime contract they immediately forget their contract and the laws, and consider that if they pay their debt it is like losing something of their own, and, instead of paying, they resort to sharp practices, special pleas, and excuses.[1]

This is mere denunciation. The whole case is weak, as the author of the hypothesis observes: πρὸς δὲ τὴν παραγραφὴν ἀσθενέστερον ἀπήντηκε διὰ τὸ πρᾶγμα τὸ πονηρόν. A similar denunciation against *diamartyria* is found in another speech attributed to Demosthenes:

> Of all methods of trial this by an exceptive affidavit [special plea] is the most unjust, and the parties who resort to it are most deserving of your displeasure, as you will clearly see by what I am about to say. In the first place, it is not necessary, as other processes are; it takes place only by the choice and desire of the party who swears the affidavit. If there is no other way of getting judgment upon disputed claims, unless you swear an affidavit of this sort, perhaps it is necessary to swear one. But, if it is possible to obtain a hearing before all tribunals without an exceptive affidavit, is not such a step a mark of recklessness and complete desperation? The legislator did not make it obligatory upon the contending parties; he allowed them to put in an exceptive affidavit, if they pleased, as if he were putting our several characters to proof, to see how far we are inclined to a reckless course of action. Observe also: if parties putting in these special pleas had their way, there would be neither courts of justice nor causes for them to try; for it is of the very essence of exceptive affidavits to put a stop to all proceedings, and to prevent questions being brought before the court; such at least is the intention of the parties who swear them. Therefore, I consider that such persons should be regarded as the common enemies of all.[2]

---

[1] Demos. xxxv. 1 ff.   [2] xliv. 57 ff.; cf. Isaeus iii. 3; vi. 43.

In the cases of Isaeus, *diamartyria* is a common proceed-ing. In one case a preposterous objection to a *diamartyria* is made:

Androcles here put in a protestation declaring that the succession was not adjudicable, thus depriving my client of his right to claim the estate and you of your right to decide who ought to be declared heir to Philocte-mon's property. He thus thinks by a single verdict and by a single suit to establish as brothers of the deceased men who have no sort of connexion with him, to place himself in possession of the estate without further legal procedure, to become the legal representative of the sister of the deceased.[1]

It so happens that we know that Chaerestratus, the claimant who uttered these words, did not win his case. In an inscrip-tion of the period he is described as the "son of Phanostra-tus," whereas if he had won he would have been described as Χαιρέστρατος Φιλοκτήμονος Κηφισιεύς.[2]

There are indications that a litigant who used a special plea felt that it was desirable to defend his action. In the Pantaenetus case[3] the speaker says that if he had failed to resort to a special plea his opponent would have been enabled to respond that if there had actually been a discharge and quittance the defendant would undoubtedly have entered a special plea.

In the second oration of Isaeus Menecles II is represented as defending his father-in-law against a charge of perjury for evidence given by the latter in Menecles' previous *dia-martyria*. There is, however, nowhere in the speech any sign or hint that the speaker felt there was any prejudice against a *diamartyria*. We may assume, then, that *diamartyria* was a normal procedure in inheritance cases and that in spite of occasional criticisms on the part of prosecutors of witnesses there is no evidence that the dicasts were in any way prej-udiced against a *diamartyria*.

The law looked with disfavor, however, upon demurrers and special pleas that were not well founded. Reckless use of them was discouraged by the imposition of substantial finan-

[1] Isaeus vi. 4.

[2] *IG²*, II, 2825. 11; cf. Wyse, *op. cit.*, p. 488.   [3] Demos. xxxvii. 1.

cial penalties. In inheritance cases contestants for an estate
had to deposit a sum of money (παρακαταβολή) amounting to
one-tenth of the value of the estate which in case of failure
was forfeit to the state.[1] In a *diamartyria*, if the prosecutor of
the witness failed to obtain at least one-fifth of the votes he
forfeited one-sixth of the amount claimed (ἐπωβελία). In case
of mere failure to convict, i.e., to obtain one-half or more
votes, he lost his deposit and fees. There is no indication that
the litigant whose witness was convicted had to pay the
ἐπωβελία.[2] In a *paragraphé*, whichever litigant lost his case
forfeited the ἐπωβελία.[3] The purpose of this unique provision
was at the same time to discourage the bringing of suits that
could be thrown out on a technicality, and also the resort to
a *paragraphé*. To balance this risk the litigant who entered a
paragraphé had the advantage of speaking first. In a *diamartyria* in inheritance suits where the heir in possession produced a witness that the estate was not ἐπίδικος the claimant
spoke first. In other cases of *diamartyria* if the plaintiff put
forward a witness the defendant spoke first.[4]

In all cases of *paragraphé* in the orators the speaker in-
variably argues the whole case as if he were afraid to rest his
case on the special plea. This situation is due in part to the
Athenian judicial system where there was no separation of
the law from the facts. The legal maxim *ad quaestionem juris
non respondent juratores: ad quaestionem facti non respondent
judices* did not hold in Athens where the dicasts were both

---

[1] Wyse, *op. cit.*, p. 374. Lipsius (*op. cit.*, p. 857) says it went to the winner of
the case, but on p. 933 he leaves it uncertain.

[2] Lipsius, *op. cit.*, p. 858, n. 41.   [3] Isoc. xviii. 2–3.

[4] It is generally assumed that the litigant who first got the ear of the jury had
an advantage. The oath of the dicasts to hear both sides impartially was intended
to check the tendency of the dicasts to give more heed to the prosecutor or plaintiff;
cf. Demos. xlv. 6: "He got the advantage of the opening speech, by reason of there
having been a special plea [*paragraphé*] and the case not coming to trial upon the
general issue; then, having read these pieces of evidence, and having made a variety
of misrepresentations to suit his case, he made such an impression on the jury, that
they would not hear me speak a single word." But some people are more impressed
by the last speaker; cf. Aristoph. *Knights* 1118, πρὸς τόν τε λέγοντ' ἀεὶ κέχηνας, and
Wasps 725, "'Twas a very acute and intelligent man, whoever it was, that happened
to say, 'Don't make up your mind till you've heard both sides.'"

juratores and *judices*. In *Apollodorus* v. *Phormio*[1] the defendant pleads that the case is not ἀγώγιμος because Apollodorus
had long ago given him a release and discharge of all and
sundry claims. A bench of judges might, after examining the
arbitration agreement and decision of the arbitrators, have
dismissed the case without more ado. But in Athens the case
had to come before a dicastery where a litigant found it difficult to confine himself to the special plea even if the grounds
on which it was based could be easily separated from the
issues of fact in the long and complicated relationship between Phormio and the family of Pasion. The author of the
hypothesis observes this feature of the case: ἅπτεται μέντοι
καὶ τῆς εὐθείας ὁ ῥήτωρ, δεικνὺς ὡς οὐκ εἶχεν ἡ τράπεζα χρήματα
ἴδια τοῦ Πασίωνος. τοῦτο δὲ πεποίηκεν, ἵνα ἡ παραγραφὴ μᾶλλον
ἰσχύῃ, τῆς εὐθείας δεικνυμένης τῷ 'Απολλοδώρῳ σαθρᾶς. It is to
be noted that Demosthenes, who composed the speech for
Phormio, explains and virtually apologizes for the special
plea: "We have put in the special plea to the action, not for
the sake of evasion and delay, but in order that, if the defendant can show by the facts that he has committed no
wrong, he may obtain in this court a final acquittal."[2] Not
only this, but he adds an elaborate explanation and justification of the law upon which the *paragraphé* is based:

You hear, men of Athens, the law mentioning among other matters for
which there shall be no right of action those of which a man has given a
release or discharge. And with reason, for if it is just that men shall not
bring fresh actions for causes that have once been tried it is far juster that
there shall be no action for claims which have been released. For a man
who has lost his cause by your verdict may possibly say that you were
deceived, but when a man has plainly decided against himself and given a
release and discharge what complaint can he prefer against himself to
entitle him to sue over again for the same matter? None surely. Therefore the framer of the statute among the cases in which there is to be no

[1] Demos. xxxvi.

[2] *Ibid.* 2. Under similar circumstances another client of Demosthenes antici-
pates possible objections as follows: "However, that none of you, men of Athens,
may suppose that I have recourse to this plea [demurrer] because I have the worst of
it on the merits of my case, I will proceed to show you that every particular of his
charge against me is false" (xxxvii. 21).

right of action first mentions those in which a man has given a release and a discharge.[1]

In this case we happen to know the result. Apollodorus created such a bad impression on the jury that he failed to obtain one-fifth of the votes and forfeited the ἐπωβελία. This information we obtain from a suit for perjury launched by Apollodorus against Stephanus, a witness for Phormio.[2] It is impossible to determine whether the special pleas or the merits of the case weighed most with the jury, but it is evident there could have been little or no prejudice against a *paragraphé* when four-fifths of the dicasts voted for Phormio. Apollodorus himself seems to have thought that he lost the case because of the *paragraphé*, if we may trust a statement of his in the perjury case against Stephanus: "He got the advantage of the opening speech by reason of there having been a special plea and the case not coming to trial on the general issue."[3] Demosthenes, who wrote the speech, did not shirk the special plea.[4] Apollodorus himself, without censure or comment, recognizes the fact that dicasts expect the whole case to be discussed: "I think, men of Athens, you are all aware, that it is your practice to look at the facts of the case as much as at the pleas which are pleaded about them."[5]

There seems to have been a reluctance on the part of litigants and their advisers to rest a special plea upon the statute of limitations alone. In all extant cases where it is pleaded there is always another reason for a special plea. For example, in *Apollodorus* v. *Phormio* the defendant pleaded not only that the claim had been outlawed but that it had been settled by arbitration. It is perhaps significant that we have in this speech a most admirable exposition of the need of statutes of limitations.

---

[1] xxxvi. 25.   [2] Demos. xlv. 6.

[3] *Ibid.;* there is implied criticism also in the words of Apollodorus in xlv. 76: "This really is the strangest thing. To this day he has never chosen to account to me for the money which he has defrauded me of, but pleads that my actions are not maintainable."

[4] The following sections deal with it: 14–16, 23–27, and 60.   [5] *Ibid.* 51.

Now please take the statute of limitations. You are bound to pay attention to all laws, but especially to this, men of Athens. For Solon, as it seems to me, framed it for no other purpose but to prevent your being harassed with false claims. He considered that five years was a sufficient time for the injured parties to recover what was due them; and he thought that length of time would be the plainest proof against those who came with false stories. And knowing also that it was impossible for the contracting parties and their witnesses to live forever, he put the law in their place, that it might be witness of the truth in favor of the destitute.[1]

This statement puts the philosophy of a statute of limitations in a nutshell. In practice the statute of limitations is used in an attempt to throw suspicion upon an outlawed claim. Delay beyond the time limit fixed by law in seeking redress would seem to show lack of confidence in one's case.

Now take the law that enacts that guarantees shall be in force for a year. And I don't insist under the statute, that I ought not to pay damages if I became surety, but I say the statute is my witness that I never was surety, and so is the plaintiff himself; otherwise he would have sued me on the guarantee in the time specified by law.[2]

It may fairly be concluded that there was a natural prejudice against a litigant who sought shelter behind the statute of limitations to avoid paying what might very well be his just debts. It was good strategy to tack onto it some other ground for demurrer wherever possible.

A distinction between special pleas may be drawn on the ground that in some the verdict is final, in others it is interlocutory.[3] The verdicts are final with respect to the persons concerned in cases περὶ ὧν μὴ εἶναι δίκας. The speaker in the Nausimachus case[4] has a law read which he seems to think embraced all grounds for final verdicts: ἀκούετε ὦ ἄνδρες δικασταὶ τοῦ νόμου σαφῶς λέγοντος ἕκαστα, ὧν μὴ εἶναι δίκας. But this is clearly an overstatement. Calhoun has pointed out that "while a number of grounds for final decrees were, in the Demosthenic period, comprehended in this law, it is clear that others were distributed throughout a great many

---

[1] Demos. xxxvi. 26–27.   [2] *Ibid.* xxxiii. 27.

[3] Calhoun, *CP*, XIII, 174; Lipsius, *op. cit.*, pp. 847 ff.; Glotz, in Darem.-Saglio, *s.v.* "Paragraphé."

[4] Demos. xxxviii. 5.

enactments."[1] A good example of a final decree is the *Apollodorus* v. *Phormio* case already discussed. If Apollodorus had been successful in this suit for perjury, he could have collected damages, either the talent he asked for or the amount suggested by Stephanus in his ἀντιτίμημα. Furthermore, he could have sued Phormio on a charge of subornation of perjury (δίκη κακοτεχνίων) for substantial damages. But under no circumstances would his success in the suit against Stephanus have enabled him to reopen the original suit against Phormio.

The case against Zenothemis in which Demosthenes also wrote the speech furnishes an example of a case in which the verdict of the court is interlocutory.[2] Zenothemis had brought a commercial suit (δίκη ἐμπορική). This type of suit involved certain advantages. It was tried before the thesmothetai during the winter months when navigation was generally suspended. Each case had to be brought to trial within a month, and the loser might be held to bail for the amount of the judgment.[3] The conditions required for a suit of this kind are thus defined in the opening paragraph, where the ground for the *paragraphé* is explained:

> The laws, men of the jury, declare that actions between shipowners and merchants shall be upon loans to Athens or from Athens, and concerning which there are contracts in writing; and if anyone sues without being so entitled, his action shall not be maintainable.[4]

Now it is manifest that if the *paragraphé* is sustained by the verdict of the court it does not mean that the original plaintiff had no recourse. All he had to do was to bring his case in the proper category and before the proper court.

The prevailing view has been that a *paragraphé* never came before an arbitrator.[5] This extreme view has not gone un-

---

[1] For examples see Calhoun, *op. cit.*, pp. 174 f ; cf. Lipsius, *op. cit.*, p. 848.

[2] Demos. xxxii; cf. Calhoun, *op. cit.*, p. 174.

[3] Lipsius, *op. cit.*, pp. 85, 631.   [4] Demos. xxxii. 1.

[5] Cf. Lipsius, *op. cit.*, p. 229: "Eine Hinausschiebung der Entschiedung konnte durch Einreden [παραγραφαί] oder Fristgesuche [ὑπωμοσίαι] oder Einigung der Parteien über einen Aufschub [ἀναβάλλεσθαι] herbeigeführt werden." Cf. p. 835: "Ist eine Einrede gegen die Klage nicht erfolgt oder zurückgewiesen, so hat . . . . der

challenged.[1] Pollux, in discussing μὴ οὖσα δίκη,[2] associates *paragraphé* with arbitration:

ἡ δὲ μὴ οὖσα δίκη οὕτως ὠνομάζετο, ὁπόταν τις παρὰ διαιτηταῖς παραγραψάμενος, καὶ ὑπομοσάμενος νόσον, ἢ ἀποδημίαν, εἰς τὴν κυρίαν οὐκ ὀφθεὶς, ἢ μὴ ἀπαντήσας, ἐρήμην ὄφλῃ, ἐξῆν ἐντὸς δέκα ἡμερῶν τὴν μὴ οὖσαν ἀντιγράφειν.

A note in the *Lexicon rhetoricum Cantabrigiense* also on μὴ οὖσα δίκη purports to quote a statement of Demetrius of Phalerum:

ἐνίους λέγει τῶν κρινομένων κακοτεχνεῖν τοῖς διώκουσιν ἀντιλαγχάνοντας τὴν μὴ οὖσαν. . . . . ἐνίους δὲ ἀσθενὲς τὸ δίκαιον ἔχοντας καὶ δεδοικότας τὴν καταδίαιταν χρόνους ἐμβάλλειν καὶ σκήψεις οἵας δοκεῖν εἶναι εὐλόγους, καὶ τὸ μὲν πρῶτον παραγράφεσθαι, εἶτα ὑπόμνυσθαι νόσον ἢ ἀποδημίαν, καὶ τελευτῶντας ἐπὶ τὴν κυρίαν τῆς διαίτης ἡμέραν οὐκ ἀπαντῶντας, ὅπως δύνωνται ἀντιλαγχάνειν, κ.τ.λ.

In these sources, and also in a scholium on Demosthenes xxi. 84, *paragraphé* and ὑπωμοσία in arbitration are more or less closely associated. Their close association in several speeches in the Demosthenic corpus has also led Lipsius and others before him to assume that we have here a different kind of *paragraphé* from that introduced by Archinus for amnesty cases and later extended to the majority of civil suits.

This combination of *paragraphé* and ὑπωμοσία with arbitration appears in *Demosthenes v. Midias*.[3] The plaintiff tells of a δίκη κακηγορίας which at an earlier stage of their litigation he had lodged against Midias. The case went to a public arbitrator, who gave his decision against Midias in default. Midias moved to have the case reopened before the arbitrator but failed to take the necessary oath. In consequence the award of the arbitrator became absolute and final.[4] In his

---

Gerichtsvorstand sie an einen öffentlichen Schiedsrichter zu verweisen." Cf. also Meier-Schömann-Lipsius, *op. cit.*, pp. 825 ff.

[1] Calhoun, *CP*, XIV, 20 ff.; Harrell, "Public Arbitration in Athenian Law," *University of Missouri Studies*, XI, No. 1, 31 f.

[2] viii. 60.   [3] Demos. xxi. 81, 83–86.

[4] *Ibid.* 86: τὴν μὲν δίαιταν ἀντιλαχὼν οὐκ ὤμοσεν, ἀλλ᾿ εἴασε καθ᾿ ἑαυτοῦ κυρίαν γενέσθαι, καὶ ἀνώμοτος ἀπηνέχθη. Cf. Kennedy, *Translation of Demosthenes*, III, 93, n. 5.

story of the arbitration Demosthenes shows that there was a παραγραφή connected with it: ἐπειδή ποθ' ἧκεν ἡ κυρία, πάντα δ'ἤδη διεξεληλύθει ταῦτα τἀκ τῶν νόμων, ὑπωμοσίαι καὶ παραγραφαί, καὶ οὐδὲν ἔτ' ἦν ὑπόλοιπον . . . . κατεδιῄτησεν.[1]

In *Apollodorus* v. *Phormio* we have a *paragraphé* case that was sent to an arbitrator.[2] Phormio had pleaded that the case not only was outlawed but had been settled by the payment of a certain sum fixed by private arbitration. As far as we know the *paragraphé* could have been filed with the Forty and passed on to the arbitrator. Indeed this was the natural thing to be done because the grounds upon which the special plea was based could not be established without an investigation involving the submission of depositions to prove the discharge.[3] This task could have been performed by the arbitrator alone. On the other hand, Phormio may have joined issue without filing a *paragraphé* with the Forty. In the informal recurrent sessions before the arbitrator there could be little, if any, advantage in the privilege of speaking first. Besides, the evidence that the case had been settled by agreement could have been introduced into the arbitration proceedings without a previous *paragraphé*. The case proves that a *paragraphé* could be heard by an arbitrator, but it furnishes no evidence as to whether it was filed with the Forty or afterward before the arbitrator. But it does show that the view of Lipsius that *paragraphé* and arbitration were mutually exclusive is untenable.[4]

Another case in the Demosthenic corpus[5] in which *paragraphé* is associated with arbitration presents unusual difficulties. It is needless to go into the details of the series of troubles in which the speaker[6] was involved in trying to force

---

[1] xxi. 84.   [2] This is apparent from Demos. xlv. 57–58.

[3] *Ibid.* xxxvi. 16–17.

[4] Cf. Calhoun, *op. cit.* There was a *paragraphé* and arbitration also in *Against Nausimachus et al.*, but in view of the very slight reference to arbitration (Demos. xxxviii. 6), the case is of no value in this discussion.

[5] xlvii.

[6] It will be convenient to call the plaintiff in the present case the "speaker" in order to avoid confusion.

Theophemus to turn over the ships' gear which he still retained after the expiry of his trierarchy. The story is badly
presented. At one stage of the case the speaker went to the
home of Theophemus in an effort to obtain the ships' gear.
Failing in this, he proceeded to make a seizure. A fight ensued in which each claimed that the other was the aggressor.[1]
Sometime later the speaker filed a δίκη αἰκίας before the
Forty, to which Theophemus responded with a cross-action
(ἀντιγραφή). Each case was sent to a separate arbitrator.[2] Pollux says: καὶ ἡ παραγραφὴ δὲ ἀντιγραφῇ ἔοικεν· διὸ καὶ προ-
εισέρχεται.[3] Schaefer,[4] without referring to Pollux, maintains
that the cross-action was tried first. Schulze[5] thinks this true
when both actions had to do with the same matter. Later
scholars do not agree.[6]

Let us see how far Pollux is justified by the present case.
Theophemus' case did come to trial first,[7] but it was due to
the fact that when the arbitrator in the case of the speaker
versus Theophemus was on the point of giving his decision
the defendant entered a *paragraphé* and a ὑπωμοσία:

προσεκαλεσάμην αὐτὸν καὶ ἔλαχον αὐτῷ δίκην τῆς αἰκίας. ἀντιπροσκα-
λεσαμένου δὲ κἀκείνου ἐμὲ καὶ διαιτητῶν ἐχόντων τὰς δίκας, ἐπειδὴ ἡ
ἀπόφασις ἦν τῆς δίκης, ὁ μὲν Θεόφημος παρεγράφετο καὶ ὑπώμνυτο, ἐγὼ
δὲ πιστεύων ἐμαυτῷ μηδὲν ἀδικεῖν εἰσῇειν εἰς ὑμᾶς.[8]

The effect of the *paragraphé* and ὑπωμοσία of Theophemus was
to block the arbitration in the case of the speaker versus
Theophemus. The speaker says that, having confidence that
he had done no wrong, he came before the court. This can
only mean that the arbitration, Theophemus versus the

---

[1] xlvii. 34 ff.

[2] *Ibid.* 45; cf. Schulze, *Prolegomenon in Demos. quae fertur orationem adv. Apaturi-
um*, pp. 19 ff.

[3] viii. 58; *s.v.* ἀντιγραφή.

[4] *Demosthenes und seine Zeit* (1st ed.), III, 2, 196.

[5] *Op. cit.*, p. 16.   [6] Cf. Lipsius, *op. cit.*, p. 860.

[7] Demos. xlvii. 39: ταύτῃ δὲ τῇ μαρτυρίᾳ πρότερος εἰσελθὼν εἰς τὸ δικαστήριον, οὐ
παραγραφομένου ἐμοῦ οὐδ' ὑπομνυμένου διὰ τὸ καὶ πρότερόν ποτε ἐφ' ἑτέρας δίκης ταῦτά
με βλάψαι, ἐξηπάτησε τοὺς δικαστάς.

[8] *Ibid.* 45.

speaker, continued to its end and that the speaker was determined to appeal the arbitrator's decision in case the award
was against him. This was precisely what happened.[1]

When we come to the nature of the *paragraphé* and ὑπωμοσία of Theophemus, we find no agreement among those who
have cared to raise the question. If Pollux is right, it might
be that Theophemus asked for an adjournment to enable him
to bring proof that he had in fact filed a cross-action. The
speaker implies that although he did not himself in fact resort
to a *paragraphé* and ὑπωμοσία, he might have done so. This
means that either in the arbitration in which he was defendant the speaker might have tried to use a *paragraphé* and
ὑπωμοσία[2] or in the arbitration in which he was plaintiff the
speaker might have tried to block the defendant's maneuver by a counter-*paragraphé* and ὑπωμοσία.[3] However, there
would still be a difficulty concerning the nature of the
paragraphé.

In Demosthenes' summary of the proceedings before the
arbitrator in his δίκη κακηγορίας against Midias[4] he speaks of
paragraphai which the arbitrator dismissed. There are two
possible explanations of the plural. Either Midias offered
more than one *paragraphé* or Demosthenes, the plaintiff, met
the defendant's *paragraphé* with a counter-*paragraphé*.[5] Either alternative excludes the normal *paragraphé*. For in the
extant λόγοι παραγραφικοί there may be several grounds for a
paragraphé but only one *paragraphé*, and it is always filed by
the defendant. Under these circumstances it looks as if we

---

[1] If Theophemus had lost and appealed, the speaker would surely have mentioned it. The fact that the speaker lost is the reason for his obscure phraseology.

[2] It is a fruitless task to speculate just how two arbitrators dealing with the same
facts could avoid being hopelessly at cross-purposes if they accepted contrary
paragraphai. The purpose of a *paragraphé* and ὑπωμοσία in Theophemus versus
the speaker would be to create such a situation.

[3] There could be no *paragraphé* in the perjury case which he is arguing; nor could
he say εἰς ὑμᾶς εἰσῇειν of his δίκη αἰκίας against Theophemus which was still pending (xlvii. 8, 10; cf. Lipsius, *op. cit.*, p. 862; Hubert, *De arbitris Atticis*, p. 40).

[4] xxi. 84.

[5] The suggestion that we have here a rhetorical plural can hardly be entertained;
cf. Calhoun, *op. cit.*, p. 25.

have here and also in the Theophemus case, since the linking of *paragraphé* and ὑπωμοσία proves that they refer to the same procedure, an entirely different kind of *paragraphé*.

Harpocration begins his definition of *paragraphé* with the words οὐ μόνον ἐπὶ τοῦ κοινοῦ καὶ γνωρίμου τίθεται παρὰ τοῖς ῥήτορσιν, which seems to indicate that the word had only one technical significance.[1] This is not such a formidable objection as it might at first sight seem to be. *Paragraphé* may be used in its etymological meaning of "notation on a document." Whatever the procedure was, it must have been available for both parties. If either party wanted an adjournment for any purpose on the eve of the arbitrator's award, how did he proceed to obtain it? Evidently an oath was required if the opponent raised an objection. It has been observed that this type of oath is always associated with a μὴ οὖσα δίκη. There must have been some record of such requests. The simplest explanation of all the phenomena involved is to regard the *paragraphé* as the record of the reasons for the adjournment noted on the pleadings of the party who made the request. As evidence of good faith in the face of opposition an oath was required. The confusion of *paragraphé* and μὴ οὖσα δίκη in the lexicographers which Calhoun has observed may be due to the fact that a belated *paragraphé* and ὑπωμοσία were not infrequently resorted to in order to have ground for having a decision *in contumaciam* set aside later.[2]

---

[1] *S.v.* παραγραφή; cf. Suidas, *s.v.*; Calhoun, *op. cit.*, p. 24, n. 1. The rest of the definition has nothing to do with legal technicalities.

[2] Harrell, *op. cit.*, p. 30.

CHAPTER V

ARBITRATION

The prevailing view is that practically all private suits were subject to arbitration.[1] The question has been raised, however, as to whether arbitration was not confined to cases within the jurisdiction of the Forty and similar cases within the jurisdiction of the polemarch, and that hence no private suits within the jurisdiction of the archon and the thesmothetai were subject to arbitration.[2] According to this theory, certain cases commonly assigned to these magistrates must lie within the jurisdiction of the Forty. Some scholars have accepted this view, but Lipsius[3] rejects it and Busolt and Swoboda[4] follow him.

In connection with the statement that all cases which came before the Forty involving more than ten drachmas were subject to arbitration, Aristotle reminds his readers of the development of the Forty from the thirty rural justices who were instituted by Peisistratus as arbitrators and justices.[5] In his account of the other boards and magistrates Aristotle says nothing about arbitrators except in connection with the polemarch, who accepted for non-citizens the same cases as the Forty did for the citizens. Consequently provision was made for participation of non-citizens in the benefits of arbitration by turning over to the Forty directly their cases which were subject to arbitration:

It is his [the polemarch's] duty to receive these cases and divide them into ten parts, and assign to each tribe the part which comes to it by lot;

[1] Cf. Meier-Schömann-Lipsius, *Der Attische Process*, pp. 1009 ff.; Lipsius, *Berichte der Königlich Sächsischen Gesellschaft der Wissenschaften* (Philol.-Hist. Classe), XLIII (1891), 58. Lipsius (*Das Attische Recht*, p. 82, n. 116; cf. p. 228) excepts suits before the ἀποδέκται and the εἰσαγωγεῖς.

[2] Bonner, "The Jurisdiction of Athenian Arbitrators," *CP*, II, 407 ff.

[3] *Op. cit.*, p. 533, n. 61.   [4] *Griechische Staatskunde*, p. 1111.

[5] *Ath. Pol.* liii. 2; cf. *supra*, I, 184–85.

after which the magistrates who introduce the cases for the tribe hand them over to the Arbitrators.[1]

Aristotle mentions arbitrators in connection with no other judicial officials or boards. His silence is not proof that *dikai* filed before other magistrates were not subject to arbitration but it is highly significant. In describing the jurisdiction of the polemarch Aristotle says that there were some *dikai* which were not subject to arbitration. These the polemarch himself introduced into court (αὐτὸς δ' εἰσάγει). Among them were suits dealing with estates and heiresses. It may fairly be concluded that these suits were not subject to arbitration when they concerned citizens and came before the archon.

The language of Aristotle describing the judicial functions of the archon definitely excludes the intervention of arbitrators in his cases: γραφαὶ δὲ καὶ δίκαι λαγχάνονται πρὸς αὐτόν, ἃς ἀνακρίνας εἰς τὸ δικαστήριον εἰσάγει.[2] Pischinger,[3] who believes that the archon and all other magistrates sent their cases through the Forty to the arbitrators, observes the difficulty and seeks to escape it by complaining of the carelessness of Aristotle in not mentioning the important process of arbitration which, according to his theory, intervened between entering a suit and the trial. But his explanation that ἀνακρίνας refers only to *graphai* assumes on the part of Aristotle even greater carelessness in expressing himself, and serves only to emphasize Pischinger's appreciation of a difficulty that called for such heroic treatment.[4] Such an unnatural, not to say impossible, interpretation of Aristotle's words is of no avail, for a client of Demosthenes, in an inheritance case, passes immediately from the *anakrisis* of the archon to the trial using exactly the same words as Aristotle: καὶ μετὰ ταῦθ' ὁ ἄρχων ἀνέκρινε πᾶσιν ἡμῖν τοῖς ἀμφισβητοῦσι, καὶ ἀνακρίνας εἰσήγαγεν εἰς τὸ δικαστήριον.[5]

Hubert[6] long ago observed that in none of the so-called

---

[1] *Ibid.* lviii. 2 (trans. Kenyon).   [2] *Ibid.* lvi. 6.

[3] *De arbitris Atheniensium publicis*, p. 39.

[4] *Ibid.*, p. 34, n. 3: "Hanc totam materiam Aristoteles minore cura aut scientia tractavit."

[5] xlviii. 31; cf. xliii. 7–8.   [6] *De arbitris Atticis et privatis et publicis*, p. 38.

inheritance cases, which are comparatively numerous in the orators, is there any mention of arbitration except in an affidavit in *Eubulides* v. *Macartatus*. The facts are briefly as follows. The estate of one Hagnias was claimed by a young man to whose mother Phylomache the estate had been adjudged in earlier litigation. In subsequent litigation the case was reopened and the estate was awarded to Theopompus, but when he died before the expiration of the προθεσμία of five years the estate was claimed by Eubulides, the minor son of Phylomache, who was now deceased. Macartatus, the son of Theopompus, was in possession. In a rather detailed account of the preceding litigation Sosicles, who is conducting the case for his son, calls for evidence that Phylomache won the first case: ὡς ἐνίκησε τοῦ κλήρου τοῦ 'Αγνίου ἡ Εὐβουλίδου θυγάτηρ Φυλομάχη.[1] But the affidavit we find inserted at this point merely proves that the decision of the arbitrator was in her favor: μαρτυροῦσι παρεῖναι πρὸς τῷ διαιτητῇ ἐπὶ Νικοφήμου ἄρχοντος, ὅτε ἐνίκησε Φυλομάχη ἡ Εὐβουλίδου θυγάτηρ τοῦ κλήρου τοῦ 'Αγνίου τοὺς ἀμφισβητοῦντας αὐτῇ πάντας. Naturally, an arbitrator's decision, if it was accepted as a final settlement of the case, would be evidence that Phylomache won her case.[2] But she did not win by an arbitrator's decision, for there is in the speech itself the statement of Sosicles to the effect that the estate was awarded to his wife by a dicastic court. In referring to the second case, which Phylomache lost, he speaks of her opponents who co-operated and took measures in common ὅπως ἀφέλωνται τὴν γυναῖκα τὴν τουτουὶ μητέρα τοῦ παιδὸς τὸν κλῆρον, ὃν αὐτῇ ὑμεῖς ἐψηφίσασθε.[3] No one who had just said that a case was settled by the verdict of a dicastic court would produce in proof of his statement the verdict of a public arbitrator. Blass suggests the substitution of δικαστηρίῳ for διαιτητῇ.[4] It is submitted that a piece of

[1] Demos. xliii. 31.

[2] It is idle to attempt to escape the difficulty by arguing that since Phylomache's victory was not in dispute this affidavit served the purpose well enough; cf. Drerup, *Jahrb.f. class. Phil.*, XXIV, 325.

[3] Demos. xliii. 30.

[4] Edition of Demos., *Commentarius criticus, ad loc.* Lipsius (*op. cit.*, p. 982) regards the affidavit as *unecht*.

documentary evidence, which has generally been viewed with suspicion because it does not confirm any statement of the speaker, should not be cited as the sole proof that inheritance cases were subject to arbitration, especially in the face of strong evidence to the contrary.

In several other cases connected with inheritance it is clearly implied that evidence might be produced that was not included in the docket.

Let Androcles, therefore, prove that the children are legitimate. . . . . His mere mention of his mother's name does not suffice to make them legitimate, but he must prove that he is speaking the truth by producing the relatives [as witnesses] who know. . . . .[1]

To prove what I say is true, his victims, though they are afraid, yet may perhaps be willing to support me by their evidence; otherwise, I will produce as witnesses those who know the facts.[2]

In another case the speaker, unable to find anyone to give positive evidence, calls an unwilling or hostile witness either to give evidence or to take an oath in disclaimer.[3] Still another speaker contemplates the possibility of the introduction of evidence by his opponent of which he has no certain knowledge: ὥστε ἂν ἐπὶ τοῦτον τὸν λόγον καταφεύγῃ καὶ μάρτυρας παρέχηται ὡς διέθετο ἐκεῖνος.[4] The fact that in these passages new evidence is contemplated shows inevitably that these were not arbitration cases, because in a hearing before an arbitrator all the evidence had to be presented.[5]

In the text of *Das Attische Recht*, Lipsius regards the inheritance cases and all other *dikai* that came before the archon as subject to arbitration.[6] In the *Nachträge und Berichtigung* at the end of his work, however, Lipsius retracts his

[1] Isaeus vi. 64.   [2] *Ibid.* viii. 42.

[3] *Ibid.* ix. 18: ἵνα ἐναντίον τούτων μαρτυρήσῃ ἢ ἐξομόσηται.

[4] *Ibid.* x. 23; cf. ix. 9.

[5] For a full discussion of the *anakrisis* cf. *supra*, I, 283 ff.; Leisi, *Der Zeuge*, p. 83; Thalheim, *Berl. Phil. Woch.*, XXIV, 1574–76.

[6] P. 228, n. 31; cf. p. 839, n. 35, where he rejects the use of expressions of a speaker indicating uncertainty as to what evidence his opponent will produce to determine whether a case came before an arbitrator or not. All such language he regarded as *hypothetische Fassung*, or, as Gomme puts it ("Two Problems of Athenian Citizenship Law," *CP*, XXIX, 128), "a rhetorical device."

earlier view and admits that inheritance cases were not subject to arbitration.[1]

If we accept the final view of Lipsius that all *dikai* except the ἔμμηνοι δίκαι[2] and the διαδικασίαι κλήρων were subject to arbitration,[3] what was the relationship of the other magistrates and boards to the arbitrators? Pischinger[4] believes that, like the cases of the polemarch, all cases must go to the arbitrators through the Forty. Suits originating with the archon or the thesmothetai would then have to go through an intolerably cumbersome procedure. This in itself is enough to arouse suspicion. According to this theory, for example, a case is entered before the archon; he holds an *anakrisis* and sends it to the Forty. From them it goes to the proper arbitrator. But this is not in accordance with the statement of Aristotle, who distinctly says that the archon brought his own cases into court, without any mention of an intervening arbitration.[5] Furthermore, in case of an appeal from an arbitrator's award, according to Pischinger, the case went back to the original magistrate—for example, to the Forty or to the archon. But this again is not in accordance with Aristotle, who says appeals went to the Forty who took them into court: παραδιδόασι (οἱ διαιτηταί in case of appeal) τοῖς τέτταρσι τοῖς τὴν φυλὴν τοῦ φεύγοντος δικάζουσιν. οἱ δὲ παραλαβόντες εἰσάγουσιν εἰς τὸ δικαστήριον.[6] To reconcile both these statements of Aristotle, Pischinger resorts to the doubtful expedient of denying the accuracy of Aristotle. Relying on Harpocration,[7] he holds that all cases which came to the arbitrators were referred back on appeal to the magistrates who first received them. But the words καὶ σημηνάμενοι (sc. οἱ διαιτηταί) παρεδίδοσαν τοῖς εἰσαγωγεῦσι τῶν δικῶν are too indefinite to support an impeachment of the testimony of Aristotle; τοῖς εἰσαγωγεῦσι may refer to the Forty as well as

[1] *Op. cit.*, p. 981.

[2] These were filed before the ἀποδέκται and the εἰσαγωγεῖς; cf. *ibid.*, p. 82.

[3] Naturally the δίκαι φόνου could not very well be subject to public arbitration.

[4] *Op. cit.*, p. 39.   [6] *Ibid.* liii. 2–3.

[5] *Ath. Pol.* lvi. 6.   [7] *S.v.* διαιτηταί.

to the original magistrates in the various cases. But, apart from this, Harpocration is as usual following Aristotle and is evidently of the opinion that he is simply reporting, not correcting him, for he adds: λέγει δὲ περὶ αὐτῶν (*sc.* τῶν διαιτητῶν) 'Αριστοτέλης ἐν 'Αθηναίων πολιτείᾳ. Lipsius[1] disagrees with Pischinger's theory that all cases went to an arbitrator through the Forty, but agrees with Pischinger in saying that cases, on appeal from an arbitrator's award, were returned to the magistrates with whom they originated. This explanation, however, fails to explain why Aristotle is silent about arbitration in the case of the archon and the thesmothetai but mentions it in the discussion of the polemarch. All difficulties disappear if one accepts just what Aristotle's words imply, that only the cases of the Forty and those of the polemarch with the exception of inheritance cases were subject to arbitration.[2]

To scholars not prejudiced by reading the extant speeches the arguments drawn from Aristotle would be convincing. "Non enim pagorum judices soli," says Pischinger, "sed etiam alii magistratus arbitris causas instruendas tradebant, id quod ex orationibus Demosthenis satis intellegitur."[3] Pischinger gives a list of cases from the orators in which public arbitration appears, assigning the cases to the magistrate he thinks proper, as follows:

I. Archontis actiones
   (1) ἐπιτροπῆς: Lysias xxxii; Demos. xxvii; xxix
   (2) κλήρου: Demos. xliii. 31
   (3) Status familiae: Demos. xl. 10
II. Thesmothetarum actiones
   (1) κλοπῆς: Demos. xxii. 27–28
   (2) Status civitatis: Lysias xxiii; Isaeus xii; Demos. lix. 60[4]

The inheritance case (κλήρου) is no longer regarded as subject to arbitration and may be omitted at once.[5] The next most important case assigned to the archon is the so-called guardianship case (δίκη ἐπιτροπῆς). Lipsius[6] maintains that guard-

---

[1] *Op. cit.*, p. 227, n. 30.   [3] *Op. cit.*, p. 34.   [5] Cf. *supra*, pp. 98 ff.
[2] *Ath. Pol.* lviii.   [4] *Ibid.*, p. 35.   [6] *Op. cit.*, p. 533, n. 61.

ianship cases came before the archon and rejects the arguments to the contrary.[1] It is to be noted that Aristotle makes no mention of guardianship suits in the list of cases he gives for the archon, but, as Lipsius justly points out, it cannot be assumed that Aristotle's list is exhaustive. But an examination of the list reveals the fact that the archon's cases are limited to suits involving the disposition of the estate (κλήρων καὶ ἐπικλήρων ἐπιδικασία), division of an estate (δατητῶν αἵρεσις), abuse of an estate (γραφὴ παρανοίας, οἴκου ὀρφανικοῦ κάκωσις), abuse of members of the family (γονέων κάκωσις, ἐπικλήρου κάκωσις, ὀρφανῶν κάκωσις), rival claims to guardianship (ἐπιτροπῆς διαδικασία). And in general the archon

has the care of orphans and heiresses and widows who on the death of their husbands declare that they are with child. . . . . He also leases out the houses of orphans and heiresses until they reach the age of fourteen and takes security for the property leased; and if the guardians fail to support his wards the archon collects the necessary funds from the guardians.[2]

The means at his disposal for carrying out these duties are a limited fine, and prosecution if he thinks a fine beyond his competence is warranted: κύριός ἐστι τοῖς ἀδικοῦσιν ἐπιβάλλειν ἢ εἰσάγειν εἰς τὸ δικαστήριον.[3]

It is to be observed that the archon's care of and responsibility for orphans ceases after their majority, and that his relations with guardians continue only during the minority of the ward. In the actions against guardians during the ward's minority he presides. As described by Aristotle, the archon's relationship to guardians is as follows. Under certain circumstances he appointed them. He decided between rival claimants for guardianship. Where injuries were done to the persons or property of wards he presided in the court which tried the case. Where a guardian refused to support his ward or to rent the real estate the archon was empowered to take action. It is of immediate interest to note that all these contacts between archon and guardian cease with the major-

[1] Bonner, CP, II, 413 ff.   [2] Arist. Ath. Pol. lvi. 6–7.
[3] Ibid.; cf. supra, I, 279 ff.; Demos. xliii. 75.

ity of the ward. While it may be freely admitted that there may have been other contacts, it is submitted that they do not go beyond the minority stage, even to the extent of presiding in court for a trial of a δίκη ἐπιτροπῆς brought by a ward on attaining manhood against a guardian for false accounting or for failure to hand in an account. Lipsius and his followers have unhesitatingly ascribed this type of suit to the archon rather than to the Forty where it naturally belongs.

In nearly all the inheritance cases in the orators the archon is mentioned as the presiding officer. In *Eubulides* v. *Macartatus*[1] the speaker in referring to an earlier suit involving the estate in litigation says ἐπειδὴ ἦγεν ὁ ἄρχων εἰς τὸ δικαστήριον, and again he says of the suit in hand that it was filed before the archon: ὁ παῖς οὑτοσὶ προσεκαλέσατο Μακάρτατον τοῦ κλήρου τοῦ Ἁγνίου εἰς διαδικασίαν, καὶ ἔλαχε πρὸς τὸν ἄρχοντα, κύριον ἐπιγραψάμενος τὸν ἀδελφὸν τὸν ἑαυτοῦ.[2] In still another case which is not an inheritance case but grew out of one the speaker in sketching the inheritance case explicitly mentions the archon as the presiding officer: ἐπειδὴ ἀνεκρίθησαν πρὸς τῷ ἄρχοντι ἅπασαι αἱ ἀμφισβητήσεις.[3] There are also several similar references in Isaeus.[4]

In contrast with this situation in inheritance cases where the archon is mentioned as the presiding officer in the bulk of the cases referred to in the orators,[5] the archon is not once referred to as the presiding officer in the eight speeches in guardianship suits. This cannot be a matter of chance or accident. It is highly significant.

In one case, *Demosthenes* v. *Onetor*, there is a reference to the archon. The passage is as follows:

[1] Demos. xliii. 8.

[2] *Ibid.* 15; cf. xliv. 1: ἀξιῶν κληρονομεῖν ὧν οὐ προσῆκεν αὐτῷ, καὶ ὑπὲρ τούτων ψευδῆ διαμαρτυρίαν πρὸς τῷ ἄρχοντι ποιησάμενος.

[3] *Ibid.* xlviii. 23.

[4] v. 18: συγχωρούντων γὰρ ἡμῶν τῷ ἄρχοντι μὴ συναριθμεῖν ἀλλὰ συγχέαι τὰς ψήφους; cf. vi. 12: ὅτε γὰρ αἱ ἀνακρίσεις ἦσαν πρὸς τῷ ἄρχοντι; xi. 33: εἰ μὲν κατ᾽ ἀγχιστείαν τῶν Ἁγνίου μετεῖναί φησι τῷ παιδὶ τοῦ ἡμικληρίου, λαχέτω πρὸς τὸν ἄρχοντα.

[5] For the list see Schulthess, *Vormundschaft nach Attischem Recht*, pp. 242 ff. It is difficult to compute the exact number of cases classified as δίκαι κλήρου which are argued or referred to in more or less detail.

It was known, men of the jury, to many of the Athenians, and it did not escape the observation of the defendant, that my guardians were grossly neglecting their duty. The discovery was indeed made very early; numerous meetings and discussions were held on the subject of my affairs, before the archon as well as other persons [τοσαῦται πραγματεῖαι καὶ λόγοι καὶ παρὰ τῷ ἄρχοντι καὶ παρὰ τοῖς ἄλλοις ἐγίγνοντο ὑπὲρ τῶν ἐμῶν]. For the value of the property left me was notorious, and it was pretty evident, that the trustees were leaving it unlet, for the purpose of enjoying the income themselves. This being so, there was not a single man acquainted with the circumstances, who did not expect that I should recover compensation from them, as soon as I came of man's estate.[1]

Here Demosthenes, trying to realize on the verdict of the court in his favor for ten talents in *Demosthenes* v. *Aphobus*, sues Onetor, the brother-in-law, to obtain a piece of property of which Onetor is the "mortgagee" on the ground of collusion between Aphobus and Onetor. Demosthenes is trying to prove to the jury that under the circumstances Onetor could not plead that he was an innocent "mortgagee" of the property because he could not fail to have been aware of the defalcations and embezzlement of his guardians, which were so well known to everybody that it was generally expected he would win his case. In that event the whole property of Aphobus would be liable to execution to satisfy the judgment. But no one regards the reference to the archon in *Demosthenes* v. *Onetor*[2] as any indication that the archon presided at a δίκη ἐπιτροπῆς,[3] because, whatever activities and discussions may have taken place before the archon, they happened during the minority of Demosthenes.

There is a case in Demosthenes which throws some light on the δίκη ἐπιτροπῆς. The situation is not easy to discover. Perhaps something like this happened. Nausimachus and Xenopithes sued their guardian, Aristaechmus, in connection with the account of the estate, ὡς γὰρ οὐκ ἀποδόντι λόγον, καὶ τοῦτο ἐγκαλοῦντες φαίνονται. λέγε αὐτὸ τὸ ἔγκλημα, ὃ τότ' ἔλαχον τῷ πατρί.[4] It seems that he settled their claims by paying three

---

[1] Demos. xxx. 6 (trans. Kennedy).   [2] *Ibid.*, just cited.

[3] Cf. Beauchet, *Histoire du droit*, II, 273; Dareste, *Les Plaidoyers civils de Demosthène*, I, 85; Schaefer, *Demosthenes und seine Zeit*, I, 270.

[4] xxxviii. 15.

talents and turned over an estate consisting of houses and
lands and a debt of one hundred staters owed the estate by
one Hermonax of Bosporus. It is not clear whether they accepted the assignment of the debt as a settlement or whether
it was to be collected for them by their former guardian. At
any rate, the plaintiffs Nausimachus and Xenopithes sued
the heirs of Aristaechmus on the ground that he himself or
someone in his behalf had collected the money: οὗτοι γὰρ
γεγράφασιν εἰς ὃ νῦν ἔγκλημα διώκουσιν, ὀφείλειν ἡμᾶς τὸ
ἀργύριον κομισαμένου τοῦ πατρὸς καὶ παραδόντος αὐτοῖς τοῦτο τὸ
χρέως ἐν τῷ λόγῳ τῆς ἐπιτροπῆς ὀφειλόμενον.[1] The defendants
demurred and entered a *paragraphé* that the case was not
actionable because there had been a release and further because the statute of limitations had run its course of five
years. The suit against the guardian was settled eight years
after the wards reached their majority. The present suit was
instituted twelve years later. The guardian Aristaechmus
had died a few months after the settlement. There are some
curious and interesting features about this case. It is an action for damages (δίκη βλάβης) and yet the defendants plead
the statute of limitations in bar of action on the part of wards
against their guardians: βούλομαι καὶ ὑμῖν τὸν νόμον εἰπεῖν,
ὅστις διαρρήδην λέγει, ἐὰν πέντε ἔτη παρέλθῃ καὶ μὴ δικάσωνται,
μηκέτ' εἶναι τοῖς ὀρφανοῖς δίκην περὶ τῶν ἐκ τῆς ἐπιτροπῆς
ἐγκλημάτων.[2] These words undoubtedly refer to a δίκη ἐπιτροπῆς. They also plead a release. In an *ex parte* statement like
this it is impossible to determine whether the guardian and
his estate were still liable after the alleged settlement for
three talents. It is true that the case was accepted by the
Forty, but against the protests of the defendants. If the
plaintiffs were right in their contention, the estate of a guardian could be sued on a claim on which he himself could not be
brought into court. This is manifestly absurd. Beauchet[3]
and others regard the δίκη ἐπιτροπῆς as a particular form of
the δίκη βλάβης. If that be so, this case with all its obscurities
goes far to show that the δίκη ἐπιτροπῆς, just as a δίκη βλάβης,

[1] *Ibid.* 14.   [2] *Ibid.* 17.   [3] *Op. cit.*, II, 303, n. 5.

came within the jurisdiction of the Forty. Lipsius[1] believes that a δίκη ἐπιτροπῆς could not be a *Schadenklage*, though he points out that a δίκη βλάβης could be used to collect a debt, and in a δίκη ἐπιτροπῆς the guardian is treated as a debtor rather than as a criminal embezzler.

In the Diogeiton case in Lysias[2] and in Demosthenes' own case against his guardians which are included in the list given by Pischinger there is no mention of the archon, though arbitration is mentioned. In brief, then, there is no evidence in the sources that guardianship cases (δίκαι ἐπιτροπῆς) came within the jurisdiction of the archon aside from such inference as may be drawn from the fact that the archon had charge of orphans and their interests during their minority. But a δίκη ἐπιτροπῆς could not be instituted by minors.[3]

The next arbitration case listed by Pischinger is labeled *status familiae*. The only extant case is *Boeotus and Pamphilus* v. *Mantias* mentioned in *Mantitheus* v. *Boeotus*.[4] The facts as given by a hostile speaker are briefly as follows. Boeotus and his brother Pamphilus grew to manhood as sons of Plangon, daughter of Pamphilus, who, so it was alleged, was the divorced wife of Mantias. These two young men on reaching manhood brought suit against their father to force him to recognize them as his sons. Sandys and Paley[5] have doubts as to the majority of Boeotus at this time. But the word αὐξηθείς and the fact that the men associated with him in laying a trap were not κύριοι but sycophants show clearly that he was no longer a minor. This case raises a number of problems that need not be discussed here.[6] Mantias was unwilling to be involved in litigation for various reasons and readily fell in with a scheme that he should tender an oath to

[1] *Op. cit.*, p. 657. [2] xxxii.

[3] At the risk of seeming κύνα δέρειν δεδαρμένην one may add another indication that there was no relationship between the arbitrators and the archon. A scholiast on Demos. xxi. 84, in speaking of arbitration, says: πολλάκις γὰρ οἱ ἀντίδικοι παρεγράφοντο. οὐ πρὸς διαιτητὴν με κρίνεσθαι δεῖ, ἀλλὰ πρὸς ἄρχοντα, ἢ θεσμοθέτην. This shows clearly that in the opinion of the scholiast the same case did not come before the archon and the arbitrator.

[4] Demos. xl. 9 ff. [5] *Demosthenes' Select Private Orations*, I, 152.

[6] Cf. Lipsius, *op. cit.*, p. 505, n. 25, for the questions at issue.

Plangon to the effect that these young men were his sons.[1]
It was understood by Mantias, however, that Plangon for the
sum of thirty minas would refuse to take the oath before the
arbitrator.[2] If she had refused to take the oath, as she had
agreed to do, Mantias would have been free of all liability:
τούτων δὲ πραχθέντων οὐδὲν ἔτι ἔσεσθαι αὐτοῖς.[3] Plangon, however, accepted the oath and declared that the young men
were the sons of Mantias. Mantias, therefore, lost the case
and introduced the plaintiffs into his phratry as his sons.
The case came before an arbitrator, but there is no definite
evidence to show which magistrate accepted the case. It has
been generally assumed that as family relations were involved
it naturally came before the archon. Lipsius does not expressly list it among the *Privatklagen* of the archon, but he approves of the list of arbitration cases given by Pischinger and
their assignment to magistrates.[4] But no one gives a name
to the suit.

There is, however, a piece of evidence which should be
considered in this connection. Boeotus ἐδικάζεθ' υἱὸς εἶναι
φάσκων ἐκ τῆς Παμφίλου θυγατρὸς καὶ δεινὰ πάσχειν καὶ τῆς
πατρίδος ἀποστερεῖσθαι.[5] The words δεινὰ πάσχειν are the
equivalent of ἕτερα πολλὰ βλάπτεσθαι used of a δίκη βλάβης.[6]
Moreover, when Mantitheus, the son of Mantias, sued the
tardily recognized Boeotus because he insisted on calling
himself Mantitheus, the suit was a δίκη βλάβης.[7] There is
practically no difference between the suits. One has to do
with paternity, the other with a family name. They both
concern family relations. If *Mantitheus* v. *Boeotus* is a δίκη
βλάβης, so also is *Boeotus and Pamphilus* v. *Mantias*.[8] As such
it came before the Forty and was subject to arbitration. This

---

[1] Demos. xl. 10.

[2] Cf. Isaeus xii. 9 for the willingness of Euphiletus' mother to take an evidentiary
oath regarding his paternity.

[3] Demos. xxxix. 3. [4] *Op. cit.*, p. 228, n. 31. [5] Demos. xxxix. 2.

[6] *Ibid.* xli. 12: cf. xxxvi. 20 for a statement of claim in a δίκη βλάβης: ἔβλαψέ με
ὁ δεῖνα οὐκ ἀποδιδοὺς ἐμοὶ τὸ ἀργύριον, ὃ κατέλειπεν ὁ πατὴρ ὀφείλοντα αὐτὸν ἐν τοῖς
γράμμασιν. Cf. Lipsius, *op. cit.*, p. 653, n. 61.

[7] Lipsius, *op. cit.*, p. 652. [8] Demos. xxxix. 2.

disposes of Pischinger's list of arbitration cases which he assigned to the jurisdiction of the archon.

Two types of cases subject to arbitration are assigned to the thesmothetai. One is the δίκη κλοπῆς. In *Euctemon and Diodorus* v. *Androtion*[1] one of the plaintiffs, in discussing the various means of redress open to aggrieved persons, mentions larceny as a crime that may be dealt with in four distinct ways. One of these was a civil action (δίκη κλοπῆς) subject to arbitration. The phraseology is suggestive: "Sue him for theft before an arbitrator [δικάζου κλοπῆς πρὸς διαιτητήν]." No mention is made in the sources of the presidency of the court which would try civil suits for larceny. The authors of *Der Attische Process* say[2] that probably (*wahrscheinlich*) the case came before the thesmothetai. In Aristotle's account of the judicial functions of the thesmothetai several *dikai* are mentioned without the slightest hint that there are others: εἰσάγουσι δὲ καὶ δίκας ἰδίας, ἐμπορικὰς καὶ μεταλλικὰς καὶ δούλων, ἄν τις τὸν ἐλεύθερον κακῶς λέγῃ. . . . καὶ τὰς δίκας τὰς ἀπὸ τῶν συμβόλων εἰσάγουσι.[3] There is nothing here to suggest a δίκη κλοπῆς.

Elsewhere, in discussing the functions of the *euthynoi* who for three days accepted charges and claims against former magistrates after their accounts had been passed, Aristotle says:

And if anyone wishes to prefer a charge, on either public or private grounds, against any magistrate who has passed his audit before the law-courts, within three days of his having so passed, he enters on a whitened tablet his own name and that of the magistrate prosecuted, together with the malpractice that is alleged against him. He also appends his claim for a penalty of such amount as seems to him fitting, and gives in the record to the Examiner. The latter takes it and hears the charge, and if he considers it proved he hands it over, if a private case, to the local justices who introduce cases for the tribe concerned, while if a public case he enters it on the register of the thesmothetai. Then if the thesmothetai accept it, they bring the accounts of this magistrate once more before the lawcourt, and the decision of the jury stands as the final judgment.[4]

[1] *Ibid.* xxii. 27–28.

[2] Meier-Schömann-Lipsius, *op. cit.*, p. 453.   [3] *Ath. Pol.* lix. 5–6.

[4] *Ibid.* xlviii. 4–5 (trans. Kenyon).

It thus appears that the bulk of the *graphai* went to the thesmothetai and the bulk of the *dikai* to the Forty. Or one might even conclude that all *dikai* not otherwise assigned went to the Forty. This view is supported by another statement in Aristotle. After discussing the cases that came within the jurisdiction of the Eleven, the εἰσαγωγεῖς, and the ἀποδέκται, he continues with a description of the duties of the Forty; πρὸς οὓς τὰς ἄλλας δίκας λαγχάνουσιν.[1] This body decided all cases under ten drachmas; other cases were handed to the arbitrators. If there was an appeal from their award, the case was referred to the Forty and by them brought to trial. The words τὰς ἄλλας δίκας are commonly taken to mean that all private suits except those previously mentioned came within the jurisdiction of the arbitrators;[2] and as far as the Greek is concerned this is the natural interpretation of the words. But the difficulty encountered in attempting to reconcile this interpretation with Aristotle's subsequent statements is practically insurmountable. Among the remaining *dikai* mentioned by Aristotle are those assigned to the three archons and the thesmothetai. Obviously all Aristotle means is that *dikai* not otherwise assigned in his treatise went to the Forty and to the arbitrators. Lipsius[3] chooses to put the δίκη κλοπῆς among the suits handled by the thesmothetai apparently because γραφαὶ κλοπῆς came within the jurisdiction of this board. Lipsius has tried to discover the grounds of distinction between the use of a criminal suit and the use of a civil suit for an act which is essentially a criminal one.[4] But whatever the circumstances of the act that permitted a civil suit for larceny, the δίκη κλοπῆς is, after all, of the same nature as the δίκη βλάβης.

Pischinger cites the case against Pancleon[5] as an arbitration case that came within the jurisdiction of the thesmothetai. In his opinion it has to do with citizenship, *status civita-*

---

[1] *Ibid.* liii. 1.

[2] Cf. Sandys, *ad loc.*; Lipsius, *Berichte der Sächischen Gesellschaft*, XLIII (1891), 54 f.

[3] *Op. cit.*, p. 438.   [4] Demos. xxiv. 113–14.   [5] Lysias xxiii.

tis. Lipsius[1] approves of the assignment to the thesmothetai. Much confusion regarding the case has arisen from the mixture of the original case against Pancleon with the proceedings to determine whether Pancleon was a slave belonging to either of two persons who claimed him. The original case against Pancleon is as follows:

It is evident that the speaker filed a suit with the polemarch, the character of which he does not specify beyond saying that Pancleon had for a long time injured him (ἀδικῶν με πολὺν χρόνον οὐκ ἐπαύετο) and that he filed a suit against him. For he proceeded to the place where Pancleon worked and summoned him to appear before the polemarch, "believing him to be a metic." Pancleon protested that he was a Plataean and so not a metic, as Plataeans had citizen rights. At the suggestion of one of his witnesses the speaker found out by questions that Pancleon claimed to be of the deme of Decelea and the tribe of Hippothoöntis. Accordingly he summoned him also before the section of the Forty which had jurisdiction over cases in which the defendant was of the tribe of Hippothoöntis.[2] It is not explained how a plaintiff could summon a man before two courts at once nor does it really matter. They are alternative summons.[3] The important thing to notice is that the speaker believed that the case would be assigned to the Forty for arbitration if the polemarch finally accepted it. Otherwise he would not have summoned Pancleon as a citizen before the Forty. The rest of the speech need not concern us. It is enough that the case against Pancleon came under the jurisdiction of the Forty and the arbitrators either directly or from the polemarch. Consequently, this case must be stricken from the list of Pischinger.[4]

Another so-called *status civitatis* case listed by Pischinger as being within the jurisdiction of the thesmothetai is men-

[1] *Op. cit.*, p. 228, n. 31.

[2] Lysias xxiii. 2: προσκαλεσάμενος αὐτὸν καὶ πρὸς τοὺς τῇ Ἱπποθωντίδι δικάζοντας.

[3] Cf. Wilamowitz, *Aristoteles und Athen*, II, 370.

[4] Cf. Gomme, "Two Problems of Athenian Citizenship Law," *CP*, XXIX, 127, n. 9.

tioned in *Theomnestus* v. *Neaera*.[1] Phrastor had married
Phano supposing that she was the daughter of Stephanus by
a former wife, but when he discovered she was really the
daughter of a notorious woman who cohabited with Stephanus, he divorced her while she was with child. Afterward
Phrastor fell ill and Phano with her mother Neaera went to
his house and nursed him. It is claimed that under these circumstances he was influenced to adopt the son whom Phano
had in the meantime borne. Accordingly pursuing this purpose, he introduced the boy to his phratry and the members
of the Brutidae, the family to which he belonged. But they
rejected him. Phrastor then entered suit (λαχόντος δὲ τοῦ Φρά-
στορος αὐτοῖς δίκην ὅτι οὐκ ἐνέγραφον αὐτοῦ υἱόν).[2] The case
came before an arbitrator and the clan members challenged
Phrastor to take an evidentiary oath that "he verily believed
the boy to be his own son by an Athenian woman lawfully
married to him." If he had sworn the solemn oath the son
would have been accepted by the clan, but he refused and
that settled the case against him. What was the nature of
the original suit which he brought against the γεννῆται? One
is inevitably reminded of *Boeotus and Pamphilus* v. *Mantias*
already discussed.[3] There a woman is tendered the oath regarding the paternity of her sons; here a man is tendered an
oath regarding the maternity of a son. Lipsius[4] regards the
latter case as coming within the jurisdiction of the thesmothetai because he considers it similar to the appeal (ἔφεσις)
from the verdict of a deme assembly striking a man from the
rolls. But the analogy is false for, so far as is known, there is
no appeal to a dicastery from the vote of a clan. The only
remedy was suit for damages (δίκη βλάβης) against the clans-
men which came before the Forty and was subject to arbitration.

Another citizenship case that came before an arbitrator
was that of *Euphiletus* v. *The Deme of Erichia*,[5] which is de-

[1] Demos. lix.   [3] *Ibid.* xl. 9 ff.; cf. *supra*, pp. 107 f.
[2] *Ibid.* 60.   [4] *Op. cit.*, p. 629.
[5] Isaeus xii, quoted by Dionysius of Halicarnassus (*De Isaeo judicium* 17).

scribed by Dionysius of Halicarnassus as an appeal to a dicastery (ἔφεσις εἰς τὸ δικαστήριον)[1] against expulsion from the deme by a διαψήφισις ordered by a decree of Demophilus of the year 346–345 B.C.[2] The case presents unusual difficulties. Lipsius classifies it as a *diké* within the jurisdiction of the thesmothetai, although the penalty in case the appeal failed was sale of the appellant into slavery.[3] But Aristotle's language seems to place such suits neither among the *graphai* nor among the *dikai*. After enumerating the *graphai* which came before the thesmothetai, Aristotle adds: εἰσάγουσι . . . . δίκας ἰδίας.[4] Wyse[5] regards it as a public case within the jurisdiction of the thesmothetai and explains the appearance of the arbitrators as an extraordinary measure due to the large number of cases that came before the thesmothetai as a result of the general διαψήφισις. An acceptable solution of the case has been proposed by Diller.[6] The date of Isaeus xii must be placed after 346–345 B.C. if it is to be classified as an appeal under the provisions of the decree of Demophilus. It has been observed that this is late for a speech of Isaeus by ten years.[7] Diller suggests that "Dionysius simply confused the pre- and post-Demophilean type of scrutiny and that the fragment of Isaeus (i.e. xii) . . . . belongs to a δίκη of the pre-Demophilean type." There is considerable evidence to support this view. Demosthenes lvii is described as ἔφεσις πρὸς Εὐβουλίδην, the demarch of Halimus. The Hypothesis of Libanius describes it as an appeal under an Athenian law providing for scrutinies of the citizen lists and appeals in the case of those rejected. The author of the law was Demophilus. Dionysius introduces his citation from Isaeus, now printed as Oration xii, in practically the same

---

[1] *Ibid.* 16. [2] Aeschin. i. 86; Harpocration, *s.v.* διαψήφισις.

[3] Lipsius, *op. cit.*, pp. 247, 415, 628–29. Cf. Gomme, *op. cit.*, pp. 130 ff., for arguments against the application of this verdict to any but persons proved to be slaves.

[4] *Ath. Pol.* lix. 5.

[5] *The Speeches of Isaeus*, pp. 716 f. [6] *TAPA*, LXIII, 193 ff.

[7] The latest date given by Thalheim (*Isaeus*, p. xxxiv) is 353 B.C. for Or. vii; cf. Wyse (*op. cit.*, p. 715), who reluctantly accepts the date after 346–345 B.C.

terms as the Hypothesis of Libanius.[1] The two speeches have been regarded as dealing with the same type of case. And yet there are marked differences. In Isaeus xii arbitrators are mentioned, but Demosthenes lvii could not have come before an arbitrator because it was proposed to introduce at the trial evidence which had not been produced before; whereas in an arbitration case all evidence had to be produced before the arbitrator.[2] The fact that there was no arbitration in the Eubulides case shows that it was not the same kind of case as the Euphiletus case. There is no direct statement in the speech against Eubulides that the defendant was liable to sale as a slave, but there are phrases that indicate that his fate would be deplorable.[3] His threat at the end to commit suicide if the verdict be against him seems to indicate that he was threatened with more than the loss of citizenship.[4] If Gomme is right in supposing that the verdict "slavery" was only for appellants who turned out to be slaves, the absence of any reference to slavery is only natural. In the Isaeus case, however, the only statement of any significance is that Euphiletus has been unjustly mistreated (ἀδίκως ὑβρίσθη), and that applies not to the effect of an adverse verdict but to the treatment which is the basis of his complaint. Obviously we have here a δίκη βλάβης just as in the cases of Boeotus and his brother, Pamphilus, and Phrastor.[5]

---

[1] Aristotle (*Ath. Pol.* xlii), in discussing the franchise, describes the appeal allowed to men rejected on scrutiny.

[2] Bonner, *Evidence in Athenian Courts*, pp. 52 ff. Gomme (*op. cit.*, p. 128) admits that new evidence was produced but adds that its importance must not be exaggerated. In view of Aristotle's statement that no evidence can be introduced in an appeal from arbitration, it is surely no exaggeration to conclude that if new evidence was introduced in a case the case had not been subject to arbitration.

[3] E.g., ἀπολέσθαι (lvii. 18).

[4] "I was left by my father an orphan. On behalf of my mother I conjure and beseech you—let the issue of this trial be, that you restore to me the right of burying her in our hereditary monuments. Do not preclude me from this—do not make me an outcast— do not sever me from communion with all my relatives, numerous as they are, and utterly destroy me. Rather than abandon them, if it is impossible for them to save me, I will kill myself, so that at least I may be buried by them in my country" (Demos. lvii. 70 [trans. Kennedy]).

[5] Cf. *supra*, pp. 107 f. and 112.

This concludes Pischinger's list of arbitration cases that he, followed by Lipsius, regarded as falling within the jurisdiction of the archon or the thesmothetai. It is clear that they all belong to the jurisdiction of the Forty and that there is nothing in the orators at variance with the natural conclusion to be drawn from Aristotle, namely, that the only arbitration cases were those which came before the Forty directly or through the medium of the polemarch.

In the Appendix to his excellent study of public arbitration in Athenian law Harrell[1] has compiled the following list of arbitration cases from the Attic orators:

1. δίκη αἰκείας (Lipsius, p. 643)   (Isoc. xx.)
                                      Demos. xlvii. Cf. sec. 45.
                                      Demos. liv.

    That this suit came under the Forty is stated in Demos. xxxvii. 33, a speech delivered *c.* 346/5 B.C. By the time of Aristotle it had evidently become one of the monthly suits; cf. *Ath. Pol.* lii. 2.

2. δίκη ἀργυρίου (Lipsius, p. 726)   (Demos. lii. Cf. sec. 14.)
                                       (Demos. xxxix. 25.)

3. δίκη ἀφορμῆς (Lipsius, p. 725)   Demos. xxxvi. Cf. sec. 12.

    Aristotle mentions (lii. 2) a monthly suit under this name. But he probably had in mind only a specific suit, not all suits of this class, since he qualifies it with a further description. There were sometimes, it seems, suits with the same name, but under different classifications; cf. 11 below. Otherwise we must assume that the Forty lost jurisdiction here as in the case of no. 1 above.

4. δίκη βιαίων (Lipsius, p. 637)   Demos. xxv. 55. Cf. sec. 58. (?)
                                    Aeschin. i, 62–63. Cf. Lipsius, p. 642,
                                    n. 21.

5. δίκη βλάβης (Lipsius, p. 652)   (Isoc. xvi.)
                                    (Isoc. xviii. Cf. secs. 11, 12.)
                                    (Hyper. iii.)
                                    (Demos. xxxviii.)

[1] *Public Arbitration in Athenian Law*, "University of Missouri Studies," XI, No. 1, 36 ff. "The list includes two classes of suits: (*a*) those containing specific internal evidence of arbitration; (*b*) those containing no specific mention of arbitration, but which may reasonably be presumed to have undergone arbitration. Suits under the latter classification have been enclosed in parentheses. The exact identification is often purely a matter of conjecture, but it is hoped this list will answer most practical purposes."

Demos. xxxix. 37. Cf. Lipsius, p. 660,
n. 89.
Demos. xlviii. Cf. sec. 48.
Demos. lii. 14.
Demos. lv. 2.

Mercantile suits of this type had to be decided within a month and therefore were not subject to arbitration. As such are probably to be recognized the following: Demos. xxxiii. 12; cf. Lipsius, p. 644, n. 28; p. 657, n. 77. Demos. xxxvii. 22; Lipsius, p. 652; p. 656, n. 74. Demos. lvi (?); Lipsius, pp. 657, 631, 633.

6. δίκη ἐγγύης (Lipsius, p. 688)   (Isaeus v, secs. 1, 31; cf. Wyse, ad. loc.)

7. δίκη ἐξούλης (?) (Lipsius, p. 664)   (Isaeus v. 22.)
(Demos. xxx.)
(Demos. xl. 34. Cf. xxi. 81.)

8. δίκη ἐπιτροπῆς   Lysias xxxii. Cf. sec. 2.
Demos. xxvii, xxviii. Cf. xxvii. 49 f.

Usually considered, e.g., by Lipsius, pp. 532 f., as coming under the archon, but without evidence. The presence of arbitral procedure in both cases points to the jurisdiction of the Forty.

9. δίκη κακηγορίας (Lipsius, p. 646)   Lysias x. 6.
Demos. xxi. 81.

10. δίκη κλοπῆς under the Forty and
subject to arbitration   Demos. xxii. 27; xxiv. 114.

11. δίκη προικός (Lipsius, p. 497, n. 101)   Demos. xl. 16–17.
Demos. xli. Cf. sec.12.

To be distinguished from the monthly suit under the same name mentioned in Arist. *Ath. Pol.* lii. 2.

12. δίκη χρέως (Lipsius, p. 725; cf. p. 717, n. 149)   Lysias *Frag.* xvi (Thalheim)
Demos. xlix. 19.

Mercantile suits of this type not subject to arbitration are: Demos. xxxiv; cf. Lipsius, p. 633; Demos. xxxv.

13. *Status Familiae vel Civitatis*   Isaeus xii. Cf. sec. 11.
Demos. xxxix. 2. Cf. xl. 9.
Demos. lix. 60.

CHAPTER VI

WITNESSES

From the time of Solomon to the present day all judges and jurors have been faced with the problem of determining the credibility of litigants and their witnesses in the cases that come before them. There are no witnesses in Homer. In the famous trial scene the litigants alone appeared. The judges were to give the award to the litigant who told the straightest story (τῷ δόμεν, ὃς μετὰ τοῖσι δίκην ἰθύντατα εἴποι).[1] In other words, the judges' decision was determined by their impressions of the relative credibility of the litigants. Solomon devised an apt and unique test of the credibility of the claimants for a child. But such a convincing test could rarely be devised.

Witnesses first appear in Hesiod.[2] In Athens witnesses were used before the time of Solon;[3] and in the time of the orators witnesses in large numbers were used on all occasions. There was one exception: when a man borrowed money from

[1] *Iliad* xviii. 508. For a discussion of the trial scene cf. *supra*, I, 31 ff. Subsequently to this discussion there appeared in 1931 the second volume of Ridgeway, *Early Age of Greece*, in which the whole question of the interpretation of the trial scene is again raised (pp. 360 ff.). Ridgeway's main point, that the metaphor of "straightness" or "crookedness" is always used of judges but never of litigants, he seeks to support by a formidable array of citations. But a negative statement about Greek usage is a bit hazardous. According to the interpretation of Ridgeway there is no statement in the description of the trial regarding the manner in which a verdict was reached. We are told that the judge who gave the best verdict got the two talents. The reader is left to guess who made the award and also to wonder on what basis such an award could be made. But Ridgeway does not realize that the interest in any trial centers not in the judges but in the litigants and their speeches. Homer shows that he is well aware of this principle and devotes the three concluding lines of the passage to the litigants and not to the judges and thereby completes his description of a trial. It was sufficient to say that the judges sat on stone seats in the agora with staves in their hands.

[2] Cf. *supra*, I, 49. For a suggestion regarding the origin of witnesses cf. *supra*, I, 41–42; Leisi, *Der Zeuge*, pp. 142–43.

[3] Cf. *supra*, I, 173 ff.

a banker he took no witnesses, for the banker had his books as evidence of the loan.[1] A client of Demosthenes remarks in a cynical vein that men borrow in private and repay in public.[2]

In the orators the litigant is always represented as summoning his opponent with two witnesses. But it is clear from Aristophanes that only one was necessary.[3]

Among citizens those only were competent witnesses who were adult males not disqualified by *atimia*. Parties to a suit were not competent witnesses in their own cases.[4] Free aliens, with one possible exception, could be witnesses in all cases but their own.[5] Demosthenes in his speech *On the Embassy* proposed to confirm some of his statements by testifying in his own behalf and rendering himself liable to a δίκη ψευδομαρτυρίων:

> To prove the truth of my statements, in the first place, I will draw up my own deposition and make myself responsible as a witness; in the next place, I call each of the other ambassadors, and will force them to do one or the other, to give testimony or swear they are unable. If they swear they are unable, I shall convict them of perjury before you clearly.[6]

But this is a mere rhetorical trick to impress the dicasts with his sincerity where he is not certain that the witnesses whom he proposes to call will testify.[7]

What interest in a suit made a person a party to it? Could a κύριος both plead and testify for a woman or a minor liti-

---

[1] Isoc. xvii. 2.   [2] Demos. xxxiv. 30.

[3] *Clouds* 1218; *Wasps* 1408, 1416. An inscription found in Decelea shows that upon the introduction of a new member into the phratry three witnesses were present (*IG*², II, 1237; Simon, *Wiener Studien*, XII, 70).

[4] Demos. xl. 58: μάρτυρες μὲν εἰσιν οὗτοι, οἷς μὴ μέτεστι τοῦ πράγματος περὶ οὗ ἡ δίκη ἐστίν; xlvi. 9: μαρτυρεῖν γὰρ οἱ νόμοι οὐκ ἐῶσιν αὐτὸν αὑτῷ οὔτ' ἐπὶ ταῖς γραφαῖς οὔτ' ἐπὶ ταῖς δίκαις οὔτ' ἐν ταῖς εὐθύναις. As Leisi (*op. cit.*, p. 28) points out, this incompetency is accidental.

[5] Cf. Leisi, *op. cit.*, p. 7, for a list of non-citizen witnesses. According to Harpocration, *s.v.* διαμαρτυρία (cf. Leisi, pp. 30 f.), a foreigner could not enter a *diamartyria* in a δίκη ἀποστασίου although metics and *isoteleis* could do so.

[6] xix. 176.

[7] Cf. Leisi, *op. cit.*, p. 28; Lipsius, *Das Attische Recht*, pp. 875–76.

gant? In Isaeus,[1] Xenocles the husband and κύριος of Phile
laid claim to the estate of Pyrrhus in her behalf and made a
diamartyria to the effect that the estate could not be claimed
by Phile's rival claimant because Phile was the legitimate
daughter of Pyrrhus.[2] Similarly in another case in Isaeus,
Chaerestratus v. *Androcles*,[3] Androcles as ἐπίτροπος of the
children of Alce claimed the estate of Euctemon in their behalf and made a *diamartyria*. It is for bearing false witness
in this *diamartyria* that he is being prosecuted in this case.
In a speech attributed to Demosthenes,[4] Leostratus was
claimant to the estate of Archiades, and his son Leochares
handled the case for his father and made a *diamartyria*. In
effect, then, Leochares made an affidavit in his own behalf
because his interest in the case was such that he could not be
included with those οἷς μὴ μέτεστι τοῦ πράγματος περὶ οὗ ἡ δίκη
ἐστίν.[5] The reason for this exception is because in matters involving the devolution of estates few persons outside those
immediately interested could be found who had enough
knowledge of the facts to risk a prosecution for false witness.

There are some cases where it is difficult to discover whether a given person has a sufficient interest in a suit to be regarded as an incompetent witness. In *Mantitheus* v. *Boeotus*[6]
the plaintiff complains that one Crito who was a witness
against him was really an opponent (οὐ μαρτυρεῖ τούτῳ νῦν
ἀλλ' ἐμοὶ ἀντιδικεῖ), but it is impossible to determine from the
speech the nature of Crito's interest in the litigation.[7] In a
bottomry case, *Chrysippus* v. *Phormio*,[8] Lampis, a ship captain, had an interest in the case because whichever party won
he might be held liable rightly or wrongly for a sum of money
said to have been intrusted to him. And yet the plaintiff com-

[1] iii. 2–3.

[2] Cf. Wyse, *The Speeches of Isaeus*, pp. 273 ff.; Lipsius, *op. cit.*, p. 859, n. 45.

[3] vi. 10, 26, 46, 53, 58; cf. Lipsius, *op. cit.*

[4] xliv. 46, 54; cf. Lipsius, *op. cit.*, p. 859.

[5] Demos. xl. 58. [6] *Ibid.*

[7] Cf. Sandys and Paley, *Demosthenes' Select Private Orations*, I, 242–43.

[8] Demos. xxxiv. 11, 46.

plains that his evidence was not offered. In another bottomry case, *Zenothemis* v. *Demon*,[1] the plaintiff laid claim to a cargo of wheat on the ground that it had been mortgaged to him by the captain, who had been drowned on the homeward voyage. But the defendant claimed that he had lent the money for the purchase of the cargo to a merchant named Protus and proposed to call Protus to give testimony. And yet Protus had an interest in the suit, for if Zenothemis got the cargo Demon would in all probability have sued Protus for the loan.

Under these circumstances it would be unwise to attach much importance to the protests of litigants against a witness on the ground of interest. In practice, at least, no one was prevented from appearing as a witness by reason of interest, unless he was actually a party to the suit, and even then he was allowed in inheritance cases to put in an affidavit, *diamartyria*, that the estate of the deceased was not subject to litigation on the ground that there was legitimate issue of the deceased alive.[2] The representatives of women or children were allowed to make a *diamartyria* under the same circumstances. The affiant in these cases was liable to a δίκη ψευδομαρτυρίων and is thus actually a witness in his own behalf.[3]

In most classes of incompetency there are virtual exceptions. Although a party to a suit could not be a witness, yet the confession of a defendant is excellent evidence. Thus a homicide might at the end of the first speech of the prosecutor withdraw from the case and go into exile. His acceptance of the penalty of exile is tantamount to a confession that he is guilty. If he returns illegally from exile he is subject to the death penalty.[4] Andocides, after confessing his guilt in the

---

[1] *Ibid.* xxxii. 30.

[2] *Ibid.* xliv. 54–55; cf. Meier-Schömann-Lipsius, *Der Attische Process*, p. 847, n. 227. It is possible that Demosthenes is not stating an actual rule of law, but is merely seeking to discredit the testimony on the ground of interest or hearsay.

[3] Isaeus iii. 3.

[4] Demos. xxiii. 28; Pollux viii. 117 excepts parricides; cf. *infra*, p. 231; Gilbert, *Const. Antiqu.*, p. 387.

mutilation of the Hermae, was excluded from the agora and the holy places. This *atimia* was inflicted by the decree of Isotimides excluding from public places those who confessed impiety. Anyone liable under this decree could be prosecuted on the basis of his confession.[1] Malefactors (κακοῦργοι), when summarily arrested, could be executed by the Eleven at once if they confessed. The confession was made before trial. Indeed, there was no regular trial in a dicastic court, as is shown by the fact that if they denied their guilt they were brought to trial.[2] But it is a mistake to take the implication of Aristotle's language or the statement of Demosthenes to mean that there was no judicial action. The point is that the Eleven could on their own authority exercise judicial functions where the accused person confessed. It is another relic of the pre-Solonian judicial power of the magistrates.[3] It is idle to suppose that the Eleven made no inquiry at all or did not discuss the case among themselves. Experience has shown that in modern times persons have for various reasons confessed to crimes which they did not in fact commit. Hence the practice of carefully checking every item in a confession before bringing the case to trial.

The unexplained failure of a party to appear for the trial was sufficient evidence for a verdict by default.[4] In a public prosecution, if the defendant fled the country his flight was regarded as a confession of guilt and he was forthwith condemned *in absentia*.[5] The prosecution in the Herodes murder case had read in court a letter written by Euxitheus, the defendant, announcing to one Lycinus that he had killed

---

[1] Andoc. i. 71; Lysias vi. 24.

[2] Arist. *Ath. Pol.* lii. 1: ἂν δ'ἀμφισβητῶσιν (the Eleven) εἰσάξοντας εἰς τὸ δικαστήριον.

[3] Cf. *ibid.* iii. 5; *supra*, I, 279 ff.

[4] Demos. xxi. 81. An appeal against a verdict by default could be taken. Often there were perfectly reasonable grounds for not appearing; cf. Meier-Schömann-Lipsius, *op. cit.*, pp. 973 ff.

[5] Lycurg. i. 117: Ἵππαρχον γὰρ τὸν Τιμάρχου οὐχ ὑπομείναντα τὴν περὶ τῆς προδοσίας ἐν τῷ δήμῳ κρίσιν, ἀλλ' ἔρημον τὸν ἀγῶνα ἐάσαντα, θανάτῳ τοῦτον ζημιώσαντες.

Herodes. Such a letter, if proved to be genuine, would amount to a confession and be conclusive evidence.[1]

A litigant always had the right to question his opponent in court.[2] These examinations are survivals of the old pre-Solonian trial before a magistrate and constitute the nearest Athenian approach to modern testimonial evidence. In the few interrogatories that have been preserved little or no information of value is discovered. In Lysias[3] the grain-dealers charged with profiteering, upon being questioned in court, admitted the charge, but they claimed they had official sanction for what they had done. Lysias' own interrogation of Eratosthenes was probably distressing for Eratosthenes and may have had some effect on the dicasts, but it produced nothing new. Eratosthenes, like the grain-dealers, admitted that he arrested Polemarchus but pleaded that he was acting under orders.[4] At best it was a rhetorical device to embarrass one's opponent rather than a means for securing information. Thus in the *Acharnians*[5] of Aristophanes the old men complain that in litigation they fall easy victims to young prosecutors skilled in the new rhetoric who "called them up and cross-examined them, setting little verbal traps." A good illustration of what Aristophanes has in mind is Socrates' examination of Meletus, who makes damaging admissions.[6] The importance attached to these interrogatories is shown by the fact that some attention was paid to them in books on rhetoric.[7] In the hands of an expert they might be useful, but they were both useless and dangerous to a man who bought his speech. For these and other reasons interrogations were abandoned by the speech-writers, although men who conducted their own cases may well have continued to use them. Technically, however, the admissions of an opponent in court could not be classed as evidence, because a δίκη ψευδομαρτυρίων could not be brought against him.

[1] Antiph. v. 53 ff. The defendant claimed the letter was a forgery.

[2] Cf. *supra*, p. 8.   [4] xii. 25.

[3] xxii. 5.   [5] 687.   [6] Plato *Apol.* 24C ff.

[7] Anaximenes xxxvi, in Spengel-Hammer, *Rhetores Graeci*, I, 94 f.

The role played by evidence in an Athenian court is quite different from its role in modern practice. If one should read merely the depositions and other documentary evidence presented at a trial in the fourth century, he would know very little about the case compared with the jury who heard the speeches also in an Athenian court; but a perusal of a transcript of the evidence in a modern trial would yield the reader as much knowledge of the facts as had the jury which gave the verdict. To put the matter in another way: In Athens the dicasts looked to the speaker for the law and facts and to the witnesses for corroboration; with us the jury looks to the witnesses for the facts and to the judge and counsel for the law and an integration of the results of examination and cross-examination of the witnesses. The litigants appear only as witnesses.

In Athens the evidentiary character of a forensic speech was well understood. The better speech-writers always had in view the credibility of the speaker. They considered it important that both the speech and the thought should by their simplicity and candor render the speaker worthy of confidence. This feature of their professional work was known as *ethopoiia*. In the hands of a skilled writer like Lysias[1] it became a most effective instrument of persuasion, for Athenian dicasts, like any other judges, were largely influenced by their opinion of the moral worth of a litigant. There was little or no chance to judge of the credibility of a witness who stood facing the dicasts while his affidavit was being read, and with a bow acknowledged it as his own. Before the period of written evidence the situation was not much better, whether the witness told his brief story of confirmation in his own way or, as is more likely, answered the questions of the litigant who called him.[2] In the absence of an opportunity to cross-exam-

---

[1] Cf. Devries, *Ethopoiia: A Rhetorical Study of the Types of Character in the Orations of Lysias*; Egger, *Mémoires de littérature ancienne*, p. 372.

[2] Aristoph. *Wasps* 962–65:

ἄκουσον ὦ δαιμόνιέ μου τῶν μαρτύρων.
ἀνάβηθι, τυρόκνηστι, καὶ λέξον μέγα·
σὺ γὰρ ταμιεύουσ' ἔτυχες. ἀπόκριναι σαφῶς,
εἰ μὴ κατέκνησας τοῖς στρατιώταις ἄλαβες.

ine witnesses the opposing litigant had to adopt other means of discrediting and impeaching witnesses.[1]

Speeches are often prefaced by promises to tell the whole truth, or by an excuse that the speaker, owing to his youth or absence from the city at a certain time, is hampered in presenting the case by lack of firsthand knowledge of the facts.[2] One of Isocrates' clients, with the purpose of discrediting his opponent's statements, introduced evidence to show that on a previous occasion he had been guilty of perjury.[3] Demosthenes even argues that the law against hearsay evidence ought in justice to be observed by prosecutors in their speeches.[4] The practice of swearing to pleadings was some check on false statements, even though the oaths were formal and did not render one liable to a prosecution of any kind.[5]

Not infrequently a man found it impossible to procure corroborative testimony and had to go into court with nothing but his bare speech.[6] That juries did believe the unconfirmed statements of a litigant is clear from a case in the Demosthenic corpus.[7] The statements of an advocate involving matters of fact were not corroborated by evidence directly though they might rest on evidence in the speech of the principal.[8] The advocate himself might be a witness.[9] Certain types of information were regularly given in a speech without direct confirmation. Thus a speaker might tell something for which his mother could vouch, with or without a challenge to accept her oath.[10]

[1] Cf. *infra*, pp. 135 f.

[2] Antiph. v. 74; vi. 14; Andoc. i. 55; Lysias i. 5; xxxi. 4; Demos. xxvii. 2; xxxviii. 6.

[3] Isoc. xviii. 52, 57.   [4] Demos. lvii. 4.

[5] Antiph. vi. 14; Demos. xxxiii. 14; Andoc. i. 55; but cf. Antiph. i. 28.

[6] Cf. Isoc. xxi; Antiph. i. Blass (*Attische Beredsamkeit*, I², 189) thinks that proof of the father's dying injunctions may have been given before the speech. This is very unlikely. Gernet (*Antiphon: Discours*, pp. 36 f.) believes that the rule requiring all witnesses to swear to the guilt or innocence of the defendant in homicide cases (Lysias iv. 4) accounts for the lack of witnesses.

[7] xliii. 9–10, 30.   [8] Isaeus iv.   [9] *Ibid.* xii. 4; Aeschin. ii. 170, 184.

[10] Demos. xxvii. 40; cf. lv. 23–24, where the speaker recites what he learned from his mother: καὶ λέγω μὲν ἅ περ ἤκουσα τῆς μητρός, οὕτως ἐμοὶ πολλὰ ἀγαθὰ γένοιτο, εἰ δὲ ψεύδομαι, τἀναντία τούτων. Cf. *ibid.* 27, where a challenge to an oath is offered.

Another type of corroboration to which speakers appeal is the knowledge of the dicasts as individuals. These appeals were rather common[1] and of some advantage, as may be inferred from efforts made to discredit them. A speaker in the Demosthenic corpus says that those who have nothing truthful to say and no evidence to produce are accustomed to appeal to the knowledge of the dicasts.[2] Sometimes the speaker apologizes for confirming by evidence matters well known to the dicasts.[3] It was customary to ask those dicasts who knew to inform their neighbors.[4] Naturally the dicasts could be called upon as confirmatory witnesses only in matters of public knowledge.[5] The private information of a few individuals among five hundred would be of little or no avail.

Women were not competent witnesses except in homicide cases.[6] As women lived a secluded life and had no contact with business or affairs, their incompetency did not materially affect the administration of justice as it would in a modern community. Besides, many of the hardships that their incompetency might have caused could be mitigated by various expedients well known to all litigants. The information possessed by a woman could be included in the speech of the litigant without confirmation, or it could come under the exceptions to hearsay evidence.[7] A woman could also take an evidentiary oath and testify if both parties were willing.[8] There is one case in which the account-books of a woman recording debts owing her were admitted.[9] Minors, like women, were not competent witnesses except in homicide

---

[1] Antiph. vi. 25; Lysias x. 1; Demos. xxi. 80; xxxiv. 50; xliv. 67.

[2] Demos. xl. 53: ὥστε περὶ ὧν ἂν μὴ ἔχῃ μαρτυρίας παρασχέσθαι, ταῦτα φήσει ὑμᾶς εἰδέναι, ὦ ἄνδρες δικασταί, ὃ πάντες ποιοῦσιν οἱ μηδὲν ὑγιὲς λέγοντες.

[3] Lysias xii. 61; cf. Demos. lvii. 33.

[4] In Demos. xl. 54 the jurors are warned not to let such appeals in this case go unchallenged.

[5] *Ibid.* xxi. 18.

[6] For women and children as witnesses in homicide cases cf. *infra*, pp. 221 ff.

[7] Cf. *infra*, pp. 130 f.   [8] Cf. *infra*, p. 159.   [9] Demos. xli. 9, 19, 24.

cases. But on reaching majority one could testify to what he knew while he was a minor.[1]

The testimony of slaves could not be produced in court unless it was given under torture.[2] A passage from Antiphon has been cited to show that the statement of a slave might be accepted as trustworthy without torture. The situation is as follows. A choregus had been informally accused of homicide by the brother of the deceased in a court where the choregus was to begin a prosecution of some officials for malversation of public moneys. It must be remembered that the suit had not yet been filed with the king archon. In answer to this informal accusation the choregus proclaimed before the same dicasts that more than fifty persons, bond and free, young and old, knew the real facts of the case, and challenged the brother of the boy to find out the facts from these individuals before he took action. He was to ἐλέγχειν τοὺς μὲν ἐλευθέρους ὡς χρὴ τοὺς ἐλευθέρους . . . . τοὺς δὲ δούλους, εἰ μὲν αὐτῷ ἐρωτῶντι τἀληθῆ δοκοῖεν λέγειν, εἰ δὲ μή, ἕτοιμος ἦ 'εκδιδόναι βασανίζειν.[3] The whole proceeding was extra-judicial. In fact the choregus hoped that as a result of this investigation there would be no prosecution.[4] Leisi[5] quotes another passage from Isocrates where Pasion the banker agreed to produce one Kittus for torture, but when the plaintiff demanded that the βασανισταί scourge and rack the slave until they got the truth out of him, Pasion objected and ἐκέλευε λόγῳ πυνθάνεσθαι παρὰ τοῦ παιδός.[6] Owing to this disagreement the questioning was dropped. If Pasion was right in his contention that there was to be no torture but a sort of formal examination for discovery ((λόγῳ μὲν ἐκέλευσε βασανίζειν, ἔργῳ δ' οὐκ εἴα)[7] in order to settle the matter in dispute without legal proceedings, we have here an attempt to have the dispute settled without a trial.

[1] Cf. Lipsius, op. cit., p. 874, n. 32.

[2] Cf. infra, pp. 223 ff.   [3] Antiph. vi. 23; cf. Lipsius, op. cit., p. 888.

[4] On this occasion, as it happened, the king archon refused to entertain the charge because it was too late for him to conclude it during his official year.

[5] Op. cit., p. 20.   [6] Isoc. xvii. 15.   [7] Ibid. 17.

Leisi[1] cites another case in the Demosthenic corpus[2] in which the confession of a slave is accepted without torture. But here again the matter is entirely private. It was not uncommon for heirs of the estate to agree to reserve the slaves as common property, to enable either party to obtain by torture or otherwise any property which he suspected the slaves were concealing.[3] In the case cited by Leisi the heirs actually did recover money stolen by a slave belonging to the deceased. They at first threatened to torture him, but when he confessed (αὑτοῦ κατεῖπε) and produced the money he had stolen, naturally they accepted his statement. These cases in no wise justify us in assuming that even by agreement of the parties statements of slaves made without torture would be accepted in court. They could of course be valid by agreement for the settlement of an issue out of court, as in the case of the claim against Pasion the banker, if the agreement to torture had been carried out and the βασανισταί like private arbitrators had given their award.[4] Such free statements of slaves might come up indirectly before a court if a party to such a settlement refused to abide by it and resorted to legal proceedings.[5]

Among commonplaces taught to students of rhetoric for use in forensic speeches were those praising or disparaging the testimony of slaves extracted by torture. In the orators these commonplaces, variously worded, appear frequently.[6] Arguments both for and against torture as a means of securing reliable evidence appear in the same orator.[7] The perusal of these commonplaces found in the extant orations will con-

---

[1] *Op. cit.*, p. 21.

[2] xlviii. 16 ff.

[3] Demos. xl. 15.

[4] Isoc. xvii. 17–18.

[5] Leisi (*op. cit.*, pp. 20 f.) incautiously seems to treat statements such as those contemplated in Antiphon vi. 23 and Isocrates xvii. 15 as evidence in court: "Aber ohne Zweifel war diese Art Beweismittel bei Einverständnis des Produkten vor Gericht zulässig, nach dem oben ausgesprochenen Grundsatz, dass das Gericht die Glaubwürdigkeit der πίστεις nicht ex officio untersucht." Lipsius (*op. cit.*, p. 888) cites only one passage and is duly cautious.

[6] Cf. Guggenheim, *Die Bedeutung der Folterung im Attischen Processe*, pp. 62 ff.

[7] Cf. Antiph. v. 31 ff. with vi. 25.

vince any reader that the Athenians attached little importance to βάσανοι. The negative side of the law should be kept
in mind. The very fact that it did not permit slave evidence
to be accepted without torture shows that they believed the
statements of slaves were not trustworthy. Furthermore, the
law did not permit a litigant to introduce the testimony of his
own slaves even if they had been put to torture by those who
made it their business to punish and whip slaves to make
them disclose some information.[1] The proper procedure was
to challenge one's opponent to put the slave to the question
under conditions to be agreed upon. Either the answers were
taken down in writing, sealed, and produced in court or those
who heard them testified in court, giving the answers in their
evidence.[2] Or a litigant might challenge his opponent to permit his slave to be put to the question.

These commonplaces regarding βάσανοι are not uttered to
discredit or to support testimony of this kind actually before
the court. For there is no single instance in the extant orations
in which βάσανοι were produced in court. A litigant praises
slave evidence when he claims that his opponent, by refusing
to accept a challenge to admit evidence extorted by the rack,
has deprived him of the most reliable kind of evidence available. Or he disparages it because he himself has refused to
accept his opponent's challenge to permit the introduction of
information extracted by torture from his own or another's
slave. There are plenty of reasons why a man should distrust
all such evidence. There is a note of insincerity about these
rhetorical commonplaces. One feels that these challenges and
counterchallenges are just moves in the game of litigation.
Only two challenges, so far as we know, were accepted, and
these were not carried out by reason of disputes as to the
terms actually agreed upon.[3] Headlam puts forward the the-

[1] Lysias i. 16–19.

[2] Demos. liii. 24–25; cf. Lipsius, *op. cit.*, p. 894; regarding the possibility of putting
slaves to the question in open court cf. *infra*, pp. 129 f.

[3] Isoc. xvii. 19, where the banker was willing to forfeit the sum of money agreed
upon if he failed to carry out the contract. Demos. xxxvii. 40 ff. shows how mis-
understandings could be promoted by a scheming litigant.

ory that there are no cases which clearly state that the answers of slaves under torture obtained by a πρόκλησις could be brought before a jury.[1] This is a plausible proposition, but the passages quoted by Headlam do not support it.[2]

On two occasions slaves were produced in court as real evidence, which in modern practice has been defined as "all evidence that is addressed directly to the senses of the jury without the intervention of the testimony of witnesses." Such "exhibits" are usually things, but persons are also included in so far as their qualities are those of things. A client of Isocrates was accused of killing a female slave.[3] To refute the charge sworn to by Callimachus, the prosecutor, and fourteen witnesses, the defendant produced the woman alive and well in court. The language of the speaker in commenting on this proof of the unreliability of Callimachus shows clearly that he realizes just the kind of evidence that was presented in the person of the female slave: τοὺς μὲν γὰρ ἄλλους ἐκ τῶν λεγομένων κρίνετε, τὴν δὲ τούτου μαρτυρίαν, ὅτι ψευδὴς ἦν, εἶδον οἱ δικάζοντες.[4] In *Nicobulus* v. *Pantaenetus* a slave named Antigenes is produced for the inspection of the dicasts to show that such a feeble old man could not have committed an assault upon Pantaenetus.[5]

It may be a matter of accident that βάσανοι do not appear in extant cases. Sometimes the evidence of a slave was intended to settle the matter at issue out of court so to speak. Such settlements would not be mentioned unless one of the parties refused to abide by the settlement and took the matter to court. However, the words of Aristophanes in the *Clouds*[6] and Aristotle's classification of βάσανοι as ἄτεχνοι πίστεις[7] show that slaves were put to the question in connection with legal proceedings. The state had power to torture slaves to secure evidence against their masters, but only on

[1] *CR*, VII, 1.

[2] Cf. Thompson, *ibid.*, VIII, 136; Lipsius, *op. cit.*, p. 889, n. 91.

[3] Isoc. xviii. 53 ff.   [4] *Ibid.* 56.   [5] Demos. xxxvii. 44.

[6] 620: κᾆθ' ὅταν θύειν δέῃ, στρεβλοῦτε καὶ δικάζετε.   [7] *Rhet.* i. 15.

rare occasions was this power exercised.[1] When slaves became informers (μηνυταί) against their masters or others they received their freedom if the charge was sustained.[2] It seems also that they might be put to the question and afterward set free.[3] Not infrequently the rack was used to extort a confession from a slave suspected of a crime, and such confessions might implicate others.[4]

Hearsay evidence was strictly forbidden in Athenian courts: οὐδὲ μαρτυρεῖν ἀκοὴν ἐῶσιν οἱ νόμοι, οὐδ' ἐπὶ τοῖς πάνυ φαύλοις ἐγκλήμασιν.[5] The witness must confine himself to matters of which he had personal knowledge: ἂν εἰδῇ τις καὶ οἷς ἂν παραγένηται πραττομένοις, ταῦτα μαρτυρεῖν κελεύουσιν (οἱ νόμοι).[6] Exceptions were allowed under certain circumstances, most commonly when the original witness was dead. In the orators this exception is frequently added to the rule (ἀκοὴν δ' οὐκ ἐῶσι ζῶντος μαρτυρεῖν, ἀλλὰ τεθνεῶτος).[7] There are few examples of the exception in the case of deceased persons,[8] but there are a number of complaints in the orators that opponents are breaking the law.[9] Plato,[10] in conformity with a genuine forensic speech, represents Socrates as promising that testimony regarding the answer of the oracle "that no one was wiser than Socrates" would be given by the brother of Chaerephon since Chaerephon, the recipient, was deceased.

It was permitted to give hearsay evidence of the statements of those who were incompetent to testify. In one of Demosthenes' cases testimony was produced that a woman

---

[1] Andoc. i. 22, 64.

[2] Lysias vii. 16; Antiph. v. 34; cf. *Tet.* A. γ. 4.   [3] Antiph. v. 31.

[4] *Ibid.* i. 20. Regarding the status of the concubine of Philoneus there has been some dispute. Guggenheim (*op. cit.*, p. 23), after a detailed discussion of the question, rightly concludes that she was a slave. Gernet (*op. cit.*, p. 43, n. 2) agrees. Lipsius (*op. cit.*, p. 895, n. 122), without giving any reason, dissents.

[5] Demos. lvii. 4.   [6] *Ibid.* xlvi. 6.   [7] *Ibid.* 7; cf. xliv. 55.

[8] Isaeus viii. 14: τίνας εἰκὸς εἰδέναι τὰ παλαιά; δῆλον ὅτι τοὺς χρωμένους τῷ πάππῳ. μεμαρτυρήκασι τοίνυν ἀκοὴν οὗτοι. Cf. *ibid.* 29; Demos. xliii. 35–36.

[9] *Ibid.* xliv. 55; xlvi. 7; lvii. 4.   [10] *Apol.* 21A.

declared that the seals on a will of her mother were genuine.[1] Normally the evidence of a woman could be presented by her κύριος.[2] The evidence of a female metic could be given by her *prostatés*.[3] A litigant could always question his opponent in court,[4] but he usually preferred to produce a witness in whose presence his opponent had made damaging admissions either voluntarily or in answer to questions.[5]

There is another class of persons consisting of men, closely associated with parties to a suit or their witnesses, whose previous statements and admissions are produced in court by the depositions of regular witnesses. In a case in Isaeus[6] the statement of one Hierocles was introduced in evidence—a statement to the effect that he had a certain will in his possession which he had received from the testator. This admission, made somewhat unwillingly by Hierocles, is used by the speaker to the disadvantage of the claimant for the estate, the son of Cleon. Another example is found in *Chrysippus* v. *Phormio*.[7] Lampis, the agent of Phormio, at first denied that he had received a certain sum of money; but later on, having been tampered with by Phormio, he virtually became his witness. Chrysippus then produced evidence of his denial of the receipt of the money in question. A curious instance is related by Aeschines.[8] He called an Olynthian named Aristophanes to give evidence that Demosthenes had approached him to substantiate a discreditable story against Aeschines. For further substantiation Aeschines also called men who were present when Aristophanes told Aeschines of Demosthenes' proposal. Leisi accepts these exceptions to the

---

[1] xli. 24. Cf. Lysias xxxii, where the woman's story, told before a group of relatives gathered to settle a δίκη ἐπιτροπῆς out of court (§§ 12 ff.), is told by the speaker and confirmed by witnesses (§ 18).

[2] Cf. *supra*, pp. 118 f.; Isaeus xii. 5; Demos. lvii. 67 ff., where husbands and relatives testify for women.

[3] Demos. xxv. 56–58. [4] Cf. *supra*, p. 122.

[5] Demos. xxx. 19–20; l. 37; lviii. 33: καί μοι κάλει Φιλιππίδην τὸν Παιανιέα, πρὸς ὃν ἔλεγε ταῦτα Θεοκρίνης οὑτοσί, καὶ τοὺς ἄλλους οἳ συνίσασι τούτῳ ταῦτα λέγοντι.

[6] ix. 6; cf. *infra*, p. 137.

[7] Demos. xxxiv. 11, 46. [8] ii. 155; cf. Leisi, *op. cit.*, p. 97.

rule against hearsay evidence,[1] and adds another category, including statements of slaves with or without torture, substantiated in court by *Solemnitätszeugen*. This is the correct classification of statements made by slaves. On one occasion Aeschines offers slaves for torture before the dicasts to establish an alibi for himself: ἄγωμεν δὲ καὶ τοὺς οἰκέτας καὶ παραδιδῶμεν εἰς βάσανον. καὶ τὸν μὲν λόγον, εἰ συγχωρήσει ὁ κατήγορος, καταλύω. παρέσται δὲ ἤδη ὁ δήμιος καὶ βασανιεῖ ἐναντίον ὑμῶν, ἂν κελεύητε.[2] In the face of a statement of the plaintiff in *Apollodorus* v. *Stephanus*,[3] βασανίζειν οὐκ ἔστιν ἐναντίον ὑμῶν, we cannot suppose, even with the support of another passage from Demosthenes[4] or Aristophanes' line κᾆθ' ὅταν θύειν δέῃ, στρεβλοῦτε καὶ δικάζετε,[5] that dicasts ever listened to the answers of a slave under torture as they listened to parole evidence and affidavits.[6] A challenge of any kind could be delivered at any time. In the Demosthenes passage the challenge was delivered for greater effect when the dicasts were assembling. Aeschines goes a step farther and delivers one in the court itself with the additional proposal that it could be carried out then and there.[7]

Exceptions to the hearsay rule were allowed, as we have seen, when the person who knew the facts was either dead or disqualified; but if a qualified person could not appear in court because of illness or absence from the country, the matter was handled in another fashion. Such testimony was

---

[1] *Op. cit.*, pp. 96 f. Lipsius (*op. cit.*) brushes all aside except where the original witness is dead.

[2] ii. 126.   [3] Demos. xlv. 16.

[4] xlvii. 17: ἔδει αὐτὸν . . . . κληρουμένων τῶν δικαστηρίων κομίσαντα τὴν ἄνθρωπον . . . . κελεύειν ἐμέ εἰ βουλοίμην βασανίζειν καὶ μάρτυρας τοὺς δικαστὰς εἰσιόντας ποιεῖσθαι ὡς ἕτοιμός ἐστι παραδοῦναι.

[5] *Clouds* 620.

[6] Guggenheim's ingenuity in trying to reconcile these passages (*op. cit.*, pp. 37 ff.) is wasted: "Wir nehmen gerne an, dass dem Redner es genügte, dass Folterung vor Gericht nicht gewöhnlich war, um für seinen Zweck behaupten zu können, sie kommen vor Gericht gar nicht vor."

[7] For the literature cf. Bonner, *Evidence in Athenian Courts*, p. 73; Lipsius, *op. cit.*, p. 892.

called ἐκμαρτυρίαι, i.e., extra-judicial depositions. The evidence of persons who were too ill to attend court, or who were absent from the city at the time of the hearings, could be taken in writing in the presence of a number of persons who afterward on the production of the document in court identified it by an attesting affidavit as the statement of the original witness.[1] The evidence was not taken by any official or a commission appointed by the court.[2] It was the business of the litigant who desired the evidence. No specified number of attesting witnesses was required, but it was wise to have more than one to avoid suspicion.

When it is a question of obtaining a written deposition [ἐκμαρτυρία] from a witness who is ill or about to go abroad, each of us summons by preference the most reputable among his fellow-citizens and those best known to us, and we always have written depositions[3] made in the presence not of one or two only but of as many witnesses as possible in order to preclude the deponent from denying his deposition at some future date.[4]

There should be two distinct parts of an *ekmartyria*, the first of which contains the facts and the name of the witness who knew them, the second the names of the attesting witnesses and a statement that the *ekmartyria* was in fact made by the extra-judicial witness.[5] A much-disputed series of depositions is found in Demosthenes.[6] In the first passage there is a deposition of one Ersicles and another of Hippias of Halicarnassus to the same effect. Then follow the words πρὸς τούσδε ἐξεμαρτύρησεν, with five names in the nominative case. In the next passage there are three depositions followed by the same words and the names of five witnesses. Lipsius is right in regarding the five depositions as *ekmartyriai* followed

---

[1] Cf. Aeschin. ii. 19: καὶ τὴν ἐκμαρτυρίαν ἀνάγνωθι τὴν Ἀριστοδήμου, καὶ κάλει πρὸς οὓς ἐξεμαρτύρησεν. Cf. Demos. xlvi. 7: τῶν δὲ ἀδυνάτων καὶ ὑπερορίων ἐκμαρτυρίαν γεγραμμένην ἐν γραμματείῳ.

[2] This is made clear by Leisi (*op. cit.*, p. 98).

[3] ἐκμαρτυρίας should be translated "extra-judicial depositions" to distinguish them from regular depositions, μαρτυρίας.

[4] Isaeus iii. 20–21 (trans. Forster). In this case an *ekmartyria* attested by only two witnesses had been denied (§§ 18, 23).

[5] Aeschin. ii. 19; Demos. xlvi. 7.   [6] xxxv. 20, 33–34.

by the names of the attesting witnesses; τούσδε are these witnesses.[1]

The lexicographers seem to identify extra-judicial evidence with hearsay, but Demosthenes carefully differentiates them.[2] The confusions between hearsay and extra-judicial evidence found in the lexicographers may be due to the fact that before the use of written testimony in 378 B.C. there could be no real distinction between the two in form. The only distinction lay in the responsibility. One might hold the sick or the absent responsible if what they said turned out to be false; or the attesting witness could be held responsible if the original witness successfully denied the *ekmartyria* attributed to him.[3] There could be no responsibility on the part of the deceased persons or those incompetent to testify, such as parties to a suit, women and slaves. Only those who reported the statements of such persons could be held responsible.[4]

The *ekmartyriai* which we know belong to the period when written testimony was required by law.[5] We hear nothing of *ekmartyria* in Antiphon, Andocides, and Lysias. And yet it must have been a hardship in many cases before 378 B.C. to be unable in some fashion to produce the evidence of persons who were ill or out of the city. Platner,[6] relying on a passage in Isaeus already quoted,[7] suggests that the testimony of the original witness was not always reduced to writing, because Isaeus says that one always provided a large number of estimable attesting witnesses. This conclusion does not fol-

[1] *Op. cit.*, p. 887, n. 84. This explanation rests upon Drerup (*Jahrb. f. cl. Phil.*, XXIV, 319), which Leisi (*op. cit.*, p. 99, n. 1) had already accepted. Cf. also Platner, *Process und Klagen*, I, 227.

[2] In Isaeus. iii. 77 ἐκμαρτυρία is loosely used of evidence which is unquestionably hearsay. The acts of a deceased person showing that he had virtually refused to recognize a woman who claimed to be his daughter are termed ἐκμαρτυρία; cf. Aeschin. i. 107 for a use of ἐκμαρτυρήσοντα in the sense of μαρτυρήσοντα.

[3] Demos. xlvi. 7: καὶ ἀπὸ τῆς αὐτῆς ἐπισκήψεως τήν τε μαρτυρίαν καὶ ἐκμαρτυρίαν ἀγωνίζεσθαι ἅμα, ἵν᾽ ἐὰν μὲν ἀναδέχηται ὁ ἐκμαρτυρήσας, ἐκεῖνος ὑπόδικος ᾖ τῶν ψευδομαρτυριῶν, ἐὰν δὲ μὴ ἀναδέχηται, οἱ μαρτυρήσαντες τὴν ἐκμαρτυρίαν.

[4] Cf. Lipsius, *op. cit.*, p. 886.

[5] Demos. xlvi. 7.

[6] *Op. cit.*, p. 226.

[7] iii. 21.

low, however, because this oration belongs to the period when all evidence was required to be written. The language of the lexicographers suggests oral statements but is not inconsistent with affidavits: καὶ ὁμοίως ἐκμαρτυρίαν λέγουσιν, ὅταν τις τὰ παρὰ τοῦ ἀπόντος εἰρημένα ἐκμαρτυρήσῃ.[1] Harpocration draws his information from Demosthenes and Aeschines and defines *ekmartyria* thus: διαφέρει τῆς μαρτυρίας, ὅτι ἡ μὲν μαρτυρία τῶν παρόντων ἐστὶν, ἡ δ' ἐκμαρτυρία τῶν ἀπόντων. As he draws his information from the later orators he has in mind only written evidence, but others, like the *Lexica Segueriana*, may go back to the period of oral evidence.

The rhetoricians paid considerable attention to the grounds upon which the credibility of witnesses might be attacked.[2] Various grounds for suspicion are urged in the orators. A client of Isocrates, after showing that his opponent was convicted of falsehood in open court on a former occasion, pertinently inquires: "Who is more likely to produce a witness of what never happened than my opponent who himself had the effrontery to give false testimony for others?"[3] Wealthy men were under suspicion of securing testimony in their favor as well as other advantages in litigation. Demosthenes[4] makes a thinly veiled suggestion to this effect in his speech against Midias. A stronger statement is found in another speech in the Demosthenic corpus.[5] Friendship or enmity for either party may render the evidence of a witness subject to suspicion.[6] Relationship of a witness to a litigant might be used in an attempt to discredit testimony. Naturally, however, in family matters relatives were the very best witnesses. In fact, failure to produce them might in some circumstances be used against a litigant.[7] A general reputation in the community for untruthfulness exposed a witness to attack.[8] One of the most effective ways of discrediting a witness was to

[1] *Lex. Seg.*, p. 248.

[2] Anaximenes in *op. cit.*, I, 48 ff.; Arist. *Rhet.* i. 15; Volkmann, *Die Rhetorik der Griechen und Römer*, pp. 186 ff.

[3] Isoc. xviii. 57.

[4] xxi. 112, 139.

[5] xliv. 3; cf. lvii. 52.

[6] Cf. Demos. xxix. 22–24; liv. 33.

[7] *Ibid.* xxx. 23; xl. 28; lii. 17.

[8] *Ibid.* xxxvii. 48; liv. 33; cf. Leisi, *op. cit.*, p. 11.

show that he had a financial interest in the suit.[1] Another exceedingly effective way of discrediting a witness was to show that he had had no opportunity of himself knowing what was contained in his affidavit. Such testimony was really hearsay evidence[2] and could be made a ground for a δίκη ψευδομαρτυρίων.

There is singularly little reference to the means at the disposal of a litigant to secure the attendance of witnesses in the various hearings of the case in which he is interested as plaintiff or defendant, whether it be a *diké* or a *graphé*. And yet it is obvious that no judicial system can function satisfactorily if witnesses cannot be obliged to appear in both criminal and civil cases. It may fairly be assumed that in a city like Athens, where men had more leisure than in modern states, one had no difficulty in securing witnesses on any occasion. The association of citizens with one another in demes, tribes, phratries, and clubs was likely to be very close compared with the conditions of life in a modern city.

On most occasions a man engaged in some transaction which might require proof in court would provide himself with reliable witnesses about whose attendance in court there could be little doubt.[3] In emergencies, however, a man had to trust to those present to give testimony in his behalf.[4] When a man called for witnesses in public in Athens there is little doubt that there would be volunteers enough and to spare.[5] It is reasonable to assume that under most circumstances a litigant would have no difficulty in securing adequate testimony without the help of the law. The difficulty would arise when a vital matter depended upon the testimony of one man who for some reason might be unwilling to testify. The earli-

[1] Demos. xl. 58.

[2] Isaeus vi. 53 ff.; Demos. xl. 59; xliv. 54; cf. *supra*, p. 130.

[3] Isaeus iii. 19: ὥστε γὰρ πάντες ὡς ὅταν μὲν ἐπὶ προδήλους πράξεις ἴωμεν, ἃς δεῖ μετὰ μαρτύρων γενέσθαι, τοὺς οἰκειοτάτους καὶ οἷς ἂν τυγχάνωμεν χρώμενοι μάλιστα, τούτους παραλαμβάνειν εἰώθαμεν ἐπὶ τὰς πράξεις τὰς τοιαύτας.

[4] Cf. Aristoph. *Clouds* 494-96. The speaker in Demos. lvii. 14 had to rely on hostile witnesses.

[5] Cf. Antiph. vi. 22 ff., where more than fifty men and boys were present when the fatal draught was administered.

est reference to an unwilling witness occurs in Isaeus,[1] where
the speaker claims that one Hierocles was witness of a fatal
assault but opines that he may be unwilling to give evidence
"detrimental to a will he is producing. But for all that, summon Hierocles that he may give his evidence before the court
or else swear to his ignorance of the fact [ἵνα ἐναντίον τούτων
μαρτυρήσῃ ἢ ἐξομόσηται]."[2] Normally, no doubt, a witness already in court would either testify or take an oath in disclaimer. There was, so far as is known, no legal penalty for a
false ἐξωμοσία. Nevertheless, many a man might well have
shrunk from taking a false oath for the sake of his reputation.[3]

It was incumbent upon the litigant himself to notify his
witnesses to be present at the arbitration or the trial. The
state did not summon witnesses sub poena. There is no evidence that a litigant took care to be in a position to prove
that he had duly notified his witnesses, but there is every
likelihood that he did.[4] If the witness did not appear or refused to take the stand, what recourse had the litigant?
Lycurgus[5] has an interesting section on witnesses.

Before the witnesses take the stand, I wish to say a few words to you.
You are not, I take it, unaware of the schemings of defendants or the en-
treaties of those trying to beg them off; but you well know that many witnesses for the sake of money or to win good-will have been persuaded either
to be forgetful or to fail to appear or to find some other excuse for not testifying. Do you, therefore, require that witnesses take the stand without
fear and that they do not attach more importance to gratitude than to
you and the city, but pay the city their debt of truth and justice and not
desert their post of duty, or touching the altar as the law requires take an
oath of disclaimer. But if they take neither course, we shall, in the interest of you and the laws and the democracy, call them to account [κλητεύ-
σομεν].

The faults for which the recalcitrant witness could be called
to account were failure to appear or, if he appeared, failure
either to testify or to take the oath in disclaimer.[6]

[1] ix. 18.

[2] The date of this speech is shortly after 371 B.C.; cf. Lipsius, op. cit., p. 876, n. 41.

[3] Demos. xix. 176; xlvii. 70.   [4] Cf. Lipsius, op. cit., p. 881.   [5] i. 20.

[6] In ten cases where the alternative was offered only three persons took the oath
of disclaimer (cf. Leisi, op. cit., p. 68).

The procedure involved in κλήτευσις is far from clear.[1] There are two passages that throw some light on the question. The plaintiff in *Apollodorus* v. *Stephanus et Neaera* says: "I shall call Hipparchus himself before you, and compel him to testify or take an oath of disclaimer according to law ἢ κλητεύσω αὐτόν."[2] Aeschines adds another step to the process: κάλει δέ μοι Ἀμύντορα τὸν Ἐρχιέα· καὶ ἐκκλήτευε, ἐὰν μὴ θέλῃ δευρὶ παρεῖναι.[3] On the basis of these two passages one might assume with considerable confidence that when it became apparent that the witness refused to testify or failed to appear, the principal appealed to the court for redress. In some fashion there was judicial action, either by the presiding officer or by the dicasts, but its nature is obscure.[4] The recalcitrant witness was fined one thousand drachmas.[5]

In the passage quoted above from Lycurgus[6] the jury is asked for assistance: ἀξιοῦτε οὖν τοὺς μάρτυρας ἀναβαίνειν. Similarly the plaintiff in *Epichares* v. *Theocrines*[7] makes a plea for help from the dicasts:

Undoubtedly, men of the jury, Theocrines and his friends have tried all they could to tamper with the witnesses, and to induce them, either by threats or persuasion, not to give evidence. However, if you will support me as you ought to do, and command them, or rather join me in compelling them, either to depose or take the oath of disclaimer, and if you will not permit them to trifle with the court, the truth will be discovered.

But in neither of these passages is judicial action contemplated. The speaker is merely trying to put pressure upon the witness by these appeals to the dicasts. As individuals the dicasts might urge the witness to take the stand, just as they might express their annoyance at what a litigant might say.[8] A verdict of a dicastery could be reached only by a formal vote.

Judicial action by a magistrate or board could only take the

---

[1] Wyse, *op. cit.*, p. 638; the word κλήτευσις does not appear in the sources (cf. Lipsius, *op. cit.*, p. 880, n. 55).

[2] *Demos.* lix. 28.   [4] Cf. Lipsius, *op. cit.*, pp. 880–81.   [6] i. 20.

[3] ii. 68.   [5] Aeschin. i. 46.   [7] Demos. lviii. 7.

[8] Cf. Socrates' frequent appeals for an uninterrupted hearing (Plato *Apol.* 27B, 30C).

form of an ἐπιβολή. But the highest ἐπιβολή recorded is fifty drachmas. Besides, an ἐπιβολή was not imposed by a magistrate in court.[1] The fine of one thousand drachmas suggests a parallel with the infliction of a similar fine upon a litigant who failed to obtain at least one-fifth of the votes. In this instance no real judicial action was required. The presiding officer forthwith recorded the fine as soon as the count of the votes showed that the losing litigant was liable under the law.[2] In the case of a defaulting witness the procedure would be much the same, with two exceptions. Upon the request of the party the witness was solemnly called upon to take the stand (κλητεύειν). If he refused, the fine of one thousand drachmas was entered in the record. The proclamation of the fine (ἐκκλητεύειν) by the herald was an unusual feature, intended, no doubt, to impress the witnesses yet to be called. In case the witness was absent, the only difference would be that the defaulting witness could protest the fine if he could show good and sufficient cause for his absence. The intervention of the litigant was required not merely to initiate the punishment of the defaulting witness but possibly to give him an opportunity to choose between the fine and a δίκη λιπομαρτυρίου or a δίκη βλάβης, either of which might be instituted against a witness. It is quite unlikely that a suit for damages could be instituted if the witness had been fined.[3]

The chief source of our information regarding the δίκη λιπομαρτυρίου is a single case, *Apollodorus* v. *Timotheus*.[4] The plaintiff relied on one Antiphanes to prove an important point in his suit:

> He prevented me by a trick from putting a deposition in the box before the arbitrator; for he kept saying that he would give evidence for me by the day of giving the award; and when the day arrived, although he was summoned from his house, (for he was not to be seen,) he failed to attend as a witness at the instigation of the defendant.

The plaintiff then and there commenced proceedings against the defaulting witness before the arbitrator. The nature of

---

[1] Cf. *supra*, I, 282 f.   [2] Cf. *supra*, pp. 56 f.; Lipsius, *op. cit.*, pp. 449–50.
[3] Cf. Bonner, *op. cit.*, pp. 42–43; Leisi, *op. cit.*, p. 49.   [4] Demos. xlix. 19.

these proceedings is wholly obscure. Apollodorus deposited the fee (a drachma) τοῦ λιπομαρτυρίου. The arbitrator did not find against the witness. There is no indication as to what the arbitrator could have done to the witness if his finding had been adverse. As it was, he waited until evening of the final day and gave his decision in favor of Timotheus. The case was appealed and came before a court. Meanwhile, Apollodorus filed a δίκη βλάβης against Antiphanes before the decision of his suit against Timotheus.[1] Just what damages he had suffered beyond the adverse decision of the arbitrator, which could be reversed if the present action was successful, and the loss of the drachma it is hard to tell. Nevertheless, he proceeds to call Antiphanes to take the stand and give his testimony under oath.[2] In the present case Antiphanes is not called as a witness in the usual way, for no affidavit of his was in the hands of the clerk. A request (ἀξιῶ) was made that he take the stand and tell (εἰπεῖν) the dicasts under oath whether he had lent a certain sum of money to Timotheus. But at this time no oral evidence was permitted in a heliastic court; all must be in writing. Neither was it the practice for a litigant to swear his own witnesses. But there is no indication that Antiphanes ever did appear in court. The whole proceeding is without parallel in the orators. Leisi regards it as "eine durch die vorausgehende Erzählung entschuldigte ungesetzliche Massregel des Apollodor."[3] It is hard to believe that Apollodorus seriously proposes something contrary to law, namely, to present oral evidence in court.[4]

The question naturally arises whether the obligation to

---

[1] *Ibid.* 20: "And now I have commenced a private action for damage against Antiphanes, because he neither gave evidence nor took an oath of disclaimer according to law. And I require him to get up and say before you on his oath, first, whether he lent Timotheus a thousand drachmas in Calauria."

[2] This was an arbitration case, and evidence not submitted at the arbitration could not normally be introduced in a court trial. For a discussion of this feature of the case cf. *supra*, p. 100.

[3] *Op. cit.*, p. 54.

[4] It is useless to indulge in speculations such as those of Rentzsch, *De Δίκη Ψευδομαρτυρίων in jure Attico*, pp. 24 ff.; cf. Bonner, *op. cit.*, p. 56; Leisi, *op. cit.*, p. 53.

testify is a duty to the state or to the individual litigant.[1] The words already quoted from Lycurgus[2] show that he believed the duty was owed the state. But since as a rule offenders against the state were prosecuted by volunteers, the means of compelling the attendance of witnesses at a trial must be initiated by the prosecutors. Consequently, there was as a rule[3] no distinction made between witnesses in public suits and witnesses in private cases.

The lexicographers suppose that a δίκη λιπομαρτυρίου was allowed only when the witness had definitely promised to be present.[4] The theory has been advanced that the witness by his promise entered into a contract. The failure to testify upon due notification of the time and the place of the hearing constituted the basis of the δίκη λιπομαρτυρίου.[5] But the decisive objection to this theory of a contract is the fact that friends, relatives, and other unwilling witnesses were compelled to take the stand or take an oath in disclaimer. In *Aphobus* v. *Phanus*[6] it is said that Aphobus had been forced in a previous case to give testimony against his uncle Demon. A better example occurs in the same speech where Aesius took

[1] Leisi, *op. cit.*, p. 38.

[2] i. 20, quoted *supra*, p. 137: ὑπὲρ ὑμῶν καὶ τῶν νόμων καὶ τῆς δημοκρατίας κλητεύσομεν αὐτούς. Photius (*s.v.* λειπομαρτύριον) describes failure to testify as an ἀδίκημα ἐφ' ᾧ γραφὴ ἦν, εἴτις ἐκλείποι μαρτυρίαν. His further statement that κλήτευσις was a form of *graphé* has some justification in the fact that the defaulting witness was fined.

[3] Cf. *supra*, pp. 25 ff., for appointed prosecutors.

[4] Pollux viii. 36: λιπομαρτυρίου δὲ (δίκη) κατὰ τῶν ἰδόντων μὲν καὶ μαρτυρήσειν ὁμολογησάντων, ἐν δὲ τῷ καιρῷ τὴν μαρτυρίαν ἐκλιπόντων. Cf. Photius, *s.v.* λειπομαρτύριον.

[5] Rentzsch (*op. cit.*, pp. 20 ff.) maintains that the agreement need not have been consummated in the presence of witnesses, citing as proof the words of Hyperides iii. 13: ὡς ὁ νόμος λέγει, ὅσα ἂν ἕτερος ἑτέρῳ ὁμολογήσῃ κύρια εἶναι. Leisi (*op. cit.*, p. 51) takes exception and maintains that witnesses were required to be present at the summons of witnesses. He finds the proof of this view in Demos. xlii. 12: κυρίας εἶναι τὰς πρὸς ἀλλήλους ὁμολογίας, ἃς ἂν ἐναντίον ποιήσωνται μαρτύρων. The reason that the arbitrator did not give judgment against Antiphanes was that there were no witnesses of his promise to testify. Lipsius (*op. cit.*, pp. 784-85) believes that Apollodorus' failure to notify Antiphanes duly until the last session (κυρία) was the cause.

[6] Demos. xxix. 19-20.

the stand against his brother Aphobus because he wished
οὔτ' ἐπιορκεῖν οὔτ' εὐθὺς παραχρῆμα δίκην ὀφλισκάνειν.[1] It is
beyond belief that Aphobus and Aesius ever promised to give
testimony which they finally gave reluctantly. It follows inevitably that a citizen upon due notification was obliged by law
to give evidence or take an oath of disclaimer. In the absence
of any indication in the sources of the nature of a legal notification it may safely be assumed that the principal must in
case of necessity be in a position to prove that the witness
had been duly summoned. In *Apollodorus* v. *Antiphanes*[2] it
would appear that Apollodorus, relying upon the frequent
promises (φάσκων ἀεί μοι μαρτυρήσειν εἰς τὴν κυρίαν) of Antiphanes to be on hand at the final session before the arbitrator,
did not summon him legally. In the meantime, so it was alleged, Timotheus had tampered with Antiphanes with the
result that he did not appear as he had promised even on the
last day of the arbitration. By that time it was no longer
possible to take the proper steps.

There are some significant differences between κλήτευσις
and δίκη λιπομαρτυρίου. The former carries a fine payable to
the treasury and so may be regarded as a means of punishing
a citizen who fails in his duty to the state by not testifying
when called upon to do so. There is no trial to impose the
penalty. The court at the instance of the principal simply
takes judicial notice of a self-evident fact and records the
fine. The litigant who has suffered by the default of his witness receives no redress. If he wishes to recover damages he
must file a δίκη λιπομαρτυρίου and take his chances of winning
his case and securing adequate damages.[3] So far as our sources
go it is clear that κλήτευσις was preferred in public suits.
Of the seven cases in which κλητεύειν is mentioned or im-

---

[1] *Ibid.* 15; the *diké* contemplated was undoubtedly a δίκη λιπομαρτυρίου.

[2] *Ibid.* xlix. 19.

[3] The δίκη λιπομαρτυρίου was τιμητός; cf. Lipsius, *op. cit.*, pp. 785 and 878 ff., whose conservative remarks about the nature and effect of this rather obscure process are preferable to the speculations of Rentzsch, *op. cit.*, p. 22.

plied,[1] only one was a private suit.[2] This is what might be
expected, for in a public case the prosecutor could only rarely
suffer such financial loss as he would in a private suit.
Normally he would let the law take its course. In a private
suit κλήτευσις was a simple and safe means of revenge, but it
carried no damages for the litigant. If he wanted to recoup
his losses he must resort to a δίκη λιπομαρτυρίου or a δίκη
βλάβης. One difference between these two is that the latter
could not be instituted until the conclusion of the case. The
only extant case is *Apollodorus* v. *Antiphanes*.[3] Here, upon
Antiphanes' refusal to testify before the arbitrator, Apollodorus at once entered a δίκη λιπομαρτυρίου. If he had won,
Antiphanes would in all probability have been obliged to
testify or to pay estimated damages. As Apollodorus did not
win, there was no way in which he could bring the vital
testimony of Antiphanes before the court, because in arbitration cases only evidence filed before the arbitrator could be
used on appeal. He could, however, bring a δίκη λιπομαρτυρίου before the decision of the appeal because the damage had
already been done before the arbitrator.

The ground for a δίκη βλάβης was in all probability not a
contract. The reasons for reaching this conclusion are not as
good as one would wish. The analogy of the δίκη βλάβης with
the δίκη λιπομαρτυρίου where no promise was required and
the inference which may be drawn from the law proposed by
Plato[4] have been regarded as sufficient grounds for the view
that no contract was required.[5] If, as has been pointed out
before, it was a duty of the citizen to go to court as a witness
when properly summoned, the liability of the witness if he
failed was *ex delicto*, not *ex contractu*.

On the basis of a passage in *Aphobus* v. *Phanus*, it has been

---

[1] Aeschin. i. 46; ii. 68; Demos. xix. 176, 198; xxxii. 30; lviii. 7, 42; lix. 28; Lycurg.
i. 20.

[2] Demos. xxxii.   [3] *Ibid.* xlix. 19.

[4] *Laws* xi. 937A: ὁ δ' εἰς μαρτυρίαν κληθείς, μὴ ἀπαντῶν δὲ τῷ καλεσαμένῳ, τῆς
βλάβης ὑπόδικος ἔστω κατὰ νόμον.

[5] Lipsius, *op. cit.*, p. 879. On p. 659 Lipsius takes the view that a δίκη βλάβης
did not lie unless the witness had promised to testify.

argued that if a litigant by having false testimony read before
a court rendered the witness liable to a δίκη ψευδομαρτυρίων,
he was himself liable to a suit for damages.[1] Leisi cautiously
remarks: "wenn wir uns auf Dem. xxix. 16 verlassen dürfen."
This caution is very commendable. For the speaker says:

> In the first place, if he really never gave this testimony, he would have
> denied it, not now for the first time, but immediately upon its being
> read in court, when denial would better have served his purpose. In the
> next place, if I had without cause exposed him to a suit for giving false
> testimony against his brother, (a charge, on which men run the risk of
> degradation, besides pecuniary penalties,) he would not have let the matter
> rest, but would have brought an action against me for damage.

Since the law required the witness to be present to acknowledge the testimony purporting to come from him or to take
an oath of disclaimer,[2] there was no possibility that an affidavit could be introduced without the knowledge and consent of the witness. The speaker in *Aphobus* v. *Phanus* was
indulging in a bit of rhetoric, hoping that a proportion of
the dicasts would be suitably impressed.

[1] Demos. xxix. 16; Leisi, *op. cit.*, p. 52; Lipsius, *op. cit.*, p. 659.

[2] Meier-Schömann-Lipsius, *op. cit.*, p. 495, n. 55; Lipsius, *op. cit.*, p. 882.

CHAPTER VII
OATHS

In origin the oath was religious, and it long preceded any idea of the formal administration of justice. Early in the history of mankind when a man's word was distrusted by his fellow-man he cast the burden of proof on higher powers and called upon the gods for assistance. The oath then was an attempt to win credence for a statement or to render a promise binding by calling the gods to witness when a simple, unsupported assertion was no longer sufficient.[1] In a primitive state of society as long as men stood in complete awe of the gods an oath in the name of the gods would have proved sufficient, for few men would have tempted Providence by swearing a false oath. But that perjury was very early practiced cannot be denied. "The Greeks especially were so prone to deceit that nothing short of very strong inculcations of the sanctity of an oath would insure its being kept."[2] In time the wording of the oath tended to become formularized and the gods who were to be called to witness were specified.[3] So that beside the informal oath there were developed fixed formulas for formal oaths for certain occasions.[4] The curse was regularly added, in which the gods were asked to send punishment upon the man who, having called the gods to witness,

[1] Cf. Hirzel, *Der Eid*, p. 2; for the place of Horkos (ὅρκος) in Greek mythology cf. Hesiod *Works and Days* 219, 804; *Theogony* 226 ff.; Stobaeus *Ecl.* i. 41, p. 978; for discussions of the etymology cf. Herodian ii. 1, p. 287. 22 (Lentz); Eustathius *Il.* ii. 338; Walde-Pokorny, *Vergl. Wörtbch. d. indoger. Sprache*, II, 502.

[2] Paley on Hesiod *Theog.* 231. The philosophers were interested in the oath and in perjury and its consequences: cf. Plato *Laws* 948B and Chrysippus in Stobaeus *Flor.* xxviii. 15 (Meineke, I, 356); cf. also Bentham's opinion of the inefficiency of oaths, quoted by Kennedy, *Demos.*, IV, 395 ff.

[3] Cf. *Il.* iii. 275 ff.; xv. 36 ff.; *Od.* v. 184 ff.

[4] For a picture of the development of the oath cf. Ott, *Beiträge zur Kenntniss des griechischen Eides*, pp. 10 f. Ott takes no account of informal oaths which must always have been a feature of the daily life of the Greeks.

then made a false statement or a promise which he did not fulfil.

According as oaths refer to future or to past time they are commonly classified as "promissory" and "evidentiary." The promissory oath is a promise on the part of the person who takes it that something either will or will not happen, at least as far as the matter lies within his power. The evidentiary oath is a statement that something either has or has not happened. This distinction is made by some late authors, and indeed it is a very convenient one in the discussion of different kinds of oaths.[1] But this classification fails to take account of all the oaths which occur in the fully developed Athenian legal system of the fifth and fourth centuries. The promissory oath appears frequently in various forms, as, for example, the oaths of officials and jurors. The evidentiary oath includes two varieties of oath. The first is the real evidentiary oath, which is a form of wager and which was used to settle a dispute with absolute finality. This oath was used as a form of trial in primitive attempts at the administration of justice. Trial by evidentiary oath is the result of a challenge and consists in tendering to an opponent an oath embodying his contentions, or in offering to take an oath embodying one's own contentions.[2] It is the same sort of at-

---

[1] Earlier writers seem not to have been interested in such a differentiation although there are many references to the oath in theory and in practice. Plato includes oaths among the ὁμολογίαι (*Rep.* 443A). Hirzel (*Der Eid*, p. 4), after a survey of the way in which different writers deal with the oath, concludes that in general the ancients thought of the oaths as promissory, although they at times in effect recognized the evidentiary oath as did Nicostratus, who gives as examples of oaths νὴ τὴν Ἀθηνᾶν ἔπραξα τάδε, οὐ μὰ τὴν Ἀθηνᾶν οὐκ ἔπραξα (Schol. on Arist., pp. 87B 30 ff. [Brandis]). Cf. also Stobaeus *Flor.* xxviii. 15 (Meineke, I, 356) in a discussion of Chrysippus' distinction between ἀληθορκεῖν and εὐορκεῖν and between ἐπιορκεῖν and ψευδορκεῖν. The classification into promissory and evidentiary oaths is the common one, although Ziebarth (*De iureiurando in iure Graeco quaestiones*, p. 42) suggests another division into the voluntary oath taken by agreement of the two parties to a suit and the obligatory oath which is prescribed by law. This division, however, takes account only of oaths which occur in legal actions. The first division here is evidentiary and so corresponds to Hirzel's first division. But the obligatory oath may or may not be evidentiary and so does not correspond to Hirzel's second division.

[2] Cf. *supra*, I, 27.

tempt to get the gods to settle a question which we find in the various forms of ordeal. Glotz[1] points out this similarity between the oath and ordeal: both put the matter of punishment upon the gods. But in ordeal the false person is punished upon the spot while in the oath the gods may postpone punishment so that it falls even upon descendants of the false swearer.[2] Sometimes the two are found together. In the *Antigone*[3] the messenger offers to undergo ordeal by fire and to swear to the truth of his story. It is not surprising that the members of a primitive society were willing to accept an oath in the name of the gods as final and as constituting a whole trial. In this oath, just as in the promissory oath, the curse was often an important part.

If we follow the course of Greek literature we find that the Greeks recognized the evidentiary oath long after it ceased to play an important part as a form of trial.[4] So in Theognis there are several references to the false evidentiary oath. One such reference in regard to a deposit of property occurs in a characteristic passage in which Theognis deals with one of his favorite topics, the late punishment of the wicked.[5] A passage in Herodotus[6] is reminiscent of this passage of Theognis. Glaucus, a Spartan who was famous for his honesty, had taken a deposit of money with suitable tokens. But later, when the sons of the depositor came to collect the deposit, he pretended to have no memory of the transaction although they produced their tokens. He told them to return later and promised that if he then had no recollection of the matter he would take an oath that he had not received the deposit.[7] That he was somewhat worried over his act is indicated by the fact that he went to Delphi to inquire of the oracle whether or not he should take an oath and thus be enabled

[1] *L'Ordalie dans la Grèce primitive*, p. 123; cf. Latte, *Heiliges Recht*, p. 6.

[2] Cf. Glotz, *op. cit.*, p. 119.   [3] 264 f.

[4] For the early history of the evidentiary oath cf. *supra*, I, 27 ff., 49 ff. For two cases of the evidentiary oath cf. the Gortyn Code ii. 11 ff.; iii. 1 ff., in Buck, *Greek Dialects;* cf. Headlam, *JHS*, XIII, 65; Bücheler and Zitelmann, "Das Recht von Gortyn," *Rhein. Mus. XL, Ergänzungsheft*, pp. 105-7.

[5] 199 ff., 1139 ff., 283 ff.   [6] vi. 86.   [7] vi. 86 β 2 and γ 1.

to keep the money. His denunciation by the priestess for
such a contemplated oath, with her promise of evil to come
upon the perjurer, had such an effect on Glaucus that he was
deterred from taking an oath. He restored the money, but
the god was not done with him; his family disappeared utterly from Sparta. If Glaucus had gone through with the oath
with the consent of the sons of the depositor, it is to be assumed that it would have settled the case, for Glaucus undoubtedly believed that if he took the oath the money would
be left in his possession. Another passage occurs in Herodotus[1] in one of those curious stories which deal with a hero or
a god who appeared to a woman in her husband's form and
became in this guise the father of her child. The wife of Ariston swore to him that it was he who had lain with her the
preceding night. The very fact that she was willing to swear
to the matter persuaded him of her good faith, and he immediately perceived that it had been a divine appearance.

Aeschylus gives us a further example of an evidentiary
oath. In this case it is a challenge to an oath which is refused.[2] The Erinyes complain that Orestes will neither take
an oath as to his innocence of the crime of matricide nor will
he tender to them an oath as to his guilt. Orestes manifestly
cannot swear to his innocence of the actual crime of killing,
for his plea is justifiable homicide.[3]

Alongside the real evidentiary oath there developed an
oath in support of testimony which for convenience may be
termed the "confirmatory" oath. This oath might be taken
either by a litigant or by a witness. In many cases this oath
was not prescribed by law but could be demanded.

In the following discussion we shall see how promissory,
evidentiary, and confirmatory oaths developed and were used
in different phases of Athenian government and administration of justice in the fifth and fourth centuries. The oath
plays a great part in Attic oratory. It is sometimes a rhetori-

[1] vi. 68 f.   [2] *Eumenides* 429 ff.

[3] In general, the commentators on this passage view the oaths as corresponding
to the oaths of the parties at the *anakrisis* (cf. Sidgwick, Blaydes, Blass, *ad loc.*).
Verrall (*ad loc.*) identifies it with the ancient purgatory oath.

cal device to strengthen a statement or to impress something upon the dicasts. The various formulas of such oaths have been extensively studied and also their artistic use.[1] There are also frequent references to the different oaths which occur in the course of a trial, such as the heliastic oath, the oaths of magistrates, the party oaths, the oaths in homicide. It is with the oaths as they occur in the orators that we are chiefly concerned. There are, however, certain passages in other authors and in inscriptions which indicate the importance of the oath in public life generally in Athens.

The curse is an important feature of the oath. Apparently the feeling was that the stronger the curse was made, so much more likely was the oath-taker to keep his oath. The curse occurs in many oaths which were required by law, and also in many incidental oaths.[2] The purport is always the same: utter destruction for the swearer and his house if he swears a false oath, many blessings for him if his oath is good.

Naturally, the promissory oath occurs in all sorts of forms in public life. There are abundant examples of treaties and public agreements which involve oaths.[3] In general the oaths which appear in such agreements contain vows of both parties to the agreement to observe certain specified conditions. Such an oath is contained in the Chalcidian decree of 446 B.C. in which the adult male Chalcidians are ordered to swear allegiance to Athens while the *bouleutai* and dicasts of Athens swear in behalf of the Athenian state to uphold certain rights of the Chalcidians which are specified in the decree.[4] The

[1] An extensive collection of the oaths in the orators has been made by Ott, *op. cit.*, pp. 39 ff. Cf. Kühnlein, *De vi et usu precandi et jurandi formularum apud decem oratores Atticos;* Blass, *Att. Bered.*, III², 384, under *Schwurformeln;* Ziebarth, *op. cit.*, pp. 10 ff.; Hofmann, *De iurandi apud Athenienses formulis.*

[2] For the formula of such a curse cf. the curse quoted in the heliastic oath (Demos. xxiv. 149; cf. also liv. 41).

[3] For a list of treaties and agreements in which oaths were involved cf. Ott, *op. cit.*, pp. 76 ff.

[4] *IG²*, I, 39; Hicks and Hill, *Greek Historical Inscriptions*, 40; Tod, *Greek Historical Inscriptions*, 42; cf. *supra*, I, 214, for the reason why the oath was sworn by the *bouleutai* and the dicasts. These two groups must here represent the whole people.

exact wording of the two oaths is given *in toto* in the decree.[1]

There are some occasional public oaths which are of the promissory type. For instance, in the decree of Demophantus, founded on a law of Solon and passed in 410 B.C. after the battle of Cyzicus, all Athenians are ordered to swear to rid the state of would-be subverters of democracy. The oath is to be taken both in the ecclesia and in the deme assemblies, apparently with the purpose of having as many as possible of the Athenians swear.[2] This decree was occasioned by the revolt of the Four Hundred. The oath was not repeated annually or at any stated periods, although there was a renewal of it after the overthrow of the Thirty in 403 B.C.[3] But that it was considered to continue in force is shown by Lycurgus in his oration against Leocrates[4] and by Demosthenes in his speech against Leptines[5] in which the jury is reminded of the decree of Demophantus.

Magistrates took an oath on entering upon office. Although they differed in details, these oaths had to do for the most part with promises to perform the duties of the office in accordance with the laws and with promises to refuse bribes. All of them were definitely of the promissory type. For instance, Aristotle[6] gives the oath of the archons. After the *dokimasia* the archons went to the oath stone and swore as follows: δικαίως ἄρξειν καὶ κατὰ τοὺς νόμους, καὶ δῶρα μὴ

---

[1] Another good example of an agreement between states is the one hundred years' treaty, of which Thucydides gives us the text (v. 47. 8), between the Athenians and their allies on the one hand and the Argives, Eleans, Mantineans, and their allies on the other hand. The treaty elaborately specifies the conditions which are to be observed on both sides and then gives the wording of the oath, listing the officials and governing bodies who are to take the oath for each state. It is a very solemn oath over a sacrifice, and the participants are each to swear the oath that is most binding in his own country (ὀμνύντων δὲ τὸν ἐπιχώριον ὅρκον ἕκαστοι τὸν μέγιστον κατὰ ἱερῶν τελείων). This means that each country involved is to use its own formulas and is to call to witness the gods customarily invoked in such oaths in that particular country, but the promise is to be the same in all cases: ἐμμενῶ τῇ ξυμμαχίᾳ κατὰ τὰ ξυγκείμενα δικαίως καὶ ἀβλαβῶς καὶ ἀδόλως, καὶ οὐ παραβήσομαι τέχνῃ οὐδὲ μηχανῇ οὐδεμιᾷ. Cf. Kennedy, *op. cit.*, IV, 393.

[2] Andoc. i. 96 ff.; for comments on the phraseology of the decree cf. *supra*, I, 214.

[3] Cf. Lycurg. i. 124 f.   [4] i. 127.   [5] xx. 159.   [6] *Ath. Pol.* lv. 5.

λήψεσθαι τῆς ἀρχῆς ἕνεκα, κἄν τι λάβωσιν ἀνδριάντα ἀναθήσειν χρυσοῦν. Afterward they had to go to the Acropolis and there swear the same oath, after which they entered upon their terms of office. On the basis of the passage in Lycurgus,[1] Gilbert assumes[2] that all Athenian officials had to take an oath before entering on their office, and this was undoubtedly the case, although it is impossible to reconstruct the oath in each instance.

Just as the magistrates swore to uphold the laws, so some of the governing and judicial bodies were required to take the oath before entering upon their duties. The oath of the *bouleutai* goes back to the time of Cleisthenes.[3] Aristotle says that the same oath still existed in his own day. Again this oath, like that of the magistrates, had to do chiefly with a promise to perform the duties of the office in the best interests of the city.[4] But another clause of the oath found in Demosthenes refers to the judicial activities of the boulé. The *bouleutai* swore not to imprison a man who produced the proper bail, except under certain conditions, i.e., treason or conspiracy for overthrow of the government.[5] This provision is wrongly attributed to Solon. Other provisions of the oath were to the effect that they would keep the laws of Solon, that they would give the best advice to the Athenians,[6] that they would reject at the *dokimasia* of the next boulé those who were not worthy to be members.[7] This is the annual oath of the *bouleutai* which they swore just as magistrates did on

[1] i. 79.   [2] *Const. Antiqu.*, p. 221.

[3] Cf. Arist. *Ath. Pol.* xxii. 2. For a discussion of the introduction of this oath cf. *supra*, I, 200, 204, and 342.

[4] Xen. *Mem.* i. 1. 18; Lysias xxxi. 1; Demos. lix. 4.

[5] Demos. xxiv. 144, 148.

[6] For the curse which was pronounced by a herald at meetings of the ecclesia and boulé against those who wilfully deceived the people or wronged them in any way cf. Demos. xviii. 282; xix. 70; xxiii. 97; Aeschin. i. 23; Din. i. 46–47. For a comic curse of this sort cf. Aristoph. *Thesmo.* 295–311, 331–50.

[7] Xen. *Mem.* i. 1. 18; Demos. lix. 4; Lysias xxxi. 1–2; Plut. *Solon* xxv. 3.

coming into office.[1] That the *bouleutai* joined in occasional oaths is evident from such oaths as were sworn in the Chalcidian decree where they with the dicasts represented the whole Athenian people. It is the same negative type of oath which is mentioned above, i.e., not to imprison a man except under certain conditions.

Before entering on their duties the members of the Heliaea took an oath which is designated as ὁ τῶν ἡλιαστῶν ὅρκος or ὁ ἡλιαστικὸς ὅρκος.[2] Naturally a great deal is heard about this oath in the orators, for the speaker frequently calls upon the dicasts to remember their oath and warns them of the danger of perjury. Often some phrase from the oath is quoted, such as πείσεσθαι τοῖς νόμοις καὶ τοῖς τοῦ δήμου ψηφίσμασι[3] or ἦ μὴν ὁμοίως ἀκροάσεσθαι τῶν κατηγορούντων καὶ τῶν ἀπολογουμένων.[4] This oath was taken annually by the whole body of heliasts[5] and is, like the oath of officials generally, a promissory oath.[6] The formula, or what purports to be the formula,

---

[1] We hear of an addition to the bouleutic oath in 410 B.C.: φησὶ γὰρ Φιλόχορος ἐπὶ Γλαυκίππου καὶ ἡ βουλὴ κατὰ γράμμα τότε πρῶτον ἐκαθέζετο καὶ ἔτι νῦν ὀμνύσιν ἀπ' ἐκείνου καθεδεῖσθαι ἐν τῷ γράμματι, ᾧ ἂν λάχωσι (Schol. on Aristoph. *Plut.* 972; cf. Gilbert, *Beiträge zur innern Geschichte Athens*, pp. 348 ff.). According to Gilbert, the reference is to assignment of places in the boulé. The evidence is not very good, but this seems to be a plausible explanation. For an addition made after the amnesty of 403 B.C. cf. *infra*, p. 154, n. 4.

[2] Demos. xxiv. 149; Hyper. iv. 40; cf. *supra*, I, 155.

[3] Din. i. 84.

[4] Isoc. xv. 21. For a collection of phrases which purport to be from the heliastic oath cf. Ott, *op. cit.*, pp. 60 ff. Ott classifies all the passages in which the dicasts are reminded of the heliastic oath according to tone and phraseology.

[5] Isoc. xv. 21. It is likely that the oath dates from the time of Solon; cf. *supra*, I, 162.

[6] The practice of swearing judges is very old. In speaking of the heroic kingship Aristotle (*Pol.* 1285B) mentions the fact that as judges the kings sometimes were sworn: καὶ πρὸς τούτοις τὰς δίκας ἔκρινον. τοῦτο δ' ἐποίουν οἱ μὲν οὐκ ὀμνύοντες, οἱ δ' ὀμνύοντες· ὁ δ' ὅρκος ἦν τοῦ σκήπτρου ἐπανάστασις. With this may be compared the provisions of the Gortyn Code that in certain cases the judge shall give his decision under oath (i. 14, 24, 36; ii. 55; v. 45). In each of these cases we are dealing with the oath of an arbitrator. Ziebarth, in Pauly-Wissowa, *s.v.* "Eid," rightly differentiates the judicial oath from that of an official. The judicial oath has a higher meaning. The judge is asking for divine aid in making his decision in case there is not enough evidence to make the matter clear otherwise.

of this oath is preserved by Demosthenes[1] in his speech against Timocrates:

Ψηφιοῦμαι κατὰ τοὺς νόμους καὶ τὰ ψηφίσματα τοῦ δήμου τοῦ Ἀθηναίων καὶ τῆς βουλῆς τῶν πεντακοσίων. καὶ τύραννον οὐ ψηφιοῦμαι εἶναι οὐδ' ὀλιγαρχίαν· οὐδ' ἐάν τις καταλύῃ τὸν δῆμον τὸν Ἀθηναίων ἢ λέγῃ ἢ ἐπιψηφίζῃ παρὰ ταῦτα, οὐ πείσομαι· οὐδὲ τῶν χρεῶν τῶν ἰδίων ἀποκοπὰς οὐδὲ γῆς ἀναδασμὸν τῆς Ἀθηναίων οὐδ' οἰκιῶν· οὐδὲ τοὺς φεύγοντας κατάξω, οὐδὲ ὧν θάνατος κατέγνωσται, οὐδὲ τοὺς μένοντας ἐξελῶ παρὰ τοὺς νόμους τοὺς κειμένους καὶ τὰ ψηφίσματα τοῦ δήμου τοῦ Ἀθηναίων καὶ τῆς βουλῆς οὔτ' αὐτὸς ἐγὼ οὔτ' ἄλλον οὐδένα ἐάσω. οὐδ' ἀρχὴν καταστήσω ὥστ' ἄρχειν ὑπεύθυνον ὄντα ἑτέρας ἀρχῆς, καὶ τῶν ἐννέα ἀρχόντων καὶ τοῦ ἱερομνήμονος καὶ ὅσοι μετὰ τῶν ἐννέα ἀρχόντων κυαμεύονται ταύτῃ τῇ ἡμέρᾳ, καὶ κήρυκος καὶ πρεσβείας καὶ συνέδρων· οὐδὲ δὶς τὴν αὐτὴν ἀρχὴν τὸν αὐτὸν ἄνδρα, οὐδὲ δύο ἀρχὰς ἄρξαι τὸν αὐτὸν ἐν τῷ αὐτῷ ἐνιαυτῷ. οὐδὲ δῶρα δέξομαι τῆς ἡλιάσεως ἕνεκα οὔτ' αὐτὸς ἐγὼ οὔτ' ἄλλος ἐμοὶ οὔτ' ἄλλη εἰδότος ἐμοῦ, οὔτε τέχνῃ οὔτε μηχανῇ οὐδεμιᾷ. καὶ γέγονα οὐκ ἔλαττον ἢ τριάκοντα ἔτη. καὶ ἀκροάσομαι τοῦ τε κατηγόρου καὶ τοῦ ἀπολογουμένου ὁμοίως ἀμφοῖν, καὶ διαψηφιοῦμαι περὶ αὐτοῦ οὗ ἂν ἡ δίωξις ᾖ. ἐπομνύναι Δία, Ποσειδῶ,[2] Δήμητρα, καὶ ἐπαρᾶσθαι ἐξώλειαν ἑαυτῷ καὶ οἰκίᾳ τῇ ἑαυτοῦ, εἴ τι τούτων παραβαίνοι, εὐορκοῦντι δὲ πολλὰ κἀγαθὰ εἶναι.

From this passage many attempts have been made to reconstruct the heliastic oath, and the general tendency is to discard the greater part of the oath as it stands in Demosthenes as the work of later writers and lexicographers who put together material found in the orators and elsewhere. Fränkel[3] reconstructs the oath on the basis of the work of Westermann.[4] He keeps the first sentence as given in Demosthenes, but adds to it two phrases, περὶ δ' ὧν ἂν νόμοι μὴ ὦσι γνώμῃ τῇ δικαιοτάτῃ and καὶ οὔτε χάριτος ἕνεκ' οὔτ' ἔχθρας, both from Demosthenes.[5] After rejecting the succeeding portion of the oath (καὶ τύραννον .... τριάκοντα ἔτη), he continues with

[1] xxiv. 149–51.

[2] Ποσειδῶ is undoubtedly a mistake. The god to be mentioned in this trinity should be Apollo; cf. Pollux viii. 122; Lipsius, *Das Attische Recht*, p. 153, n. 56; Fränkel, *Hermes*, XIII, 459 ff.

[3] *Op. cit.*, pp. 452 ff.

[4] *Commentationes de iurisiurandi iudicum Atheniensium formula*. Ott (*op. cit.*, pp. 98 ff.) follows Westermann. Hofmann (*op. cit.*, pp. 1–28), on the other hand, attempts a defense of the oath and accepts most of it. He is followed by Drerup, *Jahrb. f. cl. Phil.*, Supplbd. XXIV, 256 ff.

[5] xx. 118; xxiii. 96; xxxix. 39 ff.; lvii. 63.

the concluding passage in Demosthenes, that is, the promise to vote on the matter at issue and to listen impartially to both defendant and prosecutor, although he somewhat modifies the phraseology found in Demosthenes. He keeps also the curse, again deviating slightly from the words of Demosthenes.

Gilbert[1] follows Fränkel, but Lipsius[2] rejects the phrase καὶ οὔτε χάριτος ἕνεκ' οὔτ' ἔχθρας but rightly accepts the section on bribery from the Demosthenic passage οὐδὲ δῶρα δέξομαι κ.τ.λ.[3] He keeps the curse as it stands in Demosthenes. Lipsius does not claim that his reconstruction represents necessarily the exact wording of the oath, but he thinks the oath in all its essentials is there. The rejected portions are easily explained. Either they are repetitions in detail of the general promise to obey the laws or they consist of material which at some time for a brief period was part of the heliastic oath. For example, the passage with regard to the overthrow of the democracy is reminiscent of the addition which was made to the heliastic oath after the amnesty of 403 B.C. This oath is reported by Andocides: καὶ οὐ μνησικακήσω, οὐδὲ ἄλλῳ πείσομαι, ψηφιοῦμαι δὲ κατὰ τοὺς κειμένους νόμους,[4] but it does not occur in the oath as reported by Demosthenes. Drerup[5] believes that the parts of the oath dealing with the overthrow of the democracy and the amnesty probably belonged to the period of 410 or 403 B.C. and that the oath retained this formula year after year to keep alive in the jurors the consciousness of their duty to guard against subverters of the democracy and to preserve to the people their freedom. The

---

[1] *Beiträge*, p. 392.   [2] *Op. cit.*, p. 152.

[3] For a similar provision in an oath in a Cnidian inscription cf. Dareste-Haus-soulier-Reinach, *Recueil des inscriptions juridiques grecques* (1895), I, 170.

[4] i. 91. The passage contains two other oaths. The *bouleutai* swore: καὶ οὐ δέξομαι ἔνδειξιν οὐδὲ ἀπαγωγὴν ἕνεκα τῶν πρότερον γεγενημένων, πλὴν τῶν φυγόντων. And all Athenians were to swear: καὶ οὐ μνησικακήσω τῶν πολιτῶν οὐδενὶ πλὴν τῶν τριάκοντα καὶ τῶν ἕνδεκα (καὶ τῶν δέκα)· οὐδὲ τούτων ὃς ἂν ἐθέλῃ εὐθύνας διδόναι τῆς ἀρχῆς ἧς ἦρξεν. It may be assumed that these clauses would have some meaning for perhaps a generation or as long as there were survivors from the regime of the Thirty. After that they would cease to have point and would be dropped.

[5] *Op. cit.*, p. 261.

phrase οὐ μνησικακήσω κ.τ.λ., which would not be of any importance after, at the most, one generation, was dropped. In the same way Drerup retains the phrase καὶ τύραννον, κ.τ.λ. It would continue to bind the judges to protect the democratic constitution. Drerup considers appropriate too the clause dealing with officials, since on the proper choosing and examination of officials depends the preservation of the existing constitution. Drerup, like all the others, rejects the age-qualification clause καὶ γέγονα οὐκ ἔλαττον ἢ τριάκοντα ἔτη as having no place in the midst of the duties of the heliasts.

It is certain that the passage in Demosthenes by no means represents the heliastic oath as it was sworn in any one period, but that various details are included which would be found in the oath at every period: the promise to vote according to the laws and decrees of the Athenian people and the council of five hundred, the promise not to accept bribes, the promise to listen impartially to both sides of the case and to vote on the subject at issue,[1] the calling of the gods to witness, and the curse. In addition there are details which at some time in some form were introduced into the oath for a limited period. Here belong the provisions regarding tyranny and the overthrow of the government (especially appropriate in 410 and 403 B.C. but not long afterward), the return of exiles, distribution of property, and the *dokimasia* of officials. It is interesting to observe that these details are all in negative form. It is not necessary to believe that in any part of the passage the actual phraseology of the oath is preserved except that such a stereotyped clause as the first sentence may well have been part of the original form.[2]

---

[1] The MS reading is διαψηφιοῦμαι. A correction to ἀεὶ ψηφιοῦμαι has been suggested.

[2] For a detailed discussion of the Athenian jurors' attitude toward their oath cf. Cronin, *The Athenian Juror and His Oath* (University of Chicago, 1936), pp. 18 ff., who accepts Fränkel's reconstruction of the oath without comment. There were two parts to the oath: "I shall vote according to the laws and decrees but when laws do not exist I shall use my best judgment" and "I shall vote concerning those things which are at issue, but I shall listen impartially to both accusation and defense." In each part the second half is a qualification of the first half. Cronin believes that absolute conformance to the oath would have resulted in a severe type of justice, but that the jury having irresponsible power would consider that

The next question to be raised with regard to the jurors' oath is whether the annual oath taken by all members of the Heliaea was the only oath or whether another had to be taken at the beginning of each case by the panel of dicasts who sat on the case. Lipsius[1] thinks that the theory of an oath at the beginning of each case is based on mistaken evidence. And in fact there is no evidence for such an oath. On the contrary, the evidence of Isocrates is against such an oath: περὶ ταύτης δύ' ὅρκους ὀμόσαντες δικάζετε, τὸν μὲν, ὅνπερ ἐπὶ ταῖς ἄλλαις εἴθισθε, τὸν δ', ὃν ἐπὶ ταῖς συνθήκαις ἐποιήσασθε.[2] This refers to the annual heliastic oath and to the amnesty oath. There are many other passages in which the jurors are reminded of their oaths. In fact, on occasion the oath was read to them before they cast their votes.[3]

According to Pollux[4] and Harpocration[5] the heliastic oath was sworn at least in early times near the Ilissus and beyond the stadium at a place called Ardettus, named after a hero who had reconciled the Athenians when they were engaged in civil war.

There was an oath in connection with the award of a public arbitrator. Incidental reference is made to this by Aristotle, who, in speaking of the oath which officials took after their *dokimasia*, states that they took their oath at the same oath stone at which the arbitrators swore before giving their award: βαδίζουσι πρὸς τὸν λίθον ἐφ' οὗ τὰ τόμι' ἐστὶν ἐφ' οὗ καὶ οἱ διαιτηταὶ ὀμόσαντες ἀποφαίνονται τὰς διαίτας.[6] This might have been either a promissory or a confirmatory oath. The fact that they swore it before delivering their verdict might lead one to suppose that it was promissory, to the effect that they will act to the best of their ability in accordance with the laws in rendering their decision. On the other hand it may mean that the decision had already been made be-

---

the oath was not a strict set of rules so much as it was an ideal pattern designed to secure justice. They would therefore interpret it loosely. As long as justice was obtained the spirit of the oath was kept.

[1] *Op. cit.*, p. 153. [3] Lysias xiv. 47. [5] *S.v.* Ἀρδηττός.
[2] xviii. 34. [4] viii. 122. [6] *Ath. Pol.* lv. 5.

fore the oath was taken and that it confirmed the justice of their decision. On the whole the former seems to be the better explanation.[1] The award was always given in the official meeting place, and there is never reference to the retirement of the arbitrators to the oath stone to swear after reaching a decision and before delivering the award. If they had done so, obviously the award would have been delivered at the oath stone. The arbitrators must have taken the oath after being notified of the case by the Forty and before taking charge of the case. Harrell considers the oath another safe-guard to assure a successful arbitration.[2]

Apparently private arbitrators were not required to take an oath. Wyse believes that the parties could insist on an oath and regularly did so if a large sum was at stake.[3] There are several passages which deal with oaths in private arbitra-tion, but they are not helpful.[4] And here again it is not clear in just what the oath consisted. It was probably the same as in public arbitration.

At the age of eighteen the boy was enrolled in the deme.[5] The *demotai* under oath examined the youth and voted on the question of whether he had reached the required age and whether he was a freeman and legally born. Undoubtedly the oath of the *demotai* had to do with a promise to vote to the best of their ability and in accordance with the laws.[6] It was a promissory oath.

After enrolment on the deme register the youth took his oath of allegiance. This was partly military, partly political; in fact, it included the whole duty of a citizen and was a promissory oath. This oath seems to have been taken at the

[1] Cf. Latte, *Heiliges Recht*, p. 42.

[2] *Public Arbitration*, "University of Missouri Studies," XI, No. 1, 21 ff.

[3] *Isaeus*, p. 450. Lipsius (*op. cit.*, pp. 222 ff.) asserts that there was no oath as long as the arbitrator acted merely as διαλλακτής, but that when he gave a judg-ment as διαιτητής he took an oath. Thalheim (*Hermes*, XLI, 152 ff.) shows that the extant cases of private arbitration do not warrant such a conclusion.

[4] Isaeus ii. 31; Demos. xxix. 58; xli. 15; lii. 31.

[5] Arist. *Ath. Pol.* xlii. 1. [6] Cf. Demos. lvii. 63.

beginning of the second year of ephebic training.[1] The oath was as follows:

> I will never bring reproach upon my hallowed arms nor will I desert the comrade at whose side I stand, but I will defend our altars and our hearths, single-handed or supported by many. My native land I will not leave a diminished heritage but greater and better than when I received it. I will obey whoever is in authority and submit to the established laws and all others which the people shall harmoniously enact. If anyone tries to overthrow the constitution or disobeys it, I will not permit him, but will come to its defense single-handed or with the support of all. I will honor the religion of my fathers. Let the gods be my witnesses, Agraulus, Enyalius, Ares, Zeus, Thallo, Auxo, Hegemone.[2]

The action called *antidosis*[3] is an interesting illustration of a kind of suit which involved both a promissory and a confirmatory oath. At the preliminary hearing each of the two parties had to swear an oath that he would render an accurate inventory of his property.[4] The law required that the inventory should be given within three days of the day of the oath. The second oath occurred when the account was presented and stated that as presented it was a true and accurate inventory of the individual's possessions.[5]

As has been seen,[6] in its original form the evidentiary oath formed the entire trial and was final, i.e., it was not subject to rebuttal. But it was not possible that it should long continue to constitute necessarily the whole trial. In its surviving forms in the Attic orators we find that it might still form the whole trial and also that it might be part of a trial. Furthermore, in practically all cases it becomes subject to rebuttal. This is a natural development. The only way in which an evidentiary oath could come before a court was as

[1] Cf. Taylor, "The Athenian Ephebic Oath," *CJ*, XIII, 495 ff.

[2] Cf. Pollux viii. 105–6; Stobaeus *Flor.* xliii. 48; Lycurg. i. 76.

[3] Cf. Goligher, "Studies in Attic Law II," *Hermathena*, XIV, 481 ff.

[4] Demos. xlii. 1, 11–12.

[5] *Ibid.* 17–18. On the subject of the two oaths cf. Lipsius, *op. cit.*, p. 592; Francotte, *L'Antidosis en droit athénien;* Vollbrecht, *De antidosi apud Athenienses dissertatio*, p. 7; Böckh, *Staatsh. der Athener*, I³, 674.

[6] *Supra*, p. 146 f.

the result of a challenge. It is evident that such challenges were rarely accepted and little is heard of them except in so far as an argument is drawn from an opponent's refusal to accept a challenge to an oath.[1] It is doubtless true that sometimes an evidentiary oath was resorted to in order to settle a case without bringing it into court.

There is only one example in the Attic orators of what must have been the original use of the evidentiary oath, i.e., the oath taken as the result of a challenge to settle an entire case. In the two Boeotus speeches of Demosthenes reference is made to an earlier case which involved an evidentiary oath.[2] The case concerned the paternity of Pamphylus and Boeotus, the two sons of Plangon. Mantias, their alleged father, was sued by Boeotus for recognition as his son. Mantias desired to keep the case out of court and so had adopted the following plan. He was to give Plangon thirty minae and to challenge her to swear that the children were his. Of course, for the recompense of the thirty minae she was to refuse the challenge. But when the matter actually came up she did take the oath and swore that the children were the children of herself and Mantias. The oath settled the case. Therefore, Boeotus and Pamphylus were legally declared to be his children. The oath in this case was taken before an arbitrator, and Demosthenes says that it was taken in the Delphinium.[3] A similar oath is referred to in a case concerning the rejection of one Euphiletus from the deme list.[4] Among other proofs of Euphiletus' status the speaker declares that Euphiletus' mother had expressed her willingness to swear before an arbitrator in the sanctuary of the Delphinian Apollo an oath to Euphiletus' paternity. The alleged father of Euphiletus also was ready to swear a similar oath.[5]

There are various forms or survivals of the evidentiary oath which have a part in different legal processes. An inter-

---

[1] Cf. Bonner, *Evidence in Athenian Courts*, p. 75.

[2] Demos. xxxix. 2; xl. 10.   [3] xl. 11.   [4] Isaeus xii. 9.

[5] Cf. Lipsius (*op. cit.*, p. 228, n. 33), who believes that such an oath was taken in the Delphinium, but that it does not follow that the arbitrators had their sittings there.

esting oath occurs in connection with entrance of a child into the phratry. There were apparently different rules for different phratries.[1] There was not even uniformity about the age at which children should be admitted. Gilbert believes, however, that in general the introduction into the phratry took place in one of the early years of the child's life at the festival of the Apaturia.[2] There were two parts to the ceremony, ἀνά-κρισις and διαδικασία. At the *anakrisis* in some phratries the father took an oath to the legitimacy of the child.[3] This oath, which is evidentiary, created a presumption that the contentions of the father were true and probably at least nine times out of ten settled the matter, but the oath was subject to rebuttal if anyone had doubts about its truth.[4] In other phratries the father had to bring forward three witnesses, who swore that the boy who was being introduced was the legitimate son of the introducer by a lawfully wedded wife.[5] These are both evidentiary oaths, but that they were subject to rebuttal is shown by the second part of the ceremony, the *diadikasia*, which was concerned with a vote on the reception of the child into the phratry. Admission into the phratry served as proof of the boy's relationship and consequently of his right of inheritance.

An interesting development in the evidentiary oath is the provision attributed to Solon by which both parties to a suit might swear an oath in cases in which there was no evidence:

[1] Cf. Gilbert, *Const. Antiqu.*, p. 191.

[2] Cf. Xen. *Hell.* i. 7. 8; Schol. on Aristoph. *Achar.* 146; Suidas, *s.v.* ʼΑπατούρια.

[3] Andoc. i. 127; Isaeus vii. 16; viii. 19; Demos. lvii. 54.

[4] Cf. Ziebarth, *op. cit.*, p. 32. An analogous oath is that furnished by an inscription of Dyme, where citizenship was extended to foreigners of free birth on the payment of a talent to the state. All over seventeen years of age themselves took the oath. But if a man who was applying for citizenship had sons under seventeen, he took the oath that they were his legitimate sons and were under seventeen years of age. When they reached the age of seventeen they became citizens by reason of that oath (Collitz-Bechtel, *Sammlung der griechischen Dialekt-Inschriften*, 1614; Szanto, *Das griechische Bürgerrecht*, pp. 54, 113 f.). A Calaurian inscription furnishes another example of an evidentiary oath which admitted of rebuttal (Dareste-Haussoullier-Reinach, *op. cit.* [2d ser.], I, 104).

[5] *IG²*, II, 1237, ll. 14 f., 70 f.

δοξασταί: κριταί εἰσιν οἱ διαγινώσκοντες, πότερος εὐορκεῖ τῶν κρινομένων. κελεύει γὰρ Σόλων τὸν ἐγκαλούμενον, ἐπειδὰν μήτε συμβόλαια ἔχῃ μήτε μάρτυρας, ὀμνύναι, καὶ τὸν εὐθύνοντα δὲ ὁμοίως.[1] Up to this time the evidentiary oath had been employed only with the consent of both parties. Now the magistrate was authorized to administer the oath and, if either one or both wished to take it, to base his verdict upon it. If both parties consented to take the oath of course his position became more difficult, but he might have some basis for his decision in the attitude of the oath-takers when they swore. It is not reasonable to suppose that in every case one of the litigants would refuse to take the oath. Unfortunately the content of the oath is unknown, but it is better for the reasons outlined above[2] to suppose that the two litigants swore to the truth of their pleadings rather than that they swore that they would tell the truth during the trial.

Originally restricted to certain cases (i.e., those in which no evidence was available) in the law quoted above, the evidentiary oath soon spread to other cases and at last became the normal practice in every form of trial. It is interesting to note that Plato connects the evidentiary oath and the preliminary party oath. He attributes to Rhadamanthus the idea of tendering to both parties an evidentiary oath in the hope of obtaining a swift and trustworthy verdict. This was satisfactory in the early days when men really believed in the gods and the punishment which would come as the result of a false oath. But Plato thinks that as opinions with regard to the gods change so should the laws be changed, and that the prosecutor in a suit should write down his charges but not swear an oath, while the defendant should write down his denial and give it over to the officials without an oath. For, reflects Plato, it is a terrible thing to know that there being so many trials in the city almost half of the parties in them have perjured themselves, and therefore the members of society are constantly in contact with perjured

[1] *Lex. Seg.*, p. 242. For a full discussion of this oath and its influence upon the later preliminary party oath cf. *supra*, I, 173; Latte, *op. cit.*, pp. 24 f.

[2] *Supra*, I, 173.

people.[1] In view of this Plato proposes that all party oaths should be abolished.

There were really, then, two types of party oath in court. One party might tender an oath to the other party or offer to take one himself. The orators give many examples of such offers. Only one party took this oath, and if taken it counted as a means of proof. This kind did not occur in the homicide courts. The other kind was taken by both parties. This was the oath of the *anakrisis* in which one party always swore falsely. This oath was not at all a means of proof.[2] It is in origin evidentiary, but in its developed form it was, like the oaths of witnesses, merely confirmatory.

There were various different terms for the oaths of the parties and the witnesses in the different types of suits. Naturally these became somewhat confused. It will be convenient to list the different terms together with their original and extended uses.[3]

Both the orators and the lexicographers, who of course based their work on the orators, badly confuse the technical terms which are used for the oaths of the prosecutor and the defendant. A common word for the party oath is ἀντωμοσία. This word should strictly refer to the oath of the defendant because he swore in reply to the oath of the prosecutor, which might be called προωμοσία.[4] We find, however, in some of the lexicographers and in the orators that *antomosia* has become a quite general term for the party oath.[5] The word also is applied to the sworn accusation of the prosecutor.[6] This oath is an affirmation of the truth of the pleadings. In private suits, however, the litigants had to swear also that they would

---

[1] *Laws* 948A ff.

[2] Cf. Philippi, *Der Areopag und die Epheten*, p. 88.

[3] For a convenient listing of the terms with illustrations cf. Ott, *op. cit.*, pp. 83 ff.

[4] Pollux viii. 55; this word does not, however, occur in any other passage in Greek literature. Suidas (*s.v.* Διωμοσία and 'Αντωμοσία) makes the same distinction between these two words which Pollux makes between προωμοσία and ἀντωμοσία.

[5] Cf. Harpocration, *s.v.*; *Lex. Seg.*, p. 200; Isaeus iii. 6; v. 2, 16; ix. 1, 34; Isoc. xvi. 2.

[6] Cf. Plato *Apol.* 19B; Thalheim, in Pauly-Wissowa, *s.v.* 'Αντωμοσία.

confine themselves to the issue.[1] In the same way ἀμφιορκία is used of the oaths of both parties.[2]

An interesting use of the *antomosia* in a special kind of case is that which occurs in *diadikasia* cases; that is, in cases which deal with claims to an estate. Here each of the claimants had to present a claim to the property in question and their claims had to be strengthened by an oath. The claim is sometimes called *antigraphē*[3] and the oath is called *antomosia*, although in a *diadikasia* there is strictly neither defendant nor prosecutor. However, there are always at least two claimants who stand in the places of parties.[4]

Another evidentiary oath is the ἐξωμοσία.[5] There are many passages which illustrate two uses of this oath of denial. In the first place it was possible by an *exomosia* for a man to swear that he was unable to undertake some act or office because of poverty or illness or some similar cause.[6] Aristotle[7] speaks of the *exomosia* in connection with the selection of the ἱππεῖς. The ten *katalogeis* list the *hippeis* and turn the list over to the hipparchs and phylarchs who take the list before the council. There the former list of *hippeis* is examined and the names erased of those who have taken an oath to the effect that they are not able to act as knights. Then those in the new list are summoned and anyone who swears to his inability to serve is released. This is an excellent example of an evidentiary oath. It is an oath to fact and it is apparently final.

The other use of the word *exomosia* has to do with witnesses. A witness had either to give the evidence for which

---

[1] Arist. *Ath. Pol.* lxvii. 1.   [2] Suidas, *s.v.*

[3] Cf. Lipsius, *op. cit.*, pp. 834, 830, n. 4.

[4] Demos. xliii. 3; cf. Leist, *Der attische Eigentumsstreit im System der Diadikasien*, pp. 10 f.

[5] Cf. Pollux viii. 55; Harpocration, *s.v.* Other examples of the *exomosia* are to be found in Demos. xix. 122 f. and Aeschin. ii. 94 f. There is a jocular use of the word in Aristoph. *Eccl.* 1026 as an excuse sworn to evade duty.

[6] *Pol.* 1297A: περὶ δὲ τὰς ἀρχὰς τὸ τοῖς μὲν ἔχουσι τίμημα μὴ ἐξεῖναι ἐξόμνυσθαι, τοῖς δ' ἀπόροις ἐξεῖναι.

[7] *Ath. Pol.* xlix. 2.

he was summoned or else to swear an *exomosia*, an oath of denial to the effect that he knew nothing about the case and could give no evidence.[1] The term ἀπομνύναι is sometimes equivalent to ἐξομνύναι in this sense.[2]

Suidas[3] says that the *exomosia* could be used also in connection with an objection to the admissibility of a suit:

ἐξωμοσία· ὅταν τις φάσκῃ ἢ ὑπὲρ ἑαυτοῦ ἢ ὑπὲρ ἑτέρου ἐγκαλούμενος, μὴ δεῖν εἰσάγεσθαι δίκην· εἶτα καὶ τὴν αἰτίαν, δι' ἣν οὐκ εἰσαγώγιμος ἡ δίκη. εἰ δοκεῖ κατὰ λόγον ἀξιοῦν, ἐδίδοτο αὐτῷ ἐξωμοσίᾳ χρῆσθαι. καὶ οὕτως διεγράφετο ἡ δίκη.

Lipsius[4] agrees that *exomosia* might thus be used in later times as equivalent to ὑπωμοσία. He bases his statement on the above-mentioned passage from Pollux and on a statement of Theophrastus: ἱκανὸς δὲ καὶ δίκας τὰς μὲν φεύγειν, τὰς δὲ διώκειν, τὰς μὲν ἐξόμνυσθαι, ταῖς δὲ παρεῖναι, ἔχων ἐχῖνον ἐν τῷ προκολπίῳ καὶ ὁρμαθοὺς γραμματιδίων ἐν ταῖς χερσίν.[5] ἐξόμνυσθαι here might mean to refuse under oath to give testimony.

Again in the case of ὑπωμοσία there are two uses of the word. The first of these is an attempt under oath to delay an action by alleging absence from the city or illness or some other such excuse. Naturally, this process would usually be employed by the defendant in the case.[6] This was of course an evidentiary oath in character, but we find that this *hypomosia* had to be supported by the evidence of others.[7] In case such an oath was taken the other party, in most cases the plaintiff, could swear an ἀνθυπωμοσία, to the effect, one may judge, that there was no need for delay in the case. As has been shown above, this procedure of *hypomosia* occurs in connection with a *paragraphé* of a certain nature.[8]

[1] Pollux viii. 37, 55; Demos. xliv. 58–61; lvii. 59; Isaeus ix. 18; Lipsius, *op. cit.*, p. 880.

[2] Aeschin. i. 67; Plato *Laws* 936E. For the procedure followed by witnesses in swearing the *exomosia* cf. Lycurg. i. 20.

[3] *S.v.* ἐξωμοσία.   [4] *Op. cit.*, p. 902, n. 3.   [5] *Charac.* vi. 8.

[6] Pollux viii. 60; Harpocration, *s.v.*; Schol. on Demos. xxi. 84.

[7] Demos. xlviii. 25; lviii. 43.

[8] *Ibid.* xxi. 84; xxxix. 37; xlvii. 39; cf. *supra*, pp. 91 ff.

The second use of the word is in connection with the *graphé paranomon*. A man who objected to a proposed law or decree made a declaration under oath that he would bring a *graphé paranomon* against the originator of the law or decree.[1] Naturally this oath would result in suspension of the law until its validity was determined. Undoubtedly such an action must frequently have resulted in the dropping of the proposal.[2]

The word ὑπόμνυσθαι can be used also with the general meaning of an objection or protestation. So after the battle of Aegospotami, Euryptolemus urged that the ten generals be tried according to the decree of Cannonus, each separately. The council, on the other hand, proposed to try them all together. The assembly at first voted to follow Euryptolemus' plan, but at the objection of Menecles another vote was taken and they decided to abide by the decision of the council: ὑπομοσαμένου δὲ Μενεκλέους καὶ πάλιν διαχειροτονίας γενομένης ἔκριναν τὴν τῆς βουλῆς.[3]

Originally διωμοσία seems to have referred only to the party oath in homicide, perhaps at first only to the oath of the prosecutor.[4] Leisi[5] thinks that the term was used of an oath which if false brought down the greatest divine punishment.[6] It was a very strong and very solemn oath. As such

---

[1] Pollux viii. 56; Demos. xviii. 103; Aristoph. *Plut.* 725, ἐπομνύμενον codd.: ὑπομνύμενον corr. Girard.

[2] A remark in the *Lex. Seg.*, p. 313, indicates that the withdrawal of the proposal could also be known as *hypomosia*, but, as Thalheim has pointed out in Pauly-Wissowa, *s.v.* Ὑπωμοσία, this is probably due to a misunderstanding of Demos. xviii. 103: καίτοι πόσα χρήματα τοὺς ἡγεμόνας τῶν συμμοριῶν ἢ τοὺς δευτέρους καὶ τρίτους οἴεσθέ μοι διδόναι, ὥστε μάλιστα μὲν μὴ θεῖναι τὸν νόμον τοῦτον, εἰ δὲ μή, καταβάλλοντ' ἐᾶν ἐν ὑπωμοσίᾳ;

[3] Xen. *Hell.* i. 7. 34.   [4] Antiph. v. 88, 90, 96.   [5] *Op. cit.*, p. 59.

[6] There are many passages in which the word διόμνυσθαι occurs in the sense of a strong oath. For instance, in Demos. xviii. 286 the word is used to strengthen ἠρνεῖσθε: ἃ γὰρ εὐθενούντων τῶν πραγμάτων ἠρνεῖσθε διομνύμενοι, ταῦτ' ἐν οἷς ἔπταισεν ἡ πόλις ὡμολογήσατε. διομνύμενοι here is equivalent to ὤμοσεν in Andoc. i. 126: λαβόμενος τοῦ βωμοῦ ὤμοσεν ἢ μὴν μὴ εἶναί (οἱ) υἱὸν ἄλλον μηδὲ γενέσθαι πώποτε, εἰ μὴ Ἱππόνικον ἐκ τῆς Γλαύκωνος θυγατρός· ἢ ἐξώλη εἶναι καὶ αὐτὸν καὶ τὴν οἰκίαν, ὥσπερ ἔσται. Cf. Lysias xii. 10; Aeschin. i. 114. διόμνυσθαι is used again of an oath to relationship in Isaeus xi. 6.

it would naturally be used of the parties in homicide cases. The *diomosia* of the prosecutor consisted of three things: First, he swore to his right to prosecute; this of course involved his relationship to the deceased.[1] Second, he swore that the defendant was guilty.[2] Finally, he swore that he would confine himself in his prosecution to the matter in hand.[3] This, it will be seen, is quite different from the *antomosia* in other types of cases where the prosecutor merely swore to the truth of his pleadings. The defendant in a homicide trial, on the other hand, in his *diomosia* swore merely that he was not guilty.[4]

But the word had a wider use and was carried over to the oaths of the parties in other kinds of suits.[5] While the lexicographers recognize that the word is properly applied to the oath in homicide trials, yet they constantly show that in practice the word was used without distinction both of the oath in a homicide trial and of the oath at the *anakrisis* in other types of trial.[6]

The word was carried over from the oaths of the parties in homicide trials to the oaths of witnesses in homicide trials.[7] Naturally, then, the word came to be used also of the witness oath in other types of trials.[8] The witness oath was required before the homicide courts. In the first speech of Antiphon there are no witnesses in court perhaps because they could not swear to the guilt of the defendant.[9] In Lysias[10] the witness oath before the Areopagus is said to be obligatory:

[1] Demos. xlvii. 70 ff.; cf. Pollux viii. 118: Ἄρειος πάγος: φόνου δὲ ἐξῆν ἐπεξιέναι μέχρις ἀνεψιῶν, καὶ ἐν τῷ ὅρκῳ ἐπερωτᾶν τίς προσήκων ἐστὶ τῷ τεθνεῶτι. κἂν οἰκέτης ᾖ, ἐπισκήπτειν συγκεχώρηται. Philippi (*op. cit.*, p. 83) believes that this passage was derived from Demos. xlvii. 72, which Pollux misunderstood.

[2] Antiph. vi. 16; Lysias iii. 4; x. 11; Demos. lix. 10.   [3] Antiph. v. 11.

[4] *Ibid.* vi. 16; Lysias x. 11.   [5] Isaeus xi. 6; Demos. xl. 41.

[6] Cf. Suidas, Harpocration, Hesychius, *s.v.*

[7] Lysias iv. 4; Antiph. i. 28; v. 12, 15.

[8] Demos. lvii. 22, 39, 44; xlix. 20; Aeschin. ii. 156.

[9] Cf. Leisi, *op. cit.*, p. 58; Gernet, *Antiphon: Discours*, p. 37; Blass, *Att. Bered.*, I, 189.

[10] iv. 4.

καὶ ὅτι ἀληθῆ ταῦτα λέγω, Φιλῖνος καὶ Διοκλῆς ἴσασιν. ἀλλ᾽
οὐκ ἔστ᾽ αὐτοῖς μαρτυρῆσαι μὴ διομοσαμένοις περὶ τῆς αἰτίας ἧς
ἐγὼ φεύγω. It is probable that the same rule applied in all the
homicide courts. In each case the nature of the evidence
given under oath is clear. It was to the guilt or innocence of
the defendant. Witnesses in the homicide courts also swore
to the relationship of the prosecutor to the deceased.

There are various questions connected with the oaths of
the parties in the homicide courts. It has been maintained
that only the prosecutor swore the *diomosia* because some of
the sources speak only of the oath of the prosecutor.[1] But
other sources show that the same oath was administered to
the defense.[2] It is clear, therefore, that although the oath in
this connection is a survival of the evidentiary oath, it is so far
removed that it is no longer in any sense a means of proof.
We have here, as in other types of cases, a solemn oath on the
part of each party, one of whom must be swearing falsely. It
therefore could have no direct weight in settling the case.[3]
It may have helped to keep thoughtless charges from being
filed and have given evidence of the sincerity of each party's
conception of the circumstances. That is, the oath, while
false, may on many occasions have been sworn in good faith.
Without doubt both parties took the oath.[4]

The chief passage on *diomosia* before the Areopagus[5] gives
much information, namely, the fact that both parties took
the oath, the details of the procedure in the oath, the curse
attached to it. Demosthenes says that it is not an ordinary
oath, but one which is used for nothing else. The same oath
was taken in cases which came before the Palladium.[6] Gilbert[7] believes that this passage also proves that the oaths in
a homicide trial were taken not at the preliminary investigation but at the actual trial. He is led to believe this because
of his contention that a homicide case was referred to the

[1] Antiph. v. 11–12, 96; Lysias iii. 1, 21; Demos. xlvii. 70; lix. 10.

[2] Antiph. vi. 16; Lysias x. 11; Demos. xxiii. 63, 69; *Lex. Seg.*, p. 239.

[3] Cf. Philippi, *op. cit.*, p. 89.   [5] Demos. xxiii. 67 ff.

[4] Cf. Latte, *op. cit.*, p. 23.   [6] *Ibid.*   [7] *Op. cit.*, p. 385, n. 3.

proper court after the preliminary investigation. This being the case, the Demosthenes passage which mentions the oath as being taken at the Areopagus and at the Palladium must prove that the oaths were taken at the actual trial after the case had been referred to one of the homicide courts. Philippi[1] takes exactly the opposite position. The oaths were taken at the preliminary investigation. Inasmuch as the Demosthenes passage mentions oaths before the Areopagus and the Palladium, the *prodikasiai* must have been held in those courts and therefore the case was assigned to the proper court before the preliminary investigation.

Lipsius[2] points out that the natural course would have been to have the highly ceremonial oath at the actual trial and that some passages from the orators bear out this procedure, but that on the other hand the oath to relationship must have been taken earlier, that is, at the preliminary investigation. It is true that it seems unthinkable that the *basileus* would go ahead with the case at all unless the prosecutor had given assurance of his right to prosecute. Lipsius therefore assumes two oaths.[3]

Unfortunately we obtain little help from the orators about the matter. As has been said above, it seems absolutely necessary that the oath of the prosecutor to his relationship to the deceased should have taken place at the preliminary investigation, for in a homicide trial no one except relatives up to a certain degree was allowed to prosecute and the *basileus* would have had to be assured that a competent person was acting as prosecutor before he undertook the case.[4] By analogy with other types of cases in which we know that the *antomosiai* were sworn at the *anakrisis* it seems fair to sup-

---

[1] *Op. cit.*, pp. 87 ff.   [2] *Op. cit.*, pp. 830 f.

[3] It is interesting to see how Lipsius and Philippi each use the same passage to prove his own theory. Antiphon vi. 14 says: πολλοὶ τῶν περιεστώτων τούτων τὰ μὲν πράγματα ταῦτα πάντα ἀκριβῶς ἐπίστανται, καὶ τοῦ ὁρκωτοῦ ἀκούουσι. Philippi takes this to mean that the same people were present both at the trial and at the preliminary investigation. Hence they heard the oath of the preliminary investigation. Lipsius, on the other hand, thinks that the passage must mean that the oath was taken at the trial.

[4] Cf. *supra*, I, 114 f.

pose that in homicide cases also the oaths were sworn at the preliminary investigation. In fact, the two oaths correspond: in other cases the parties swore to their pleadings; in homicide cases they in effect did the same thing, the prosecutor swearing to the guilt of the accused, the defendant to his own innocence. It may be suggested that, while undoubtedly the party oaths were sworn at the preliminary investigation in homicide cases, it is quite possible also that these oaths, with a solemn sacrifice, were repeated at the actual trial. Since it is substantially the same oath on both occasions ancient authors do not make any distinction. That such is the case is borne out by the passage of Demosthenes cited above in which we are told that the oath over the solemn sacrifice was taken both in the Areopagus and in the Palladium:

ἴστε δήπου τοῦθ' ἅπαντας, ὅτι ἐν Ἀρείῳ πάγῳ, οὗ δίδωσ' ὁ νόμος καὶ κελεύει τοῦ φόνου δικάζεσθαι, πρῶτον μὲν διομεῖται κατ' ἐξωλείας αὐτοῦ καὶ γένους καὶ οἰκίας ὅ τιν' αἰτιώμενος εἰργάσθαι τι τοιοῦτον, εἶτ' οὐδὲ τὸν τυχόντα τιν' ὅρκον ἀλλ' ὃν οὐδεὶς ὄμνυσ' ὑπὲρ οὐδενὸς ἄλλου, στὰς ἐπὶ τῶν τομίων κάπρου καὶ κριοῦ καὶ ταύρου καὶ τούτων ἐσφαγμένων ὑφ' ὧν δεῖ καὶ ἐν αἷς ἡμέραις καθήκει, ὥστε καὶ ἐκ τοῦ χρόνου καὶ ἐκ τῶν μεταχειριζομένων ἅπαν, ὅσον ἔσθ' ὅσιον πεπρᾶχθαι. . . . . καὶ τῷ μὲν διώκοντι ὑπάρχει ταῦτα, τῷ δὲ φεύγοντι τὰ μὲν τῆς διωμοσίας ταῦτά. . . . . καὶ γὰρ ἐνταῦθ' [in the Palladium] ὑπόκειται πρῶτον μὲν διωμοσία, δεύτερον δὲ λόγος, τρίτον δὲ γνῶσις τοῦ δικαστηρίου, κ.τ.λ.[1]

This leads to another question: whether the same oath was taken in all the homicide courts, or at least in the Areopagus, the Palladium, the Delphinium, and in Phreatto. Philippi states[2] that the oath was taken in all four courts. He is apparently not including the Prytaneum, in which, although there might be a *diomosia* of the prosecutor, there certainly could not be a *diomosia* of the defendant, inasmuch as the defendant was either an animal, an inanimate object, or an unknown person. Now in a very rhetorical passage Demosthenes speaks as follows:

οὗ γὰρ οὐ κλῆσις, οὐ κρίσις, οὐ μαρτυρία συνειδότος, οὐ διωμοσία, ἀλλ' ἀπ' αἰτίας εὐθὺς ἡ τιμωρία γέγραπται, καὶ αὕτη ἣν ἀπαγορεύουσιν οἱ νόμοι, τί ἂν ἄλλο τις εἴποι; καίτοι ταῦτα πάντ' ἐπὶ πέντε δικαστηρίοις γίγνεται προστεταγμένα τοῖς νόμοις.[3]

[1] Demos. xxiii. 67-71. [2] *Op. cit.*, p. 87. [3] xxiii. 63.

Doubtless his statement is true for all five courts as far as the prosecutor is concerned, but, as has already been pointed out, it cannot be true of the *diomosia* for the defendant in the Prytaneum nor can there have been any oath for the defendant in some of the cases before the Delphinium court in which cases of justifiable homicide were tried. In his detailed description of the five homicide courts Demosthenes specifically mentions the oath which is to be sworn by the plaintiff and the defendant in cases before the Areopagus and the Palladium, but when he turns to the court of the Delphinium there is no reference to the *diomosia*.¹ And in other passages where we have references to the oaths of the parties in homicide cases the reference is always to the courts of Areopagus and Palladium.² In connection with his discussion of the Delphinium, Demosthenes mentions the case of Orestes who, as Demosthenes says, admitted that he had killed his mother, but insisted that his deed was justifiable.³ Justifiable homicide carried no moral guilt with it. In fact, the killer was not even polluted. This leads us to a consideration of the passage in Aeschylus⁴ in which the Erinyes complain that Orestes will neither take an oath nor tender one. The explanation is obvious. Since he is admittedly the slayer he cannot take an oath that he is not guilty. The only thing that he can do is to plead that his act was justifiable.

In cases, then, which ultimately came before the three homicide courts, Areopagus, Palladium, and in Phreatto, at the preliminary investigation both the prosecutor and the defendant took oaths, the prosecutor to the effect that he was a relative in the proper degree to the deceased and that the defendant was guilty, the defendant to the effect that he was

---

¹ For Demosthenes' description of the Delphinium cf. xxiii. 74: τρίτον δ' ἕτερον πρὸς τούτοις δικαστήριον, ὃ πάντων ἁγιώτατα τούτων ἔχει καὶ φρικωδέστατα, ἄν τις ὁμολογῇ μὲν κτεῖναι, ἐννόμως δὲ φῇ δεδρακέναι. τοῦτο δ' ἐστὶ τοὐπὶ Δελφινίῳ.

² Cf. Antiph. i. 28; Lysias x. 11; Demos. xlvii. 70; lix. 9.

³ xxiii. 74: λογιζόμενοι δ' ὅτι μητέρ' Ὀρέστης ἀπεκτονὼς ὁμολογῶν θεῶν δικαστῶν τυχὼν ἀποφυγγάνει, νομίσαι δίκαιόν τιν' εἶναι φόνον· οὐ γὰρ ἂν τά γε μὴ δίκαια θεοὺς ψηφίσασθαι.

⁴ *Eumen.* 429.

not guilty. These oaths were probably repeated over a solemn blood sacrifice in the homicide court at the beginning of the actual trial. In most cases before the Delphinium and at the Prytaneum (both of which incidentally are purely ceremonial courts) the prosecutor alone swore as to his relationship with the slain person and as to the guilt of the defendant.

There is some evidence for two other oaths during the course of a homicide trial. A statement is found in the *Lexica Segueriana*[1] to the effect that a second oath, apparently a repetition of the oath which occurred at the beginning of the trial, was taken after the first speeches of the prosecutor and the defendant:

διωμοσία· ὅρκος ἐστίν, ὃν ὤμνυον οἱ φόνου ἀγῶνα διώκοντες ἢ φεύγοντες· ἀμφότεροι γὰρ ὤμνυον μετὰ τὸ εἰπεῖν τὸν πρότερον λόγον· ὁ μὲν ἦ μὴν ἀληθῆ κατηγορηκέναι καὶ δικαίως, ὁ δὲ ἦ μὴν ἀληθῆ ἀπολελογῆσθαι καὶ δικαίως· ὤμνυον δὲ καὶ πρὶν εἰπεῖν τὸν αὐτὸν ὅρκον ἀμφότεροι, ἐπενεχθείσης ἤδη τῆς ψήφου, εἰ μὴ δικαίως νενικηκέναι, ἐξώλειαν ἑαυτῷ ἐπαρώμενος, εἰ ἐξηπάτησεν.

This passage is accepted by Mederle.[2] Together with the oath which the winner of the case took after the trial was over to the effect that as many of the judges as had voted in his favor had voted justly and that no false statements had been made there would have been three oaths.[3] There is, however, no other evidence for the oath after the first speeches, and it seems extremely unlikely that any such oath was sworn. The writer of the foregoing passage may have confused it with the right of the defendant to withdraw after the first speech or, as Lipsius thinks,[4] he may have made some wrong inference from the passage cited below from Aeschines. Philippi does not deal with this alleged oath at all. The oath of the winner after the trial, however, may be accepted on the testimony of Aeschines, although this is the only reference to such an oath. It is accepted by Lipsius and by Mederle:

[1] P. 239.

[2] *De iurisiurandi in lite Attica decem oratorum aetate usu*, pp. 23 f.

[3] Aeschin. ii. 87.   [4] *Op. cit.*, p. 833, n. 17.

ἢ πῶς οὐκ εἰκότως οἱ πατέρες ἡμῶν ἐν ταῖς φονικαῖς δίκαις ταῖς ἐπὶ
Παλλαδίῳ[1] κατέδειξαν, τέμνοντα τὰ τόμια τὸν νικῶντα τῇ ψήφῳ ἐξορκίζεσθαι,
καὶ τοῦτο ὑμῖν πάτριόν ἐστιν ἔτι καὶ νῦν, τἀληθῆ καὶ τὰ δίκαια ἐψηφίσθαι
τῶν δικαστῶν ὅσοι τὴν ψῆφον ἤνεγκαν αὐτῷ, καὶ ψεῦδος μηδὲν εἰρηκέναι,
εἰ δὲ μή, ἐξώλη αὐτὸν εἶναι ἐπαρᾶσθαι καὶ τὴν οἰκίαν τὴν αὐτοῦ, τοῖς δὲ
δικασταῖς εὔχεσθαι πολλὰ καὶ ἀγαθὰ εἶναι;

Still another oath is connected with homicide trials, the
oath of the relatives on granting *aidesis* to a homicide who is
in exile. The nature of this oath is not specified, but from the
fact that no oath is required from phratry members in case
there are no relatives and the phratry members have to act
on the granting of *aidesis*, it is a safe guess that the oath was
to substantiate the claims of the relatives to relationship with
the deceased. The oath is mentioned in the fragment of the
homicide laws of Draco as they appeared in the revision of
409–408 B.C.[2]

There remains the question of the persons to whom the
party oath in other cases was administered. Philippi[3] suggests that outside of homicide cases the introductory oath
was administered only to the plaintiff. But the very name
antomosia argues for an oath of the defendant. Further, there
are several passages which disprove Philippi's statements.
Isaeus seems definitely to refer to a preliminary oath of both
parties: ἑκατέρῳ οὖν ἡμῶν, ἐξ ὧν ἀντωμόσαμεν σκεψάμενοι, ψηφί-
σασθε.[4] Antiphon refers to the oath of the defendant: πῶς οὖν
εὔορκα ἀντομωμοκὼς ἔσται φάσκων εὖ εἰδέναι, κ.τ.λ.[5]

Whether witnesses in other than homicide trials were
regularly sworn has been a matter of much dispute. Diogenes
Laertius states that no evidence was given in Athens without

---

[1] ἐπὶ Παλλαδίῳ is considered a gloss by Lipsius. Cf. Philippi (*Rhein. Mus. f. Phil.*,
XXIX, 10), who believes that the gloss was added by someone who remembered
Demos. xlvii. 70: ὥστ' εἰ διομεῖ ἐπὶ Παλλαδίῳ αὐτὸς καὶ ἡ γυνὴ καὶ τὰ παιδία καὶ
καταράσεσθε αὐτοῖς καὶ τῇ οἰκίᾳ, χείρων τε δόξεις πολλοῖς εἶναι, κἂν μὲν ἀποφύγῃ σ',
ἐπιωρκηκέναι, ἐὰν δὲ ἕλῃς, φθονήσει. Inasmuch as the passage continues with some
remarks about unjustifiable homicide as opposed to justifiable homicide, it may well
be a gloss. It seems that if such a procedure was followed in one homicide court it
might well be in all of them.

[2] For a full discussion of the matter cf. *supra*, I, 112 ff.   [4] ix. 34.

[3] *Op. cit.*, p. 89.   [5] i. 8; cf. Lipsius, *op. cit.*, p. 830, n. 4.

oath. Speaking of Xenocrates, he says: ἦν δὲ καὶ ἀξιόπιστος σφόδρα, ὥστε μὴ ἐξὸν ἀνώμοτον μαρτυρεῖν, τούτῳ μόνῳ συνεχώρουν Ἀθηναῖοι.¹ But this cannot be correct. In fact, in the Herodes murder trial, in which the defendant was tried as a *kakourgos* and not as a homicide, he complains that he must submit to the evidence of witnesses who had taken no oath, whereas if he had been tried as a homicide it would have been necessary for the witnesses to be under oath.² This may be mere rhetoric on the part of the speaker to indicate that in the present suit the witnesses have not taken the very solemn oath which they would have had to take before a homicide court. From all the references to witness oaths before the non-homicide courts, it is apparent that they were considered of slight importance. Such oaths were administered not by the magistrates but by the parties, and it seems to have been the privilege of a party to administer such an oath to his opponent's witnesses if he desired to do so. Witnesses were not always sworn, but any witness might take an oath.³ A witness might in court take an oath of any one of the three following varieties: (1) an oath as the result of a challenge; (2) a voluntary oath to make his evidence more impressive in the interest of a friend; (3) possibly an oath at the instance of the party for whom he appeared, as the result of a suspicion that he would prove adverse.

In two cases there are references to oaths to be sworn by witnesses in court.⁴ Lipsius argues from these that there could have been no regular witness oath as in these two cases there would then be two oaths from the witness regarding the same matter.⁵ Leisi⁶ agrees with this and disagrees with Bonner,⁷ who, without arguing that there was such a double oath, yet sees no objection to it inasmuch as the second oath would have been much more impressive in character and would have been administered only with the consent of the

---

¹ iv. 2. 7.   ² Antiph. v. 12.

³ Bonner, *Evidence in Athenian Courts*, pp. 76 ff.; Lipsius, *op. cit.*, pp. 884 f.

⁴ Demos. xlv. 57 f.; liv. 26.   ⁶ *Der Zeuge*, p. 64.

⁵ *Op. cit.*   ⁷ *Op. cit.*, p. 77.

witness. Hence the two cases do not prove Lipsius' point, although he is undoubtedly correct in his main contention that there was no regular witness oath.[1]

There is some dispute about the necessity of oaths in extra-judicial depositions. It was possible for a witness because of illness or absence from the city to give his testimony in writing in the presence of witnesses. This is called ἐκμαρτυρία.[2] This document could subsequently be produced in court accompanied by affidavits of the witnesses who had heard the testimony given. There are two parts to such testimony then, the extra-judicial deposition and the affidavits of the attesting witnesses. That there was no oath involved is agreed upon by Bonner,[3] Leisi,[4] and Lipsius.[5] Glotz,[6] however, believes that an oath was required. But in view of the fact that the witness ran the same danger of a suit for false evidence as he would run in any other case it does not seem likely that an oath was required any more than if he were present in the court. The theory that there was an oath rests upon the procedure in an inscription which deals with procedure in Cnidos where οἱ ἐκμαρτυροῦντες are ordered to take an oath.[7]

In his classification of oaths, in addition to promissory and evidentiary oaths, Hirzel takes account of a third type which he calls the *Echtheitseide*, that is, an oath as to genuineness. This oath he refers to the present as opposed to the evidentiary oath which he refers to the past and the promissory oath which he refers to the future.[8] By his *Echtheitseide* Hirzel is referring to the institution of Eideshelfer or, as we call them for lack of a better term, "oath-helpers" or "compurgators."

---

[1] There are many references to the witness oath in non-homicide cases, although it was not obligatory; cf. Isaeus ix. 19, 24; xii. 9 f.; Aeschin. ii. 156; Demos. xviii. 137; xxix. 54; xlv. 58; lii. 28; liv. 26; lvii. 22, 36, 39, 44, 56; Xen. *Apol. of Soc.* xxiv.

[2] Cf. *supra*, pp. 132 ff.   [3] *Op. cit.*, p. 26.   [4] *Op. cit.*, p. 66.

[5] *Op. cit.*, p. 887.   [6] In Darem.-Saglio, *s.v.* "Jusjurandum."

[7] Dittenberger, *Sylloge*[3], 953; Collitz-Bechtel, *op. cit.*, 3591; Dareste-Haussoulier-Reinach, *op. cit.*, X, ll. 24 ff.

[8] *Op. cit.*, p. 6. Hirzel is wrong in referring the evidentiary oath only to the past, for it may refer to the present status of a matter equally as well.

Compurgation has regularly been treated as an independent institution. But it is really a development of the evidentiary oath, and many of its peculiarities become clear only if this fact is recognized. In the various legal systems the evidentiary oath was early felt to be insufficient and, as has been seen to be the case in the Athenian legal system, it survived in modified forms in only a few instances. Frequently the oath of the principal had to be supported by auxiliary oaths varying in number according to the matter at issue.[1] This form of trial was especially common in the Middle Ages,[2] and a description of the details of the practice in that period may serve to clarify the institution as it appears in Greek legal systems. In German law the co-swearers were known as *Eideshelfer*, in English as oath-helpers or compurgators.[3] Under both systems the helper swore merely to his confidence in the principal's oath.[4] It had nothing whatever to do with the fact

[1] Thayer, *A Preliminary Treatise on Evidence at the Common Law*, p. 24; Schröder, *Lehrbuch der deutschen Rechtsgeschichte*, p. 83.

[2] Grimm, *Deutsche Rechtsaltertümer*, II, 495 ff.

[3] A late Latin word. The institution was quite unknown in Roman law. In English law the institution itself is known as "compurgation" or "wager of law." German law, aside from the term *Eideshelfer*, uses the Latin names *consacramentales* and *coniuratores* and designates the institution *Eidhilfe*. The institution was in use in France also in the case of heretics (cf. Du Cange, *Glossarium*, *s.v.* "Compurgator"). The oath was as follows: "Ego talis juro per Deum et haec sancta quattuor Evangelia, quae in manibus meis teneo, me firmiter credere quod talis non fuit Insabbatus, Valdensis, vel Pauperum de Lugduno, neque Haereticus credens errorum erroribus, et credo firmiter eum in hoc jurasse verum."

[4] In both England and Germany oath-helpers were apparently first used in criminal suits, for all the earliest cases belong to this kind of action (cf. Grimm, *op. cit.*, II, 491). In later times, however, trial by compurgation was admitted in civil suits, in England surviving chiefly in cases of detinue and debt. In an action of debt, unless the plaintiff relied on a sealed document, the defendant as a rule might wage his law (cf. Pollock and Maitland, *The History of English Law before the Time of Edward I*, II, 214). The institution early fell into disuse in criminal suits in England. There from the beginning it was used both in ecclesiastical courts (*ibid.*, I, 443) and in the king's courts as an optional form of trial alongside trial by jury. In the fourteenth century a citizen had a choice between the Great Law and a jury of twelve (*ibid.*, II, 634–36). The institution had nearly disappeared by the latter half of the eighteenth century, but as late as 1824 a case appeared in which a debtor demanded compurgation and the practice was not officially discontinued until 1833, when further use of it was forbidden by an act of Parliament (cf. Thayer, *op. cit.*). In Germany in the Middle Ages compurgation was restricted almost en-

at issue. Any freeman might wage his law.[1] Slaves, not being competent to take an oath, were consequently not allowed as oath-helpers. It is generally believed that in the earlier stages of the institution a man had as oath-helpers only his own relatives. Naturally the relatives would be most keenly interested, since the accusation, if not disproved, might cause a feud.[2] It was also a matter of duty.[3] As time went on, however, the right to take the oath was extended to neighbors and friends. Naturally only people who knew the principal well—relatives, neighbors, intimate friends—could be admitted as oath-helpers.[4] It was always a distinctly partisan institution. Oath-helpers had to be of age.[5] As a general rule women could not act as oath-helpers.[6] The rank of an oath-helper might depend on that of his principal, or on that of the person injured, for instance on that of the deceased in a homicide case.[7] In the beginning oath-helpers must always have been on the side of the defendant. It is of course a very natural growth of the institution that the privilege should eventually be extended to the plaintiff as well,[8] just as in the case of the evidentiary oath of the principal.

---

tirely to criminal suits. The oath-helpers in civil suits gradually faded into witnesses who testified from their own knowledge (Schröder, *op. cit.*, p. 715). A case in which *Eideshelfer* were used in the year 1548 shows that the institution in Germany lasted until a late period.

[1] Only a freeman was capable of paying *Wergeld* (Grimm, *op. cit.*, II, 495 ff.). The only exception to the rule that any freeman might be tried by compurgation is found in Salic law where it is stated that only nobles were allowed trial by compurgation, although any freeman could be tried in that way if the plaintiff gave his consent.

[2] Pollock and Maitland, *op. cit.*, II, 600.   [4] *Ibid.*, p. 83.

[3] Schröder, *op. cit.*, p. 70.   [5] Grimm, *op. cit.*, II, 543.

[6] *Ibid.*, I, 563. There are exceptions to this rule. In the ecclesiastical courts of England a woman strengthened her cause with women oath-helpers. Among certain Germanic peoples also women could support the oath of a litigant, as, for example, among the Lombards and Burgundians (*ibid.*, II, 495).

[7] *Ibid.*

[8] In English law there is no case cited by Thayer or by Pollock and Maitland in which the oath-helpers aided the plaintiff until the later stages of the institution when it had begun to be used in civil suits (Pollock and Maitland, *op. cit.*, II, 634–

The procedure was quite simple. In England when the litigant was permitted to wage his law the court fixed the number of compurgators which he must produce,[1] since the number varied according to the importance of the case.[2] As the institution developed the method of choosing the oath-helpers changed. At first the selection lay entirely with the party to the suit,[3] but later they were chosen by the adversary or the judge. But under this later procedure the litigant always retained the right to reject those who were chosen if he could satisfactorily support his refusal to accept them. The oath-helper, on the other hand, had the right to refuse to take oath if he was unable to reconcile it with his conscience.[4] In the primitive stages of every legal system there is apparent a great fear of committing perjury. Herein, as in the case of the evidentiary oath of the parties, consist the safeguards which made the institution a sounder means of proof than it seems to be. When the trial took place the oath was administered to the litigant by the adversary in early times and in later times by the judge. The litigant repeated it word for word. Then the oath-helpers had to swear, at first, it seems, jointly, but in later times singly.[5] By the individual oath it was made to appear a more personal and solemn thing. The content of the oath is much the same in both systems. In English courts they swore: "The oath is clean that ———

36; cf. Grimm, *op. cit.*). In Germany also the *Eideshelfer* seem originally to have aided the defendant exclusively, although later they appear even in homicide cases on the side of the plaintiff. An old law is mentioned by Meister according to which the plaintiff in a homicide trial could with two *Eideshelfer* swear that the defendant was guilty (cf. Meister, *Rhein. Mus.*, LXIII, 575, n. 1).

[1] Pollock and Maitland, *op. cit.*, II, 610.

[2] An interesting illustration of this is the different number of oath-helpers required by the three laws in London in the thirteenth century (*ibid.*, pp. 634–36). Twelve seems to have been the normal number in both the Germanic and the English systems (cf. *ibid.*, p. 600; Thayer, *op. cit.*, p. 90; Schröder, *op. cit.*, p. 358). Only rarely was the oath with one helper sufficient (Grimm, *op. cit.*, I, 285). Occasionally as many as three hundred oath-helpers are found.

[3] Schröder, *op. cit.*, pp. 83, 384; Pollock and Maitland, *op. cit.*, I, 140.

[4] Schröder, *op. cit.*, p. 83; Pollock and Maitland, *op. cit.*, I, 140.

[5] Schröder, *op. cit.*, p. 354.

hath sworn,"[1] although it might also take a less positive form, i.e., they might swear that the oath was true to the best of their knowledge.[2] In the Germanic system they swore that the oath of the principal was *rein und unmein*.[3] So in neither system is an oath-helper ever found who swore to the fact, although there are undeniably cases in which the fact was known. That the procedure was highly ceremonial is shown by the fact that great emphasis was put upon the form of the oath as sworn by the oath-helper.[4] The compurgator who swore to the innocence of a person who was really guilty was not liable to a charge of perjury. There is no action and consequently no penalty for a false oath. The idea seems to have been that such punishment was the affair of the gods. A man could, however, be convicted of giving false evidence. But in compurgation the oath-helper swore to his own belief, not to the facts of the case which presumably he did not know. He would not, therefore, be liable to a charge of giving false evidence.

The institution of compurgation in England and Germany was never developed further than this. The oath-helpers never swore to anything except their confidence in the principal. It is true that they appear sometimes on one side of the case, sometimes on the other. It is true also that they must have known the facts on many occasions. But this in no wise changed the character of their oath.

[1] Pollock and Maitland, *op. cit.*, I, 140.

[2] *Ibid.*, II, 600. Cf. the formula used in London, thirteenth century: "Quod secundum scientiam suam iuramentum quod fecit fidele est." This does not, however, imply any knowledge at all of the fact, i.e., it does not mean that they have positive knowledge that the oath is true, but merely that they know of nothing which makes it untrue.

[3] Schröder, *op. cit.*, p. 83: "Die Eideshelfer hatten nicht die objektive Wahrheit, sondern nur die subjektive Reinheit des Haupteides zu beschwören." Cf. Grimm, *op. cit.*, II, 495 ff. and 541: "Eideshelfer schwuren nicht dass eine That wahr sei, sondern dass der, dem sie halfen, einen echten Eid ablege."

[4] At the use of a wrong word the oath "bursts" and the adversary wins (cf. Pollock and Maitland, *op. cit.*, II, 600; Schröder, *op. cit.*, p. 358). There are further specifications as to the physical attitude in which an oath must be taken. Often the helper must grasp the arm or shoulder of his principal as he speaks the oath (Grimm, *op. cit.*, II, 551; cf. II, 129).

Although the institution was so well known in medieval law no one had observed any instance of it in the legal systems of the ancient Greeks until in 1895 Zitelmann[1] declared that he had found some cases of oath-helpers in the great Gortyn inscription. He was followed by various scholars who pointed out additional examples of the institution elsewhere in Greece,[2] and the whole matter was subjected to a careful study by R. M. E. Meister,[3] who collected and discussed all the previously alleged occurrences of the institution and added a few new examples. Although the examples of the institution in Greece are non-Athenian, they are worth some consideration as a background for the survivals which occur in the Athenian system.

Before examining the various passages adduced by Meister and his predecessors in support of the existence of the institution in Greece it will be well to point out that oath-helpers as a distinct class of witnesses are not mentioned by any Greek author. Nor does any certain technical name for them occur in Greek inscriptions.[4] No definite reference to the institution is found in the Attic orators, and the lexicographers who confine themselves to the explanation of what occurs in the orators are silent. Not even Pollux, who devotes his entire eighth book to legal terminology, mentions them. Neither Plato nor Aristotle, who were both versed in legal history,

[1] Bücheler and Zitelmann, "Das Recht von Gortyn," *Rhein. Mus.*, XL, *Ergänzungsheft*, Comment. by Zitelmann, p. 76.

[2] Ziebarth, *op. cit.*, pp. 40 f.; in Pauly-Wissowa, *s.v.* "Eid"; Gilbert, *Beiträge*, pp. 468 f.; R. Meister, *Berichte der Sächs. Ges. der Wiss.* (Phil.-Hist. Cl.), XLVIII (1896), 35 ff.; Wyse, in Whibley, *Comp. to Greek Studies*[4], p. 467; Glotz, *Solidarité de la famille dans le droit criminel en Grèce*, pp. 288 ff.

[3] *Rhein. Mus.*, LXIII, 559 ff.; cf. Cauer's review, *Woch. f. kl. Phil.*, XXVI, 766.

[4] The word ὀμωμόται, which is preserved in two inscriptions (Collitz-Bechtel, *op. cit.*, 4964, 5092), has often been considered a technical designation for this class of witnesses, and ὀρκομόται (*ibid.*, 4969; Fougères, *Bull. corr. hell.*, XVI, 577) has been interpreted as a variant for ὀμωμόται. But all four inscriptions are fragmentary and unintelligible and it is not possible to make any deductions from them alone. Meister rejects ὀρκομόται as oath-helpers on the ground that this word is used unmistakably of jurors in the Oeanthea-Chaleion inscription (*op. cit.*, p. 579). The nearest approach to a word for the institution is the verb συνεκσομόσασθαι (Collitz-Bechtel, *op. cit.*, 4986).

has any designation for them. Aristotle makes the following statement in regard to the different kinds of witnesses: εἰσὶ δὲ αἱ μαρτυρίαι αἱ μὲν περὶ αὑτοῦ αἱ δὲ περὶ ἀμφισβητοῦντος καὶ αἱ μὲν περὶ τοῦ πράγματος αἱ δὲ περὶ τοῦ ἤθους, ὥστε φανερὸν ὅτι οὐδέποτ᾽ ἔστιν ἀπορῆσαι μαρτυρίας χρησίμης.[1] That is, Aristotle makes a division into witnesses of fact and witnesses to character. But although it is generally admitted that the institution of oath-helpers in the German and English sense was unknown in Athenian law, most scholars have accepted the phrase αἱ μαρτυρίαι περὶ τοῦ ἤθους as referring to *Eideshelfer*. But Aristotle is describing the law as it existed in his day. Hence it is not probable that he would discuss an obsolete type of witness. Those who argue that the phrase has reference to oath-helpers use as proof the fact that Aristotle places these witnesses on a par with witnesses of fact (he calls them both χρησίμη, i.e., a decision might be based on the evidence of either), but that German *Leumundszeugen*, the counterpart of our familiar character witnesses who testify to the general reputation of a defendant, are never on a par with witnesses of fact. But in this case the analogy with German law is valueless. For English law puts character witnesses on precisely the same plane with witnesses of fact. Furthermore, character evidence, although not quite in the English sense, was well known at Athens and might be admitted even in the Areopagus.[2] It is then inconceivable that Aristotle refers to compurgation which was not known at Athens in his day. That he refers to character evidence is borne out by the following sentence which Meister fails to quote: εἰ μὴ γὰρ κατὰ τοῦ πράγματος ἢ αὑτῷ ὁμολογουμένης ἢ τῷ ἀμφισβητοῦντι ἐναντίας, ἀλλὰ περὶ τοῦ ἤθους ἢ αὑτοῦ εἰς ἐπιείκειαν ἢ τοῦ ἀμφισβητοῦντος εἰς φαυλότητα.[3] Obviously there is no indication here of an oath either to a fact or to the truth of an-

---

[1] *Rhet.* i. 15. 18.

[2] Bonner, *Evidence in Athenian Courts*, pp. 18, 83 f.

[3] Sandys translates: "For if we have no evidence as to the fact, either in agreement with our own side of the case or opposed to that of the adverse party, at all events (we shall be sure to find plenty) as to character, ... to establish, that is, either our own respectability or the opponent's worthlessness."

other man's oath. The witness, regularly unsworn in Athenian practice, simply testifies to the ἐπιείκεια or φαυλότης of the party. It is clear, then, that Aristotle is not only not using a special designation for oath-helpers but is not even speaking of oath-helpers.

Meister[1] recognized two distinct classes of oath-helpers in Greek law: (1) those who swore that the principal's oath was good (this class corresponds precisely to compurgation in English and Germanic law as described above); (2) those who swore the same oath as the principal in support of his contentions (this class is entirely unknown to the English and Germanic systems). The former class need have no knowledge of the fact; the latter must. The oaths consequently are quite different in content, the common feature being that they join the principal in his preliminary oath in denial or affirmation and that in both cases the oaths are final. The ordinary witness, if sworn at all, had no part in the preliminary oath taken by the litigants, but swore to matters within his knowledge which were considered germane to the issue; frequently he had no knowledge of the main issue, the guilt or innocence of the defendant. Still another factor may be noted. In many cases no witnesses could be found to swear that the defendant did not commit the crime with which he was charged. For example, Euxitheus, the defendant in the Herodes murder trial, was the last person seen in company with Herodes.[2] So no one could swear that he was not the murderer.

The problem, then, is to discover if possible whether Class 2 develops from Class 1. Although Meister has recognized the two distinct classes in Greek law, he has failed to consider this question in detail, thus confusing his argument.

Of the examples given by Meister there are only two cases of *Eideshelfer* which correspond to the English and German systems, i.e., relatives who swear to the truth of the defendant's oath. One occurs in an inscription from Egyptian

---

[1] *Op. cit.*, pp. 579 ff.; cf. Bücheler and Zitelmann, *op. cit.*, p. 76; Ziebarth, *op. cit.*, pp. 40 f.

[2] Antiph. v. 22.

Thebes belonging to the second century B.C.[1] Two brothers, Heracleides and Nechutes, were charged with wounding. They were ordered to take an evidentiary oath to the effect that they themselves did not cause the wound, and did not know who did (this probably means, as Meister suggests, that they were not accomplices). In support of this oath their brothers swear that it is true (ἀληθῆ τὸν ὅρκον εἶναι). ἀληθῆ is used in the same sense as the German *rein und unmein* and the English "good," that is, it merely expresses the helper's confidence in the principal and implies no knowledge of the facts. The oath-helpers could not have had knowledge of the facts unless the time of the crime was specified and they could prove an alibi for the defendants. This, however, is only incidental. The fact that they swear merely that the oath of the defendants is true proves that they are oath-helpers in the only sense of the term known in German and English law. It is interesting to note that they are the closest relatives of the defendants. Relationship was one of the qualifications for the first type of oath-helper. Apparently the oath of the defendants with their oath-helpers decided the case. If the helpers failed to take it, the defendants were to be brought before the *epistatés* (ἔρχεσθαι ἐπὶ τὸν ἐπιστάτην) for trial on the merits of the case.

This form of compurgation is illustrated also by a passage from the *Politics* in which Aristotle, commenting on the absurdity of ancient laws, uses as an illustration a law of Cyme: ἂν πλῆθός τι παράσχηται μαρτύρων ὁ διώκων τὸν φόνον τῶν αὐτοῦ συγγενῶν, ἔνοχον εἶναι τῷ φόνῳ τὸν φεύγοντα.[2] The phrase τῶν αὐτοῦ συγγενῶν has sometimes been construed as dependent upon φόνον and so has been considered to have reference to the universal rule in Greece that only a relative of a murdered man could prosecute the murderer.[3] But if it is joined with πλῆθος μαρτύρων, which is the natural interpreta-

[1] Revillout and Wilcken, *Revue égyptologique*, VI, 11; Wilcken, *Griechische Ostraka aus Aegypten und Nubien*, II, 1150. Cf. Meister, *op. cit.*, p. 575.

[2] 1269A; cf. Meister, *op. cit.*, pp. 573 ff.

[3] Glotz, *op. cit.*, pp. 47 ff., 425 ff.

tion,¹ one of the important characteristics of the original *Eideshelfer* would be fulfilled. In any case there is no real difficulty in recognizing oath-helpers in the πλῆθός τι μαρτύρων. It may be objected that there is no mention of an oath, the indispensable feature of the institution. But the objection cannot be sustained. For this is a murder trial and at Athens all witnesses in murder trials were sworn so that Aristotle would scarcely think it necessary to mention the oath which his readers would assume. Aristotle describes them as μάρτυρες, which seems to show that he did not recognize them as oath-helpers. But if he had realized that he was criticizing the institution of oath-helpers, he would not have used the word μάρτυρ, but some circumlocution, since his readers could not have known that he meant oath-helpers. With his knowledge of legal institutions it is remarkable that Aristotle was ignorant of the institution of oath-helpers, but in the face of this passage it is better to admit his ignorance than to make a desperate effort to defend his knowledge.²

The fact that stress is put on the quantity also makes for their being oath-helpers. If they were fact witnesses, number would be of comparatively little importance. Reliability, not quantity, is the *desideratum* in testimonial evidence. It is scarcely possible that they could be fact witnesses, for murder is usually committed with the greatest secrecy. The only reason for demanding a certain number of eyewitnesses would be a practice of determining the case without letting the defendant be heard in his own defense. This is just what happens in the case of oath-helpers. If the party produces the required number he wins the case. It is inconceivable that the law required a fixed number of eyewitnesses in order to establish a prima facie case. If they are oath-helpers, the pas-

¹ Cf. Jowett's translation: "At Cumae there is a law about murder, to the effect that if the accuser produce a certain number of witnesses from among his own kinsmen, the accused shall be held guilty." Cf. also Newman, *ad loc.*: "Witnesses from the number of his own kinsmen."

² Cf. Wyse (*op. cit.*), who says that Aristotle is wrong. Meister weakens his argument by trying to defend Aristotle.

sage furnishes an illustration of oath-helpers as used on the side of the plaintiff. The number was fixed in court.[1]

These two cases exhaust the Greek instances of *Eideshelfer* as they appear in Germanic and English practice. In the other cases cited by Meister and his predecessors the so-called oath-helpers swear not that the oath is good, but they swear the same oath as the principal. In other words, owing to their knowledge of facts they are able to join the principal in a solemn oath. They thus differ fundamentally also from regular witnesses in that the combination oath, like the ancient evidentiary oath, settled the case. The opponent is not allowed to say a word. The unity and finality of the oath indicate a distinct development of oath-helpers unknown to other systems. All of Meister's examples of this class are taken from the laws of Gortyn.

An alleged case of *Eideshelfer* which has occasioned an enormous amount of discussion is that of the ἐπωμόται, which an alien plaintiff in Oeanthea or Chaleion was allowed to choose under certain conditions:

Αἴ κ' ἀνδιχάζωντι τοὶ ξενοδίκαι, ἐπωμότας ἐλέστω ὁ ξένος ὠπάγων τὰν δίκαν ἔχθος προξένω καὶ ϝιδίω ξένω ἀριστίνδαν, ἐπὶ μὲν ταῖς μναϊαίαις καὶ πλέον, πέντε καὶ δέκ' ἄνδρας, ἐπὶ ταῖς μειόνοις ἐννέ' ἄνδρας.[2]

The word ἐπωμόται has been regarded as referring to additional jurors by many scholars.[3] Buck,[4] Hitzig,[5] and Ott[6] in-

---

[1] Meister (*op. cit.*, p. 575, n. 1) cites an excellent analogy in a German law to the effect that a plaintiff in a homicide case could with two oath-helpers swear that the defendant was guilty of a murder. Apparently the verdict was based on this oath and the defendant was not heard in his own defense.

[2] Hicks and Hill, *op. cit.*, 44; Tod, *op. cit.*, 34; Collitz-Bechtel, *op. cit.*, 1479.

[3] Oikonomides, Λοκρικῆς ἀνεκδότου ἐπιγραφῆς διαφώτισις; Rangabé, *Antiquités helléniques*, 356b; Röhl, *Inscrip. Gr. Ant.*, 322; Kirchhoff, *Phil.*, XIII, 1 ff.; Dareste, *REG*, II, 318; Eduard Meyer, *Forschungen zur alten Geschichte*, I, 307; Roberts, *Introduction to Greek Epigraphy*, 232; Dittenberger, *Inscr. Gr. Sept.*, III, 333; Hicks and Hill, *op. cit.* Several of these scholars had expressed their opinions before the idea of oath-helpers in Greek law had become established.

[4] *Greek Dialects*, 56, p. 218.

[5] *Altgriechische Staatsverträge über Rechtshilfe*, pp. 13, 45.

[6] *Op. cit.*, p. 120. It is difficult to discern whether Buck and Hitzig conceive of these sworn men as additional jurors or as an entirely new court. Ott asserts that

terpret the word as "sworn men with judicial functions." A
small group of scholars who have argued the case in detail
interpret the word as "oath-helpers."[1] Their arguments are
as follows: ἐπωμόται cannot mean additional jurors; no instance of a partial jury thus specially selected occurs elsewhere; if the chosen ones are additional judges, who decides
whether they are chosen according to the conditions? They
cannot be fact witnesses since they are chosen (ἐλέστω).

The last argument is sound. They cannot be witnesses of
fact. With regard to the other arguments, in the first place in
Greek as in English law,[2] trial by wager of law is often an
alternative for trial with witnesses. In any case the oath-
helpers are not brought in after the jury has already reached
its decision. It is inconceivable that the plaintiff would not
be allowed the benefit of oath-helpers from the beginning
even if there were fact witnesses. Again, although *Eideshelfer*
are admittedly partisans, yet in this case the ἐπωμόται must
not include the πρόξενος and Ϝίδιος ξένος of the litigant, the
only two people whom there would be much possibility of his
knowing well. For, by the terms of the treaty, if a man has
made a sojourn of more than a month in Oeanthea or
Chaleion he must submit to the regular courts and cannot
be tried before the ξενοδίκαι. This restriction, which constitutes the most important argument against *Eideshelfer*, is disregarded by both R. Meister and R. M. E. Meister. It is
impossible to see why the right to choose fifteen or nine
Eideshelfer is not just as great or even more of a preference
accorded to one side than the right to choose some jurors.
R. M. E. Meister argues that if the men are additional jurors
they will sit along with the ξενοδίκαι and so there will be no
one to decide whether the conditions specified for the choice
of them have been complied with or not. This argument is

---

the word means merely "jurors" and is not a compound ἐπ-ωμόται, but comes from
ἐπόμνυμι, meaning "to swear to a thing."

[1] R. Meister, *op. cit.*, pp. 35 ff.; R. M. E. Meister, *op. cit.*, pp. 561 ff.; Gilbert,
Jahrb. f. cl. Phil., Supplbd. XXIII, 468 ff.

[2] Cf. the Theban case, *supra*, pp. 181 f.

quite untenable, for the ξενοδίκαι would naturally decide the matter.

To the fact that there are odd numbers in both cases no importance has been attached by either writer. The numbers are too large for fact witnesses, as has been said. It is also too much to suppose that an alien who had been in the place less than a month could get so many *Eideshelfer*, exclusive, be it observed, of the only two men who could be supposed to know him well, his host and his πρόξενος. Thus Meister's argument against fact witnesses militates against *Eideshelfer* also. But if the ἐπωμόται are considered as a new group of jurors (odd in number, so that there cannot be an equal number of votes on both sides), there is then described by the inscription an extremely fair means of dealing with the case. The plaintiff, an alien, is given a fair deal by being allowed to choose them. His opponent is treated fairly because the citizens chosen by the alien are not likely to be influenced to the disadvantage of their fellow-citizen. There is no objection to this interpretation either from a linguistic or from a legal standpoint. It is interesting to note in connection with this the last part of the same inscription. In a case in which a citizen proceeds against a fellow-citizen in accordance with the terms of the συμβολαί the magistrates are to choose from the worthiest men jurors (ὁρκωμόται), who on oath are to decide the case by a majority decision. However, another treaty cited by Hitzig[1] supports this interpretation. The inscription deals with a treaty between Gortyn and Lato in Crete. In suits between citizens of the two places the Gortynian plaintiff brings action at Lato and vice versa and the plaintiff chooses his own judges (δικαστὰνς ἑλέσθω ὁ ἀδικιόμενος). The situation is precisely the same as that at Oeanthea and Chaleion.

To summarize: There existed in Greece two distinct forms of the institution of oath-helpers: those who swore to their confidence in the oath of the principal (they might or might not have knowledge of the facts of the case) and those who swore a joint oath with the principal to the facts. Together

---

[1] *Op. cit.*, p. 27. For the text of the decree cf. *Bull. corr. hell.*, XXVII, 219 ff.

with the character witnesses found in Aristotle[1] there are then three types of witnesses who assist the principal otherwise than by merely testifying to the fact. This third class may also, as Class 2, have developed from the original oath-helper. The attitude of both types (i.e., Class 1 and Class 3) toward the litigant is obviously the same, for both have implicit confidence in his honesty. Between the two there is undoubtedly a psychological connection, but only confusion results from failure to recognize the fact that they are not the same. No Greek writer has identified them either explicitly or implicitly. There is no feature that is common to all three types of witnesses. The first two swear in the preliminary oath although they swear to different things. The first and third signify their confidence in the principal, although one swears and the other takes no oath. It is quite reasonable, then, to treat the second and third types as separate developments of the original oath-helper, inasmuch as each type has a point in common with the original oath-helpers.

The procedure followed in connection with the two types of *Eideshelfer* was apparently the same although the content of the two oaths was different. The numbers are much smaller than those as a rule found in the English and German systems. There they might be several hundred in number. But in Greek law they range from one in one part of a case at Gortyn to four in another division of the same case. The extant examples, however, are very few and doubtless larger numbers were often required. Definite numbers are required for specific cases by law. In the laws of Gortyn the number varies with the importance of the individual injured. This tallies with Germanic and English law. They are found on the side both of the defendant and of the plaintiff. As a rule they are chosen by the litigant, but they might be designated by the court. They are found in both civil and criminal suits. In one case the oath includes a solemn curse, and perhaps it always did so as was the case with the earliest type of evidentiary oath.

It was assumed at the beginning of the discussion of the

[1] Cf. *supra*, pp. 180 f.

institution of *Eideshelfer* that it is an outgrowth and strengthened form of the evidentiary oath.[1] This has long been recognized by investigators in the field of Germanic law. But writers on the history of the Greek institution have failed to
recognize the connection. A man's own oath which at first
had sufficed to clear him without further inquiry gradually
came to be felt as insufficient proof of his innocence. So the
sworn confidence of his relatives and later of friends was
added.[2] Glotz, who treats the institution only as a part of
the evolution of family solidarity, explains its development
in the following way.[3] He maintains that at first the oath-
helpers are relatives of the party and so occupy the same
position as avengers of blood. Hence in origin the institution
is merely a declaration of family solidarity. The relative who
is especially injured becomes the chief avenger and the others
are more or less auxiliary. From this comes the fact that only
the accuser or the accused ever has oath-helpers to confirm
his oath. That is to say, a witness never has an oath-helper
to substantiate his statements. The only difficulty with
Glotz's solution is the fact that as a usual thing in the earliest
stage of the institution oath-helpers are found only on the
side of the defendant. Glotz's argument admits of them on
both sides from the very beginning, perhaps even as arising
on the side of the avenger or plaintiff. It is not impossible,
however, partially to reconcile the two views given above.
Perhaps at first a man was allowed to clear himself by an
oath. This is felt as insufficient. Then family solidarity steps
in and the relatives support the defendant. That is, family
solidarity explains the fact that at first relatives are always
the oath-helpers. This limits the institution in its beginnings
to the defendant's side, or to what Glotz would designate the
passive solidarity of the family.

The remainder of Glotz's argument is undoubtedly correct. When families of the γένος are split apart, oath-helpers

[1] *Supra*, p. 175.

[2] Schröder, *op. cit.*, p. 83; Pollock and Maitland, *op. cit.*, II, 600; Grimm, *op. cit.*,
II, 495 ff.

[3] *Op. cit.*, pp. 288 ff.

are chosen in one of two ways. They may be limited to the closest relatives without regard to number or the number may be restricted without specification as to the degree of relationship. The next stage is when the origin is forgotten and neighbors and friends are called on.

But whatever may have been its origin, the psychology of the institution is perfectly clear—the partisan spirit which continued to be its dominant characteristic as long as it lasted. Gilbert suggests[1] that it arose out of such situations as the trial scene depicted on the shield of Achilles,[2] where, after describing the dispute, the poet adds λαοὶ δ' ἀμφοτέροισιν ἐπήπυον, ἀμφὶς ἀρωγοί. To say that it had its origin in such a situation is slightly misleading, as it does not account for the fact that originally the oath-helpers were relatives. But the argument that there is the same feeling, that is, the partisan spirit, in both is quite true. Glotz[3] objects to the use of this passage in the evolution of the institution on the ground that the oath-helper always appears in the character of a subordinate, but that ἀρωγός implies a protector rather than a supporter. Besides, the ἀρωγοί of Homer have no practical influence, as they are not really participants in the trial. Of course, his contention is correct that they are not really oath-helpers, but the word has such a definite partisan signification that it is not going too far to say that the psychology back of the Homeric scene is the same as that behind compurgation. Two other passages are of interest in determining the meaning of ἀρωγός.

> ἀλλ' ἄγετ', Ἀργείων ἡγήτορες ἠδὲ μέδοντες,
> ἐς μέσον ἀμφοτέροισι δικάσσατε, μηδ' ἐπ' ἀρωγῇ,
> μήποτέ τις εἴπησιν Ἀχαιῶν χαλκοχιτώνων.[4]

There is no protection implied here; it is mere partiality.

> ὑμεῖς δὲ μαρτύριά τε καὶ τεκμήρια
> καλεῖσθ', ἀρωγὰ τῆς δίκης ὀρκώματα.[5]

[1] *Jahrb. f. cl. Phil.*, Supplbd. XXIII, 469, n. 1.

[2] *Il.* xviii. 497 ff.; cf. esp. l. 502. [4] *Il.* xxiii. 573 ff.

[3] *Op. cit.*, pp. 292 f. [5] Aesch. *Eumen.* 485 f.

Here the idea of partisanship is not as distinct as that of mere aid.

A false oath could not be punished by legal process. Such punishment was left to the gods. It is natural that no action should be brought for an evidentiary oath, for it was taken as the result of a challenge and the other party agreed to accept it as final. Apparently very little account was taken of the party oaths. One of these was almost always false. The false evidence of witnesses who gave testimony under oath could be dealt with by δίκη ψευδομαρτυρίων.[1] In the case of the promissory oath there were various ways of dealing with the problem. For instance, an official who was guilty of misconduct in office was not tried for having sworn a false oath, but for malfeasance in office.

There are found in Athenian law a few kinds of oaths which seem to be survivals of the institution of oath-helpers. The survival of compurgation in the procedure of διαμαρτυρία has been pointed out.[2] In cases before the Areopagus no person could give evidence unless at the beginning of the trial he had taken an oath either as to the innocence or as to the guilt of the defendant.[3] In this oath we see the development of the oath-helper into the regular witness. He still swears the preliminary oath along with his principal, but later in the case he presents his testimony just as an ordinary witness of fact. So his oath is not final. One step farther and the preliminary oath with the principal would be abandoned and nothing would be left but the witness of fact.

Another oath which is analogous to the oath of oath-helpers is that which was sworn preliminary to a murder trial to the relationship of the prosecutor to the murdered man. This is the same oath as that which the principal swears, and it is sworn along with the principal. With the joint preliminary oath, however, the analogy ends, for it was not final. Even women and children, as has been argued above, were allowed

[1] Cf. *infra*, pp. 261 ff.   [2] Cf. *supra*, pp. 82 f.

[3] Lysias iv. 4; Bonner, *Evidence in Athenian Courts*, pp. 28 ff.; Leisi, *op. cit.*, p. 57; *supra*, pp. 166 f.; Latte, *op. cit.*, p. 32.

to take oath to establish the relationship of the prosecutor to the deceased.[1]

The voluntary oath which might be offered in defense of a litigant has in common with oath-helpers sworn confidence in a man.[2] This oath seems generally to have been taken by relatives.[3]

There are then in Attica a few survivals of the institution. Meister, failing to see these survivals, asserted:

> In Attika hat sich keine Spur von ihnen gefunden, wie leicht erklärlich ist: Eideshelfer sind auf kleinere Verhältnisse zugeschnitten, wo einer den anderen kennt; in der grossen Stadt und bei entwickelten Verkehrs-verhältnissen können sie nicht vorkommen.[4]

It is interesting to note that in England, one of the greatest commercial countries in the world, the institution was not abolished until 1833.

[1] Cf. *infra*, pp. 221 f.

[2] Ziebarth, *op. cit.*, p. 41; cf. Meier-Schömann-Lipsius, *Der Attische Process*, p. 899, n. 379, for plentiful examples of the oath.

[3] Ziebarth gives an illustration of this oath which Meister (*op. cit.*, p. 578) has conclusively shown to be false. For the text of the inscription see Collitz-Bechtel, *op. cit.*, 1478; Dareste-Haussoulier-Reinach, *op. cit.*, pp. 180 ff.; Michel, *Recueil d'inscriptions grecques*, 285.

[4] *Op. cit.*, p..581.

CHAPTER VIII

HOMICIDE

In the discussion of the Athenian homicide courts great prominence has been given to the influence of pollution on homicide procedure.[1] The idea of pollution often tends to become confused with the doctrine of ποινή, or the recompense which was due the murdered man. The desire for vengeance was very active from the earliest times, but the pollution doctrine, it is now conceded, did not exist in the Homeric period.[2] In that period homicide was entirely the concern of the relatives of the slain man and might be dealt with in several ways: the homicide, in fear of being slain, might go into exile; or he might be caught before he could escape and consequently lose his life; or he might be able to effect a settlement with the family of his victim. Homer furnishes abundant examples of each of these procedures. It is clear that in none of the cases was the slayer of interest to anyone except the relatives. A homicide who had fled from his native land was hospitably received in other lands and suffered no deprivations other than loss of native land, for the slayer was beyond the vengeance of his victim's relatives. On the other hand, if he managed while remaining in his own land to appease the relatives with a satisfactory payment, he was allowed to stay without being molested and to remain in possession of his property and privileges. The punishment exacted from the slayer served both as a satisfaction to the family for its loss and also as recompense to the slain man. There is no suggestion that the slayer was polluted or that his presence had any effect on the state or on his associates. It was, like most early legal transactions, a matter solely for

[1] The procedure in homicide trials has been discussed at length *supra*, I, 110 ff. There are, however, disputed details of homicide practice which call for fuller discussion. An attempt is made here to set forth the various arguments involved.

[2] Cf. *supra*, I, 15 f., 53 ff.

the criminal and the family of the victim. The slaying of kin, on the other hand, met with utter condemnation in the Homeric period just as it did in later times.[1]

It is interesting to see how the Homeric attitude toward homicide is reflected in the historical period, when new ideas about homicide had developed and the state had taken over the actual prosecution. The *poiné* principle remained very active. In fact, the dying man is often represented as demanding *poiné*.[2] But the relatives of the victim might no longer kill the homicide if he remained in the state. Although the initiation of the prosecution still rested primarily with the relatives, the homicide had to be dealt with through a court. This innovation was obviously calculated to end blood feud.

If a man obtain a conviction for murder, even then he gets no power over the condemned, who for punishment is given up to the laws and to persons charged with that office; he may behold the condemned suffering the penalty which the law imposes, but nothing further.[3]

In this witnessing of the execution Lipsius[4] sees a survival of the old blood vengeance. So, although the state had imposed certain restrictions, the relatives and not the state continued to be considered the injured parties in homicide. The homicide might be slain only if, having been interdicted, or having been tried and condemned, he then entered the forbidden places. And in this case not only the relatives, but anybody, might either slay or arrest him. Here the pollution principle is seen to be at work. But so far as the relatives are concerned, the idea back of all this is *poiné* or compensation.[5] When it became a matter of pollution anyone could act.

As in the Homeric period so in later times exile was not

---

[1] Cf. *infra*, pp. 201 f., 216 f. The question of homicide in Homer has been treated at great length by many writers: cf. *supra*, I, 15 ff.; Philippi, *Der Areopag und die Epheten*, pp. 3 ff.; Glotz, *La Solidarité de la famille dans le droit criminel en Grèce*, pp. 47–222; Lipsius, *Das Attische Recht*, pp. 6 ff.; Treston, *Poiné*, pp. 11–26; Calhoun, *Growth of Criminal Law in Ancient Greece*, pp. 15–24.

[2] Cf. *infra*, pp. 195 f.   [3] Demos. xxiii. 69.   [4] *Op. cit.*, p. 603.

[5] Even the procedure before the Prytaneum must be viewed as an attempt to secure recompense for the deceased rather than to rid the country of polluted objects.

purificatory. It doubtless was, to begin with, just a means of self-preservation for the homicide. It became, through lack of other means, a means of securing *poiné* for the murdered man. The exiled homicide seems to have been considered polluted in other cities in historical times no more than in the Homeric period, although a homicide is occasionally represented as begging for purification from his foreign host.[1]

Pardon (αἴδεσις) and a return from exile could be granted the convicted homicide only by relatives of the slain man or, in cases where there were no relatives, by members of the phratry.[2] This shows that the object of the exile was *poiné*, not purification. Otherwise, the state religion would have settled the term of exile and would have awarded the pardon and the family would not have been concerned. As it is, the state could do nothing about the pardon. In Homer ἀειφυγία was apparently the rule, there being no distinction between different kinds of homicide. In historical times only premeditated homicide admitted of no pardon.[3] An interesting question with regard to return from exile is raised by the procedure in Phreatto. It was not primarily because he was polluted that the homicide was not allowed to land; he had not completed the *poiné* and had not secured a pardon from the relatives.

That the purpose of exile for homicide was for *poiné* is very clearly shown by a passage of Demosthenes[4] in which Demosthenes explains the purpose of the law which provided that a convicted homicide in exile should not be molested as long as he kept away from the border market, the games, and the Amphictyonic sacrifices.

[1] Cf. Adrastus in Herod. i. 35 ff.; Jason and Medea in Apol. Rhod. iv. 693 ff.; Orestes in Aesch. *Eumen.* 448 ff. It is noteworthy that in each of these cases the suppliant had slain a blood relative—a horrible crime even in the Homeric period. Cf. *Il.* ix. 458 of Phoenix:

> τὸν μὲν ἐγὼ βούλευσα κατακτάμεν ὀξέι χαλκῷ·
> ἀλλά τις ἀθανάτων παῦσεν χόλον, ὅς ῥ' ἐνὶ θυμῷ
> δήμου θῆκε φάτιν καὶ ὀνείδεα πόλλ' ἀνθρώπων,
> ὡς μὴ πατροφόνος μετ' Ἀχαιοῖσιν καλεοίμην.

This passage is suspected and is omitted from some texts.

[2] *IG*[2], I, 115.   [3] *Ibid.*   [4] xxiii. 37 ff.

The legislator thought it only right that the murderer should have the power of removing from the land of the murdered man to a land where none has been injured and of dwelling there in security. So he made his law to provide for this and also to prevent the endless avenging of misfortunes. In order to do this he banished the culprit from everything in which the deceased in his lifetime had a part.

There is no idea of pollution here.

Thus it can be seen that in regard to exile the state did not interfere with *poiné* for homicide.[1] The family, not the state, gave pardon. Homicides were always excluded from amnesty laws.[2]

The idea of *poiné* is emphasized in the passages which represent the dying man as enjoining it upon the surviving relatives to secure vengeance for him. A client of Antiphon[3] tells how his father before he died told him to get vengeance for him for his death at the hands of his wife. It is interesting to note that in this case the speaker says that if men who are mortally wounded can do so before they die, they summon their relatives and friends and ask them to exact vengeance. If this is impossible they write letters and summon their slaves and call them to witness at whose hands they died. The important idea in this whole passage is recompense for the slain man. There is no mention of pollution. Another case is that of Agoratus. Dionysodorus summoned his brother and wife and brother-in-law to prison before he died and charged them and all his friends to punish as a murderer Agoratus who had given false information which led to his condemnation. Dionysodorus also admonished his wife to charge their unborn child to take vengeance on Agoratus.[4] In this passage Treston translates the phrase τοῖς φίλοις by "all his kindred." It is more natural to understand the words as referring not to relatives but to friends. Two explanations may be suggested for the inclusion of friends. They may have

---

[1] For the question of a legal term of exile cf. *infra*, pp. 229 ff.

[2] For the text of the amnesty law cf. Gertrude Smith, "The Prytaneum in the Athenian Amnesty Law," *CP*, XVI, 345; for the literature on the subject of the law cf. Busolt, *Griech. Gesch.*, II, 159, n. 1.

[3] i. 29 f.   [4] Lysias xiii. 42.

been included, because if members of the phratry they could join in the prosecution. Or they may have been included as witnesses of the dying man's request. There is an excellent statement in Antiphon about the expectation of the deceased that he would receive *poiné*.[1]

On the other hand, a man fatally wounded might forgive his slayer and release him from guilt and forbid his relatives to take vengeance. In fact, if he had once given release the relatives were barred from further action. Demosthenes is the chief authority on this subject.[2] He plainly states that in case a slain man, before dying, has released his slayer it is not lawful for his relatives to prosecute. The man who has been released by his victim is at once absolved from all penal consequences. The reference is plainly to a release from any sort of homicide, although the preceding passage is concerned only with unpremeditated homicide. Treston[3] agrees that the reference is to any kind of homicide, but Müller[4] thinks it refers to manslaughter only. According to Lipsius,[5] this passage proves that the premeditated homicide could be pardoned only by the murdered man before he died; his relatives could not do it. Lipsius thus would apparently agree that the passage refers to any kind of homicide. In this case again there is no question of pollution. The dying man by giving release to the guilty man declared that he wished no *poiné*. So apparently nothing further was ever done in such cases. Treston[6] says that the homicide was completely freed. Not even a charge of involuntary homicide could be brought. For the dying man's release did not merely reduce the charge to one of justifiable or accidental slaying, but it furnished full pardon.

The question of the legality of the practice of giving material compensation or blood money to the family of the deceased in the historical period has been much discussed.

[1] ii. δ. 11. In ii. γ. 10 the murdered man is represented as being a suppliant for vengeance.

[2] xxxvii. 59.   [4] *Eumenides*, p. 127.

[3] *Op. cit.*, p. 176.   [5] *Op. cit.*, p. 604.   [6] *Op. cit.*, p. 177.

Because of the fact that such practice was well established in the Homeric period and that the family continued to be regarded as the party chiefly concerned in dealing with homicide, some scholars have argued that the *wergeld* system continued to be thoroughly recognized in fifth- and fourth-century Athens. The ancient references to the subject are not conclusive.[1] In Demosthenes,[2] Theocrines is criticized by the speaker for accepting a sum of money from his brother's slayers and dropping further prosecution. The passage, however, is not conclusive, for Theocrines' act in so doing may have been legal and his condemnation by the speaker for such action mere rhetoric. A puzzling passage occurs in another speech of Demosthenes:[3]

> This, I presume, you will all acknowledge, that other people have suffered wrongs before now, of a more grievous nature than pecuniary wrongs; (for example, unintentional homicides, and outrages on what is sacred, and many similar things, are perpetrated;) yet in all these cases the injured parties are finally and conclusively barred, when they have come to a settlement and given release [ἀλλ' ὅμως ἁπάντων τούτων ὅρος καὶ λύσις τοῖς παθοῦσι τέτακται τὸ πεισθέντας ἀφεῖναι]. This rule of justice is so universally binding that when a man has convicted another of involuntary[4] homicide and clearly proved him to be "polluted," yet if he afterwards condones the crime and "releases" him, he has no longer the right to force the same person into exile.

It is possible but quite unlikely that the word πεισθέντας should refer to material compensation.[5]

A third passage used by Glotz in support of his argument that private settlement was legal, unfortunately for his theory, does not refer to homicide. It is the famous passage in the *Frogs* of Aristophanes[6] where Aeschylus' verse ἥκω γὰρ

---

[1] The practice of giving material compensation for homicide is mentioned by Harpocration, *s.v.* ὑποφόνια, and is quoted from Dinarchus Κατὰ Καλλισθένους and Κατὰ Φορμισίου. But in our ignorance of how ὑποφόνια is there mentioned no conclusion can be drawn as to the legality of the practice.

[2] lviii. 28.   [3] xxxvii. 58; cf. xxxviii. 21 ff.

[4] Kennedy, reading ἑκούσιον,—an emendation of Reiske—translates "intentional." The Oxford and Teubner texts read ἀκούσιον.

[5] Cf. Paley and Sandys, *Select Private Orations of Demosthenes*, I, 147, and Dareste, *Les Plaidoyers Civils de Démosthène*, I, 271.

[6] 1154-68.

ἐς γῆν τήνδε καὶ κατέρχομαι is attacked by Euripides on the ground of redundancy. Euripides argues that κατέρχομαι cannot be used of Orestes because Orestes came back secretly without having duly appeased those who had authority to permit his return (λάθρα γὰρ ἦλθεν, οὐ πιθὼν τοὺς κυρίους). But the Aeschylean passage to which Euripides is referring occurs at the beginning of the *Choephoroi*[1] when Orestes is returning from Phocis and before the murder of his mother. The passage has nothing to do with a return from exile for homicide.

On the basis of these passages Glotz[2] holds that even in case of murder private settlement without trial was legal in historical Athens. Philippi, on the other hand, argues[3] that private settlement was illegal and that it is absurd to think the penalty for homicide could be paid with money. After a searching study of the above-mentioned passages and of the arguments of Glotz, Treston,[4] on the basis of his earlier argument that the doctrine of pollution was incompatible with any further continuation of the *wergeld* system,[5] reaches the following plausible conclusion. Private settlement was permitted by law or custom whenever a release had been formally granted by the victim before death or, in the absence of a charge, could be assumed. Otherwise private settlement was a sin, a religious quasi-criminal offense. Hence it was legally invalid and the offender was liable to prosecution.[6]

There is abundant evidence of the persistence of the doctrine of *poiné* through all periods of Greek history. And this principle explains fully why originally the relatives alone are

---

[1] 3.   [2] *Op. cit.*, p. 315.   [3] *Op. cit.*, pp. 148 f.

[4] *Op. cit.*, pp. 173 ff. *et passim.*   [5] *Ibid.*, p. 123.

[6] Cf. Dareste, *Les Plaidoyers civils de Démosthène*, II, 140, n. 24, who admits "transaction" for earlier times but says that in the age of Demosthenes "la vieille tradition commençait à n'être plus comprise, et d'autres idées se faisaient jour." Beauchet (*Histoire du droit privé*, I, 15) argues that the murderer can oftentimes appease the relatives by paying blood money, corresponding to the *wergeld* of the ancient Germans. Busolt-Swoboda (*Griech. Staatsk.*, p. 531) asserts that the receiving of money for the purchase of blood guilt was forbidden. Hermann-Thumser (*Lehrb. der griech. Staatsalt.*, I, 357) says that only in unpremeditated homicide could the relatives forego legal procedure and content themselves with a money payment.

concerned in homicide and continue to be the chief actors in
homicide cases. But, although it does not appear at all in
the Homeric period, the doctrine of pollution must have appeared very shortly thereafter in homicide, and it had considerable effect on homicide procedure.[1] The effect of pollution is a favorite talking-point on the part of the orators, and
this very fact may have given undue emphasis to the importance of pollution.[2] After trying to have Demosthenes
charged with murder, Midias made no objection to his
participation in various events.[3] This indicates to Demosthenes that Midias did not think him really guilty of homicide. Again in the speech on the murder of Herodes, Euxitheus, the defendant, says that often the presence of people
with unclean hands has wrecked a ship. His own innocence
is proved, however, by the fact that whenever he was present
voyages were fair and sacrifices were good.[4] But even the
fear of pollution could not bring about a situation which allowed others than the family and perhaps the phratry members of the victim to initiate a prosecution for homicide before one of the homicide courts, and there are indications that
a man who had committed homicide was not legally considered polluted until the relatives of the slain had pronounced a formal interdict against him. It is not to be supposed in the first speech of Antiphon that the stepmother,
although her husband had begged for vengeance against her,
had been considered polluted during all the years before the
son reached his majority and was able to prosecute. And
again in Antiphon vi the choregus makes a great deal of the
point that his prosecutors associated with him between the
time of the death of the boy and the bringing of the accusation, thus indicating his freedom from pollution, even in the
eyes of the relatives of the victim. Furthermore, in this case
the *basileus* refused to accept the case for trial because his

---

[1] Treston (*op. cit.*, p. 159) well says that Athenian homicide laws are a combination of clan traditions and religious influence from Delphi.

[2] In the tetralogies Antiphon warns the jurors that by wrongful acquittal they
will involve themselves in pollution (ii. a. 3; iii. γ. 11; ii. γ. 10).

[3] Demos. xxi. 114.   [4] Antiph. v. 82 ff.

term of office was too near its end. There was apparently,
then, no ban against the murderer until the king archon had
accepted the case for trial and the interdict had been pronounced. In this case the choregus went ahead with his lawsuits, the very thing which his opponents were trying to prevent by bringing the homicide charge, and won his case.

In the Agoratus case the suit was not entered until several
years after the alleged offense. Agoratus was not, in the
meantime, banned from various pursuits. It may be argued
here that this is not primarily a homicide case. But Dionysodorus had enjoined it upon his relatives and friends to get
vengeance for his death on Agoratus as his slayer. And although Agoratus was not banned from public places and was
not officially polluted, yet in the minds of people in general he
was considered a murderer. He joined the group at Phyle and
he also joined the procession of the Peiraeus party to the
citadel. His legal right to do so is apparently unquestioned.
But the men refused to associate with him, or even to speak
to him, on the ground that he was a known murderer.[1] He
was exceedingly roughly treated by the entire group. At
Phyle they would even have put him to death if the general
had not intervened. Agoratus was very well known and had
been instrumental in the deaths of many men of the democratic party. The aversion to him is then to be explained not
only by the fact that he was a murderer but also by the fact
that he was a foe of the democratic party who had later
sought to get into the good graces of the democratic party
when it came back into power. The argument, then, that he
was polluted and hence was avoided is largely rhetorical. He
was an object of the same hatred which fell upon the Thirty.

But once the interdict was pronounced, the accused was
considered polluted and he was barred from public places.
This does not mean that he did not continue to live at home
and to go on with his private business so long as it did not
concern the state or take him into public places from which
he was banned by the interdict. The whole matter of pollution in homicide looks like a sort of legalized pollution which

[1] Lysias xiii. 77 ff.

was foisted upon homicide procedure by religion for various reasons. It had considerable to do with the forms of the procedure, but very little to do with the punishment.

The slaying of kindred must be treated separately, for the spilling of kindred blood even from the earliest times was looked upon with horror.[1] The feeling which is represented by the tragedians against Orestes as a matricide is older than the doctrine of pollution attaching to anyone who spilled human blood. For example, Phoenix, in telling his story to Achilles, explains that public opinion and the reproaches of men who would call him parricide restrained him from slaying his father.[2] In the Homeric period, then, murder of kin not only brought about the exile of the slayer just as other homicide did but as a sin against one's own clan it also carried with it a social stigma which does not seem to have been the case with other homicide. This is noticed also in the case of the slaying of a guest or of one who has a claim upon the hospitality of another.[3] The laws of the family and of hospitality forbade slaying within the group, although the slayer of kin, like any other slayer, might be granted release by his victim. This feeling that kin murder is far worse than the slaying of one outside the group persists in the stories of Greek mythology and elsewhere. The story of Adrastus in Herodotus[4] il-

[1] The question has been raised as to whether, if an infant was exposed and died, any pollution resulted to those who were responsible for the exposure. It is now generally admitted that although infanticide was not forbidden by law, yet it was practiced very rarely, if at all, in fifth- and fourth-century Athens. Cf. Glotz, in Darem.-Saglio, *s.v.* "Expositio"; Van Hook, *TAPA*, LI, 144 f.; Bolkestein, *CP*, XVII, 222 ff.; Gomme, *The Population of Athens in the 5th and 4th Centuries B.C.*, pp. 75 ff. Nowhere, however, is the practice condemned even by philosophers. It was viewed as a matter which concerned only the family. The father of the dead child is the only one to bring a charge, and he is responsible for the death. The state is silent. Nowhere is there any suggestion of pollution. This is further indication of the comparatively small emphasis which was placed on pollution.

[2] *Il.* ix. 459 ff.; cf. *supra*, p. 194, n. 1; *supra*, I, 16 f.

[3] Cf. the case of Eumaeus, who refuses Odysseus' wager to kill him if he is found not to have told the truth (*Od.* xiv. 402 ff.; *supra*, I, 16). In like manner Glaucus and Diomedes refuse to fight with each other when they discover that they are hereditary guest-friends (*Il.* vi. 119 ff.).

[4] i. 35 ff.

lustrates the point. Although it is told of a non-Greek, yet it is entirely Greek in feeling. Adrastus had killed his brother, and although the act was involuntary (ἀέκων), yet he had been banished by his father. He afterward, again by an involuntary act, slew the son of Croesus who was both his purifier and his host. His horror at his act was so great that he slew himself upon the tomb of Croesus' son. Such a feeling would have been unthinkable except in the case of kin murder or murder of a guest-friend.

There are references to special atonement for kin murder. For example, Theseus is said to have established the Isthmian festival in atonement for the slaying of Sciron, although Sciron was a great rascal who richly deserved killing.[1] In this case Plutarch specifically says that the atonement was made because it was kin murder (διὰ τὴν συγγένειαν). But a heavy atonement might be exacted for the slaying of one who was not a kinsman. In recounting the story of the slaying of Iphitus by Heracles, Plutarch says that Heracles' slavery to Omphale was atonement for this murder. Iphitus was brother to Iole whom Heracles loved.[2]

It would seem from Antiphon[3] that any alleged homicide had a right to go into exile after he had made his first defense speech. The speaker there says that the privilege is granted ἅπασι. This privilege is mentioned also by Demosthenes.[4] But a curious passage in Pollux, in which there is unfortunately text difficulty, according to one text states that flight was possible except in cases of parricide.[5] It is difficult to understand the source of this statement, for it does not seem likely that the murderer of kin would have been refused this privilege.

There are, then, two elements which are of great importance and which constantly occur in the references to homi-

[1] Plut. *Theseus* xxv.

[2] *Ibid.*, vi; cf. Apollodorus ii. 6. 2 f.; *Od.* xxi. 23 ff.; Soph. *Trach.* 270 ff.

[3] v. 13.   [4] xxiii. 69.

[5] viii. 117 (Bethe): μετὰ δὲ τὸν πρότερον λόγον ἐξῆν φυγεῖν [πλὴν] εἴ τις γονέας εἴη ἀπεκτονώς.

cide. There is the *poiné* which belongs to the slain man and which his relatives must secure for him, and there is the pollution which attaches to the slayer. In the case of pre-meditated homicide the offense was considered so great that it admitted of no leniency. Either the death or the lifelong exile of the slayer was necessary as a *poiné* for his victim. So here there is no question of purification in his own land, for *aidesis*[1] was impossible unless granted by the victim and there was no reconciliation. In cases of unpremeditated homicide after the homicide had completed the *poiné* he underwent ceremonial purification on returning to his own land.[2]

With regard to justifiable homicide there has been much dispute as to whether or not the slayer was considered pol-luted and therefore had to undergo rites of purification. It is certain that no *poiné* was involved. In the laws of Draco it is expressly stated[3] that if a man in self-defense kills another who is unjustly carrying off his property by force there shall be no punishment (νηποινεὶ τεθνάναι). That is to say, the slain man has no claim on *poiné*. In like manner in the decree of Demophantus[4] it is declared that if anyone overthrows the democracy or holds any office when the democracy has been overthrown, he is to be considered an enemy of the Athenians and may be slain νηποινεί. In accordance with a law of Solon cited in Demosthenes[5] it is permissible to slay or to wound or to bring before the Eleven by *apagogé* a thief by night. Like-wise the slayer of an opponent in the games is not a wrong-doer.[6] Also death in war brings no guilt to the slayer and a man who slew an adulterer caught with his wife or mother or sister or daughter or concubine was not liable to punishment.[7] Further, there was a law that if a person died while being treated by a physician the physician should not be considered a murderer.[8] These provisions are attributed, some to Solon,

---

[1] Demos. xxi. 43; cf. Philippi, *op. cit.*, p. 143.

[2] Demos. xxiii. 72.   [3] *IG*², I, 115, ll. 37 f.

[4] Antiph. i. 96; cf. Bolkestein, Ὅσιος en Εὐσεβής (Amsterdam, 1936), p. 93.

[5] xxiv. 113.   [6] Demos. xxiii. 54.   [7] Lysias i.

[8] Antiph. iv. γ. 5: ὁ μὲν ἰατρὸς οὐ φονεὺς αὐτοῦ ἐστιν, ὁ γὰρ νόμος ἀπολύει αὐτόν.

some to Draco. It seems clear that there were laws which specified certain kinds of slaying which were considered justifiable and which involved no punishment, i.e., the dead man did not deserve and could not expect *poiné*.

Plato enumerates as not liable to punishment a list of homicides similar to that which is found in the orators.[1] It is permissible to kill: (1) the thief by night; (2) the footpad whom one kills in self-defense; (3) anyone who forces a woman or a boy in love; (4) the adulterer; (5) anyone whom one kills in defense of father, mother, children, brothers, or mother of his own children. Elsewhere Plato mentions accidental deaths in games and contests or in war or practice for war and the death of a man while under a physician's care as not being liable to punishment.[2]

From the foregoing examples it is quite clear that there were certain kinds of homicide which were viewed as legitimate. But the question still remains and has been much debated as to whether these homicides, although they involved no punishment for the slayer, did nevertheless bring pollution upon him which necessitated a ceremonial purification. Was it always necessary to undergo purificatory rites when one had shed human blood, no matter what the provocation or the intent?

It is reasonable to suppose that the physician may be eliminated. He has done nothing to further the death of the patient, and, in fact, he has presumably done everything in his power to save the patient's life. He can in no way be considered polluted. Yet the Athenians thought it necessary to protect him by law from the possibility of being attacked as a homicide. The passage seems quite specific. He is not a φονεύς.

Very frequently in the orators the word καθαρός or some equivalent expression is found applied to men who have committed justifiable or accidental homicide. For instance,

---

[1] *Laws* 874B–C.

[2] *Ibid.* 865A f. For a list of crimes for which it was legal to slay cf. Kahrstedt, *Studien zum öffentlichen Recht Athens*, Teil I: "Staatsgebiet und Staatsangehörige in Athen," p. 162.

in the passage cited above from Andocides[1] the slayer of a
man who attempted to overthrow the government is declared ὅσιος and εὐαγής. Likewise in Demosthenes[2] the man
who by mistake kills a friend in war is declared καθαρός. So
also in Lycurgus[3] the slayer of the traitor to the government
is pronounced καθαρός. And Plato uses this term of justifiable
homicide.[4] The question is whether καθαρός and its apparent
synonyms ὅσιος and εὐαγής mean merely that the slayer was
free from guilt or whether they mean that in addition to freedom from guilt he could also dispense with ceremonial purification. Drerup argues that any kind of homicide involved
pollution,[5] and according to Philippi's argument[6] καθαρός does
not mean that the justifiable homicide was excused from a
religious-symbolic purification. Anyone who shed human
blood was impure and must undergo purification. Philippi
cites the analogy of the purification of Apollo after the slaying
of the dragon, and, further, the analogy of Plato[7] who stipu-
lates that the one who kills accidentally in contests or in war
shall be καθαρός after he has been purified by the Delphic law
governing such matters (καθαρθεὶς κατὰ τὸν ἐκ Δελφῶν κομισ-
θέντα περὶ τούτων νόμον). Philippi reaches the conclusion
that καθαρός as it appears in the orators is used in a juristic,
not a religious, sense, and is used as the opposite of μὴ καθαρὸς
τὰς χεῖρας φόνου. Purification, then, was not abandoned, although atonement had no part in δίκαιος φόνος. Although
the dead man and his relatives are prevented by law from
seeking atonement, still the person of the slayer must be
cleansed by purification. Gilbert[8] likewise asserts that anyone who had shed human blood was unclean and that there-

[1] i. 96; cf. καθαρὸς τὰς χεῖρας (i. 95).

[2] xx. 158; xxiii. 55.   [3] i. 125.   [4] *Laws* 874B–C.

[5] *Jahrb. f. cl. Philol.*, Supplbd. XXVII, 282. Drerup comments on the inexactness
of the phrase φόνος δίκαιος, for the emphasis is always on the fact that homicide
under certain circumstances is not punishable and the technical term for this is
νηποινεὶ τεθνάναι (Demos. xxiii. 60).

[6] *Op. cit.*, pp. 62 f. Cf. Hermann, *Staatsalt.* § 104. 15, 16; Schoemann-Lipsius,
Gr. Alt., II⁴, 364; Maetzner, on Lycurg. i. 125.

[7] *Laws* 865A f.   [8] *Const. Antiq.*, p. 387.

fore even one who had committed justifiable homicide had to
undergo purification. Lipsius[1] states that the fact that justifiable homicide was not punishable does not mean that religious purification was dispensed with. He points out that
Draco's law says only that such homicide shall not be punished. It does not say that the slayer shall be καθαρός. Taking up the use of καθαρός in the orators, Lipsius expresses the
opinion that the belief in pollution and the indispensability
of purification had weakened very much and that in practice
the purification was omitted. Treston,[2] basing his statement
on Plato, asserts that purgation in historical Greece was required of the perpetrators of justifiable homicide. This, in his
opinion, confirms his own view that homicide purgation was
a sacred and solemn symbol of reconciliation between the
slayer and his native gods rather than a placation of ghosts
or an expiation offered to the gods. It symbolizes the reinstatement of the slayer in society.

It is very difficult to decide this matter. As the passages
stand it is tempting to interpret them as meaning that the
justifiable homicide is without pollution and that his pure
state is emphasized, particularly in the passage of Andocides,
by the three words καθαρός, εὐαγής, ὅσιος, all of which could
easily be understood to refer to absence of pollution. In the
Andocides passage this is especially tempting because the
contrast of the condition of the slayer and the slain is emphasized. The traitor is to be allowed to be killed νηποινεί,
i.e., he can expect no vengeance (the customary privilege of
the slain) in the form of the punishment of the slayer. The
slayer, on the other hand, is not subject to the usual dis-
ability of the slayer, i.e., he suffers no punishment and is subject to no pollution. In fact, the decree contains an oath in
which the Athenians swear that they will consider ὅσιος in the
sight of the gods (πρὸς θεῶν καὶ δαιμόνων) anyone who kills a
man who has a part in an attempt to overthrow the democracy. This phrase does not seem possible if the slayer is still
to be considered polluted and in need of ceremonial purification. Interesting as this suggestion is, it must however re-

[1] *Op. cit.*, p. 618.   [2] *Op. cit.*, p. 153.

main a mere suggestion. The word καθαρός can mean either "without legal guilt" or "unpolluted." Conservative religion may have continued to insist on purification whenever blood was spilled, but if this is the case, Lipsius must undoubtedly be correct in insisting that the formality of purification ceremonies was often dispensed with, so that for all practical purposes καθαρός as used in the orators does mean "unpolluted." Certainly failure to perform such rites would have had no influence on the position of the justifiable homicide in society since law proclaimed him guiltless. In many cases of justifiable homicide there can have been no trial at all. It is inconceivable in many cases that a man who killed a traitor would be tried; and so with many other types of homicide which the lawgiver declared justifiable or accidental. This fits in with the general thesis expressed above that at present too much prominence is given to the pollution doctrine in homicide. The *poiné* doctrine, which was of great significance before the pollution doctrine appeared, remained of paramount importance throughout the history of the Athenian homicide courts. It is very doubtful whether much attention would be paid to pollution if the law had once declared that a particular type of homicide was undeserving of *poiné*. On the other hand, religious scruples may often have led to purification.[1] This seems to have been religious practice rather than the actual bidding of the law.

Homicide was not considered by the Greeks nearly as serious a wrong as many crimes which today are viewed as far less heinous.[2] As has been said, it remained fundamentally a matter for the family to handle. This must always be considered in discussing prosecution. It is clearly stated in the homicide code of Draco that if a homicide case was brought before the king archon for reference to one of the five homicide courts, the only persons who were permitted to initiate proceedings were relatives up through the degree of first cousin.[3] In the actual prosecution, however, all relatives

---

[1] Cf. Antiph. vi. 4, where a man is said to purify himself if he kills his own slave.

[2] Cf. Calhoun, *Growth of Criminal Law*, p. 85.   [3] Cf. *supra*, I, 115.

and even members of the phratry participated (συνδιόκεν δὲ
καὶ ἀνεφσιὸς καὶ ἀνεφσιῶν παῖδας καὶ γαμβρὸς καὶ πενθερὸς καὶ
φράτερας).[1] This provision is substantiated by Demosthenes,[2]
where the speaker is expressly told by the exegetes not to
bring the case before the *basileus* on the ground that he is
neither the relative nor the master of the dead woman.
Again, in Plato's *Euthyphro*, Socrates assumes that the dead
man in consequence of whose death Euthyphro proposes to
bring action against his father before the *basileus* must of
course have belonged to Euthyphro's household, for otherwise Euthyphro would not bring action.[3]

In each of these cases, from the fact that the action is before the *basileus*, the court concerned would be one of the five
homicide courts. These courts were always characterized by
a very archaic procedure, and it is not at all surprising to find
that before them the practice continued of allowing only relatives of the victim to prosecute. Homicide procedure, being
religious in origin, was highly conservative and change would
not be expected. Furthermore, these courts had been
founded, not for the purpose of insuring the prosecution of
homicide, but rather for the purpose of differentiating the
types of homicide and thereby procuring for the slayer, if
guilty, a more equitable punishment. The lawgiver laid emphasis on the treatment and status of the criminal, not on
making homicide a matter of concern to people in general.
It is tempting, however, to suggest that in lack of relatives
phratry members could initiate proceedings, even before the
homicide courts. The laws clearly state that members of the
phratry might join in the prosecution after it had been
started and they also grant to selected phratry members,
when there are no relatives, the right to extend *aidesis* to
those who are convicted of unpremeditated homicide. Kahrstedt[4] states that phratry members could actually initiate a

---

[1] *IG*², I, 115, ll. 21 ff.   [2] xlvii. 69–70.   [3] *Euth.* 4B.

[4] *Op. cit.*, p. 245: "Schon o.S. 161 war der Satz zu erwähnen, dass bei Mordpro-
zessen nächst den Angehörigen die φράτορες des Getöteten die Verfolgung einzuleiten
berechtigt sind insofern als bei einem Fehlen naher Verwandter ein Ausschuss
der φράτορες eintritt. Das ist kein Prozess, den die Phratrie als solche führt, da

homicide process in lack of close relatives, but he cites no proof for this assertion. It seems, however, a reasonable position to take in view of the above-mentioned extension to phratry members of privileges in homicide prosecution. Indeed, if there were no relatives of the victim, how could the criminal ever have been brought to trial and convicted in the first place—at least before one of the homicide courts— and thus made eligible to *aidesis*? The question must remain unsettled, especially in view of the fact that the notices about the homicide courts are comparatively few and have reference to the regular procedure and not to the exceptions to it.

In regard to prosecution the question arises as to whether it was obligatory for relatives of the slain man to prosecute. It is obvious that, if a slain man on dying had given a formal release to the murderer, nothing further was done. But if, on the other hand, the dying man made a formal charge to his relatives to secure vengeance for him, the relatives considered this a solemn obligation.[1] And for premeditated homicide there is no question but that the relatives always felt an obligation to prosecute unless release had been given. But the real problem lies in the question of involuntary homicide. Treston[2] insists that in such cases no trial or formal proceedings of any kind were necessary unless the dying man had made a formal charge to his relatives to prosecute. He bases his statement on Lysias xiii. 41 and 78, which passages merely prove that if such a charge were made the relatives felt a solemn obligation to act. They do not prove that in the absence of such a charge the relatives felt no such obligation. Treston assumes that whenever a trial for involuntary homicide took place either one of two things had happened: (1) the accused had denied the guilt and refused "private compensation" or (2) the dying man had charged his relatives to prosecute. There is unfortunately no evidence for this statement, but in the absence of such evidence it seems best to

---

die betr. φράτορες von den Epheten, d.h. Areopagiten selbst ausgewählt werden; es ist nur ein Prozess einzelner privater φράτορες."

[1] Antiph. i. 29–31; Lysias xiii. 41, 92.   [2] *Op. cit.*, p. 146.

assume that some action was taken. Treston assumes that
only in case of a formal charge was there any pollution for
the slayer. He is undoubtedly correct in this statement. But
once the formal charge had been made, the alleged guilty man
was considered polluted until his innocence was proved, or,
if found guilty, until he had undergone the proper penalty
and had secured *aidesis*.

It is obvious from the foregoing that as long as the homicide courts were resorted to for redress for homicide only the
relatives could initiate proceedings or perhaps phratry members in cases where there were no relatives. Accordingly, it
would seem impossible that there could be a γραφὴ φόνου, that
is, that anyone who wished to do so could bring a prosecution
for homicide. Various scholars have pointed out that homicide cases never ceased to be *dikai*. Kahrstedt[1] has stated
this very simply and clearly. Glotz[2] likewise holds this view,
and Ranulf[3] says, "There was a δίκη φόνου, but not a γραφὴ
φόνου." But in view of a passage of Pollux,[4] in which homicide is included in a list of public prosecutions, Treston[5] has
argued in some detail the question as to whether or not homicide cases could be brought before a heliastic court by anyone
who wished to do so. Such procedure would not be in accordance with the laws of Draco, and since it is recognized nowhere except in the passage of Pollux, Pollux' statement must
be otherwise explained. Treston explains it as a confusion
with γραφὴ ἀσεβείας, which could be brought by any citizen
against a relative of a slain man who had failed to "proclaim"
and to prosecute the slayer.

It is possible that the early attitude toward homicide as
the affair of the relatives persisted in the fifth and fourth centuries to such an extent that no legislation was ever passed
which permitted the homicide to be dealt with directly by

[1] *Op. cit.*, p. 161.   [2] *Op. cit.*, p. 425.

[3] *Jealousy of the Gods and Criminal Law at Athens*, p. 19.

[4] viii. 40: γραφαὶ δὲ, φόνου καὶ τραύματος ἐκ προνοίας, καὶ πυρκαϊᾶς. καὶ φαρμά-
κων, κ.τ.λ.

[5] *Op. cit.*, p. 260.

others than relatives of the victim.[1] Glotz[2] asserts that since homicide cases never ceased to be *dikai*, doubtless the state sometimes left crimes unpunished for lack of an accuser.[3] It is quite possible that occasionally there were no relatives or phratry members and sometimes, even if there were such persons, they may have had no interest in prosecuting. There was no statute of limitations for the prosecution of homicide,[4] and the fact that in both of the extant cases[5] in which a charge is laid upon the relatives to prosecute the case was not brought to trial for some years lends color to the view that only relatives could prosecute and that generally others outside the family were not concerned with bringing suit if the relatives failed to prosecute. Certainly here the fear of pollution played little or no part. However, it is difficult to suppose that the state would not devise some means by which, in the absence of a relative willing to prosecute, a notorious homicide could be prevented from staying in the city unpunished. Philippi[6] concludes that it is inconceivable that the state would not make provision for a crime which could not be tried by the common procedure. Furthermore, the procedure before the regular homicide courts was a long and tedious process and much of it was thoroughly anti-quated. Even the relatives of a slain man may have desired something simpler.

As long as the homicide courts were used homicide continued to be the affair of the relatives. But what process might be used which could be brought by any interested person, so that the homicide might indirectly be brought to justice for his crime? In the *Lexica Segueriana*,[7] φονεῖς are included among those who could be dealt with by the sum-

---

[1] Cf. the Twelve Tables, which make no provision for manslaughter.

[2] *Op. cit.*, p. 425.

[3] Thucydides (viii. 65–66), in his account of political murders during the revolution of the Four Hundred, describes a different situation in which homicide went unpunished not because of lack of prosecutors but because of the terror of those who should have prosecuted.

[4] Lysias xiii. 83; cf. Lipsius, *op. cit.*, p. 853, n. 24.

[5] Antiph. i; Lysias xiii. [6] *Op. cit.*, p. 106. [7] P. 250, ll. 4 ff.

mary process of *apagogé*. In a passage of Demosthenes,[1] after an elaborate description of the five homicide courts the speaker continues by saying that there is a sixth method of dealing with homicide:

> If a man has been ignorant of all the other courses, or if the times within which they must each be pursued have gone by,[2] or if for any reason whatever he does not choose to adopt these methods of prosecution, but sees the homicide walking about in the temples and the market, it is lawful to carry him off to prison [ἀπάγειν ἔξεστιν εἰς τὸ δεσμωτήριον], but not to his own house, or where he pleases, as you have allowed. And when he is brought to prison, he will suffer nothing there before trial, but, if he is found guilty, he will be punished with death.

In actual fact, among the scanty number of homicide cases which have come down to us we find that two were certainly handled by *apagogé*.[3] In the Herodes case,[4] Euxitheus, a Mytilenean, was accused of the murder of Herodes and was summarily arrested and tried as a *kakourgos* before the Eleven. In the Agoratus case[5] the speaker accused Agoratus of the judicial murder of Dionysodorus. Agoratus had been summarily arrested and was being tried before the Eleven.[6]

It seems clear, then, that *apagogé* was a possible method of

---

[1] xxiii. 80.

[2] Apparently the reference here is to the fact that because of time required by the preliminary investigations the *basileus* could not accept a homicide case during the last three months of his term.

[3] It has been suggested that Menestratus was brought to trial by *apagogé* as a homicide for his activities under the Thirty (Lysias xiii. 56). According to the terms of the amnesty, however, only those who had slain αὐτοχειρίᾳ could be tried for homicide (Arist. *Ath. Pol.* xxxix. 5). It has therefore been argued that whatever procedure was used the charge was not φόνος (Gernet and Bizos, *Lysias*, I, 186 f.). Furthermore, it has been suggested that since he was a citizen the procedure for homicide could not be *apagogé* (*ibid.*; cf. also Gernet, *Revue des études grecques*, XXXVII [1924], 277, n. 3.) Thalheim, however, supposes that Menestratus was brought to trial by *apagogé* (Frohberger-Thalheim, *Ausgewählte Reden des Lysias*, p. 75).

[4] Antiph. v.   [5] Lysias xiii.

[6] Lycurgus (i. 112) says that when Phrynichus had been killed by Apollodorus and Thrasybulus they were caught and placed in prison (ἀποτεθέντων) by the friends of Phrynichus. If this story were true, the process here referred to would be *apagogé* (cf. Jebb, *Attic Orators*, I, 57, n. 1). According to the accounts of Thucydides (viii. 92), Lysias (xiii. 71), and Plutarch (*Alcib.* xxv. 10), the slayer of Phrynichus escaped.

dealing with homicide and that since *apagogé* was open to ὁ βουλόμενος it was possible for any interested citizen to prosecute for homicide under certain conditions. Now by what methods and under what conditions could a non-relative prosecute? In the above-quoted passage from Demosthenes the words ἀπάγειν ἔξεστιν εἰς τὸ δεσμωτήριον seem to provide for the use of *apagogé*. But the question is: Was such a method open to anyone in this case? It would seem that a proclamation had already been issued by the relatives against the homicide. Otherwise how could he be called ἀνδροφόνος? In this case, then, proceedings had actually been started. For some reason, however, the prosecution had failed to proceed in the regular way before the homicide courts.[1] But seeing him about in public places anyone who wished dealt with him by *apagogé*.[2] It may be suggested that the long-drawn-out process before a homicide court was frequently found irksome and that the other method would regularly be resorted to in case the homicide appeared in the places from which he was banned even during the three months of preliminary investigations. In this case action might be taken by the relatives. Or somebody else after the relatives had pronounced the interdict might choose to deal with the proclaimed homicide by this summary method. This form of *apagogé* may be called ἀπαγωγὴ ἀτίμων, i.e., against those who have been deprived of certain rights but are caught exercising them. This was probably the only possible form of procedure against parricides whose relatives would be expected to excommunicate them. Otherwise, if the relatives continued to allow the parricide to live with them they were subject to γραφὴ ἀσεβείας.

Treston[3] believes that such an indictment against the relatives of the slain man who had failed to proclaim and to pros-

---

[1] It may be suggested that a proclamation at the grave such as that recommended by the exegetes in Demos. xlvii. 69 was sufficient to brand a man ἀνδροφόνος. In this case, however, the exegetes specifically stated that the murderer should not be mentioned by name at the grave.

[2] Cf. Sorof, "Die ἀπαγωγή in Mordprocessen," *Jahrb. f. cl. Phil.*, XXIX (1883), 111.

[3] *Op. cit.*, p. 260.

ecute the slayer involved, if successful, a verdict of murder against the slayer. Demosthenes reports a case in which Diodorus' uncle was charged with impiety by Androtion for not prosecuting Diodorus on a charge of parricide. Diodorus makes the following statement: "If Androtion had succeeded in his prosecution of my uncle I, as a convicted parricide, should have been deprived not only of my property but of my life: nay, even to die, which is the common lot of all, would not for me have been easy."[1] Certainly no specific trial for parricide is referred to here. The alleged parricide would have been charged only indirectly in the course of the γραφὴ ἀσεβείας, but the trial of the uncle on that charge would necessarily have involved a review of and a decision on the guilt of the nephew.

On the other hand, it seems unlikely that another passage of Demosthenes[2] refers to the γραφὴ ἀσεβείας as a method of dealing with homicide, as Treston[3] interprets it. In this case the prosecutor was told by the exegetes not to bring a charge of homicide against Euergus and Theophemus before the *basileus*, but to wait and get vengeance in some other way. Treston argues that "the other way" is the γραφὴ ἀσεβείας, and that if such a charge had been brought against a relative of the nurse who had met with a violent death the charge would have involved a verdict of murder or of manslaughter against Euergus and Theophemus. In view of the fact that the nurse was a freedwoman and probably had no relatives of status which would enable them to bring suit in her behalf, this explanation is impossible. "The other way" referred to may well be *apagogé*.

Very frequently homicide is connected with some other crime such as robbery or housebreaking or kidnapping. The case would then come under the heading of κακούργημα and the homicide could be dealt with by *apagogé* by anyone who had knowledge of the offense. In this case naturally there is no interdict. The homicide is imprisoned until the trial takes place before the Eleven. In such a case doubtless the em-

---

[1] xxiv. 7.   [2] xlvii. 70.   [3] *Op. cit.*, pp. 260 f.

phasis was placed upon the κακούργημα and not upon the homicide. In case of conviction death was the penalty.[1]

There is still another kind of homicide which might be dealt with by *apagogé*. In case a non-citizen committed homicide and was tried at Athens, he was seized by *apagogé* and held prisoner until the time of his trial.[2] The reason for this is easy to see. Since the man was not a citizen, exile from Athens would be of little consequence to him. In such cases the non-citizen was allowed bail.[3]

Aside from the γραφὴ ἀσεβείας and *apagogé* there were doubtless other methods by which an interested person could bring a slayer to justice in behalf of a victim who was not his relative. Caillemer[4] thinks that the institution of a γραφὴ φό-νου by Solon would have been inconsistent with the laws of Draco, but he admits that other methods of dealing with homicides were allowed and suggests that some homicides could undoubtedly be brought to justice by the process of *eisangelia*.[5] As a further method the γραφὴ ὕβρεως may be suggested. In case of maltreatment of a slave by his master any interested citizen might bring a γραφὴ ὕβρεως.[6] It has been

[1] Sorof (*op. cit.*, pp. 106 ff.) insists that the charge in Antiphon v was *Raubmord*. From the absence of the formula ἐπ' αὐτοφώρῳ in this case which appears in Lysias xiii. 85 as an indispensable condition for the apprehension of a homicide by *apagogé*, Sorof concludes that at the time of the case represented in Antiphon v a homicide could not be brought to trial by *apagogé*. In order to do that some other crime must be charged to him which came under the νόμος κακούργων. But probably at the time of the revision of the constitution after the restoration of democracy a provision was introduced that a homicide caught ἐπ' αὐτοφώρῳ could be tried by *apagogé*. This is a plausible suggestion, for it is inconceivable that a homicide caught ἐπ' αὐτοφόρῳ would be allowed to go. However, the charge against him might not be φόνος.

[2] Antiph. v and Lysias xiii.

[3] Meuss (*De ἀπαγωγῆς actione apud Athenienses*, pp. 27 ff.) admits *apagogé* only when the slayer was a foreigner.

[4] In Darem.-Saglio, *s.v.* φόνος.

[5] Cf. the review of Glotz, *La Solidarité*, by Dareste, in *Jour. des Savants*, 1905, p. 66, where he explains that at least in the time of Demosthenes any citizen could bring an *eisangelia*, or political action, before a heliastic court, and it was always easy to class a murder as a political crime. It is true that the process came to be widely employed for the most trivial offenses (cf. *supra*, I, 309).

[6] Aeschin. i. 17; Demos. xxi. 46; Hyper. *Frag.* 120; Lycurg. *Frag.* 74; Kahrstedt, *op. cit.*, p. 327.

argued convincingly by Morrow[1] that the same procedure
could be used against the master who killed his slave.

From the foregoing discussion it is obvious that the old
homicide courts did not furnish the sole means of bringing
an alleged homicide to trial. However, how far the ancient
feeling that homicide was the affair of the relatives of the
homicide persisted and how many homicides remained untried must remain a problem. Unsuccessful *graphai* in which
the prosecutor failed to obtain at least one-fifth part of the
votes involved the payment of a fine by the prosecutor, and
this fact must certainly have restrained possible prosecutors
to some extent from engaging in suits which according to the
traditional point of view were none of their business. If pollution played so small a part as would seem to be the case, the
citizens would continue to be more or less unconcerned about
homicide outside of their own families.

A question of prosecution arises in connection with kin
slaying. If the murderer did not flee from the city, the only
person who could prosecute him before one of the homicide
courts was the kinsman of the slain man, who was also the
kinsman of the homicide. But at least in this case the state
could do something about failure to prosecute. In the Androtion case of Demosthenes a charge of impiety (γραφὴ ἀσεβείας)
was brought against a man for association with his nephew
who was a parricide and not because he failed to prosecute.
But the resulting trial would involve necessarily a discussion
of the homicide. Treston[2] believes that such a case brought
in really a trial of the homicide and would end with a verdict
for or against him. Glotz[3] says that there is never indication
of kin prosecuting kin for homicide. The δήμου φάτις caused
an excommunication equivalent to a sentence of exile.
Aidesis was not possible for kin slaying. The homicide had to
leave his country, at least for a time, and if he returned he had
no further communication with his family.[4] Kin slaying resulted in complete disinheritance. For securing some kind of

---

[1] *CP*, XXXII, 210 ff.

[2] *Op. cit.*, pp. 260 f.

[3] *Op. cit.*, pp. 436 f.; cf. Ranulf, *op. cit.*, I, 19.

[4] Glotz, *op. cit.*, pp. 234 f.

action in kin slaying the state had the γραφὴ ἀσεβείας as a weapon.[1]

In ancient Athens, as far as can be determined, there was nothing corresponding to the modern coroner or coroner's jury. At the present time, when an individual dies a certificate from a physician stating the cause of death is required. If there is a suspicion that the deceased has met with foul play, there must be a coroner's inquest to determine the cause of death and if possible to discover the person or persons responsible. The Athenian procedure was widely at variance with the modern system. There were three exegetes or interpreters belonging to the family of the Eumolpidae whose duty it was to expound religious and ceremonial laws and to give advice in problems touching religious matters. It seems that it was a common practice to resort to these officials for advice if one was doubtful about the correct procedure in homicide cases. In Plato's dialogue *Euthyphro*, Euthyphro's father is represented as sending for advice to the exegetes after the murder of his slave at the hands of a hired man.[2] In this case the inquirer is the master of the murdered man. We do not know what advice the exegetes gave, for the hired man died from neglect before the messengers to the exegetes returned. Likewise, in the speech of Demosthenes against Euergus and Mnesibulus, the plaintiff, after the death by violence of an old woman who had formerly belonged to the family, but who had been freed by the plaintiff's family, repaired to the exegetes for advice.[3] The plaintiff is neither a relative nor the master of the dead woman. In this case the exegetes gave very definite advice. The speaker had told them all the details of the case, the connection of the woman, i.e., the former slave, now free, with the family, and how she lost her life in the house of the speaker in defense of his property. The exegetes advised that a spear should be carried in the funeral procession and a proclamation should be pronounced at the tomb and that thereafter the tomb should be guarded for three days: πρῶτον μὲν ἐπενεγκεῖν δόρυ ἐπὶ τῇ ἐκφορᾷ, καὶ προ-

---

[1] *Ibid.*, p. 442.   [2] *Euth.* 4C.   [3] xlvii. 68 ff.

αγορεύειν ἐπὶ τῷ μνήματι, εἴ τις προσήκων ἐστὶ τῆς ἀνθρώπου, ἔπειτα τὸ μνῆμα φυλάττειν ἐπὶ τρεῖς ἡμέρας.[1] The nature of the proclamation has been a matter of much dispute. It has been understood by some as a proclamation, given at the tomb by a relative of the deceased and containing an interdict against the murderer.[2] But others have understood it as an attempt made at the burial to find out if there is some relative who can prosecute.[3] It is hardly possible to interpret the Greek in this way, especially in view of the passage immediately following in which προαγορεύειν is used again: ὀνομαστὶ μὲν μηδενὶ προαγορεύειν, τοῖς δεδρακόσι δὲ καὶ κτείνασι, εἶτα πρὸς τὸν βασιλέα μὴ λαγχάνειν. Here it is clear that the proclamation is against the homicides, although the exegetes warn the speaker against calling the homicides by name. The proclamation is to be general, merely against τοῖς δεδρακόσι δὲ καὶ κτείνασι.

The following interpretation may be suggested. If it is possible to find a connection (προσήκων) of the woman, he is to make a proclamation at the tomb against the homicides by name, bidding them stay away from the forbidden places. This is merely a statement of the general law in such cases. But if no connection is found, the speaker of the present speech is to pronounce an interdict, but without naming the homicides. But he is to proceed no further with the case. In this case the deceased is a freed woman. She would therefore

[1] *Ibid.* 69.

[2] Kennedy's translation of the passage is noncommittal, but he adds a note: "This was a proclamation giving notice to the homicide to keep away from the tomb, and from all public places and sacrifices. It was followed, in case of a prosecution, by another notice, given in the market-place, warning the party accused to appear and answer the charge." Auger, quoted by Kennedy, translates: "Et qu'un des parents annonce au meurtrier, de ne pas approcher au tombeau." Dareste (*op. cit.*, I, 377) interprets in like manner: "D'abord s'il existe un parent de cette femme, il doit paraître aux obsèques une pique à la main, et debout sur la tombe prononcer l'interdiction du coupable, puis garder la tombe pendant trois jours."

[3] Cf. Pabst, quoted by Kennedy: "Und am Grabe ausrufen: ob irgend ein Anverwandter von der Frau vorhanden sei." Likewise Treston (*op. cit.*, p. 182) says: "To carry a spear in front of the funeral procession, and at the tomb to publicly inquire [προαγορεύειν] if the woman had any relative, and to watch the tomb for three days!"

have no relative of citizen status who could act for her. Her natural protector or *prostatés* would be the man who had freed her and who had formerly been her master. But in this case her protector is dead and the law therefore cannot be literally fulfilled. The present speaker is the son of the woman's dead *prostatés*, and it is because of this relationship to her that he goes to the exegetes to find out if there is anything that he can do about the matter. On the ground that the woman neither belonged to his family nor was his slave, the exegetes advise him not to prosecute. However, they do advise him to pronounce the interdict, not against anyone by name, but only τοῖς δεδρακόσι καὶ κτείνασι. He is allowed to do this only in case a προσήκων of the woman fails to appear. Philippi[1] sees in the προσήκων not a relative (who, being either slave or freedman, could not possibly prosecute) but the *prostatés*. Obviously in this case neither the relative nor the *prostatés* is a possible prosecutor. So the whole act is merely a ceremony to appease the dead woman. It could not possibly lead to an actual trial.[2] In the first mention of the interdict the exegetes are expounding the general law. In the second reference they are telling the speaker what he is actually to do in this particular case. This case is concerned with a freedwoman. In case of a murdered citizen who had no relatives it is not so easy to determine what is done. This is the only actual instance which has come down to us of an interdict pronounced at the tomb of a murdered person and unfortunately it concerns a non-citizen. It has been shown that whatever its content was, it was a pure formality and led to nothing.

Schoemann[3] supposes that there were three proclamations, the first one by the relatives at the tomb, the second by the relatives in the agora at the time of the presentation of the case, and the third by the king archon on his acceptance of the case. Philippi[4] objects to this on the ground that there is

---

[1] *Op. cit.*, p. 99. [2] Cf. *ibid.*, pp. 98 f.

[3] *Antiquit.*, pp. 289 f.; but cf. Schoemann-Lipsius, *op. cit.*, I⁴, 508 f.

[4] *Op. cit.*, pp. 69 f., 99.

only one case of the proclamation at the grave and that it is
pure ceremony. No real accusation could come from it, and
in quite exceptional circumstances it might be made by others
than the relatives. This proclamation was merely to appease
the dead. He believes that there was only one real proclamation, the one after the *basileus* had accepted the case.[1] This is
a reasonable point of view. The proclamation at the tomb
has the characteristics of a very ancient ritual. It may be suggested that the spear which is carried out in the procession
to the grave is an emblem of hostility and that its purpose is
to show the hostility of the relatives of the deceased toward
the murderer and their intention perhaps to prosecute him
whoever he may be. This is the view of the lexicographers.[2]
Perhaps the proclamation forbade the murderer to approach
the tomb.[3] This proclamation apparently has nothing to do
either with pollution or with state intervention in homicide,
but is rather a survival of a very ancient ritual, an assurance
to the deceased that his relatives will obtain the *poiné* which
is due to him and a warning to the murderer of their intention.

There is considerable evidence available, on the other
hand, for the interdict in the agora before the beginning of a
homicide trial. According to a passage in the homicide laws
of Draco, the interdict had to be made by relatives within the
degree of first cousins: προειπεῖν τῷ κτείναντι ἐν ἀγορᾷ ἐντὸς
ἀνεψιότητος καὶ ἀνεψιοῦ.[4] Again in Antiphon's speech on the
Choreutes the relatives of the dead chorus boy are the ones
who decide to prosecute the choregus and to have the interdict pronounced against him.[5] Now in the *Constitution of
Athens* Aristotle in a discussion of the duties of the *basileus*
makes the following statement: καὶ ὁ προαγορεύων εἴργεσθαι
τῶν νομίμων οὗτός ἐστιν.[6] This statement led Lipsius[7] to think

---

[1] Cf. Gilbert (*Const. Antiqu.*, p. 385, n. 1), who agrees with Philippi.

[2] Cf. Harpocration, *s.v.* ἐπενεγκεῖν δόρυ ἐπὶ τῇ ἐκφορᾷ; Pollux viii. 65; *Lex. Seg.*,
p. 247, l. 30.

[3] Cf. Kennedy, *ad loc.*   [4] *IG²*, I, 115; this is repeated in Demos. xliii. 57.

[5] vi. 34–36.   [6] lvii. 2.   [7] *Op. cit.*, p. 810.

that the proclamation was actually pronounced by the *basileus*, and indeed this may have been the case. This does not alter the fact, however, that it was the relatives who instigated the action while the *basileus* acted as their mouthpiece for the proclamation.[1]

The general purport of the proclamation against the homicide is given in several passages. Demosthenes says[2] that the homicide was to be excluded from "lustrations, cups, drink-offerings, from temples and the market place." The purpose of this interdict is twofold: to forbid the presence of the murderer in certain public places and thus to avoid spreading pollution and also, as a part of the *poiné* due to the victim, to prevent the participation of the murderer in anything in which the deceased would have taken part during his lifetime. So both stages in the history of homicide procedure are represented in this proclamation: the early period, when there was no pollution connected with homicide but recompense had to be secured, and the later period when still only the relatives could prosecute, but when it was necessary to guard the state against the pollution which a murderer could spread abroad.

There are some debated points in regard to evidence before the homicide courts, particularly regarding the admission of women and children and slaves as competent witnesses. On the basis of a passage in Demosthenes it has been convincingly argued that in cases of homicide women, and children as well, regularly appeared in the capacity of witnesses.[3] In this case the only witnesses to the assault on the freedwoman were the wife and children of the defendant. The plaintiff admits that he and his wife and children might take a solemn oath in the Palladium but they would thereby be in danger of incur-

---

[1] Pollux (viii. 90) doubtless drew his account from Aristotle. For the view of Philippi, who thinks that the relatives made the proclamation on the order of the *basileus*, cf. *supra*, I, 114, n. 1.

[2] xx. 158.

[3] xlvii. 69 ff.; cf. Bonner, "Did Women Testify in Homicide Cases at Athens?" *CP*, I, 127 ff.; "Evidence in the Areopagus," *ibid.*, VII, 453; Leisi, *Der Zeuge*, pp. 17 ff.; Lipsius, *op. cit.*, p. 874, n. 20.

ring the odium of perjury. Hence, being averse to taking a
false oath, he let the matter drop. Undoubtedly the oath
here contemplated was an oath to substantiate a claim to
relationship with the deceased. It is beyond doubt, then, that
women and children had the right to appear publicly and to
take solemn oaths. But the further question arises of the capacity in which they would have appeared if they had taken
the oath: as joint prosecutors, as regular witnesses, or as
special witnesses to the fact of relationship. The expounders
virtually call them witnesses when they say: ἐπειδὴ αὐτὸς μὲν
οὐ παρεγένου, ἡ δὲ γυνὴ καὶ τὰ παιδία, ἄλλοι δέ σοι μάρτυρες οὐκ
εἰσίν. Eyewitnesses must have been necessary for securing a
conviction, and it is assumed that a conviction was possible.
If they were joint prosecutors, they could not appear as
witnesses. But in any event in the contemplated oath they
would have sworn to the same thing which the prosecutor
swore to in his *diomosia* and would thus be virtually witnesses.[1] Plato's rules regarding competency of witnesses afford by implication a striking confirmation of the view that
women were competent witnesses in homicide cases. Women
over forty years of age are to have a general right to give
evidence in any case, and slaves and children are to be allowed under special restrictions to testify in homicide cases.[2]
Plato has here started with the Athenian practice which admitted women to testify in cases of homicide, and extends
this right to "infants" and to slaves.[3] Next he proceeds to
increase the privileges of women by allowing them to testify
in any case, provided they are over forty years of age. It is
true that there are no instances where women actually testified in homicide cases, but, as has been pointed out,[4] in none
of the few homicide cases with which the extant speeches deal
could a woman have been involved as a witness. A woman
appears as defendant in Antiphon i, and in Lysias i a woman

---

[1] Bonner (*CP*, I, 129 f.) refutes Mederle's contention (*De juris jurandi in lite
Attica decem oratorum aetate usu*, p. 29) that the oath of the wife was a regular
evidentiary oath. As an oath on the question of relationship it can hardly be an
evidentiary oath.

[2] *Laws* 937A–B.   [3] Cf. Bonner, *op. cit.*, p. 131.   [4] *Ibid.*, p. 132.

appears, but as wife of the defendant and paramour of the slain man she naturally is not brought in as a witness.

In Antiphon[1] the choregus, previously to a regular accusation, had been informally charged with homicide in a court where he was to be a prosecutor on the following day. On two successive days in the presence of dicasts and spectators he challenged his accuser to take witnesses and go to those who were present when the alleged poison drink was administered. He said that more than fifty men and boys were present and offered to furnish a list of their names. This proceeding was to take place before the formal charge was made and was intended to show the relatives of the boy that there was no ground for bringing the charge. Consequently the boys were not witnesses in the legal sense at this stage of the inquiry but some of them were doubtless among the witnesses called a short time earlier in the speech.

On the basis of a single sentence in Antiphon it is quite generally assumed that a slave could give evidence for the prosecution in the case of homicide. The passage is as follows:

εἴπερ γὰρ καὶ μαρτυρεῖν ἔξεστι δούλῳ κατὰ τοῦ ἐλευθέρου τὸν φόνον, καὶ τῷ δεσπότῃ, ἂν δοκῇ, ἐπεξελθεῖν ὑπὲρ τοῦ δούλου, καὶ ἡ ψῆφος ἴσον δύναται τῷ δούλῳ ἀποκτείναντι καὶ τῷ ἐλευθέρῳ, εἰκός τοι καὶ ψῆφον γενέσθαι περὶ αὐτοῦ ἦν, καὶ μὴ ἄκριτον ἀποθανεῖν αὐτὸν ὑφ’ ὑμῶν.[2]

---

[1] vi. 19, 22 ff.

[2] Antiph. v. 48. Leisi (*op. cit.*, p. 21) also quotes a sentence from Antiphon as follows: οὐ γὰρ ἐπὶ ταῖς τοιαύταις μαρτυρίαις βασανίζονται (οἱ δοῦλοι), ἀλλ’ ἐλεύθεροι ἀφίενται, ii. γ. 4. This passage really has no bearing on the question. In the first speech of the prosecutor we are told that the slave of the murdered man was mortally wounded, but still able to speak and tell the bystanders who the murderer was (ii. α. 9). These witnesses were to be produced to tell what the dying slave said. This would be hearsay testimony under one of the categories permitted in Athenian courts, as Leisi himself elsewhere points out (*op. cit.*, p. 96; cf. *supra*, p. 130 ff.). In his reply the defendant tries to show his skill by confusing the issue with attacks on the credibility of the slave's statement, which he calls μαρτυρία in the sense of information. He ends his attacks by saying: ἀπιστουμένων δὲ καὶ τῶν ἄλλων δούλων ἐν ταῖς μαρτυρίαις (οὐ γὰρ ἂν ἐβασανίζομεν αὐτούς) πῶς δίκαιον τούτῳ μαρτυροῦντι πιστεύσαντας διαφθεῖραί με; ii. β. 7. These words show clearly that the statements (μαρτυρίαι) of slaves are not accepted without torture. When the prosecutor returns to the information gained from the slave, he confuses the matter still further by saying that in such information as that given by the slave it was not the practice to torture the slave but to set him free. This points clearly to an information

But this view has not gone unchallenged. From a modern standpoint homicide is the most serious crime in the calendar. And so we are not at first surprised that an exception should be made in the matter of a slave's competency in an effort to use every available means to convict a slayer. But the Athenians took no such serious view of homicide. If the relatives failed to prosecute, a slayer might not be brought to trial at all for the homicide.[1] Furthermore, the general attitude of freemen to slaves in the ancient world should be fully realized by those who would put them on a par with freemen as witnesses in homicide cases. Slaves were sold, beaten, and half-starved at times. In all actual cases in the orators we hear of nothing but evidence extracted by torture. In the southern section of the United States less than three-quarters of a century ago slaves were held by civilized and cultured people. And yet under no circumstances whatsoever could a slave be a competent witness against a white man.[2] We must be wary of any theory that Athenian citizens would have permitted their lives and liberties to be endangered by a slave testifying in any kind of a case.

The statement in Antiphon is a mere *obiter dictum*, as lawyers say. A slave was indeed said to be cognizant of some facts which pointed to the guilt of the defendant, but the prosecution never thought of producing him as a witness. In fact, they got possession of him and put him to death instead of using him as an informer or allowing the defendant to put him to the question. Against this conduct on the part of the prosecution the defendant protested in rather ponderous and

---

(μήνυσις), but since the informer was dead it could only be an ante-mortem statement reported by those who heard and as such was permitted (cf. Thiel, *Antiphons Erste Tetralogie*, pp. 81 ff.). The reference to the slave's information as μαρτυρία is but another instance of lack of precision in the use of technical words. The only witnesses in the case were those who reported the statements of the slave.

[1] Cf. *supra*, pp. 210 ff.

[2] "Any negro or mulatto, bond or free, shall be a good witness in pleas of the commonwealth for or against negroes or mulattoes, bond or free, or in civil pleas where free negroes or mulattoes shall alone be parties, and in no other cases whatsoever" (*Acts of Virginia General Assembly, Code*, Vol. I [1814], c. 283, 4).

pompous fashion by pointing out that a slave had some protection under the law and some rights and so should not be put to death with impunity. Among the rights of the slave was the right μαρτυρεῖν for the prosecution in a homicide case. As was long ago suggested by Platner, μαρτυρεῖν is used loosely for μηνύειν. For the purposes of the speaker the argument is not weakened if μαρτυρεῖν equals μηνύειν.[1] Anyone familiar with Athenian legal terminology will scarcely deny that an argument based upon the notion that a word is always used in its technical sense rests upon an insecure foundation. Law was administered by amateurs; the speeches upon which we have to rely are not so much legal disquisitions clothed in the exact terminology of modern counsel as rhetorical addresses to a panel of dicasts whose knowledge of law and procedure must not be overestimated. It was inevitable that the technical and the literary signification of words should be occasionally confused. This is particularly true of μάρτυς and μαρτυρεῖν, as Guggenheim has shown.[2]

In this connection it should be observed that slave evidence is to be allowed only in case it is against the defendant in a homicide case. This is suspiciously like an information (μήνυσις) which could only be against someone. It would be quite as important, for example, to use the testimony of a slave to establish an alibi and free his master or another from a charge of homicide. But it is evident that the problem cannot be settled by attempts to prove that μαρτυρεῖν is the equivalent of μηνύειν. Leisi[3] is correct in urging that "Alles, was Gug-

---

[1] *Der Process und die Klagen* (1824–25), I, 215; Guggenheim, *Die Bedeutung der Folterung im Attischen Process* (1882), pp. 3 ff. These arguments were rejected by Meier-Schömann-Lipsius, *Der Attische Process*, pp. 875 ff. Bonner (*Evidence in Athenian Courts* [1905], p. 34) revived the case against slave witnesses. Wyse (*CR*, XX [1906], 59) approves, as does Thiel (*op. cit.*, p. 81). Leisi (*op. cit.*, pp. 12 ff., 21, n. 1), while adhering to the view of Lipsius, makes some important concessions. Bonner (*CP*, VII, 453 ff.) answers the objections of Leisi. Lipsius (*op. cit.*, pp. 873 f.) maintains his former position but makes an important concession which will be discussed later. Thus the matter stands.

[2] *Die Bedeutung*, pp. 7 ff. E.g., if one insists upon the technical meaning of these words wherever they occur, he could prove that a party to a suit could be regarded as a witness for his opponent.

[3] *Op. cit.*, p. 22.

genheim, S. 11 f., und Bonner, *Evidence*, S. 34–38, dagegen anführen, macht die Annahme, dass Antiphon daselbst μαρτυρεῖν auch wieder für μηνύειν brauche, *möglich*, aber nicht absolut *notwendig*." Leisi quotes as decisive a provision in Plato's *Laws*[1] as follows: δούλη δὲ καὶ δούλῳ καὶ παιδὶ φόνου μόνον ἐξέστω μαρτυρεῖν καὶ συνηγορεῖν. But this provision of Plato differs from the rule deduced from Antiphon in one very important respect. Plato would permit a slave to give evidence either *for* or *against* a defendant charged with homicide. It is extremely hazardous to assume that Plato is following Attic law here or elsewhere. Lipsius dismisses the possibility.[2] Plato's proposal to let slaves συνηγορεῖν is quite incompatible with Athenian practice.[3] In the minor homicide courts whose procedure is set forth in the laws of Draco, the right to join in the prosecution (συνδιώκειν) is extended from blood relatives only to relatives by marriage and phratry members.

But the decisive objection to the theory that slaves could give evidence against a defendant charged with homicide is the fact that there is no trace of such evidence in the orators.[4] In most of these cases slaves appear. In the first oration of Lysias an adulterer was slain by the woman's husband who discovered the liaison and trapped the adulterer through information furnished by his wife's maid.[5] The relatives of the slain man claimed that he was not an adulterer at all but was enticed into the house and slain without justification. Now if the claim of the prosecution was true, the girl could have been put on the witness stand to refute the story which her master said she told him and be a witness against him. It is easy to

[1] 937A.

[2] *Op. cit.*, p. 874, n. 32: "Unverwertbar für attisches Recht ist die Vorschrift von Platon *Ges.* 937A wegen des letzteren Zusatzes und des weiter Folgenden."

[3] Cf. Wyse, *CR*, XX, 59.

[4] All Antiphon's six speeches, including the three sets of practice speeches, and Lysias i, xii, and xiii are wholly concerned with homicide. There are at least three other references to proceedings in homicide cases: Demos. xlvii. 68 ff.; lix. 9 f.; and Isoc. xviii. 52 ff.

[5] i. 18 ff.

dismiss this possibility by saying that a slave girl would not voluntarily contradict her master. Quite true, but the explanation only serves to show how wholly impracticable it would be to obtain from a slave trustworthy evidence against the master.

In the Herodes murder case we have at least one slave who could have appeared against the defendant. The charge of the prosecution, if we may trust the statements of the defendant, was based upon information furnished by a slave under torture. This slave was a member of the crew of the ship which took Herodes and Euxitheus to Methymna and then returned to Mytilene where Herodes and his relatives lived. The slave was purchased by the prosecution[1] and made a statement incriminating Euxitheus. The slave, however, according to the story of the defendant, finding that he was to be put to death anyway, changed his story and so exonerated the defendant.[2] The slave upon whose story the prosecution relied is called τὸν μηνυτήν, ᾧ πιστεύοντες ἐμὲ διώκουσι.[3] It must occur to any reader that, if the slave were a competent witness, the prosecution would have produced him for they had him in their power. But it does not require much ingenuity to discover more than one reason for their not doing this, especially if the defendant's story of the torture is true. But if the slave were really a competent witness who could appear in court and tell his story,[4] it is simply inconceivable that the defendant did not protest that instead of torturing him the prosecution should have produced him as a witness. Instead of availing himself of this safe and reasonable means of throwing discredit upon the case of the prosecution, he argues that the slave should have been turned over to him-

[1] Antiph. v. 47.　　　　[2] Ibid. 32 ff.

[3] Ibid. 34; cf. 36, 47. When Herodes disappeared, and did not return to the vessel in which he and Euxitheus, the defendant, were sailing, Euxitheus offered to send his own servant to Mytilene with the news and to set further inquiries on foot. His words, καίτοι οὐ δήπου γε κατ' ἐμαυτοῦ μηνυτὴν ἔπεμπον εἰδώς (24), show that if the servant had anything incriminating to report it would be as an informer and not as a witness.

[4] At this time evidence was still oral, and evidence in homicide courts was always oral (cf. Bonner, CP, VII, 450 ff.; Lipsius, op. cit., p. 884).

self for questioning under torture.[1] His friends also had proposed the same course by way of challenge when they heard
about the prosecution's dealing with the slave.[2] Is it possible
that a defendant whose words have been interpreted to mean
that slaves were competent witnesses in homicide cases
should have failed to invoke the law in his own behalf? A
shrewd and able counsel like Antiphon would surely not have
failed his client so completely.

Leisi is properly impressed by the absence of any reference
to slaves as actual witnesses in homicide cases and suggests
that the law merely permitted slaves to testify; it did not
forbid their being tortured according to the practice in other
cases. Here is his final conclusion:

> Im allgemeinen gilt aber eine auf der Folter abgenommene Aussage
> für zuverlässiger als ein Zeugnis. Diese Regel wird sich auch auf das
> Zeugnis von Sklaven erstrecken, und daraus wird es sich erklären, warum
> wir weiter nichts von Sklavenzeugnis hören. Das ganze Institut macht
> den Eindruck von einem Residuum einer frühern Gerichtsordnung, das
> aus religiöser Scheu vor Änderung der alten geheiligten Satzungen an
> den Blutgerichtshöfen bestehen blieb.[3]

In a word the law was obsolete even in the time of Antiphon.
It had disappeared without leaving a trace in legal practice.

There is, however, another case in point with which neither
Leisi nor Lipsius was familiar. In *Theomnestus* v. *Neaera*[4]
there is a brief account of a homicide trial. Some time before
the present trial Stephanus, the husband of Neaera, prosecuted Apollodorus, the brother-in-law of the plaintiff, in the
Palladium for homicide. In support of this charge, which was
proved in court to be false, Stephanus produced some slaves
as witnesses, representing them as Cyrenaeans (παρασκευα-
σάμενος ἀνθρώπους δούλους καὶ κατασκευάσας ὡς Κυρηναῖοι
εἴησαν). Here at least is a case where there were no obstacles
to producing these slaves in court if they were indeed competent witnesses. Their testimony was against the defendant
and they were obviously in the control of the prosecutor. If
they were competent, why did Stephanus in pressing a doubtful case incur an additional risk by pretending that they were

---

[1] Antiph. v. 36.   [2] *Ibid.* 34.   [3] *Op. cit.*, p. 23.   [4] Demos. lix. 9 f.

freemen? Quite apart from the other considerations, this case alone is sufficient to show that slaves were not competent witnesses in homicide cases. Lipsius, in the text of *Das Attische Recht*, says: "Ausgeschlossen von dem Zeugnisrechte sind also zunächst die Sklaven mit der leicht verständlichen Ausnahme von Blutprozessen, wenn ihr Zeugnis den eines Mordes Angeklagten belastet."[1] In the note, however, he suggests in reference to the Stephanus case, to which his attention was called by Bonner, that the exception applied only to murder trials in the Areopagus: "So liegt die Annahme sehr nahe, dass die Ausnahme nur für Mordklagen vor dem Areopag gegolten hat." He gives not the slightest hint why an exception should be made in cases before the Areopagus. The *obiter dictum* upon which alone the whole theory rests does not even occur in a speech before the Areopagus. It would have been much better to abandon the theory altogether than to try so unconvincingly to salvage a shred. It is beyond belief that the Athenians should accept the testimony of a slave like that of any other witness against a man charged with homicide but bar, unless given under torture, his statement as to who began a brawl.

Before dealing with the problems of punishment for homicide, it will be convenient to summarize the punishments for the different types. Any slayer, including the kin slayer, might be granted release by his victim, and in such cases no trial ensued. But if a slayer was not released and remained to stand his trial, after the first speeches of the parties he was allowed to go into exile if he chose. In case he stayed and the trial was completed, equal votes secured his acquittal.[2] If acquitted, he made a thank-offering to the Σεμναί.[3] If convicted of premeditated homicide he was put to death. If convicted of unpremeditated homicide he was sent into exile until he obtained *aidesis*.

For premeditated homicide no *aidesis* was possible. A murderer who had not been granted release by his victim and who had gone into exile before the court pronounced judg

---

[1] P. 873.   [2] Antiph. v. 51.   [3] Paus. i. 28. 6.

ment would never receive *aidesis* from his victim's relatives.[1] But in cases of φόνος ἀκούσιος there is a question as to whether there was a legal term of exile after the expiration of which the relatives were compelled to grant *aidesis* or whether the relatives of the slain man had full power to decide whether the homicide's application for *aidesis* should ever be granted. It is the opinion of most scholars that there was a legal term of banishment, although there is not agreement as to its length. Gilbert[2] states that there was such a legal term, but admits that its duration cannot be estimated. Philippi[3] distinguishes two possible situations, that is, when an agreement is made with relatives of the slain and when no such agreement is made. In this second case most scholars fix the term at one year, basing their conclusion on the word ἀπενιαυ-τισμός, which is found in the scholia and lexicographers, which they take to mean a period of one year. But this word does not necessarily mean only one year.[4] Philippi thinks that the legal term must have exceeded a year in consideration of a passage from Antiphon: ἐπί τε γὰρ τῇ τούτου διαφ-θορᾷ ἀβίωτον τὸ λειπόμενον τοῦ βίου διάξω, ἐπί τε τῇ ἐμαυτοῦ ἀπαιδίᾳ ζῶν ἔτι κατορυχθήσομαι.[5] Philippi does not, however, venture an opinion on the exact duration of the exile. Treston[6] speaks also of a legal term of exile and, relying on Plato, thinks that the term of exile was normally one year. Glotz,[7] on the other hand, does not believe that the Athenians fixed the length of ἀπενιαυτισμός. It is difficult to rely on Plato, for he has four classes of homicide instead of the two of Athenian law, ἑκούσιος and ἀκούσιος, and he has four penalties, one-year, two-year, three-year exile, and death. In the absence of further evidence, however, it does not seem likely that the Athenian state, after intervening in homicide, would have

---

[1] Cf. Philippi, *op. cit.*, pp. 143 ff.; Demos. xxi. 43; xxxvii. 58 ff.

[2] *Op. cit.*, p. 382.   [3] *Op. cit.*, pp. 114 ff.

[4] Cf. Plato *Laws* 868E: τριετεῖς ἀπενιαυτήσεις διατελεῖν.   [5] iii. β. 10.

[6] *Op. cit.*, pp. 211 ff. Cf. the one year exile of Theseus for the slaying of the Pallantidae (Euripides *Hipp.* 37).

[7] *Op. cit.*, p. 309.

permitted an angry family to refuse the involuntary slayer reinstatement in his country for a long period of time or even to doom him to lifelong exile. But yet Draco's law seems to make it clear that the pardoning power rested entirely with the relatives. If they agreed to grant pardon it was granted. If one relative refused the pardon was stopped. One might argue, however, that there was a legal term after the expiration of which the family could no longer refuse to pardon.

As long as the wilful murderer who had escaped into exile or the man exiled by the court for involuntary homicide and not yet pardoned remained in exile and avoided the places stipulated by law, he was protected from being molested. It was a punishable offense to kill him.[1] His slayer was subject to the same laws as any other slayer. But if a homicide was caught in any of the forbidden places, he could be killed with impunity or taken for execution to the thesmothetai or informed against.[2]

[1] Demos. xxiii. 38, 29 ff., 51 ff.; *IG²*, I, 115.

[2] For a discussion of the punishments for homicide cf. Gilbert, *op. cit.*, p. 387.

CHAPTER IX

APPEALS, PARDONS, AND NEW TRIALS

Aristotle regards the ἔφεσις εἰς δικαστήριον as one of the most significant democratic features of the constitution of Solon.[1] The word ἔφεσις means in Attic procedure a "reference" of a case from any judicial officer, body, or board to a dicastery.[2] If the *ephesis* depends upon the volition and action of the losing party in the original proceedings, it is to all intents and purposes an "appeal" as it is known in Anglo-American law and practice. But if the *ephesis* is required by law, it is in no sense an appeal. These two meanings are not always distinguished in the sources.[3] Aristotle in attributing so much importance to *ephesis* has in mind not only the Solonian *ephesis* but all the cases of *ephesis*, whether appeals or references required by law, that he mentions in his book. In consequence, there has been considerable difference of opinion regarding the meaning of *ephesis* in its various occurrences in literary and epigraphical sources.

Solon's *ephesis* is the earliest example of a real appeal,[4] but long before his day magisterial decisions could be reversed or quashed. In the pre-Draconian system the Areopagus, the sovereign body in the state, had the task of supervising the laws[5] and seeing that the magistrates in both their executive and their judicial capacities paid heed to the laws. The authority clearly implied the right to nullify the verdict of a

[1] *Ath. Pol.* ix. 1; cf. Plut. *Solon* xviii. 2; *supra*, I, pp. 159 ff.

[2] In the following discussion of *ephesis* a number of suggestions are drawn from the unpublished doctoral dissertation of John D. Ralph, *Ephesis in Athenian Courts* (University of Chicago, 1936).

[3] Cf. Pollux viii. 62.

[4] Cf. Lipsius, *Das Attische Recht*, p. 28; Thalheim, in Pauly-Wissowa, *s.v.* Ἔφεσις; Busolt-Swoboda, *Griech. Staatsk.*, p. 851.

[5] Arist. *Ath. Pol.* iii. 5: ἡ δὲ τῶν Ἀρεοπαγιτῶν βουλὴ τὴν μὲν τάξιν εἶχε τοῦ διατηρεῖν τοὺς νόμους.

magistrate contrary to a specific law. Such action would naturally be taken by the Areopagus at the instance of an Areopagite, who became aware of the character of the verdict in question. His source of information might very well be the aggrieved party. But such informal complaints to Areopagites were not appeals because there was no constitutional machinery for presenting the case to the Areopagus. Nevertheless, there is the germ of an appeal. It must be admitted that these virtual appeals to the supreme authority in the state were infrequent and of little value to the oppressed masses. So long as laws were unwritten and uncertain the ordinary citizen had little chance of having a "crooked decision"[1] of an aristocratic magistrate reversed. The code of Draco takes an important step toward mitigating abuse of magisterial judicial authority:

ἡ δὲ βουλὴ ἡ ἐξ Ἀρείου πάγου φύλαξ ἦν τῶν νόμων, καὶ διετήρει τὰς ἀρχὰς ὅπως κατὰ τοὺς νόμους ἄρχωσιν. ἐξῆν δὲ τῷ ἀδικουμένῳ πρὸς τὴν τῶν Ἀρεοπαγιτῶν βουλὴν εἰσαγγέλλειν, ἀποφαίνοντι παρ' ὃν ἀδικεῖται νόμον.[2]

Solon seized upon this principle and applied it in his own constitution by permitting an appeal to the Heliaea, just as he developed freedom of prosecution, another of his three great democratic features, from a germ found in Draco's laws.[3]

Of the proceedings involved in a Solonian appeal we know practically nothing. In case the magisterial verdict was upheld, the Heliaea had the right to increase the penalty.[4] It is to be assumed that if within a time limit no steps were taken by a dissatisfied litigant, the magistrates' verdict became final.

The commonly accepted view that the Solonian ἔφεσις εἰς τὸ δικαστήριον was a real appeal has not gone unchal-

[1] Hesiod *Works and Days* 219–21, 250; cf. *Il.* xvi. 386 ff.

[2] Arist. *Ath. Pol.* iv. 4. Regarding the authenticity of this section there can be little doubt; cf. *supra*, I, 145.

[3] Cf. *supra*, I, 157 ff., 166.

[4] Lysias x. 16; cf. Busolt-Swoboda, *op. cit.*, pp. 851, 1151; Busolt, *Griech. Gesch.* (1895), II, 285, n. 1.

lenged. Wilamowitz[1] asserts that ἔφεσις means that the magistrate had to refer to the Heliaea all penalties beyond a limit fixed by the various laws dealing with particular offenses. There is no support for this view in the only law we have regarding judicial action by the Heliaea: δεδέσθαι δ' ἐν τῇ ποδοκάκκῃ ἡμέρας πέντε τὸν πόδα, ἐὰν προστιμήσῃ ἡ ἡλιαία.[2] This law of Solon answers fully the view that the verdict of the magistrate is not a verdict of first instance.[3] The Heliaea, if it upheld the verdict of a magistrate, had the power to impose an additional penalty, just as an English court of appeal may increase the penalty of the lower court if it rejects the appeal.[4] In this law of Solon the Heliaea adopts and supplements the verdict of the magistrate. Adcock, after pointing out the relative unimportance of cases such as that referred to in Lysias x. 16, continues: "We may then suppose that the magistrates judged cases regularly with the help of a meeting of citizens."[5] If this means that a magistrate presided in the Heliaea when his own cases came up for appeal it is wholly reasonable.[6] But if it means that in the

---

[1] *Arist. und Athen*, I, 60.

[2] Law of Solon, Lysias x. 16. Lipsius (*Berichte der Königlich Sächsischen Gesellschaft der Wissenschaften* [Philol.-Hist. Classe], L [1898], 157) rightly rejects Wilamowitz' supposition without discussion. In *Das Attische Recht*, p.30, n. 94, he suggests that the court had the power to supplement the penalty fixed by law rather than the penalty imposed by the magistrate. No doubt the magistrate did inflict the penalties prescribed by law, so the suggestion of Lipsius does not alter the situation.

[3] Steinwenter, *Die Streitbeendigung durch Urteil, Schiedsspruch und Vergleich nach griechischem Rechte*, p. 71: "Das ἐφιέναι ist dann eben nichts anderes als die Erklärung der Partei, dass sie den Beamtenspruch nicht als bindend anerkenne, sondern die Entscheidung des ordentlichen, des Geschworenengerichtes verlange. Gewiss liegen dann zwei 'Erkenntnisse' vor, das des Beamten und jenes der Heliaia, aber man kann nicht gut von einer zweiten Instanz sprechen und auch nicht von einer Appellation, da die Heliasten keine eigentliche Kassation oder Reformation vornehmen." The further statement that the mere existence of the right of appeal (*die Tatsache der Ephesis*) renders the magistrate's verdict ineffective (*wirkungslos*) might be amplified as follows: the magistrate's verdict is not a verdict because an appeal lies, and so there can be no appeal because there is no real verdict. The conclusion is obvious.

[4] For further examples of penalties imposed upon an unsuccessful appellant cf. *supra*, I, 179.

[5] *CAH*, IV, 56.   [6] Cf. Busolt-Swoboda, *op. cit.*, p. 1151.

first trial of all cases the Heliaea participated, it is less de-
fensible than the supposition of Wilamowitz.

The Solonian appeal disappeared from Athenian practice
when the Heliaea was organized into dicasteries and the magistrate lost practically all judicial power. But with the institution of public arbitrators appeals were restored.[1] A real
remnant of the pre-Solonian power of the magistrates to decide cases finally on their own authority[2] is found in the competence of the Forty to pronounce final judgment on cases
involving not more than ten drachmas. All other cases filed
with them were turned over to the public arbitrators.[3]

The first duty of the arbitrator was to try to secure some
settlement or compromise that would be satisfactory to both
parties. Of the method of procedure in this first stage we have
no information in the sources. Doubtless, like private arbitrators, they sought "what was in the interest of all," to use
a phrase of Isaeus.[4] In any event, the agreement effected was
as binding as any contract and could be pleaded in bar of any
future action in the same matter. Failing in this endeavor,
the arbitrator ceases to be a διαλλακτής and becomes a real
δικαστής capable of rendering a verdict in accordance with
the law and the facts. The proceedings, as may be inferred
from Aristotle's account, are now practically the same as
those of a regular court and include depositions, challenges,
and laws; but they are spread over several meetings and are
less formal. On a set day the arbitrator delivered his award
(γνῶσις). On the selfsame day the defeated litigant must decide whether he would abide by the verdict (ἐμμένειν τῇ
διαίτῃ) or appeal (ἐφιέναι εἰς τὸ δικαστήριον).[5] A litigant
suffered no real hardship by being allowed so brief a time in
which to come to a momentous decision. In most cases both
parties must have guessed the verdict sometime in advance.
If there was no appeal, the arbitrator, before the end of the
final day, filed his verdict in the office of the Forty.[6] The

---

[1] For the institution cf. *supra*, I, 347 ff.   [2] Arist. *Ath. Pol.* iii. 5.

[3] *Ibid.* liii. 2.   [4] ii. 30.   [5] Demos. xl. 31.

[6] *Ibid.* xxi. 85. The identity of τῶν ἀρχόντων in this passage, long uncertain, has
been satisfactorily settled; cf. Lipsius, *op. cit.*, p. 68, n. 61; p. 627, n. 2.

Forty or, rather, the four concerned in the case—i.e., the four representing the tribe of the defendant[1]—certified the verdict. The importance of the notation by the Forty is seen in the efforts of Midias to persuade these officials μεταγρά-φειν.[2] The effect of the filing and the notation was to make the award a matter of record as the verdict of the Forty. The verdict was now as final and effective as their verdict in cases involving ten drachmas or less. It settled the case as effectively and finally as the verdict of a dicastery. If the defeated party failed to satisfy the judgment, the winner could levy on his goods and chattels or eject him from his real estate by a δίκη ἐξούλης.

But if, on the other hand, an appeal was entered, all the evidence and other documents in the case were sealed up in separate receptacles and sent to the four in charge of the case, who introduced it into a dicastery. As in modern appeals the evidence was the same as that heard by the court of first instance.[3]

Lipsius in 1898 wrote: "Dass ἔφεσις vom Spruch des Diaiteten Appellation ist, wird wohl von keiner Seite mehr bestritten."[4] This remained true until 1925 when the thesis of Wilamowitz that there was no appeal in Attic law was revived by Steinwenter, who, in regard to arbitration, says: "Wäre also die Heliaia ein Berufungsgericht, dann müsste der öffentliche Diaitet ordentlicher Richter erster Instanz sein und in seinem Amte bliebe vom schiedsrichterlichen Element nicht viel mehr als der Titel übrig."[5] The answer is emphatically that the arbitrator was, when he gave his

---

[1] Arist. *Ath. Pol.* liii. 2: καὶ τὴν γνῶσιν τοῦ διαιτητοῦ γεγραμμένην ἐν γραμματείῳ προσαρτήσαντες, παραδιδόασι τοῖς τέτταρσι τοῖς τὴν φυλὴν τοῦ φεύγοντος δικάζουσιν.

[2] Demos. xxi. 85. Ulpian on this passage says the four signed the verdict: ἔδει τὴν διαιτηθεῖσαν δίκην ὑπογραφῆναι παρὰ τῶν ἀρχόντων. Steinwenter (*op. cit.*, p. 64) suggests that each wrote ἀνέγνων.

[3] Arist. *Ath. Pol.* liii. 3: οὐκ ἔξεστι δ' οὔτε νόμοις οὔτε προκλήσεσι οὔτε μαρτυρίαις ἀλλ' ἢ ταῖς παρὰ τοῦ διαιτητοῦ χρῆσθαι ταῖς εἰς τοὺς ἐχίνους ἐμβεβλημέναις. For exceptions to this rule which are apparent rather than real cf. Bonner, *Evidence in Athenian Courts*, pp. 55 f.

[4] *Berichte der Sächsischen Gesellschaft*, L (1898), 157.

[5] *Op. cit.*, pp. 68 f.

award, an "ordentlicher Richter erster Instanz." As has been pointed out, the public arbitrator was a διαλλακτής so long as he sought a settlement by agreement. Failing this, he became a one-man court and decided the case on its merit according to the law and the evidence, and, like the dicasts, gave his award under oath.[1] These two distinct and separately exercised functions of the arbitrator (διαλλακτής and δικαστής) are clearly and succinctly set forth by Aristotle in the words ἐὰν μὴ δύνωνται διαλῦσαι, γιγνώσκουσι.[2]

Another indication of the judicial character of the arbitrator is shown by the fact that if a witness properly summoned did not appear, the litigant could at once file a δίκη λιπομαρτυρίου against him before the arbitrator. In the only known case, *Apollodorus* v. *Timotheus*,[3] Antiphanes, a witness for the plaintiff, was charged with λιπομαρτυρίου. Apollodorus says the arbitrator refused to give a decision against Antiphanes, the defaulting witness (οὐ κατεδιήτα). It is impossible to say why the arbitrator did this. The best suggestion is that Apollodorus, relying on the promises of the witness to appear and testify, did not summon him properly.[4] Beyond this it is unprofitable to speculate what the arbitrator could have done had he adjudicated the case. Leisi's guess is as good as any:

Über das Urteil ist es schwer, eine Vermutung aufzustellen; vielleicht enthielt es für den Beklagten die Alternative, die Gebühren des Klägers zurückzuerstatten und jetzt noch Zeugnis abzulegen, oder bei Unterlassung der Aussage eine grössere Busse, vielleicht an den Kläger, zu bezahlen; diese Busse wird wohl schätzbar gewesen sein, wie Meier, *Att. Proc.* 500, will.[5]

[1] Arist. *Ath. Pol.* lv. 5; Harrell, *Public Arbitration* ("University of Missouri Studies") pp. 21 f.

[2] Arist. *Ath. Pol.* liii. 2. Occasionally private arbitration closely approximated public arbitration in this respect: ἐκεῖνοι δ' εἶπον ἡμῖν, εἰ μὲν ἐπιτρέποιμεν αὐτοῖς ὥστε τὰ δίκαια διαγνῶναι, οὐκ ἂν ἔφασαν διαιτῆσαι· .... εἰ δ' ἐάσομεν αὐτοὺς γνῶναι τὰ συμφέροντα πᾶσιν ἔφασαν διαιτήσειν (Isaeus ii. 30).

[3] Demos. xlix. 19.

[4] Lipsius, *op. cit.*, p. 785. Leisi's suggestion (*Der Zeuge*, p. 51) that the promise to appear was not made before witnesses is to be rejected because a δίκη λιπομαρτυρίου would lie whether the witness promised or not. Cf. *supra*, pp. 141 f.

[5] *Op. cit.*, p. 52.

Nothing shows more clearly that an arbitrator was a real judge than the provision for redress in case a litigant felt he had been wronged by an arbitrator: ἔστιν δὲ καὶ εἰσαγγέλλειν εἰς τοὺς διαιτητὰς ἐάν τις ἀδικηθῇ ὑπὸ τοῦ διαιτητοῦ, κἄν τινος καταγνῶσιν ἀτιμοῦσθαι κελεύουσιν οἱ νόμοι· ἔφεσις δ᾽ ἐστὶ καὶ τούτοις.[1] The nature of the wrongs contemplated is not specified, but it is clear that the *eisangelia* was not based upon the award itself, for that could be appealed. The grievances must have arisen out of the conduct of the case. In the forensic speeches the litigants have little to say about irregularities permitted or committed by the arbitrator in the conduct of the case. Apollodorus, in prosecuting Stephanus for perjury, says that when the original case came to trial on appeal an important document was not to be found in the ἐχῖνος. His suspicion, however, was not directed against the arbitrator but against the section of the Forty in charge of the case in whose custody the documents were kept.[2] Unfairness might be exhibited in granting or refusing continuances or failing to check obstructive tactics on the part of a litigant. It is wholly unlikely that the arbitrator would refuse to file and seal up any deposition or document offered. In any event, the severity of the penalty prescribed by law, complete *atimia*, shows that ample precautions were taken to prevent the abuse of the unusual judicial powers granted to a single individual. As there is no trace of an *euthyna* for arbitrators,[3] this impeachment was all the more necessary. The purpose in having it brought before the assembled arbitrators was to have the matter first examined by men familiar with the duties of an official arbitrator.

Lipsius[4] regards the words ἔφεσις δ᾽ ἐστὶ καὶ τούτοις as proof that a condemned arbitrator had a right of appeal, but, as we shall see, similar phraseology in the case of *dokimasia*[5] does not, in the face of other considerations, mean that there

---

[1] Arist. *Ath. Pol.* liii. 6.

[2] Demos. xlv. 57–58.

[3] Lipsius, *op. cit.*, p. 232, n. 46.

[4] *Ibid.*, p. 231.

[5] Arist. *Ath. Pol.* xlv. 3; lv. 2; cf. *infra*, pp. 243 f.

was an appeal.[1] In the only recorded case of an adverse verdict by a board of arbitrators[2] the case did come before a dicastery, but there is no sure indication whether it was a matter of routine required by law or an appeal by Straton.[3] Demosthenes' account of the disfranchisement of the arbitrator Straton is given in a way to bring out the animosity of Midias against Straton.[4] An example is the virtual suppression by Demosthenes of the action of the dicastery who confirmed the verdict against Straton. If Straton was able to obtain μήτε συγγνώμης μήτε λόγου μήτε ἐπιεικείας μηδεμιᾶς,[5] the dicastery was not less blameworthy than Midias. Under these circumstances it is not to be expected that the story of Demosthenes would be of any assistance in determining whether ἔφεσις was an "appeal" or a "reference." Since he almost ignores the action of the dicastery in order to fasten all blame on Midias, it is not to be expected that there would be any allusion to an appeal to a dicastery by Straton.

Thus far there is nothing decisive in favor of either "appeal" or "reference" in this type of case. But there is one consideration that cannot be lightly dismissed even if it be not decisive. It is wholly contrary to Athenian ideas and practices to permit a group such as the arbitrators, assembled neither by election nor by lot nor subject to account at the end of the year, to impose such a severe penalty. The right of appeal may have proved to be a sufficient guaranty against abuse of delegated judicial power,[6] but a better guaranty was to make the verdict subject to review by a dicastery. If the verdicts of the *boulé* beyond five hundred drachmas had to be

---

[1] In favor of appeal in impeachments of arbitrators is the appeal from the decisions of individual arbitrators. These, however, dealt only with civil or private cases and involved no severe penalties.

[2] Demos. xxi. 81 ff.

[3] The words καὶ τοῦτ' ἐχαρίσασθ' αὐτῷ (*ibid.* 91), as was pointed out first by Fränkel (*Die attischen Geschworenengerichte*, pp. 73–74, n. 4), mean that the verdict of *atimia* was confirmed by a dicastery. Dobree's emendation ἐχαρίσαθ' αὐτῷ has not found favor, though King in his edition of 1901 prints it in his text.

[4] Cf. Ulpian on Demos. xxi. 83: σαθρόν ἐστιν ὅλον τὸ περὶ τὸν Στράτωνα μέρος.

[5] xxi. 90.   [6] Cf. Harrell, *op. cit.*, pp. 15 ff.

referred to a court, there is every reason to suppose that the same would be required in a sentence of *atimia* imposed by the board of arbitrators. The immediate effect of a sentence of *atimia* was the suspension of the arbitrator. Ulpian[1] says that his award in the case out of which the *eisangelia* arose was quashed. If this be true, this case would have to be referred *de novo* to another arbitrator.

One is interested to inquire how far arbitration was a success. On the basis of a passage in Demosthenes it is argued that the majority of cases were appealed: καίτοι ἄτοπον δοκεῖ μοι εἶναι, εἰ οἱ μὲν ἄλλοι, ὅταν οἴωνται ἀδικεῖσθαι, καὶ τὰς πάνυ μικρὰς δίκας εἰς ὑμᾶς ἐφιᾶσιν.[2] This is perhaps about what we should expect. If a litigant refused to accept a settlement where he would gain at least a modicum of his claims, he would most likely reject an adverse verdict on the merits of the case. But inevitably when two men had agreed to accept a settlement worked out by the arbitrator as διαλλακτής, there could be no question of an appeal. Hence we may assume that the success of arbitration lay in the activity of the arbitrators as διαλλακταί rather than as δικασταί.[3]

When the judicial function of the boulé was reduced to inflicting penalties of not more than five hundred drachmas, the boulé was required by law to send to a dicastery all cases which in its opinion called for a more severe penalty:

ὁ δὲ δῆμος ἀφείλετο τῆς βουλῆς τὸ θανατοῦν καὶ δεῖν καὶ χρήμασι ζημιοῦν, καὶ νόμον ἔθετο, ἄν τινος ἀδικεῖν ἡ βουλὴ καταγνῷ ἢ ζημιώσῃ, τὰς καταγνώσεις καὶ τὰς ἐπιζημιώσεις εἰσάγειν τοὺς θεσμοθέτας εἰς τὸ δικαστήριον, καὶ ὅ τι ἂν οἱ δικασταὶ ψηφίσωνται, τοῦτο κύριον εἶναι.[4]

There is no specific mention in Aristotle of a τέλος within which the boulé was supreme. The law as cited by Aristotle merely forbids the boulé to impose fines (χρήμασι ζημιοῦν) and the reader is left to suppose that all penalties in the way of fines (ἐπιζημιώσεις) must come before the dicastery. But

---

[1] *Op. cit.*   [2] xl. 31.

[3] One is reminded of Aristotle's distinction between an arbitrator and a judge in the *Rhetoric* i. 13. 19: ὁ γὰρ διαιτητὴς τὸ ἐπιεικὲς ὁρᾷ, ὁ δὲ δικαστὴς τὸν νόμον· καὶ τούτου ἕνεκα διαιτητὴς εὑρέθη ὅπως τὸ ἐπιεικὲς ἰσχύῃ.

[4] Arist. *Ath. Pol.* xlv. 1.

an incident in a Demosthenic speech shows that the boulé could fine up to five hundred drachmas on its own authority.[1] No importance is to be attached to the fact that the conclusions and decisions of the boulé to be referred to a dicastery are called καταγνώσεις, ἐπιζημιώσεις, and κρίσεις.[2] In effect καταγνώσεις, ἐπιζημιώσεις, and κρίσεις were mere recommendations arrived at by discussion and voting. The procedure is described by the speaker in the above-mentioned speech,[3] where the words καὶ ἐπειδὴ ἐν τῷ διαχειροτονεῖν ἦν ἡ βουλὴ πότερα δικαστηρίῳ παραδοίη ἢ ζημιώσειε ταῖς πεντακοσίαις, ὅσου ἦν κυρία κατὰ τὸν νόμον show that the defendant had no option in the matter. It depended entirely on the boulé to determine whether the case was to be ἐφέσιμος, i.e., subject to transfer to a dicastery, or settled by a fine of five hundred drachmas. The thesmothetai, on receiving the recommendation of the boulé, automatically referred the matter to a dicastery. The recommended penalty (Strafantrag) is analogous to the τίμημα proposed by a private prosecutor.[4] When the case came to trial in a dicastery one or more members of the boulé conducted the prosecution.[5]

Everybody is agreed that the transfer of the recommendation of the boulé to a dicastery is not an appeal. But it has been maintained[6] that fines within the τέλος of the boulé were subject to appeal on the basis of the following passage in Aristotle:[7]

κρίνει δὲ τὰς ἀρχὰς ἡ βουλὴ τὰς πλείστας, μάλισθ' ὅσαι χρήματα διαχειρίζουσιν· οὐ κυρία δ' ἡ κρίσις, ἀλλ' ἐφέσιμος εἰς τὸ δικαστήριον.

[1] Demos. xlvii. 43, quoted below. This is confirmed by a decree probably about 423 B.C. (IG², I, 76, ll. 58 ff.). It has been pointed out by Wilamowitz (op. cit., II, 196) that ἐπί in composition in ἐπιζημιώσεις means fines "over and above," "in addition to" the permitted fine; cf. Lipsius, op. cit., p. 45, n. 137.

[2] Cf. Arist. op. cit. xlv. 1, quoted above; Lysias xxii. 3.

[3] xlvii. 43; cf. Busolt-Swoboda, op. cit., p. 1046, n. 2.

[4] Cf. Demos. xliii. 75, where the ἐπιβολή of a magistrate beyond his τέλος is called τίμημα.

[5] Lysias xxii. 3.

[6] Lipsius, op. cit., p. 198; Busolt-Swoboda, op. cit., p. 1046.

[7] Ath. Pol. xlv. 2.

ἔξεστι δὲ καὶ τοῖς ἰδιώταις εἰσαγγέλλειν ἣν ἂν βούλωνται τῶν ἀρχῶν μὴ χρῆσθαι τοῖς νόμοις. ἔφεσις δὲ καὶ τούτοις ἐστὶν εἰς τὸ δικαστήριον, ἐὰν αὐτῶν ἡ βουλὴ καταγνῷ.

The trial of officials here mentioned would seem to have arisen out of the monthly audits required of officials. These audits were conducted by the *logistai* of the senate chosen by lot from the senate,[1] as distinguished from the annual auditors allotted from the general citizen body. Presumably they handled the monthly audits much the same way as the annual ones were handled by the other *logistai*. If the auditors found nothing wrong, they so reported to the senate and the official was given, so to speak, a clean bill of health. If the auditors were not satisfied, or if a private individual brought a charge of illegality (μὴ χρῆσθαι τοῖς νόμοις), the senate tried the case. One would naturally suppose that in these cases also, although they affected officials only, the judicial power of the boulé would be the same as in cases involving private citizens, viz., its authority would be final in fines of five hundred drachmas or less.

If the passage refers to a real appeal we have here a distinction in the treatment of officials and ordinary citizens before the boulé, about which Lipsius is rightly disturbed. But he nevertheless perseveres in his opinion, "Wiewohl man nicht einsieht, warum allein bei den Beamten der Appellation gegen solche Bussen gedacht wird."[2] There is no parallel to such a distinction. It is wholly out of accord with the general Athenian attitude toward official responsibility to give appeal to an official condemned by the boulé and deny it to the rank and file of citizens. The theory of Lipsius involves two serious objections. A τέλος is fixed within which we are told that the boulé is κυρία.[3] Just what does κυρία mean? Aristotle constantly uses κύριος in the sense of "having full authority." Of the ἀποδέκται he says: τὰ μὲν μέχρι δέκα δραχμῶν ὄντες κύριοι, τὰ δ' ἄλλ' εἰς τὸ δικαστήριον εἰσάγον-

---

[1] *Ibid.* xlviii. 3: κληροῦσι δὲ καὶ λογιστὰς ἐξ αὐτῶν οἱ βουλευταὶ δέκα τοὺς λογιου-μένους ταῖς ἀρχαῖς κατὰ τὴν πρυτανείαν ἑκάστην.

[2] *Op. cit.*, p. 198, n. 67.   [3] Demos. xlvii. 43, quoted above.

APPEALS, PARDONS, AND NEW TRIALS 243

τες ἔμμηνα.[1] There is no doubt of the meaning of κύριοι here[2] or of κύριοι as used of decisions of the dicasteries.[3] Surely κυρία has in Demosthenes xlvii. 43 the same meaning as elsewhere, where it is used to characterize judicial authorities and their decisions.

The other objection is the discrimination in favor of an official whom the senate thinks guilty as contrasted with an ordinary citizen similarly situated. The apparent difficulty is easily dissolved by interpreting ἐφέσιμος to refer not to κρίσεις within the τέλος, of which Aristotle makes no mention, but to those that exceeded five hundred drachmas, where there was no appeal but an obligatory reference.

Aristotle mentions *ephesis* in connection with the *dokimasia* of the newly chosen members of the boulé and the nine archons. The outgoing boulé conducted this scrutiny first: δοκιμάζει δὲ καὶ τοὺς βουλευτὰς τοὺς τὸν ὕστερον ἐνιαυτὸν βουλεύσοντας καὶ τοὺς ἐννέα ἄρχοντας. καὶ πρότερον μὲν ἦν ἀποδοκιμάσαι κυρία, νῦν δὲ τούτοις ἔφεσίς ἐστιν εἰς τὸ δικαστήριον.[4] Aristotle seems to say here that *ephesis* in his day was permitted only to those who were rejected. In other words, this was a real appeal. But in a later and more elaborate statement he puts the matter in a different light:

δοκιμάζονται δ' οὗτοι πρῶτον μὲν ἐν τῇ βουλῇ τοῖς πεντακοσίοις, πλὴν τοῦ γραμματέως, οὗτος δ' ἐν δικαστηρίῳ μόνον, ὥσπερ οἱ ἄλλοι ἄρχοντες (πάντες γὰρ καὶ οἱ κληρωτοὶ καὶ οἱ χειροτονητοὶ δοκιμασθέντες ἄρχουσιν), οἱ δ' ἐννέα ἄρχοντες ἔν τε τῇ βουλῇ καὶ πάλιν ἐν δικαστηρίῳ. καὶ πρότερον μὲν οὐκ ἦρχεν ὅντιν' ἀποδοκιμάσειεν ἡ βουλή, νῦν δ' ἔφεσίς ἐστιν εἰς τὸ δικαστήριον, καὶ τοῦτο κύριόν ἐστι τῆς δοκιμασίας.[5]

Lipsius[6] alone among the scholars who have dealt with *dokimasia*[7] does not believe that the nine archons were required to undergo two scrutinies. But the contrast between the officials who appeared ἐν δικαστηρίῳ μόνον and the nine archons

[1] *Ath. Pol.* lii. 3. [2] Lipsius, *op. cit.*, p. 100.

[3] Arist. *Ath. Pol.* xlv. 1; cf. Plato *Crito* 50B; Andoc. i. 88.

[4] *Ath. Pol.* xlv. 3. [5] *Ibid.* lv. 2. [6] *Op. cit.*, pp. 271 f.

[7] Busolt, *Die griechischen Staats- und Rechtsaltertümer*, p. 223; Busolt-Swoboda, *op. cit.*, pp. 470, 1045; Hermann-Thumser, *Lehrbuch der griechischen Staatsaltertümer*, p. 607.

who were scrutinized πρῶτον μὲν ἐν τῇ βουλῇ .... καὶ πάλιν
ἐν δικαστηρίῳ leaves no doubt that the *dokimasia* in the
court was obligatory and not the result of appeal. But the
matter is finally settled by a passage in Demosthenes: ᾤετο
ὁ Σόλων .... τοὺς μὲν θεσμοθέτας τοὺς ἐπὶ τοὺς νόμους κληρου-
μένους δὶς δοκιμασθέντας ἄρχειν ἔν τε τῇ βουλῇ καὶ παρ' ὑμῖν
ἐν τῷ δικαστηρίῳ.[1] So precise an expression as δὶς δοκιμασθέντας
is quite inappropriate if the second *dokimasia* depended upon
occasional appeals. Still further confirmation not hitherto
noticed in this connection may be found in Aristotle's
account of the procedure in *dokimasia*. After the candidate-
elect answers the questions put to him and produces his
witnesses, the official in charge asks:

"Does anybody wish to bring a charge against this man?" And if
any accuser is forthcoming, he is given a hearing and the man on trial
an opportunity of defense, and then the official puts the question to a show
of hands [ἐπιχειροτονία] in the Council or to a vote by ballot [ψῆφος] in the
Jury-court; but if nobody wishes to bring a charge against him, he puts the
vote at once; formerly one person used to throw in his ballot-pebble, but
now all are compelled to vote one way or the other about them, in order
that if anyone being a rascal has got rid of his accusers, it may rest with
the jurymen to disqualify him.[2]

This passage shows the manner of voting in the boulé and
the dicastery when an accuser appears, a show of hands in
the boulé and a ballot in the dicastery. This process applies
both to those who are scrutinized in the dicastery only and
to those scrutinized first in the boulé, then in the dicastery.
But the words ἐὰν δὲ μηδεὶς βούληται κατηγορεῖν, εὐθὺς δίδωσι τὴν
ψῆφον show that in all cases the dicastery alone can finally
accept a candidate.

The double *dokimasia* required both of members of the
boulé and of the nine archons effectively disposes of the question of an appeal. *Ephesis* in both cases means obligatory
reference to a court.[3] Aristotle's statement that there was

[1] xx. 90; cf. Cloché, *REG*, XXXIV, 240, n. 1.

[2] Arist. *Ath. Pol.* lv. 4 (trans. Rackham).

[3] Lipsius, in his preoccupation with the theory that *ephesis* in Aristotle always
means "appeal," brushes aside too lightly the opposing arguments.

ephesis for those rejected by the boulé[1] is, as we have seen, apparently inconsistent with his later statement that the dicastery is the final authority in *dokimasia:* καὶ τοῦτο (τὸ δικαστήριον) κύριόν ἐστι τῆς δοκιμασίας.[2] The discrepancy, apparent rather than real, may be due to the brevity and succinctness of the statement. It was quite as important from the standpoint of democracy that a dicastery should check the acceptances as well as the rejections of the boulé to prevent undesirable citizens getting into office by bribing intending accusers: ἵνα, ἄν τις πονηρὸς ὢν ἀπαλλάξῃ τοὺς κατηγόρους, ἐπὶ τοῖς δικασταῖς γένηται τοῦτον ἀποδοκιμάσαι.[3]

Athenian magistrates were permitted to fine anyone who obstructed them either actively or passively in the performance of their official duties.[4] If the fine (ἐπιβολή) exceeded a fixed limit (τέλος), the magistrate had to take the matter to a dicastery, which could either confirm or remit the fine. It has been argued that even a fine within the *telos* could be appealed. There is no direct evidence to support this view; but there are some indications that deserve consideration.[5] In the law cited by Demosthenes the only reference to the court is when the sum exceeds the *telos*, and then it becomes and is called a *timema*. There is no mention of an *ephesis*. Also in point is a case in Lysias which has already been discussed,[6] and it is unnecessary to repeat the arguments used there. So far as this case goes, it may be confidently asserted that there is no feature of the case that cannot easily be explained by assuming that in this case the *epibolé* was beyond the competence of the magistrate and required court action to confirm it. The fact that the defendant nowhere

---

[1] *Ath. Pol.* xlv. 3.   [2] *Ibid.* lv. 2.   [3] *Ibid.* 4.

[4] Demos. xliii. 75: ἐὰν δέ τις ὑβρίζῃ ἢ ποιῇ τι παράνομον, κύριος ἔστω (ὁ ἄρχων) ἐπιβάλλειν κατὰ τὸ τέλος. ἐὰν δὲ μείζονος ζημίας δοκῇ ἄξιος εἶναι, προσκαλεσάμενος πρόπεμπτα καὶ τίμημα ἐπιγραψάμενος ὅ τι ἂν δοκῇ αὐτῷ, εἰσαγαγέτω εἰς τὴν ἡλιαίαν.

[5] The argument drawn from a decree (*IG²*, II, 1177) of the deme Piraeus is not pertinent. The fine in this case to be imposed is not the normal fine as in the case of other magistrates. Here the demarch is instructed and empowered to inflict a fine in case of certain infractions and to take the matter to court. In point of fact, by the terms of the decree he becomes a public prosecutor and the *epibolé* is a *timema*.

[6] ix; cf. *supra*, I, 279 ff.

explicitly mentions this feature of the case is no objection to this view. In fact, the words οὔτε εἰς δικαστήριον εἰσελθόντες τὰ πραχθέντα[1] imply very clearly that the action of the generals was not κυρία until taken to a court by them and not by the defendant by way of appeal. The case finally reached the court by an *apographé*[2] brought by someone who hoped to profit by it.

The word ἔφεσις occurs in an inscription of 446–445 B.C. recording the terms granted to the Chalcidians after their unsuccessful attempt to secede from the empire. The so-called resolution of Archestratus, an amendment to the act of settlement, is as follows:

Ἀρχέστρατος εἶπε· τὰ μὲν ἄλλα καθάπερ Ἀντικλῆς· τὰς δὲ εὐθύνας
Χαλκιδεῦσι κατὰ σφῶν αὐτῶν εἶναι ἐν Χαλκίδι καθάπερ Ἀθήνησιν Ἀθηναίοις,
πλὴν φυγῆς καὶ θανάτου καὶ ἀτιμίας. περὶ δὲ τούτων ἔφεσιν εἶναι Ἀθήναζε
ἐς τὴν ἡλιαίαν τὴν τῶν θεσμοθετῶν κατὰ τὸ φσήφισμα τοῦ δήμου.[3]

The word εὐθύνας here has not the technical Athenian meaning of "audit" but means "legal punishment." There are three possible procedures suggested by *ephesis* here: it may mean appeal in the true sense, as Lipsius believes;[4] it may mean that sentences of death, banishment, or *atimia* imposed in local courts must be taken to Athens for review by a dicastery; it may mean that cases involving the penalties of death or exile or loss of civil and political rights, whether τίμητοι or ἀτίμητοι, were reserved cases to be tried in Athens in the first instance.

Pseudo-Xenophon devotes considerable space to a discussion of Athenian judicial control of the empire. The text of the first sentence of the passage is evidently corrupt, but the significant parts of the discussion are abundantly clear.

With regard to the allies, the popular party has a hatred for, and brings, as appears, malicious accusations against the best men among them, knowing that the ruler must in any case be hated by the ruled, and that if the

---

[1] Lysias ix. 11.   [2] Lipsius, *op. cit.*, p. 299.

[3] *IG*², I, 39; Hicks and Hill, *Greek Historical Inscriptions*, 40; Tod, *Greek Historical Inscriptions*, 42; Dittenberger, *Sylloge inscriptionum Graecarum*², 17.

[4] *Op. cit.*, p. 970.

rich and responsible classes in the cities become strong, the ascendancy of
the democratic party at Athens will endure for but a very short time; for
this reason, then, they deprive the good of their civil rights and property,
and get them exiled, and put them to death, and they help on the bad.[1]

It is clear from these words that the Athenians in their own
courts condemned individual allies to disfranchisement,
banishment, death, and heavy fines: τοὺς μὲν χρηστοὺς ἀτι-
μοῦσι καὶ χρήματα ἀφαιροῦνται καὶ ἐξελαύνονται καὶ ἀποκτείνουσι.
Kalinka takes the words χρήματα ἀφαιροῦνται to refer to confiscation of property that followed or rather was included
in the sentences of banishment and death. The order of the
words is against this view as well as the fact that a sentence
of death or exile against a citizen of a subordinate state
condemned for high crimes or misdemeanors surely included
confiscation of property. Consequently, there was no occasion to mention it.

In the amendment of Archestratus we find no mention of
confiscation of property, merely banishment, death, and disfranchisement, but the amendment must be read in connection with the decree of Diognetus where in the oath of the
boulé and the dicasts property is mentioned: οὐδὲ χρήματα
ἀφαιρήσομαι ἀκρίτου οὐδενός.[2]   It would seem likely rather
that the words χρήματα ἀφαιροῦνται refer to ruinous fines such
as are contemplated in Aristophanes: τῶν δὲ συμμάχων ἔσειον
τοὺς παχεῖς καὶ πλουσίους, αἰτίας ἂν προστιθέντες.[3]   Here there
can be little question of anything but a fine. In any event,
the passage in Pseudo-Xenophon shows that the penalties

---

[1] *Const. of Athens* i. 14 ff. (trans. Brooks, using text of Kalinka).

[2] *IG²*, I, 39, ll. 8–9.

[3] *Peace* 639–40. A passage in the *Wasps* 287–89 also refers to wealthy and influential inhabitants of the Thraceward cities who were suspected of being dis-
affected and were harassed by perpetual persecutions, as Rogers points out:

> καὶ γὰρ ἀνὴρ παχὺς ἥκει
> τῶν προδόντων τἀπὶ Θρᾴκης·
> ὃν ὅπως ἐγχυτριεῖς.

Starkie, following Müller-Strübing, attempts to identify the ἀνὴρ παχύς with
Thucydides, but the arguments are far from convincing. Cf. also *Knights* 262 ff.,
and Antiph. v. 78, where a wealthy citizen of Mytilene is said to have emigrated to
Aenus to escape the sycophants.

of disfranchisement, banishment, and death were imposed
upon guilty citizens of subordinate cities by Athenian courts.

We learn from the Archestratus amendment that there
was an *ephesis* to Athens for natives in case of serious crimes
involving penalties of death, banishment, and disfranchisement. Lipsius believes that *ephesis* here as elsewhere means
appeal, not reference. The passage of Pseudo-Xenophon already quoted is a general statement that the Athenians banished, executed, and disfranchised citizens of the subordinate
state. But in a later passage where he ironically justifies this
system of judicial control he says: "While remaining at home,
without sending out ships, they manage the allied cities and
protect the commons while they ruin their opponents in the
courts." He means, of course, the Athenian courts. The alternative to trial at Athens is trial in the local courts. "If
each of the allies tried their lawsuits at home, out of hatred
for Athenians, they would have destroyed those of their own
people most friendly to the Athenian commons."[1] In brief,
by this system the Athenians protected pro-Athenians from
death, banishment, or disfranchisement by sentence of the
local court and at the same time saw to it that they had the
opportunity to punish anti-Athenians by imposing these
severe penalties in their own courts. The only certain way
to carry out such a system without fail was to reserve all such
cases for trial in Athens. According to Pseudo-Xenophon,
this is precisely what they did: τοὺς συμμάχους ἀναγκάζουσι
πλεῖν ἐπὶ δίκας Ἀθήναζε.[2] If Pseudo-Xenophon is right,
ephesis in the Chalcidian act of settlement means not appeal
but obligatory reference. It is true Pseudo-Xenophon is writ-

[1] *Const. of Athens* i. 16. Opinion is divided as to whether or not a democratic
form of government was the rule in Athenian dependencies; cf. Kalinka, *Die
Pseudoxenophontische* Ἀθηναίων Πολιτεία, pp. 151, 153; Walker, *CAH*, V, 471–72;
Robertson, *CP*, XXVIII, 50–53. But in any event there was always a more or less
dangerous pro-Spartan and oligarchic group. Athens' judicial restrictions were
intended to prevent or check *stasis*.

[2] *Const. of Athens* i. 16; cf. Athenaeus ix. 407*b*; καθ' ὃν δὲ χρόνον θαλασσοκρατοῦντες
Ἀθηναῖοι ἀνῆγον εἰς ἄστυ τὰς νησιωτικὰς δίκας. It was common Greek practice to
oblige subordinate states to try their cases in the courts of the sovereign state; cf.
Herod. v. 83.

ing twenty years later than the Chalcidian decree and there may have been changes, but the decree says explicitly that the *ephesis* was κατὰ τὸ φσήφισμα τοῦ δήμου. This is taken to mean that *ephesis* in such cases by a general law was applicable to all subordinate cities.[1] The case of Mende, where upon the suppression of a revolt in 423 B.C. the Mendeans were permitted to try in their own courts any of their citizens suspected of causing the revolt, is an exception that proves the rule.[2]

It is clear that there was considerable current criticism of the Athenian judicial restrictions in overseas communities. The Athenian apologist in Sparta on the eve of the war devotes a paragraph to the charge that imperial Athens was fond of adjudication (φιλοδικεῖν).[3] His defense rests entirely upon the reciprocity involved in suits under specific treaties which Athens had negotiated both with her allies and with others (ἐν ταῖς ξυμβολαίαις δίκαις). Nothing is said about criminal cases. If the *ephesis* to Athens was optional, it is difficult to see why neither the fifth-century apologist nor Isocrates[4] in the fourth century said so. It would not have afforded a complete rejoinder to criticism either current or retrospective, but it would have confused the issue in favor of Athens. No rhetorician worthy of the name could have missed it.

The only sure way for the Athenians to be certain that these special cases would actually be brought before their courts was to make the *ephesis* obligatory. It was not enough

[1] Robertson, *Administration of Justice in the Athenian Empire* ("University of Toronto Studies in History and Economics," Vol. IV, No. 1), p. 55, discusses the question with a citation of the literature.

[2] Thuc. iv. 130. 7.   [3] *Ibid.* i. 77; cf. Bonner, *CP*, XIV, 284–86.

[4] The impression one gains from Isocrates is that overseas cases were tried in Athens not at the option of the litigants concerned but by the will of Athens; cf. Isoc. iv. 113; xii. 63, 66. The last passage is as follows (trans. Norlin): "For example, in the present instance, if they bring up the fact that the lawsuits of the allies were tried in Athens, is there anyone so slow of wit as not to find the ready retort that the Lacedaemonians have put to death without trial more of the Hellenes than have ever been brought to trial and judgment here since the founding of our city?" The passages cited above from Aristophanes convey the same impression.

to rely upon appeal. There could be no certainty that such cases would be appealed. It may at first sight seem certain that no man would fail to appeal against such severe penalties. But it would be rash to assume that means could not be found to dissuade a man from appealing a sentence of *atimia*. If courts could be found to disfranchise a man, means would not be lacking to put pressure upon him to submit to the decision. With the death penalty it would be otherwise; no man would submit to death if an appeal might save him. But an appeal could be prevented in another way. The Athenian boulé on more than one occasion[1] condemned a man to death *ultra vires* and executed him without referring the matter to a dicastic court as the law required. What the boulé could do in Athens an overseas court could certainly do. These risks might have been avoided by a strict system of supervision and reprisals, but in such cases an ounce of prevention is worth a pound of cure. It was simpler to follow the Greek theory of political and judicial subordination and compel "their dependents to sail to Athens for the adjudication of suits," as Pseudo-Xenophon says they did. These various considerations should dispose of overseas appeals.

There remains a further problem. Just how was it possible to determine what cases came under the exception? Where the law fixed the penalty as either death, or exile, or *atimia*, the matter would be simple; but where the penalty was assessed by court, it would be necessary to wait until the trial was over and then send the case to Athens for retrial. A much surer and more practical procedure would be not to allow the local courts to go through the motions of trying such cases. Where the law provided one of the forbidden punishments or the prosecution asked for it as the *timema*, at the *anakrisis* or preliminary inquiry the case could be assigned for trial in Athens.[2] This is precisely the procedure of the *boulé*.

---

[1] Arist. *Ath. Pol.* xl. 2; cf. Lysias xxii. 2.

[2] The entire conduct of the *anakrisis* could scarcely be in the hands of Athenian officials, for it would have been necessary for them to handle all criminal cases, a formidable task. Cf. Lecrivain, in Darem.-Saglio, *s.v.* "Ephesis": "On sait que, dans la première ligue maritime, Athènes a réservé à ses héliastes le jugement de tous

It did not try a serious case but recommended a suitable penalty and sent the case to a dicastery.[1]

Unfortunately there is only one recorded case in which a crime committed overseas was tried in Athens.[2] Euxitheus, a citizen of Mytilene, was tried by the process of *apagogé* for the killing of Herodes, who appears to have been an Athenian citizen resident in Mytilene.[3] Probably he was one of those who emigrated from Athens as a settler on confiscated land. That there was some official investigation of the disappearance of Herodes cannot be questioned. No freeman could be tortured without official sanction and supervision. It was quite otherwise with the slave who was the property of the relatives of Herodes. Euxitheus was never himself present at any inquiry so far as is known from his own account. This was due in part to the fact that he had gone to Aenus, where his father resided, without any notion that he would be suspected. Furthermore, the torture of the slave at first and the torture of the freeman were intended in all probability to secure a confession of their guilt or complicity. When this failed to solve the disappearance of Herodes, the suspicions of his friends were directed toward Euxitheus. The letter,[4] whether genuine or forged, and admissions of a slave constituted the basis of action.[5] But this case gives no real help in determining whether the investigation was conducted by local or Athenian overseas officials. There is a wide divergence of opinion as to the identity of τοῖς ἄρχουσι in section 47, but we may be certain that the investigation of the disappearance of an Athenian resident in Mytilene after the

---

les procès et délits qui ont trait aux institutions fédérales. Il en est de même des crimes privés qui entraînent la peine de mort, l'atimie, l'exil; *l'instruction de l'affaire peut avoir lieu dans la ville soumise, mais le jugement appartient aux héliastes,* présidés par les archontes thesmothètes."

[1] Cf. *supra*, pp. 240 f.   [3] Cf. Jebb, *Attic Orators*, I, 55.

[2] Antiph. v.   [4] Antiph. v. 53.

[5] It is interesting to observe that Euxitheus meets it not by questioning the writing but by *eikota* arguments; cf. Bonner, *Evidence in Athenian Courts*, p. 80. On two occasions it was claimed that slaves could detect changes made in documents they had written (Demos. xxix. 21; xxxiii. 17 ff.).

revolt would not be trusted wholly to local officials.[1] But even if it could be shown that they were Athenian overseas officials, it is of little value, because the crime involved not natives of Mytilene but a native and an Athenian. The case affords no help in determining the procedure in overseas crimes involving natives only.

The matter may be approached from another angle. If Athens required certain reserved cases to be tried in Athens, there must have been some agency to see that the law was enforced. It is known that Athens had a very large number of overseas officials.[2] Among these overseas officials the ἐπίσ-κοποι receive considerable attention from the lexicographers,[3] but all they tell us is that these men were sent to the subordinate cities ἐπισκέψασθαι τὰ παρ' ἑκάστοις or τὰ τούτων πράγματα. To this information, which is mostly etymological, Aristophanes adds a valuable hint. In the *Birds*[4] an *episkopos* appears with a pair of voting urns, saying that he has been chosen by lot and showing his credentials. It is an ill business extracting information about Attic legal institutions from a comedy, but the association of an *episkopos* with judicial ballot boxes at least justifies the surmise that in the subordinate cities the *episkopos* had some relation to the imperial judicial system. He is introduced merely as a figure common

---

[1] Lipsius (*op. cit.*, p. 873, n. 23) contends that the reference is to the Eleven, while the view that the Athenian magistrates resident in Mytilene are meant is advanced by Böckh, *Staatsh. d. Athener*, I, 480, n. *e*; Busolt, *Griech. Gesch.*, III, 227; Fränkel, *De condicione, jure, jurisdictione sociorum Atheniensium*, p. 17; Gilbert, *Const. Antiq.*, p. 432, n. 1. Robertson (*op. cit.*, pp. 57–64) has a full discussion of Athenian overseas officials. *IG²*, I, 60 reads δεχομένους instead of the restoration ἐπιμελητάς or ἐπισκόπους known to Robertson in 1924.

[2] Arist. *Ath. Pol.* xxiv. 3 puts the number at seven hundred. This number has aroused much suspicion. The latest editors, Kenyon (Oxford) and Opperman (Teubner), both query it. Sandys accepts it without question and lists enough types of overseas officials to quiet any doubts. Apart from cleruchies which had officials, there were well-nigh one hundred and forty subordinate cities in the empire (Meritt and West, *Harvard Studies*, XXXVII, 98). Kalinka (*op. cit.*, pp. 168 f.) thinks the number none too large. It may be an accidental repetition in round numbers of the number of home officials. But in any event the number must have been very large, perhaps more than seven hundred.

[3] Cf. Robertson, *op. cit.*, p. 60, for full citations.   [4] 1032 and 1053.

throughout the Athenian Empire.¹ It has been plausibly suggested that the *episkopoi* were charged with the task of checking the lists of criminal cases and making sure that those in which the law required or the prosecution demanded a forbidden penalty were sent to Athens for trial.² But even if this conjecture be unacceptable, its rejection in no way invalidates the conclusion that *ephesis* in the overseas cases meant reference and not appeal.³

The ecclesia, as the supreme body in the state, exercised the pardoning power which in modern states is the privilege of monarchs or presidents. In the exercise of this power the ecclesia quashed or annulled the verdicts of the dicasteries. Alcibiades, for example, when charged with impiety, was condemned to death *in absentia* by a dicastery.⁴ Later the assembly voted his return.⁵ Dorieus, a Rhodian, became a rebel and joined the Spartans during the Peloponnesian War. He was summoned to Athens for trial and, failing to appear, was condemned *in absentia*.⁶ Xenophon does not say that he was tried by a dicastery, but it was the general practice of Athens to try traitors from overseas before a court presided over by the thesmothetai.⁷ Eventually Dorieus was captured in a naval engagement and taken to Athens. According to law, the sentence already passed upon him could have been executed without further ado. But, owing to the fact that he was a famous athlete, he was released by the assembly.⁸ Beyond this we cannot follow the case. It is idle to inquire what was Dorieus' status in the future. At all events his sentence of death was quashed by the assembly. This was not at all an appeal in the regular sense, but rather a pardon granted to

¹ Cf. Robertson, *op. cit.*, p. 61. Whatever view one may take of the *Birds*, it reflects a number of the features of the Athenian imperial system.

² *Ibid.*, p. 62.

³ For a discussion of reference to Athens of cases from subordinate cities under the second Athenian Empire cf. *supra*, I, 317.

⁴ Thuc. vi. 61. 7; for details cf. *supra*, I, 301 f.

⁵ Thuc. viii. 97. 3.   ⁷ Cf. Robertson, *op. cit.*, p. 68.

⁶ Xen. *Hell.* i. 5. 19.   ⁸ Paus. vi. 7. 4–5.

a convicted rebel permitted to appear before the assembly[1] as a prisoner of war to make a plea for pardon. No doubt the friends who were instrumental in saving him from immediate execution brought the case before the assembly and supported his plea.

Antiphon[2] refers to a different type of case, where the Hellenic treasurers were all condemned for peculation. All but one, Sosias, were executed before it was discovered that none of them was guilty. Normally one would expect that the discovery of new evidence would result in a new trial and acquittal if the dicastery deemed the evidence reliable. But in this case the evidence was presented to the ecclesia and Sosias was released from the custody of the Eleven.

τοῦ δ' ἑνὸς τούτου (Σωσίαν ὄνομά φασιν αὐτῷ εἶναι) κατέγνωστο μὲν ἤδη θάνατος, ἐτεθνήκει δὲ οὔπω· καὶ ἐν τούτῳ ἐδηλώθη τῷ τρόπῳ ἀπωλώλει τὰ χρήματα, καὶ ὁ ἀνὴρ ἀπήχθη ὑπὸ τοῦ δήμου τοῦ ὑμετέρου παραδεδομένος ἤδη τοῖς ἔνδεκα.[3]

Here the ecclesia reverses a court verdict on the basis of new evidence.

In the cases of Dorieus and Alcibiades the question of their guilt or innocence played no part in the action of the assembly. Dorieus was released because the Athenians admired his athletic prowess. There was so little certainty of the guilt of Alcibiades in the first place that his enemies feared to try him while the army recruited for the Sicilian campaign was still in the city. The reasons for his recall were political. Sosias, however, was proved to be innocent to the satisfaction of the ecclesia. To this extent the case resembles a retrial rather than a pardon.

The amnesty laws passed in Athens on rare occasions granted pardons in wholesale fashion, with a few traditional exceptions,[4] to all who were wholly or partially disfranchised (ἄτιμοι) by the courts. Sometimes the *atimia*, complete or

---

[1] *Ibid.*: ὡς δὲ ἐς ἐκκλησίαν συνελθόντες ἄνδρα οὕτω μέγαν καὶ δόξης ἐς τοσοῦτο ἥκοντα ἐθεάσαντο ἐν σχήματι αἰχμαλώτου, μεταπίπτει σφίσιν ἐς αὐτὸν ἡ γνώμη καὶ ἀπελθεῖν ἀφιᾶσιν.

[2] v. 69-70.   [3] *Ibid.* 70.

[4] For the exceptions to the amnesty law cf. *supra*, I, 104 ff.

partial, was prescribed by legal enactment as a punishment.[1] Again, if a man failed to pay fines or damages assessed by a court he finally became *atimos*.[2] In these types of cases the unsuccessful defendant is restored by the amnesty to all the rights and privileges of full citizenship and his property is exempt from execution.

Besides the quashing of court verdicts, the amnesty law halted pending suits that might have exposed the unsuccessful defendant to *atimia*. As we should say, the case was nolprossed by action of the ecclesia. The only cases of this class mentioned in the decree of Patroclides were γραφαὶ περὶ εὐθυνῶν which had been accepted by the *euthynoi* but had not yet been brought before a dicastery.[3]

The intervention of the ecclesia in the case of Lysimachus of the Scaffold already discussed[4] presents some interesting features in this connection. Aristotle[5] gives the impression that the condemnation of Lysimachus by the boulé was the occasion for the enactment of the law restricting the powers of the boulé by depriving it of the right to inflict the death penalty, imprisonment, or fines. But it is more likely to have been the occasion of the re-enactment of the law after the revolutions. Eumelides is said to have rescued Lysimachus almost from the hands of the executioner who was on the point of carrying out the sentence of the boulé. According to Aristotle, a trial was subsequently held in a dicastery and Lysimachus was acquitted. At the same time a law was passed or revived restricting the judicial powers of the boulé. On what authority did Eumelides act? It is not likely that even the most determined citizen could force his way into prison and rescue a condemned criminal for whom the jail officials would be responsible with their lives. It is more likely that the matter was first brought up in the ecclesia. Perhaps on the motion of Eumelides, Lysimachus was turned over to the proper authorities (the thesmothetai) and tried before a dicastery. To insure against further *ultra vires* actions on the

---

[1] Andoc. i. 74 ff.   [3] *Ibid.* 78.

[2] *Ibid.* 73.   [4] *Supra*, I, 337.   [5] *Ath. Pol.* xlv. 1.

part of the boulé the law was re-enacted.[1] Here the ecclesia interfered not to quash a verdict but to insure that a man illegally condemned should be tried by due process of law. Indeed, the dicastery might have reached the same verdict as the boulé and have condemned Lysimachus to death.

The doctrine of the finality of *res judicata* and *autre fois acquit* prevailed in Athens as in modern communities: οἱ νόμοι δὲ οὐκ ἐῶσι δὶς πρὸς τὸν αὐτὸν περὶ τῶν αὐτῶν οὔτε δίκας οὔτ' εὐθύνας οὔτε διαδικασίαν οὔτ' ἄλλο τοιοῦτ οὐδὲν εἶναι.[2] But Euxitheus, a client of Antiphon, claims that if the prosecutors fail to convict him as a malefactor (κακοῦργος) for killing Herodes, they can try him again as a homicide for the same offense. Indeed, he himself asks for an acquittal because he is being tried illegally as a *kakourgos*, and he expresses his willingness to submit to a trial for murder.[3] As the prosecution had put death as the *timema*,[4] Euxitheus would, on the second trial, be put twice in jeopardy of his life. There is a theoretical distinction enough to save the rule of *res judicata* in law, but little practical difference between the two trials. When Euxitheus says ἔπειτα τίμησίν μοι ἐποίησαν, τοῦ νόμου κειμένου τὸν ἀποκτείναντα ἀνταποθανεῖν,[5] his slender justification for drawing a distinction between death by *timesis* and death by law is that in the former case the jury might convict and choose a lesser penalty proposed by the defendant himself. Hence the slain man would be deprived of his due. Antiphon relies upon the religious feeling he hopes to stir to obscure the sophistry of his plea. But *ex parte* statements must be dealt with cautiously. There is no certainty that if acquitted Euxitheus could have been tried again,[6] nor does the case show for certain that a man could be placed twice in jeopardy for the same offense.

The procedures for examining the accounts of retiring

[1] For the tendency of the boulé to overstep its power cf. *supra*, I, 338-39.

[2] Demos. xx. 147. Plato (*Crito* 50B) refers to the law ὃς τὰς δίκας τὰς δικασθείσας προστάττει κυρίας εἶναι. Cf. Demos. xviii. 224; xxix. 55.

[3] Antiph. v. 94-96.   [4] *Ibid.* 10, 59, 63, 85.   [5] *Ibid.* 10.

[6] Cf. *supra*, pp. 211 ff., for a discussion of *apagogé* in murder trials.

officials present a curious feature which seems on the face of it to transgress the principle of *res judicata*. The *logistai*, in addition to the financial accounts, investigated offenses which were punishable with a fine. Aristotle[1] mentions three: peculation (κλωπῆς), acceptance of bribes (δώρων), and maladministration (ἀδικίου).[2] This list of offenses seems exhaustive, as Lipsius holds.[3] Each official was brought before a court for discharge or trial in connection with his accounts. If the *logistai* and the *synegoroi* found no fault with the official's accounts and actions in office, they took him before a court and recommended his discharge. The herald, however, asked τίς βούλεται κατηγορεῖν.[4] If any irregularities were discovered by the *logistai* or disclosed by a volunteer prosecutor, there was a regular trial with fines in case of conviction.

But neither the sealed discharge nor a conviction fully released the former official. He had still to face possible charges, private and public, before the *euthynoi*. Aristotle is quoted to facilitate discussion of some important points:

κληροῦσι δὲ καὶ εὐθύνους, ἕνα τῆς φυλῆς ἑκάστης, καὶ παρέδρους δύο ἑκάστῳ τῶν εὐθύνων, οἷς ἀναγκαῖόν ἐστι ταῖς ἀγοραῖς κατὰ τὸν ἐπώνυμον τὸν τῆς φυλῆς ἑκάστης καθῆσθαι, κἄν τις βούληταί τινι τῶν τὰς εὐθύνας ἐν τῷ δικαστηρίῳ δεδωκότων, ἐντὸς τριῶν ἡμερῶν ἀφ᾽ ἧς ἔδωκε τὰς εὐθύνας, εὔθυναν, ἄν τ᾽ ἰδίαν ἄν τε δημοσίαν, ἐμβαλέσθαι, γράψας εἰς πινάκιον λελευκωμένον τοὔνομα τό τε αὐτοῦ καὶ τὸ τοῦ φεύγοντος καὶ τὸ ἀδίκημ᾽ ὅ τι ἂν ἐγκαλῇ, καὶ τίμημα ἐπιγραψάμενος ὅ τι ἂν αὐτῷ δοκῇ, δίδωσιν τῷ εὐθύνῳ· ὁ δὲ λαβὼν τοῦτο καὶ ἀνακρίνας, ἐὰν μὲν καταγνῷ, παραδίδωσιν τὰ μὲν ἴδια τοῖς δικασταῖς τοῖς κατὰ δήμους, τοῖς τὴν φυλὴν ταύτην εἰσάγουσιν, τὰ δὲ δημόσια τοῖς θεσμοθέταις ἐπιγράφει, οἱ δὲ θεσμοθέται, ἐὰν παραλάβωσιν, πάλιν εἰσάγουσιν τὴν εὔθυναν εἰς τὸ δικαστήριον καὶ ὅ τι ἂν γνῶσιν οἱ δικασταί, τοῦτο κύριόν ἐστι.[5]

The phrase τῶν τὰς εὐθύνας ἐν τῷ δικαστηρίῳ δεδωκότων should include not only those who received a discharge from the court on the recommendation of the *logistai* but those who had been tried either at the instance of the *logistai* or at the

---

[1] *Ath. Pol.* liv. 2.

[2] The meaning of ἀδικίου is not explicit. Kenyon renders it "unfair dealing"; Rackham translates "maladministration." The offenses contemplated cannot be serious in Athenian estimation for the only penalty they carry is a fine.

[3] *Op. cit.*, pp. 104 ff.   [4] Aeschin. iii. 23.   [5] *Ath. Pol.* xlviii. 4–5.

instance of a private citizen and had been either acquitted or fined.[1] If this be true, a retiring official was subject to a double accounting for his official acts. It must be assumed that there was a clear-cut division between the jurisdiction of the *logistai* and *synegoroi* and that of the *euthynoi*. It is difficult to see how a retiring official could be given a discharge by one court and again before the final release of himself and his property[2] run the risk of condemnation as a former official without violating the principle of *res judicata*. This difficulty has been recognized.[3] But it is not enough to say that the action of the court was "perfunctory" in the case of a man who "had rendered his accounts," involving as it did the possibility of trial by a court for peculation or bribery or maladministration. The trial would be just as thorough as any normal Athenian trial was. It would be strange, indeed, to grant a man a discharge by verdict of the court finding in his favor in a trial prosecuted by the *synegoroi* of the *logistai* or a private prosecutor, and then in effect say to him: "The verdict in these cases is not final as it is in others, and we reserve the right for three days to hale you before another court if any prosecutor appears, whether the charge has already been brought before or not." Assuredly this is not the right explanation. There were two quite different examinations; Wilamowitz calls the first λόγος and the second εὔθυνα.[4] This distinctive terminology is not always used. For example, in the passage quoted above,[5] the first stage is called εὔθυναι. But quite apart from the terminology, the distinction to which Wilamowitz draws attention is valid. When the *logistai* had finished their task, the *euthynoi* for a space of

<hr/>

[1] The unsuccessful defendant who paid his fine had as truly passed his account as the official who had been acquitted or discharged without trial.

[2] For the restrictions put upon ὑπεύθυνοι cf. Aeschin. iii. 21.

[3] Koch, *De Atheniensium logistis euthynis synegoris*, p. 7; cf. also Lipsius, *op. cit.*, pp. 105, 293.

[4] *Op. cit.*, II, 232 ff.

[5] Arist. *Ath. Pol.* xlviii. 4–5. For a full discussion of the terminology cf. Koch, *op. cit.*, pp. 15 ff.

three days received charges against the retiring magistrate.[1] On receiving a written charge the *euthynos* and his assessors examined it (ἀνακρίνειν). If it had to do with accounts and vouchers, or peculation, or bribery, or any instance of maladministration, for which the retiring official had already been acquitted or convicted, they naturally would do nothing about it. If, however, it dealt with some fault of omission or commission outside this range, private cases were turned over to the proper section of the Forty, and public cases to the thesmothetai. Owing to the insistence upon a technical meaning for such words as καταγνῷ and ἀνακρίνας, some misapprehension regarding the functions of the *euthynoi* has arisen.[2] The *euthynoi* and their assessors examined the records of the case in the *logisterion*, and if they determined that the charge did not violate the principle of *res judicata*, they turned it over to the proper official for *anakrisis* and trial.[3]

It is much better to assume that the Athenians in this fashion avoided putting a man twice in jeopardy than to conclude with Lipsius: "Freilich lag darin ein gewisser Abfall von dem Rechtsgrundsatze, dass niemand zweimal wegen derselben Sache zur gerichtlichen Verantwortung gezogen werden dürfe."[4]

An apparent exception to the *res judicata* rule occurs when

---

[1] The phrase εὔθυναν ἄν τ' ἰδίαν ἄν τε δημοσίαν ἐμβαλέσθαι is a curious one. Koch (*op. cit.*, p. 5, n. 1) points out that εὔθυναι in the plural is used of rendering accounts. The singular has the meaning of "penalty," "damages," and also "the charge," as in Lysias x. 27; xi. 9. Andoc. i. 73, cited by Liddell and Scott (1925), is not a parallel, because it has the plural. In Aristotle it simply means "file a charge, public or private"; cf. Rackham, Kenyon, *ad loc.*

[2] The editors vary between ἀναγνούς, read now by Kenyon and Rackham, and ἀνακρίνας, read by Sandys, Thalheim, and Opperman. ἀνακρίνας is preferable, but it does not refer to the regular *anakrisis*, for there was no *anakrisis* in the ordinary sense. That was conducted by the thesmothetai or the Forty. It seems unnecessary to say that an official read a document filed with him, but undoubtedly the accuser and the accused were interviewed, as ἀνακρίνας suggests.

[3] The word καταγνῷ in Aristotle and κατεγνωσμέναι in Andoc. i. 78, ὅσων εὔθυναί τινές εἰσι κατεγνωσμέναι ἐν τοῖς λογιστηρίοις ὑπὸ τῶν εὐθύνων, do not mean that these officials were real judges of the case. They simply reached a conclusion unfavorable to the official in the sense that he must in their opinion stand trial.

[4] *Op. cit.*, pp. 293 and 953, where is cited the passage from Demosthenes quoted *supra*, p. 256, in which εὔθυναι are mentioned.

a man who had sued for an estate unsuccessfully might renew his claim on another ground. This was done in *Eubulides v. Macartatus*.[1] Glaucus and Glaucon claimed the estate of Hagnias under a will which the court decided was false. Later they pushed their claim as relatives along with others and were successful. Such a situation must have been a bit bewildering to the common man, but it was according to law. When the speaker says οὐκ οἴονται δεῖν οὔτε τοῖς νόμοις τοῖς ὑμετέροις πείθεσθαι οὔτε τοῖς γνωσθεῖσιν ἐν τῷ δικαστηρίῳ[2] he is merely trying to arouse prejudice in the minds of those dicasts who might be puzzled and annoyed by the situation. For if the matter was actually *res judicata* the procedure was to file a *paragraphé*, but in this case this was not done.

Provision for a new trial on the appearance of new evidence especially in criminal cases is a well-known feature of modern criminal justice, but in Athens little is heard of it. In the case of Sosias already discussed the ecclesia itself discharged the condemned man. The case was not sent to a dicastery for retrial as might have been expected. But the ecclesia as sovereign body in the state could do as it pleased. The only check was a γραφὴ παρανόμων against the man responsible for such a measure as that which freed Sosias and others. In the archon's court for the settlement of conflicting claims to an estate (διαδικασία) there is a notorious case in which new evidence appeared. Dicaeogenes II died without issue. After his death Proxenus, an uncle of the deceased, produced a will according to the terms of which his own son Dicaeogenes III was adopted as son of the deceased and became heir to one-third of the estate. The rest of the estate was divided among the four sisters of the deceased who were next of kin. This distribution of the estate, though made without litigation, was sanctioned by the archon.[3] Twelve years later Dicaeogenes III produced another will according to which he was adopted as heir to the entire estate. A dicastery approved the will and the sisters lost their shares.[4]

---

[1] Demos. xliii. 4 ff.   [2] *Ibid.* 6.

[3] Isaeus v. 6: τῶν δὲ λοιπῶν ἑκάστη τὸ μέρος ἐπεδικάσατο τῶν Μενεξένου θυγατέρων.

[4] *Ibid.* 7 ff.

In a sense this is not a new trial as a jury did not "probate" the first will, but the estate was legally distributed.

In American courts new trials are constantly granted because of technical objections. Such objections played no part in Athenian courts. However, as it was the practice of litigants in arguing a special plea to deal with the whole case on its merits, a dicastery frequently heard the merits of a case discussed twice. But this does not amount to a new trial or a rehearing as we understand it.[1]

In certain cases a successful suit for perjury against an opponent's witnesses enabled the litigant to reopen the case. Suits for perjury (δίκαι ψευδομαρτυρίων) present some interesting problems which have not been satisfactorily solved. It seems desirable to review some of these difficulties at this point to enable the reader to understand the conditions under which the Athenian system regularly permitted a case to be retried.[2]

All suits for perjury must be announced and filed before the votes of the dicasts were counted.[3] As a result of this requirement a successful litigant might sue the witnesses of his opponent. Such a case is mentioned by a client of Lysias.[4] This case presents some unusual features that must have occurred but rarely. Lysistheus had accused Theomnestus of throwing away his shield. Theomnestus was acquitted but he sued Dionysius, one of the witnesses who had testified at the trial that the charge was true. Again he won and the witness was disfranchised. One can easily understand the motive back of the action of Theomnestus even if he was sure that the prosecution had failed when he denounced the witness. Any dereliction in one's military duty was a serious business. Politicians thought it worth while to try to injure

[1] Only in the process of legislation is an insistence upon a fixed meticulous procedure found. If this procedure was not observed the legislation could be attacked by a γραφὴ παρανόμων; cf. Gilbert, *op. cit.*, pp. 299–301.

[2] For the sake of convenience we speak of a δίκη ψευδομαρτυρίων as a suit for perjury, but the suit included not only false evidence but also illegal evidence; cf. Demos. xlvii. 1–3.

[3] Arist. *Ath. Pol.* lxviii. 4.   [4] x. 22 ff.; cf. Leisi, *op. cit.*, pp. 122 f.

an opponent's reputation by such charges where there was so far as we can see no chance of a conviction. Even an acquittal did not still suspicion.[1] Under these circumstances one can easily see that nothing would help so much to dispel any lingering suspicion as a verdict against one of the witnesses against him. It may very well have been the case that Theomnestus was taking no chance on the outcome of the case and was prepared to lay the basis for a new trial.

The lodging of an ἐπίσκηψις before the dicasts voted must have presented some difficulties to the litigant. Would his denunciation of witnesses show the dicasts that he had little confidence in his case? Or would the denunciation of witnesses injure the litigant who produced them?[2] The law seemed to encourage suits for perjury by inflicting no penalties beyond the loss of the fees in case of failure.[3]

The *timema* in perjury suits has caused some difficulties. Lipsius[4] was so much impressed by the emphasis laid upon deceiving the people in perjury cases that he argued that a false witness could be attacked by a γραφὴ συκοφαντίας. This conjecture has the advantage of accounting for penalties that are normally only associated with a *graphé*. But nowhere in the orators or other legal literature is there the slightest hint that anyone but a prosecutor was ever regarded as a sycophant. The hard-pressed defendant often sought to arouse the sympathy of the dicasts by exclaiming συκοφαντοῦμαι, but he is always referring to the tactics of his opponent and never to his witnesses.[5]

The *timema* is sometimes referred to in language that seems to indicate that *atimia* as well as damages could be inflicted for perjury.[6] The frequent use of ἁλίσκομαι instead of ὀφλισ-

---

[1] See the taunting words addressed to Theomnestus by the present speaker (x. 9).

[2] Cf. Leisi, *op. cit.*, p. 126; Calhoun, *CP*, XI, 376, n. 7.

[3] Demos. xlvii. 2; cf. Lipsius, *op. cit.*, p. 783.

[4] *Op. cit.*, p. 782.   [5] Cf. Calhoun, *CP*, XI, 372.

[6] Demos. xxix. 16: δίκην ἄν μοι βλάβης ἔλαχεν, εἰ ψευδομαρτυρίων ὑπόδικον αὐτὸν ἐποίουν κατὰ τἀδελφοῦ οὐ προσῆκον, ἐν ᾗ καὶ περὶ χρημάτων καὶ περὶ ἀτιμίας ἄνθρωποι κινδυνεύουσιν. Antiph. ii. δ. 7: οἱ μὲν γὰρ ἀτιμοῦνταί τε καὶ χρήμασι ζημιοῦνται, ἐὰν μὴ τἀληθῆ δοκῶσι μαρτυρῆσαι.

κάνω points to a criminal rather than a civil suit.¹ It is a certainty that a man thrice "convicted" of perjury was disfranchised. It is generally agreed that this penalty was inflicted in accordance with a specific law.

There are two leading cases in which *atimia* is mentioned. Some clients of Isaeus were prosecuting one Leochares for perjury in an ἐπιδικασία. When the votes had been emptied out for counting it became apparent that Leochares had lost his case.² An agreement was reached by which Dicaeogenes, in whose behalf Leochares had committed perjury, gave up his claim to the estate. Later in the speech the plaintiffs claimed that it had been possible for them to have disfranchised the defendant: ἐγγενόμενον ἡμῖν αὐτὸν ἐπειδὴ εἵλομεν τῶν ψευδομαρτυρίων ἀτιμῶσαι οὐκ ἐβουλήθημεν.³ In itself this case presents no real difficulty. The *atimia* anticipated could very easily be the result of the inability of the defendant to pay the damages that might have been imposed. Even the talent asked as damages in *Apollodorus* v. *Stephanus*⁴ was a large sum of money quite beyond the means of the ordinary citizen. In the Theomnestus case in Lysias, already mentioned, the reference to *atimia* is not so easily explained,⁵ although several explanations are possible. Lipsius⁶ believes that in cases where *atimia* is mentioned the speaker has in mind nothing more than disfranchisement resulting from the defendant's inability to pay heavy damages. This *rednerische Übertreibung* is not uncommon in other cases where heavy fines or damages are likely to be incurred.⁷ But the difficulty in this case lies in the consideration that no jury would be likely to award heavy damages when the plaintiff had won

---

¹ Isaeus v. 14: ἐπειδὴ οἱ μάρτυρες ἑάλωσαν. Cf. Andoc. i. 7; Lysias xix. 4; Plato *Laws* xi. 937C; Hyper. ii. 12.

² Isaeus v. 17–18; for the difficulties raised by this passage as to the method of counting cf. Wyse, *The Speeches of Isaeus*, p. 423; Lipsius, *op. cit.*, p. 926, n. 98.

³ Isaeus v. 19.   ⁵ x. 22: τὸν μαρτυρήσαντα ἠτίμωσεν.

⁴ Demos. xlv. 46.   ⁶ *Op. cit.*, p. 256, n. 54.

⁷ Cf. Isoc. xvi. 47: τῶν γὰρ αὐτῶν τιμημάτων ἐπιγεγραμμένων οὐ περὶ τῶν αὐτῶν ἅπασιν ὁ κίνδυνός ἐστιν, ἀλλὰ τοῖς μὲν χρήματα κεκτημένοις περὶ ζημίας, τοῖς δ' ἀπόρως ὥσπερ ἐγὼ διακειμένοις περὶ ἀτιμίας.

his case and suffered no damage. It would be a case rather for the imposition of merely nominal damages. Böckh[1] long ago suggested that *atimia* could be imposed by the dicasts as an additional penalty, προστίμημα. This view has found considerable favor,[2] but there are objections to it. Lipsius points out that so far as we know *atimia* was always imposed by law and not by the verdict of the dicasts. Coming back to the Lysias case,[3] we find that had Theomnestus been convicted of throwing away his shield on the evidence of the witness Dionysius, he would have suffered *atimia*.[4] This situation at once suggests that a witness whose false evidence exposed a citizen to *atimia* himself suffered *atimia* upon conviction. It may have been part of the same law that imposed *atimia* for the third offense.[5] It is true that both Andocides and Hyperides speak of *atimia* only for the third offense, but this need not invalidate the suggestion.

A successful perjury suit, whether the damages were nominal or substantial, was a necessary step toward a suit for subornation of perjury (δίκη κακοτεχνιῶν) against the litigant who produced false testimony.[6] Beyond these general statements nothing is known about the suit. It may be surmised that as in a δίκη ψευδομαρτυρίων the main case would be again argued before the jury, but in neither instance is there a real retrial of the case.

---

[1] *Kleine Schriften*, IV, 123.

[2] Wyse, *op. cit.*, p. 426; Leisi, *op. cit.*, p. 132; Hermann-Thalheim, *Lehrbuch der Griechischen Rechtsaltertümer*[4], p. 136, n. 3.

[3] x; cf. *supra*, pp. 261 f.   [4] Cf. Andoc. i. 74.

[5] There is no doubt that *atimia* was the immediate result of the conviction, as is shown by Lysias x. 24–25 (trans. Lamb): "Remember that there you have presented him with a rich and goodly gift [his success in securing the condemnation and disfranchisement of Dionysius, the other witness in the previous trial]: in that respect, who would not pity Dionysius for the disaster that overtook him, after he had proved himself a man of the highest valour in times of danger, who on leaving the court remarked that that was our most calamitous campaign, in which many of us were killed, and those who saved their arms had been condemned for false witness at the suit of those who threw theirs away; and that it had been better for him to be killed on that day than return home to meet with such a fate?" (i.e. *atimia*).

[6] Demos. xlvii. 1; xlix. 56.

The immediate effect of a successful perjury suit upon the main case was not the same in all instances. Where a claim to an estate (ἐπιδικασία) was met by a *diamartyria* a conviction for perjury merely left the way open to press the claim in court.[1] The defeated party could still press his claims in a *diadikasia*.[2] A will was invalidated by convicting the witnesses of perjury.[3]

In cases involving the disposition of estates (κλήρων) in Athens there is evidence that convictions for perjury invalidated judgments and opened the way for new trials.[4] It is perhaps a matter of chance that there is no instance of a δίκη κακοτεχνιῶν in the extant forensic literature. In one case in Isaeus when one witness to a will had been convicted the holder under the will to which the witnesses testified compromised and agreed to yield up a portion of the estate involved.[5] In another case in Isaeus[6] a litigant says: "The law ordains that, if there is any conviction for perjury, the action claiming an estate must be heard over again." Plato[7] would allow a δίκη ἀνάδικος if more than half the witnesses were convicted of perjury. The scholiast on this passage says: οὐκ ἐπὶ πάντων δὲ τῶν ἀγώνων ἐγίγνοντο ἀνάδικοι αἱ κρίσεις, ἀλλ' ὥς φησι Θεόφραστος ἐν ζ' Νόμων, ἐπὶ μόνης ξενίας καὶ ψευδομαρτυριῶν καὶ κλήρων. It is generally believed that this list is not complete. The scholiast merely selects serious cases in which the defendant had lost his liberty, his citizen rights, or an estate carrying valuable family rights for which no damages in a δίκη ψευδομαρτυριῶν or a δίκη κακοτεχνιῶν would be adequate compensation. It has been conjectured that where life or liberty or citizenship rights or family property rights were involved a new trial was allowed as a result of a successful action for perjury.[8] There is no proof for this extremely plausible theory, for, as has been pointed out, the evidence for a

[1] Cf. Wyse in Whibley, *Companion to Greek Studies*, p. 397; Isaeus v. 17.

[2] Cf. Isaeus vi. 52; Leisi, *op. cit.*, p. 32; Lipsius, *op. cit.*, p. 856, n. 38.

[3] Isaeus v. 12 ff.   [5] v. 12–14, 17–18.

[4] *Ibid.*, 12–14; xi. 45–46.   [6] xi. 45–46.   [7] *Laws* xi. 937C–D.

[8] Leisi, *op. cit.*, p. 133; Lipsius, *op. cit.*, pp. 955 ff.

δίκη ἀνάδικος in the orators is limited to the disposition of estates. In support of this theory it has been pointed out[1] that upon the denunciation (ἐπίσκηψις) of a witness or witnesses in serious cases the penalty was not exacted until the perjury suit had been settled. But where the penalty consisted in damages it was enforced without waiting for the outcome of the perjury suit. The suspension of severe penalties points clearly to a possible remedy if the suit for perjury was successful. It is to be understood that the *atimia* in question must have been incurred by a legal enactment and was not merely the result of inability to pay a money penalty. A representative list of cases in which the penalty was complete *atimia* is given by Andocides (i. 74). In the following sections he gives examples of partial *atimia*: ἄλλοι αὖ κατὰ προστάξεις, οἵτινες οὐ παντάπασιν ἄτιμοι ἦσαν. It is not easy to see why the arguments, such as they are, for allowing a new trial in cases of complete *atimia* would not also apply to partial *atimia*.[2]

There are but slight indications in the sources regarding the number of witnesses to be convicted before a new trial could be granted. Plato[3] would require that more than one-half of the witnesses should be convicted of perjury before there could be a new trial. Moreover, there should be ἀμφισβήτησις and διαδικασία to determine how far the perjured testimony influenced the verdict of the jury.

Turning to the orators, we find the prosecution of witnesses often a matter of strategy to procure better terms from the winner of the suit.[4] As he was faced with a δίκη κακοτεχνιῶν

[1] Leisi, *op. cit.*, pp. 126 f.

[2] Lipsius (*op. cit.*, p. 957) conjectures that false testimony could be attacked in public cases by the original prosecutor or anyone else and a new trial allowed where a criminal escaped punishment by means of perjured testimony. Some support for this view is found in the fact that if the defendant in a γραφὴ ξενίας secured his acquittal by bribery, he could be attacked by an indictment for bribery (γραφὴ δωροξενίας (Arist. *Ath. Pol.* lix. 3). A successful prosecution for bribery would undoubtedly invalidate the verdict of the bribed dicasts.

[3] *Laws* xi. 937C–D; for the moment we defer the discussion of the applicability of Plato's suggestion to the Athenian system.

[4] Demos. xlvii. 49.

it was in his interest to protect his witnesses from prosecution. So the loser was sometimes able to obtain terms by dropping further prosecution of witnesses already denounced.[1]

On the basis of a statement in Isaeus[2] it has been argued that a judgment was nullified by the conviction of a single witness.[3] The passage is as follows: κελεύει δ' ὁ νόμος, ἐὰν ἀλῷ τις τῶν ψευδομαρτυρίων, πάλιν ἐξ ἀρχῆς εἶναι περὶ αὐτῶν τὰς λήξεις. Lipsius objects that the law "ist zu wenig präzis gefasst, um einen sicheren Schluss zu rechtfertigen"[4] and refers to perjury prosecutions in another case in Isaeus.[5] The case in outline is as follows.[6] When Dicaeogenes III produced a second will granting him all the estate of Dicaeogenes II, Polyaratus, husband of the eldest sister of Dicaeogenes II, made an ἐπίσκηψις but died πρὶν ἐπεξελθεῖν οἷς ἐπεσκήψατο τῶν μαρτύρων. Later Menexenus II, son of a sister of Dicaeogenes II, brought a successful action for perjury against Lycon, who had been one of the witnesses to the genuineness of the second will (ἐπεξήει τοῖς καταμαρτυρήσασιν ἡμῶν καὶ ἐκείνου τὰ ψευδῆ). Dicaeogenes III became alarmed and made a bargain with Menexenus to accept his share of the estate, abandon the other relatives, and τοὺς δὲ μήπω ἑαλωκότας τῶν μαρτύρων ἀφεῖναι. But Dicaeogenes III failed to carry out his part of the bargain and all the heirs joined in an attack on him ἐπειδὴ οἱ μάρτυρες ἑάλωσαν. The plural μάρτυρες is used here and in the following section, although the conviction of only one witness, Lycon, is mentioned. If the statement is correct, Menexenus II must have proceeded with the prosecution of the rest of the witnesses when he found the bargain was broken.[7] But whether all the witnesses were prosecuted or not makes little difference, for it was clearly the intention

---

[1] Isaeus v. 12–13.   [2] xi. 46.

[3] Gide and Caillemer, in Darem.-Saglio, s.v. ἀναδικία; Leisi, op. cit., p. 134.

[4] Op. cit., p. 958.   [5] v. 9, 12 ff.

[6] For a fuller statement cf. supra, p. 260.

[7] Wyse (op. cit., p. 421) seems to doubt the correctness of the plural, but Lipsius (op. cit., p. 958, n. 12) accepts it.

of both Polyaratus and Menexenus to prosecute more than
one witness.[1] But it will be readily granted that it is not the
number but the importance of the witness who gave false
testimony that counted in persuading the jury. Plato, as we
have seen,[2] wished to have the effect of the denounced testimony determined. Lipsius accepts Plato's suggestion regarding an inquiry into the effect of the denounced evidence upon
the verdict of the court:

> Wohl aber liesse sich denken, dass der Gerichtsvorstand, der für Haupt-
> und Zeugnisklage der gleiche war, darüber zu befinden oder eine Ent-
> scheidung der für letztere bestellten Richter herbeizuführen hatte, in-
> wieweit das bei dieser beigebrachte Beweismaterial eine Wiederaufnahme
> der Hauptsache rechtfertige.[3]

It is wholly contrary to the spirit of the Athenian judicial
system to delegate to any official real judicial powers such as
Lipsius contemplates. The alternative suggestion that the dicasts who condemned the witnesses should determine whether
the testimony did in fact influence the verdict in the main
issue would require two trials: the first to determine whether
the evidence denounced was in fact false and the second to
determine whether the false evidence was of such character
as to warrant a new trial. The only parallel to this double
trial is in the criminal cases where the dicasts after finding a
defendant guilty proceeded to determine the degree of punishment. But this parallel is too remote. The difficulty requires no such heroic treatment as the alternatives suggested
by Lipsius. It is much better to accept the law cited by
Isaeus[4] and conclude that the conviction of even one witness
was sufficient to warrant a new trial. It would be quite possible to find matters proved by witnesses in the extant
speeches that were so unimportant that they might easily
have been omitted. But we must remember that the litigant
had to think not only of convicting a witness of perjury but
of winning his case when he was granted a new trial. He
could not afford to reopen the case with the conviction of a

---

[1] Isaeus v. 9, 12 ff.   [2] *Supra*, p. 266.   [3] *Op. cit.*, p. 960.
[4] xi. 45, quoted *supra*, p. 265. Cf. Calhoun, *TAPA*, LXV (1934), 86.

wholly unimportant witness. Here is where the common sense
of an amateur system triumphs over our modern technicalities. It was, however, sound sense for a litigant to go to trial
with as many convictions for perjury as he could compass,
even if the law required only one.[1]

When a litigant lost a case by default he could, for good
and sufficient reasons, have the case reopened within two
months of the delivery of judgment. A claim that his absence
from court was unavoidable and justifiable must be supported by an oath. If the other party contested the claim, a
court would have to decide. If the defendant could not establish his claim, judgment given in default could be executed
forthwith. Otherwise the plaintiff had the right to renew
the suit. If the defendant claimed that his failure to appear
was due to the fact that he had not been properly summoned,
he had to bring a successful suit for false summons against the
individual who had made oath that he had duly summoned
the defendant. The γραφὴ ψευδοκλητείας was τίμητος. A third
conviction entailed *atimia*. Lipsius[2] gives the reader a wrong
impression when he says that the death penalty could be
inflicted. The case he cites was very unusual. In *Apollodorus*
v. *Nicostratus*[3] the plaintiff tells how he had on a former occasion prosecuted Arethusius, the brother of Nicostratus,
for ψευδοκλητεία. According to the story of Apollodorus, after
the indictment had been filed and the *anakrisis* had been
completed, Arethusius had destroyed his flower gardens and
had made an aggravated assault upon himself one night on
the way between the city and the Piraeus. After the conviction of the defendant the dicasts, evidently incensed by the
story of the murderous assault, tried to induce Apollodorus
to change his *timema* to the death penalty, but in the end accepted the penalty of a talent offered by the defendant. The
passage is as follows: καὶ ἐν τῇ τιμήσει βουλομένων τῶν δικαστῶν θανάτου τιμῆσαι αὐτῷ, ἐδεήθην μὲν ἐγὼ τῶν δικαστῶν μηδὲν
δι' ἐμοῦ τοιοῦτον πρᾶξαι, ἀλλὰ συγχωρῆσαι ὅσον περ αὐτοὶ

[1] Cf. Leisi, *op. cit.*, pp. 134–35.

[2] *Op. cit.*, p. 447.   [3] Demos. liii. 17–18, 26.

ἐτιμῶντο, ταλάντου.[1] There is no indication here that Apollodorus had ever asked for the death penalty. If the jury had condemned the defendant to death it would have been only because pressure was put by the dicasts upon Apollodorus to change his *timema* to one of death. But when he says he refused to ask for the death penalty because he did not wish that it could be said that he, a naturalized citizen, was the cause of the death of a native Athenian, it seems clear that he had not demanded the death penalty. He had already entered the *timema* before the aggravated assault and destruction of property which alone could have justified such a severe penalty. Consequently, it is misleading to say that a simple case of γραφὴ ψευδοκλητείας might carry the death penalty. The actual penalty in the only extant case was one talent.

The incident shows, in spite of obvious exaggeration, that individual dicasts might in considerable numbers protest against the proposed penalties of the prosecutor and the defendant and ask for something different. But such participation by the dicasts does not amount to an official participation in an increase or decrease in the penalty proposed by the prosecution.

[1] Demos. liii. 18; cf. *infra*, p. 274.

CHAPTER X

EXECUTION OF JUDGMENTS

When the verdict of a court required a defeated litigant to pay anything to the plaintiff in the way of damages or debt, it was the business of the successful litigant to execute the judgment.[1] In the case of a successful *apographé* also it was the business of the prosecutor to recover the property. This provision was no doubt due to the fact that the prosecutor received three-fourths of the property recovered.[2] Otherwise confiscations were the business of public officials.

If the subject of a suit was the ownership of a particular piece of property, personal or real, the loser was granted a fixed period of time within which to make restoration. If he failed to do so, he became $\dot{\upsilon}\pi\epsilon\rho\dot{\eta}\mu\epsilon\rho\sigma s$ and the winner might seize personal property or make formal entry upon real estate ($\dot{\epsilon}\mu\beta\dot{\alpha}\tau\epsilon\upsilon\sigma\iota s$). If the formal entry was not recognized, the litigant could bring an action of ejectment or ouster ($\delta\dot{\iota}\kappa\eta$ $\dot{\epsilon}\xi\sigma\dot{\upsilon}\lambda\eta s$). Thus a successful suit was not infrequently the cause of more litigation. The experience of Demosthenes with his guardians is a good example. First Demosthenes obtained a verdict against one of them, Aphobus, for ten talents.[3] Aphobus tried unsuccessfully to convict Phanus, one of Demosthenes' witnesses, of perjury.[4] If the prosecution had been successful, it could have been used by Aphobus and the other guardians to effect a favorable settlement; or if Demosthenes sued the other guardians, the verdict against the witness would have been a formidable weapon for the defense. The next step was Demosthenes' entry upon a piece of real estate. Onetor, the brother-in-law of Aphobus, claimed that the property was pledged to him as security for

---

[1] For the possible participation of the demarch cf. *supra*, I, 322.

[2] Cf. Lipsius, *Das Attische Recht*, pp. 299 ff., 944.

[3] xxvii–xxviii.   [4] xxix.

the dower of his sister, the divorced wife of Aphobus. The final step was an action of ejectment against Onetor to test his claim.[1]

Assaults not infrequently resulted from attempts to execute judicial judgments. Naturally, a defeated defendant was more likely to resist the plaintiff whom he regarded as his personal enemy than an officer of the court backed by the law. Consequently, they sometimes came to blows, and resultant actions for assault and battery were frequent. Two excellent examples of such cases occur in a Demosthenic speech. The speaker was charged by the state with recovering some ship's gear from one Theophemus. Being authorized by law to make a seizure, he did so and came to blows with Theophemus. The speaker later filed a suit for assault and battery.[2] Theophemus responded with a cross-action of the same nature. The latter came to trial first, and the verdict of the court was in favor of Theophemus, who in due time proceeded to collect the damages awarded. If the story of the speaker[3] is to be believed, the men making this seizure for Theophemus invaded the quarters of the women and killed an old freedwoman who had tried to resist them. This was of course a most unusual case in so far as the homicide was concerned.[4]

Banishment was a severe punishment in the ancient world. A man expelled from the social and political group to which he belonged found great difficulty in establishing himself.[5] A court might in some cases sentence a defendant to *atimia*, full or partial loss of civil rights. For example, partial *atimia* was the penalty for failure on the part of a prosecutor to

---

[1] xxx–xxxi.

[2] xlvii. 45; cf. 39 *et supra*.

[3] *Ibid.* 52 ff.

[4] Cf. *supra*, pp. 217 ff.

[5] The nearest approach to banishment in the modern world is the deportation of undesirable aliens. This form of punishment for criminal aliens is not uncommon in the United States. Banishment for life or a term of years was practiced at Athens in homicide cases (cf. *supra*, I, 118 ff.). A man who evaded trial for a serious offense was normally condemned to death *in absentia*. He might, like Alcibiades, be pardoned eventually, but in the meantime he lived in exile. An exile who returned without due permission before the allotted time elapsed was liable to the death penalty.

obtain at least one-fifth of the votes in a criminal case or to carry through a prosecution once begun. He was forbidden by law to engage in similar prosecutions in the future. It is not known how such punishments were enforced. Magistrates and judicial boards intrusted with criminal prosecutions might be furnished with a list of such penalized prosecutors, in which case it would be an easy matter to refuse their indictments. In any event, if such a prosecutor's indictment was accepted, we may be sure that the defendant or his friends would become aware of his predicament and insist that the indictment be quashed. Naturally, it would help the alleged criminal only for the moment as there were plenty of qualified prosecutors to conclude the prosecution if the evidence warranted it.[1]

In cases of *atimia* either imposed by the courts or arising from failure to pay a fine, the enforcement of the penalty frequently gave rise to further litigation in the form of *endeixis* against a man exercising forbidden rights. Andocides selects some for special mention to show how varied they were. The list includes deprivation of the right to be a councilor, to bring a public suit, to speak in the assembly, to enter the market place, to sail to the Hellespont or to Ionia. The number of persons laboring under these and other disabilities was considerable, as may be inferred from the practice of pardoning them in times of great national danger.[2] Athens possessed no police force to enforce these restrictions. Indeed, no conceivable force in the fifth century B.C., except possibly the Spartan secret police (κρυπτεία), could have been effective. The volunteer prosecutor in the guise of an informer animated by personal or political hostility was under the circumstances the most efficient instrument available.

Pains and penalties were either fixed by law (ἀτίμητοι) or determined by the court (τιμητοί). It is indicative of the popular character of Athenian criminal justice that a choice of penalties was given the jury in the majority of cases. The

---

[1] Cf. Antiph. vi. 36 f. for an attempt to disqualify by a charge of homicide a particularly dangerous prosecutor.

[2] Andoc. i. 73 ff.

trial of Socrates furnishes a good example of what could happen in an Athenian trial. The prosecutor and the defendant each proposed a penalty, between which the dicasts must choose. There was no further alternative. But the convicted defendant might change his recommended penalty, as did Socrates upon the advice of friends.[1] The prosecutor also could change the penalty originally set down.

> When it came to the question of punishment, the jurors were inclined to pass sentence of death upon him; I begged them, however, not to do anything of the sort at my instance, but to consent to the fine which they themselves proposed, a talent—not that I had any desire to spare Arethusius, (for he well deserved death for what he had done to me,) but that it might not be said, that I, the son of Pasion, who had been created citizen by a decree of the people, had caused the death of an Athenian.[2]

The jurors here tried to put pressure on Apollodorus to change his original *timema*. They themselves could not change it.[3]

Corporal punishments were exacted by the state. The first Athenian code was found to be too severe. Solon was undoubtedly expressing current public opinion especially of the lower classes when he

> repealed the laws of Draco, all except those concerning homicide, because they were too severe and their penalties too heavy. For one penalty was assigned to almost all transgressions, namely death, so that even those convicted of idleness were put to death, and those who stole salad or fruit received the same punishment as those who committed sacrilege or murder. . . . . And Draco himself, they say, being asked why he made death the penalty for most offenses, replied that in his opinion the lesser ones deserved it, and for the greater ones no heavier penalty could be found.[4]

Later ages approved the abolition of the Draconian severity as is shown by the epigram of Demades, a contemporary of Demosthenes much given to phrase-making: "Draco's laws were written not with ink, but with blood."[5] The impression made by Demades' epigram is shown by its application to the indictments of that stern and righteous prosecutor Lycurgus,

[1] Plato *Apol.* 38B.   [3] Cf. Lipsius, *op. cit.*, pp. 253 f.

[2] Demos. liii. 18.   [4] Plut. *Solon.* xvii.   [5] *Ibid.*

who was said to have written his indictments "not in ink but in death."[1]

Imprisonment at Athens was both precautionary and penal. It is an accepted fact that persons accused of flagrant crimes were incarcerated until their trial and criminals condemned to death were imprisoned until execution.[2] But the use of imprisonment as a penalty for crime among the Athenians has been generally denied by scholars.[3] Barkan, however, strongly affirms that imprisonment was used as a penalty in itself.[4] It was clearly an additional penalty inflicted upon a thief,[5] and persons sentenced to a fine could be incarcerated until the fine was paid.[6] A state debtor who failed to pay his debt by the appointed time could be imprisoned. If he persevered in his refusal to pay, he could be kept in prison indefinitely, even for life; this imprisonment would, in fact, constitute his punishment. It is logical to suppose, therefore, that imprisonment was regarded as an alternative penalty.[7]

Demosthenes speaks of imprisonment as a corporal penalty: "In the first place, men of the jury, it would not have been lawful for you to determine what penalties corporal or pecuniary a man should suffer [ὅ τι χρὴ παθεῖν ἢ ἀποτεῖσαι], for in the expression 'corporal penalty' is included imprisonment [ἐν γὰρ τῷ παθεῖν καὶ ὁ δεσμὸς ἔνι]."[8] In the same speech he says: "People have been imprisoned ere now both for debts and upon judgments [καίτοι καὶ ἐπὶ χρήμασιν ἤδη τινὲς

[1] Ps.-Plut. *Vita Lycurgi* 10.

[2] Antiph. v. 69; Xen. *Hell.* i. 7; Plut. *Phocion* xxxvi.

[3] Schoemann, *Gr. Alterth.*, I, 533; Thonissen, *Le droit pénal de la république athénienne*, p. 114; Thalheim, in Pauly-Wissowa, *s.v.* δεσμωτήριον; Gilbert, *Const. Antiq.*, p. 414.

[4] *CP*, XXXI, 338 ff.

[5] Demos. xxiv. 105; cf. Barkan for the argument that ἐν ποδοκάκκῃ δεδέσθαι and ἐν ξύλῳ δεδέσθαι are the same and refer not to exposure in public in an uncomfortable position but to harsher punishment within the prison walls.

[6] Demos. xxi. 47; cf. xxv. 46; xxxiii. 1; liii. 11; lvi. 4.

[7] There are many references to the unpleasantness of long imprisonments (*ibid.* xxiv. 125, 135; xxv. 61; Dinarchus ii. 2).

[8] xxiv. 146.

ἐδέθησαν καὶ ἐπὶ κρίσεσιν]."¹ The author of the speech
Against Alcibiades, attributed to Andocides, lists imprisonment in the category of penalties such as exile and death.²
And again in Demosthenes the speaker says: "For the courts
of justice decide all questions that are brought to trial and
they are empowered to pass sentence of imprisonment or any
other sentence that they please."³ When Socrates was asked
to propose a counterpenalty he says: "What penalty shall I
propose? Imprisonment? And why should I live in prison
[καὶ τί με δεῖ ζῆν ἐν δεσμωτηρίῳ], a slave to those who may be in
authority?"⁴ Here Socrates is clearly referring to life-im-
prisonment, and he goes on to say that a money fine would be
the same thing (ταὐτόν) for, having no money, he would have
to remain in prison.⁵ And Lysias remarks: "For Andocides
. . . . committed himself to prison having assessed the penalty at imprisonent if he failed to hand over his attendant."⁶
All of these passages, together with the frequent use of the
word τιμησάμενος, seem to furnish conclusive evidence that
imprisonment was a normal penalty in Athens. When the
evidence is weighed, concludes Barkan,⁷ it seems indisputable
that imprisonment was a penalty per se in Athens and was
probably used even more frequently than the sources indicate.

The death penalty was obligatory in the case of murder,⁸
high treason, temple robbery, κακουργήματα which included
κλέπται, λωποδύται, ἀνδραποδισταί, τοιχωρύχοι, and βαλαντιοτόμοι,⁹ and certain offenses in connection with the grain
supply.¹⁰

---

¹ *Ibid.* 132; cf. 92; li. 4.

² Andoc. iv. 3 f. The fact that the speech is spurious does not detract seriously
from its authority in a statement of this nature; cf. Jebb, *Attic Orators*, pp. 131 f.;
Blass, *Attische Beredsamkeit*, pp. 332 ff.

³ xxiv. 151.   ⁵ Cf. Schanz *ad loc.*   ⁷ *Op. cit.*, p. 341.

⁴ Plato *Apol.* 37C.   ⁶ vi. 21.   ⁸ Cf. Lipsius, *op. cit.*, p. 603.

⁹ Cf. *ibid.*, p. 78; *supra*, pp. 214 f. In the case of κακουργήματα the death penalty
was obligatory only if the criminal confessed (Arist. *Ath. Pol.* lii. 1).

¹⁰ Demos. xxxiv. 37; xxxv. 50; Lycurg. i. 27. It seems clear that death was the
penalty by law for treason, though the dicasts may have had to determine sometimes

Stoning was a natural form of community vengeance upon a public wrongdoer who had openly injured the community.[1] It was originally a form of community self-help in which even the unarmed men and the women could participate. There are references to stoning in the Heroic period;[2] they are all examples of community self-help. Some appearance of judicial action was taken in Argos before stoning for a military offense. In Thucydides' account of the attempted stoning of Thrasyllus, the Argive general, there is a hint that military offenders were tried and stoned if found guilty.[3] Euripides[4] represents the city of Argos as voting in assembly whether or not Orestes and his sister should be stoned to death (εἰ χρὴ θανεῖν νὼ λευσίμῳ πετρώματι). There is no indication that stoning was ever a legal punishment in Athens. The instances of community stoning mentioned can only be classified as lynching.[5]

It is interesting to note that Plato in the Laws harks back to early Greece and introduces stoning in a curious form in his ideal state where slayers of mothers, fathers, children, and brothers are concerned:

> If any man be convicted of such a murder, and of having slain any of the persons named, the officers of the judges and magistrates shall kill him and cast him out naked at an appointed cross-roads outside the city; and all the magistrates, acting on behalf of the whole State, shall take each a stone and cast it on the head of the corpse.[6]

It is the community character of the punishment that appealed to Plato, as may be seen in the provision that each

---

just what constituted treason (Thuc. i. 138. 6; Xen. Hell. i. 7. 20–22; Demos. xviii. 38; xx. 79).

[1] Hirzel ("Die Strafe der Steinigung," Abhandlung d. Königl. Sächs. Gesellsch. d. Wissensch., LVII, 225 ff.) has collected and studied all the instances of stoning in the ancient world. Barkan (Capital Punishment in Ancient Athens, pp. 41 ff.) has confined himself to the Greek instances of stoning.

[2] Cf. supra, I, 26, 206.

[3] Thuc. v. 60; cf. Hirzel, op. cit., p. 238.   [4] Orestes 46 ff.

[5] Plut. Solon xii; schol. on Aristoph. Knights 447. For the confusion of names in Herod. ix. 5 and Demos. xviii. 204 cf. Barkan. op. cit., p. 45, n. 2; cf. the proposed stoning of Dicaeopolis in the Acharnians 295.

[6] 873B (trans. Bury).

magistrate shall cast a stone in behalf of the citizens to free the community from pollution. There is no indication that the culprit was executed by stoning.

Three different methods of inflicting the death penalty in Athens are mentioned in the sources. They are precipitation into the *barathron* or a convenient rocky chasm,[1] *apotympanismos* (ἀποτυμπανισμός), and poisoning by hemlock (κώνειον). In the following pages the order in which these punishments were introduced and the nature of *apotympanismos* will be discussed.[2]

Execution by precipitation from a high rock or tower into a chasm was a primitive and widespread practice which can be authenticated for several places. Pausanias[3] says that there was a law in Elis to the effect that any woman found at the Olympic games was to be cast from Mount Typaeum. Similarly, criminals were thrown from a high rock in Delphi,[4] in Sparta,[5] and in Thessaly.[6] Though there is no recorded case of legal execution in Athens at any time by casting condemned criminals into the *barathron*, it is very likely that it was so used. The killing of the envoys of Darius by hurling them into the *barathron* suggests at once that the Athenians treated them as they did their own condemned criminals.[7]

The lack of any definite statement regarding the *barathron* has led some scholars to believe that the *barathron* was not used as a place of execution but as a receptacle for the bodies of criminals otherwise executed.[8] There are three passages

---

[1] This method of execution has been denied by some authorities.

[2] The question of the disposal of the bodies of executed criminals (cf. Hager *Jour. of Phil.*, VIII, 1 ff.), the prohibition of burial in Attica, and the location of the *barathron* and the *orygma* are beyond the scope of this discussion.

[3] v. 6. 7.

[4] Aeschin. ii. 142; cf. Plut. *Moral.* 557A, who tells of the execution of Aesop at Delphi.

[5] Paus. iv. 18. 4.

[6] Zenob. 87: ἐν Θεσσαλίᾳ τόπος ἐστὶ Κόρακες, ὅπου τοὺς κακούργους ἐνέβαλλον.

[7] Herod. vii. 133.

[8] Cf. Barkan, *op. cit.*, p. 60, for the literature and a discussion of the problem. Cf. Gernet, *REG*, XXXVII, 268 ff., for a complete refutation of the view that the *barathron* was never used as a place of execution.

involved in the problem. Miltiades was brought to trial on a capital charge of deceiving the people; Xanthippus was the prosecutor.[1] In referring to this trial Plato says: Μιλτιάδην δὲ τὸν Μαραθῶνι εἰς τὸ βάραθρον ἐμβαλεῖν ἐψηφίσαντο.[2] On the face of it, the statement seems to mean that Miltiades, if convicted, was to be executed by being cast into the *barathron*. If it merely means that his body was to be disposed of by being thrown into the *barathron*, why was a vote necessary to authorize it?[3] Moreover, the following words, καὶ εἰ μὴ διὰ τὸν πρύτανιν, ἐνέπεσεν ἄν, clearly indicate that the *prytaneis* saved him from death, for he was fined, not executed. Xenophon, in speaking of the so-called decree of Cannonus, uses the words ἀποθανεῖν εἰς τὸ βάραθρον ἐμβληθέντα.[4] Here there is no doubt of the meaning of the Greek.[5]

All indications point to the *barathron* as the earliest form of legal execution in Athens. An ancient scholiast and a number of the lexicographers[6] describe the *barathron* as a rocky chasm fitted with spikes and hooks. It would seem that they were designed to tear and lacerate the body so as to insure death.

The next method of inflicting capital punishment to be discussed is known as ἀποτυμπανισμός. Until recently it has been interpreted as "beating to death with a club."[7] In a book published in 1923, however, Keramopoullos presents an entirely different view, based upon excavations in Phalerum. In one grave were found seventeen skeletons with iron collars

---

[1] Herod. vi. 136, quoted *supra*, I, 207.   [3] Cf. Gernet, *op. cit.*, p. 271.

[2] *Gorgias* 516E.   [4] *Hell.* i. 7. 20, quoted *supra*, I, 205.

[5] The MS reading is ἀποθανόντα εἰς τὸ βάραθρον ἐμβληθῆναι. However, the scholiast on Aristoph. *Eccl.* 1081 quotes Xenophon as reading ἀποθανεῖν εἰς τὸ βάραθρον ἐμβληθέντα, which is adopted by both the Oxford and the Teubner texts. Those who believe that the *barathron* was not a place of execution accept the MS reading and regard the *Gorgias* passage as inconclusive.

[6] Schol. on Aristoph. *Plutus* 431; Suidas, Photius, *s.v.* μητραγύρτης; Pollux viii. 71; Harpocration, *s.v.* βάραθρον.

[7] Cf. Lipsius, *op. cit.*, p. 77, n. 101; Caillemer, in Darem.-Saglio, *s.v.*; Thalheim, in Pauly-Wissowa, *s.v.* Hermann-Thalheim (*Gr. Rechtsalt.*, p. 141, n. 5) adopt the view of Pollux viii. 71 that τύμπανον or τύπανον was the "machine" upon which the condemned criminal was bound for execution.

around their necks and cramp irons to which bits of wood still adhered about their ankles and wrists. Keramopoullos believes that they were executed criminals.[1] There are several possible methods of execution with these implements. The new Liddell and Scott *Lexicon* translates ἀποτυμπανισμὸς as "crucifixion." According to Herodotus,[2] the Athenians crucified a Persian enemy who had by impious deeds polluted a temple. The words ζῶντα πρὸς σανίδα διεπασσάλευσαν[3] mean "crucify" in the oriental manner by driving spikes through the hands and feet. For this meaning of διαπασσαλεύω is quite clear in a passage in Aristophanes[4] where the word is used of a skin pegged out on the ground. But there is no evidence that the Athenians ever crucified their own criminals in this manner.

Keramopoullos, however, from archaeological evidence reconstructs an execution of the following fashion.[5] The criminal was stripped and fastened to a wide, upright plank by means of five iron bands encircling his ankles, wrists, and neck. From the condition of the skeletons it would seem that the neck-band was the tightest and supported most of the weight of the body. Thus the criminal hung for many days, exposed to heat and cold, hunger and thirst, birds and insects, until he finally expired, his agony having been prolonged inhumanly because no blood was let as in a Roman crucifixion. Keramopoullos remarks that this form of punishment was altogether unworthy of the Athenian civilization, and he explains its existence by saying that it was not a product of the great period of fifth-century Athens but of ancient times.

---

[1] Ὁ Ἀποτυμπανισμὸς (Βιβλιοθήκη τῆς ἐν Ἀθήναις Ἀρχαιολογικῆς Ἑταιρείας, No. 22). Gernet (*op. cit.*, pp. 261 ff.) completely accepts the conclusions of Keramopoullos regarding *apotympanismos*. Keramopoullos' findings, however, are vigorously attacked on archaeological grounds by Arvanitopoulos, Μέθοδος πρὸς ἔρευναν τοῦ Ἀττικοῦ ποινικοῦ δικαίου (Volo, 1923).

[2] vii. 33.   [3] Cf. ix. 120: σανίδι προσπασσαλεύσαντες ἀνεκρέμασαν.

[4] *Knights* 369–71:   ἡ βύρσα σου θρανεύσεται.
δερῶ σε θύλακον κλοπῆς.
διαπατταλευθήσει χαμαί.

[5] *Op. cit.*, pp. 108 ff.

This harsh and inhuman law was a part of an ancient legislation which, for general traditional reasons in later times, the Athenians preserved with reverence and firmness as a shield of their democratic organization. It seems preferable, however, to regard death as brought about by strangulation rather than by a bloodless crucifixion.

There is in Aristophanes[1] an excellent burlesque of *apotympanismos*. Mnesilochus, on being discovered among the female celebrants of the Thesmophoria, is fastened by order of the *prytanis* to some kind of upright wooden contrivance called σάνις or τύμπανον.[2] The one who fastened him up is ordered to mount guard and allow no one to approach. Mnesilochus asks the guard to loosen the nail and then complains that instead of loosening he has tightened it.[3] Later Mnesilochus complains that he is dying with throat-cutting agonies.[4] On the basis of these words we might conclude that the criminal condemned to death by *apotympanismos* was strangled by tightening with a ἧλος a collar such as Keramopoullos discovered. A similar modern method of execution is the Spanish garotte.[5]

It is worth while to re-examine the literary sources to see whether there is any evidence to show how soon death occurred. Plutarch[6] reports a story by Duris, the Samian, to the effect that when Pericles reduced Samos in 439 B.C. he had the Samian officers and marines fastened to planks (σανίσι προσδήσας) and exposed to the public. At the end of ten days their skulls were crushed. It is clear that this was not a case of *apotympanismos*. The word προσδήσας suggests rather a

---

[1] *Thesmoph.* 930 ff.; cf. Gernet, *op. cit.*, p. 264, n. 1.

[2] Cf. *Thesmoph.* 1123 f. and the use of κρεμάζω in 1026, 1053, 1110.

[3] 1003 f.: χάλασον τὸν ἧλον. . . . . οἴμοι κακοδαίμων, μᾶλλον ἐπικρούεις σύ γε.

[4] 1053 f.: ὡς ἐκρεμάσθην λαιμότμητ' ἄχη.

[5] Webster, *Unabridged Dictionary, s.v.* "Garotte": "A Spanish mode of execution by strangulation, with an iron collar affixed to a post and tightened by a screw until life becomes extinct."

[6] *Pericles* xxviii.

parallel to fastening in the stocks.[1] Aristophanes[2] speaks distinctly of nails in his burlesque of *apotympanismos*, and Demosthenes[3] uses προσηλῶσθαι as a synonym of ἀποτυμπανίζεσθαι. Plutarch refuses to believe the story of Duris and says it was invented by Duris to throw discredit upon the Athenians. If the Athenians practiced *apotympanismos* as Keramopoullos conceives it, why did the execution of the Samians in the manner described by Plutarch seem a discredit to the Athenians? We can only conclude that in Plutarch's mind the cruelty consisted in the long duration of the execution. But Keramopoullos' reconstruction of *apotympanismos* is even more cruel.

The execution of the poet Antiphon by *apotympanismos* at the hands of Dionysius the tyrant is of interest. Aristotle, speaking of shame, says:

> And they are more likely to be ashamed when they have to be seen and to associate openly with those who are aware of their disgrace. Wherefore the tragic poet Antiphon, when he was about ἀποτυμπανίζεσθαι by order of Dionysius, seeing that those who were to die with him covered their faces as they passed through the gates, said, "Why cover your faces? Is it because you are afraid that one of the crowd should see you tomorrow?"[4]

Does Aristotle mean that by the morrow, being dead, they would no longer feel shame at the prospect of a disgraceful death? This seems to be the natural meaning of the passage.[5]

On archaeological grounds Keramopoullos dates the graves as pre-Solonian and regards this type of punishment as an

---

[1] According to a law of Solon, if the ecclesia denied an appeal it had the authority to add five days in the stocks as an additional penalty. It was no doubt a severe and ignominious punishment, but there was no intention that it should result in the death of the criminal; cf. Demos. xxiv. 105; *supra*, I, 179. δέω is also the normal word for imprisonment because no doubt the prisoners were always put in irons, as in the case of Socrates in Plato *Phaedo* 59E–60B.

[2] *Thesmoph.* 1003.   [3] xxi. 105.   [4] *Rhet.* ii. 6. 27.

[5] Cf. Barkan, *op. cit.*, pp. 66 ff. It must be recognized that the passage in Aristotle may mean that once fastened to the death plank they would no longer be able to cover their heads in shame for they would be naked. Aeschin. ii. 181 f., cited *infra*, p. 286, proves nothing concerning the duration of suffering.

innovation of Draco.[1] If the date of Keramopoullos be accepted, how are we to account for the proposed execution of Miltiades at a later period by precipitation into the *barathron?* The situation with regard to capital punishment may be reconstructed as follows. In the pre-Draconian period the *barathron* was used as a place of execution. In the early legislation, perhaps that of Solon when all the laws of Draco except those dealing with homicide were repealed, *apotympanismos* was introduced as another means of execution.[2] At a later period the decree of Cannonus[3] was passed specifying the death penalty by precipitation into the *barathron* in cases where the ecclesia voted to apply it. It was well known in 406 B.C. as a form of trial and execution where the accused had aroused the indignation of the populace. That the decree of Cannonus was notorious, as Xenophon says,[4] is also clear from the scene in the *Ecclesiazusae*[5] which would otherwise have been unintelligible to the Athenian audience:

> τουτὶ τὸ πρᾶγμα κατὰ τὸ Καννωνοῦ σαφῶς
> ψήφισμα, βινεῖν δεῖ με διαλελημμένον.

Here Aristophanes has reference to the form of the trial and not to the punishment. But there are other references to the *barathron* as a place of execution still in use in the latter part of the fifth century. Plutarch[6] reports that on leaving the assembly, where a measure of importance to the city and sponsored by Themistocles had been defeated, Aristides said that "there was no safety for the Athenians unless they threw both Themistocles and himself into the *barathron*." Whether

---

[1] Here again Arvanitopoulos (*op. cit.*, pp. 17–22) refuses to follow the dating of Keramopoullos because of the unscientific manner in which the various excavations were conducted.

[2] The earliest-known certain instance of *apotympanismos* occurred during the Sicilian Expedition, when the eldest brother of Agoratus was caught making signals to the enemy and by order of the general Lamachus was executed by *apotympanismos* (Lysias xiii. 67).

[3] Cf. *supra*, I, 205.

[4] *Hell.* i. 7. 20: ἴστε δὲ, ὦ ἄνδρες Ἀθηναῖοι, πάντες ὅτι τὸ Καννωνοῦ ψήφισμά ἐστιν ἰσχυρότατον.

[5] 1089–90.   [6] *Aristides* iii.

a trial or a lynching was contemplated, the *barathron* was conceived of as a place of death. In the *Knights*,[1] Agoracritus questions the reformed Demus:

AGORACRITUS: But answer this;
                If any scurvy advocate should say,
                "Now please remember, justices, ye'll have
                No barley, if the prisoner gets off free,"
                How would you treat that scurvy advocate?

DEMUS: I'd tie Hyperbolus about his neck,
                And hurl him down into the Deadman's Pit.

Gernet[2] regards the tying of Hyperbolus to the neck of the advocate as referring possibly to the use of a weight to insure death of the precipitated criminal or some other detail of the execution. In any event, it is the death of the advocate and not the disposition of his body that is contemplated. In the *Clouds*,[3] and likewise in the *Plutus*,[4] when references are made to the *barathron* it is suicide which is contemplated. All these references to the *barathron* are quite intelligible when one reflects that in the time of Aristophanes there was always the possibility that it might be used as a place of execution by vote of the ecclesia as was proposed in 406 B.C.

Poisoning by the administration of hemlock (κώνειον) was used and possibly introduced by the Thirty. The evidence adduced by Lipsius[5] is not very strong. Hemlock is mentioned by Aristophanes in the *Frogs*,[6] produced in 405 B.C., as a means of committing suicide used by women.[7] Hence the view that execution by poison was, as Gernet and Glotz put it, *suicide par tolérance*.[8] If hemlock was introduced by the Thirty it must have received legal recognition in the legislation of the restored democracy. Socrates was executed by

---

[1] 1357 ff. Hager (*Jour. of Phil.*, VIII, 1 ff.) believes that here and in other passages Aristophanes used *barathron* only in a metaphorical sense.

[2] *Op. cit.*, p. 271, n. 4.   [3] 1450.   [4] 431.

[5] *Op. cit.*, p. 77, n. 101; cf. Barkan, *op. cit.*, p. 77.

[6] 117 ff. When Dionysus is seeking a path to the lower world, hanging, leaping from a high tower, and hemlock are all recommended.

[7] 1051.   [8] Gernet, *op. cit.*, p. 267; Glotz, *L'Ordalie*, p. 91.

hemlock in 399 B.C., and a certain Menestratus was executed by *apotympanismos* a considerable time after the overthrow of the Thirty.[1] Hemlock became the normal method of execution,[2] and *apotympanismos* was reserved for certain types of crime specified by law. It is altogether unlikely that a prosecutor could demand a certain kind of execution. In the indictment of Socrates the *timema* is death. It is true, however, than the court may have decided whether the crime charged did in fact fall within the category punishable by *apotympanismos* or by hemlock.

It is difficult to construct from the sources a list of crimes punishable by *apotympanismos*.[3] Normally we are simply told that a man was put to death, but in a few cases the manner of his execution is specified. A client of Lysias says that two of the brothers of Agoratus were executed by *apotympanismos:*

> Now Agoratus, gentlemen, had three brothers. One of them, the eldest, was caught in Sicily making traitorous signals to the enemy, and by Lamachus' order he was executed on the plank. . . . . The third was arrested here by Phaenippides as a clothes-stealer [λωποδύτην ἀπήγαγε], and you tried him in your court: you condemned him to death, and consigned him to execution on the plank.[4]

The use of the word λωποδύτης, cloak-snatcher, at once suggests the class of criminals known as malefactors (κακοῦργοι), which included thieves (κλέπται), kidnappers (ἀνδραποδισταί), house-breakers (τοιχωρύχοι), purse-snatchers (βαλαντιοτόμοι), and cloak-snatchers (λωποδύται). The inclusion of κλέπται is to be explained by the fact that they are caught ἐπ' αὐτοφώρῳ.[5] The eldest brother of Agoratus could be classified as a traitor, as could the hirelings of Philip also. Two passages in Demosthenes bear upon this question. On one occasion, speaking of

---

[1] Lysias xiii. 56.

[2] Barkan (*op. cit.*, pp. 73–78) has collected considerable information about the source, preparation, and physical effects of hemlock.

[3] Gernet (*op. cit.*, pp. 276 ff.) has a very satisfactory discussion.

[4] xiii. 65–66 (trans. Lamb).

[5] Lipsius, *op. cit.*, p. 320; cf. Gernet, *op. cit.*, pp. 279 ff.

the hirelings of Philip in Athens, he says: "These men who
have sold themselves to Philip you should detest and execute
by *apotympanismos*."[1] On another occasion he says: "If
Philip had heard that those who spoke thus at that time were
put to death by *apotympanismos* as soon as they returned
here, he would have acted differently."[2] We have here cases
which look like treason. Gernet[3] warns us that all we have
here is rhetorical exaggeration, but it is not likely that Demosthenes would invoke a punishment not in accordance
with the law.[4] There are furthermore the words of Aeschines
when on trial for treason (προδοσία) which involved the death
penalty.

> With all loyalty I have served the city as her ambassador, alone sub-
> jected to the clamour of the slanderers, which before now many a man
> conspicuously brave in war has not had the courage to face; for it is not
> death that men dread but a dishonoured end. Is he not indeed to be pitied
> who must look into the sneering face of an enemy, and hear with his ears
> his insults? But nevertheless I have taken the risk, I have exposed my
> body to the peril.[5]

The following may be regarded as a probable list of criminals executed by *apotympanismos:*

I. κακοῦργοι.

II. προδόται caught in the act, as was the brother of
Agoratus when signaling to the enemy.[6]

III. To these criminals we may add those who were subject to summary arrest because they were caught in the act
of exercising certain forbidden privileges, as, for example,
murderers and traitors who returned from exile without permission. It is to be observed that all of these cases fall within
the process of *apagogé*. In other words, anyone caught in the

---

[1] viii. 61.   [3] *Op. cit.*, pp. 276 f.

[2] xix. 137.   [4] Cf. Barkan, *op. cit.*, p. 71.

[5] ii. 181 f. (trans. Adams). Aeschines is referring to *apotympanismos*, a public
execution, rather than to hemlock, which seems to have been administered within
the prison walls.

[6] Lysias xiii. 67. The passages in Demos. viii. 61; xix. 137, are mere attempts to
arouse his audience against the pro-Macedonian politicians by classifying them as
προδόται technically caught in the act of betraying their country. Even so interpreted the passages furnish some indication that προδόται were included in the list.

act of stealing, betraying his country, or, after going into exile for murder or treason, returning without legal permission was executed by *apotympanismos*.

IV. There is the problem of the execution of convicted murderers, which Gernet regards as insoluble.[1] It is probable that they also were executed by *apotympanismos*. In Lysias[2] it is said that one Menestratus was tried as an ἀνδροφόνος and executed by *apotympanismos*.[3] It is known that the nearest relatives of the murdered man had the privilege of being present at the execution; and the words of Aeschines quoted above at once suggest *apotympanismos*. In speaking of the way Midias treated his enemies Demosthenes says:

> Having but one object in view, to destroy me by every possible means, he would leave no stone unturned, as if it were right that any person who has been insulted by Midias, and determines to obtain redress instead of holding his tongue, should be utterly exterminated and not allowed to rest, should even stand convicted of desertion of post, and be exiled on a charge of murder, and all but crucified [ἐφ' αἵματι φεύγειν καὶ μόνον οὐ προσηλῶσθαι].[4]

[1] *Op. cit.*, p. 265, n. 3.

[2] xiii. 56; cf. *supra*, I, 212 f., for earlier proceedings concerning Menestratus.

[3] Gernet (*op. cit.*, p. 277) suggests that he might have been brought to trial by the process of *apagogé*.

[4] xxi. 105 (trans. Kennedy).

CHAPTER XI

ESTIMATES OF ATHENIAN JUSTICE

It is a difficult matter to form an adequate opinion of the effectiveness of the Athenian system of justice. One of the main difficulties in such an investigation is the fact that we hear only one side of a case and rarely know what the verdict was. It is always easy to quote the opinions of modern lawyers and philologians. Rogers, who spent his leisure hours for years with Aristophanes, has this to say:

> I must record my opinion as an English lawyer, that it would be difficult to devise a judicial system less adapted to the due administration of justice. A large assembly can rarely if ever form a fit tribunal for ascertaining facts or deciding questions of law. Its members lose their sense of individual responsibility to a great extent, and it is apt to degenerate into a mere mob, open to all the influences and liable to be swayed by all the passions which stir and agitate popular meetings.[1]

From among the philologians we may select the considered estimate of Wyse, editor of the speeches of Isaeus:

> There is no evidence that the Athenian judges were often bribed or terrorized or intentionally dishonest. Neither did the discretion granted them in the absence of a statute become an instrument of oppression. This danger, though real enough, was diminished by the number and representative character of the judges, who were not likely to treat as criminal, acts tolerated by public opinion. But the speeches of the orators are a convincing proof, if proof be needed, of the vices inherent in such a system. The amount of injustice done cannot now be estimated, but it is sufficient condemnation of the courts, that appeals to passion and political prejudice, insinuating sophistry, and outrageous misrepresentations of law were judged by shrewd and experienced observers suitable means to win a verdict. No development of law was possible; nothing excited the suspicion and mistrust of the judges so much as a display of legal subtlety. .... The conclusions of a court were bare affirmations or negations, not discriminating between law and fact, applicable only to a particular case and based on reasons which were known only to the individual voters, and perhaps not always to them. And these decisions, such as they were, could

[1] Introd. to Aristoph. *Wasps*, pp. xxvi f.

288

not bind another court, for in theory and practice the courts were equal and independent, each being a committee of the sovereign people supreme and irresponsible.[1]

Contemporary writers had plenty of fault to find with the Athenian system, though mainly for different reasons than those offered by modern jurists and philologians. Pseudo-Xenophon, writing in the last quarter of the fifth century, complains of the congestion of the courts, caused by the fact that

in the first place, they have to keep a greater number of festivals than any of the Greek cities, during which there is less possibility of any of the city's business being transacted, and in the second place have to give a decision upon more lawsuits, prosecutions, and audits than the rest of mankind put together.[2]

Comedians were not slow to jest about litigation in Athens. "You Athenians do nothing but try cases," says one of the characters in the *Peace* of Aristophanes.[3] In the *Clouds*, when Athens was pointed out on a map of Greece, Socrates refused to believe it, for he saw no juries in session.[4]

These jests need not be taken too seriously, for Aristophanes as well as Pseudo-Xenophon must have had a better idea of the causes of this flood of litigation than the casual modern reader of the ancient sources would suspect. "For, not even at present," says Pseudo-Xenophon, "when sitting through the year, do they avail to keep evildoers in check, owing to the largeness of the population."[5] But there were other reasons than the size of the population. Much Athenian litigiousness was due to certain features of their legal and political system which are wholly unknown to modern systems.

The annual scrutiny, *dokimasia*, of elected and allotted magistrates was in the majority of cases a matter of form and

[1] In Whibley, *Companion to Greek Studies*⁴, p. 473.

[2] *Const. of Athens* iii. 2 (trans. Brooks). [3] 505.

[4] 207 f. Cf. *Birds* 39–41; Telecleides *Amphictyons, Frag.* 2: "But, oh ye who are best of all citizens at blackmail and litigation, cease your cannibalistic lawsuits" (trans. Norwood).

[5] *Op. cit.* iii. 6.

could have been finally disposed of by a board of scrutineers (e.g., the outgoing members of the boulé), but democracy as conceived in the ancient world would delegate no real power to any board, no matter how constituted. Provision was made for the intervention of the courts either to confirm the findings of the retiring council in the case of the nine archons and the new council or in the case of all other officials to deal with the scrutiny from the beginning.[1] The vote on the recall (ἐπιχειροτονία) of the magistrates each prytany permitted a volunteer accuser to intervene if he had a grievance.[2] On the expiry of the official year all officers in the administration had to submit their accounts. Only the courts could grant final release. Here again the volunteer was invited to participate. But even this was not considered sufficient guaranty. For three days *euthynoi* sat before the statues of the eponymous heroes of the tribes and received any kind of case against the retiring magistrates. Private suits, *dikai*, were handed to the Forty; criminal charges, *graphai*, to the thesmothetai. These elaborate provisions must have created an atmosphere of suspicion which fostered litigation and encouraged all kinds of charges.

The peculiar Athenian system of legislation which made the mover personally responsible for the law or decree he sponsored by means of the *graphé paranomon* was the cause of an extraordinary amount of litigation. The personal liability did not extend beyond a year, but the legislation could be assailed at any time. Naturally the mover was always involved. The attack on the law was still in effect an attack on him by his political opponents or their henchmen.

A feature of the Athenian system of taxation was responsible for a type of litigation unknown in modern times. If a citizen appointed to perform one of the more costly liturgies felt that someone else was more able to assume the burden, he might challenge him to perform it or to exchange properties with the challenger, who would then perform the liturgy.

---

[1] Arist. *Ath. Pol.* xlv. 3; lv. 2; Lipsius, *Das Attische Recht*, p. 271.

[2] Cf. Lipsius. *op. cit.*, p. 295.

This was known as *antidosis*.[1] If both proposals were rejected the matter came before the court by way of an interpleader, *diadikasia*.[2]

The Athenians understood quite well the importance of the prosecutor in the administration of criminal justice. "Both the laws and the courts are powerless," says Lycurgus, "without someone to bring offenders to justice."[3] Solon solved the problem of how to initiate prosecutions by permitting volunteers to prosecute. Under the pre-Solonian oligarchy the injured party alone had the right to seek justice against the wrongdoer. If the state was injured by high crimes and misdemeanors, the magistrates and the members of the Areopagus took the necessary steps to bring the wrongdoers to justice upon information furnished them. Solon's famous provision permitting anyone who pleased to prosecute any wrongdoer, whatever its merits, was responsible for a number of abuses, the chief of which was sycophancy in the Greek sense. The Athenians were well aware of the evils that developed from this provision. The comedies of Aristophanes and the forensic orations abound in denunciations of the sycophants. A number of measures were adopted to restrain them, but they were never suppressed. Both the advocates and the critics of democracy recognized the necessity of having volunteer prosecutors. Aristotle, who was not hostile to democracy, selects for approval three outstanding democratic features of the Solonian constitution. Of these the second is τὸ ἐξεῖναι τῷ βουλομένῳ τιμωρεῖν ὑπὲρ τῶν ἀδικουμένων.[4] And yet Aristotle was as aware as any Athenian could be of the abuses of the system which were fully developed when he was writing. Pseudo-Xenophon, a caustic critic of democracy and all its ways, finds fault with the congestion of the courts but has nothing to say about volunteer prosecutors. Plato offers no substitute for the volunteer prosecutor but accepts him, as the following words show:

[1] Cf. Goligher, "The *Antidosis*," *Hermathena*, XIV, 481 ff.

[2] For a discussion of other unusual aspects of Athenian litigiousness cf. Bonner, *Lawyers and Litigants*, pp. 96–112.

[3] i. 4.   [4] *Ath. Pol.* ix.

Worthy of twice as much honor as he [who does no wrong], and more, is the man who, in addition, consents not to wrongdoers when they do wrong; for while the former counts as one man, the latter counts as many, in that he informs the magistrates of the wrongdoing of the rest. And he that assists the magistrates in punishing, to the best of his power,—let him be publicly proclaimed to be the Great Man of the State and perfect, the winner of the prize for excellence.[1]

And Isocrates, when proposing a return to the ancient democracy, approved of the volunteer prosecutor.[2]

Athens was not the only democracy that suffered from sycophants. According to the laws of Charondas, "those convicted of sycophancy were to go about crowned with tamarisk." The laws of Charondas were fitted to democratic constitutions in various Sicilian cities.[3] Aristotle[4] associates the excesses of demagogues and sycophants as frequent causes of the overthrow of democracy. It is quite plain that the abuses for which the volunteer prosecutor was responsible were inherent in democracy.[5]

In democracy as organized in Athens, there was no place for elected or appointed public prosecutors to bring to justice all alleged criminals. On occasion special prosecutors or advocates, *synegoroi*, as they were called, were chosen to handle

---

[1] *Laws* 730D.

[2] vii. 42. In modern communities the public prosecutor often prevents the prosecution of alleged criminals by refusing for one reason or another to take action. The result is that many criminals escape indictment to say nothing of conviction. Again in some jurisdictions prosecutors or judges reduce a charge to a less serious category. Sometimes this is done to induce the criminal to plead guilty to the lesser crime with a lighter sentence. More often, however, bribery and dishonest local politicians are involved. None of these abuses is found in Athens. A volunteer prosecutor might be bribed, but there was no assurance that another might not push the charge. Nor could the criminal expect leniency in the classification of his crime. For all judicial officials were held strictly responsible for their official acts.

[3] Cf. Diodorus xii. 11–12; for a list of these cities cf. *supra*, I, 69–70.

[4] *Pol.* 1304B. 20.

[5] In the words of Plutarch, "Not only as Simonides says 'on every lark must grow a crest' but also in every democracy must spring up a false accuser" (*Timol.* 37; Bergk, *Frag.* 68; cf. Lofberg, *Sycophancy*, p. 10, n. 53).

prosecutions which were regarded as particularly important.[1] One is obliged to admit that if neither the friends nor the critics of democracy ever suggested changing Solon's famous provision its excellencies must have more than counter-balanced the evils that grew out of it. Its success was due to the high sense of civic duty developed in the Athenian citizen body as compared with modern political communities.

The greatest offense of the Athenian system in the eyes of modern critics lies in the large popular juries. But one must remember that in Greek political theory democracy and popular juries are inseparable. In Athens, Pseudo-Xenophon says, cases are tried ἐν τῷ δήμῳ.[2] A man was not a real citizen unless he shared in political office and the administration of justice. Aristotle defines a citizen as one who has the right to take part in the deliberative or judicial administration of the state.[3] In a democracy such a theory leads to large popular courts whose shortcomings were recognized both by political theorists and by the oligarchic opponents of democracy. Plato does not construct in the *Republic* an ideal judicial system, but he makes it clear that he believes that judges should be experts and not cross-sections of the citizens drafted for the work. "In this state and in this only shall a shoemaker be a shoemaker and not a pilot also, and a farmer be a farmer and not a dicast also."[4] But in the *Laws*, a more practical treatise, he accepts the normal Greek view with few reservations.

Every magistrate must also be a judge of some things. . . . . In the judgment of offenses against the state the people ought to participate, for when anyone wrongs the state they are all wronged, and may reasonably complain if they are not allowed to share in the decision. . . . . And in private suits, too, as far as possible, all should have a share; for he who

[1] The manner in which Pericles handled the prosecution of Cimon shows that ancient like modern prosecutors were not without fault. Cf. advocates in Aristophanes, *supra*, pp. 27 ff.

[2] *Op. cit.* i. 19.

[3] *Pol.* 1275A, 1281B. Aristotle extends the word "office" (ἀρχή) to include membership in a democratic assembly.

[4] *Rep.* 397E.

has no share in the administration of justice, is apt to imagine that he has no share in the state at all.[1]

Plato indicates very clearly his distrust of large popular courts, as the following words show: "Where courts are noisy and disorderly, as in a theater, clapping or hooting in turn this or that orator, the legislator should allow them to ordain the penalties only for the smallest offenses."[2] Aristotle, however, with some hesitancy maintains that the multitude, with all its defects, is a better judge than a superior few:

> For the many, of whom each individual is but an ordinary person, when they meet together may very likely be better than the few good, if regarded not individually but collectively, just as a feast to which many contribute is better than a dinner provided out of a single purse.[3]

But doubts assail him:

> Whether this principle can apply to every democracy, and to all bodies of men, is not clear. Or rather, by heaven, in some cases it is impossible of application; for the argument would equally hold about brutes. . . . . But there may be bodies of men about whom our statement is nevertheless true. And if so, the difficulty which has been already raised, and also another which is akin to it—viz. what power should be assigned to the mass of freemen and citizens, who are not rich and have no personal merit —are both solved. There is still a danger in allowing them to share the great offices of state, for their folly will lead them into error, and their dishonesty into crime. But there is a danger also in not letting them share, for a state in which many poor men are excluded from office will necessarily be full of enemies. The only way of escape is to assign to them some deliberative and judicial functions.[4]

Aristotle, in reporting the institution of pay for the dicasts, says:

> Pericles was the first to institute pay for service in the lawcourts, as a bid for popular favor to counterbalance the wealth of Cimon. . . . . Some persons accuse him of thereby causing a deterioration in the character of the juries, since it was always the inferior people who were anxious to submit themselves for selection as jurors, rather than the men of better position.[5]

---

[1] *Laws* 767A–768B (trans. Jowett).   [2] *Ibid.* 876B.

[3] *Pol.* 1281B (trans. Jowett).   [4] *Ibid.*   [5] *Ath. Pol.* xxvii. 4 (trans. Kenyon).

It seems likely that Aristotle has in mind a criticism of Plato, who in the *Gorgias*[1] represents Socrates as saying:

I should like to know whether the Athenians are said to have been made better by Pericles, or, on the contrary, to have been corrupted by him; for I hear that he was the first who gave the people pay, and made them idle and cowardly and encouraged them in the love of talk and of money.

The rejoinder of Callicles that Socrates must have heard that from the philo-Spartan set shows that his was the view of the conservatives who, if not openly antidemocratic, were at least strongly opposed to the extreme type of democracy developed in Athens.

It has been objected that the verdicts of Athenian courts are mere affirmations or negations. Hippodamus, in his constitution, proposed that every dicast "should have a tablet on which he might not only write a simple condemnation, or leave the tablet blank for a simple acquittal; but, if he partly acquitted and partly condemned, he was to distinguish accordingly."[2] Aristotle roundly condemns the proposal because in practice it would be unworkable. How could votes of this kind be counted?

In the fifth century when the same dicasts were assigned to one court for a whole year a certain amount of bribery was possible. But few would have the means to bribe a sufficient number of dicasts to make sure of an acquittal. Aristotle says that bribery began after the introduction of pay and that Anytus in 409 B.C. was the first to employ bribery.[3] It is known that suggestions were being made in the late fifth century to ameliorate the notorious congestion of the courts. Pseudo-Xenophon[4] objects to the proposal that the number of courts be increased by decreasing the number of dicasts in each panel because of the increased danger of bribery. But in any event the method of assigning dicasts to the various courts in the fourth century must have rendered bribery practically impossible. This is the period in

[1] 515E.   [2] Arist. *Pol.* 1268A.

[3] *Ath. Pol.* xxvii; cf. Diodorus xiii. 64. 6; Plut. *Coriolanus* xiv.

[4] *Op. cit.* iii. 6–7.

which all the forensic speeches except those of Antiphon fall.
It is clear that in spite of the doubts voiced by some scholars
bribery had no effect on the administration of justice in
Athens.[1]

In one respect at least the Athenian system challenges
favorable comparison with the best of the modern systems.
Practically all civil disputes were submitted to arbitration.
The arbitrator was a man of experience and at first attempted
to induce the parties to reach a settlement acceptable to
both. Failing this, he gave a judgment on the merits of the
case which was subject to appeal. In consequence of this
system a litigant in a civil suit had an opportunity to present
his case in the most informal manner to a single judge of age
and experience where rhetoric played no part in the case,
and where the reasons for the decision were doubtless set
forth. Moreover, he was twice given the opportunity to
avoid having his case tried in a popular court. It is not now
possible to tell how successful arbitration was, but it is to be
noted that on several occasions the speaker tells the court
that an attempt had been made to settle the case without
trial. In the settlement of estates, however, there was no
arbitration, and in no other class of case could a large jury
be so ineffective. The modern reader of the speeches of
Isaeus dealing with the devolution of estates can follow most
of them only with a family tree of the persons involved.
Indeed, one speaker was so aware of this difficulty that he
had thought of using some such device in court but abandoned the idea because he realized that only a portion of the
dicasts could see the writing. Under these circumstances miscarriages of justice could scarcely be avoided.

In the so-called *graphé paranomon* the Athenians had a
parallel to a function of the Supreme Court of the United
States.[2] Any citizen who deemed that a law or a decree was
illegal could institute a criminal action against it. If the
action was brought within a year, the sponsor was personally

[1] Gilbert, *Const. Antiqu.*, p. 415, n. 4.

[2] Cf. Thomas Goodell, *Yale Review*, II, 64 ff.

liable. The entry of the suit at once suspended the law or decree in question. If the legislation was found to be illegal by the court, it thereby became null and void. In the United States only the person directly wronged can appeal to the courts for protection against what he claims is an unconstitutional law. But his suit raises the question indirectly. The rule of precedents, however, enables any citizen wronged in the same manner to avail himself of the benefit of the court decision because no one will take action against him. Hence the law complained of becomes unconstitutional only indirectly. Moreover, it constantly happens that a part of a law may become unconstitutional while other parts must wait for victims to challenge them. The great advantage of the Athenian system lay in the fact that the constitutionality of legislation could be raised and finally settled before any citizen suffered wrong. Public advocates were always chosen to defend the law, but any citizen could speak for or against the law. The court, like any other dicastery, was a cross-section of the people and so represented public opinion. Here again the Athenian system compares favorably with a modern system.

Witnesses were not so important in Athens as in a system where the court hears the facts as told by witnesses and summed up by counsel. Athenian dicasts heard the facts of the case from the litigant himself with supporting testimony at various points. In the fifth and early fourth centuries witnesses were questioned by the litigants. Later they merely acknowledged affidavits prepared beforehand. In neither system was there any provision for cross-examination. In the absence of cross-examination a litigant could venture upon questions and produce affidavits that would be dangerous if the witness was subject to cross-examination. But the lack of cross-examination is not so serious a matter as it would be in a modern system, for such pieces of evidence as are extant are quite simple and brief. The nearest approach to cross-examination was the questions addressed by a litigant to his opponent, but here again the extant orations furnish no such examples as Socrates' examination of Meletus. Nor is it surprising. A man who bought his speech from some logograph would be running serious risks if he undertook to question a clever opponent.

It is not to be expected that litigants will in open court criticize the dicasts upon whom their success or failure in their litigation depends. In forensic theory the dicasts did no wrong. The unscrupulous prosecutors were responsible for all miscarriages of justice. Few litigants had the hardihood of the Platonic Socrates, who roundly condemned the common practice of bringing weeping children and female relatives into court.

Perhaps there may be some one who is offended with me as he calls to mind how he himself on a similar or even less serious occasion had recourse to prayers and supplications with many tears, and how he produced his children in court together with a posse of friends and relatives; whereas I who am probably in danger of my life will do none of these things. Perhaps this may come into his mind and he may vote in anger because he is displeased. I say these things ought not to be done; if they are done you ought not to permit them.[1]

He further protests against the practice of allowing popular prejudice to influence verdicts. He observes:

My conviction, if I am convicted, will be due not to my accusers, but to longstanding calumnies and prejudices. These have convicted many a good man, and it is not likely that my case will prove an exception.[2]

Andocides shows some boldness in comparing the deliberations of the boulé with the decisions of the dicasts. He remarks:

The boulé is less likely than you to make a mistake, for they deliberate at leisure and are liable to be blamed and held in ill repute by the rest of the citizens. But there is no one to find fault with you. For it is your right to dispose of matters that come before you well or ill as you please.[3]

Here and there in current literature we find criticisms of the Athenian judicial system. Pseudo-Xenophon[4] asserts that the Athenians are less concerned with justice in their courts

---

[1] Plato *Apol.* 34C.   [3] Andoc. ii. 19.
[2] *Ibid.* 28A–B.   [4] *Ath. Pol.* i. 18.

than with what is advantageous to themselves. This view may be dismissed as the normal oligarchic attitude. Of more importance is a later admission in which he points out to interested oligarchs that there is little chance of overthrowing such a democracy.

Someone might retort that after all no one has been unjustly disfranchised at Athens, to which I reply that there are some who have been unjustly disfranchised, but only a few. However, it will need more than a few to make an attack upon the democracy at Athens, the truth of the case being that men who have been justly disfranchised do not take it to heart, but only those who have suffered unjustly. Now, how could anyone suppose that the majority would have suffered unjustly at Athens, where it is the people who hold the official posts? No, it is for misconduct in office, or in speech or act, for such reasons as these that men are disfranchised there. From these considerations one must not think that there is any danger from the disfranchised class at Athens.[1]

Aristophanes, according to prevailing opinion, devoted the *Wasps* to a criticism of the Athenian dicasteries. "Mr. Grote," says Rogers, "is merely stating the popular view as well as his own, when he says that the poet's purpose was to make the dicasts monsters of caprice and injustice." But Rogers has rightly divined the real purpose of the *Wasps*. It is really an attack on the demagogues who exploited the dicasts for their own political purposes. But a comedy must have humor. This is furnished mainly by Philocleon, whose name at once suggests the relationship between the dicasts and the reigning demagogue. He is a grotesque exaggeration of the normal dicast who is so admirably and admiringly represented in the chorus—the Marathonian heroes whom Aristophanes delighted to honor.

We the only true-born Attics, of the staunch heroic breed,
Many a time have fought for Athens, guarding her in hours of need;
When with smoke and fire and rapine forth the fierce Barbarian came,
Eager to destroy our wasps-nests, smothering all the town in flame,
Out at once we rushed to meet him: on with shield and spear we went,
Fought the memorable battle, primed with fiery hardiment;
Man to man we stood, and, grimly, gnawed for rage our under lips.
Hah! their arrows hail so densely, all the sun is in eclipse![2]

---

[1] *Ibid.* iii. 12–13.　　　[2] Aristoph. *Wasps* 1077–90; cf. 230–39.

Of Philocleon one of the slaves says in explaining the plot:

> I'll tell you the disease old master has.
> He is a LAWCOURT-lover, no man like him.
> Judging is what he dotes on, and he weeps
> Unless he sit on the front bench of all.[1]

And again:

> He of us all, I ween,
> Was evermore the austerest, and most keen.
> Alone no prayers he heeded:
> Whene'er for grace they pleaded,
> He bent (like this) his head,
> *You cook a stone*, he said.[2]

The fact that *The Wasps* obtained the second prize is significant. If the judges and the audience had thought that Aristophanes was attacking democracy in one of its fundamental principles, or if they had taken his jests seriously, his play would have received a rough reception. Support is lent to this interpretation of Rogers by Isocrates, who in the fourth century deplores the same situation.

> Who of the friends of democracy is not pained to see the numbers of citizens standing around the courts hoping to be drawn for service in order to secure the means of subsistence?[3]

> I am surprised that you are unable to realize that no class is more ill disposed to democracy than the vicious politicians and demagogues. Seeing a portion of the citizen body, owing to their poverty and dependence upon the income from attendance at courts and assemblies, obliged to be at their beck and call they rejoice at the increase of impeachments, indictments and other vexatious litigation which they encourage.[4]

The Athenians were fond of oratory, and there were plenty of skilled speakers ready to gratify their desire. Thucydides puts into the mouth of Cleon a striking condemnation of Athenian preoccupation with oratorical displays:

> Misled by clever speakers the people make dangerous concessions to the subject states. The sophisticated members of the assembly ought rather to give good advice than to seek occasions for the display of eloquence and cleverness and become rivals in oratory for popular applause. In such rhetorical contests the city gives away the prizes to others while she takes the risk upon herself. And you are to blame for ordering these contests

---

[1] *Ibid.* 87–90.   [2] *Ibid.* 277–81.   [3] vii. 54.   [4] viii. 129–30.

amiss. When speeches are to be heard you are too fond of using your eyes, but where actions are concerned you use your ears. You are slaves of each paradox and contemptuous of the familiar. Not a man of you but would be an orator if he could. In a word you are at the mercy of your ears and sit like spectators attending a performance of sophists rather than counsellors of state. Do not hold out a hope which eloquence can secure. . . . . Do not be misled either by pity or by the charm of words. . . . . Our charming orators will have another occasion for display where the issues are not so serious.[1]

This attitude toward oratory rendered the large popular juries particularly unfitted for dispensing justice. It is not surprising that men of the older generation thought that those skilled in rhetoric could make the worse appear the better reason. Again and again defendants deplore their inability to speak in public. On the eve of the trial of Socrates a friend urging him to make a good preparation for his defense inquires, "Do you not see that the Athenian dicasts frequently become angry and put innocent men to death and frequently acquit those guilty of wrong, moved to pity by their eloquent speeches?"[2] One is not so much impressed by these complaints when it is recalled that all the litigants who voice them are using speeches composed for them by experts. Neither is it to be forgotten that the speech of the prosecutor also may be composed by an expert. But be that as it may, rhetoric was a weapon which gave a litigant an undue advantage. It is interesting to note that the people themselves were suspicious of the new rhetoric. Thucydides, in his famous characterization of Antiphon, says that

although he did not come before the assembly or willingly take part in any public contest but was under suspicion with the people on account of his reputation for cleverness yet he was the one man most able to help any who were involved in contests either in court or before the assembly in case they sought his advice.[3]

[1] Thuc. iii. 38. (paraphrased) The whole Mytilenaean episode well illustrates the characteristics of the Athenians which Cleon here attributes to them. At first they condemned the whole male population to death, the normal procedure in dealing with revolting allies (iv. 122, 6). In a second vote they decided to put to death only those who were proved guilty of the revolt. Viewed from another angle, the whole incident is a striking illustration of the essential mildness of the Athenian character.

[2] Xen. *Apol.* 4.   [3] viii. 67.

Plato takes high ground in his condemnation of rhetoric in the courts. In his dialogue named after the famous Sicilian rhetorician Gorgias, Socrates inquired:

"What is rhetoric, Gorgias?"[1]
"Rhetoric is the art of persuasion in courts and other assemblies about the just and the unjust" [replied Gorgias].
"And what sort of persuasion does rhetoric produce in courts of law and other assemblies about the just and the unjust? Is it the sort of persuasion which gives belief without knowledge or that which gives knowledge?"
"That which produces belief only."
"The rhetorician, then, need have no real knowledge; he has only to discover some way of persuading the ignorant that he has more knowledge than those who know" [concluded Socrates].

To the same effect is a passage in the *Theaetetus* of Plato.

Orators and lawyers persuade men by their art and make them think whatever they like, but they do not instruct them. Do you imagine that there are any teachers in the world so clever as to be able to convey to others the truth about acts of robbery and violence of which they were not eyewitnesses while a little water is flowing in the hourglass?[2]

In theory this view is correct, no doubt, but it is wholly impractical. How else can a litigant put his case before a court than by words?

Courts may err either on the side of laxity or on the side of severity. Isocrates in the *Areopagiticus* by implication criticizes the laxity in the administration of justice in his own day:

For they saw that in cases of contract the judges were not in the habit of indulging their sense of equity but were strictly faithful to the laws; and they did not in trying others seek to make it safe for themselves to disobey the law, but were indeed more severe on defaulters than were the injured themselves, since they believed that those who break down confidence in contracts do a greater injury to the poor than to the rich. . . . .[3]

In another speech Isocrates plainly sets forth the animosity of the poverty-stricken masses toward men of wealth:

[1] *Gorgias* 454B, E; 459B, C. The passage is paraphrased.

[2] 201B.   [3] vii. 33–34.

Some jurors are so savage and so hostile that because of their envy and their poverty they are enemies not of wickedness but of success, and hate not only the most moderate citizens but the most righteous conduct. This is bad enough. But they even side with wrongdoers on trial and acquit them, while they put to death those whom they envy if they can.[1]

Demosthenes also finds fault with the light-hearted irresponsibility of the dicasts of his day:

You, O Athenians, acquit men who are guilty and plainly proved to be guilty of the gravest offenses, if they merely say one or two witty things, and some fellow-tribesmen chosen to be their advocates petition for them: should you even convict any one, you fix the penalty at five-and-twenty drachmas.[2]

Apparent laxity may have justification in the fact that there was no high authority to exercise clemency or grant pardons in the Athenian system. Accordingly the large popular courts had to exercise these powers and take account of extenuating circumstances. In these conditions an acquittal may amount to a pardon. And a large popular jury was well suited to exercise these functions.

Over-severity in a democratic system of justice cures itself more readily than laxity. It is felt that it is better to let ten guilty men go free than to punish one innocent man. The code of Draco provided death as the penalty for a long list of crimes. Solon, with full popular support, repealed all the laws of Draco except the homicide laws, because they were "written in blood." In only a few cases was the death penalty obligatory by laws. Otherwise it was left to the dicasts to determine the penalty. In England at the beginning of the nineteenth century over two hundred crimes were capital by law. If a jury found a man guilty, the law took its course unless the criminal was pardoned. To be sure all this is changed now, but the fact remains that until the beginning of the nineteenth century the administration of criminal justice in England was in all probability quite as severe as it was in fifth-century Athens. In one extant case, the trial and execution of the generals in 406 B.C., there was a miscarriage of justice due to the passions aroused in the people

[1] xv. 142.   [2] xxiii. 206.

generally as well as the relatives of the seamen who perished.[1]
The Athenians themselves soon recognized their mistake and
took measures to bring to justice those who were regarded
as mainly responsible for the prosecution.

One of the most remarkable instances of national self-
restraint was the amnesty of 403. The victorious democracy
had at its mercy many of the men responsible for the execution of fifteen hundred adherents of democracy during the
tyranny of the Thirty, and yet they decided to let bygones
be bygones. The amnesty was always a matter of just pride
to Athenians of later generations. Aristotle[2] took occasion to
remark on the Athenian law against would-be tyrants. They
and their descendants were disfranchised.

Modern critics of the Athenian judicial system naturally
compare it with contemporary systems. Grote[3] alone has
recognized that modern standards should not be used entirely
in estimating the effectiveness of the administration of justice in Athens. He reminds us that "the distinction between
powers administrative and judicial, so highly valued among
the more elaborate governments of Europe, since the political speculations of the last century, was in the early history
of Athens almost unknown." In England before the distinction between judicial and administrative powers was in force
an alleged criminal was much more harshly treated than an
Athenian citizen in like circumstances. Thayer says:

> In England the king in criminal cases was no mere ordinary party to an
> action: the procedure was heavily weighted in his favor. In treason and
> felony the accused could not have counsel; later when witnesses could be
> had for the crown, the accused could not have them; and still later when
> he also could have them, his witnesses could not be sworn.[4]

[1] Xen. *Hell.* i. 7. 16 ff.; cf. Thuc. vii. 48. 3. In his refusal to withdraw from
Sicily before the final disaster without authorization from home, Nicias recognized
how volatile and easily influenced the Athenians were in their dealings with defendants in matters affecting the nation. One is tempted to think that Thucydides
has in mind the fate of the generals after the battle of Arginusae.

[2] *Ath. Pol.* xvi.   [3] *History of Greece*, V, 237.

[4] *Preliminary Treatise on Evidence at the Common Law*, p. 157.

In a note Thayer cites a case in the year 1565 in which a robber was on trial. There were no witnesses for the prisoner at the bar, only for the crown. Other cases are also cited to the same effect. An Athenian, although he must plead his own case, could have a speech written for him and could have counsel and witnesses. His rights in these respects were the same as the prosecutor's.

Grote points out an aspect of the Athenian system of popular courts that usually escapes notice.

> To make the rich and powerful effectively amenable to justice has indeed been found so difficult everywhere, until a recent period of history, that we should be surprised if it were otherwise in Greece. . . . . Now the dikasteries were inaccessible both to corruption and to intimidation: their number, their secret suffrage, and the impossibility of knowing beforehand what individuals would sit on any particular case prevented both the one and the other. And besides that the magnitude of their number, extravagant according to our ideas of judicial business, was essential to this tutelary effect—it served farther to render the trial solemn and the verdict imposing on the minds of parties and spectators, as we may see from the fact that in important causes the dikastery was doubled or tripled. Nor was it possible by any other means than numbers to give dignity to an assembly of citizens of whom many were poor, some old, and all were despised individually by the rich brought before them. . . . . These numerous dikasteries offered the only organ which Grecian politics could devise for getting redress against powerful criminals, public as well as private, for obtaining a sincere and uncorrupt verdict.[1]

Solon, in allowing an appeal to the Heliaea, had in mind this very situation, and a perusal of Demosthenes' indictment of Midias will convince any reader that only a court that was so large that it could neither be bought nor be intimidated could deal with such a man as Midias.

The general respect accorded the Areopagus as a court might seem to indicate that a select body, including the former archons who had stood the test of the *euthyna*, might have been a satisfactory group from which to draw panels for both criminal and civil cases; but the reforms of Ephialtes and Pericles show clearly that democracy was determined to control both administrative and judicial powers. For, as

[1] *Op. cit.*, V, 237 ff.

Aristotle[1] observes, the control of the courts made the people sovereign of the state.

There is no doubt that the large popular courts of Athens, subject to personal and political prejudices, swayed by oratory, deceived by unscrupulous prosecutors and uncontrolled by expert judges, deserve the strictures of Rogers. But we leave to the reader to decide whether after all it was not as good a system as Greek democracy could devise to protect the rights of the humblest of its citizens. "In the eyes of the law," says Pericles, "all are on an equality as regards the settlement of their private disputes."[2]

[1] *Ath. Pol.* ix.   [2] Thuc. ii. 37; cf. Hyper. iv. 36 quoted *supra*, pp. 49 f.

I

GENERAL INDEX

(For cases in the orators see Index of Passages)

ἄδεια, 68

ἀδικία, 3, 5 f.

Adrastus, 194 (n. 1), 201 f.

Adultery, 51 f., 67, 203, 204, 226

Advocates, private, 8 ff.: types of, 8; οἱ ὑπεραπολογούμενοι, 8 f.; law against payment of, 10 ff.; relationship of, to prosecutor, 10, 11 f.; in fourth century, 12 f.; contemporary opinion of, 13; extant cases, 13 f.; club members as, 20 f.; as co-prosecutors, 38; nature of testimony of, 124

Advocates, public, 25 ff., 292 f.: in trial of Cimon, 26 f.; in trial of Antiphon, 27; types of cases, 27 ff.; contemporary opinion of, 27, 29; in treasury prosecutions, 28, 30 ff.; bribery of, 31, 33; relation of, to officials, 33 f.; synegoroi of logistai, 35 f., 257 ff.; in fourth century, 36 f.; Hyperides as advocate, 36 f., 38; in citizenship cases, 37; in revision of laws, 37, 297; representing deme, 37 f.; representing tribe, 37 f.

Aeschines, trial of, 132, 286

Aeschylus, trial of, 4

Aidesis: oaths in, 172; granted by relatives, 194; granted by phratry members, 194, 208 f.; in premeditated homicide, 203, 229 f.; in unpremeditated homicide, 210, 229, 230; in kin murder, 216

αἵρεσις δατητῶν, 103

ἀκίνδυνος, 59 ff.

Alcibiades, pardon of, 253, 254, 272, n. 5

Amnesty: decree of Patroclides, 48, 82,

255; institution of *paragraphé*, 77 f.; appeals to, 81; cases contrary to, 81 f.; oaths after, 154 f.; homicides excluded, 195; pardons to ἄτιμοι, 254 f., 273; as national self-restraint, 304

ἀμφιορκία, 163

ἀμφισβήτησις, 266

ἀνάκρισις: origin of, 7 f.; evidence at, 17; in financial audit, 35; right of official to reject case, 57 f.; in phratry entrance, 160; oaths at, 162, 166, 167 ff.; in allied states, 250

Andocides, trial of, 21, 38, 39, 81, 120 f.

ἀνθυπωμοσία, 164

Antidosis, 158, 290 f.

ἀντιγραφή: in fourth century, 76; in Pancleon case, 78 f.; in Theophemus case, 94; claim to estate, 163

Antiphon: as logograph, 16; trial of, 27, 34; execution of, 282

ἀντιτίμημα, 91

ἀντωμοσία, 162 f., 168 f.

Anytus: bribery of jury by, 10 f., 295; in trials of Socrates and Andocides, 38; fate of, 65

ἀπαγωγή: of κακοῦργοι, 3, 121, 203, 212, 214 f.; of homicides, 7, 81, 211 ff.; of sycophants, 71; indictment in, 75 (n. 2); ἀτίμων, 213; of non-citizens, 215; punishments in, 286

ἀπογραφή: function of, 41; favored by sycophants, 50; against Agoratus, 66; in Polyaenus case, 246; execution of judgment, 271

ἀποδέκται, 242 f.

Apollodorus, as advocate, 11 f., 13, 14

ἀπόφασις, 37

ἀποτυμπανισμός: nature of, 279 ff.; date of introduction, 282 f.; crimes subject to, 285 ff.

Appeals. See ἔφεσις

Arbitration: evidence in, 17, 58, 100, 238; in Callimachus case, 51, 54, 77; in *paragraphai*, 91 ff.; cases subject to, 97 f.; in inheritance cases, 98 ff.; *status civitatis* in, 102, 111 f., 116; *status familiae* in, 102, 107 ff., 116, 159; classification of extant cases, 102 ff., 115 f.; in δίκη ἐπιτροπῆς, 102 ff.; in δίκη κλοπῆς, 102, 109 f.; in δίκη λιπομαρτυρίου, 139 f.; oaths in, 156 f.; appeals in, 235 ff.; success of, 240, 296

Arbitrators: relation of, to Forty and other officials, 97 f., 101 f.; oath of, 156 f; *ephesis* in impeachment of, 238 f.

Archestratus, amendment of, 246 ff.

Archinus, law of, 77 ff., 81

Archon: in arbitration, 97 f., 101 ff.; cases under, 103 ff.

Archons: oath of, 150 f.; *dokimasia* of, 243 ff.

Areopagus: jurisdiction of, 4, 7; in Harpalus case, 37; oaths before, 167 ff.; appeal to, 232 f.; position of, 305

Aristides, 283

Aristogiton, 37, 49, 55, 70

Ariston, 148

ἀρωγοί, 189 f.

Assault: affected individual, 40; in Theophemus case, 94; in Arethusius case, 269 f.; in attempts to execute judgments, 272. See δίκη αἰκίας

ἀτιμία: for military offenses, 5, 264; for perjury, 21, 261 ff.; for debt, 22, 57, 61, 255, 263 f., 273; for dropping case, 24, 58 f., 61, 272 f.; for failure to win fifth part of votes, 50, 56 f., 272 f.; disqualified witnesses, 118; for impiety, 121; of arbitrators, 238, 240; appeals, 250; pardons, 254 f., 273; new trials, 265 f.; for ψευδοκλητεία,

269 f.; enforcement of, 272 f.; types of, 272 f.

Audit. See εὔθυνα

βάραθρον: nature of, 278 f.; early origin of, 278, 279; in decree of Cannonus, 283; late use of, 283 f.

βάσανοι, 126 ff., 132, 224 ff.

βασιλεύς, in homicide cases, 168, 199 f., 207 f., 214 f.

βλάβη. See δίκη βλάβης

Blackmail, by sycophants, 50 ff.

Blood money, 196 ff., 209

βούλευσις, 82

Bottomry cases, 119 f.

βουλή: in trial of Antiphon, 27; oath of, 151 f.; limitation of powers of, 239 f., 240 ff., 250 f., 255 f.; *logistai* of, 241 f.; *dokimasia* of, 243 f.; comparison of, with dicasteries, 298

Bribery: law against, 10 f.; of witnesses, 21 f., 264 ff.; of officials, 33, 35, 43; of prosecutors, 33, 60, 62; in Harpalus case, 37; of dicasts, 50, 56, 295 f.

Callias (Andocides i. 121), 21, 56

Callixenus, trial of, 64 f., 66, 67, 70. See Generals, trial of

Cannonus, decree of, 3, 5, 165, 283

Cephalus, 38

Cephisius, 21, 38, 56

Chalcidian decree: oath in, 149 f., 151; appeal in, 246, 248 f.

Challenge: to give up slaves for torture, 128 f., 132; to evidentiary oath, 158 f.

Charmides, 53

Charondas, laws of, 292

Cimon, trial of, 15, 22, 26, 43

Citizenship cases, 37, 41, 59 f., 110 ff., 116

Cleisthenes, 5, 6, 46, 151

Cleon, 28, 44

Cleophon, 64

Clubs: as aid to litigant, 10, 11, 19 ff.; law against, 10 f.; of sycophants, 54

of magistrates, 243 f., 289 f.; appeals in, 243 ff., 290

Dorieus, 253, 254

Draco, laws of: institution of suits, 1 ff.; on homicide, 4, 7, 203 f., 207, 220, 226; litigation under, 7; appeals under, 233; severity of, 274, 303

Duris, 281 f.

Ecclesia: appeal to, 8, 37, 233 f., 305; trial of Generals before, 9, 27, 64 f., 66, 67, 70; *probolai* before, 24 f., 63 ff., 69 f.; κυρία ἐκκλησία, 67; pardoning power of, 253 ff.

Eisagogeis, 5

εἰσαγώγιμος, 75 f., 164

Eisangelia: under Draco, 7, 233; abuse of, 16 (n. 5); confusion of, with *euthyna*, 26 f.; of Antiphon, 27; of Generals, 27; of sycophants, 63 f., 66, 70; of homicides, 215; of arbitrators, 238

ἐκμαρτυρία: nature of, 132 ff.; oaths in, 174

Eleven, jurisdiction of, 75 (n. 2), 78, 121, 203

Elpinice, 26

ἐμβάτευσις, 271

Embezzlement, 30 ff., 35

ἔμμηνοι δίκαι, 101. *See* Suits, monthly

ἔνδειξις, 71, 78, 80, 81, 273; in *apagogé*, 75, n. 2

ἔφεσις: in citizenship cases, 37, 112 f.; in arbitration, 110, 235 ff.; meaning of, 232; before Solon, 232 f.; under Solon, 232, 233 ff.; of magistrates' decisions, 232 ff.; of boulé decisions, 239 f., 240 ff.; in *dokimasia*, 243 ff.; in Athenian empire, 246 ff.

ἐπιβολή, 138 f., 245 f.

ἐπιδικασίαι κλήρου: not subject to *paragraphé*, 79; under archon, 103; perjury in, 263, 265

ἐπιμεληταὶ τοῦ ἐμπορίου, 62

ἐπίσκηψις, 77, 262, 266

Episkopoi, 252 f.

ἐπιχειροτονία, 27, 290

ἐπωβελία: as check on litigation, 58; in special pleas, 80, 87, 89

ἐπωμόται, 184 ff.

ἐργαστηρία συκοφαντῶν, 54

Ethopoiia, 123 f.

Euryptolemus, 9, 165

εὐθυδικία, 75

εὔθυνα: of Cimon, 26 f.; Trial of Dog, 28 f.; treasury prosecutions, 30 ff.; types of, 34; officials in charge of, 35; procedure in, 35 f., 256 ff.; abuses of, 43 f.; of magistrates, 57 f.; none for arbitrators, 238; monthly, 241 f.; cause of litigation, 290

εὔθυνοι: right of, to reject case, 57 f.; functions of, 109, 255, 257 ff., 290

Euthyphro, 208, 217

Evidence: in arbitration, 17, 58, 100; confessions as, 120 ff., 127, 130; importance of, in Athenian courts, 123; hearsay, 124, 125, 130 ff., 134, 136; of women, 125, 221 ff.; of minors, 125 f., 221 ff.; of slaves, 126 ff., 132, 223 ff.; persons as evidence, 129; written, 134 f., 140; extra-judicial, 134 ff.; introduction of new, 260 f.

Exegetes, 208, 213 (n. 1), 214, 217 ff.

ἐξωμοσία, 137, 163 f.

Exile, 272. *See* Homicide

Fines: aid in paying, 22; for failure to win fifth of votes, 25, 55, 56 ff., 71, 80, 87, 89, 139, 216; share to prosecutor, 40 f.; for dropping suit, 58 ff.; inflicted by magistrate, 103, 245; in κλήτευσις, 138 f., 142 f.; inflicted by boulé, 240 ff. *See* ἐπιβολή, ἐπωβελία

Forgery, 56

Forty, the: as check on litigation, 58; *paragraphé* under, 93; functions of, 97 ff., 101 f., 110; relation of, to arbitrators, 97 f., 101 f., τέλος of, 110; list of arbitration cases, 115 f.; procedure of, in cases, 235 f., 290

Four Hundred, revolution of, 11, 19, 20, 21, 47, 150

INDEX OF PASSAGES IN THE ORATORS

(The numbers in italics refer to pages in this book)

III

INDEX OF PASSAGES IN ARISTOPHANES

IV

INDEX OF PASSAGES IN ARISTOTLE

CPSIA information can be obtained at www.ICGtesting.com
Printed in the USA
BVOW08*1749300915

420058BV00014B/45/P

THE ADMINISTRATION OF
JUSTICE FROM HOMER
TO ARISTOTLE

BY

ROBERT J. BONNER, Ph.D., Litt.D.

Professor of Greek, University of Chicago
Formerly of the Ontario Bar

AND

GERTRUDE SMITH, Ph.D.

Associate Professor of Greek, University of Chicago

VOLUME I

Συνέχει πόλεις τὸ τοὺς νόμους σῴζειν καλῶς.
—Euripides

The Lawbook Exchange, Ltd.
Clark, New Jersey

ISBN 978-1-58477-117-3 (Set)
ISBN 978-1-61619-367-6 (Vol. I)
ISBN 978-1-61619-368-3 (Vol. II)

Volume I © copyright 1930 by The University of Chicago
Volume II © copyright 1938 by The University of Chicago

Lawbook Exchange edition 2001, 2014

The quality of this reprint is equivalent to the quality of the original work.

THE LAWBOOK EXCHANGE, LTD.
33 Terminal Avenue
Clark, New Jersey 07066-1321

*Please see our website for a selection of our other publications
and fine facsimile reprints of classic works of legal history:*
www.lawbookexchange.com

Library of Congress Cataloging-in-Publication Data

Bonner, Robert Johnson, 1868-1946.
   The administration of justice from Homer to Aristotle/ by Robert J.
Bonner and Gertrude Smith.
       p. cm.
   Originally published: Chicago : University of Chicago Press, c1930-1938.
   Includes bibliographical references and index.
   ISBN 1-58477-117-8 (cloth : alk. paper)
   1. Justice, Administration of (Greek law)--History. I. Smith, Gertrude,
Ph.D. II. Title.

KL4345.B66 2000
347.38--dc21   00-050693

Printed in the United States of America on acid-free paper

THE ADMINISTRATION OF JUSTICE
FROM HOMER TO ARISTOTLE

THE UNIVERSITY OF CHICAGO PRESS
CHICAGO, ILLINOIS

—

THE BAKER & TAYLOR COMPANY
NEW YORK

THE CAMBRIDGE UNIVERSITY PRESS
LONDON

THE MARUZEN-KABUSHIKI-KAISHA
TOKYO, OSAKA, KYOTO, FUKUOKA, SENDAI

THE COMMERCIAL PRESS, LIMITED
SHANGHAI

THE ADMINISTRATION OF
JUSTICE FROM HOMER
TO ARISTOTLE

BY

ROBERT J. BONNER, Ph.D., Litt.D.

Professor of Greek, University of Chicago
Formerly of the Ontario Bar

AND

GERTRUDE SMITH, Ph.D.

Associate Professor of Greek, University of Chicago

VOLUME I

Συνέχει πόλεις τὸ τοὺς νόμους σώζειν καλῶς.
—Euripides

THE UNIVERSITY OF CHICAGO PRESS
CHICAGO · ILLINOIS

PREFACE

The administration of justice constituted a very vital element in the Athenian scheme of government. All officials and governing bodies and boards had more or less important judicial functions to perform. In the processes of government the courts constantly intervened in a fashion quite unknown in a modern state. In the last resort they enforced the responsibility of magistrates, passed upon proposed legislation, ratified treaties providing for reciprocity in litigation between the contracting states, and by means of the γραφὴ παρανόμων protected the constitution and exercised a salutary control over professional politicians.

The materials available for tracing the development of Athenian legal institutions are comparatively meager and inadequate. The main source is Aristotle's *Constitution of Athens*. The later chapters, portraying the system introduced about the middle of the fourth century, leave little to be desired. This portion of the treatise might well have served as a textbook on practice and procedure for young men desirous of becoming professional speech-writers. But when one turns to the preceding review of Athenian constitutional history for information about the earlier period, where our other sources afford the least assistance, disappointment awaits him.

Aristotle is fully aware of the importance of Solon's judicial reforms. Two of the three most important democratic features of the constitution which he particularly emphasizes are legal—freedom of prosecution and the appeal to the Heliaea. And yet he has nothing to say about the organization of the Heliaea, and his paragraph on the Areopagus is confined to vague generalities. One of the reasons for this neglect of detail may be his lack of interest in judicial history. He was chiefly concerned with the constitution as he saw it in his own day. The story of its development was a comparatively minor matter. But indications are not lacking that reliable material for reconstructing the πάτριος πολιτεία,

even if Aristotle had wished to do so, were not available. It
was much discussed in the late fifth century when it became
a political catch word and a party slogan. But it is extremely
doubtful if even the would-be reformers knew much about it.
The revolutionists of 411 B.C. were under the impression that
the constitution of Cleisthenes was "not really democratical
but closely akin to that of Solon" (Aristotle, *Constitution of
Athens* xxix. 3), if one may judge from the amendment of
Cleitophon to the decree of Pythodorus providing for a constitutional commission.

Cleisthenes was responsible for some extremely important
judicial reforms. Among them, in all probability, were the
reorganization of the Heliaea and the organization of the
boulé of Five Hundred. But Aristotle dismisses the subject
with the mention of the oath of the boulé and a reference to
some "new laws."

In the age of Pericles the heliastic courts were highly
organized and played an increasingly important rôle in the
state. But all the information Aristotle vouchsafes is that the
dicasts numbered 6,000 and received pay. One would like to
know precisely what prerogatives of the Areopagus were distributed among the assembly, the boulé, and the heliastic
courts. And no ancient source has a word to say about the
functions of the board of Thirty appointed in 453–452 B.C.
which, it seems likely, was second in importance to the thesmothetae alone. These and other omissions, such as the date
of the establishment of public arbitration, would seem to indicate that Aristotle was not much interested in legal history.
For there could not have been the same lack of evidence for
the fifth century as for the early period.

The work of Aristotle, however, contains so much new
material that its recovery renewed and stimulated interest
in Athenian judicial history. Much attention has been devoted to special topics in monographs, dissertations, and
articles in journals and dictionaries of antiquities. But the
only attempt to trace continuously the development of the
Athenian judiciary is Lipsius' "Einleitung" to *Das Attische
Recht und Rechtsverfahren*. Though very brief, it is an admir-

able outline of an important phase of Athenian institutional history. Constant use has been made of it in the following pages, which are offered as a contribution to Greek judicial history.

The earlier chapters of the present volume are devoted to a detailed discussion of the origin and development of legal processes among the Greeks down through the age of the law-givers. They constitute a necessary background for a history of the Athenian judiciary, which is essentially an account of the development of the Solonian Heliaea into the highly or-ganized dicasteries of the fourth century. The Solonian Heliaea is itself the direct descendant of the Homeric *agora*, which on occasion meted out justice to public offenders.

In the chapters devoted to the Athenian system, the main theme is the machinery employed for administering justice. But matters which belong more properly to practice and pro-cedure have not been wholly excluded. The choice of topics to be treated in the present volume has in some cases been more or less arbitrary; but it is our intention in the near future to deal with some of the topics here omitted, as well as others in the general field of Greek judicial history.

Some of the views set forth in the following pages are more or less speculative and conjectural. In dealing with a subject where adequate evidence is lacking, one inevitably has recourse to assumptions and conjectures. As a method of procedure they have a place particularly in the investigation of institutions, provided an effort is made to control conjec-tures by giving due attention to antecedents in earlier prac-tice and survivals in later practice. Institutions arise and de-velop most frequently by a process of evolution, and rarely disappear without leaving some trace or influence, even where revolution has intervened.

On some of the topics discussed in the following pages we have already individually published articles in *Classical Phi-lology*, and we desire to thank the editors of this journal for permission to make use of this material. In no sense, how-ever, have these articles been reprinted. The material con-tained in them has always been reorganized, amplified, brought up to date, and adapted to the needs of the present volume.

We wish to thank Professor John Adams Scott, of Northwestern University, for his critical examination of the chapter on the Heroic Age and for the helpful suggestions which his expert knowledge of Homer enabled him to offer. He is in no sense, however, to be held responsible for opinions expressed on controversial points. Thanks also are due Professor A. P. Dorjahn, of Northwestern University, for reading the first five chapters in manuscript and for various suggestions during the progress of the work. We are indebted to our colleague, Professor Carl Darling Buck, for the note on the word ἡλιαία, page 157.

Miss Smith gratefully acknowledges the very material aid afforded her by a grant for research from the Council of Learned Societies.

ROBERT J. BONNER

GERTRUDE SMITH

UNIVERSITY OF CHICAGO

TABLE OF CONTENTS

CHAPTER I

THE HEROIC AGE

In his description of the four types of kingdoms Aristotle gives the following picture of that of the Heroic Age:

There is a fourth species of kingly rule—that of the heroic times—which was hereditary and legal, and was exercised over willing subjects. For the first chiefs were benefactors of the people in arts or arms; they either gathered them into a community, or procured land for them; and thus they became kings of voluntary subjects, and their power was inherited by their descendants. They took the command in war and presided over the sacrifices, except those which required a priest. They also decided causes either with or without an oath; and when they swore, the form of the oath was the stretching out of their scepter.[1]

Thucydides also is describing the kingship of heroic times when he says that formerly there had been hereditary kingships based on fixed prerogatives: πρότερον δὲ ἦσαν ἐπὶ ῥητοῖς γέρασι πατρικαὶ βασιλεῖαι.[2] Aristotle is interested in the kingship itself rather than in the political organization of society in the Heroic Age. But from Homer it is possible to obtain a fairly complete picture of the state of affairs in early Greece. For the threefold division of society Homer uses the names which were current in later times. There was the clan (γένος), all the members of which claimed descent from a common ancestor.[3] Aside from the γένος there were the phratry (φρήτρη) and the tribe (φῦλον), which appear only as military divisions in Homer. When the Greeks were assembled to go

---

[1] *Politics*, 1285b; cf. also his succeeding summary: "These, then, are the four kinds of royalty. First the monarchy of the heroic ages; this was exercised over voluntary subjects, but limited to certain functions; the king was a general and a judge, and had the control of religion." Jowett's translation.

[2] Thucydides i. 13. 1.

[3] *Iliad* xiii. 354. Cf. Glotz, *La solidarité de la famille dans le droit criminel en Grèce*, pp. 12 ff. According to Cary, *Cambridge Ancient History*, III, 582 ff., the γένος had no official importance and was not a subdivision of the phratry. In Athens it was an aristocratic organization indicative of wealth and high birth and hence had considerable power.

I

to battle with the Trojans in the second book of the *Iliad*, they were organized by tribes and phratries.[1] It has regularly been assumed, owing to the later use of the terms φρήτρη and φῦλον, that in Homeric society the military organization was based on the political organization and that the phratry was composed of a group bound by common religious rites which developed into an organization for the defense of life and property. The tribe was a larger unit, originally including the members of one community.[2] However this may be, the importance of the phratry in public estimation is indicated by the Homeric line,

ἀφρήτωρ ἀθέμιστος ἀνέστιός ἐστιν ἐκεῖνος.[3]

At the head of the Homeric state was a chief (βασιλεύς); and next to him, a council composed of other less powerful chiefs, likewise called βασιλεῖς.[4] Finally there was an assembly composed of all freemen, which met irregularly to hear the plans presented to it by a chief.

The king is regularly spoken of as "Zeus-born" or "Zeus-nurtured"; and the kings of whom Homer makes mention trace their descent to a god either immediately, as in the case of Achilles, or more remotely, as in the case of Agamemnon. The obedience of the people to their kings in the first

---

[1] *Il.* ii. 362. Elsewhere in Homer φῦλον occurs only in such phrases as φῦλον ἀνθρώπων, φῦλον γυναικῶν, φῦλον θεῶν. The organization of the army in Athens in the historical period was by tribes.

[2] Botsford, *The Athenian Constitution*, pp. 95 ff., attributes to the tribe a much smaller part than to the phratry in the synoecism of communities later into organized political cities.

[3] *Il.* ix. 63.

[4] Myres, *Political Ideas of the Greeks*, pp. 64 ff., argues plausibly that the Homeric poems describe the conditions and customs of the thirteenth and twelfth centuries. In the following discussion no attempt will be made to distinguish between earlier and later portions of Homer. The fully developed Homeric society will be described. Fanta's entire argument about the Homeric state is used to prove earlier and later portions of the two poems (*Der Staat in der "Ilias" und "Odyssee"*). Bréhier, *Rev. historique*, LXXXV, 1 ff., differentiates between the age of (1) the early *Iliad* and (2) the later portions of the *Iliad*, and the *Odyssey*. According to his theory, the quasi-feudal age of the earlier period, when the state was not yet in existence and the social organization depended only on fealty to a chief and his family, gives way to an organized aristocracy of the later period.

instance was probably due to this reputed divine descent. Each chief was suzerain to a group of lesser chiefs, who, in their turn, were suzerain to a group of subordinates. So a chief is described as more or less kingly according as he had more or fewer *basileis* subordinate to him.[1] For instance, Agamemnon is described as more kingly (βασιλεύτερος) than Achilles.[2] The kingship was in general hereditary, although a family might be set aside and another king chosen.[3] Since this was the case, a king had to have many personal qualities aside from his wealth in order to maintain his authority. Different qualifications are mentioned as desirable,[4] in connection with various Homeric chiefs; for example, good generalship, eloquence, wise counsel, superiority in athletics, proficiency in the arts and crafts. The king might, of course, lack some of these qualities. Agamemnon, for instance, showed no prowess in athletics. When a king became old, he could be represented in war by his son, as in the case of Peleus and Achilles. The outward sign of the kingship was the scepter, which was inherited and which was carried by the king in council. The scepter of Agamemnon is represented as being of divine workmanship.[5] The revenues of the king came from various sources. The people gave him land, called his τέμενος. In addition, frequent gifts were expected from his people; and in sumptuous public entertainments for his guests the people were often called upon to

[1] So the chief king might be described as βασιλεύτατος, *Il.* ix. 69. Cf. Glotz, *La cité grecque*, pp. 45 f. Nillson, "Das Homerische Königtum," *Sitzungsberichte d. preuss. Akad. d. Wissenschaften*, Phil. Hist. Kl. 1927, p. 27, says that the royal power in the *Iliad* consists primarily in military command. When the great military enterprises ceased, the lesser chiefs were no longer so closely connected with the king but became more independent (p. 37).

[2] *Il.* ix. 160. Cf. Glotz, *Solidarité*, p. 12. The wealth of the chieftains was doubtless gained by force. Cf. Moreau, "Les assemblées politiques d'après l'*Iliade* et l'*Odyssée*," *Rev. d. études grecques*, VI, 236 ff.

[3] Cf. the threat to remove Telemachus from the succession in Ithaca, *Od.* i. 386; cf. xi. 174 ff.

[4] The good king is like a gentle father to his people (*Od.* v. 7 ff.). Helen describes Agamemnon as both a good king and a good warrior (*Il.* iii. 179).

[5] Cf. *Il.* ii. 101 ff.

contribute.[1] Further, from war and from marauding expeditions the largest share of the booty went to the king.[2] In the loosely organized state of Homeric society there were many duties which the king had to perform personally. He had to provide for the entertainment of guests and for the protection of guests and suppliants. His earliest function as village chief in the earliest stage of society was doubtless the superintendence of the sacrifices for the community. This is one of his important functions in Homer.[3] The king had charge of foreign relations, and it was he who made official visits to other cities and negotiated with them.[4] The arbitral and judicial functions of the king were important.[5] In war the king was the leader, and he had absolute authority. This is shown most strikingly in the case of Agamemnon, the chief leader of the Greek forces before Troy. Nobody questioned his authority, and disrespectful criticism of him was viewed with disfavor even by the common people.[6] The chief also had the duty of avenging those of his followers who were slain in battle. In this case he stood in the position of a relative to his followers. This duty involved also the general

---

[1] Cf. Odysseus at the court of Alcinous, *Od.* viii. 390 ff.; cf. also xix. 197.

[2] E.g., the gift of more goats to Odysseus in the Cyclops adventure (*Od.* ix. 160).

[3] Cf. Agamemnon in charge of the sacrifice before the duel of Paris and Menelaus, *Il.* iii. 271 ff.

[4] Cf. the visit of Odysseus and Menelaus to Troy prior to the Trojan War, *Il.* iii. 205 ff.

[5] Fanta, *op. cit.*, p. 58, says that the king never appears as the real or single judge in the *Iliad* or the *Odyssey*. Arete is represented as settling the disputes even of men (*Od.* vii. 74). There is no doubt that this is viewed as a surprising situation. Arete's capacity here is obviously that of arbitrator. Cf., on the judicial powers of the king in the Homeric period, Glotz, *Études sociales et juridiques sur l'antiquité grecque*, p. 5, and Bréhier, *Rev. historique*, LXXXIV, 30, who says that the king does not draw judicial power from Zeus, but guards the customs of the city and this only in religious and military spheres, outside of which he has no judicial authority. Cf. p. 32: "Tout ce qui est dans les états modernes du ressort de la justice criminelle ou des tribunaux civils était tranché souverainement par un accord entre les particuliers. Cet accord n'était souvent que le résultat d'une longue lutte qui pouvait ensanglanter la cité pendant plusieurs générations, etc." Cf. also, *ibid.*, LXXXV, 21.

[6] Cf. the case of Thersites, *Il.* ii. 212 ff.

protection of his followers at all times.[1] Absolute as the authority of the king would appear to be from this summary, it is nevertheless not to be supposed that there were no limitations on his power. In the first place he would not venture to disturb the time-honored customs and privileges of the people. And a more definite check is to be found in the advice and opinions of the Council of Elders and the general assembly.[2]

The Council of Elders (γέροντες) was composed of the petty chiefs. It is probable that the number of the members of the council was not fixed but depended on the number that the king wanted to consult.[3] Obviously the council of the most prominent chieftain in a community would be composed of the foremost men. Before Troy the council was composed of all the other leaders together with Agamemnon as chief. Of course, many of these chiefs in their own communities at home were scepter-bearing kings, but in the army they gave way to Agamemnon as the most kingly. These lesser chieftains also were reputed to be of divine origin. In general they exhibited the same characteristics, that is, they were good generals, orators, and counselors. The ostensible function of the boulé was to act as a consultative and advisory body. The king seems frequently to have laid his plans before the boulé before they were brought before the general assembly. Since the king selected his council, he naturally was the one who summoned it. The council had no actual power to restrict the authority of the king, but in practice it must have had considerable influence in this regard. He must often have listened to the wisdom of the boulé and have accepted it, even though he had to disregard his own plans. On the other hand, there was nothing to hinder him from carrying through his own designs even if the whole council disapproved.[4] He took his counselors' opinions under con-

[1] Cf. Fanta, *op. cit.*, pp. 64 ff.   [2] Cf. Nillson, *op. cit.*, p. 28.

[3] Cf. Moreau, *op. cit.*, pp. 236 ff.

[4] Moreau, *op. cit.*, p. 249. The king might bring any matter before the council but was not forced to submit any.

sideration, but himself made the final decision.[1] With Botsford it seems fair to say that the strength or weakness of the
boulé depended very largely on the character of the king.[2]
The members of the council are called βουληφόροι.[3]

The popular assembly was composed of all adult free male
members of the community. It cannot be assumed that the
right to call an assembly belonged to the king alone. No one
questioned the authority of Telemachus to call a meeting to
deal with the suitors; and yet it is certain that this point
would have been raised by the suitors, who were anxious to
prevent the intervention of the people, if the sole right to
summon the assembly belonged to the king.[4] At a later time
Penelope proposed to have Laertes appeal to the people;[5]
and the suitors themselves, after their attempt to waylay and
kill Telemachus, were in dread of another appeal to the people which might result in their banishment.[6] Both Nestor
and Odysseus expressed surprise that the people did not interfere to protect Penelope and Telemachus.[7] Aegyptius, the
father of one of the suitors but a friend of Odysseus, clearly
intimates that anyone who had important news might summon a meeting of the people:

[1] Cf. Agamemnon's taking of Briseis and the straits in which his act left the
army (Il. i. 318 ff.). On the other hand, he yielded with regard to Chryseis. Another
instance is the treatment of Polydamas by Hector as a result of his opposition,
although Hector was obviously in the wrong (Il. xviii. 285 ff.).

[2] Op. cit., p. 118.   [3] Il. i. 144.

[4] Od. ii. 6 ff.; cf. iii. 137; xvi. 361 ff.; also Il. i. 53; xix. 34. It is surprising to
learn that the assembly of the second book of the Odyssey is the first meeting since
the departure of Odysseus. Fanta, op. cit., p. 87, regards this as proof that the king
regularly summoned the assembly. There is a strong temptation to regard the
statement of Aegyptius as a rhetorical exaggeration. Moreau, op. cit., p. 214, remarks: "Il est sans doute extraordinaire qu'Ithaque ait passé vingt ans sans agora,
et si j'osais, je dirais volontiers que je n'en crois rien." Finsler, "Das Homerische
Königtum," Neue Jahr. für Phil., XVII, 321, sees, in the meeting, "die Wiederkehr
geordneter Zustände." This seems to be correct. The interests of the suitors had
made it desirable that there should be no meetings.

[5] Od. iv. 735 ff. There is no indication that Laertes had special authority during
the absence of Odysseus, whose representative was Mentor (Od. ii. 225 ff.).

[6] Od. xvi. 375 ff.

[7] Ibid., iii. 214 ff.; xvi. 95 ff.

νῦν δὲ τίς ὧδ' ἤγειρε; τίνα χρειὼ τόσον ἵκει
ἠὲ νέων ἀνδρῶν, ἢ οἳ προγενέστεροί εἰσιν;
ἠέ τιν' ἀγγελίην στρατοῦ ἔκλυεν ἐρχομένοιο,

. . . .

ἦέ τι δήμιον ἄλλο πιφαύσκεται ἠδ' ἀγορεύει;[1]

It would seem, then, that the right to summon an assembly was open to all, both chieftains and common people.[2] But not always was an assembly formally summoned. It was the natural instinct of Greeks to resort to the place of assembly, even without special summons, when anything happened that concerned the whole community. Thus the Ithacans, on hearing of the slaughter of the suitors, assembled of their own accord in the agora.[3] They went there automatically since it was the one certain place for information and discussion. It was the common daily meeting place.[4]

Formal meetings were held at irregular intervals. After Telemachus called the people to assembly, Aegyptius is represented as saying that the assembly had not met in Ithaca since the departure of Odysseus twenty years before.[5] But the assembly could be summoned whenever there was a matter to put before it. For example, at the beginning of the second book of the *Iliad* Agamemnon dispatches heralds to call the people to assembly so that he may make trial of their spirit. The Achaeans assemble with the utmost eagerness and promptness. Evidently, assembly meetings were of great interest to the army.[6] Achilles calls a meeting of the people to discuss the plague.[7] Doubtless he sent out heralds just as Agamemnon did. Alcinous calls an assembly of the Phaeacians to inform them of the arrival of a stranger whom they are to entertain and afterwards to escort home.[8] All

[1] *Ibid.*, ii. 28 ff.

[2] Cf. Moreau, *op. cit.*, p. 213, and Finsler, *op. cit.*, p. 327.

[3] *Od.* xxiv. 420.

[4] This may be inferred from the remark about Achilles that during the period of the wrath he did not frequent the man-ennobling assembly (*Il.* i. 490). This is better than to suppose that the called assemblies were so frequent that his absence during the few days of his wrath was a matter for remark.

[5] *Od.* ii. 26 f.   [6] *Il.* ii. 86 ff.   [7] *Ibid.*, i. 54.   [8] *Od.* viii. 4 ff.

three of these meetings are called for the purpose of giving information to the people, and the first two particularly for getting the reaction of the people to the subject in hand. The assembly afforded a means of communicating information and orders to the people, who were eager for news and could always be counted upon to assemble readily. The person who called the assembly was not necessarily the one who introduced the business before it.[1] The consultative and deliberative character of the assembly develops later, but is firmly established in the time of Homer, as evidenced by the case of the assembly called by Achilles wherein various people gave their opinions with regard to the plague and the course to be followed. That the speakers were not necessarily chieftains is illustrated by the case of Thersites, who was apparently a common soldier—the only one named in the *Iliad*.[2] On more than one occasion he had ventured to criticize the chieftains in the assembly. Apparently, then, after the business had been brought before the meeting, anyone had a right to speak in approbation or criticism. The man of the common people, however, had to be careful of his words, for the chieftains did not take kindly to criticism from their inferiors. It is noteworthy that nobody questioned the right of Thersites to speak; the criticism is directed altogether against what he says.

Fanta[3] argues that there was a second assembly, called θῶκος, in which the king, surrounded by his chiefs, gave orders to the people or informed them about public matters. There was no opportunity for discussion. Some scholars regard the word as another designation of the council of chiefs, the βουλή.[4] Moreau[5] rejects both of these theories on the ground that θῶκος means merely "sitting"; hence it may refer to any seated assembly, and therefore should not be regarded as having any such exact meaning as either of these two

[1] Cf. *Il*. x. 203. For some examples of topics treated by the assembly, cf. Moreau, *op. cit.*, pp. 227 ff.

[2] *Il*. ii. 212 ff.   [3] *Op. cit.*, p. 77.

[4] Buchholz, *Die homerischen Realien*, Vol. II, Part I, Section I, § 4; Glotz, *La cité*, pp. 54 and 59.

[5] Moreau, *op. cit.*, pp. 209 f.

theories would attribute to it, especially in view of the lack of detail in any of the passages in which θῶκος occurs. At any rate, there is no need to suppose that there was a third assembly.[1]

In this period, deliberative, executive and judicial functions were not yet distinct. The political organization of the Homeric state had developed from such patriarchal communities as the one described in the case of the Cyclopes.[2] The authority of the father under such a system had developed into the authority of the king in the Homeric state. Naturally there are found in Homer no laws in the sense in which the Xenophontic Pericles defined them: πάντες γὰρ οὗτοι νόμοι εἰσὶν οὓς τὸ πλῆθος συνελθὸν καὶ δοκιμάσαν ἔγραψε φράζον ἅ τε δεῖ ποιεῖν καὶ ἃ μή.[3] But there were, nevertheless, definite ideas of ἅ τε δεῖ ποιεῖν καὶ ἃ μή, though they had not yet been formulated in codes and constitutions. And the notion of orderliness and of obedience to the prevailing standards of right and justice was expressed by such words as εὐνομίη, εὐηγεσίη, and εὐδικίη.

The θέμιστες were the nearest approach to laws. Strictly speaking, they were pronouncements of the king indicating in an authoritative fashion what was right and proper (θέμις) in a particular set of circumstances. A θέμις was given only to properly qualified men, and to them it transmitted the pleasure and advice of the gods.[4] Such men were the kings, of course. The king held a scepter, a hereditary symbol of power; he acquired communion with the gods through ritual acts, and he summoned meetings of the whole people before whom he made known his decisions.[5] It will be seen from

[1] For the meaning of the word θῶκος and the passages in which it occurs, cf. Ebeling, Lexicon Homericum, s.v.

[2] Vinogradoff, Outlines of Historical Jurisprudence, Vol. II: The Jurisprudence of the Greek City, p. 1.

[3] Xen. Mem. i. 2. 42.

[4] Maine, Lectures on the Early History of Institutions, p. 35: "Among the Achaeans of Homer the chief has ceased to be priest, but he is still judge; and his judicial sentences, θέμιστες, or 'dooms,' however much they may be drawn in reality from preexisting usage, are believed to be dictated to him from on high."

[5] Myres, op. cit., p. 138.

this that originally all decisions were regarded as divinely inspired, but in the Homeric period the notion of a divine source had largely disappeared.[1] None of these inspired judgments is recorded in the poems.

Along with θέμις, δίκη shared the general idea of justice, and is used to supplement the Homeric legal vocabulary. δίκη strictly represents the application by the human agent of the θέμις, which comes from the gods. Since his application may be wrong, there being a multiplicity of θέμιστες, it is possible to speak of crooked judgments (σκολιαὶ θέμιστες). The particular θέμις which fits a particular case has not been applied, but some other θέμις which does not fit. Glotz[2]

---

[1] Cf. Gilbert, *Beiträge zur Entwickelungsgeschichte des griechischen Gerichtsverfahrens*, p. 463.

[2] *Solidarité*, pp. 21 ff. He sees in θέμις family law of a supernatural and mysterious origin, and in δίκη custom which regulates interfamily relations, also of divine origin but less mysterious in its workings than θέμις. Cf. *Études*, pp. 3 ff. For the dependence of law on religion, cf. *ibid.*, pp. 1 ff. Sandys discusses the two words as follows (*Encyclopaedia Britannica*, article "Greek Law," p. 501): "Diké (δίκη), assigned by Curtius (*Etym.* 134) to the same root as δείκνυμι, primarily means 'a way pointed out,' a 'course prescribed by usage,' hence 'way' or 'fashion,' 'manner' or 'precedent.' In the Homeric poems it sometimes signifies a 'doom' of law, a legal 'right,' a 'lawsuit'; while it is rarely synonymous with 'justice,' as in *Od.* xiv. 84, where 'the gods honor justice.'

"Various senses of 'right' are expressed in the same poems by themis (θέμις), a term assigned (*ib.* 254) to the same root as τίθημι. In its primary sense *themis* is that which 'has been laid down'; hence a particular decision or 'doom.' The plural *themistes* implies a body of such precedents, 'rules of right,' which the king receives from Zeus with his sceptre (*Il.* ix. 99). *Themis* and *diké* have sometimes been compared with the Roman *fas* and *jus* respectively, the former being regarded as of divine, the latter of human origin; and this is more satisfactory than the latest view (that of Hirzel), which makes 'counsel' the primary meaning of *themis*."

Ehrenberg, *Die Rechtsidee im frühen Griechentum*, rejects, as does Hirzel (*Dike, Themis und Verwandtes*), both of the etymologies given above. θέμις he assigns to the root θεμ- as found in such words as θεμέθλα, θεμείλια, and asserts that the word originally meant "hill," then "the holy hill," then the chthonic deity dwelling in the hill, then the oracle, and finally the heavenly command. Consequently the word signified the command of Zeus and was extended to the commands of kings and judges (pp. 41 ff.). δίκη is connected with δικεῖν and means "a throw," signifying the cast of a vote which decides a dispute (pp. 70 ff.). On the two words, cf. also E. Weiss, *Griechisches Privatrecht*, I, 19 ff.; Steinwenter, *Die Streitbeendigung durch Urteil, Schiedsspruch und Vergleich nach griechischem Rechte*, pp. 32 ff.; Meyer, *Geschichte des Altertums*, II, 82 f.; Bréhier, *Rev. historique*, LXXXIV, 30; Hirzel, *op. cit.*, pp. 53, 94; Maine, *Ancient Law*, pp. 4 f.; Finsler, *op. cit.*, p. 329. For examples of θέμις and δίκη, cf. Myres, *op. cit.*, pp. 126 ff. and 169 ff.

explains the relationship of the two words by saying that θέμιστες are inspired, spontaneous judgments while δίκαι refer to judgments which are based on custom. The abstract idea of justice is expressed not by θεμιστοσύνη but by δίκη. And a person who refuses to do what is right is ἀθέμιστος; but a righteous man is δίκαιος, not θεμιστός. Θεμιστεύω, in the sense of "pronounce judgment," occurs, but δικάζω is the more common word. Κρίνω is also used of the exercise of judicial functions, in such phrases as κρίνωσι θέμιστας.

Crimes and criminals are unknown to Homer.[1] The conception of crime as a wrong which was a menace to society was not yet formulated, though it is dimly foreshadowed in the feeling of abhorrence for the fomenter of civil strife so well voiced by Nestor:

ἀφρήτωρ ἀθέμιστος ἀνέστιός ἐστιν ἐκεῖνος
ὃς πολέμου ἔραται ἐπιδημίου ὀκρυόεντος.[2]

The administration of justice, then, necessarily was largely an informal matter in Homer, carried out mainly by the two parties involved, whom we should call the prosecutor and the defendant. The commonest method of obtaining redress was probably by self-help. In modern criminal law, self-help in the form of self-defense against aggression plays an important rôle subject to certain restrictions.[3] But in the Homeric age there were no restrictions upon the exercise of self-

[1] Levi, *Delitto e Pena nel Pensiero dei Greci*, p. 38, finds one exception: "Un solo tipo di degenerato, come direbbesi ora, ricorda l'Iliade: Tersite." But Thersites cannot fairly be called a criminal.

[2] *Il.* ix. 63 f.

[3] Anyone may resist attacks upon himself or his property. But the law requires that the resistance shall not be more than is sufficient for the purposes of self-defense; for the prevention of a wrong, not its redress, is the object of self-defense. But in the case of certain wrongs the common law allows true remedial self-help. One may expel a trespasser, retake goods of which he is the rightful owner, or abate a nuisance. So far as assisting another to defend himself is concerned, it is certain that a person may always defend those whose relation to him implies protection. It has even been held that a man may defend anyone; but his right to assist is no greater than the other's right to defend himself. In practice these rights are materially restricted by the prohibition against carrying weapons. The example of Sir Frederick Pollock is followed in using the English equivalent of the expressive German *Selbsthülfe*. The distinction between self-defense and self-help which he points out has no application here (*The Law of Torts*, p. 181).

help save such as were imposed by the individual's own weakness. The general custom of carrying arms greatly facilitated recourse to this method of obtaining redress. Relatives and friends were always expected to espouse the cause of the injured. Even wrongdoers could count on the assistance of their kinsmen. Odysseus, in his character of Cretan refugee, wondered why Telemachus was not aided in his troubles by his brothers:

οἷοί περ ἀνὴρ
μαρναμένοισι πέποιθε, καὶ εἰ μέγα νεῖκος ὄρηται.[1]

And later, disguised as a beggar, he said to the suitors, "Many an infatuate deed I did, giving place to mine own hardihood and strength, and trusting to my father and my brethren."[2] Within his own household the master punished his servants even to the extent of inflicting death.[3] And, like the Cyclopes, each man θεμιστεύει παίδων ἠδ' ἀλόχων.[4] It was the duty of the father to avenge the wrongs of those who were under his protection, including the servants.[5]

There are various specific cases in Homer in which the injured party sought redress by self-help. For instance, adultery, seduction, or rape was punished by the husband or nearest relative in the case of a free woman, by the master in the case of a slave. It is probable that Aegisthus' adultery with Clytemnestra is regarded as aggravating the murder of Agamemnon, and his death at the hands of Orestes is an expiation of the seduction as well as of the murder.[6] That the punishment would have been so severe if the sole fault of Aegisthus had been adultery is doubtful. It is clear that the injured relative might exact a fine from the adulterer, as

[1] *Od.* xvi. 97 f.

[2] *Ibid.*, xviii. 139 f.

[3] Odysseus punished with death the goatherd and faithless maidservants (*Od.* xxii. 457 ff.).

[4] *Od.* ix. 114 f. Cf. *Il.* ix. 447 ff., where Amyntor curses his son and drives him into banishment for debauching his concubine.

[5] One of Odysseus' charges against the suitors was that they had debauched the female servants.

[6] *Od.* i. 35 ff.

Hephaestus did in the lay of Demodocus.¹ Anteia, the wife of Proetus, falsely accused Bellerophon of improper proposals and insisted that her husband should slay him. Accordingly Proetus took steps to compass his death by guile after banishing him.² The fact that Proetus sought to bring about his death in such a roundabout fashion strongly suggests that slaying was not the customary punishment for adultery in Homeric Greece and was not considered justifiable.³ On the other hand, Proetus may have resorted to a trick through fear of the power of Bellerophon. Amyntor punished his son Phoenix for debauching his concubine by cursing and banishing him.⁴ One of the explicit charges which Odysseus made against the suitors before he proceeded to slay them was δμωῆσιν δὲ γυναιξὶ παρευνάζεσθε βιαίως. This amounts to rape if, indeed, βιαίως is to be taken literally, but it probably means merely "in defiance of decency,"⁵ for, in view of the fact that these women are afterward punished for unchastity, one should not look for the precision of an Athenian indictment in Odysseus' charge. The conduct of both suitors and servants was an intolerable insult to the master and called for redress.⁶

Robbery in the form of cattle-lifting and piracy was extremely common. Against piracy, the individual, even when aided by his friends, had but slight means of protection. Both piracy and cattle-lifting on a large scale were matters for the community as a whole to redress. Against ordinary steal-

¹ *Ibid.*, viii. 266 ff. Glotz, *Solidarité*, p. 383, finds in the passage a similarity to the Gortyn code which makes provisions for pecuniary settlement with the injured husband. Vinogradoff, *op. cit.*, p. 234, deals with the case at some length. The whole transaction is explained as "the substitution of a convention with Poseidon for the convention with Ares, as originally proposed by Poseidon." Treston, *Poine*, p. 58, uses this case to prove that there was in Homeric times among the Pelasgians a distinction between cases in which slaying was justifiable and those in which it was not. The suggestion that there was a prescribed μοιχάγρια renders it likely that the killing of an adulterer was not justifiable. Cf. Gernet, *Rev. d. études grecques*, XXX (1917), 249 ff.; Calhoun, *The Growth of Criminal Law in Ancient Greece*, pp. 62 ff. and 69 ff.

² *Il.* vi. 160 ff. Cf. Treston, *op. cit.*, p. 59.

³ Cf. Treston, *op. cit.*, p. 58.

⁴ *Il.* ix. 454 ff.   ⁵ *Od.* xxii. 37.   ⁶ *Ibid.*, xxii. 418.

ing a man had some chance of protecting himself. If, under cover of mist or darkness, his sheepfolds or herds were raided, he might trace the lost animals and seek to recover them.[1] But the mere finding of stolen animals would not suffice if the robber who operated by stealth was prepared to resort to force. Iphitus lost his life in trying to recover some stolen horses from Heracles.[2] But the vigilant owner might surprise the thief in the act, and men were not infrequently wounded in protecting their cattle and sheep.[3]

Self-help in another form in a case akin to robbery is seen in the action of Achilles after the taking of Briseis.[4] Realizing his inability to recover Briseis by force, he refrained from battle. The subsequent losses of the Greeks compelled Agamemnon not only to offer to return Briseis but also to add many valuable gifts.

There is an intimation of self-help in Achilles' impulse to slay Agamemnon at the first suggestion of the taking of Briseis.[5] His desire was overruled by Athena's timely intervention. This situation arose in the midst of a violent quarrel between Achilles and Agamemnon. Assault and battery arising out of disputes and quarrels of various kinds must have been of common occurrence among men who habitually carried arms. For example, a quarrel about boundary stones, such as is described in a simile of the *Iliad*, might easily lead to a personal encounter.[6] Threats of violence no doubt often caused men to refrain from insisting on their rights.[7]

It has been observed that the redress sought by the injured person included not merely the restitution of property destroyed, stolen, or withheld, but also substantial damages.[8]

[1] *Il.* iii. 10 f. Autolycus, the maternal grandfather of Odysseus, was a skilful thief (*Od.* xix. 396).

[2] *Od.* xxi. 22 ff.   [4] *Il.* i. 320 ff.

[3] *Ibid.*, xvii. 471 ff.   [5] *Ibid.*, i. 188 ff.

[6] *Ibid.*, xii. 421 ff.; cf. the fight between Irus and Odysseus, *Od.* xviii. 1 ff.

[7] Laomedon is said by threats of violence to have defrauded Apollo and Poseidon of their wages (*Il.* xxi. 435 ff.).

[8] Such damages were known as τιμή, ποινή, and more specifically μοιχάγρια. Cf. Ferrini, *Quid conferat ad iuris criminalis historiam Homericorum Hesiodorumque*

The suitors offered to make terms on this basis; and the Trojans agreed to return Helen and her treasures, together with suitable damages, if Menelaus slew Paris in the duel.[1] To these examples cited by Lipsius may be added the offer of Antilochus[2] to pay reasonable damages as well as to restore the prize he wrongfully won from Menelaus in the chariot race. When the suitors proposed that Telemachus send his mother back to her father, he refused to dismiss her against her will, partly because her dowry would have to be restored, together with a substantial sum in the way of damages. It is true that the words κακὸν δέ με πόλλ᾽ ἀποτίνειν Ἰκαρίῳ may refer to the restitution of the dowry only; but the next line, ἐκ γὰρ τοῦ πατρὸς κακὰ πείσομαι, seems to indicate that more than mere restitution is contemplated.[3] In effect, the wager in the trial scene and the μοιχάγρια in cases of adultery amount to damages.[4]

Of self-help in obtaining redress for the killing of relatives there is a number of instances. Thirteen homicides are mentioned apart from the slaying of the suitors and of the followers of Aegisthus and Agamemnon.[5] The typical wanderer from his native country is the fleeing homicide,[6] and the typical trial-scene pictured on the shield of Achilles arises out of a homicide. There is no trace in the poems of the later conception that homicide involves the pollution both of the

---

poematum studium, p. 17. Cf. the Hesiodic use of ἀμοιβή, *Works and Days*, 333. On the question of ποινή, cf. Lipsius, *Das Attische Recht*, pp. 7 ff.

[1] Cf. the version preserved by Herodotus (ii. 118) according to which an embassy under Menelaus demanded the return of Helen and the stolen property as well as τῶν ἀδικημάτων δίκας. Cf. *Il.* iii. 205 ff. for the embassy.

[2] *Il.* xxiii. 591 ff.

[3] *Od.* ii. 132 ff. There is a possibility that τοῦ πατρός may refer to Telemachus' own father. At any rate, the words πόλλ᾽ ἀποτίνειν suggest a penalty. Lipsius, *op. cit.*, p. 10, n. 29, thinks the dowry alone is in question. Cf. *Il.* ix. 634, where the words are used of paying blood-money.

[4] Cf. *infra*, pp. 31 ff. Fanta, *op. cit.*, p. 84, wrongly regards πεῖραρ as referring to the deposit (*Il.* xviii. 501).

[5] *Od.* iv. 536.

[6] *Il.* xxiv. 480. When Odysseus desires to conceal his identity and account for his wandering from Crete, he pretends that he slew a man (*Od.* xiii. 259).

slayer and of those who associated with him.[1] Eumaeus, the swineherd, comes close to this conception, so far as the slayer himself is concerned. The disguised Odysseus had prophesied that Eumaeus' master was on the point of returning, and he offered to permit Eumaeus to slay him if the prophecy should not be fulfilled. Eumaeus refused the wager saying:

Aye, stranger, so should I indeed win fair fame and prosperity among men both now and hereafter, if I, who brought thee to my hut and gave thee entertainment, should then slay thee, and take away thy dear life. With a ready heart thereafter should I pray to Zeus, son of Cronos.[2]

The suitors even propose to seek the counsel of the gods regarding the contemplated murder of Telemachus.[3]

Outside of the circle of the dead man's kinsmen and friends,[4] there is no indication of any popular sentiment against ordinary homicide. Odysseus, in his character of Cretan refugee, had told a tale to Eumaeus in which he represented himself as the slayer of the son of Idomeneus. It would be hard to imagine a more cowardly murder than this. And yet Eumaeus receives the supposed murderer with all the respect due a stranger in accordance with the prevailing customs.[5] Several homicides are mentioned who were living as honored members of communities to which they had come as exiles. The slaying of parents, however, met with universal condemnation. Phoenix, the aged companion of

---

[1] There are some instances of ceremonial purification (cf. *Il.* i. 313; vi. 266 ff.; etc.), but there is no indication that the feeling extended to homicide particularly. For a discussion of the subject, cf. Drerup, *Homerische Poetik*, Vol. I: *Das Homerproblem in der Gegenwart*, p. 147; Ferrini, *op. cit.*, pp. 22 f.; Glotz, *Solidarité*, pp. 228 ff.; Lipsius, *op. cit.*, p. 9, n. 25; Gillies, "Purification in Homer," *Class. Quar.*, XIX, 71 ff.; Gardikas, τὸ ποινικὸν καὶ ἰδία τὸ φονικὸν δίκαιον παρ' 'Ομήρῳ, 'Αθηνᾶ (1919), pp. 209 ff.; Treston, *op. cit.*, p. 112; and Calhoun, *op. cit.*, p. 16. The Theoclymenus episode (*Od.* xv. 223 ff.) shows quite clearly that no pollution was involved. Nor is the acceptance of blood-money compatible with the pollution idea. For the age of Hesiod, cf. *infra*, p. 53.

[2] *Od.* xiv. 402 ff. (Murray's translation):

ξεῖν', οὕτω γάρ κέν μοι ἐϋκλείη τ' ἀρετή τε
εἴη ἐπ' ἀνθρώπους ἅμα τ' αὐτίκα καὶ μετέπειτα,
ὅς σ' ἐπεὶ ἐς κλισίην ἀγαγον καὶ ξείνια δῶκα,
αὖτις δὲ κτείναιμι φίλον τ' ἀπὸ θυμὸν ἐλοίμην·
πρόφρων κεν δὴ ἔπειτα Δία Κρονίωνα λιτοίμην.

[3] *Od.* xvi. 402.   [4] *Ibid.*, iii. 310; iv. 535.   [5] *Ibid.*, xiii. 259 ff.

Achilles, tells of his feud with his father and of his design to
slay him. But, owing to his fear of "the people's voice and
the many reproaches of men," who would call him parricide,
he refrained.[1] In later Greek story Orestes slew his mother
Clytemnestra. In Homer it is not explicitly stated that he
was responsible for her death, but it is assumed, for she died
with Aegisthus and no other cause for her death is given.
But the honor Orestes won for avenging his father's murder
does not imply public approval of matricide under any circumstances.[2] And we may be sure that the wife who com-
passed the death of her husband would be freely condemned.
Menelaus has nothing to say of Clytemnestra's share in the
plot against Agamemnon; Aegisthus alone is responsible for
his death.[3] Nestor, too, seems to lay the blame of her treachery to her husband upon Aegisthus and the μοῖρα θεῶν,
though he does call her στυγερή.[4] Agamemnon's spirit speaks
bitterly of her and says she has brought disgrace not only
upon herself but upon her whole sex.[5] He does not say explicitly that she murdered him but implies that she had at
least planned the murder. As a rule men shrank from slaying
a guest. Heracles' murder of Iphitus is aggravated by the
fact that Iphitus was his guest.[6] And the refusal of Eumaeus
to accept Odysseus' wager, which has already been quoted,
affords further evidence of this prevailing sentiment.[7]

The idea that murder is a menace to society is modern;
in Homer it is regarded as the concern of the relatives alone
and such partisans as they can assemble. Public sentiment
not only tolerated blood-feuds but even demanded that men
should avenge the death of their kinsmen.[8] Shame and dis-

[1] Il. ix. 459 ff.; cf. Buchholz, op. cit., II, 83.

[2] Od. i. 298.   [4] Ibid., iii. 269 ff., 310.

[3] Ibid., iv. 518 ff.   [5] Ibid., xi. 429 ff.

[6] Ibid., xxi. 27 ff.:

ὅς μιν ξεῖνον ἐόντα κατέκτανεν ᾧ ἐνὶ οἴκῳ,
σχέτλιος, οὐδὲ θεῶν ὄπιν αἰδέσατ' οὐδὲ τράπεζαν,
τὴν ἥν οἱ παρέθηκεν.

[7] Ibid., xiv. 402 ff.

[8] On the blood-feud, cf. Glotz, Solidarité, pp. 47 ff. and 94 ff.

grace were the portion of him who failed to take vengeance on the slayer of brother or son, while honor and glory awaited him who performed this duty.[1] And fortunate were they who left behind them near kinsmen to punish their slayers.[2] Some scholars, influenced by the later Athenian practice of confining within certain limits of relationship the right to institute legal proceedings against a slayer, have sought for traces of a similar practice in Homer. Leist[3] attempts to show that the blood-feud did not extend beyond cousins; other kinsmen and relatives by marriage participated only as assistants. To make his point, he is obliged to translate ἔται by "cousins" in one passage and "brothers" in another. Naturally the nearest relatives took the leadership if they were in a position to do so.[4] There is no doubt that if Menelaus had returned home earlier he would not have waited for Orestes to avenge Agamemnon.[5] But in the absence of near relatives distant kinsmen and even friends would readily take up the blood-feud.[6] The question as to the right to exact vengeance could arise in practice only in cases where an agreement to accept blood-money was reached. Such an

[1] *Od.* xxiv. 433:

> λώβη γὰρ τάδε γ'ἐστὶ καὶ ἐσσομένοισι πυθέσθαι,
> εἰ δὴ μὴ παίδων τε κασιγνήτων τε φονῆας
> τισόμεθ'.

Cf. Orestes (*Od.* i. 298).

[2] *Od.* iii. 196:

> ὡς ἀγαθὸν καὶ παῖδα καταφθιμένοιο λιπέσθαι
> ἀνδρός.

Cf. *Il.* xiv. 485.

[3] Leist, *Gräco-italische Rechtsgeschichte*, p. 42; κασίγνητοί τε ἔται τε, *Od.* xv. 273; ἔται καὶ ἀνεψιοί, *Il.* ix. 464. The scholiast defines ἔται as συγγενεῖς. Ferrini, *op. cit.*, p. 19, defines them as persons closely associated with the family who aid in time of trouble, i.e., as ἀοσσητῆρες rather than συγγενεῖς. Cf. Glotz, *La cité*, p. 43.

[4] Lipsius, *op. cit.*, p. 7: "Der Kreis der zur Blutrache verpflichten Verwandten erscheint nicht genau begrenzt; zunächst sind es natürlich Söhne, Brüder, Väter, aber auch Vettern und wenigstens an einer Stelle auch die entfernteren Verwandten." Among the more distant relatives may be mentioned grandnephews and great-grandnephews (*Il.* ii. 665).

[5] *Od.* iv. 546 ff.:

> ἢ γάρ μιν ζωόν γε κιχήσεαι, ἤ κεν 'Ορέστης
> κτεῖνεν ὑποφθάμενος.

Cf. *Od.* iii. 309.

[6] *Ibid.*, xxiii. 119. Cf. Achilles and Patroclus.

agreement could satisfactorily be made only with someone who could give a reasonable guaranty that the slayer would not be molested. The only specific instance of an agreement to accept a blood-price occurs in the trial scene on the shield of Achilles. The relationship is not mentioned.[1]

Homicide among relatives was commonly settled by banishment. Normally the exile seems to have been in no danger if he afterward met a kinsman of his victim. There must have been a number of such possibilities on the expedition against Troy. Medon, the illegitimate son of Oïleus, who slew his stepmother's brother, must have met his half-brother Ajax, the nephew of his victim.[2] But sometimes a family feud arose and the life of the slayer was in danger. Thus Tlepolemus, who slew his great-uncle, fled with a large number of followers owing to the threats of his relatives: ἀπείλησαν γάρ οἱ ἄλλοι ‖ υἱέες υἱωνοί τε βίης Ἡρακληείης.[3] Althea is said to have called down curses on her son Meleager, who had slain her brother; but Meleager was neither slain nor banished.[4]

In the case of homicides outside of the family the first instinct of the slayer was to flee. The more important the victim, the more serious was the predicament of the slayer: δεινὸν δὲ γένος βασιλήιόν ἐστι ‖ κτείνειν. Even if the slain man was a humble person with few to avenge him, the only sure safety lay in flight.[5] The fate of the various homicides mentioned in the poems seems to indicate pretty clearly that voluntary banishment was the usual issue.[6] Eight of the thirteen went into exile. These figures are, of course, not entirely conclusive, because there is but little occasion for mentioning those who fell victims to the vengeance of enraged kinsmen, or those who paid the blood-price.

[1] Il. xviii. 498.   [2] Ibid., xv. 332 ff.   [3] Ibid., ii. 665.

[4] Ibid., ix. 565.   [5] Od. xvi. 401; xxiii. 118 ff.

[6] Odysseus, in his character of Cretan exile (Od. xiii. 259), is included in this list. The others are as follows: Medon, Il. xiii. 696; xv. 332; Lycophron, ibid., xv. 431; Epigeus, ibid., xvi. 573; Patroclus, ibid., xxiii. 85 ff.; an unnamed Aetolian, Od. xiv. 378; Theoclymenus, ibid., xv. 271; Tlepolemus, Il. ii. 655 ff.; all these were banished. Aegisthus was slain. The unnamed slayer in the trial-scene paid blood-money. Heracles (Od. xxi. 27), Meleager (Il. ix. 565), and Orestes were not molested. The slaying of the suitors is not included in this list.

When men of rank were concerned in a homicide, the resulting feud might involve so many as to amount to civil war. Tlepolemus, to avoid a disastrous feud, gathered his faction together and founded a settlement in Rhodes.[1] Civil war would have been the result of the feud between Odysseus and the relatives of the suitors had they not become reconciled. When once the fugitive got away, he did not seem as a rule to be in any danger. Twice the fleeing slayer is called a suppliant. But what he asks for is not protection but shelter, or assistance in continuing his flight. Theoclymenus professed to fear pursuit, but apparently his fears were groundless.[2] But the passage indicates that fugitive homicides were sometimes pursued by relatives of their victims. The lot of the murderer banished for life must often have been hard. The spirit of Patroclus speaks bitterly of his banishment, though he found in Peleus a noble patron and in Achilles a loving comrade.[3] Aegisthus is the only murderer who suffered death. He had committed a dastardly murder, and Nestor suggests that if Menelaus had slain him he would have denied him funeral rites. Menelaus himself gives no hint of such an intention, had he forestalled Orestes in slaying Agamemnon's murderer.[4] Three homicides paid no penalty. Heracles slew a stranger whose death could have been avenged only by war.[5] Meleager's distinguished services in saving his city from sack probably enabled him to defy the machinations of his incensed mother;[6] the punishment of Orestes by avenging furies is unknown to Homer.[7]

[1] Il. ii. 655.
[2] Od. xv. 271.
[3] Il. xxiii. 85 ff.
[4] Od. iii. 256 ff.; iv. 547.
[5] Ibid., xxi. 28; cf. Il. xvi. 58–59,

τὴν ἂψ ἐκ χειρῶν ἕλετο κρείων Ἀγαμέμνων
Ἀτρεΐδης ὡς εἴ τιν' ἀτίμητον μετανάστην,

for the position of a stranger.

[6] Il. ix. 565 ff.

[7] Murderers are spoken of in one passage as men seized by a grievous curse:

ὡς δ' ὅτ' ἂν ἄνδρ' ἄτη πυκινὴ λάβῃ, ὅς τ' ἐνὶ πάτρῃ
φῶτα κατακτείνας ἄλλων ἐξίκετο δῆμον.

(Il. xxiv. 480–81). The ἄτη is best taken as that which caused the homicide. The notion of ἄτη following a homicide seems to belong to a later period. But Homer does mention curses called down upon wrongdoers (Il. ix. 453 ff., 565 ff.; Od. ii. 135).

The acceptance of blood-money seems to have been comparatively rare. Apart from the trial scene pictured on the shield of Achilles, which arose out of an agreement to settle a homicide for a blood-price, there is no specific case. A man who has settled with the slayer of a brother or a son for a large sum is cited in a simile of the *Iliad*[1] as an instance of commendable, though perhaps unusual, self-restraint. We do not know what considerations induced relatives to accept blood-money. There is no trace of a tendency to put pressure on relatives to induce them to forego the blood-feud. Neither is there any indication that the circumstances under which the homicide was committed were ever taken into account. The modern classification of homicide as justifiable and excusable was unknown. The distinction between involuntary homicide (φόνος ἀκούσιος) and voluntary homicide (φόνος ἐκούσιος) belongs to a later period.[2] Patroclus committed the homicide for which he was banished, οὐκ ἐθέλων. This case shows further that not even extreme youth saved one from the penalties of manslaughter.[3]

There is no reliable clue to the origin of the practice of taking blood-money.[4] It has been suggested that it was to defray the expenses of sacrifices to appease the spirit of the dead. There is a hint of this in Achilles' promise to share with the spirit of Patroclus the ransom he received for Hector's body.[5] Neither is there any trace of the modern idea of compensation measured by the damages suffered by surviving relatives.[6]

[1] ix. 632 ff.   [2] Cf. *infra*, p. 53.

[3] εὖτέ με τυτθὸν ἐόντα Μενοίτιος ἐξ Ὀπόεντος
ἤγαγεν ὑμέτερόνδ᾽ ἀνδροκτασίης ὑπο λυγρῆς,
ἤματι τῷ ὅτε παῖδα κατέκτανον Ἀμφιδάμαντος
νήπιος, οὐκ ἐθέλων, ἀμφ᾽ ἀστραγάλοισι χολωθείς.
—*Il.* xxiii. 85 ff.

In a modern court such a homicide might be adjudged excusable if, indeed, the perpetrator was of an age at which he could be tried at all. Under seven years there is no liability; between seven and fourteen there is a rebuttable presumption of incapacity for entertaining a criminal intent.

[4] Cf. Drerup, *op. cit.*, p. 146.

[5] *Il.* xxiv. 595; cf. Bréhier, *De graecorum judiciorum origine*, pp. 38 f.

[6] Lord Campbell's act of 1846 enabled the wife, husband, parent, and child to collect the actual damages suffered by the death of one who was killed by somebody's

It is clear that the idea of self-help on the part of an individual easily develops into community self-help in cases in which the state is injured directly or indirectly through one of its citizens. The popular sentiment against wrongdoers, which is revealed in community action and which lies at the base of the conception of criminal law, was active in the time of Homer. There are numerous cases in which wrongdoers committed acts which affected the whole community alike. A common example of this class of offender is the man who, by committing depredations upon a neighboring people, involved his fellow-citizens in responsibility. Neither the king nor the council ever undertook to punish the offender. Normally, such offenses were punished, if at all, by the people. Even in a Homeric community, public opinion was quickly crystallized[1] and easily translated into action through the medium of the popular assembly. In any free community, public opinion is always a latent power. Odysseus, in his character of Cretan refugee, bears testimony to the power of public opinion—χαλεπὴ δ' ἔχε δήμου φῆμις—that forced him to go to war in Troy.[2] Some scholars have hastily dismissed community action in such cases as a resort to lynch law.[3] But, however much apparent justification may be found for this view in the differences between the orderliness and precision of modern legal machinery and the rough-and-ready methods of a primitive people, it is based upon a misconception.

"wrongful act, neglect, or default." Similar statutes in this country have added a *solatium* to the actual damages. But the principle has nowhere been extended so as to include homicides of every kind.

[1] There was practically no restriction upon freedom of speech. Cf., however, the Thersites episode. Jebb, "Ancient Organs of Public Opinion," *Essays and Addresses*, pp. 139 ff., points out how the poet keeps us informed of the trend of public opinion by constantly quoting remarks or conversations that sum up the sentiments of a crowd.

[2] *Od.* xiv. 239.

[3] Cf. Lipsius, *op. cit.*, p. 6; Gilbert, *op. cit.*, p. 447. Finsler, *op. cit.*, pp. 321 ff., recognizes fully the judicial power of the people but treats it only incidentally: "Eine richterliche Gewalt hat, wie ebenfalls schon erwähnt worden, der Demos, wenn er den Eupeithes an Leib und Gut straffen will, oder die Freier Halitherses mit Busse und Mentor mit Vernichtung bedrohen." Cf. Calhoun, *op. cit.*, p. 23. Cf. Glotz, *La Cité*, p. 66, for lynch law.

The terms "mob violence" and "lynch law" are properly applied only to the acts of people who usurp the functions of the regular courts. Sporadic instances of this type of mob violence occasionally occur in certain parts of the United States. Another type of popular justice was exemplified in the settlement of the west, where isolated communities sprang up mushroom-like far in advance of the line of settlement. It required time for the establishment of the forces of law and order in these distant and often temporary settlements. Meanwhile committees known as "vigilantes" were organized to protect life and property. Such expedients were mere stop-gaps to tide the community over the time that must elapse before the government could establish its courts. They were usually justifiable under the circumstances, but they were always illegal. They were never steps in the path of political progress. In the absence of any provision for the punishment of public offenders,[1] the early Greeks were obliged to take measures for their own protection. If they met together and acted after due deliberation, they constituted a popular court quite as much as the Athenian assembly that tried Miltiades.[2] The essential difference between the Assembly of the Ten Thousand which tried Xenophon for aggravated assault and the mob of soldiers that attacked the market clerks is that in the former case they acquainted themselves with the facts while in the latter many of the participants were entirely ignorant of the cause of the attack.[3]

The practice of determining an issue by shouting rather than by ballot or show of hands is not an evidence of mob violence. The Spartans in the fourth century continued to express their opinion by shouts for or against a proposal in the Apella. Only in case of doubt did they resort to a formal division.

When an outrage was committed by a member of another

---

[1] The king, in his capacity of general, might punish breaches of discipline; cf. *Il.* xii. 248.

[2] Herodotus vi. 136. This is the first trial before the assembly of which we have any account. Cf. Lipsius, *op. cit.*, p. 180.

[3] Xen. *Anabasis* v. 7. 19 ff.; v. 8. 1 ff.

community, the injured person might himself seek to recover his property by presenting a claim to the community
to which the stranger belonged. But that such a course involved considerable risk is clear from the fate of Iphitus,
who was slain by Heracles while seeking to recover some
stolen horses.[1] As a rule, the whole community took up
these claims and took steps to obtain compensation. Thus
Odysseus, when a mere lad, was sent by his father and the
Council of Elders to Messenia to obtain redress for the theft
of a number of sheep by Messenians.[2] The attitude of a community toward a marauder who thus exposed them to claims
for damages is well illustrated by the measures taken by the
Ithacans to punish Eupeithes, who, by joining in a Taphian
raid against the Thesprotians, a friendly people, had rendered
the Ithacans liable to claims for redress. It was only the
intervention of Odysseus that saved him from death and confiscation of property.[3] Failing redress by peaceful means, the
injured people usually resorted to reprisals. The accruing
booty was divided by the elders acting as a court of claims
and was distributed among those who had suffered loss of
property.[4]

The line of demarcation between a deliberative assembly
and a judicial assembly is ill defined.[5] A fair example of a
meeting of the people which contemplated the possibility of
judicial action is that summoned by Telemachus to deal with
the suitors.[6] Telemachus brings up what is apparently a
private grievance; but as Halitherses hinted, it really concerned the whole people.[7] And the event proved that this
was the case, for Odysseus later demanded that they make

---

[1] *Od.* xxi. 22 ff.   [2] *Ibid.*, xxi. 16 ff.

[3] *Ibid.*, xvi. 420 ff. This incident will receive fuller treatment in the discussion
of the judicial power of the people.

[4] *Il.* xi. 685 ff. Cf. Lécrivain, "Le droit de se faire justice soi-même et les
représailles," *Mémoires de L'Academie des Sciences de Toulouse* (1897), p. 277.
Lécrivain and the writers whom he quotes dismiss the Homeric period with a mere
reference to the mission of Odysseus and the raid of Nestor.

[5] Cf. *Od.* ii. 28, and Euripides *Orestes*, 870 ff., where the trial of Orestes is
represented as being held before the Argive assembly.

[6] Cf. Glotz, *Solidarité*, p. 16.   [7] *Od.* ii. 45; 166 ff.

good the material losses occasioned by the constant feasting of the suitors.[1] Three speakers presented the case against the suitors, and four addressed the assembly in their favor. Telemachus did not ask for the punishment of the suitors or for the restitution of his property.[2] At best he hoped to be able to induce or force them to leave the palace. ἀλλὰ πολὺ πρὶν φραζώμεσθ' ὥς κεν καταπαύσομεν· οἱ δὲ καὶ αὐτοὶ παυέσθων, says Halitherses, one of Telemachus' active supporters.[3] But the threats of the suitors deterred the people from taking any active measures.

As a result of the slaughter of the suitors Odysseus was himself charged with offenses against the community. After disposing of the bodies of the slain suitors, the people resorted to the ἀγορά. Eupeithes, the father of Antinous, was the first speaker. He began, not by asking aid in avenging the deaths of the suitors, but by asking for the punishment of Odysseus as a public offender: ὦ φίλοι, ἦ μέγα ἔργον ἀνὴρ ὅδε μήσατ' Ἀχαιούς.[4] Speeches against the proposal of Eupeithes were made by partisans of Odysseus. Halitherses pointed out that the men richly deserved their fate, and Medon, the herald, a forced adherent of the suitors, expressed his conviction that the gods were on the side of Odysseus.[5] Finally a majority decided to slay Odysseus. By a curious reversal of fortune Eupeithes now led the people against the man who years before had saved him in a similar predicament.[6] Our information about this case is meager. The people met in the absence of the king and reached a decision with which he was not in accord. But there is no hint that they exceeded their powers. The implication is, rather, that they yielded to the persuasions, and not the power, of Odysseus in allowing the guilty man to go free. Judging from the orderly

[1] *Od.* xxiii. 356.

[2] He does, indeed, suggest restitution, but in a very guarded manner. Cf. *Od.* ii. 74.

[3] *Od.* ii. 167.   [4] *Ibid.*, xxiv. 426.   [5] *Ibid.*, xxiv. 439 ff.

[6] *Ibid.*, xvi. 420 ff. Cf. *supra*, p. 24. As has been pointed out, it was the practice to hold the whole community responsible for cattle-lifting, even when only a few participated.

procedure against Odysseus, we may assume with some degree of confidence that Eupeithes was treated in much the same way. Paris, like Eupeithes, had, by carrying off Helen, exposed his people to reprisals on the part of the Greeks. Hector[1] has this situation in mind when he says:

> ἀλλὰ μάλα Τρῶες δειδήμονες· ἦ τέ κεν ἤδη
> λάινον ἔσσο χιτῶνα κακῶν ἔνεχ' ὅσσα ἔοργας.

Stoning was a common mode of executing the death penalty in antiquity generally.[2] The suitors, in threatening to fine Halitherses for aiding and abetting Telemachus, contemplated the use of the judicial powers of the people for their own ends. No doubt they possessed sufficient ascendancy over the people to secure their acquiescence in the punishment of Halitherses, though the charge against him could not have appealed to any considerable number of them.[3]

The Homeric ἀγορά as the medium of community self-help was the prototype of the Athenian ἡλιαία. The φῆμις δήμου eventually became the κῦρος δήμου.[4]

In Homeric times a common method of bringing a dispute to an issue was by means of a wager.[5] The wager takes various forms. There are traces of challenge to battle as a means of settling disputes. This is in effect a wager. After the chariot race Achilles proposed to give Eumelus the second prize of a mare because, owing to an accident, he had lost his leading position and had been compelled to drop out.

---

[1] Il. iii. 56 f.

[2] Cf. Hirzel, "Die Strafe der Steinigung," Abhandl. d. Königl. Sächs. Gesellschaft, Phil. Hist. Kl., XXVII, 225 ff.

[3] αἴ κε νεώτερον ἄνδρα παλαιά τε πολλά τε εἰδὼς
παρφάμενος ἐπέεσσιν ἐποτρύνῃς χαλεπαίνειν
αὐτῷ μέν οἱ πρῶτον ἀνιηρέστερον ἔσται

. . . .

σοὶ δέ, γέρον, θωὴν ἐπιθήσομεν

(Od. ii. 188 ff.). Finsler, op. cit., p. 322, thinks that in the case of Mentor also judicial proceedings were contemplated (Od. xxii. 216 ff.). In such examples of community action as the foregoing, Calhoun, op. cit., pp. 20 ff., sees the beginnings of criminal law.

[4] Cf. Aristotle Ath. Pol. xxxv. 2.

[5] Cf. Bréhier, De graecorum iudiciorum origine, pp. 91 ff.

But Antilochus protested and claimed the mare because he was second in the race:

τὴν δ' ἐγὼ οὐ δώσω· περὶ δ' αὐτῆς πειρηθήτω
ἀνδρῶν ὅς κ' ἐθέλησιν ἐμοὶ χείρεσσι μάχεσθαι.[1]

In view of this challenge to combat, Achilles yielded and gave Antilochus the mare. The award was at once protested by Menelaus on the ground that Antilochus had won by a foul, and the dispute was finally settled by a challenge to Antilochus to take an evidentiary oath, which is also a species of wager. At first Menelaus called upon the chiefs to arbitrate impartially (μηδ' ἐπ' ἀρωγῇ) between himself and Antilochus, but immediately he rejected his own suggestion in favor of a challenge to take an evidentiary oath.[2] Trial by evidentiary oath consists in tendering to an opponent an oath embodying his contentions, or in offering to take an oath embodying one's own contentions.[3] Antilochus refused to take the oath, and without more ado the prize went to Menelaus. The oath which Menelaus purposed to have Antilochus take was to the effect that he did not win by a foul. Had Antilochus ventured to take the oath at the risk of being δαίμοσι

---

[1] Il. xxiii. 553 f.; Cf. Bréhier, De graecorum iudiciorum origine, p. 96.

[2] Il. xxiii. 574 ff.

[3] Bonner, Evidence in Athenian Courts, p. 74. This form of trial is found in the primitive stages of many legal systems. It was known in Germanic law (Grimm, Deutsche Rechtsaltertümer, II, 495 ff.); in Anglo-Saxon law it was occasionally allowed (Thayer, A Preliminary Treatise on Evidence at the Common Law, pp. 24 f.); and in Massachusetts colony a white man was permitted by law to swear an evidentiary oath in answer to the accusation of an Indian (1 Prov. Laws Mass. 151 [1693-94]). After the heroic period various references to the evidentiary oath are found. Theognis makes several references to the false evidentiary oath (199 ff., 1139 ff.); Aeschylus gives an instance of a challenge to an evidentiary oath which was refused (Eumenides, 429 ff.); and Herodotus in two instances refers to this type of oath (vi. 68 f. and vi. 86). Various references are made to it in the Gortyn code (ii. 11 ff.; iii. 1 ff.; ix. 51 ff.). Cf. Headlam, "The Procedure of the Gortynian Inscription," Jour. of Hellenic Studies, XIII, p. 65, and Bücheler and Zitelmann, Das Recht von Gortyn, ad. loc. An interesting type of the evidentiary oath is the oath of the Athenian father to the legitimacy of a son on his introduction into the phratry (Isaeus, vii. 16). A change attributed to Solon allowed both parties to take the oath in cases in which no other evidence was available. (Cf. infra, pp. 173 ff.) From this doubtless arose the oath of the parties preliminary to a trial. On the whole question of the evidentiary oath, cf. Gertrude Smith, The Administration of Justice from Hesiod to Solon, pp. 55 ff.

ἀλιτρός, he would have been entitled to the prize according to the terms of the challenge. This is implied in Menelaus' assertion during the race, οὐδ' ὡς ἄτερ ὅρκου οἴσῃ ἄεθλον. No money wager is required in this kind of trial, but Antilochus expresses his willingness to pay the usual damages. This offer is, of course, quite gratuitous, but it serves to show how firmly fixed was the custom of demanding damages along with the restitution of an article wrongfully taken. Menelaus' words, εἰ δ' ἄγ' ἐγὼν αὐτὸς δικάσω, are commonly taken to mean that he proposes to act as judge—and that, too, in his own case. Now Menelaus had rejected his own proposition to submit the dispute to the arbitration of the chiefs lest people should criticize him and say, "Menelaus, by constraining Antilochus with false words, has gone off with the prize." Trial by evidentiary oath was preferred expressly because the result would be just (ἰθεῖα) and because there would be no chance for a decision ἐπ' ἀρωγῇ. Under these circumstances Menelaus' words cannot be interpreted to mean that he intended to be judge in his own case. He would, doubtless, have been ready to agree with Plato[1] that the gods, and not men, are the judges in this kind of trial. The confusion arises from pressing the meaning of δικάσω too closely, owing to a desire to preserve a distinction between the active and middle voices. Menelaus simply means to say, "I'll make my right in the matter clear." As a matter of fact, the chiefs who are asked to criticize his proposal are the only persons who can be regarded as judges. This is the only specific instance in Homer of the tendering of an evidentiary oath. Autolycus, the maternal grandfather of Odysseus, who is said to have excelled all men in stealing and swearing, was apparently able to escape responsibility, when charged with theft, by taking an oath. He was able to shape an oath so craftily that he could seem to say one thing and yet mean another.[2] Hermes, in the Homeric hymn, offered to swear that he had not stolen the cattle.[3]

---

[1] *Laws*, 948 B.

[2] *Od.* xix. 396; cf. *Il.* x. 267; Ovid *Met.* xi. 313.

[3] *Hymn to Hermes*, 304.

The above-mentioned ways of dealing with wrongdoers—
self-help, community action, the evidentiary oath—are more
or less informal. It is obvious that as soon as a community
possesses any form of organization it will provide some means
for the formal settlement of disputes between citizens.[1]
Where the dispute was not the result of violence, the parties
showed a disposition to resort to amicable means of settlement. Unquestionably, voluntary arbitration was the first
step in a systematic administration of justice. This, too,
must at first have been an informal procedure. For instance,
in the dispute over the second prize in the chariot race described above, Menelaus at first called upon the chiefs to
arbitrate impartially between himself and Antilochus.[2] But
a more formal stage had already been reached in the time of
the Homeric Greeks. They had a system of challenge and
wager for the purpose of inducing a reluctant opponent to
submit to arbitration. It was only a question of time until
arbitration became obligatory in case either party desired it.
Naturally the disputants would seek to obtain the services
of a person who had a reputation for impartiality and wisdom, without regard to rank or official position. Even a
woman, Arete, queen of the Phaeacians, acted as an arbitrator.[3] But the prestige of the king must have marked him as
the natural arbitrator. And it is the arbitral functions of
the Homeric kings that Aristotle[4] has in mind when he says
that they tried cases (τὰς δίκας ἔκρινον). Homer, it is true,
nowhere pictures a king dispensing justice. But this is a mere
accident, for Idomeneus proposed to Ajax to submit their
dispute to Agamemnon.[5] Minos, settling disputes in the
spirit land, certainly had his prototype in such kings as Nestor, who περὶ οἶδε δίκας, and Sarpedon, who Λυκίην εἴρυτο

---

[1] Modern investigators are not agreed as to the kind of provision that was made.
Thonissen, *Le droit pénal de la république athénienne*, p. 23, conveniently summarizes
the different views: (1) Parties chose arbitrators who had no power to enforce
their awards; (2) judges were chosen from among the γέροντες, and they had the
power to enforce their decisions; (3) the judges were really magistrates and represented the king. Finsler, *op. cit.*, pp. 320 f., 329, denies that a king ever acted as
judge.

[2] Cf. *supra*, pp. 26 ff.   [4] *Politics*, 1285b.

[3] *Od.* vii. 74.   [5] *Il.* xxiii. 485.

δίκῃσί τε καὶ σθένει ᾧ.[1] Everywhere in ancient times kings
and tyrants exercised judicial functions.[2] Deioces of Persia
and Peisistratus[3] of Athens administered justice as arbitrators. Accordingly we are justified in assuming that the Homeric ruler, whether a Zeus-nourished king or the official head
of an aristocratic government, was constantly called upon to
act as arbitrator. From a royal arbitrator to a court of γέροντες is not a far cry. In the *Iliad* the chiefs are called δικασπόλοι. The term occurs only once in the *Odyssey*, where
Telemachus is called δικασπόλος by his grandmother.[4] Clearly it was an established practice to refer disputes to the lesser
chiefs acting either individually or in a body.[5] An ambitious
aristocracy would not fail to recognize the advantages that
would accrue to it from the establishment of a regular court
of arbitration to which disputants might refer their differences. In the Greek camp before Troy there was a place in or
adjoining the ἀγορά which was set apart for the administration of justice[6] and which was provided with seats for the
judges.

The appearance of a trial-scene on the shield of Achilles
as a typical incident of public life, and two similes drawn
from judicial activities point to some sort of judicial organization.[7] Court sessions were probably held with some degree

[1] *Od.* iii. 244; *Il.* xvi. 542.

[2] Among the Lydians, Persians, Egyptians, and Hebrews. Herod. i. 14, 96–97, 100; ii, 129; II Sam. 15:2.

[3] Arist. *Ath. Pol.* xvi. 5; cf. Stesagoras of the Chersonese, Herod. vi. 38.

[4] *Il.* i. 237 ff.; *Od.* xi. 184 ff.

[5] *Od.* xii. 439–40. Some think that the trial scene (*Il.* xviii. 497 ff.) has reference to a sitting of the whole council. Cf. Glotz, *La Cité*, pp. 57 f., and Ferrini, *op. cit.*, p. 40.

[6] *Il.* xi. 807; xviii. 497, 504.

[7] Treston, *op. cit.*, p. 40, supposes that the elders in the trial-scene constituted a Pelasgian court. The Achaean kings never really functioned as δικασπόλοι,, but the elders were the real judges. In fact, the kings knew little and cared less about these Pelasgian courts. The elders were the tribal chiefs, whose main function was to arbitrate in cases of interclan or interphratry disputes. Inside of each clan there would be similar assemblies for jurisdiction in intraclan disputes (pp. 82 ff.). Treston's insistence on the distinction between Pelasgians and Achaeans has led him into many errors. Cf. Calhoun, *op. cit.*, p. 18, n. 10.

of regularity, and might last all day.[1] There is no indication that recourse to such a court was obligatory. Doubtless the tendency of public opinion was to support the man who was willing to arbitrate his differences with a fellow-citizen. The interests of the aristocracy would be materially advanced by fostering such a tendency.[2]

There are several examples of challenge and wager as an inducement to arbitration. When Idomeneus and Ajax had a dispute regarding the identity of the leader in the chariot race, the Cretan warrior said, "Come then, let us wager a tripod or a caldron and make Agamemnon, Atreus' son, our umpire, which mares are leading."[3] And when Eumaeus, the swineherd, refused to believe the disguised Odysseus when he asserted that his master would return, Odysseus offered to stake his life against a suit of clothes that he spoke the truth. The parties to a challenge entered into a solemn agreement, confirmed by oath, to abide by the decision.[4] The famous trial-scene on the shield of Achilles is another instance of arbitration on challenge and wager.[5] Like all the scenes represented on the shield, this really combines a series of pictures;[6] that is to say, several pictures would be required to illustrate the poet's description. The text of the passage is as follows:

[1] *Il.* xvi. 387 f.; *Od.* xii. 439.

[2] By the time of Hesiod the processes of arbitration had become practically compulsory. *Works and Days*, 35 ff. Cf. *infra*, pp. 43 ff.

[3] *Il.* xxiii. 485. Lang, Leaf, and Myer's translation.

[4] *Od.* xiv. 391 ff.; cf. *ibid.* xvi. 102 f.

[5] Among the important discussions of the trial-scene are the following: Ferrini, *op. cit.*, pp. 42 ff.; Hofmeister, *Zeitschrift für vergleichende Rechtswissenschaft*, II, 443 ff.; Bréhier, "La royauté homérique," *Rev. historique*, LXXXIV, 27 ff.; Glotz, *Solidarité*, pp. 115 ff.; *La Cité*, p. 57; Bonner, "Administration of Justice in the Age of Homer," *Class. Philol.*, VI, 24 ff.; Lipsius, *Leipziger Studien zur classischen Philologie*, XII, pp. 225 ff.; Leaf, *Translation of the Iliad* (1883), p. 516; *Companion to the Iliad* (1892), p. 312; edition of the *Iliad*, ad. loc.; Maine, *Ancient Law*, pp. 385 f.; Myres, *op. cit.*, pp. 198 ff.; Busolt-Swoboda, *Griechische Staatskunde*, I, 332 ff.; Treston, *op. cit.*, pp. 34 ff.; Calhoun, *Criminal Law*, pp. 18 f.; *Proceedings of the Classical Association*, XVIII, p. 93; Ehrenberg, *op. cit.*, p. 55; Croiset, "La scène judiciaire représentée sur le bouclier d'Achille," *Rev. d. études grecques* XXXII, 96 ff.; Steinwenter, *op. cit.*, p. 34, n. 3.

[6] Dareste, *Annuaire des études grecques*, XVIII, 91.

497 λαοὶ δ' εἰν ἀγορῇ ἔσαν ἀθρόοι· ἔνθα δὲ νεῖκος
ὠρώρει, δύο δ' ἄνδρες ἐνείκεον εἵνεκα ποινῆς
ἀνδρὸς ἀποφθιμένου· ὁ μὲν εὔχετο πάντ' ἀποδοῦναι
500 δήμῳ πιφαύσκων, ὁ δ' ἀναίνετο μηδὲν ἐλέσθαι·
ἄμφω δ' ἱέσθην ἐπὶ ἴστορι πεῖραρ ἐλέσθαι.
λαοὶ δ' ἀμφοτέροισιν ἐπήπυον, ἀμφὶς ἀρωγοί·
κήρυκες δ' ἄρα λαὸν ἐρήτυον· οἱ δὲ γέροντες
ἥατ' ἐπὶ ξεστοῖσι λίθοις ἱερῷ ἐνὶ κύκλῳ,
505 σκῆπτρα δὲ κηρύκων ἐν χέρσ' ἔχον ἠεροφώνων·
τοῖσιν ἔπειτ' ἤισσον, ἀμοιβηδὶς δὲ δίκαζον.
κεῖτο δ' ἄρ' ἐν μέσσοισι δύω χρυσοῖο τάλαντα,
508 τῷ δόμεν, ὃς μετὰ τοῖσι δίκην, ἰθύντατα εἴποι.[1]

In disputed matters the following translation embodies the interpretations which are advocated in the subsequent discussion.

"But the folk were gathered together in the place of assembly. And there strife had arisen and two men were contending about the blood-price of a slain man. The one avowed that he had paid all and the other denied that he had received anything, declaring it to the people. And both were eager to gain a decision by arbitration. The folk applauded both, aiding either side. Heralds restrained the folk. And the elders sat on polished stones in a sacred circle, and they held in their hands the staves of clear-voiced heralds. Before them[2] then they [the elders] jumped up and gave their decisions in turn [or the litigants jumped up and made their pleas in turn]. And two talents of gold lay in their midst to be given to the one who should most justly plead his cause before them."

The passage fairly bristles with difficulties, and the various problems involved have been the subjects for interminable debate. There are certain large problems of vital importance which must be settled first; that is, the most plausible explanation must be determined. The most important point, and the one on which there is the greatest lack of unanimity, is the question of the point at issue. According to one view, lines 499–500 should not be translated as above[3] but mean, rather, "the one claimed that he was paying it all (i.e., promised to pay it), but the other refused to accept anything." Then the question at issue is, "*must* the avenger accept the blood-money or *might* he claim blood for blood?"[4]

---

[1] *Il.* xviii. 497 ff.   [2] Or τοῖσιν may mean "with the scepters."

[3] The scholiast agrees with the foregoing translation.

[4] Leaf, *Journal of Hellenic Studies*, VIII (1887), 122 ff.; Croiset, *op. cit.*

This theory implies that in some way the homicide itself is in issue and also involves the question of a compulsory wergeld system. It may be admitted that linguistically this interpretation is possible, but Lipsius argues strongly against it.[1] A minor difficulty lies in the word πάντα, line 499. A man who insisted on his right to pay a blood-price could scarcely be said to promise to pay *all*. But there is a more serious difficulty. There is nothing in Homer to show that relatives could be forced to accept blood-money; neither is there any evidence of a growing popular sentiment in favor of a settlement.[2] Quite the contrary is the case. Banishment, as we have seen, is the usual fate of the slayer. Moreover, the acceptance of blood-money is cited as an example of self-restraint.[3] But it by no means follows that the passion of the man was restrained if he accepted blood-money under compulsion; his heart might still be seething with anger and a desire for revenge. Surely the poet is thinking of a man who acted of his own free will. Leist[4] assumes that when the homicide was ἀκούσιος the relatives were obliged to accept money. Unfortunately for this theory, in the only instance of φόνος ἀκούσιος, the slayer, Patroclus, a mere youth, was banished.[5] As far as the evidence of the poems goes, the distinction between φόνος ἀκούσιος and φόνος ἑκούσιος played

[1] Dareste, *Nouvelles études d'histoire du droit*, p. 6, is unconvinced by the criticisms of the view of Leaf by Lipsius in *Leipziger Studien* (1890), pp. 228 ff.

[2] In view of the killing of Aegisthus, Leaf's statement is surprising. "There is, I believe, no case in the poems where blood is ever exacted for blood," *op. cit.*, p. 124.

[3] *Il.* ix. 632–37:
κai μέν τίς τε κασιγνήτοιο φονῆος
ποινὴν ἢ οὗ παιδὸς ἐδέξατο τεθνηῶτος·
καί ῥ' ὁ μὲν ἐν δήμῳ μένει αὐτοῦ πόλλ' ἀποτείσας,
τοῦ δέ τ' ἐρητύεται κραδίη καὶ θυμὸς ἀγήνωρ
ποινὴν δεξαμένῳ. σοὶ δ' ἄλληκτόν τε κακόν τε
θυμὸν ἐνὶ στήθεσσι θεοὶ θέσαν εἵνεκα κούρης
οἴης.
Leaf (*op. cit.*, p. 124) cites this passage to prove that the payment of a fine instead of exile was the recognized course.

[4] *Gräco-italische Rechtsgeschichte*, pp. 330 ff.

[5] This case has already been discussed in some detail, *supra*, p. 21.

no part in determining the fate of the slayer; neither is it a necessary assumption to explain the trial scene.

It has been suggested that it is difficult to account for the deep popular interest in the trial unless the homicide is the issue. The tremendous interest in the proceedings is evidenced by line 497.[1] But if it is assumed that the present suit is connected with an earlier feud, the popular interest in the case easily becomes clear. This brings us to the second theory, i.e., that before the present trial a man had been killed and an agreement was reached to make a money settlement for the blood-feud which arose. The shield scene represents the dispute as to whether this money has been paid or

---

[1] Myres, *op. cit.*, pp. 200 ff., has a detailed theory about the identity of λαοί in various lines. In line 497 it refers merely to the orderly organized groups of society; in line 502 it is not the whole assembly but merely the kinsmen of the principals (this explains their partisanship); and in line 503 it is again the whole assembly. In line 500, δήμῳ, he asserts, means the whole countryside, i.e., the whole crowd of onlookers. It seems impossible to see any distinction between the four. Gilbert suggests that the people were *Eideshelfer* (*Beiträge*, p. 469, n. 1). Others believe that they decided to which of the elders the two talents should go. Various attempts have been made to explain the excitement of the λαοί. Glotz, *Solidarité*, p. 118, says that it is due to the fact that if the wergeld had not been paid as contracted, hostilities would begin all over again. This gives sufficient motive for their excitement, but there are other considerations also which must be mentioned. Maine speaks of the trial (*Ancient Law*, p. 386) as a "striking and characteristic, but still only occasional feature of city life." This would explain the interest of the people to some extent. Treston, on the other hand (*op. cit.* p. 42), argues that a wergeld dispute was one of the commonest occurrences of tribal life. The interest is to be explained by the fact that "the folk" are the wider kinsmen of plaintiff and defendant. In a note on the primitive character and informality of Homeric justice, Calhoun says: "The picture is not that of a court assembled by an official to try a case. It is of the people—and the gerontes—assembled in the agora, where they go every day that their presence is not demanded elsewhere, exactly as the Athenians did in the fifth century. The gerontes occupy their customary seats of honour, and the people throng hither and thither, but when an interesting or notorious dispute comes before the gerontes, or before one or more of them, a circle is quickly formed. Then the heralds who are regularly in attendance upon the gerontes have to preserve order. Sooner or later any dispute of more than trivial character was bound to find its way into the agora and to the gerontes, for the simple reason that the disputants were bound sooner or later to come face to face with one another in the agora" (*Proceedings*, p. 93, n. 2). Vinogradoff, *op. cit.*, p. 90, makes an interesting comparison of the partisanship of the people in this scene with the interest of phratry members in hearing appeals concerning citizenship before five appointed συνήγοροι (*IJG*, II, xxix, pp. 200 ff.). The elders in the Homeric scene correspond to the five συνήγοροι.

not. The defendant claims that he has paid the entire sum; the plaintiff denies that he has ever received payment.[1] In view of other matters in the passage now to be discussed, this seems to be the correct interpretation.

The ἴστωρ (l. 501) has been variously identified as a witness, as the king, as the chairman of the γέροντες.[2] The scholiast regards the ἴστωρ as a witness; and Leaf followed him in his first theory (1883) and translated "and each one was fain to obtain consummation on the word of his witness." Recently this theory was revived by Treston,[3] who thinks that the relation of the verse to its context is distinctly in favor of the interpretation "witness." He assumes that the witnesses were included among the people and were brought forward to testify as to the actual transference of property. They would therefore be, in effect, compurgators. An objection urged by Dareste is fatal to this theory.[4] If the case was to be decided by the testimony of a witness, what need was there of pleas by the parties or of discussions by the elders? In 1902 Dareste explained the ἴστωρ as the sole judge while the elders were assessors.[5] This is a possible explanation although there is no mention of a presiding officer of the council of elders in connection with an arbitration.[6] Idome-

[1] This view is followed by Glotz, Lipsius, Bonner, Calhoun, Treston, Maine and Bréhier. Treston misunderstands Lipsius (op. cit., p. 39, and elsewhere). He credits Lipsius with maintaining that "the trial in question was a murder-trial—a decision of homicidal guilt or innocence; he therefore holds that the two talents of gold were the actual Wergeld." It is true that Lipsius interprets the talents as Wergeld; but as to the point at issue, he says as follows: "Zwei Männer streiten auf dem Markte über das Sühngeld für einen erschlagenen Mann; der eine behauptet, es ganz erlegt, der andere, nichts empfangen zu haben."

[2] ἴστωρ means the "expert," the "one who knows." It could, of course, be used of one who gives judgment or of a witness.

[3] Op. cit., p. 43. Cf. also, Gardikas, op. cit., p. 210.

[4] Annuaire des études grecques, 1884, pp. 94 ff.

[5] Nouvelles études d'histoire du droit (1902), p. 11. Cf. Meyer, op. cit., II, 357.

[6] After the Pylians had made a successful raid on the Eleans, the king selected a portion of the plunder to recoup losses he had suffered at the hands of the Elean raiders. The elders, acting as a court of claims, divided the remainder among those who had lost property. If the king acted in this case, he is not distinguished from the nobles (Il. xi. 670 ff.).

neus, in the dispute between himself and Ajax, proposed Agamemnon as the arbitrator; while Menelaus, in his dispute
with Antilochus, offered to submit the matter to the 'Αργείων
ἡγήτορες ἠδὲ μέδοντες.[1] But Dareste's earlier view (1884)
that ἐπὶ ἴστορι merely means "by arbitration" is the most
satisfactory.[2] Leaf adopted this view in his later writings
(1892 and 1902); and it has since been followed by Bonner,
Busolt, Calhoun, Lipsius[3] and Steinwenter.[4]

Line 506 is not free from difficulty, although the theory
that it refers to the litigants has been rather generally abandoned—i.e., "they (the litigants) hurried forward and pleaded each his cause in turn." So it was explained by Doeder-
lein and Heyne. It is obvious that ἤισσον suits the eager
litigants better than it suits the judicial elders; but two objections may be urged: the abrupt change of subject necessitated by this interpretation, and the fact that δίκαζον would
have to be considered as equivalent to δικάζοντο. It is said
that δικάζω in the active is never used of a litigant.[5] To maintain this rule, however, in one instance Menelaus must be
considered both plaintiff and judge in the same case.[6] In the
shield picture the poet is describing a variety of incidents in
connection with a trial in public. And it is certainly surprising that the only line which deals with the proceedings should
be devoted to the process by which a decision is reached
which is of little interest in comparison with the pleas of the
parties. But, so far as the legal interpretation of the passage
is concerned, it is of no consequence whether the line refers to
the litigants or the elders. The scholiast refers the line to the
action of the judges.

---

[1] Il. xxiii. 485, 573.

[2] Annuaire des études grecques, XVIII, p. 95: "L'ἴστωρ et les γέροντες sont seule
et même chose." (So also Lipsius, Leipziger Studien [1890], p. 231.)

[3] Lipsius says that ἴστωρ is identical with the group of elders. Myres advances
a curious theory, i.e., that it refers to the one who gave the final decision and that
this man, as shown by line 508, was someone who gave voluntary and effective help
from the agora, whose decision the elders agreed to adopt as better than their own.

[4] Op. cit., p. 36.

[5] Cf. Laurence, "Judges and Litigants," Jour. of Philol., VIII (1879), 125 ff.

[6] Il. xxiii. 570. Cf. supra, p. 28.

The next point is the significance and destination of the two talents. Lipsius' view has already been noted, that they constituted a genuine wergeld deposited in court by the defendant, to be reclaimed by him if successful, otherwise to go to the plaintiff.[1] Lipsius admits that two talents is a small sum for the price of a slain man. In the only other case where blood-money is mentioned, the amount is said to have been large: "Yet doth a man accept recompense of his brother's murderer or for his dead son: and so the slayer for a great price abideth in his own land."[2] It is pointed out that the close relationship, that of brother or son, accounts for the largeness of the sum. But even if we accept the assumption that in the trial scene the slain man is a distant relative of the plaintiff, the sum is still too small. Two talents are the fourth prize in a chariot race in which the first is a tripod and a woman, the second a mare, and the third a caldron. Surely a freeman is of more value than a female slave.[3] Indeed, a woman or a tripod is the usual prize in a chariot race;[4] and a tripod or a caldron is an ordinary wager in a trivial dispute between Ajax and Idomeneus.[5] Was the life of a man held so lightly by even a distant relative? Surely lifelong banishment could not be commuted for so small a sum. Busolt is of the opinion that a wergeld could easily be small in view of the fact that there would be taken into consideration the property of the murderer, the personality and relationship of the deceased, and the circumstances under which the murder occurred. It is perhaps true that the

[1] Lipsius, *Das Attische Recht*, p. 4; Busolt-Swoboda, *op. cit.*, p. 333, follows Lipsius.

[2] *Il.* ix. 632 ff.

[3] *Il.* xxiii. 262–70. These women not only were skilled in handiwork (ἔργα ἰδυίας) but possessed personal charms (αἳ κάλλει ἐνίκων φῦλα γυναικῶν [*Il.* ix. 130]).

[4] *Il.* xxii. 164. This phase of the question is treated by Ridgeway, *Jour. of Philol.*, X, 30 ff. In a later paper, *Jour. of Hellenic Studies*, VIII, 133, he discusses the value of the Homeric talent and shows that it is not too large a sum for a reward to the best judge. He finds that the talent is equal in value to an ox. The results of these investigations tend to confirm the objection that two talents are quite insufficient for the blood-price.

[5] *Il.* xxiii. 485.

amount of the wergeld would, in any case, be fixed in some proportion to the property owned by the murderer; but there is no indication, as has been observed before, that any account was taken of the kind of homicide.

A second theory sees in the two talents a court fee. So Glotz argues.[1] Treston[2] makes them a kind of advocate's fee deposited by the litigants to encourage the advocates to give a proper exposition of the unwritten codes of the tribes. He is therefore compelled to provide advocates, and he assumes that two of the elders acted in this capacity. Myres[3] sees in the talents a customary fee to go to someone who gives a voluntary decision from the agora, this decision being adopted by the elders as better than their own. Obviously Myres is anticipating the difficulty which arises if it is assumed that the talents are to go to one of the elders, that is, the difficulty of deciding to which one they shall go. Maine compares the procedure described here with the payment of a *sacramentum* in archaic Roman law. This was a wager, offered by the plaintiff and accepted by the defendant, which went to the state. The large sum in Homer as compared with the trifling amount of the *sacramentum* he accounts for by supposing that the Homeric scene represents fluctuating usage rather than usage consolidated into law. The two talents, according to his theory, were deposited by the two litigants and were destined for the judge "who shall explain the grounds of his decision most to the satisfaction of the audience."[4] Beyond this point it is impossible to follow the proceedings. It would seem necessary to confine the contest for the prize to those of the judges whose opinion agreed with the verdict; otherwise the people might reach a conclusion at variance with that of the council. For we may be sure that the merits of the case would play a large part in the popular decision. Such a result would assuredly defeat the purpose of the arbitration. On the other hand, if the prize must be assigned to one of the majority judges, what is the basis of the decision? In a case involving a question of fact (that is,

[1] *Solidarité*, p. 128; *La Cité*, p. 57.

[2] *Op. cit.*, p. 89.   [3] *Op. cit.*, p. 207.

[4] *Ancient Law*, p. 386. Cf. the scholiast; Brehiér, *Rev. historique*, LXXXIV, 29.

was the money paid as alleged?) there could be but little
difference between the affirmative opinions in point of merit.
Laurence[1] has emphasized this feature of the theory in a vein
of mild and well-deserved satire. He points out that if the
theory is correct there must have been two trials: one in
which the merits of the suit were adjudged, and a second one
to judge the merits of the respective judgments. Furthermore, it is quite conceivable that the spectators would not
have been unanimous in their awarding of the prize, and it is
incongruous to suppose that they would have had the duty
of rewarding the elders. Lastly, the amount of the reward
is quite disproportionate to the services rendered by the
elders. It is doubtless to avoid all of these incongruities that
Leist, Leaf, and other followers of Maine have, without sufficient warrant, assumed that the homicide itself is in issue.
This would allow some considerable variety of reasons for
reaching the same conclusion; but it involves a difficulty
quite as serious, for everything in the poems, as has been
pointed out, indicates that the relatives always decided
whether they would accept the blood-price or not.

But the line is capable of quite another rendering.
Lipsius has shown that, in accordance with Homeric usage,
δίκην εἰπεῖν may be rendered "plead a cause." He cites
᾽Αχιλῆα δίκῃ ἠμείψατο, "answered Achilles with a claim of
right," and δίκας εἴροντο ἄνακτα, "they were asking the king
concerning their rights." To these may be added ἐπὶ ῥηθέντι
δικαίῳ "a (fair) claim of right." Both explanations may be
linguistically correct,[2] but Lipsius finds in μετὰ τοῖσι a decisive argument: "Die Bedeutung der Präposition aber lässt
nur die Wiedergabe mit 'vor,' 'bei' zu und verbietet die
Gleichsetzung mit einem Genetiv." μετὰ τοῖσι simply
means "in court." The two talents, then, must go to the
man in whose favor the verdict was given.[3]

[1] *Op. cit.*, pp., 125 ff.

[2] But compare the remarks of Laurence, *op. cit.*, p. 128, based on the assertions
of Shilleto that the ordinary usage of δίκην εἰπεῖν is not "to pronounce judgment"
but "to plead a cause," and that indeed there is no instance of the phrase being used
in any but the latter sense.

[3] Cf. the parody of this passage in Lucian *Piscator*, 41.

Although Maine is wrong about the destination of the two talents, he is undoubtedly correct in thinking them a sort of wager. As a wager a talent is not excessive.[1] The tripod or the caldron which are mentioned in the proposed wager between Ajax and Idomeneus might cost more than two talents apiece, as may be inferred from the prize list in the chariot race.[2]

The wager has been compared with the *poena sponsionis et restipulationis* of Roman law which went to the successful litigant. In Attic law it survives in a modified form in the παρακαταβολή, deposited by the plaintiff and forfeited in case of failure either to the state or to the defendant, according to the nature of the case.[3] In effect the wager corresponds to the damages which, according to Homeric practice, usually accompanied restitution and redress.

The most plausible explanation of the trial-scene seems, then, to be as follows. A man had been killed sometime before the trial, and his kinsmen and friends rallied to take vengeance on the slayer, whose friends also supported him in great numbers. Finally the bulk of the community was ranged on one side or the other. A compromise seemed advisable, and an agreement to settle the blood-feud for a sum of money was reached. The scene on the shield presents the principals disputing about the payment. The one claims that he has paid the money in full; the other denies it. In the market place each man, surrounded by his partisans who had sided with him in the earlier stages of the feud, tells his side of the case to those within hearing. At length one challenges the other to stake a talent apiece and refer the dispute to arbitration. An agreement to abide by the verdict is made and confirmed by oaths. The talents constituting the wager are deposited before the elders seated in the place of justice, each with a scepter, the emblem of the judicial office. Around them surge the partisans so closely that the heralds are

---

[1] The wager theory is followed by Maine, Bonner, Calhoun, and by Fanta (*op. cit.*, p. 86).

[2] *Il.* xxiii. 262 ff.

[3] Meier and Schoemann, *Der Attische Process*, 815 ff.

obliged to restrain them. The litigants then present their cases amid the applause of their partisans. The two talents were awarded to the winner of the suit. Thus the trial-scene conforms to the common practice of settling a dispute by wager.

An obvious and weighty objection to other current interpretations of the trial-scene is that each of them represents a form of trial without parallel in Homeric practice. But the wager theory is well exemplified in the proposed settlement of the dispute between Idomeneus and Ajax by wager and arbitration. The tendency to back one's opinion by a wager is universal. Men still on occasion settle disputes as Idomeneus proposed to do. Furthermore, a trial based on a wager of money has marked affinities with other primitive forms of trial. In the trial by battle men risk loss of life or limb. In the trial by evidentiary oath there is the risk of divine punishment. In each of these three types the litigant stakes and risks something. Each appeals to a universal human instinct.

Witnesses are nowhere mentioned in Homer in connection with arbitrations. The gods in whose names oaths were sworn are called μάρτυροι or ἐπιμάρτυροι. They are not only witnesses but sureties or guarantors of the compact or treaty, because they punish perjurers.[1] For the person in whose interest they act they are protectors. Zeus is called the μάρτυρος of strangers, because, when called upon to witness a wrong done to the stranger, he punishes the wrongdoer.[2] Here we have the origin of human witnesses and sureties. In place of gods, men are summoned to the making of a contract to insure its provisions being carried out. But this stage was not reached in the age of Homer.[3] Occasionally the word μάρτυρος is used of those who are familiar with some event or situation,[4] but they are not summoned either as formal or as

---

[1] *Il.* iii. 274 ff.; vii. 76; cf. Nägelsbach, *Homerische Theologie*, p. 265.

[2] *Od.* xvi. 423.

[3] In the "Song of Demodocus" (*Od.* viii. 266 ff.) Poseidon offered to be surety for Ares. This passage is of late origin but preserves a link in the process of development.

[4] *Il.* i. 338; ii. 302.

general witnesses. The word μαρτυρίη in the *Odyssey* is not used in a technical sense,[1] though not far from it.

Some scholars regard the omission of testimonial evidence as purely accidental.[2] The fact that witnesses are known in the age of Hesiod is an unsafe ground for inference regarding the Homeric age, since the judicial system that prevailed in the time of Hesiod is considerably more advanced than that of the age of Homer. In addition to the statements of the parties the Homeric arbitrator had to rely upon what Gilbert aptly calls his *eigene Combination* (resourcefulness), or the voluntary evidentiary oath of one of the parties.[3]

Regular judicial processes were developed from the arbitral functions of the chiefs and elders (ἡγήτορες ἠδὲ μέδοντες). Even in the Homeric period there are unmistakable indications that arbitration had become a regular and normal proceeding. Odysseus, in relating his escape from Charybdis on the timbers of his wrecked ship, says:

> ἦμος δ' ἐπὶ δόρπον ἀνὴρ ἀγορῆθεν ἀνέστη
> κρίνων νείκεα πολλὰ δικαζομένων αἰζηῶν
> τῆμος δὴ τά γε δοῦρα Χαρύβδιος ἐξεφαάνθη.[4]

This is highly significant. The chiefs and elders, instead of waiting for calls for their services as arbitrators, held more or less regular sittings in the agora to settle the disputes of all who might appear before them. In the course of a single session lasting the better part of a day they disposed of many cases (κρίνων νείκεα πολλά). Several considerations impelled the authorities to facilitate in this fashion recourse to arbitration. In matters of religion the Homeric community acted as a group to secure the favor of the gods by public sacrifices.[5] In war they had to co-operate for protection against their neighbors who were always potential enemies. Quarrels and strife between individuals tended to weaken

---

[1] *Od.* xi. 325. πάρος δέ μιν (Ariadne) Ἄρτεμις ἔκτα Δίῃ ἐν ἀμφιρύτῃ Διονύσου μαρτυρίῃσι.

[2] Gilbert, *op. cit.*, p. 467; Buchholz, *op. cit.*, p. 87.

[3] Cf. the judgment of Solomon, I Kings 3:16 ff.

[4] *Od.* xii. 439 ff.

[5] Cf. the description of the sacrifice to Poseidon by Nestor and the Pylians, *Od.* iii. 5 ff.

the solidarity of the group. It was clearly in the public interest to reduce as far as possible these potential sources of danger to the community. And so it was only natural that public opinion should increasingly favor arbitration as an effective means of settling disputes. Furthermore, it was in the interests of the ruling class to foster and encourage arbitration. The settlement of disputes in this fashion would increase their political power and enhance their prestige in the eyes of the community. Another important factor in the situation was the force of habit and example. In due time the practice of resorting to arbitration tended to become a recognized custom; and custom in primitive communities readily hardens into law such as existed before the period of the codes.

It is not easy to determine with any degree of certainty the point at which arbitration became in practice obligatory. In the seventh century written codes made their appearance in various parts of Greece. A striking feature of these codes is the exercise of judicial functions by magistrates.[1] In the matter of judicial machinery and procedure the codes, as a rule, simply recorded current practice. Novelty was usually confined to the substantive law. Obviously, for a considerable period before the codification of the law it had been the duty of magistrates to adjudicate cases. The earliest datable code is the Athenian code of Draco in 621 B.C. By this time the thesmothetae[2] had been instituted as special judicial officers to aid the regular magistrates. The institution of this board implies a fully organized judicial system in which the magistrates κύριοι ἦσαν τὰς δίκας αὐτοτελεῖς κρίνειν.[3] A similar inference has been drawn from the archon's proclamation guaranteeing the security of property rights.[4] The archon as chief annual magistrate may go back to 682 B.C. It may fairly be assumed that the archon in his capacity as judge simply continued the judicial functions of the later king-

[1] Cf. Meyer, *op. cit.*, II, 572. Cf. *infra*, p. 77.

[2] Cf. *infra*, pp. 85 ff.

[3] Aristotle *Ath. Pol.* iii. 5.

[4] *Ibid.*, lvi. 2. Cf. Busolt, *Griechische Geschichte*, II, 169; Lipsius, *Das Attische Recht*, p. 11. Cf. *infra*, p. 62.

ship. If this be true, a virtual compulsory legal process had
been evolved in Athens about the beginning of the seventh
century. This time falls well within the period which for
convenience may be called the "age of Hesiod," about 750–
650 B.C. The chief source for this period is Hesiod's *Works
and Days*, supplemented by the prooemium to the *Shield of
Heracles* based on Hesiod's *Catalogue of Women*. These
sources enable us to recover some of the main features of the
Boeotian judicial system as Hesiod knew it.

Hesiod reveals a much more advanced stage of legal development than is found in the Homeric poems. It was customary for litigants to substantiate their statements with
testimonial evidence. "Even when dealing with your brother," says Hesiod, "summon a witness but do it with a smile."[1]
The smile was intended to cover the insistence on what might
under the circumstances be regarded as a useless, if not in-
sulting, formality. Hesiod had learned this lesson from his
experience with his own brother. That witnesses might give
their testimony under oath is made plain by the poet's denunciation of the witness who knowingly commits perjury
and thereby does an injury to justice: "But whoever deliberately lies in his witness and forswears himself, and so hurts
Justice and sins beyond repair, that man's generation is left
obscure thereafter."[2] The statement that "retribution for
perjury attends crooked decisions"[3] may refer either to the
witness oath or to the oath of a party, evidentiary or confirmatory. It seems likely that some provision had been
made for the regular administration of justice in Boeotia.
Within each district the petty chiefs composing the dominant
aristocracy met with more or less regularity in the chief city
and adjudicated disputes. Thither flocked the country peo-

[1] Hesiod, *Works and Days*, 371.

[2] *Ibid.*, 282 ff.: (Evelyn-White's translation)

ὃς δέ κε μαρτυρίῃσι ἑκὼν ἐπίορκον ὀμόσσας
ψεύσεται, ἐν δὲ δίκην βλάψας νήκεστον ἀασθῇ,
τοῦ δέ τ' ἀμαυροτέρη γενεὴ μετόπισθε λέλειπται.

[3] *Ibid.*, 219:

αὐτίκα γὰρ τρέχει Ὅρκος ἅμα σκολιῇσι δίκῃσιν.

Cf. Lipsius, *op. cit.*, p. 11, n. 41.

ple from the villages either as litigants or as listeners; and a
city agora on court day must have presented a scene strikingly similar to that pictured on the shield of Achilles.[1] It is
interesting to note that the processes of law were open to
strangers as well as to citizens.[2] Access to the courts of a
foreign city was commonly regulated by special treaties.

Hesiod warns his brother of the dangers of indulging the
litigious spirit that was characteristic of the period:

Perses, lay up these things in your heart, and do not let that Strife
who delights in mischief hold your heart back from work, while you peep
and peer and listen to the wrangles of the court-house [νείκε' ὀπιπεύοντ'
ἀγορῆς]. Little concern has he with quarrels and courts [νεικέων τ' ἀ-
γορέων τε] who has not a year's victuals laid up betimes, even that which
the earth bears, Demeter's grain. When you have got plenty of that, you
can raise disputes and strive to get another's goods [νείκεα καὶ δῆριν
ὀφέλλοις‖ κτήμασ' ἐπ' ἀλλοτρίοις].[3]

This picture presents an element in litigation not found in
the age of Homer. Court sessions in the agora had become
so usual and frequent that those who resorted there regularly
as onlookers and listeners spent so much time that they were
in danger of neglecting their own affairs. This is perhaps not
entirely incompatible with the situation as disclosed in the
Homeric poems, but the suggestion that one may acquire a
taste for litigation on his own account in the hope of acquiring other people's property implies quite a different system.
One is inevitably reminded of the denunciation of the sycophants and the evil influences of the agora upon the young
men, which are found in the orators.[4] Under a system of
purely voluntary arbitration one could scarcely hope to get
possession of other people's property by going to law. The
proposed victim had only to refuse to submit the dispute or
quarrel to arbitration.

Those who give judgments in the court sessions of the

[1] Hesiod, *Works and Days*, 27. Askra, the poet's native place, belonged to
Thespiae (Lipsius, *op. cit.*, p. 11). But cf. Steitz, *Werke und Tage des Hesiods*, p. 32.

[2] Hesiod, *Works and Days*, 225 ff., 327; cf. Glotz, *Solidarité*, pp. 220 ff.

[3] Hesiod, *Works and Days*, 27 ff., Evelyn-White's translation.

[4] Isocrates vii. 48; cf. Aristophanes, *The Clouds*, 991; *The Knights*, 1373 ff.;
Plato *Theaetetus*, 173c.

agora are constantly described as "bribe devouring kings" (δωροφάγοι βασιλῆες) who oppress the people by their "crooked decisions" (σκολιῇσι δίκῃσι).[1] These repeated charges cannot be based solely upon Hesiod's own experience with his brother. Obviously, bribery and crooked decisions constituted a general abuse. The nobles could not have made a practice of accepting bribes and rendering corrupt decisions as arbitrators. Even a few known instances of corruption would seriously interfere with sessions of arbitrators in the agora. But a general reputation for accepting bribes and rendering crooked decisions would have made recourse to arbitration a comparatively rare occurrence. No community would voluntarily continue to submit its differences to men who were notoriously corrupt. The remedy was in their own hands. They could easily choose impartial judges from the populace and ignore the sessions of the nobles.

Hesiod's litigation with his brother Perses bears out the conclusion that the adjudication of cases by the nobles had to be accepted and their judgments respected. The brothers had divided their inheritance. But Perses was dissatisfied. Profiting by the lessons he had learned in the agora, he entered suit, so to speak, and won a larger share of the patrimony. The judgment of the court, influenced by bribes, was duly enforced.

> ἤδη μὲν γὰρ κλῆρον ἐδασσάμεθ', ἀλλὰ τὰ πολλὰ
> ἁρπάζων ἐφόρεις μέγα κυδαίνων βασιλῆας
> δωροφάγους οἳ τήνδε δίκην ἐθέλουσι δίκασσαι.[2]

But even so, Perses was not satisfied and proposed to engage in further litigation. Hesiod, instead of refusing to appear

---

[1] Hesiod, *Works and Days*, 220 f.:

> τῆς δὲ Δίκης ῥόθος ἑλκομένης, ᾗ κ' ἄνδρες ἄγωσι
> δωροφάγοι, σκολιῇς δὲ δίκῃς κρίνωσι θέμιστας,

and 263 f.:

> ταῦτα φυλασσόμενοι, βασιλῆς, ἰθύνετε δίκας,
> δωροφάγοι, σκολιέων δὲ δικέων ἐπὶ πάγχυ λάθεσθε.

The βασιλῆες are not kings but nobles (Steitz, *op. cit.*, p. 33). Cf. *Works and Days*, 38 f., 248 ff.

[2] Hesiod, *Works and Days*, 37–39. ἀλλὰ τά (l. 37) is Guyet's emendation for ἄλλα τε of the MSS; Schoemann emended the MSS reading ἐθέλουσι δίκασσαι (l. 39), to ἐθέλοντι δίκασσαν.

again before the judges, as he might have done had they been arbitrators, was content to appeal to his brother to settle their dispute by impartial award (ἀλλ' αὖθι διακρινώμεθα νεῖκος ‖ ἰθείῃσι δίκῃς).[1] In effect he is proposing arbitration by agreement as an alternative to submitting the case to the adjudication of the nobles. This seems to be the natural interpretation of Hesiod's account.[2] Other explanations that have been suggested do not alter the situation materially.[3] If Hesiod really believed that the chiefs accepted bribes and rendered corrupt judgments, it is hard to understand why he should ever have consented even once to accept them as arbitrators. If Homeric views and practices still prevailed, he could have refused to do anything further or he could have proposed other arbitrators. As he did neither in the first case, one is constrained to believe that he had no choice in the matter.

It is generally agreed that the administration of justice in the age of Hesiod is much more advanced than in the age of Homer.[4] But Steinwenter has objected to the use of the phrase "compulsory process of law" to characterize this development. Regarding the picture in the *Theogony* of Hesiod[5] of the ideal king dispensing justice (διακρίνοντα θέμιστας ‖ ἰθείῃσι δίκῃσιν), he remarks as follows: "Danach beruht aber die Unterwerfung der Parteien unter dem Spruch des Königes nicht auf einem staatsrechtlichen Im-

---

[1] *Ibid.*, 35–36. For the meaning of αὖθι (*here*), see Steitz, *op. cit.*, p. 32; Hays, "Notes on the *Works and Days* of Hesiod" (University of Chicago dissertation, 1918) takes it in a temporal sense.

[2] The scholiast read ἐθέλουσι δικάσσαι and understands that a second suit is pending. Cf. Scholium on line 39: δωροφάγους: οἶά τε πρόθυμους ὄντας καὶ αὖθις δικάζειν τῷ Πέρσῃ καὶ τῷ Ἡσιόδῳ διὰ τὴν τῶν δώρων ἐλπίδα. So also Steitz, *op. cit.*, p. 24; Schwartz, *Charakterköpfe aus der antiken Literatur*, p. 8.

[3] Ehrenberg, *op. cit.*, p. 63, assumes that Hesiod has appealed the case. Steinwenter, *op. cit.*, p. 41, also thinks that the case was reopened by Hesiod but finds it difficult to decide on the nature of the issue. Kirchhoff, *Hesiodos' Mahnlieder an Perses*, p. 43, believes that the case has been heard but not yet decided; cf. Wilamowitz, *Hesiodos Erga*, p. 46.

[4] Lipsius, *Das Attische Recht*, pp. 10 ff.; Steinwenter, *op. cit.*, p. 42. Bonner, *Class. Phil.*, VII, 17, first used the expression "compulsory process of law." Bréhier, *Rev. historique*, LXXXV, 12 ff.

[5] 81 ff.

perium, welches das Urteil als Amtsbefehl erscheinen liesze, sondern nur auf der Kraft der Argumente und der Ehrfurcht oder wohl auch Furcht vor den Königen."[1] From a strictly legal and constitutional point of view this is quite true. Indeed, there could not be a *staatsrechtliches Imperium* until the lawgivers had reduced current practices and customs to writing, with such additions as they deemed desirable. But there is a danger of missing important developments in the early judicial history of the Greeks if we insist too rigidly upon the application of modern legal and constitutional standards. The judicial powers exercised by the authorities during the age of Hesiod were not conferred upon them by the action of any sovereign body in the state. They were derived rather from tradition, custom, and precedent. The important point was that the Boeotian peasants submitted to their judgments, as Steinwenter points out. "Die 'krummen Sprüche' der bestochenen Richter hat der Bauer eben anzuerkennen, weil er sich vor dem Adeligen ducken musz, nicht aber weil eine mit Zwangsgewalt ausgestattete Rechtsordnung es gebietet."[2] This statement is not essentially different from the view set forth above. It is to be regretted that the form of trial described by Hesiod cannot be designated by some convenient term that would mark it off both from Homeric arbitration and from the more highly developed Athenian legal process of the fourth century. Since the expression "compulsory process of law" has implications for the modern reader even beyond the Athenian conception of a legal process, it may be better to use the designation "obligatory arbitration."[3] It emphasizes the degree of compulsion achieved by growing custom backed by public opinion and fostered by the government. It carries also the idea of equitable settlement inherent in arbitration as distinguished from strict legal adjudication.

---

[1] Steinwenter, *op. cit.*, p. 41.

[2] *Ibid.* The rather narrow interpretation Steinwenter puts upon *wahre Judikationsgewalt* is shown by the fact that he finds only the beginnings of real judicial power in the code of Draco.

[3] Bonner, *Lawyers and Litigants in Ancient Athens*, p. 31.

It is useless to speculate how proceedings were initiated[1] or how judgments were executed. Even in fourth-century Athens these duties devolved upon the parties in the first instance. It may be observed that in the age of Homer there could be no real assurance that an award of an arbitrator would be enforced. Even agreements fortified with oaths and sureties might not avail. In the end the only compelling forces were custom and public opinion. In a closely knit ancient community a man could not lightly disregard these powerful forces.

The practice of settling a dispute by means of an evidentiary oath was still in common use. This is made clear by the following couplet:

βλάψει δ' ὁ κακὸς τὸν ἀρείονα φῶτα
μύθοισιν σκολιοῖς ἐνέπων, ἐπὶ δ' ὅρκον ὀμεῖται.[2]

Tzetzes explains this passage as meaning that a man deprives another of some property and, when called to account, swears that he is innocent, just as Hermes offered to swear that he did not steal the cattle of Apollo. Even if the *Hymn to Hermes*, in which the dispute between Hermes and Apollo is described, is considerably later than the poems of Hesiod, it may be safely used to add some details to the picture of legal procedure in the age of Hesiod. For it no doubt reflects in the main the practice in vogue down to the period of written codes. Apollo, on discovering the loss of the cattle, at once set out to trace them and secure witnesses to establish the identity of the culprit.[3] So important was testimonial evidence that rewards for information leading to the finding of the thief were sometimes offered.[4] If witnesses could be produced, the accused had the option of returning the

---

[1] It has been suggested that royal heralds were used to summon witnesses and parties (Thonissen, *Le droit pénal de la république athénienne*, p. 31).

[2] *Works and Days*, 193 f.; cf. 322.

[3] *Hymn to Hermes*, 185 ff.

[4] *Ibid.*, 264 ff., where Hermes says,

οὐκ ἂν μηνύσαιμ', οὐκ ἂν μήνυτρον ἀροίμην.

Cf. Hesiod *Frag.*, 153, where he is said to have offered Battus (cf. *Hymn to Hermes*, 87 ff.) a reward for information in order to test him.

booty with suitable damages or of facing almost certain defeat in court. Apollo, though he was unable to secure a witness, confidently charged Hermes with the theft. Irritated by the accusations, Hermes threatened to bring the matter before Zeus, and offered to swear that he was innocent. It is not stated that Apollo agreed to accept the oath as decisive, as did Menelaus when he challenged Antilochus to swear that he had not won the race by a foul. At any rate, the case was taken before Zeus for adjudication:

> αἶψα δ' ἵκοντο κάρηνα θυώδεος Οὐλύμποιο
> ἐς πατέρα Κρονίωνα Διὸς περικαλλέα τέκνα.
> κεῖθι γὰρ ἀμφοτέροισι δίκης κατέκειτο τάλαντα.[1]

The words δίκης τάλαντα are commonly explained as the scales of justice, but the view of Ridgeway[2] that τάλαντα were sums of money deposited by the litigants as in the trial pictured on the shield of Achilles seems preferable. In this

[1] *Hymn to Hermes*, 322 ff.

[2] "Homerica," *Jour. of Philol.* XVII, 111 f. He points out that κατέκειτο recalls κεῖτο in the Homeric trial-scene in the sense of "deposited":

> κεῖτο δ' ἄρ' ἐν μέσσοισι δύω χρυσοῖο τάλαντα.

In the *Iliad* (viii. 69 ff.; xxii. 209 ff.) Zeus uses scales to weigh the fates of men, never to decide a dispute between gods. "Scales of justice" are not mentioned in Homer. But against this interpretation may be urged the consideration that although Apollo and Hermes are said to have resorted to Zeus because (γάρ) their talents had already been deposited, the story contains no previous mention of this fact. Indeed such a possibility seems to be excluded. On the other hand, ἀμφοτέροισι, which is quite appropriate if the reference is to a deposit of money, is without point in a reference to scales of justice. Furthermore, Zeus does not use the scales as he does in the *Iliad*, but proceeds to pronounce judgment after hearing the pleas of the litigants. Later poets used δίκης τάλαντα in the sense of "scales of justice." But this may be due to a misapprehension. The poet, using the expression to indicate that they joined issue before Zeus as judge, added δίκης to make this clear. Later writers, thinking the reference was to the scales of Zeus, perpetuated the phrase δίκης τάλαντα in the sense of "scales of justice":

> οὐ γὰρ ἀφαυρῶς
> ἐκ Διὸς ἰθείης οἶδε τάλαντα δίκης·
> —*Anth. Pal.* vi. 267. 3 f.

Cf. Aesch. *Agam.*, 250.

The passage thus interpreted, however, furnishes no support for the view that the Homeric talents went to one of the judges, as Ridgeway argues. Cf. Ferrini, *op. cit.*, p. 45; also Bréhier, *Rev. historique*, LXXXIV, 29, who says that the talents were destined for Zeus if he gave a decision agreeable to the parties. The parties were not obliged to submit to the sentence.

case, however, the talents are not wagers. Under compulsory arbitration, wagers were not needed to induce an unwilling opponent to appear in court. Among primitive peoples customs are not easily discarded; they are more likely to be modified and adapted to changed conditions. On the introduction of compulsory arbitration the custom of depositing wagers was continued, though the need for it no longer existed. It may very well have been that for a time the money went to the successful litigant as a species of damages, but its conversion into court fees could not long have been delayed when the aristocracy controlled the courts. Under these circumstances damages would be assessed by the court.[1]

After the payment of the money into court, Apollo proceeded to plead his case. Hermes denied the charge and affirmed his innocence with an oath.[2] Apparently this was not an evidentiary oath, for Hermes was not acquitted as he would have been had Apollo agreed to stake the issue on an oath. The oath was simply a means of lending weight to the litigant's plea.

Courts did not, on their own motion, take cognizance of wrongs done to individuals on the theory that they were a menace to society. Hesiod, it is true, constantly insists that wrongdoing of individuals would inevitably bring down the wrath of the gods upon the whole community.[3] Such passages as this and his reference to the popular outcry against those who thwarted the ends of justice show that public opinion in his day was active just as in the Homeric age, and might manifest itself in popular action.[4] Thus the same spirit which has been discussed in the Homeric age as lying at the basis of criminal law is apparent in the time of Hesiod, although there is as yet no organized criminal law.[5]

For various wrongs which Hesiod mentions—ill treat-

---

[1] Glotz, *Solidarité*, p. 149, regards the lyre given by Hermes to Apollo as damages. Zeus in his decision said nothing about damages. Hermes gave the lyre of his own free will. The incident throws no light on the purpose of the talents.

[2] *Hymn to Hermes*, 383–84; cf. 274 ff.

[3] *Works and Days*, 240; cf. Thonissen, *op. cit.*, p. 26.

[4] Hesiod, *Works and Days*, 220.   [5] Cf. *supra*, p. 22.

ment of strangers, suppliants, parents, or orphans[1]—redress
could usually be obtained most easily by legal proceedings.
Hesiod's dispute with his brother regarding the division of
their patrimony was in the first instance settled in court.

But, side by side with obligatory arbitration, voluntary
arbitration flourished just as it did under the highly organized judicial system of Athens. Thus Hesiod proposed to his
brother to submit their differences to arbitration rather than
to resort again to the court of "bribe-devouring kings."[2]

Self-help continued to play an important part in the redress of wrongs. An injured man always sought to gain partisans among his kinsmen and neighbors. Hesiod emphasizes
the folly of relying too much on one's relatives, and the
advantages of being on good terms with neighbors. Then, in
time of need neighbors will come in haste to assist. Relatives are likely to be more deliberate.[3] In all probability
self-help is implied in the statement that a man who has good
neighbors will never lose his cattle;[4] that is to say, they will
aid him in recovering stolen animals by the use of force.
They could be useful as witnesses by identifying the raider.
Custom required that witnesses should accompany a man
when he searched the premises of the suspected thief.[5]

In case of adultery the injured husband would naturally
exact satisfaction from his wife's paramour without recourse
to the courts, either by slaying him, as did Hyettus,[6] or by
forcing him to pay substantial damages (μοιχάγρια), like
Hephaestus in the lay of Demodocus. The slayer of an adulterer, however, became involved in a blood-feud with the
relatives. There was a possibility of litigation in case the
compensation agreed upon was not paid, as in the trial-scene.

[1] Hesiod, *Works and Days*, 327 ff., warns his brother against these wrongs as
well as against adultery. They are severely punished by the gods.

[2] *Ibid.*, 35 f.   [3] *Ibid.*, 342 ff.; cf. Glotz, *Solidarité*, pp. 193 ff.

[4] *Works and Days*, 348.

[5] Apollo made a thorough search of the abode of Maia (*Hymn to Hermes*,
246 ff.). Hermes objected that the search was conducted without witnesses (*ibid.*,
372; cf. 385 f.); cf. Glotz, *op. cit.*, pp. 203 ff.

[6] Hesiod *Frag.*, 144.

In cases of homicide the Homeric practice was followed. Thus Amphitryon, who slew Electryon, his kinsman and father-in-law, went into banishment in Thebes. His wife Alcmene, daughter of Electryon, accompanied him. Later she induced him to avenge the death of her brothers. It would seem that his going into exile freed him from any fear of vengeance at the hands of the other relatives of his victim. Only in this way can we reconcile Alcmene's strong desire for vengeance on her brother's slayers with her loyalty to the man who slew her father.[1] All homicides were regarded alike. Hyettus, who slew Molurus, whom he surprised in adultery with his wife, was obliged to flee from Argos to Orchomenus, notwithstanding the ample excuse for slaying Molurus.[2]

It is clear from the foregoing that through the age of Hesiod, at least, homicide was still viewed wholly as the concern of the relatives of the victim. On the other hand, from the earliest period there was a growing feeling that any action that was opposed to the good order and well-being of the state should be punished by the state. It is obvious, then, that the germs of criminal law are to be found while homicide was still entirely a matter for the family to deal with. The conception of crime and the origin of criminal law, then, are not to be found in actions for homicide.[3] This being the case, it remains to consider two things in connection with homicide. When did the doctrine of pollution, attached to the homicide, become current; and why did the state undertake the settlement of homicide cases?

The notion that homicide involved pollution was not known in the Homeric age, but it was firmly established in the time of Draco. Between these two periods there is little evidence by which the exact time of the appearance and the development of the doctrine can be fixed. By the time of Aeschylus the idea had already assumed an air of great an-

---

[1] *Shield of Heracles*, 9 ff., 80 ff.

[2] Hesiod *Frag.*, 144. Calhoun, *Criminal Law*, p. 26, uses this fragment to show that the idea of pollution from homicide was not widespread in the age of Hesiod.

[3] Cf. Calhoun, *Proceedings*, pp. 87 ff.; *Criminal Law*, pp. 16 ff. and 26 ff.

tiquity. It is difficult to account for this unless it is supposed that the doctrine had been widely disseminated long before Aeschylus' day. In the amnesty law which was passed before the reforms of Solon, those are specifically excluded from the benefits of the amnesty who are in exile as the result of conviction for homicide by any of the homicide courts.[1] Certainly the exclusion of these Athenians is due solely to the fact that their presence would pollute the soil of Attica. They would not be excluded to prevent blood-feud, because at this time the state had control in homicide cases. In the code of Draco there is a provision that anyone could prosecute a homicide who illegally returned to Attic soil.[2] Here, again, the reason is undoubtedly pollution. The fact that Draco embodied the idea in a law indicates that the doctrine was a familiar and established one. The familiarity of the idea of pollution in the second half of the seventh century is then firmly established. It is often said on far slighter evidence that moral pollution resulting from homicide was familiar to the Greeks of Hesiod's day. The statement is based on the following arguments. Two of the Greek prefaces to the *Shield of Heracles* state that Amphitryon went into exile in Thebes in accordance with a custom requiring those who started a πόλεμος ἐμφύλιος to undergo purification for a period of three years. In the poem itself nothing is said about pollution or purification.[3] A scholiast to *Iliad* ii. 336 mentions purification in an account of the sack of Pylos by Heracles and says that Hesiod tells the story in the *Catalogue*. It cannot, of course, be assumed that Hesiod mentioned purification. In his summary of the *Aethiopis* of Arctinus,[4] Proclus says that Achilles was obliged to go to Lesbos in order to be freed from the pollution resulting from the slaying of Thersites. Calhoun[5] attacks this passage as evidence for the Hesiodic age on the ground that we do not know under what

---

[1] Plutarch *Solon*, xix. Cf. *infra*, pp. 104 ff., for a discussion of the amnesty law.

[2] *CIA* i. 61.

[3] *Shield of Heracles*, Hypotheses Δ, ll. 13 ff.; E, ll. 12 ff.

[4] Kinkel, *Epici Graeci*, 33.9 ff. The *fluorit* of Arctinus is 750 B.C.

[5] *Criminal Law*, p. 28.

circumstances the slaying occurred or how much of the pollution idea was due to Proclus, who had frequently encountered it in the treatment of homicide by later authors. Calhoun places far too much emphasis on this passage. No matter which way it be interpreted, it is in no way essential to his thesis. It is true that the evidence is not as certain as it would be if Arctinus' text were extant. Yet it seems more probable that Proclus told the story as he found it than that he introduced the episode from his familiarity with the idea of pollution in later authors.[1] In any event, in view of the thorough familiarity with the doctrine by the end of the seventh century, the doctrine of moral pollution must have become widely current among the Greeks very shortly after the time of Hesiod, if not actually in his day. The exact date is of slight consequence.[2]

There appear to be two reasons for the intervention of the state in homicide cases.[3] The first is the idea of pollution attaching to the homicide which has just been discussed. As the doctrine of pollution spread, the state was bound, for self-protection, to find some means of ridding the land of a polluted person in case relatives of the victim failed to act.

The other motive for state intervention is the prevention of blood-feud. Homicide is not viewed as an injury to the state until it is felt that the death of the victim has in some way injured the state. In the aristocratic society of Homeric times it was impossible that the death of a man of the people, for instance, should mean anything to the ruling class. Vengeance for his death was the business solely of his family. The state would not be concerned even if the homicide led to a blood-feud. Similarly, if a member of one of the noble families was slain, the family, with its innate feeling of soli-

---

[1] Cf. Halliday, review of Calhoun, *Class. Rev.*, XLI, 181.

[2] Cf. Bréhier, *Rev. historique*, LXXXV, 13; Glotz, *Études*, pp. 38 ff. The idea of pollution from homicide and the subsequent purificatory rites are closely bound up with the cult of Apollo Catharsios, which does not appear in Homer. The conception of miasma is closely associated with the chthonic powers, the worship of which did not interest Homer. Farnell, *Greek Cults*, IV, 298, regards the post-Homeric development of cathartic ceremonies in connection with the ritual of Apollo as a revival of the ghost cult which existed in pre-Homeric times.

[3] Cf. Meyer, *op. cit.*, II, 575.

darity, would set about obtaining requital. It is true that each family might enlist its friends, and the affair might develop into a kind of civil war involving the destruction of many on both sides. But it was always the family that led. There was for a long time apparently no thought of peaceful adjudication of the matter. There was only one thing to be done—the family must obtain vengeance for its injured member. But in the fact that people generally took sides in the homicide of an important person may be seen the foreshadowings of state intervention. The nearest approach to this situation in Homer is the action of the assembly which determined the fate of Odysseus after he had slain the suitors. The strong popular feeling aroused was undoubtedly due to the wholesale character of the slaughter. There came a day, however—it is impossible to say just when—when long-continued blood-feud came to be recognized as a distinct menace to the welfare of the state. Then the state definitely assumed control. This is well brought out by the Argive statute to which Euripides refers:

> "By exile justify, not blood for blood.
> Else one had aye been liable to death
> Still taking the last blood-guilt on his hands.[1]

It is at this time that various types of homicide were differentiated.

[1] *Orestes*, 515 ff.

CHAPTER II
THE UNIFICATION OF ATTICA[1]

In the Heroic Age, Attica, according to tradition, was divided into a number of petty principalities[2] loosely organized for defensive purposes under the suzerainty of the kings of Athens. Each community had its own magistrates and town hall (πρυτανεῖον) and managed its local affairs, including the administration of justice, independently of Athens. But unifying forces were at work.[3] Similarity of language and institutions facilitated the formation of groups of smaller communities for defensive or religious purposes, such as the Tetrapolis of Marathon, Oenoe, Tricorythus, and Probalinthus. The tribal system also advanced the cause of unity. The four Ionic tribes, said to have been introduced by Ion, were local. Each included within its boundaries several πόλεις. As the organization of the military forces was on a tribal basis, the citizens of different communities were closely associated in war under the leadership of the tribal kings (φυλοβασιλεῖς).[4] The final step in the process was taken by Theseus, who succeeded, without the employment of force, in bringing the nobles together into Athens, which became the capital city; the common people for the most part continued to reside in the country,[5] but

[1] Aristotle added to his historical account of the development of the Athenian constitution a convenient summary of the most important political changes (*Ath. Pol.* xli). As legal and constitutional changes are generally closely connected, Aristotle's summary marks the most important milestones in Athenian judicial history down to the restoration of democracy in 403. In the main, Aristotle's division into periods will be followed in the succeeding chapters.

[2] According to Philochorus (quoted by Strabo ix. 1.20), there were twelve cities in Attica. Cf. De Sanctis, *Storia della repubblica Ateniese*[2], pp. 26 ff.; Busolt, *Griechische Geschichte*, II[2], 69 ff.; *Cambridge Ancient History*, III, 577 ff.; Busolt-Swoboda, *Staatskunde*, II, 776, n. 4, for bibliography on the *Synoikismos* of Attica.

[3] De Sanctis, *op. cit.*, pp. 28 ff.

[4] Meyer, *Geschichte des Altertums*, Vol. II, sec. 205.

[5] Thucydides ii. 15. 2. Cf. *CAH*, III, 579; De Sanctis, *op. cit.*, p. 23.

resorted to the capital for litigation and the exercise of such political rights as they possessed in the reorganized state. Henceforth, all inhabitants of Attica were Athenians. Such is the story of the unification of Attica that was current in the fifth century.

In Homer, Athens is the most important city of Attica. In fact, it is the only one mentioned in the catalogue. It is described as a "well-built town" with "broad streets."[1] Its inhabitants are the "folk of Erechtheus." Sunium[2] was included within its territories as the epithet ἄκρον 'Αθηνέων seems to indicate. Marathon is mentioned in the *Odyssey* in connection with Athens, but with no indication of its relationship.[3] The archaeological evidence confirms the testimony of Homer that Athens was the most important city in the peninsula.[4] Thucydides accepts the common tradition regarding the political situation in Attica. As evidence of the independence of the cities of Attica, he cites the fact that they sometimes made war on each other.[5] The festival known as ξυνοίκια he regards as having been instituted by Theseus in commemoration of the unification of Attica. Aristotle accepts the tradition regarding Theseus. His treatment of the early constitution is available only in excerpts; but in his summary of the constitutional changes in Athens, he starts with the settlement of Ion and the institution of the four tribes.[6] The theory has been advanced that the festival ξυνοίκια was in commemoration, not of the union of Attica, but of the union of four groups settled in villages on and beside the Acropolis to form the city of Athens.[7] Others believe

---

[1] *Iliad* ii. 546 ff.:

οἳ δ᾽ ἄρ᾽ 'Αθήνας εἶχον, ἐϋκτίμενον πτολίεθρον.

Odyssey, vii. 80:

ἵκετο δ᾽ ἐς Μαραθῶνα καὶ εὐρυάγυιαν 'Αθήνην.

[2] *Od.*, iii. 278.   [3] *Od.*, vii. 80.   [4] De Sanctis, *op. cit.*, p. 29.

[5] ii. 15. For further evidence on this point, see De Sanctis, *op. cit.*, pp. 24 ff.; Meyer, *op. cit.*, sec. 223.

[6] Aristotle *Ath. Pol.* xli. 2. Cf. *Fragmenta* in the edition of Thalheim (Teubner, 1909), p. 107.

[7] Wachsmuth, *Rheinisches Museum*, XXIII, 181. He thinks that Thucydides refers only to a political union which was celebrated in the Panathenaea. Cf. *Die Stadt Athen*, i, 453. Cf. Wilamowitz, *Aus Kydathen*, pp. 116 ff.

that the *Synoecia* had nothing to do with the unification either of Athens or of Attica, but was an annual reunion of families, resembling the Apaturia.[1]

Thucydides puts the date of the unification very early in Attic history. The achievement of Theseus he regards not as the consummation of a long-continued movement toward unity but as the carrying out, at one stroke, of a great political conception by a man of vision and power. The unification, according to Thucydides, was accomplished without the use of force,[2] though the characterization of Theseus as a powerful king carries the suggestion that force was available. It is now generally believed that Theseus' success was the culmination of a long-continued process. The available evidence seems to support the view that the process began as early as 1000 B.C. And it may have continued for two or even three centuries.[3]

The Athenians were very fond of connecting Theseus with democracy. Isocrates[4] goes so far as to say that Theseus established a modified form of democracy; and an orator contemporary with Demosthenes[5] speaks in a similar strain. Euripides in the *Supplices*[6] puts into the mouth of Theseus a vigorous condemnation of tyranny and a laudation of the reign of law. The oligarch of Theophrastus[7] denounces Theseus as the source of all the ills of the state. Plutarch[8] quotes Homer's designation of the inhabitants of Athens as "the people (δῆμος) of Erechtheus," as evidence that Theseus

[1] De Sanctis, *op. cit.*, p. 24.

[2] The peaceful character of the unification is confirmed by the fact that all inhabitants of Attica were made citizens; there were no *perioeci* as in Sparta. Cf. *CAH*, III, 579.

[3] De Sanctis, *op. cit.*, pp. 34 ff.; *CAH*, III, 580; Bury, *History of Greece*, p. 170; Meyer, *op. cit.*, sec. 224; Busolt-Swoboda, *op. cit.*, II, 777, put the date in the middle of the eighth century at the latest.

[4] *Panathenaicus*, 129, 131; *Helen*, 35.

[5] [Demosthenes] lix. 75.

[6] 429. The passage is quoted *infra*, p. 68. Cf. also 352 f.

καὶ γὰρ κατέστησ' αὐτὸν (τὸν δῆμον) ἐς μοναρχίαν
ἐλευθερώσας τήνδ' ἰσόψηφον πόλιν.

[7] *Characters* xxix (xxvi). 11. 25 ff.

[8] *Theseus*, xxv. *Il.* ii. 547.

"displayed a leaning toward the multitude and had given up his absolute rule." Democratic propagandists[1] seized upon and fostered this tradition, just as they magnified the services of Solon, in the interests of democracy. It was highly desirable to furnish democracy with an ancient and honorable lineage. In government and in law, ancestral and time-honored usages and institutions commanded general respect in Athens, as elsewhere both in the ancient and in the modern world.

The unification of Attica must have involved some constitutional changes. In his enumeration of the eleven changes in the Athenian constitution, Aristotle lists Theseus' reorganization as the first. He describes it as "a slight deviation from absolute monarchy."[2] Some details of the reorganization effected by Theseus and the concessions he made to the nobles and the lower classes are found in Plutarch. For himself the king retained the leadership in war and guardianship of the law; "to the nobles he committed the care of religious rites, the supply of magistrates, the teaching of the laws, and the interpretation of the will of Heaven. For the rest of the citizens he established a balance of privileges, the noblemen being thought to excel in dignity, the husbandmen (Γεωμόροι) in usefulness, and the handicraftsmen in numbers."[3] This reference to the importance of numbers and the promise of equality made to the lower classes would seem to indicate that Plutarch had in mind a popular assembly. There was provision for assemblies of the people in the local communities, for Theseus, in his canvass from community to community in the interests of his project, must have on occasion addressed the assembled inhabitants. Plutarch evidently was familiar with Aristotle's treatment of Theseus, but his main source was the traditional conception of early Athenian

[1] Pausanias (i. 3. 3) saw a painting representing Democracy, Demos, and Theseus in a group. He mentions the story that Theseus τὸν καταστήσαντα ᾿Αθηναίοις ἐξ ἴσου πολιτεύεσθαι with the comment κεχώρηκε δὲ φήμη καὶ ἄλλως ἐς τοὺς πολλοὺς ὡς Θησεὺς παραδοίη τὰ πράγματα τῷ δήμῳ.

[2] *Ath. Pol.* xli. 2: ἡ ἐπὶ Θησέως γενομένη (πολιτεία) μικρὸν παρεγκλίνουσα τῆς βασιλικῆς.

[3] *Theseus* xxiv. xxv (Perrin's translation).

history as it appeared in Istrus' summary of the Atthi-
dographers.[1] On the whole, Plutarch's reconstruction is not
very wide of the mark. In order to induce the petty chiefs
to give up their independence, Theseus must have promised
them concessions which resulted in the establishment of a
modified oligarchy. And whatever degree of participation
in the affairs of the state[2] was permitted to the common
people, it was inevitable that their concentration in Athens
should have enabled them to voice their aspirations and exert
their influence more effectively. This appears in the success
of Menestheus[3] in appealing to the populace for support in
his efforts to supplant Theseus.

The Athenians claimed the credit of being the first to
establish regular legal processes in Greece.[4] The fundamental requirement of a regular legal process is that it should
be compulsory. An aggrieved person must have the power
to force the one who has wronged him in person or in property to appear before a court, which holds regular sittings
when the need arises. In the settlement of disputes and the
punishment of wrongdoers, much the same system was in
vogue under the early kingship as is pictured in the Homeric
poems: voluntary arbitration for civil cases, self-help for
homicide and other wrongs to person and property, and action by the assembled people against dangerous public offenders.

As has already been pointed out, the change from voluntary to obligatory arbitration in Boeotia seems to follow the

---

[1] Busolt, *Geschichte*, II, 57.

[2] Plutarch *Theseus* xxv. 1: ἔτι δὲ μᾶλλον αὐξῆσαι τὴν πόλιν βουλόμενος ἐκάλει πάντας ἐπὶ τοῖς ἴσοις.
   Aristotle *Ath. Pol.*, Heraclidis Epitoma, 3: Θησεὺς δὲ ἐκήρυξε καὶ συνεβίβασε τούτους ἐπ' ἴσῃ καὶ ὁμοίᾳ.

[3] Plutarch *Theseus* xxxii.

[4] Aelian *Vera historia* iii. 38: Δίκας δοῦναι καὶ λαβεῖν ηὗρον Ἀθηναῖοι πρῶτοι.
   Cicero *Pro Flacco*, 26, § 62: "Adsunt Athenienses, unde humanitas, doctrina, religio, fruges, jura, leges ortae atque in omnes terras distributae putantur."
   Isocrates (*Panegyricus*, 40) claims great antiquity for the homicide trials: οἱ γὰρ ἐν ἀρχῇ περὶ τῶν φονικῶν ἐγκαλέσαντες καὶ βουληθέντες μετὰ λόγου καὶ μὴ μετὰ βίας διαλύσασθαι τὰ πρὸς ἀλλήλους ἐν τοῖς νόμοις τοῖς ἡμετέροις τὰς κρίσεις ἐποιήσαντο περὶ αὐτῶν.

change from the Heroic kingship to an aristocratic form of government.[1] Much the same situation developed in Attica, as may be seen in Aristotle's reconstruction of early Athenian history. The oath,[2] sworn by the archons against accepting bribes, is the same as was sworn in the days of Acastus, the first regent or archon under the new régime which usurped the chief functions of the kingship. The annual proclamation[3] of the archon assuring security of property to the citizens is at least as early as 683–682, the year in which the annual archonship was established.[4] But there is no reason why it may not be as old as the oath. The nobles who at first restricted, and then abolished, royalty naturally desired popular support. The promise of honest government and security of property was well calculated to conciliate and reassure the people who might have some misgivings regarding the new government. Security of property is one of the foundation stones of organized society. But no government would bind itself to respect the person or property of a citizen who tried to subvert it. The proclamation of the archon must have meant that no citizen would be deprived of his property without cause. The modern formula would be "without due process of law." And it is not too much to assume that in view of such a proclamation a government would not fail to bring before the sovereign body in the state any citizen suspected of designs to overthrow it. In effect this would amount to the institution of some sort of public trial

[1] Cf. *supra*, pp. 44 ff.

[2] Aristotle *Ath. Pol.* iii. 3: τεκμήριον δ' ἐπιφέρουσιν ὅτι οἱ ἐννέα ἄρχοντες ὀμνύουσιν ὥσπερ ἐπὶ 'Ακάστου τὰ ὅρκια ποιήσειν, ὡς ἐπὶ τούτου τῆς βασιλείας παραχωρησάντων τῶν Κοδριδῶν ἀντὶ τῶν δοθεισῶν τῷ ἄρχοντι δωρεῶν.

Op. cit., vii. 1: οἱ δ' ἐννέα ἄρχοντες ὀμνύντες πρὸς τῷ λίθῳ κατεφάτιζον ἀναθήσειν ἀνδριάντα χρυσοῦν, ἐάν τινα παραβῶσι τῶν νόμων. ὅθεν ἔτι καὶ νῦν οὕτως ὀμνύουσι.

Op. cit., lv. 5: ἀναβάντες δ' ἐπὶ τοῦτον ὀμνύουσιν δικαίως ἄρξειν καὶ κατὰ τοὺς νόμους, καὶ δῶρα μὴ λήψεσθαι τῆς ἀρχῆς ἕνεκα, κἄν τι λάβωσι ἀνδριάντα ἀναθήσειν χρυσοῦν.

[3] *Op. cit.*, lvi. 2: Καὶ ὁ μὲν ἄρχων εὐθὺς εἰσελθὼν πρῶτον μὲν κηρύττει, ὅσα τις εἶχεν πρὶν αὐτὸν εἰσελθεῖν εἰς τὴν ἀρχήν, ταῦτ' ἔχειν καὶ κρατεῖν μέχρι ἀρχῆς τέλους. Cf. Busolt-Swoboda, *op. cit.*, II, 787–88, for judicial functions of early archonship.

[4] Busolt, *op. cit.*, II, 135; Meyer, *Gesch. des Altertums*, II, sec. 228; Busolt-Swoboda, *op. cit.*, II, 786.

before the ancient aristocratic council—the Areopagus.[1] Similarly, security of property against one who, to quote Hesiod,[2] "might stir up quarrels and strife to secure the possessions of another" could only be assured by invoking the aid of the magistrates. Let us take a simple case, a quarrel about boundary stones.[3] The victim of his neighbor's encroachment, upon the failure of amicable means of settling the dispute, must have had the privilege of appearing before the archon with a petition for protection of his property. The magistrate could not act on *ex parte* information. The alternative was to have both parties before him. The result would be a legal process ($\delta i \kappa \eta$) and a verdict. If the verdict was not obeyed, recourse could again be had to the magistrate to implement the promise in his proclamation. These proceedings were all doubtless more or less informal in an age when the administrative and judicial functions of magistrates were not differentiated and neither the substantive laws nor the rules of procedure had been reduced to writing.

Another clear indication of the antiquity of the Athenian legal process is afforded by the designation of the court fees as $\pi\rho\upsilon\tau\alpha\nu\epsilon\hat{\iota}\alpha$. Lipsius believes that there is indicated a connection with an early court in the Prytaneum that cannot now be identified.[4] But it is possible to be more specific than Lipsius was willing to be.

The homicide court in the Prytaneum, consisting of the king archon and the tribe kings ($\phi\upsilon\lambda\upsilon\beta\alpha\sigma\iota\lambda\epsilon\hat{\iota}s$), was in the historical period a purely ceremonial tribunal. It was in operation as early at least as the time of Draco, who provided in his homicide laws for the trial of animals or inanimate things that caused the death of a human being.[5] But, as

---

[1] Cf. *infra*, p. 169.   [2] *Works and Days*, 33 f.   [3] *Il.* xii. 421 ff.

[4] Lipsius, *Das Attische Recht*, p. 25; Keil, *Die Solonische Verfassung*, pp. 108 ff., identifies it with the court in the Prytaneum, mentioned in the amnesty law of Solon, which he thinks judged those accused of tyranny. But he is in error. The court mentioned in the amnesty law dealt with unknown murderers only. Tyrants were tried by the Areopagus. Cf. *infra* pp. 104 ff.

[5] Pausanias (vi. 11. 6), in describing the action of the Thasians against a statue that fell on a man and killed him, says they followed Draco, who provided in his homicide laws that if an inanimate object caused the death of a human being it

Draco was doubtless including in his legislation an ancient practice, it is reasonable to assume that the court is of great antiquity. But it is not to be supposed that the court was originally formed for a purely ceremonial purpose. It is obviously a relic of a very early court with wider jurisdiction and greater powers. It may go back to the institution of the Ionic tribes. The heads of the tribes (φυλοβασιλεῖς) must have outranked the Homeric Council of Elders attached to the suzerain king in Athens. It is quite unlikely that their co-operation with the king in the Council of Elders was confined to such religious and ceremonial functions as those of the court in the Prytaneum. It is more reasonable to suppose that they shared in a much wider range of judicial functions. The Prytaneum was always the seat of the highest officials in Athens.[1] When compulsory process of law was substituted for arbitration and the government undertook to provide machinery for the administration of justice, it is only natural that the king and the phylobasileis sitting in the Prytaneum should participate. The fees for the services thus rendered were euphemistically called "gifts" (δῶρα). They belong to the γέρα given to the Homeric kings both by the community and by individuals.[2] Whether all such offerings were designated as τὰ πρυτανεῖα (i.e., things belonging

---

should be cast beyond the borders. Cf. Treston, *Poine*, pp. 91, 197 ff., 246 ff. Cf. Busolt-Swoboda, *op. cit.*, II, 792, for the early history of the phylobasileis: "Dieses Gericht (Prytaneum) war zweifellos eine Überrest einer einst ausgedehntern richterlichen Tätigkeit."

[1] Aristotle *Ath. Pol.* iii. 5; Thucydides ii. 15.

[2] Schöll, *Hermes*, VI, 23, developed a suggestion originally made by Boeckh in the 1817 edition of his *Staatshaushaltung der Athener*, I, 216, and repeated in the third edition by Fraenkel (I, 216): "Schon der Name der Prytaneien als Gerichtsgelder beweiset, dass diese ehemals den Prytanen als Richtern im Prytaneion wie ein Richtersold erlegt wurden, woraus ihre Mahlzeiten theilweise mochten bestritten worden." The identification of these judges in the prytaneum as the prytaneis of the Naucrars cannot be accepted.

So Meyer (*op. cit.*, sec. 225, A,) remarks, "Aus den Geschenken an den König sind später die Gerichtsgebühren erwachsen, so in Athen die πρυτανεῖα die von den Kolakreten, den Finanzbeamten des ältesten Staats, verwaltet werden." For the original functions of the Kolakretae, see *ibid.*, sec. 209. For their subsequent history, see Boeckh, *op. cit.*, I, 216. Cf. Busolt-Swoboda, *op. cit.*, II, 788, n. 1, on the implications of πρυτανεῖα.

to the Prytaneum) is not known. Possibly the term came to be applied to court fees exclusively because these were the most common, if not the only, "gifts" presented by individuals to the royal judges in the Prytaneum. Originally, the offerings were in kind, chiefly foodstuff. The kolakretae were the officials who took charge of them and prepared the public meals for the officials and the guests of the state. It is significant in this connection to recall that in the fifth century the kolakretae paid the Athenian dicasts out of a fund provided in part from the court fees (τὰ πρυτανεῖα).[1] The motives of the state in interfering in homicide cases can be more conveniently treated at a later stage in connection with a full discussion of the homicide courts.[2] But it is evident that the functions of the king archon and the phylobasileis in the Prytaneum in Aristotle's time point to a more vital participation on the part of these officials in the earliest steps taken by organized society to mitigate blood-feuds that tended to disrupt it, or to obviate the dangers of pollution. When a member of a phratry was slain, it was only natural that in some cases the immediate relatives should desire the advice or aid of their phratry.[3] Evidence in support of the view that members of a phratry actively participated in questions arising out of the murder of one of its members is found in the homicide laws of Draco. It was provided that where a murderer in exile was eligible for pardon (αἴδεσις) at the hands of the relatives of his victim, the members of the phratry might grant the pardon if there were no surviving relatives. Similarly, phratry members were permitted to join in the prosecution of a murderer.[4] It has been suggested that where murders involved persons of different tribes, intervention on the part of the phylobasileis may have occurred.[5] Naturally the king would act as chairman of such a commis-

[1] Aristophanes *Wasps*, 695, with Starkie's note.

[2] Cf. *infra*, p. 103.

[3] Cf. De Sanctis, *op. cit.*, pp. 49 f.

[4] Cf. *CIA* i. 61. 21 ff.: συνδιόκεν δὲ καὶ ἀνεφσιὸς καὶ ἀνεφσιõν παῖδας καὶ γαμβρὸς καὶ πενθερὸς καὶ φράτερας.

[5] Cary in *CAH*, III, 584; cf. Treston, *op. cit.*, p. 91.

sion. These considerations point strongly to a time when the king and the phylobasileis presided over the earliest homicide trials in the Areopagus.

Plutarch, in his account of the unification of Attica, touches upon the provisions made for the administration of justice. The nobles became administrators of justice (διδά-σκαλοι τῶν νόμων), while the king was intrusted with the guardianship of the laws in the interest of the common people.[1] These provisions are suspiciously like the later Athenian system projected back into early times. Provision was always made for the guardianship of the laws, whether by Areopagus or nomophylakes or nomothetae. Before the age of written codes, supervision over laws could most easily be exercised by hearing informal complaints against the decisions of the eupatrid judges. But an aristocratic kingship could not afford to run the risk of alienating the nobles by reversing their judgments in the interest of the masses.

The concentration of political power in Athens as the capital and the increase in the numbers of the city populace must have eventually hastened the development of some sort of legal process. If the conclusions drawn from the archon's annual proclamation and the suggested antecedents of the court of the Prytaneum are correct, the traditional claim that the Athenian legal process was an early development seems entirely warranted. It is at least as early as the establishment of the annual archonship (683–682 B.C.) and may very well go back to the earlier struggles between the king and the aristocracy in the establishment of a government in which the powers of the kingship were exercised by the archons.[2]

---

[1] Plutarch *Theseus*, xxiv and xxv.

[2] "Mit der Einsetzung des Archons unter Akastos ist dessen Stelle in der Liste der lebenslänglichen Erbkönige (bezw. Archonten) ganz unvereinbar. Da Akastos als zweiter in der Reihe der dreizehn lebenslänglichen und erblichen Eponymoi erscheint, so müszte er etwa um die Mitte des 11 Jahrhunderts gelebt haben. Aber der relativ junge Charakter des Archontenamtes und die noch um die Mitte des 7 Jahrhunderts aktuelle Bedeutung der Eidopfer unter Akastos verbieten es, das Amt über die Mitte des 8 Jahrhunderts hinauszurücken."—Busolt-Swoboda, *op. cit.*, II, 789.

CHAPTER III

THE LAWGIVERS

Under the rule of the early aristocracy in Greece, the magistrates administered an unwritten customary law. The common people, dissatisfied by reason of the uncertainties of the interpretation and administration of the law, demanded the substitution of a set of rules binding upon all judges, in place of the body of vague customary laws which could be modified and interpreted to suit the interest of the ruling class —the bribe-devouring kings of Hesiod.[1] Whether in every case concessions were extorted by the people, or whether they were the result of an act of grace on the part of the aristocracy to forestall the danger which they saw was coming, is uncertain and immaterial. At any rate, there was general codification of the laws in Greece in the course of the seventh century.[2] Contemporary opinion about the necessity for codified laws and the resultant advantages and disadvantages is voiced on the one hand by Hesiod, a member of the lower classes, who had suffered from the maladministration of justice, and on the other hand by Alcaeus and Theognis, nobles who had lost their privileges through the new state of affairs. Theognis makes strikingly clear the attitude of the nobles toward the new powers and privileges of the common people. There is no hope for the city in which the power has been transferred from the nobles (οἱ ἀγαθοί) to the commons (οἱ κακοί) :

> Our commonwealth preserves its former frame
> Our common people are no more the same.
> They, that in skins and hides were rudely dress'd,

[1] *Works and Days*, 38 f.

[2] The codification of law in Greece is so important a step in the evolution of the judiciary and judicial practice and procedure that it has been thought best for the proper appreciation of the work of Draco to discuss in some detail the work of the lawgivers that appeared relatively about his time elsewhere in Greece. For the contributions of the lawgivers toward the development of criminal law, cf. Calhoun, *Criminal Law*, pp. 107 ff.

Nor dreamt of law nor sought to be redress'd
By rules of right, but in the days of old
Flock'd to the town like cattle to the fold,
Are now the brave and wise. And we, the rest
(Their betters nominally, once the best),
Degenerate, debased, timid, and mean!
Who can endure to witness such a scene?
Their easy courtesies, the ready smile, ·
Prompt to deride, to flatter and beguile!
Their utter disregard of right or wrong,
Of truth or honor![1]

Theognis had a personal cause for grievance in the confiscation of his property.[2] Fifth-century opinion is represented by the following statement of Euripides:

No worse foe than the despot hath a state,
Under whom, first, can be no common laws,
But one rules, keeping in his private hands
The law: so is equality no more.
But when the laws are written, then the weak
And wealthy have alike but equal right.
Yea, even the weaker may fling back the scoff
Against the prosperous, if he be reviled;
And, armed with right, the less o'ercomes the great.[3]

Among modern writers, who deal with the matter merely from a historical point of view, Maine sees in the codes a means of protection against the degeneration and corruption of customary usages. Pollock, on the other hand, declares that codification may sometimes arrest the normal development of law, and cites as an example the Roman Twelve Tables, which, he says, "went near to stereotype an archaic and formalist procedure."[4]

---

[1] 53 ff. (Frere's translation). Cf. Alcaeus, *Frag.* 59 (Hiller-Crusius).

[2] Cf. 1197 ff.:

Ὄρνιθος φωνήν, Πολυπαΐδη, ὀξὺ βοώσης
ἤκουσ', ἥτε βροτοῖς ἄγγελος ἦλθ' ἀρότου
ὡραίου· καί μοι κραδίην ἐπάταξε μέλαιναν,
ὅττι μοι εὐανθεῖς ἄλλοι ἔχουσιν ἀγροὺς
οὐδέ μοι ἡμίονοι κύφων' ἕλκουσιν ἀρότρου
τῆς (μάλα μισητῆς) εἵνεκα ναυτιλίης.

[3] *Supplices*, 429 ff. (Way's translation).
[4] Maine, *Ancient Law*, with notes by Pollock, pp. 16 and 25.

It is not a matter of accident that the codification began in the colonies rather than on the mainland of Greece. It is only natural that the colonists, freed from the restraints of conservatism at home, should be more progressive and more inclined to embark upon social and political reforms. Moreover, the different physical conditions in the colonies necessitated considerable adaptation of, and addition to, the laws of the homeland. In modern times the tendency on the part of self-governing colonies to make political and social innovations is well illustrated in the case of Australia and New Zealand, which have worked out important experiments in democracy.[1] In the Greek colonies, codification was sometimes rendered imperative because the colonists were recruited from different cities with divergent systems of customary law.[2] Hence, no single set of customary laws could be entirely satisfactory to all the citizens.

It is interesting to note that the first codes were made in the western colonies, which were farther from Greece than the eastern colonies both in distance and in the difficulty of the voyage. The western colonies were settled by Ionians, Dorians, and Achaeans. Each of these races produced its own lawgiver: Zaleucus in Achaean Locris,[3] Charondas in Ionian Catana, and Diocles in Dorian Syracuse.[4] The adop-

[1] Cf. Bryce, *Modern Democracies*, II, 166 and 329.

[2] Sometimes the lawgiver was intrusted also with the framing of a constitution. Cf. *infra*, p. 134.

[3] Aristotle (*Pol.* 1274*a*. 25) refers to Onomacritus the Locrian, who was wrongly regarded by some (probably the reference is to Ephorus; cf. Newman, *The Politics of Aristotle*, II, 377) as the first person of note to draw up laws. He may be identical with the Athenian oracle-monger of the age of Peisistratus. Cf. Newman, *op. cit.*, II, 379.

[4] Diodorus xii. 19; xiii. 35. Cf. Meyer, *Geschichte des Altertums*, II, 566 ff., for data on the lives of the various lawgivers. Cf. also articles "Charondas," "Diokles," "Lykurgos," "Drakon," in Pauly-Wissowa; Busolt-Swoboda, *Staatskunde*, pp. 369 ff. For Zaleucus and Charondas, cf. Mühl, "Die Gesetze des Zaleukos und Charondas," *Klio*, XXII, pp. 105 ff., 432 ff.; Adcock, "Literary Tradition and Early Greek Codemakers," *Cambridge Historical Journal*, II, No. 2, 95 ff. The laws of Zaleucus and Charondas were generally regarded as the oldest written laws in Greece. They must have been written before the middle of the seventh century. To the seventh century belong also Androdamas, Philolaus, Pheidon, Draco (traditional date 621 B.C.). Pittacus and Solon belong to the early years of the sixth

tion of the laws of Charondas by the Ionian (Chalcidian) cities of Italy and Sicily is specifically mentioned by Aristotle.[1] These cities included Naxos, Zancle, Mylae, Himera, in Sicily; Rhegium, and possibly also Cyme, in Italy. Zaleucus' laws were adopted also in Sybaris, and those of Diocles in other Sicilian cities. The fact that the Ionian colonies adopted the laws of Charondas suggests the possibility that the laws of Zaleucus were to be found in the other Achaean colonies of the west, and those of Diocles in the Dorian colonies. The mixed colony of Thurii (founded 443 B.C.) is said by Diodorus to have adopted the laws of Charondas. Other authorities say that the colony adopted the laws of Zaleucus. Since the laws of Zaleucus were in use in the neighboring colony of Sybaris, it seems more likely that his code would be the one adopted in Thurii.[2]

Some of the western codes found their way into eastern Hellas. The code of Charondas was introduced even into the island of Cos[3] and in Mazaka, a city of Cappadocia.[4] The Chalcidians of Thrace (Euboean Chalcidians) are said to have summoned Androdamas from Chalcidian Rhegium to formulate laws for them. It is quite possible that he introduced the code of Charondas, which was in force in his native city, although his name is connected with homicide laws which are not mentioned in the code of Charondas.[5] Other cities in Asia Minor and the islands produced their own lawgivers. Pittacus of Mytilene established a code of laws for his native city;[6] and there is a bare reference to Aristides, the lawgiver of Ceos.[7] The code about which the

---

century. For the dispute about the date of Diocles, cf. Freeman, *History of Sicily*, III, 722 ff. Later Syracusan lawgivers are said by Diodorus·to have been regarded merely as interpreters of Diocles' laws because of the ancient dialect in which they were written.

[1] *Pol.* 1274a. 23 ff.; cf. Heracl. Pont. *de reb. pub.* 25. 4.

[2] Diodorus xii. 11; Athenaeus xi. 508a.; Suidas *s.v.* Ζάλευκος. For a detailed discussion of the question, cf. Busolt, *Geschichte*, III, 534, n. 1.

[3] Herondas 2. 46 ff.   [4] Strabo xii. 2. 9.   [5] Aristotle *Pol.* 1274b. 23 ff.

[6] *Ibid.*, 1274b. 18; cf. Plutarch *Sept. Sap. Conv.*, 13; Alcaeus, frag. 42.

[7] Heracl. Pont., 9.

most is known belongs to the city of Gortyn on the island of Crete.[1] The name of the lawgiver—if the large fragment is the work of an individual—is unknown.

Various cities in the homeland had their own lawgivers. The institutions of Sparta were attributed to Lycurgus. But Spartan laws were not reduced to writing.[2] Athens is commonly supposed to have received her first code of laws at the hands of Draco.[3] Philolaus of Corinth made laws for the Thebans,[4] while the Corinthians themselves were provided with laws by Pheidon.[5] The exact situation in Megara is not known; but from the statements of Theognis,[6] it is evident that a democracy must have prevailed there for a time,

[1] Collitz-Bechtel, *SGDI*, 4991; Comparetti, *Monumenti Antichi*, III, 93 ff.; Dareste, Haussoullier, Reinach, *Recueil des inscriptions juridiques grecques*, I, 352 ff.; Michel, *Recueil d'inscriptions grecques*, 1333; Solmsen, *Inscriptiones Graecae ad inlustrandos dialectos selectae*, 30; Kohler and Ziebarth, *Das Stadtrecht von Gortyn;* Buck, *Greek Dialects*, pp. 261 ff.; Gertrude Smith, *The Administration of Justice from Hesiod to Solon*, pp. 32 ff.

The code of Gortyn belongs mainly to the fifth century. But there are fragments of it which go back to the seventh century. Furthermore, Crete, like Sparta, is a type of arrested development. The social and political organization of the cities abounded in archaic survivals even in the age of Ephorus and Aristotle. The code seems to be a restatement, with additions and amendments, of articles and chapters of a prior code. So, in point of development, there is justification for comparing it with the legal system of Athens in the seventh and sixth centuries. It is noteworthy that there is no mention of homicide. It may be suggested that another portion of the code, not now extant, dealt with this subject. Or, possibly, self-help in homicide was still practiced and the state had not yet assumed control. For the mention of blood-money in fragments of the earlier codes, cf. *infra*, p. 79. Cf. Wyse, in Whibley, *Companion to Greek Studies*, p. 379.

[2] For the various theories about Lycurgus, cf. Ehrenberg, *Neugründer des Staates*, pp. 7 ff.

[3] Ancient writers ascribed to Athens the invention of lawsuits (Aelian *V. H.* iii. 38; cf. Lipsius, *Das Attische Recht*, p. 1, and *supra*, p. 61). This does not mean, however, that they were the first Greeks to have a written law. According to Strabo (vi. 1. 8), the western Locrians were the first Greeks to establish written laws. Cf. Scymnus of Chios, 312 ff.

[4] Aristotle *Pol.* 1274*b*. 2.   [5] *Ibid.*, 1265*b*. 12 ff.

[6] 289 ff.

> Νῦν δὲ τὰ τῶν ἀγαθῶν κακὰ γίνεται ἐσθλὰ κακοῖσιν
> ἀνδρῶν· ἡγέονται δ' ἐκτραπέλοισι νόμοις·
> αἰδὼς μὲν γὰρ ὄλωλεν· ἀναιδείη δὲ καὶ ὕβρις
> νικήσασα δίκην γῆν κατὰ πᾶσαν ἔχει.

Cf. 53 ff., quoted *supra*, p. 67.

during which the people acquired a written code of laws from some unknown lawgiver.

There are examples of lawgivers from all classes of society, but the majority were drawn from the middle class. The nobility naturally were opposed to codification, inasmuch as it deprived them of many privileges. Aristotle declares that the best lawgivers belonged to the middle class. In proof of this statement he offers, as examples, Solon, Lycurgus, and Charondas.[1] The accounts of Zaleucus' rank are contradictory. According to one story, the laws were given to him in a dream by Athena while he was a poor shepherd.[2] But in the account given by Diodorus, he is described as ἀνὴρ εὐγενὴς καὶ κατὰ παιδείαν τεθαυμασμένος.[3] Pittacus was not himself of noble family, but he married a daughter of the tyrant Penthilus.

In some cases the task of establishing a code of laws was intrusted to one of the citizens, specially chosen. Occasionally he was vested also with some high office. So at Athens, Draco was a special thesmothete in 621 B.C., the year to which his legislation is generally assigned. Solon, chosen as διαλλακτής to revise the laws and constitution, was appointed archon.[4] Pittacus is an illustration of an extraordinary magistrate intrusted with the making of laws. He was appointed supreme ruler of the city (αἰσυμνήτης) for a period of ten years in order to restore civil peace. In general, with regard to the other lawgivers, there is no information about the circumstances under which they were appointed or about the official positions which they held. It is hardly to be supposed that a foreigner called in to establish a code of laws would be clothed with any political authority.[5]

The earliest laws were generally believed to be of divine

---

[1] *Pol.* 1296a. 18 ff.; cf. *Ath. Pol.*, v; Plutarch *Solon*, i, xiv, and xvi; *Lycurgus*, iii; *Cleom.*, x.

[2] Scholiast, Pindar *Olymp.* 10. 17.   [3] xii. 20.

[4] Cf. F. D. Smith, *Athenian Political Commissions*, pp. 13 f., who sees in these two lawgivers the beginning of the commission principle.

[5] Cf. Androdamas, who came from Rhegium to make laws for the Chalcidians in Thrace.

origin.[1] For example, Zeus was responsible for the Cretan laws, since Minos and Rhadamanthus received their inspiration directly from him.[2] The laws of the western Locrians were said to have been communicated to Zaleucus by Athena in a dream,[3] after he had been appointed to frame a code of laws in answer to the response of the Delphic oracle.

There are many tales of the visits of lawgivers to foreign countries for the purpose of studying the institutions of other cities, both customary and recorded. For instance, Zaleucus is reported by Ephorus to have taken his laws from Cretan, Spartan, and Athenian sources.[4] According to Plutarch,[5] Lycurgus studied the institutions of Crete, Ionia, Egyptian cities, and perhaps of Libya, Iberia, and India. Herodotus states that the Spartan institutions came from Crete.[6] Before drawing up his code, Charondas examined the laws of many peoples and chose from them the best.[7]

[1] There appears always to have been a feeling that there was some inspired person responsible for the laws. Cf. the famous personification of the laws in *Crito*, 50a ff.

[2] Plato *Laws*, 624. Beloch (*Griechische Geschichte*, I, 1, 350) believes that these early codes were really all attributed to gods—even that of Draco. So the Cretans referred their laws to Minos; and, as he was reduced from a god to a hero, they said that the laws were given to him by Zeus. The Lacedaemonians considered their laws a revelation of the god of light. Tyrtaeus believed that they came from Delphi. This is due to the story which grew up after Lycurgus had been reduced to a hero that he received the sanction for his laws from the Delphic oracle. In the same way Zaleucus is the "Hellstrahlende" and Charondas the "Helläugige" —both sun-gods. Diocles of Syracuse was a god, since he had a temple in Syracuse and was worshiped as a hero at Thebes. Philolaus is also a figure of mythology. The most ancient laws of Athens were attributed to Draco, the serpent god, who was worshiped under the names of Erechtheus and Cecrops on the Acropolis and who was regarded as the founder of the state. Cf. Mühl, *op. cit.*, pp. 107 f., for a criticism of Beloch.

[3] Scholiast, Pindar *Olymp.* 10. 17. Cf. Plutarch, *De se ips. laud.*, 11.

[4] Strabo, vi. 1.8. Meyer believes that in this statement Ephorus was wrong. Gilbert (*Beiträge*, pp. 478 f.), on the other hand, argues that Ephorus' statement is sound, inasmuch as identical provisions are found in Cretan and in Locrian law and also in Athenian and Locrian law. But according to this method of reasoning, all of the early codes could be assumed to be related, for similar provisions occur in many of them.

[5] *Lycurgus*, iv.   [6] i. 65 ff.

[7] With these tales may be compared the alleged embassy of the Romans to Athens at the time of the decemviral legislation. In modern times it was long the

The early codes were doubtless based on traditional and customary law.[1] In procedure this dependence on customary law would be most marked. In the case of homicide, there would be a tendency to adhere to the existing practice, inasmuch as the procedure was ritualistic. Religious conservatism would tend to prevent innovations. It is quite obvious that Draco followed the practice of the time in his homicide laws.[2] It may well be, also, that the procedure used at Cyme in homicide trials, that is, the evidentiary oath with oath helpers,[3] represents customary practice which was seized upon by the legislator and introduced into the code. It is quite probable that the tendency, observable in homicide cases, to make use of a procedure which was already familiar, spread to other types of cases also. No specific instances of the perpetuation of customary law can be recognized as such. On the other hand, there are indications that early legislation was more than a mere record of customary law. The fact that in general the lawgivers were regarded as inspired would seem to indicate that their laws were to some extent different from the customary law. New conditions, both political and social, had to be met by many new provisions. Thus Charondas is said to have invented many new regulations.[4]

---

prevailing view that such an embassy never occurred. On the other hand, Cicero mentions one law of Solon which was adopted by the decemvirs (*De leg.* 2. 25. 64: "Quam legem (Solonis) eisdem prope verbis nostri decemviri in decimam tabulam coniecerunt." Cf. 2. 23. 59). Other ancient writers accept the story of the embassy, e.g., Dionys. Hal. *Antiq. Rom.* x. 51 ff.; Livy iii. 31. Hofman, *Beiträge zur Geschichte des griechischen und römischen Rechts*, pp. 1 ff., argues convincingly in favor of Greek influence on the Twelve Tables, and his conclusions are accepted by Beauchet, *Histoire du droit privé des Athéniens*, I, xxiii. Cf. Jefferson Elmore, "The Purpose of the Decemviral Legislation," *Class. Philol.*, XVII, 138.

[1] In some cases there would be some written material available for the lawgiver. The work of the thesmothetae, for instance, may have afforded Draco some written material as a basis for his work. Their task consisted partly in recording judicial decisions. Cf. *infra*, p. 85.

[2] Cf. *infra*, p. 111.

[3] Cf. *infra*, p. 79. Cf. Gertrude Smith, *Administration of Justice from Hesiod to Solon*, pp. 79 f.

[4] Diodorus xii. 11. According to Aristotle (*Pol.*, 1325a), it was the duty of a good legislator to examine his state and the nature of his people, and likewise their relations with neighbors, in order to satisfy their needs by his laws.

The reluctance of the Greeks to alter, or even to criticize, their laws is probably due in part to the general belief in their divine origin. At any rate, there are provisions in some of the codes which rendered it extremely difficult to change the laws. There was a requirement in Locris that if anyone wished to introduce a new law or to change an old one, he had to argue the matter with a rope about his neck before the Council of One Thousand. If the council voted against him, he was choked to death on the spot.[1] Only one law was so changed during a period of two hundred years.[2] Diodorus ascribes a similar provision to Charondas.[3] He says that only three laws were ever changed by this procedure at Thurii. The same reluctance to change laws is shown in Athens by the elaborate procedure provided in the fourth century for changes and amendments.[4] The advisability of changes in the laws was much debated by the theoretical law-givers and political theorists. The Pythagoreans held that it was better to abide by the ancient laws.[5] One of the charges made by the opponent of tyranny in the famous political debate reported by Herodotus is that tyrants alter the an-cestral laws.[6] So also Cleon, as well as other speakers in Thucydides, declares that it is better to keep the laws un-changed.[7] The fact that a law is ancient and unchanged is cited by the orators as a proof of its excellence.[8] The theo-retical lawgivers do, however, advocate alteration under cer-tain conditions. Aristotle objects to allowing the laws to re-main for a long period of time without change. But where the advantage of the new law is trifling, it is much better to retain the old law without alteration. Frequent changes in the laws tend to produce contempt for law and result in dis-obedience.[9]

[1] Demosthenes xxiv. 139; Polybius xii. 16; Stobaeus *Flor.* 44. 21.

[2] Demosthenes xxiv. 139 ff.   [3] xii. 17.

[4] For the process involved, cf. Gilbert, *Constitutional Antiquities*, pp. 301 ff.

[5] Aristox. *Frag.* 19; Müller, *Fr. Hist. Gr.*, II, 278.

[6] iii. 80.   [7] iii. 37. 3; i. 71. 3.   [8] Antiphon v. 14; vi. 2.

[9] *Pol.*, 1268b ff. Cf. Plato, *Laws*, 634; *Polit.*, 295e ff.

The work of the lawgiver was made possible by the discovery and diffusion of the art of writing.[1] The laws were
regularly recorded on the walls of some public building or on
separate *stelae* set up in a public place. The extant fragment
of the laws of Draco belongs to the fifth century, but in early
times the laws of Draco, like those of Solon, were published
on pillars of wood or bronze called κύρβεις or ἄξονες. According to later Greek writers, the κύρβεις were three-cor-
nered, the ἄξονες four-cornered. The former contained religious laws, while the latter contained civil law.[2] But it may
be seen from earlier writers that the two were identical and
that the names were used interchangeably, κύρβεις referring
to their shape and ἄξονες to the fact that they could be turned
around.[3] Weiss believes that the laws in the stoa were on
stone while the wooden originals were kept in the Prytaneum.[4] Other old laws were inscribed on the inside walls of
the stoa. The laws of the Areopagus were set up so that the
court had them before their eyes when trying a case. The
laws of Gortyn are known from the original inscription. The
fragments belonging to the earlier period were probably parts
of the walls of the temple of Pythian Apollo, inasmuch as
they were found on the site of that building. It is generally
supposed that the laws of the second period were engraved
on the inner wall of a sort of courthouse.[5] Aside from copies
on wood and stone, there must also have been documentary
copies. A reference to the singing of Charondas' laws[6] and another reference to the νομῳδός in Mazaka, where Charondas'
laws were introduced,[7] make it seem not improbable that
there was provision in some cities for the regular repetition
of the laws at intervals in order to familiarize the citizens

---

[1] Maine, *op. cit.*, pp. 12 f.

[2] *Etymologicum magnum* and Suidas under κύρβεις. Cf. Sondhaus, *De Solonis Legibus*, p. 4, with diagram.

[3] Aristotle *Ath. Pol.*, vii; Plutarch *Solon*, xxv.

[4] Egon Weiss, *Griechisches Privatrecht*, I, 34 ff. Cf. Gilbert, *op. cit.*, pp. 140 ff.

[5] Cf. Wyse, in Whibley, *Companion to Greek Studies*, p. 466.

[6] Athenaeus 14. 619*b*.   [7] Strabo xii. 2. 9.

with them.[1] The νομῳδός appears also to have interpreted the laws, being somewhat similar in character to the ἐξηγητής at Athens.

On the whole, the information gained from the codes about the actual administration of justice is rather slight. The extant fragments, however, indicate that judicial functions were assigned to the regular magistrates assisted by secretaries, and to special judicial officers. The sole traces of courts composed of a group of judges before the legislation of Solon are in the code of Charondas,[2] but nothing is known about their organization or jurisdiction. The popular assemblies in democracies and the senates in oligarchies apparently participated to some extent in the administration of criminal law. The Areopagus at Athens, for instance, acted in the twofold character of an administrative and a judicial body. The fact that the fragments of the Draconian and Gortynian codes are devoted almost entirely to procedure makes it seem probable that considerable emphasis was laid on it in the codes generally. Aristotle singles out for especial mention the so-called ἐπίσκηψις of Charondas in connection with actions for perjury which he was the first to institute.[3] According to Polybius, Zaleucus permitted self-help in case a slave had been carried off.[4]

A noteworthy feature, because novel at this time, is the fixing of penalties. No longer is the punishment left to the arbitrary will of the judge.[5] According to later standards, the punishments provided by these early lawgivers were exceedingly severe.[6] The severity of Draco's laws became proverbial. The orator Demades said they were written, not in ink, but in blood.[7] The severity of Charondas' punishments may be illustrated by the provision of the death pen-

---

[1] Freeman, op. cit., II, 60, believes that the laws were often in verse that they might be more easily remembered.

[2] Aristotle Pol. 1297a. 21 ff.   [3] Pol. 1274b. 7.

[4] xii. 16. Calhoun, op. cit., p. 117, believes that neither Zaleucus nor Charondas made any notable advance in criminal law.

[5] Strabo vi. 1. 8.   [6] Aristotle Pol. 1274b. 17.   [7] Plutarch Solon, xvii.

alty for entering the assembly wearing a sword. He himself broke the law and committed suicide.[1] The same story is told of Diocles of Syracuse, whose punishments also were notoriously harsh.[2] On the other hand, the punishments imposed by the Gortyn code were regularly fines. Charondas also provided fines for various offenses. He attempted to force the citizens to perform their civic duties by the imposition of fines for failure to act as jurors. He laid greater fines upon rich offenders in this regard than upon the poor.[3] One of the mimes of Herondas records a law of Charondas regarding assault on a slave girl by a freeman.[4] The penalty was double the amount of the injury. It is interesting to compare with this the fine of five drachmas imposed by the Gortyn code for a similar offense.[5] In the same mime of Herondas there is a list of fines for assault, house-breaking, and arson:

$$\text{ἢν θύρην δέ τις κόψῃ,}$$
$$\text{μνῆν τινέτω, φησί· ἢν δὲ πὺξ ἀλοιήσῃ,}$$
$$\text{ἄλλην πάλι μνῆν, ἢν δὲ τὰ οἰκί' ἐμπρήσῃ,}$$
$$\text{ἢ ὅρους ὑπερβῇ, χιλίας τὸ τίμημα}$$
$$\text{ἔνειμε, κἢν βλάψῃ τι, διπλόον τίνειν.}$$

This illustrates very well the minute provisions (ἀκρίβεια) of Charondas' laws upon which Aristotle comments;[6] for example, ἀλοιήσῃ is further defined by πύξ. Punishments were often vindictive. For example, the adulterer, according to the code of Zaleucus, was blinded.[7] In the laws of Charondas it was provided that a deserter should be placed in the agora for three days in women's clothes. A sycophant had to appear publicly with a crown of tamarisks.[8]

So far as can be determined from the scanty fragments, there is no attempt in the codes to classify laws according to their subject matter. Civil, criminal, religious laws, and

---

[1] Diodorus xii. 19.   [2] Diodorus xiii. 33 and 35.

[3] Aristotle *Pol.* 1297a. 15 ff. Cf. Mühl, *op. cit.*, p. 115. For graduated fines for failure to attend meetings of assembly and council, cf. *Ath. Pol.* iv. 3; xxx. 6. Attempts to enforce performance of civic duties have been made in some modern states. Cf. compulsory voting in Argentina (Bryce, *op. cit.*, I, 196).

[4] 2. 46 ff.   [5] 2. 9.   [6] *Pol.* 1274b. 7.

[7] Aelian *V. H.* xiii. 24.   [8] Diodorus xii. 12.

rules which have merely to do with the moral life of the citizens are thrown together indiscriminately.[1] Noteworthy is the absence of provisions regarding homicide in the fragments of the codes of the majority of the lawgivers. This omission may be due to accident. It is possible, however, that in many places homicide was dealt with entirely by relatives of the deceased and was not yet considered a matter for interference on the part of the state. The fact that such provisions do not appear in the most complete of the codes, the Gortynian, may be due to the loss of part of the code, inasmuch as mention is made of blood-money in the fragments of the earlier code. The only homicide laws of which any details are known are those of Draco, the Athenian lawgiver.[2]

Several of the lawgivers are known to have made provisions regarding marriage and divorce. So Androdamas legislated about heiresses, as did the Gortyn code. There was a law of Charondas that an heiress should claim her nearest male relative in marriage. If he failed to marry her, he was obliged to pay her 500 drachmas as a dowry. This law was later changed so that the relative was obliged to marry her. The law which permitted a woman to divorce her husband and to live with whomever she pleased was also changed.[3] There are various provisions in the Gortyn code dealing with the status and privileges of the divorced woman.[4]

[1] Demosthenes divides laws into two kinds: those which regulate our dealings with one another and those which regulate our dealings with the state (xxiv. 192). Cf. Hippodamus who, according to Aristotle (*Pol.* 1267b. 22), divided laws into three kinds, corresponding to three sets of actions: assault, trespass, or death. Maine (*op. cit.*, p. 13) explains the apparent attempt at classification in the Twelve Tables as due to Greek influence.

[2] No homicide laws are mentioned in the codes of any of the other lawgivers except Androdamas, who legislated for the Chalcidians in Thrace. Aristotle mentions an ancient law of Cyme providing for oath helpers in a homicide case. *Pol.* 1269a. Cyme in Italy is a Chalcidian city, and, according to Aristotle, all Chalcidian cities adopted the laws of Charondas. If, then, Aristotle is referring to Italian Cyme and not Cyme in Asia Minor, also a Chalcidian colony, it is tempting to suggest that this law is a part of the code of Charondas either in its original form or as it was modified to suit the conditions in Cyme. If that be true, Androdamas' homicide laws probably have the same origin.

[3] Diodorus xii. 18.   [4] 2. 45 ff.; 3. 44 ff.; 8. 20 ff.; 11. 46 ff.

A great effort was made to protect the interests of children. The parents were still permitted to expose children, but the rights of those who were allowed to live were scrupulously guarded. Charondas is supposed to have attached great importance to the family as the basis of the life of the state.[1] A widower who brought a stepmother into his house was forbidden to take part in the councils of state.[2] The property of orphans was cared for by the father's people, while the orphans themselves were brought up by the mother's relatives. The father's relatives presumably would administer the estate carefully on the chance that it would come to them if anything befell the orphans. The cost of the education of the sons of all citizens was borne by the state according to Charondas' regulations.[3] In the Gortyn code, the uncles on both sides managed the property of an heiress.[4]

There were various laws regarding the limitation of the number of the citizens. Pheidon, the Corinthian, fixed the number of families and of the citizens.[5] The νόμοι θετικοί of Philolaus at Thebes were passed as a means of keeping the number of families unchanged.[6] Lycurgus fixed the number of households and of lots, but apparently did not limit the number of citizens, for there was a law at Sparta encouraging the growth of the population.[7]

The increasing importance of slavery made provisions regarding slaves necessary. Slavery would naturally be a problem of great importance in the colonies where a conquered people was reduced to servitude. With the introduction of manufactures, the mother-cities were forced to resort to the importation of slaves in large numbers since there were no longer sufficient free laborers available.[8] Few specific pro-

[1] Aristotle Pol. 1252b. 14.

[2] Diodorus xii. 12. 1.   [4] Gortyn code 12. 28 ff.

[3] Ibid., xii. 12. 4.   [5] Aristotle, Pol. 1265b. 12 ff.

[6] Cf. Newman, op. cit., II, 381. He agrees with Hermann (Gr. Ant., III, sec. 65, 2) that, by permitting adoption, Philolaus in effect introduced testation in Thebes.

[7] Plutarch Agis v. 1; Aristotle Pol., 1270b; Plato Laws, 740d.

[8] Cf. Bury, History of Greece, p. 118.

visions about slaves are known. Zaleucus permitted self-help in the recovery of a stolen slave,[1] and Charondas fixed the penalty, as did the Gortyn code, for the rape of a slave girl.[2] This seems to indicate that the slave was coming to be recognized as such a valuable asset that certain provisions were passed to protect him. There was also constant danger that a freeman might be kidnapped and sold as a slave, and certain provisions were included in the codes in regard to this matter. Slavery for debt is freely recognized in the codes, but a man sold into slavery for debt was readmitted to all the rights and privileges of a free citizen on the payment of the debt. The ransomed man who failed to pay back the price of his ransom was reduced to slavery.[3] In Athens the evil of slavery for debt was finally abolished by Solon.[4]

There were a few laws regulating the transfer and disposition of property. In the earliest period there was a marked tendency to keep property in the hands of the landed classes. Thus a Locrian[5] law forbade the sale of private property (οὐσία) unless the owner was able to prove that he had suffered misfortunes great enough to necessitate it. At Athens before the time of Solon it was impossible to alienate property from relatives by will. All provisions about heiresses and adoption were intended to prevent property from going out of the family. Solon's permission to alienate property by will shows the reaction which took place in the course of time against this state of affairs. He also limited the amount of land which a citizen might possess.[6] There are many provisions in the Gortyn code limiting the size of gifts which could be made.[7]

The new demands of the times made necessary some regulations for suits arising out of business relations. Some such

---

[1] Polybius xii. 16.   [2] Herondas 2. 46 ff.   [3] Gortyn code 6. 46 ff.

[4] Cf. Grote, *History of Greece*, III, 94 ff.

[5] Aristotle *Pol.* 1266*b*. 19; cf. Büchsenschütz, *Besitz und Erwerb*, p. 32, n.

[6] Cf. Aristotle *ibid*. It is not until later, in the provisions suggested by the theoretical lawgivers, that equality of property is emphasized. Cf. *ibid.*, 1266*a*. 39 ff.

[7] 10. 15 ff.

provisions are credited to Zaleucus.[1] The code of Charondas discouraged the granting of credit by not allowing a man to institute proceedings against another whom he had trusted and who had failed to make payment.[2] A law of Pittacus provided that a contract was not binding unless executed before the magistrates as witnesses.[3]

The sumptuary legislation of the early lawgivers was passed partly in a democratic spirit to prevent display by wealthy families and partly to improve the morals of the citizens. An old Achaean inscription[4] gives explicit directions about the apparel of a corpse and the display permitted at the burial. There are also various provisions about excess in drinking and association with evil companions. Similar laws are attributed to Charondas.[5] Pittacus[6] attempted to discourage drunkenness by imposing a greater penalty upon those who had committed wrong while drunk than upon those who were sober. Zaleucus also attempted to restrict ornamentation in dress.[7] Various laws were passed also with regard to the conduct of women. Zaleucus limited the number of attendants of a woman who appeared in public, and forbade her departure from the city after nightfall.[8] Such laws are attributed also to Aristides of Ceos.[9]

[1] Diodorus xii. 21.

[2] Stobaeus *Flor.* 44. 22.

[3] *Ibid.*

[4] Dittenberger, *Sylloge,*[2] No. 468.

[5] Diodorus xii. 12. 3.

[6] Aristotle *Pol.* 1274*b*. 19 ff.

[7] Diodorus xii. 21.

[8] *Ibid.*

[9] Heracl. Pont., 9.

CHAPTER IV

THE PRE-SOLONIAN JUDICIARY

Draco, the Athenian lawgiver, "adapted his laws to a constitution which already existed."[1] Aristotle describes the political situation before the time of Draco as follows:

The magistrates were elected according to qualifications of birth and wealth. At first they governed for life, but subsequently for terms of ten years. The first magistrates, both in date and in importance, were the King, the Polemarch and the Archon. The earliest of these offices was that of the King, which existed from ancestral antiquity. To this was added, secondly, the office of Polemarch, on account of some of the kings proving feeble in war; for which reason Ion was invited to accept the post on an occasion of pressing need. The last of the three offices was that of the Archon, which most authorities state to have come into existence in the time of Medon. Others assign it to the time of Acastus, and adduce as proof the fact that the nine Archons swear to execute their oaths "as in the days of Acastus," which seems to suggest that it was in his reign that the descendants of Codrus retired from the kingship in return for the prerogatives conferred upon the Archon. Whichever way it be, the difference in date is small; but that it was the last of these magistracies to be created is shown by the fact that the Archon has no part in the ancestral sacrifices, as the King and Polemarch have, but only in those of later origin. So it is only at a comparatively late date that the office of Archon has become of great importance, by successive accretions of power. The Thesmothetae were appointed many years afterwards, when these offices had already become annual; and the object of their creation was that they might publicly record all legal decisions, and act as guardians of them with a view to determining the issues between litigants. Accordingly their office, alone of those which have been mentioned, was never of more than annual duration. So far, then, do these magistracies precede all others in point of date.

At that time the nine Archons did not all live together. The King occupied the building now known as the Bucolium, near the Prytaneum, as may be seen from the fact that even to the present day the marriage of the King's wife to Dionysus takes place there. The Archon lived in the Prytaneum, the Polemarch in the Epilyceum. The latter building was formerly called the Polemarcheum, but after Epilycus, during his term of

[1] Aristotle *Politics*, p. 1274*b*: Δράκοντος δὲ νόμοι μὲν εἰσί, πολιτείᾳ δ' ὑπαρχούσῃ τοὺς νόμους ἔθηκεν.

office as Polemarch, had rebuilt it and fitted it up, it was called the Epilyceum. The Thesmothetae occupied the Thesmotheteum. In the time of Solon, however, they all came together into the Thesmotheteum. They had power to decide cases finally on their own authority, not, as now, merely to hold a preliminary hearing. Such then was the arrangement of the magistracies. The Council of Areopagus had as its constitutionally assigned duty the protection of the laws; but in point of fact it administered the greater and most important part of the government of the state, and inflicted personal punishments and fines summarily upon all who misbehaved themselves. This was the natural consequence of the facts that the Archons were elected under qualifications of birth and wealth, and that the Areopagus was composed of those who had served as Archons; for which latter reason the membership of the Areopagus is the only office which has continued to be a life-magistracy to the present day.[1]

Along with the political functions of the king the three archons inherited judicial functions which tended to overshadow their other duties.[2] The assignment of judicial functions to the magistrates was characteristic of Greek legal systems. The archons did not sit as a body, but each archon adjudicated the cases assigned to him.[3] They had, in a sense, final jurisdiction, for not until the reforms of Solon was provision made for an appeal from the decisions of the magistrates to the heliaea.[4] No doubt a survival from a period when the jurisdiction of the archon was much wider is to be found in his proclamation, on entering office, to the effect that "whatever anyone possessed before he entered into office, that he shall possess and hold until the end of his

---

[1] *Ath. Pol.*, iii. Kenyon's translation.

[2] In the case of the polemarch, this can be definitely shown. Before the time of Cleisthenes there are several instances of Athenian generals in chief command in battle in place of the polemarch. Cf. Thompson, "The Athenian Polemarch," *Transactions of the American Philological Association, 1894,* p. xviii. At the battle of Marathon the position of the polemarch was purely honorary, a mere survival of the real power which he once possessed. Judicial duties tended to confine him to the city. When the Athenians began to send out commercial and colonizing expeditions, the generals must have assumed the actual command. Thompson concludes that the time when the polemarch lost his actual command cannot be determined, but the development of the στρατηγία must have begun about the end of the seventh century.

[3] In later times the archons performed certain functions as a college. Cf. *Ath. Pol.* iii. 5: ἐπὶ δὲ Σόλωνος ἅπαντες εἰς τὸ θεσμοθετεῖον συνῆλθον; also lxiii. 1: τὰ δὲ δικαστήρια κληροῦσιν οἱ θ ἄρχοντες κατὰ φυλάς.

[4] *Ath. Pol.* ix. 1. Cf. *infra*, p. 151.

term."[1] The archon judged mainly cases in which the family was involved, that is, cases of injured parents, orphans, or heiresses. His jurisdiction was concerned also with civil suits, especially those dealing with property. The polemarch was for foreigners what the archon was for citizens, and the *archon basileus* conducted cases connected with religion. In particular, he was the presiding officer in homicide courts, which were of a religious nature because of the pollution involved.

Aristotle is the sole important authority for the origin and institution of the thesmothetae. The purpose of their creation was ὅπως ἀναγράψαντες τὰ θέσμια φυλάττωσι πρὸς τὴν τῶν ἀμφισβητούντων κρίσιν.[2] This is not a very explicit statement; Aristotle is probably etymologizing. Modern scholars have argued that their duty was either to reduce to writing the customary law in an authoritative form or to record the legal principles underlying the decisions either of themselves or of other judicial officers.[3] Either view presents difficulties. It is possible, however, that they were both judicial officers and in a sense also legislators.[4] It is quite natural that as

[1] *Ibid.*, lvi. 2; cf. Bury, *History of Greece*, p. 171; Busolt-Swoboda, *Staatskunde*, pp. 783 ff; Meyer, *Geschichte des Altertums*, II, 348.

[2] *Ath. Pol.* iii. 4. A similar statement appears in the *Lexica Segueriana* (Bekker, *Anecdota*, I 264) and in Harpocration, *s.v.* θεσμοθέται.

[3] Cf. Lipsius, *Das Attische Recht*, p. 12, n. 44; Busolt, *Geschichte*, II, 177; Ziehen, *Rheinisches Museum*, LIV, 335 ff.; Wilamowitz, *Aristoteles und Athen*, I, 245; Sandys, on Aristotle, *ad loc.*; Botsford, *Athenian Constitution*, p. 129; Bury, *op. cit.*, p. 176; Ledl, *Studien zur älteren Athenischen Verfassungsgeschichte*, p. 269; *CAH*, III, 593; Meyer, *op. cit.*, II, 347; De Sanctis, *op. cit.*, p. 133; Busolt-Swoboda, *Staatskunde*, pp. 802 f.; Ehrenberg, *Die Rechtsidee im frühen Griechentum*, p. 107.

[4] There is by no means general agreement on the original functions of the thesmothetae. De Sanctis, *op. cit.*, p. 133, says: "L'essenziale nella loro operosità sarebbe sempre la giurisdizione e non la codificazione." Busolt, on the other hand, *Staatskunde*, p. 802, n. 2, says: "Es ist sehr fraglich, ob die Thesmothetai je ein selbständig richtendes Kollegium bildeten," and contends that their original functions were twofold: (1) to record the Thesmia (θέσμια); (2) to guard the θέσμια (i.e., they were θεσμοφύλακες). In the latter capacity, they stood in close connection with the Areopagus, and this duty explains why their annual office was continued from year to year. This part of Busolt's argument is unconvincing. It would seem that in the years between 621 (legislation of Draco) and 594 (legislation of Solon) they would have had practically nothing to do. And after his legislation, Solon extracted a promise from the people that his laws should remain in force for ten years. At this time, furthermore, we are expressly told that the guardianship of the laws

the city grew and judicial business increased, the need should be felt for additional officials to take care of the litigation which did not fall under the jurisdiction of any of the three archons.[1] To relieve the archons, the college[2] of the thesmothetae was created, presumably to take over cases which were not connected with the official duties of the three archons.[3] With their institution there came into existence, alongside of the magistrates with judicial functions, a body of special judicial officers. A definite attempt was thus made to systematize more highly the administration of justice. This practice is characteristic of other Greek judicial systems. In

---

was in the hands of the Areopagus. Under these circumstances the continuity of the office of the thesmothetae is somewhat difficult to explain unless they had some other function. It is curious, as De Sanctis observes, that if they were wholly a legislative body there is no trace of their activities preserved. Cf. Myres, *The Political Ideas of the Greeks*, p. 219, who thinks that the records of the thesmothetae were not published at first. Aristotle says that the thesmothetae originally occupied the *thesmotheteon* alone. In the time of Solon the other archons joined them there (ἐπὶ δὲ Σόλωνος ἅπαντες εἰς τὸ θεσμοθετεῖον συνῆλθον). It is quite clear that Aristotle understood that all nine archons (ἅπαντες) had full judicial powers (κύριοι . . . . ἦσαν . . . . κρίνειν).

[1] The various theories which have been advanced regarding the number and origin of the thesmothetae have no bearing on this discussion. It has been suggested that they originated as πάρεδροι or assistants to the other magistrates and were made independent judicial officers to take over part of the judicial business of these magistrates. Cf. Gilbert, *Constitutional Antiquities*, p. 113; Lecoutère, *L'archontat athénien*, p. 114; Myres, *op. cit.*, p. 215. This theory is inconsistent with their later activity as a college. Bury, *History of Greece*, p. 176, suggests that "the number of six was determined by the fact that they originated in a compromise between the orders, three being Eupatrids, two Georgi, and one a Demiurgos." De Sanctis, *op. cit.*, p. 137, contends that the number was not originally six, but that new thesmothetae were added as the number and importance of the cases which came before them increased.

[2] De Sanctis, *op. cit.*, p. 136, asserts that the thesmothetae did not act as a college, but separately. He argues also that the even number of six is opposed to their acting as a college. Grote believes that the thesmothetae sometimes acted as a board, sometimes individually (*History of Greece*, III, 74). Lipsius, *op. cit.*, p. 68, n. 60, is right in contending that they acted only as a college.

[3] It is quite possible that the thesmothetae came into existence at the time when the archonship was made an annual office. Busolt, *Geschichte*, II, 177, asserts that the institution could not have been created until the seventh century, so that Aristotle is correct in placing the institution after the beginning of the annual archonship. In 630 (attempt of Cylon) there were nine archons (Thucydides i. 126). So they must have been instituted about the middle of the seventh century.

the Gortyn code, for instance, the κόσμοι, or chief magistrates, had special judicial functions. For example, the κόσμος ξένιος in his character as judge, seems to be parallel to the polemarch at Athens. Aside from the κόσμοι, there were special judicial officers, referred to always as δικασταί. They correspond in a general way, in so far as they were specially appointed for judicial purposes, to the thesmothetae. This is a normal development which was bound to take place with the expansion of the state and the consequent growth of litigation.

In applying customary law to specific cases and recording their decisions, the thesmothetae were, in a sense, legislators, because, as has been well said, "in the absence of a written code, those who declare and interpret the laws may be properly said to make them."[1] It may be suggested that the practice of recording judicial decisions was new at the time of their institution, and that their name is due to the novelty of the custom now followed by all magistrates. Aristotle employs the word θέσμια. The more common form θεσμοί, analogous to the θέμιστες of Homer, includes both general laws and particular sentences.[2] The two ideas are not yet distinguished. General law is conceived only in its application to some particular case. "The thesmothetae, therefore, received their name not merely from the fact that they made law by administering it, but from being the first to lay it down in written decisions."[3]

The advantage of this explanation is that it accounts for the later twofold function of the thesmothetae in the fifth and fourth centuries. Aside from their strictly judicial business which included a large variety of cases, they had general supervision of the laws and directed their annual revision.[4] These duties were a natural outgrowth of their early

[1] Thirlwall, *History of Greece*, II, 17, quoted by Sandys, *op. cit.*, p. 8.

[2] Grote, *op. cit.*, III, 75.

[3] Kenyon, *Aristotle's Constitution of Athens*, p. 8. Cf. De Sanctis, *op. cit.*, p. 133; "Testmoteta è in realtà ogni giudice in quanto afferma dei principî di diritto applicandoli al caso speciale."

[4] Gilbert, *op. cit.*, p. 302.

activities as makers and recorders of judicial decisions. In the fifth and fourth centuries the thesmothetae were mainly concerned with criminal cases. Civil suits ordinarily came before the Forty and the εἰσαγωγεῖς. In the early period, cases that intimately concerned the whole public were dealt with by the body most representative of public opinion. Thus, in Homer the assembly was the normal medium for the expression of such public will as there was.[1] Under the aristocracy in Athens in the pre-Solonian period the Areopagus was the most suitable body for taking public action. Now the jurisdiction of the thesmothetae must have fallen between that of the Archons and that of the Areopagus. This would include both criminal and civil suits.[2]

The sovereignty of the state was vested in a council which represented the ruling aristocracy. Whether this council is identical with the Areopagus is a question that was discussed as early as the time of Aristotle. Some believed that the Areopagus was the creation of Solon; others that it was the outgrowth of the Homeric Council of Elders.[3]

As to Solon, he is thought by some to have been a good legislator, who put an end to the exclusiveness of the oligarchy, emancipated the people, established the ancient Athenian democracy, and harmonized the different elements of the state. According to their view, the council of the Areopagus was an oligarchical element, the elected magistracy, aristocratical, and the courts of law, democratical. The truth seems to be that the council and the elected magistracy existed before the time of Solon, and were retained by him, but that he formed the courts of law out of all

---

[1] Cf. *supra*, p. 22.

[2] Aristotle's words τὴν τῶν ἀμφισβητούντων κρίσιν (*Ath. Pol.* iii. 3) may indicate, as De Sanctis believes (*op. cit.*, p. 136), that the majority of the cases which originally came before them were civil suits. It may be a matter of accident that, in divesting themselves of a part of their duties as litigation increased, they tended to reserve criminal cases for themselves and to turn over civil suits first to the δικασταὶ κατὰ δήμους and later to other officials, namely the Forty and the εἰσαγωγεῖς. Cf. *infra*, p. 348. The revival of the circuit judges in 453–452 B.C. was for the express purpose of giving other officials relief from civil actions (cf. De Sanctis, *op. cit.*, p. 136). Many of these would have come under the jurisdiction of the thesmothetae. Calhoun, *Criminal Law*, pp. 102 f., attributes the taking away of civil suits from the thesmothetae to the great expansion and systematization of the criminal law which took place in the first half of the fifth century.

[3] Aristotle *Politics*, 1273*b* ff. Jowett's translation.

the citizens, thus creating the democracy, which is the very reason why he is sometimes blamed.

In modern times this problem has occasioned much discussion because of the apparent contradictions in some of the ancient sources and the difficulty of interpreting them.[1] The majority of these ancient sources, however, are subsequent to Aristotle. Their evidence and many of the speculations of modern scholars on the subject were superseded by the recovery of Aristotle's *Constitution of Athens*, which confirms his statement in the *Politics*, if confirmation is needed. In his account of the constitution before the time of Draco, Aristotle gives the following description of the Areopagus:

> The Council of Areopagus had as its constitutionally assigned duty the protection of the laws; but in point of fact it administered the greater and most important part of the government of the state and inflicted personal punishments and fines summarily upon all who misbehaved themselves. This was the natural consequence of the fact that the Archons were elected under qualifications of birth and wealth, and that the Areopagus was composed of those who had served as Archons; for which latter reason the membership of the Areopagus is the only office which has continued to be a life-magistracy to the present day.[2]

Before the time of Solon, there existed only one council, which had both judicial and deliberative functions.[3] This council was a lineal descendant of the Homeric boulé.[4] The dispute as to whether it was called ἡ ἐν Ἀρείῳ πάγῳ βουλή in

[1] For the ancient sources, which treat the Areopagus mainly as a homicide court, cf. *infra*, p. 92. For a summary of the later literature on the subject, cf. Busolt-Swoboda, *Staatskunde*, p. 794, n. 2. For a convenient summary of modern theories on the subject, cf. Ledl, *op. cit.*, pp. 286 ff. Cf. also Treston, *Poine, A Study in Ancient Greek Blood-Vengeance*, pp. 269 ff.

[2] *Ath. Pol.* iii. 6. Kenyon's translation. The scholars who attack the theory that the Areopagus existed before Solon's time reject this passage as an interpolation on the basis of its similarity to the description of the Areopagus under Solon.

[3] Cf. *Ath. Pol.*, iv, for the alleged Draconian council. Cf. *infra*, pp. 136 ff.

[4] Actually as the most representative group in the aristocracy, the council is comparable to the Homeric assembly which dealt with offenses affecting the whole community. It would appear that the arbitral functions of the ancient boulé and the spontaneous judicial functions of the assembly are in a measure combined in the aristocratic council at Athens. For example, it would be the natural body to try cases of homicide, treason, and impiety. In the ancient traditions the Areopagus appears as a famous homicide court.

the early period is of no moment.[1] It is possible that at the time when a second council, the boulé, was instituted, the Council of Elders received the name of Areopagus, by which it was known in later times. It may also be true that the council thus received its name in the time of Solon and that on this account its institution was ascribed to him. There was, however, a marked tendency among Athenians to refer their ancient institutions to Solon, and to this tendency may be due the idea that the Areopagus was instituted by him.[2]

Before the unification of Attica the local chiefs did not resort to Athens[3] "to take counsel with the king except in times of national danger." But when Theseus dissolved the local councils and established a central council in the capital, there must have been large additions to its permanent membership. Not only were the independent kings in Attica included, but a proportion, if not all, of the members of the local senates. The resulting powers and prestige of this council enabled it eventually to substitute for the kingship an aristocratic oligarchy governed by magistrates drawn from its own membership. On the expiration of their tenure of office they naturally resumed their former status as members of this council. This explains why, in the later period, the archons, although they were no longer drawn from the mem-

[1] Cf. Headlam, *Class. Rev.*, VI, 295: "The later council of the Areopagus was then the representative of an older Council, the origin of which was lost in antiquity, but which was doubtless descended from the Homeric Council of Elders. It is, however, not so clear that we must follow him (Aristotle) in calling the old Council by the name which it had in later times. If, as seems most probable, there was only one Council then it would certainly be called ἡ βουλή; it may have been connected with the Ἀρείος πάγος; if so, the name is not incorrect; but, if I am right in supposing that there was no older authority than Solon, Aristotle's use of the name for the early period means nothing more than continuity of existence, and does not tell us anything of the earlier usage. Without then necessarily accepting the statement that the Council had always been called after the Areopagus, we may consider it as almost certain that the Council of the Areopagus was substantially identical with the early Council."

[2] Busolt-Swoboda, *Staatskunde*, pp. 794 ff., gives as the normal development in the Greek state the continuance of the Council of Elders from the time of the oligarchy as an executive and judicial body alongside the Council of the democracy. So in Athens the old council continued as the Areopagus alongside the Council of Four Hundred. Cf. De Sanctis, *op. cit.*, pp. 140 ff.

[3] Thucydides ii. 15.

bership of the council (Areopagus), became members on the expiration of their term of office. With the growth of trade and commerce, land ceased to be the sole form of wealth. The political importance of the *nouveaux riches* secured for them the right to participate in the magistracies along with the eupatrids. And so the membership of the senate came to be recruited on the basis of birth and wealth.[1]

Such an explanation of the origin of the Areopagus fully recognizes the historical continuity of institutions and depends upon the authority of Aristotle, whose critical knowledge of the history of Athenian institutions makes him a more reliable source of information than any of the other ancient writers who discussed the history of the Areopagus.

The chief evidence which has been used against the foregoing view is that of Pollux to the effect that Draco instituted the ephetae who sat in all five homicide courts and that, in addition to them, Solon instituted the Council of the Areopagus: Δράκων δ' αὐτοὺς κατέστησεν ἀριστίνδην αἱρεθέντας· ἐδίκαζον δὲ τοῖς ἐφ' αἵματι διωκομένοις ἐν τοῖς πέντε δικαστηρίοις. Σόλων δ' αὐτοῖς προσκατέστησε τὴν ἐξ Ἀρείου πάγου βουλήν.[2] On the basis of this statement, Ledl[3] makes a distinction between the court of the Areopagus and the Council of the Areopagus, declaring that Pollux is correct in supposing that the court existed in the time of, and prior to, Draco, but that the institution of the council must be attributed to Solon. At the same time he admits that Pollux is wrong in assigning the ephetae as judges to the court of the Prytaneum. In view of Pollux' blunder in making the Prytaneum an ephetic court, it is better to say that he is in error also with regard to the court of the Areopagus than to try to explain his reference to it as Ledl does, for Ledl is forced, in the end, to admit that the ephetae never sat in the court of the Areopagus, but rather that a pre-Solonian council sat there, whose duties were divided by Solon between the Council of the Areopagus and the Council of the Four Hundred, the judicial

[1] Aristotle *Ath. Pol.* iii. 6: ἡ γὰρ αἵρεσις τῶν ἀρχόντων ἀριστίνδην καὶ πλουτίνδην ἦν, ἐξ ὧν οἱ Ἀρεοπαγῖται καθίσταντο.

[2] viii. 125.   [3] *Op. cit.*, pp. 296 f.

functions being chiefly assigned to the Areopagus. His argument fails to recognize that the Areopagus of Solon's time was nothing more than a development of this pre-Solonian council to which were assigned all of the judicial functions, which Ledl admits formerly belonged to the pre-Solonian council, as well as some of the executive-administrative functions. By failing to recognize this continuity, he is led to reject the testimony of Aristotle in favor of the inferior testimony of Pollux, whose statement regarding the ephetic composition of the Areopagus during the time of Draco is admittedly wrong. There is obviously, then, no justification for accepting his other statement regarding its institution by Solon when it is at variance with the evidence both of the *Politics* and of the *Constitution of Athens*. Ledl is unduly skeptical in refusing to admit that the court was also a council of state. It was characteristic of Greek states that administration of justice was very closely connected with the government, and magistrates and governing bodies regularly exercised judicial functions. If, then, there was a court sitting on the Areopagus, it is more than likely that it was a political body as well.

The antiquity of the homicide functions of the Areopagus is attested by the myths which represent it as a homicide court. In a fragment of Hellanicus there are collected all the mythical trials for homicide which were believed to have taken place before the Areopagus.[1] This account is found also on the Parian Marble,[2] in Euripides,[3] Demosthenes,[4] and Pausanias.[5] And the name of the hill was attributed to the fact that Ares was the first to be tried there.[6] Plutarch believed that the Areopagus was in existence before the time of Solon:

[1] Scholiast on Euripides *Orestes*, 1648.

[2] *Ep.* 3.

[3] *Electra*, 1258 ff. For dramatic purposes Aeschylus, in the *Eumenides*, changed the order given by the other writers and represented the court as being first instituted to try Orestes.

[4] xxiii. 65 f. [5] i. 28. 5.

[6] Pausanias, *ibid.* Cf. Suidas, Ἄρειος πάγος.

Now most writers say that the Council of the Areopagus, as I have stated, was established by Solon. And their view seems to be strongly supported by the fact that Draco nowhere makes any mention whatsoever of Areopagites, but always addresses himself to the "ephetai" in cases of homicide. Yet Solon's thirteenth table contains the eighth of his laws recorded in these very words: "As many of the disfranchised as were made such before the archonship of Solon, shall be restored to their rights and franchises, except such as were condemned by the Areopagus, or by the ephetai, or in the prytaneium by the kings, on charges of murder or homicide, or of seeking to establish a tyranny, and were in exile when this law was published." This surely proves to the contrary that the council of the Areopagus was in existence before the archonship and legislation of Solon. For how could men have been condemned in the Areopagus before the time of Solon, if Solon was the first to give the council of the Areopagus its jurisdiction? Perhaps, indeed, there is some obscurity in the document, or some omission, and the meaning is that those who had been convicted on charges within the cognizance of those who were Areopagites and ephetai and prytanes when the law was published, should remain disfranchised, while those convicted on all other charges should recover their rights and franchises. This question, however, my reader must decide for himself."[1]

An attempt has been made to explain the statement of Pollux quoted above by supposing that during the time of Draco all homicide trials came before the ephetae and that Solon restored jurisdiction in cases of premeditated homicide to the Areopagus. But it is quite unlikely that Draco should have taken a function of such prime importance from the chief governing body of the state. The Athenians were too conservative in matters involving religion to do anything of this sort.[2] The natural conclusion from the foregoing evidence is that the Areopagus in Draco's time and before Draco's time had charge of cases of premeditated homicide in addition to the other cases which had always come within their jurisdiction.[3] The king was chairman of his council.

[1] *Solon*, xix. Perrin's translation. Plutarch doubtless knew the homicide laws only in their revised form of 409–408 B.C.

[2] Cf. Freeman, *The Work and Life of Solon*, p. 55: "The utmost that can be conjectured with any probability is that for a time the Areopagus deputed trial for wilful murder to a court of fifty-one of its members, and that Solon restored the old order of trial by the whole body." For an explanation of the source of Pollux' error, cf. *infra*, p. 100.

[3] Cary in *CAH*, III, 590, says that the judicial functions of the Areopagus were confined to criminal actions.

Consequently, the magistrates who succeeded him must have presided over its deliberations. The evidence for this conclusion is found in the participation of the king archon in the deliberations and verdict of the Areopagus acting as a homicide court. The amnesty law shows that the king archon presided at other judicial sessions of the Areopagus as well as at homicide trials.[1] This practice is a survival from the time when the king and his council administered justice. Conservatism explains why the *archon basileus* rather than the archon exercised this royal prerogative.

The title "boulé" shows clearly that the Areopagus was primarily a deliberative body, but there is no information regarding its sessions available. In its capacity as a deliberative body it is possible that the college of archons, like the later prytaneis of the Senate of Five Hundred, constituted a presiding committee under the chairmanship of the archon. Other possibilities readily suggest themselves, but, in view of our total lack of information on the subject, speculation is futile.[2]

Beyond Aristotle's statement that "the Areopagus administered the greater and most important part of the government," nothing is known about its functions—deliberative, administrative, and executive. It elected the magistrates and, by virtue of its guardianship of the laws, must have exercised some control over them during their incumbency of office. Foreign relations, including the negotiation of treaties and the making of peace and war, would naturally be included in τὰ πλεῖστα καὶ τὰ μέγιστα, as well as some control over the finances of the state, such as providing and allotting funds for war, for public buildings, for the celebration of religious festivals, and for the public service in general. Its service to the state on the eve of Salamis was really a resumption in a small way of the early financial functions which in the fifth century had been given to the Council of Five Hundred. To Aristotle we are indebted for an account of

---

[1] Cf. *infra*, p. 109; cf. Vinogradoff, *op. cit.*, p. 181.

[2] *CAH*, III, 589–90. For retention of the name βουλή, cf. Busolt-Swoboda *Staatskunde*, p. 795; De Sanctis, *op. cit.*, p. 143.

this instructive incident. When the generals were utterly at a loss how to meet the crisis and made proclamation that everyone should see to his own safety, the Areopagus provided a donation of money, distributing eight drachmas to each member of the ships' crews, and so prevailed on them to go on board. This timely action enabled the Athenians to fight the Battle of Salamis.[1]

Great importance has always been attached to the due administration of the law on the part of the magistrates.[2] In pre-Solonian Athens the responsibility of seeing that the magistrates enforced the law rested with the Areopagus, which "had as its constitutionally assigned duty the protection of the laws." Its authority was enforced by the infliction of suitable pains and penalties. The guilt or innocence of a person accused before the Areopagus was ascertained by a more or less formal inquiry. No source contains information about procedure before the Areopagus in non-homicide cases. It can only be surmised that the Areopagus acted as the result of information laid by one of its members. The original informant would usually be the person who had suffered from the failure of a magistrate to observe and uphold the laws. If he appeared at all, he would be a complaining witness and an Areopagite would be the nominal prosecutor. These surmises explain very naturally a provision of the code of Draco. It is specified that the Areopagus was to see that "the archons governed according to the laws." Any person who was wronged might lay information before the Areopagus, indicating what law had been transgressed.[3] This is a privilege of prime importance comparable with the right of petition in modern times. It meant that an aggrieved person need not depend upon enlisting the interest and efforts of an Areopagite in order to get justice; he had the right to appear in person before the assembled council and state his case. This was the means adopted by Draco to insure the

[1] *Ath. Pol.* xxiii. 1. Cf. *infra*, p. 251.

[2] Since the days of Solon officials everywhere have been sworn to uphold the law.

[3] *Ath. Pol.* iv. 4. Cf. *infra*, p. 166.

enforcement of his laws.[1] Draco thus recognized the right of the injured person to take the initiative in his own case.

One is immediately confronted with the question as to whether the control of the Areopagus extended to the judicial decisions of the magistrates. Aristotle says that "the archons had power to decide cases finally on their own authority, not as now, to hold a preliminary hearing merely."[2] This is Kenyon's version. But there is more in Aristotle's statement than can be expressed in a translation. Aristotle is comparing the pre-Solonian archon with the archon of his own day who was little more than a clerk. As a judge, he could only decide on the question of his own jurisdiction; his decision did not affect the main issue. αὐτοτελεῖς κρίνειν must be understood as the opposite of προανακρίνειν. Hence, we get the idea of an independent judgment regarding the whole matter at issue. There was no provision for an appeal in each and every case, such as was granted by Solon to a regularly constituted court of appeal. But Aristotle's words do not mean that the Areopagus could not, in the exercise of its function as guardian of the laws, nullify or reverse the decision of a magistrate who had failed to observe the law. The only difference between annual magistrates and other rulers, such as kings and tyrants, lies in the full responsibility of the former. The substitution of annual magistrates for the life-tenure kingship in Athens meant that the magistrates were fully responsible to the sovereign body in the state, viz., the Areopagus. There is no indication that the aristocracy had developed an elaborate procedure of accounting like the democratic εὔθυνα; but even if the means of insuring responsibility of magistrates for their official acts were less formal, we may be certain they were not less effective.

The language of Aristotle further indicates that the Areopagus dealt with offenders *contra bonos mores*. To the same effect is the statement of Isocrates that the early Athenians

---

[1] This was always a prime concern of all ancient legislators.

[2] *Ath. Pol.* iii. 5: κύριοι δ' ἦσαν καὶ τὰς δίκας αὐτοτελεῖς κρίνειν καὶ οὐχ ὥσπερ νῦν προανακρίνειν.

gave the Areopagus the task of insuring good behavior on the part of the citizens.[1] For the more effective carrying-out of this purpose the city was distributed by wards (κῶμαι) and the country by demes. The Areopagites inspected the life of each citizen and brought the disorderly (ἀκοσμοῦντες) before the council. Some the council warned, some it threatened, and others it punished suitably. This is a rather fanciful picture, but it reflects the traditional view that the Areopagus exercised censorial powers. But the Areopagus was more than a *censor morum;* it was a criminal court. There are no records of its activities in this capacity except in the amnesty law where it is mentioned, according to the most natural interpretation, as the court which tried those who attempted to establish tyranny.[2] It was undoubtedly the court that dealt with treason and other crimes that endangered the safety of the state.

The Areopagus, then, is nothing more than the old aristocratic senate which developed out of the Council of Elders of the Homeric age. Its twofold function, judicial and political, is quite in accord with the system in vogue in other states. For example, the Council of Elders in Crete, composed of those who had held the office of κόσμος, acted both as a council of state and as a court.[3] At Sparta, the Gerousia, the main function of which was political, was also a court which dealt with criminal cases.[4]

A discussion of the Areopagus inevitably involves an examination of the identity and institution of the ephetae, who tried cases of homicide in the Palladium, the Delphinium, and in Phreatto. The question of the origin of this body and

---

[1] *Areop.*, 46: ἀλλὰ διελόμενοι τὴν μὲν πόλιν κατὰ κώμας, τὴν δὲ χώραν κατὰ δήμους, ἐθεώρουν τὸν βίον τὸν ἑκάστου, καὶ τοὺς ἀκοσμοῦντας ἀνῆγον εἰς τὴν βουλήν. ἡ δὲ τοὺς μὲν ἐνουθέτει, τοῖς δ᾽ ἠπείλει, τοὺς δ᾽ ὡς προσῆκεν ἐκόλαζεν. For the use of committees by the Areopagus, cf. *infra*, p. 258.

[2] Lipsius, *op. cit.*, pp. 23 and 33, has a different view of the amnesty law (cf. *infra*, p. 106). De Sanctis, *op. cit.*, p. 149, takes the correct view of the Areopagus in the amnesty law.

[3] Cf. Gilbert, *Griechische Staatsaltertümer*, II, 221.

[4] Cf. Gilbert, *Constitutional Antiquities*, p. 80.

its relation to the Areopagus presents peculiar difficulties because of the meager ancient evidence on the subject.[1] An ancient source mentions an age qualification according to which the ephetae were required to be above fifty years of age.[2] There are examples of preference being given to men over fifty years of age, in view of which some scholars have accepted the fifty-year requirement in the case of the ephetae. An example of the fifty-year qualification is found in a law of Solon which gave precedence in speaking before the assembly to those who had passed this age.[3] It is claimed, also, that men over fifty years of age were preferred as ambassadors.[4] In view of the fact that there was no such qualification for members of the Areopagus who tried the most serious homicide cases, it is quite unlikely that there was such a requirement in the case of the ephetae who sat in the minor homicide courts. The age qualification occurs only in two late lexicographers. In all probability it is the result of confusion with the number of the ephetae, which is indubitably established for the time of Draco as fifty-one.[5] When

[1] On the ephetae, cf. Lange, "Die Epheten und der Areopag vor Solon," *Abhand. d. sächs. Gesellschaft d. Wissen.*, 1874, pp. 178 ff.; Philippi, *Der Areopag und die Epheten;* De Sanctis, *op. cit.*, pp. 169 ff.; Busolt-Swoboda, *Staatskunde*, pp. 803 ff.; Gilbert, *Beiträge*, pp. 491 ff.; Miller, article "Ephetai" in Pauly-Wissowa; Lipsius, *op. cit.*, p. 15; Treston, *op. cit.*, pp. 263 ff.; Glotz, *Solidarité*, pp. 299 ff.; Myres, *op. cit.*, p. 227; Vinogradoff, *op. cit.*, pp. 187 ff.

[2] Suidas and Photius, *s.v.* ἄνδρες ὑπὲρ ν′ ἔτη γεγονότες καὶ ἄριστα βεβιωκέναι ὑπόληψιν ἔχοντες οἱ καὶ τὰς φονικὰς δίκας ἔκρινον.

[3] Aeschines *Tim.* xxiii: τίς ἀγορεύειν βούλεται τῶν ὑπὲρ πεντήκοντα ἔτη γεγονότων. Cf. *Ctesiph.* iv; Gilbert, *Constitutional Antiquities*, p. 294.

[4] Plutarch *Pericles*, xvii; *CIA* i. 40. 17. Poland, *De legationibus Graecorum publicis*, p. 52, contends that there was once a law forbidding men to be sent on embassies who were not at least fifty years of age, but that the law early fell into disuse. Krech, *De Crateri ψηφισμάτων συναγωγῇ*, p. 36, n. 48, believes that there never was such a law, but that it was customary to send the older men on such missions. If there had been a law to this effect, there would be no reason for the inclusion of the age specification in the inscription.

[5] *CIA* i. 61. Zonaras, p. 926, erroneously gives the number as eighty. There is no known historical reason for the number fifty-one, and the attempts to explain it have been many and ingenious. Lange, *op. cit.*, pp. 204 ff., believes that the Areopagus was composed of fifteen men from each of the four pre-Cleisthenean tribes and that the ephetae consisted of the same body minus the nine archons. Müller (Introduction to Aeschylus' *Eumenides*) suggested that the number included five

once confusion arose, comparison with other age qualifications would tend to confirm it.

Quite a simple and natural explanation of the origin of the ephetae lies ready to hand. The ephetae were really a commission of the Areopagus. The odd number at once suggests the analogy of the later popular courts of two hundred and one and of five hundred and one.[1] The tendency of institutions to persist in more or less modified form, even when political conditions are fundamentally changed, points in the same direction. The ephetae are the prototype of the popular courts. The odd number is intended to prevent a tie. It is uncertain whether the *archon basileus* was one of the fifty-one ephetae or whether he merely acted as the presiding officer. In favor of the former view it may be argued that, since he voted in the Areopagus, he voted in the courts of the ephetae also. It cannot be assumed that he voted in addition to the fifty-one ephetae, for that would have destroyed the old number. If he voted at all, it was as an ephetes. On the other side it may be argued that as the chairman of the popular courts did not vote, so the *archon basileus* did not vote in the ephetic courts. The sharp distinction made between the *archon basileus* and the ephetae in the Draconian code has led many to believe that he was not an ephetes.

A fragment of Philochorus also suggests that the ephetae were recruited from the Areopagus.

ἐκ γὰρ τῶν ἐννέα καθισταμένων ἀρχόντων Ἀθήνησι τοὺς Ἀρεοπαγίτας ἔδει συνεστάναι δικαστάς, ὥς φησιν Ἀνδροτίων ἐν δευτέρᾳ τῶν Ἀτθίδων· ὕστερον δὲ πλειόνων γέγονεν ἡ ἐξ Ἀρείου πάγου βουλή· τουτέστιν ἐξ

---

from each of the Cleisthenean tribes with the addition of the *archon basileus*. Schoemann, *Antiq. jr. publ.*, p. 171, advanced the theory that the ephetae were a combination of twelve men chosen from each of the four pre-Cleisthenean tribes, and three exegetae. A variation of Schoemann's theory is a substitution of the *archon basileus* and his two paredroi for the exegetae. The attempt to identify the ephetae with the naucraroi has met with slight approval.

[1] Headlam, *Class. Review*, VI, 252 and 297, suggests that the court of the fifty-one ephetae must have been the model for the later popular courts with panels of odd numbers. Neither Headlam himself nor subsequent writers recognized the importance of the suggestion for the solution of the much vexed question of the institution of the ephetae. Cf. Wilamowitz, *Aristoteles und Athen*, I, 251, n. 137; Gilbert, *Griechische Staatsaltertümer*, I, 137, n. 1.

ἀνδρῶν περιφανεστέρων πεντήκοντα καὶ ἑνός. Οὐ παντὸς ἀνδρὸς ἦν εἰς τὴν ἐξ Ἀρείου πάγου βουλὴν τελεῖν· ἀλλ' οἱ παρ' Ἀθηναίοις πρωτεύοντες ἔν τε γένει καὶ πλούτῳ καὶ βίῳ χρηστῷ, κ.τ.λ.[1]

It is obvious that Androtion, knowing the original number of ephetae, who in his time had of course been replaced by dicastic courts, thought that the membership of the Areopagus was fifty-one; and it is also obvious that he was, in this passage, making an attempt to distinguish between the ephetae (i.e., τοὺς Ἀρεοπαγίτας δικαστάς) and the Council of the Areopagus. At any rate, the passage indicates that Androtion considered the ἐφέται Areopagites.[2]

The ephetae could not continue to be a single group of fifty-one specific individuals. Owing to possible illness, if for no other reason, there could be no assurance that any body of fifty-one men would always be available for service when required, if, indeed, an odd number was always required.[3] The only means of assuring the attendance of the full complement of fifty-one would be to draw them from a larger body as need arose. Obviously this group was the Areopagus. Some confirmation of this is to be found in a statement of Pollux, to the effect that before Solon the ephetae sat in the Areopagus: ἐδίκαζον δὲ τοῖς ἐφ' αἵματι διωκομένοις ἐν τοῖς πέντε δικαστηρίοις.[4] Pollux' error in regard to the Areopagus is quite natural if the ephetae were drawn from the membership of the Areopagus. As to the method of selection, there

---

[1] *F.H.G.* (ed. Müller), I, 394.

[2] Headlam, *op. cit.*, p. 251, considers that the passage makes a clear distinction between Ἀρεοπαγῖται δικασταί and ἡ ἐξ Ἀρείου πάγου βουλή. The ἐφέται would be the πεντήκοντα καὶ εἷς, and these were taken from the ex-archons. The ἐφέται were not identical with the council. Freeman, *op. cit.*, p. 53, follows Headlam and says: "According to Androtion they [the ephetae] were chosen from ex-archons, that is, from the Areopagus." Freeman fails to note that the theory that the ephetae were really commissions of the Areopagus, which had been hinted at by Headlam, was developed by Gertrude Smith, *The Administration of Justice from Hesiod to Solon*, p. 17. Cf. S. B. Smith, "The Establishment of the Public Courts at Athens," *TAPA*, LVI, 110. In Treston's opinion (*op. cit.*, pp. 269 ff.) the pre-Solonian Areopagus was not really distinguishable from the ephetae.

[3] If the law providing for acquittal in case the vote was even was in force, an odd number could be dispensed with on occasion. Cf. *infra*, p. 239.

[4] Pollux viii. 125. The five homicide courts were the Areopagus, the Palladium, the Delphinium, in Phreatto, and the Prytaneum.

can be little doubt that it was by lot, which was often employed in oligarchic constitutions.[1]

The etymologies of ἐφέτης commonly given do not support this interpretation.[2] Another derivation—from ἐφίεσθαι—may be suggested. If the word be understood in the passive sense, it can mean "men sent out as a commission" from a larger body. There may be some difficulty in understanding the word passively, since nouns in -της, denoting agent, are regularly active in force. It is not impossible, however, that the noun should have come from the verbal in -τος and that under the influence of names of other officials ending in -της, it was changed by analogy from ἔφετος to ἐφέτης. This explanation of the word is supported by the word ἀφέτης, which is used passively of a freed slave.[3]

References to a class qualification are found in the passages quoted from Pollux and Androtion. Possibly Pollux derived his statement that they were chosen ἀριστίνδην,

[1] The membership of the ephetae could have been varied from time to time, for the number of Areopagites must regularly have been more than two hundred. Cf. S. B. Smith, *op. cit.*, p. 114, n. 39.

[2] The word occurs in the sense of chief in Aeschylus' *Persae*, 79; but this is of no assistance here. Pollux regarded the ephetae as a court of appeal, thus deriving the name from ἐφέσιμος. This description of the court Lipsius pronounces impossible both linguistically and on the ground of the facts in the case (*op. cit.*, p. 15, n. 53). He himself derives the word from ἐφίεσθαι (connected with ἐφετμή) and defines it as *Anzeiger des Rechts*, equivalent apparently to the later ἐξηγητής. Schoemann much earlier had claimed this same etymology for the word, but explained it as their determination of how the accused was to be dealt with in individual cases (*De Areopago et ephetis*, pp. 7 f.). But Philippi has shown that such a name might apply equally well to any college of judges (*Der Areopag und die Epheten*, p.213). He himself accepts Lange's explanation (*De ephetarum Atheniensium nomine*, pp. 11 ff.) that the word is a compound of ἐπί and ἔταις, i.e., "representatives of the citizens standing in the condition of relationship to one another." According to this view, however, they would constitute an administrative council as well as a homicide court, which was not the case. There is no evidence that as ephetae they had any functions aside from their activity as a homicide court. De Sanctis' view that they had to do with granting permission for religious purification is not deserving of serious consideration (*op. cit.*, pp. 169 f.). Ledl, *op. cit.*, pp. 335 f., derives the word from ἐφιέναι in the sense that the ephetae permit an objection of the defendant to the plaintiff's conception of the act; i.e., they determine whether he shall be tried on a charge of murder or involuntary or justifiable homicide.

[3] Athenaeus, 271 F: Μύρων δὲ ὁ Πριηνεὺς ἐν δευτέρῳ Μεσσηνιακῶν πολλάκις, φησίν, ἠλευθέρωσαν Λακεδαιμόνιοι δούλους καὶ οὓς μὲν ἀφέτας ἐκάλεσαν, κ.τ.λ.

from the law of Draco.[1] But if this is the case, he has mis-interpreted the law: τούτους δὲ οἱ πεντήκοντα καὶ εἰς ἀριστίνδην αἱρείσθων. The word ἀριστίνδην refers not to the class from which the ephetae were chosen but to that from which they were to choose a certain number of phratry members. If Pollux' statement be accepted at its face value, it can only be understood to mean that the institution came into exist-ence before the *nouveaux riches* were included in the aristoc-racy. But the *nouveaux riches* before the time of Draco were eligible for magistracies. Hence, they could not be excluded from the Areopagus. The explanation must be that the old qualification continued to be used after the *nouveaux riches* were admitted to office, but was understood to include all members of the aristocracy whether by wealth or by birth.

There are no means of determining whether a fresh group of ephetae was drawn for each case or whether others were selected to fill the gaps due to death, illness, or other causes, leaving the personnel the same as far as possible. The anal-ogy of the popular courts does not help. The practice differed at different periods.[2]

According to Plutarch, the Alcmaeonidae who were in-volved in the curse of Cylon were tried by a court of three hundred selected from the aristocracy.[3] This has led to the belief on the part of some scholars that there was in Athens a second council, composed of three hundred members.[4] But there is no evidence whatever for any further activity on the part of such a body, and it is much more plausible to sup-pose that a special court was provided for this very impor-tant case.[5] Vinogradoff says, "In a sense the tribunal of the

---

[1] Pollux viii. 125: ἐφέται τὸν μὲν ἀριθμὸν εἰς καὶ πεντήκοντα, Δράκων δ' αὐτοὺς κατέστησεν ἀριστίνδην αἱρεθέντας.

[2] Cf. Lipsius, *op. cit.*, pp. 137 f. Cf. *infra*, p. 242.

[3] *Solon*, xii.   [4] Cf. Philippi, *op. cit.*, pp. 240 ff.

[5] Cf. Wilamowitz, *op. cit.*, II, 55: "Schliesslich erzwang die Gemeinde doch eine Abrechnung; aber sie geschah bereits durch ein grosses Ausnahmegericht von 300 Standesgenossen." Cf. the boulé of the partisans of Isagoras which Cleomenes tried to establish in a later attack on the Alcmaeonidae at Athens (Herodotus v. 72). It also consisted of three hundred members. Cf. Sandys, *Aristotle's Constitu-tion of Athens*, p. 1.

300 representatives of the Eupatrid clans (ἀριστίνδην αἱρεθέντες) may be said to have been an enlarged and extraordinary commission of Ephetae appointed to try the accomplices of Kylon or their slayers."[1] The Areopagus could hardly have been large enough to make up such a court even if it were included entire, and Vinogradoff's statement can be true only in the sense that to certain representatives of the Areopagus were added other eupatrids to bring the number up to three hundred.

The earliest mention of the ephetae occurs in the homicide laws of Draco. Both this document and the amnesty law of Solon[2] show that the distinction between different kinds of homicide was drawn and that the five courts existed at least as early as Draco's time, for the purpose of dealing with the different types of homicide. Pollux[3] attributes the institution of the ephetae to Draco; but because Draco was the first to codify the laws, much was attributed to him which undoubtedly corresponds with earlier practice. This was probably the case with the ephetae. Their antiquity is attested by the archaic nature of the courts in which they sat. The desirability of recognizing extenuating circumstances and of differentiating the various types of homicide was in all probability a motive for state intervention. Religion was another factor which led to the intervention of the state. As soon as the idea was conceived that homicide involved pollution, the slayer was regarded as a public menace and society took measures to rid itself of his presence, provided the family refused to act.[4] The development was possibly as follows: homicides who had slain unintentionally or who felt that their acts were justifiable began to resort to temples for refuge or purification and claimed protection on these grounds; but as litigation and political activity increased, it

---

[1] *Op. cit.*, p. 181.   [2] Plutarch *Solon*, xix, quoted *infra*, p. 105.

[3] Pollux viii. 125.

[4] Cf. *supra*, pp. 53 ff. Cf. Glotz, *Solidarité*, pp. 227 ff.; Gilbert, *Beiträge*, pp. 508 ff. Treston, *op. cit.*, p. 263, connects the institution of the various Athenian homicide courts with the synoecism of Attica. Cf. Myres, *op. cit.*, p. 108, who attributes state control in homicide to the development of the *polis*.

was not convenient to assemble the whole senate for each one of these cases. So while the whole body sat on the most important homicide cases—that is, murder—they drafted sections from their own number to deal with the less important cases.[1] It would be natural to try the suppliants on the spot. Hence the committee would try the case where the suppliant had taken refuge. This is obviously what Photius means when he describes the ephetae as ἄνδρες οἵτινες περιιόντες ἐδίκαζον.[2] Just as in later times each heliastic court represented the whole body of dicasts, so the ephetae represented the Areopagus. A passage from Photius describing the ephetae as ἄριστα βεβιωκέναι ὑπόληψιν ἔχοντες supports this view. As members of the Areopagus they would be ex-archons, and as such would have passed a successful *dokimasia* and audit before their admission. Therefore the description may be accepted as it stands rather than as a perversion of Pollux' ἀριστίνδην, as it is usually understood.[3]

The chief evidence for the functioning of the Prytaneum —the fifth homicide court—in pre-Solonian Athens occurs in the so-called "amnesty law" which was passed prior to the introduction of Solon's reforms. From the text of the amnesty law which was re-enacted after the battle of Aegospotami in 405 B.C., as it appears in the decree of Patrocleides, and from the Solonian amnesty law, as it is found in Plutarch, · it is possible to determine with reasonable certainty the original text of the law. The decree of Patrocleides contains the following provision:

πλὴν ὁπόσα ἐν στήλαις γέγραπται τῶν μὴ ἐνθάδε μεινάντων, ἢ ἐξ Ἀρείου πάγου ἢ τῶν ἐφετῶν ἢ ἐκ Πρυτανείου ἢ Δελφινίου ἐδικάσθη ἢ ὑπὸ τῶν βασιλέων, ἢ ἐπὶ φόνῳ τίς ἐστι φυγὴ ἢ θάνατος κατεγνώσθη ἢ σφαγεῦσιν ἢ τυράννοις.[4]

This law is expressly said to be a replica of the amnesty law which was passed on the eve of the Persian War. The latter

---

[1] There could be different sections, but not concurrent sessions, since the presence of the *archon basileus* was required at each session of each of these courts.

[2] *S.v.* ἐφέται. The passage is thus quite intelligible and there is no need to emend περιιόντες to π' ὄντες, in accordance with Zonaras' account of the number. Cf. *supra*, p. 98.

[3] Cf. Meyer, *Geschichte des Altertums*, II, 579.   [4] Andocides i. 78.

was undoubtedly a repetition of the Solonian law. Plutarch's version of the Solonian law is as follows:

ἐπιτίμους εἶναι πλὴν ὅσοι ἐξ Ἀρείου πάγου ἢ ὅσοι ἐκ τῶν ἐφετῶν ἢ ἐκ πρυτανείου καταδικασθέντες ὑπὸ τῶν βασιλέων ἐπὶ φόνῳ ἢ σφαγαῖσιν ἢ ἐπὶ τυραννίδι ἔφευγον ὅτε ὁ θεσμὸς ἐφάνη ὅδε.[1]

The three laws were substantially the same. The following may be suggested as the correct text of the provision in question:

πλὴν ὁπόσα ἐν στήλαις γέγραπται τῶν μὴ ἐνθάδε μεινάντων, ἢ ἐξ Ἀρείου πάγου ἢ τῶν ἐφετῶν ἢ ἐκ πρυτανείου ἐδικάσθη ὑπὸ τῶν βασιλέων, ἢ ἐπὶ φόνῳ τίς ἐστι φυγὴ ἢ θάνατος κατεγνώσθη ἢ σφαγεῦσιν ἢ τυράννοις.[2]

It may be translated:

Except whatever names have been written on stelae of those who have not remained here or those upon whom sentence has been passed by the Areopagus or the Ephetae or the Prytaneum under the chairmanship of the kings, that is to say, if a verdict of exile or death has been rendered for murder, manslaughter or tyranny.

There is obviously reference to the Areopagus acting as a murder court,[3] while the phrase ἐκ τῶν ἐφετῶν refers to the three courts—the Palladium, the Delphinium, and in Phreatto in which the judges were the fifty-one ephetae. In the time of Andocides the words could not have been understood otherwise. The chief problem in interpreting the law lies in determining the functions and composition of the court called

---

[1] *Solon*, xix. It is in accordance with the practice of ancient writers not to quote a document verbatim, but to give the substance of it in language which conforms to their own style. Plutarch is no exception to this rule. Cf. Flickinger, *Plutarch as a Source of Information on the Greek Theatre*, pp. 10 ff. It is probable, then, that the passage in Andocides is an actual quotation of the law, while the words of Plutarch, as appears from the context, are in the nature of an exegetical paraphrase rather than a reproduction of the exact text of the law.

[2] For the reasons for the departures from the text of Andocides, cf. Gertrude Smith, "The Prytaneum in the Athenian Amnesty Law," *Class. Philol.*, XVI, 346 ff. ἢ Δελφινίου, being included in τῶν ἐφετῶν, is undoubtedly a gloss and should therefore be omitted, while the ἢ preceding ὑπό was probably occasioned by the rough breathing.

[3] It has been shown, *supra*, p. 88, that the Areopagus was functioning all through the pre-Solonian period. Plutarch's statement that no Areopagus existed before Solon's time occasioned much of the discussion about that body. For the question as to whether Plutarch had read the *Ath. Pol.*, compare G. H. Stevenson, "Ancient Historians and Their Sources," *Jour. Philol.*, XXXV, 219 ff.

Prytaneum. Three theories have been advanced. The first is based mainly on the order of words. The first offenses (φόνος and σφαγή) were naturally assigned to the first-named judicial bodies, the Areopagus and the ephetae. The Prytaneum alone, then, is left as the tribunal which dealt with tyrants. The statement of Herodotus[1] that at the time of the Cylonian rebellion the prytaneis of the naucraries were in charge of affairs at Athens has given rise to the view that the Prytaneum court was composed of these prytaneis, who exercised judicial functions in the extraordinary case of a revolution, although they were ordinarily an administrative body. Meyer is the most vigorous exponent of this theory.

Freilich stand ihnen [the Areopagites] als Gegengewicht der Rath im Prytaneion gegenüber, der aus den Vorstehern der 48 Naukrarien, der Unterabtheilungen der Phylen, mit den Phylenkönigen an der Spitze, gebildet war. Ihm präsidirte, wie es scheint, in der Regel der Archon, der im Prytaneion sein Amtslocal hatte (Arist. *Ath. Pol.* iii. 5), bei Gerichtssitzungen aber der König.[2]

He regards this council as identical with the prytaneis mentioned by Herodotus and also with the court of the Prytaneum mentioned in the amnesty law. But, even if Herodotus' statement is accepted, there is no evidence that the prytaneis of the naucraries acted as a judicial body. The adherents of Cylon were to have undergone trial, but there is not the slightest evidence that Herodotus meant that the prytaneis of the naucraries were to act as their judges.[3]

Another group of scholars likewise hold that cases of treason came before a court at the Prytaneum. But this court they maintain to have been composed of the nine archons. Lipsius insists that the nine archons would form a natural body for dealing with political offenses.[4] In his opinion it

---

[1] Herodotus v. 71.

[2] *Geschichte des Altertums*, II, 354 ff. Cf. Schöll, "Die Speisung im Prytaneion zu Athen," *Hermes*, VI, 21; Müller, *Eumenides*, p. 157, n. 13. Gilbert, *Constitutional Antiquities*, p. 123, n. 2 (cf. p. 125), identifies the judges of the Prytaneum court with the prytaneis or standing committee of Draco's new council.

[3] For the discussion of the naucraroi and the correctness of Herodotus' statement, cf. *infra*, pp. 129 ff.

[4] *Op. cit.*, p. 24. Cf. Philippi, *op. cit.*, pp. 217 ff., and Lange, *op. cit.*, pp. 223 ff.

was probably not an extraordinary, but a permanent, court. There is no evidence, however, that the archons acted in a body as a court on any occasion. Thucydides' language in describing the affair of Cylon does not imply any trial at all.

ἀναστήσαντες δὲ αὐτοὺς οἱ τῶν Ἀθηναίων ἐπιτετραμμένοι τὴν φυλακήν, ὡς ἑώρων ἀποθνῄσκοντας ἐν τῷ ἱερῷ, ἐφ' ᾧ μηδὲν κακὸν ποιήσουσιν, ἀπαγαγόντες ἀπέκτειναν· καθεζομένους δέ τινας καὶ ἐπὶ τῶν σεμνῶν θεῶν τοῖς βωμοῖς ἐν τῇ παρόδῳ ἀπεχρήσαντο.[1]

Busolt advanced the theory that the Prytaneum here mentioned was composed, as in later times, of the king archon and the phylobasileis, but that in early times this court was an important state court which tried serious political cases, including attempts at tyranny. He explains the reappearance of the reference to this function of the court in the decree of Patrocleides as merely a formal repetition, inasmuch as at that time (404 B.C.) such cases came before the popular assembly or before a popular court.[2] Only in the pre-Solonian period did it have such extensive powers, while by the fourth century it had become a sham court (*Scheingericht*). Busolt is undoubtedly correct in maintaining that the Prytaneum of the amnesty law is the court which in the time of Aristotle sat in judgment on unknown murderers, animals, and inanimate objects which had caused the death of human beings.[3] There is no trace of a court called Prytaneum other than this court of the phylobasileis and the king archon. Busolt is also correct in supposing that, although in historical times it had become a purely ceremonial court, concerned only with homicide, yet originally it had been an important state court.[4] The diminution in its powers antedates the legislation of Draco, its important functions having been turned over to the Areopagus. That the law of Solon should refer back to the distant period when this court was prominent seems quite unlikely. Furthermore, homicide is the chief topic of the passage under discussion.

Of the five Athenian homicide courts, four are mentioned

[1] i. 126.   [2] *Staatskunde*, p. 793.

[3] Cf. Lelyveld, *De infamia iure Attico commentatio*, pp. 57 ff.; Verdam, *De senatu Areopagitico*, pp. 18 ff.

[4] Cf. *supra*, p. 64, and *infra*, p. 117.

in the amnesty law either directly or by implication—the Areopagus and the three ephetic courts. In this context the Prytaneum must be the fifth homicide court. No legislator subsequent to Draco would, in a list of homicide courts, mention the Prytaneum, meaning some other court of the same name but different functions and possibly a different personnel, without distinguishing it specifically from the homicide court. Furthermore, the Prytaneum could not reasonably be omitted from a provision which excluded all homicides from the benefits of the amnesty, for it dealt with unknown murderers who constituted a not unimportant category of homicides.

No more serious political crime could be committed in a Greek community than an attempt to establish a tyranny. The Cylon incident shows, if proof is required, that the Athenians had the normal Greek attitude toward subverters of the government. It is futile to imagine that such a crime could be dealt with by any but the most authoritative body in the city. According to Aristotle, in the early period this body was the Areopagus:

> The Council of the Areopagus had as its constitutionally assigned duty the protection of the laws; but in point of fact it administered the greater and most important part of the government, and inflicted personal punishments and fines summarily upon all who misbehaved themselves.[1]

Apparently, all criminal matters were in the hands of the Areopagus. Aristotle says that the Areopagus in the time of Solon dealt with those who tried to overthrow the government:

> Solon assigned to the Areopagus the duty of superintending the laws so that it continued as before to be the guardian of the constitution in general. It kept watch over the citizens in all the most important matters and corrected offenders, having full power to inflict either fines or personal punishment. The money received in fines it brought up into the Acropolis without assigning the reason for the punishment. It also tried those who conspired for the overthrow of the state, Solon having enacted a process of impeachment to deal with such offenders.[2]

[1] *Ath. Pol.* iii. 6 (Kenyon's translation). The passage refers to the period before the time of Draco.

[2] *Ibid.*, viii. 4.

In 462 B.C., according to the account given by Aristotle, Themistocles expected to be tried for treason before the Areopagus.[1] This expectation furnished the motive for his participation in the overthrow of the power of the Areopagus.[2] After the Battle of Chaeronea the Areopagus arrested and put to death (λαβοῦσα ἀπέκτεινε) political wrongdoers.[3] If, then, as seems beyond question, the Areopagus dealt with subverters of the established order, there is no need to posit a court at the Prytaneum other than the homicide court. Would-be tyrants were tried by the Areopagus.[4]

Several theories have been advanced with regard to the identity of "the kings." Some scholars have construed the phrase ὑπὸ τῶν βασιλέων solely with ἐκ πρυτανείου and hold that it has no reference to the other courts named.[5] According to this interpretation, the reference is to the king archon and the phylobasileis who composed the ceremonial court of the Prytaneum.[6] Justification for this view is found in the language of the homicide laws of Draco, where τοὺς βασιλέας refers to the king archon and the phylobasileis in activities outside the Prytaneum court.[7]

The amnesty law, then, specifies those wrongdoers who

[1] *Ibid.*, xxv.

[2] Compare the reference to this story in the argument to the *Areopagiticus* of Isocrates in the Didot edition of the *Oratores Attici*, II. 484.

[3] Lycurgus *Con. Leocratem*, 52.

[4] Vinogradoff, *op. cit.*, p. 181: "The duty of prosecuting persons conspiring to obtain tyranny was entrusted to the Areiopagus by the decree of Patrocleides in 405 B.C." He says that the presiding judge in such trials was the king archon.

[5] Cf. Verdam, *op. cit.*

[6] *Ath. Pol.*, lvii. Sauppe offers a very curious explanation of the kings. The phylobasileis must be understood, who had jurisdiction over involuntary homicide. This crime was judged in the Palladium. Therefore, since no mention is made of the Palladium either in the law of Solon or in the decree of 404 B.C., the phrase must refer to the Palladium, and the following words, ἐπὶ φόνῳ τίς ἐστι φυγή, apply to involuntary homicide. In order to make this explanation plausible, Sauppe retains ἤ before ὑπὸ τῶν βασιλέων and deletes ἤ before ἐπὶ φόνῳ. The remainder of the decree refers to decisions made by the heliastic courts concerning civil strife and would-be tyrants. *Symbolae ad emendandos oratores atticos additae sunt* (Göttingen, 1874).

[7] Cf. *infra*, p. 118. In the Draconian code the reference to the group is to its capacity as an advisory body in the investigation preliminary to a homicide trial.

are to be excluded from reinstatement because they have been exiled by any one of the five homicide courts for homicide or by the Areopagus for an attempt on the government. The Areopagus is thus mentioned in two capacities, as a homicide tribunal and as the court before which a grave political offense was tried.[1]

The situation with regard to the homicide courts in pre-Solonian Athens may then be summarized as follows: At the Areopagus were heard trials for murder and also, in later times at least, for malicious wounding and for arson.[2] The fifty-one ephetai sat in the Palladium, which tried unpremeditated homicide; in the Delphinium, where cases of justifiable homicide were tried; and in Phreatto, a court which sat to try for premeditated homicide men who were already in exile for unpremeditated homicide. The fifth homicide court, the Prytaneum, dealt with unknown murderers, animals, and inanimate objects which had caused the death of human beings. This ceremonial court was composed of the king archon and the phylobasileis.[3]

The laws of Draco dealing with homicide constitute the main source of our information regarding practice and procedure in Athenian homicide courts during, and previous to, the time of Draco. Practically nothing is known about Dra-

[1] Stahl, *Rhein. Mus.*, XLVI (1891), 250, 481, contended that the Areopagites judged cases of tyranny, but for this purpose sat in the Prytaneum. Verdam, *op. cit.*, took exception to this view and saw in the mention of the Areopagus merely a court which sat at the Areopagus for the trial of a political offense. In his opinion there is no reference to the Areopagus as a murder court.

[2] Aristotle *Ath. Pol.*, lvii; Pollux viii. 117-20.

[3] Ancient writers attempted to date the institution of these various courts. Pausanias (i. 28. 8 ff.) places the institution of the Palladium at the time of the return of the Trojan heroes from Troy, the institution of the Delphinium at the time of Theseus in connection with the slaying of Pallas and his sons, the institution of the court in Phreatto to the time when Teucer defended himself against the charge of slaying Ajax, and the Prytaneum he regards as originating in the ceremonial act of judging the ax which was used to slay the bull at the altar of Zeus Polieus. In vi. 11. 6, however, Pausanias, in describing the action taken by the Thasians against the statue of Theagenes which fell on a man with fatal results, seems to attribute the institution of the Prytaneum to Draco, who in his homicide laws made the provision that an inanimate object which caused the death of a person should be cast beyond the borders. Pausanias doubtless realized that Draco was putting an existing practice into writing.

co's laws except those concerning homicide. This is due to
the fact that, although Draco made a complete code which
was in use until the reforms of Solon, Solon repealed all but
the homicide laws.[1] These continued in use and were revised
and republished in 409–408 B.C. Owing to their close connection with religion and the well-known religious conservatism of the Athenians, it is fairly certain that only such modifications were made as were necessary to adapt them to the
changed judicial system. The inscription is badly mutilated;
but with the aid of passages from Demosthenes[2] a tolerably
certain restoration of the major part of the inscription has
been achieved.[3] The sections of the code dealing with unpremeditated and justifiable homicide, as restored, are so
complete that the procedure can be followed from accusation
to verdict.

Draco, to a large measure, was simply reducing to writing
the practices that prevailed in Athens in his own time.[4] This
is shown by the omission from his code of certain essential
matters. For example, he fails to indicate the nature and
purpose of the oath taken by the relatives of the deceased
when they started the prosecution. This oath must already
have been in use.[5] His omission of the formula of the inter-

[1] Aristotle, *Ath. Pol.* vii. 1. Cauer in 1889 ("Uber die Gesetzgebung Drakons" *Verhandl. der 40. Philol. Vers. zu Görlitz* [1890]) limited Draco's work to the homi-cide laws. Linforth, *Solon the Athenian*, p. 276, follows this theory. Some scholars, on the other hand, consider Draco a wholly legendary name to which the work of the thesmothetae was attached. Garofalo, *Les Νόμοι de Dracon*. Cf. Glotz, *Soli-darité*, p. 301, n. 2.

[2] xxiii. 28, 37, 44, 51, 53, 60; xliii. 57.

[3] *CIA* i. 61; Dareste, Haussoullier, Reinach, *Recueil des inscriptions juridiques grecques*, II (No. 21), 1; Michel, *Recueil*, No. 78; Dittenberger, *Sylloge*, No. 52; Roberts-Gardner, *Introduction to Greek Epigraphy*, II, 25; Köhler, *Hermes*, II, p. 27; Philippi, *Jahrb. f. Phil.*, CV, 577; *Der Areopag und die Epheten*, pp. 333 ff.; Hicks and Hill, *Greek Historical Inscriptions*, No. 78; Bergk *Philologus*, XXXII, 669; Ziehen, *Rhein. Mus.*, LIV, pp. 321 ff.; Ledl, *Wiener Studien*, XXXIII, 1 ff. Cf. Treston, *op. cit.*, pp. 192 ff. For a discussion of the laws of Draco, cf. Busolt-Swoboda, *Staatskunde*, pp. 805 ff.

[4] Busolt-Swoboda, *Staatskunde*, p. 808, point out that although the work of Draco depends on older practices, yet it shows a great development over the Homeric period.

[5] *CIA* i. 61. 16 ff. The words τὸν ὅρκον are used as if it were a familiar oath.

dict to be pronounced against an alleged murderer shows that the interdict was already known and used.[1] Similarly his failure to mention the participation of the king archon in the interdict is further evidence to the same effect.[2] The text of the document with restorations is as follows:[3]

Διόγν[ε]τος Φρεάρριος ἐγραμμάτε[υε
Διοκλῆς ἔρχε

῎Ε]δοχσεν τῆι βουλῆι καὶ τõι δέμο[ι]· ᾽Ακα[μ]αντ[ὶς ἐπρυτάν]ευε,
[Δι]ό[γ-
νετος ἐγραμμάτευε, Εὐθύδικο[ς ἐπεσ]τάτε, [Χσ]ε[νοφ]άνες ε[ἶ]πε· [τ]ὸ[ν
5 Δράκοντος νόμον τὸμ περὶ τõ φ[όν]ο ἀν[α]γρα[φ]σά[ν]τ[ον οἱ ἀ]ν[α-
γρ]αφε̂-
s τὸν νόμον, παραλαβόντες παρὰ τõ [βασιλέος μετὰ τõ γραμμ]ατέο-
s[4] τῆς βουλῆς ἐστέλει λιθίνει κα[ὶ κ]α[τ]α[θ]έ[ν]τ[ον πρόσθεν τ]ê[ς] στο-
ᾶς τῆς βασιλείας, οἱ δὲ πολεταὶ ἀ[π]ομ[ισθοσάντον κατὰ τὸν νό]μο-
ν, οἱ δὲ ἐλλενοταμίαι δόντον τὸ ἀ[ργύριον.
10 Πρõτος ἄχσον·

Καὶ ἐὰμ [μ᾽] ἐκ [π]ρονο[ία]ς [κ]τ[ένει τίς τινα, φεύγεν, δ]ι-
κάζεν δὲ τὸς βασιλέας αἰτ[ι]õ[ν] φό[νο] ê [ἐάν τις αἰτιᾶται ὡς[5] βου]λ-
εύσαντα, τὸς δ[ὲ] ἐφέτας διαγν[õναι· Αἰδέσασθαι δ᾽ ἐὰμ μὲν πατέρ] ê-
ι ê ἀδελφὸ[ς] ê ὑε̂ς, ἅπα[ντας, ê τὸ[ν κ]ο[λύοντα κρατ̂εν· ἐὰν δὲ μὲ
ho]ῦ-
15 τοι δσ[ι, μ]έ[χ]ρ᾽ ἀ[ν]εφ[σι]ότ[ε]τος κ[αὶ ἀνεφσιõ, ἐὰν ἅπαντες
αἰδέσα]σ-
θαι ἐθέλοσ[ι], τὸν hό[ρκ]ον [ὀμόσαντας· ἐὰν δὲ τούτον μεδ᾽ hε̂ς ἔι, κτε-

---

[1] *Ibid.*, ll. 20 ff. It is, of course, possible that there was no standardized formula for the interdict. Cf. Demosthenes, xx. 158; Pollux viii. 66.

[2] *Ibid.*, ll. 20 ff. Aristotle says expressly that the king archon made the proclamation (*Ath. Pol.* lvii. 2; cf. Pollux viii. 90). In view of the conservative character of procedure in homicide courts it is likely that Aristotle is right for the early period also.

[3] The text is given here according to Dareste, *op. cit.* This text is followed in general by Dittenberger, *op. cit.*

[4] Dittenberger in his third edition reads here: παρὰ τõ κατὰ πρυτανείαν γραμματέος, following Köhler.

[5] Treston reads μὴ βουλεύσαντα and translates the first three lines of the passage: "And if a man slays a man not with intent to kill, let him be put on trial (φεύγειν), and let the 'Kings' judge of the causes of death, or, if anyone accuses a person of slaying without deliberation (μὴ βουλεύσαντα), let the Ephetae adjudicate." The first part of the sentence then refers to accidental killing in which there was no guilt attaching to the human agent, but in which it was necessary to prove that an animal or inanimate object had caused the death. The second part refers to manslaughter (*op. cit.*, pp. 195 ff.).

νει δὲ ἄκο[ν], γ[ν]ōσ[ι δ]ὲ h[οι πεν]τ[έκοντα καὶ hε̂ς hοι ἐφέται ἄκοντα
κτε̂ναι, ἐσέσθ[ο]ν δέ[κα hοι φράτερες ἐὰν ἐθέλοσιν· τούτος δ]ὲ [ho-
ι πεντέκο[ν]τ[α καὶ] hε̂ς ἀρ[ι]σ[τίνδεν hαιρέσθον· Καὶ hοι πρό]τε[ρ-
20 ον κτέ[ν]α[ντες ἐν τ]ō[ιδε τōι θεσμōι ἐνεχέσθον. Προειπε̂ν δὲ τōι] κ-
τέ[ναντι ἐν ἀ]γορ[α̂ι, ἐντ]ὸ[ς ἀνεφσιότετος καὶ ἀνεφσιō· συνδιόκε]ν
δὲ [καὶ ἀνε]φσ[ιὸς καὶ ἀνεφσιō̂ν παι̂δας καὶ γαμβρὸς καὶ πενθερὸ]ς [κ-
αι φ[ρά]τ[ε]ρ[ας . . . .
. . . . τὸς πεκτέκοντα κα]ὶ
25 hένα . . . .   hὸν ἂν φ]όνο
hε[λ]ōσ[ι   Ἐὰν δέ τις] τ-
ὸ[ν ἀνδροφόνον κτένει ἒ αἴτιος ε̂ι φόνο, ἀπεχόμενον ἀγορα̂ς ἐφ]ο-
ρί[α]ς [καὶ ἄθλον καὶ hιερὸν ἀμφικτυονικὸν, hόσπερ τὸν Ἀθεναι̂]ον [κ-
[τέναντα ἐν τοι̂ς αὐτοι̂ς ἐνέχεσθαι· διαγιγνόσκεν δὲ τὸς ἐφ]έτα[ς.
30 Τὸς δὲ ἀνδροφόνος ἐχσει̂ναι ἀποκτένεν καὶ ἀπάγεν ἐν] τε̂[ι] ἐμε[δ-
[απει̂, λυμαίνεσθαι δὲ μέ, μεδ' ἀποινα̂ν, ἒ διπλο̂ν ὀφέλεν hόσ]ο[ν ἂν κ-
[αταβλάφσει . . . .
. . . . Ἐὰν δέ τις ἄρξαντ]α χε[ρ-
ὸ[ν ἀδίκον κτένει . . . . ἐὰν] ἀέκον κ-
35 τέ[νει, δικάζεν δὲ τὸς βασιλέας αἰτιο̂ν φόνο, διαγνο̂ναι δ]ὲ τὸς ἐ-
[φέτας. Καὶ κατὰ ταὐτὰ φόνο δίκας εἶναι δōλον κτέναντι] ἒ ἐλεύθ-
ε[ρ]ο[ν. Ἐὰν δέ τις φέροντα ἒ ἄγοντα βίαι ἀδίκος εὐθὺς ἀμυν]όμενο-
ς κτ[ένει, νεποίνει τεθνάναι.
. . . .
47 . . . . . hὸς ἂν . . . . ἒ μετ]απ[ο]έ-
48 σει] . . . . .

"Diognetus of Phrearrhus was secretary
"Diocles was archon

"The resolution of the senate and the assembly. The tribe Aca-
mantis was the prytanizing tribe, Diognetus was secretary, Euthydi-
5 cus was chairman, Xenophanes made the motion. Let the commissioners obtain the law of Draco regarding homicide from the king
and the secretary of the Boulé and publish it on a stone stele. Let
them set up the stele before the King's Portico. Let the Poletae hire
the work done according to law and let the Hellenotamiae furnish
the money.
10 "First axon.
"If anyone kills a man without premeditation or if anyone is
charged with plotting homicide, he shall be exiled, the kings shall decide
the nature of the homicide and the ephetae shall give the verdict.
"If there is a father or a brother or sons let them grant pardon to
the homicide, if all agree. Otherwise the one who opposes it shall
15 prevent the pardon. But if there are no such relatives, then let the
relatives up to and including the first cousins exercise the right of

pardon, if all are willing to pardon, after taking the oath. But if there is none of these and the man committed homicide without premeditation and the Fifty-one, i.e. the Ephetae, have decided that he slew without premeditation, let ten phratry members admit him to the country if they are willing. And let the Fifty-one choose these phratry
20 members on the basis of birth. And let those who slew before this law was enacted be liable under this law.

"The relatives up to and including first cousins shall pronounce the interdict against the homicide in the agora.

"And the cousins and the children of cousins and the sons-in-law and the fathers-in-law and phratry members shall join in the prosecution.

27 "If anyone slays a homicide or is responsible for his death while he keeps away from border markets and games and Amphictyonic rites he shall be liable to the same punishment as the one who kills an
30 Athenian. The ephetae shall give the verdict. It shall be permitted to slay homicides and also to hale them into court in their own land, but not to abuse them or to extort blackmail. The punishment for such an offense shall be double the damages.

"If one slays another who is the aggressor (i.e. in a quarrel)
35 . . . . . if the slaying is unpremeditated, the kings shall decide the nature of the homicide and the ephetae shall render the verdict. The same procedure shall be followed whether a slave is killed or a free man.

"If a man while defending himself kills another on the spot who is unjustly and forcibly carrying off his property there shall be no punishment for the slaying."

The first step in a trial for unpremeditated homicide was a public proclamation in the agora forbidding the accused to frequent the market place and temples. The purpose of this interdict was to protect from pollution all public places and all religious ceremonies. The proclamation was made by the king archon at the instance of a near relative of the deceased. The code makes no mention of the king archon in this connection, but Aristotle says expressly that in his time the king archon made the proclamation.[1] In view of the conservative character of the procedure in the homicide courts, it is quite likely that Aristotle is right even for the earlier period. The

[1] *Ath. Pol.* lvii. 2: καὶ ὁ προαγορεύων εἴργεσθαι τῶν νομίμων οὗτός (ὁ βασιλεύς) ἐστιν. Pollux viii. 90, doubtless drew his account from Aristotle: προαγορεύει (ὁ βασιλεύς) δὲ τοῖς ἐν αἰτίᾳ ἀπέχεσθαι μυστηρίων καὶ τῶν ἄλλων νομίμων. Philippi, who wrote before the discovery of Aristotle's treatise, rejects the statement of Pollux, explaining it on the ground that the relatives could make the proclamation only on the order of the king archon after they had laid the charge before him.

silence of the code on the subject is to be explained by the fact that the king archon in pre-Draconian times was in the habit of making this and similar proclamations regarding polluted persons.[1] The interdict was omitted because, no doubt, it was an ancient and well-known formula. Its general purport is found in several passages.[2]

The exact degree of relationship of those who were permitted to initiate proceedings has been a matter of some dispute: προειπ͂εν δὲ τ͂οι κτέναντι ἐν ἀγορ͂αι ἐντὸς ἀνεφσιότετος καὶ ἀνεφσῖο.[3] But the interpretation of Lipsius seems the most plausible. On the basis of a passage of Demosthenes, ἐὰν δὲ μηδετέρωθεν ͂η ἐντὸς τούτων,[4] he asserts that ἐντός may mean "up to and including." ἐντός in this case is equivalent to μέχρι in the phrase preceding: ἐὰν δὲ μὴ ͂ωσι πρὸς πατρὸς μέχρι ἀνεψῖων παίδων. Wyse has conclusively shown that μέχρι may, and sometimes must, mean "up to and including."[5] Those who participated in the accusation, then, were father, brother, son, the children of brothers and sisters, uncles, and first cousins. The addition of the concrete ἀνεφσῖο after ἀνεφσιότετος is intended to restrict definitely the meaning of the abstract ἀνεφσιότης, which might easily be understood in a wider sense than the relationship of first cousin. While participation in the initial accusation was narrowly restricted, all relatives, and even members of the phratry, joined freely in the prosecution: συνδιόκεν δὲ καὶ ἀνεφσιὸς καὶ ἀνεφσιὸν παῖδας καὶ γαμβρὸς καὶ πενθερὸς καὶ φράτερας.

The interdict was followed by the preliminary investigation in which "the kings"[6] decided *prima facie* on the kind

---

[1] *Supra*, p. 111.

[2] Demosthenes xx. 158: χέρνιβος εἴργεσθαι τὸν ἀνδροφόνον, σπονδ͂ων, κρατήρων, ἱερ͂ων, ἀγορ͂ας. Cf. Pollux viii. 66.

[3] 20 ff.

[4] xliii. 51. Lipsius, *op. cit.*, p. 557; *Jahresbericht über die Fortschritte der klassischen Altertumswissenschaft*, XV, 291.

[5] *The Speeches of Isaeus*, pp. 566 ff. Philippi contends that ἐντός can mean only "within the circle of" or "up to and not including" and that the second of these two meanings must be accepted for this passage (*Der Areopag*, pp. 70 ff.). Cf. Busolt, *Geschichte*, II, 230; Dareste, *op. cit.*, p. 15; De Sanctis, *op. cit.*, p. 181.

[6] By "the kings" are to be understood the king archon and the phylobasileis. Cf. *infra*, p. 117.

of homicide which had been committed, thus determining
before which court the trial should take place: δικάζεν δὲ
τὸς βασιλέας αἰτιὸν φόνο.[1] It is known that in later times three
investigations were made in three successive months and
that the case was finally tried on the last three days of the
fourth month.[2] In the fifth and fourth centuries the preliminary investigations were called προδικασίαι. It was on
the basis of the evidence produced at these investigations
that the assignment of a case was made to a particular court.
Undoubtedly the term προδικασία reflects the word δικάζειν
as it is used in the present inscription. At the actual trial
the fifty-one ephetae served as judges: τὸς δὲ ἐφέτας διαγνῶναι.

Four theories have been advanced as to the identity of
the kings mentioned here: (1) all of the nine archons, or at
least the first three;[3] (2) the phylobasileis or kings of the
pre-Cleisthenean tribes;[4] (3) the archon basileus alone;[5] (4)
the archon basileus and the phylobasileis combined.[6] Against
the first of these theories it may be objected that such a
designation of the archons in an official document after the
institution of the annual archonship is unthinkable. If the
phrase were so understood when the law was copied down
for practical uses in 409–408, it would surely have been
changed, for at that time the king archon presided in homicide courts and would naturally alone be thought of. Another objection to the theory is that a court of the nine archons under the presidency of the king archon is inconceivable. In such a case the archon eponymous would naturally
have held the presidency. The second of the four theories is
negligible since the king archon must have been included
whether he presided alone or in conjunction with the phylobasileis. The third theory is to be rejected for linguistic rea-

[1] 11 f. Cf. Philippi, op. cit., p. 85.

[2] Antiphon vi. 42; Pollux viii. 117.

[3] Curtius, Berichte d. Berl. Akad. (1873), pp. 288, 290.

[4] Wachsmuth, Stadt Athen, I, 469 ff.

[5] Köhler, Rhein. Mus., XXIX, 8; Lange, op. cit., p. 43; Philippi, op. cit., pp. 233
ff.; Busolt, Geschichte, II, 159, n. 1; Gilbert, Beiträge, p. 489, n. 2.

[6] Schoemann, Jahr. f. kl. Phil., CXI, 153 ff.; CXIII, 16 ff.; Lipsius, Das Attische
Recht, p. 26; Treston, op. cit., pp. 195 ff.

sons, although an attempt has been made to explain the plural by referring it to "the king-archons in succession."[1] Scholars have been tempted to follow this view because it is expressly stated in one of the later speeches of Antiphon, whose career ended in 411 B.C., that the king archon conducted the preliminary investigation in homicide cases.[2] There is no reference to the phylobasileis in the passage. This is not, however, conclusive proof that the king archon acted alone. Even though the phylobasileis participated in determining the jurisdiction of the case, yet subsequently the king had to prepare the case for trial and bring it before the court. In this the king acted alone, and it is to this function that Antiphon is referring. The fourth theory, the combination of the king archon and the phylobasileis, is supported by the plural number and by the fact that there are no other kings to whom the plural number could refer. The following development may be suggested. After the unification of Attica, at least, the phylobasileis were members of the Council of Elders but, as a group, outranked the other members of the council in importance. In addition, from the time of the formation of the Ionic tribes, the phylobasileis formed an important state court, probably for the settlement of intertribal disputes. They were summoned by the king and sat under his presidency. Long before the state interfered in homicide cases generally, the court of the phylobasileis, it may be conjectured, heard homicide cases which involved members of different tribes. They are thus very early definitely connected with homicide cases. As members of the Council of Elders, it is reasonable to suppose that the king might at any time use them for consultation in regard to any business that he might wish to bring before the council. This would include all sorts of state matters and also, from time to time, various matters connected with homicide.[3] In this capacity the phylobasileis were an advisory committee.

[1] Cf. the plural βασιλῆς in Plato, *Menexenus*, 238 D, which has regularly been understood to refer to the king archons. Cf. Shorey, *Class. Philol.*, V, 361.

[2] vi. 42.

[3] Compare the Homeric trial-scene, which is connected with homicide, *supra*, p. 32.

With the coming of the idea of pollution and the interference of the state in homicide, definite courts were established for the trial of different degrees of homicide. The phylobasileis continued to act as an advisory committee in the preliminary investigation; that is, they helped to determine the nature of the homicide and consequently the proper jurisdiction for the case. The king archon, however, like his royal predecessor, brought the case before the council (the Areopagus) or before one of the newly established courts after proper preparation.

Certain types of homicide cases never came before a court. If the murderer were unknown or the death were due to an accident through the agency of an animal or an inanimate object, the case could go no farther. There could be no real trial. The phylobasileis constituted the group that determined that an object or an animal had been the cause of the death. They thereupon pronounced sentence upon the polluted animal or object and had it conveyed beyond the borders. Against the unknown murderer the interdict was pronounced. The phylobasileis under the presidency of the archon basileus came to be known in this capacity as the Prytaneum—the fifth homicide court.

Draco does not specify the place of the trial for unpremeditated homicide, but unquestionably it was the Palladium, just as it was in later times. τῶν δ' ἀκουσίων καὶ βουλεύσεως, κἂν οἰκέτην ἀποκτείνῃ τις ἢ μέτοικον ἢ ξένον οἱ ἐπὶ Παλλαδίῳ.[1] Banishment for an indeterminate period was the penalty. The person banished had to keep away, not only from Attica, but also from pan-Hellenic gatherings: ἄθλων καὶ ἱερῶν. Under certain conditions the exile could be terminated.[2] If the deceased had a father or a brother or a son, they might readmit the murderer to the country provided that all of these relatives agreed on the pardon. But if there were no such relatives, the circle was widened to include first cousins. Again, the consent of all was necessary to make the pardon effective. There was a further provision, namely, that the

[1] Aristotle *Ath. Pol.* lvii. 3; Demosthenes xxiii. 71; Harpocration, *s.v.* βουλεύσεως; Philippi, *op. cit.*, pp. 29 ff.

[2] Cf. Demosthenes xliii. 57.

relatives were required to take an oath. The nature of the oath is not specified, doubtless because it was an oath which had long been in use. It is obviously intended to substantiate the claims to relationship with the deceased,[1] as is shown by the fact that it was not required of the phratry members who, in case the deceased left no relatives at all, exercised the pardoning power, αἴδεσις.[2] Ten members were chosen ἀριστίνδην by the fifty-one ephetae for the purpose of considering a pardon. The provision with regard to the pardon of murderers is made retroactive, granting return from exile on the same terms to those convicted before the enactment of Draco's law as well as after.[3] So long as a convicted murderer or one accused of homicide and interdicted[4] remained in banishment and avoided gatherings which Athenians might be expected to frequent, he was protected from violence as was any other Athenian living abroad. Whoever killed him was liable to punishment, like any homicide, if he returned to Athenian territory. But if an exiled homicide re-entered Attica before his banishment was terminated, he was liable to be put to death.

This section of the code has caused some misapprehension. Heraldus long ago suggested that the exile could be slain only if he resisted arrest.[5] This suggestion was due to the conviction that civilized Athenians would not think of killing a man in cold blood without a good and sufficient reason. Thalheim[6] expressed surprise that, although killing

---

[1] A similar oath was in later times required of prosecutors in homicide cases, Demosthenes xlvii. 72.

[2] CIA i. 61. 16 ff. ἐὰν δὲ τούτων μηδ᾽ εἷς ᾖ, κτείνῃ δὲ ἄκων, γνῶσι δὲ οἱ πεντήκοντα καὶ εἷς οἱ ἐφέται ἄκοντα κτεῖναι, ἐσέσθων δέκα οἱ φράτερες ἐὰν ἐθέλωσιν. Premeditated murder could not, of course, be pardoned even by the relatives. The penalty was death or ἀειφυγία.

[3] It is interesting to compare this with the code of Gortyn, which is never retroactive.

[4] Demosthenes xxiii. 29 ff. argues that ἀνδροφόνους in this passage means "convicted murderers" only. But this view is disproved not only by Lysias' use of the word (x. 7), but also by Demosthenes' own usage in a later section of the same speech (80). Cf. Lipsius, p. 943, n. 4.

[5] Kennedy, Demosthenes, Orations, III, 176, n. 2, cites Heraldus with approval.

[6] Rechtsalterthümer, p. 50. Maltreatment was forbidden because it might be employed to extort blackmail.

was permitted, physical abuse was forbidden. Some[1] have taken ἀπάγειν to mean "enslave." Others have held that the right to kill or to arrest was confined to the relatives of the murdered man. These misapprehensions are due in part to the fact that the primitive method of dealing with an outlaw by killing him on sight and the more civilized method of arrest and inquiry before execution are set forth as alternatives in the same section. Death was the penalty for unlawful return from banishment. In accordance with primitive custom, it could be exacted by anyone who cared to take the risk of killing a desperate man. Or the alleged criminal could be turned over by anyone to the proper authorities for execution after suitable inquiry into the facts. We may be sure that even in the age of Draco few citizens would prefer the first alternative. It is clearly implied in Demosthenes' discussion of the section that in the fourth century the death penalty was regularly exacted by the thesmothetae. As the offense was not the original homicide, but the unlawful return from exile, there can be no question of limiting the right of action to relatives of the victim.[2] Neither can there be any question of enslaving the exile, because, being a murderer, he was polluted.[3]

The discussion regarding the authenticity and interpretation of this section of the code has obscured one of its most significant features from the standpoint of Athenian judicial history. In permitting any citizen to slay a returning exile, Draco is no doubt incorporating in his code an ancient practice. But the alternative provision for arrest by anyone and a trial before a magistrate marks a distinct step in advance. It is intended to meet the requirements of a more enlightened age. The state now intervenes and executes the outlaw not

---

[1] Dareste, Haussoullier, Reinach, *op. cit.*, I, 18. Cf. Usteri, *Aechtung und Verbannung im Attischen Recht* (1903), p. 9.

[2] Dareste, Haussoullier, Reinach, *op. cit.*, I, 18. This view has been generally rejected. Cf. Lipsius, *op. cit.*, p. 604; Usteri, *op. cit.*, p. 9.

[3] Demosthenes xxiii. 31-32, understands ἀπάγω to mean "take into custody and deliver to the authorities by the summary process known as ἀπαγωγή." Cf. Gilbert, *Constitutional Antiquities*, p. 387; Lipsius, *op. cit.*, p. 604.

for the original crime—homicide, but because, being polluted, he is a public menace. Usteri finds a different reason
for state intervention. He thinks that in defying the law
the exile has outraged the community. "Der zur Verbannung
Verurteilte, der im Lande bleibt oder unbefugt dahin zurück-
kehrt, vergeht sich damit gegen die Gesetze, somit gegen die
gesamte Bürgerschaft, und nicht nur gegen die Familie, die
durch seinen Totschlag betroffen wurde."[1] But the invariable
practice of excluding from amnesty[2] all homicides in exile supports the view that pollution is an important reason for the
intervention of the state. Once the notion that the shedding
of blood involved pollution became current, it was inevitable
that communities should take steps to protect themselves
adequately from the danger of close association with murderers. Draco's provision marks the public interest in the
matter. The citizen who makes the arrest and prosecutes the
culprit represents the whole community. It is an exception to
the prevailing rule that only the individual wronged had the
right to prosecute.

It may be objected that the citizen who thus takes an
outlaw into custody is an informer rather than a prosecutor,
because the exile may already have been condemned in a
court of law. But the condemned murderer is guilty of a
new infraction of the law in returning to Attica. Consequently the authorities must always have taken steps to satisfy
themselves that the man arrested was guilty of a breach of
the law. This procedure would involve proof of his identity
and of the fact that he was arrested in Attic territory, in case
of denial on his part. Such an inquiry, be it never so simple
and informal, must be regarded as a trial. The citizen who
brought the accused before a magistrate and proceeded to
establish the facts was really a prosecutor representing the

[1] Usteri, *op. cit.*, p. 9.

[2] Cf. Plutarch (*Solon*, xix) for the Solonian amnesty law which was repeated
on the eve of the Persian War and after the Battle of Aegospotami (Andocides i.
78.). Homicides were excluded from the benefits of the amnesty after the overthrow of the Thirty (Aristotle *Ath. Pol.* xxxix. 5.). Cf. Bonner, *Class. Philol.*,
XIX, 175.

community. The action thus instituted exhibits all the essential features of a normal public action.[1]

There are indications that this was not the only departure in the code from the rule that the victim alone could prosecute one who had wronged him. The law forbade maltreatment or blackmail of the exile, under pain of paying double damages. The procedure was doubtless set forth in the lacuna (seventy-nine letters missing) found at this point in the inscription (l. 31). In the version of the section which is quoted by Demosthenes the provision appears as follows: εἰσφέρειν δ᾽ ἐς τοὺς ἄρχοντας, ὧν ἕκαστοι δικασταί εἰσι, τῷ βουλομένῳ. τὴν δ᾽ ἡλιαίαν διαγιγνώσκειν.[2] The reference to the heliaea[3] shows that the section is not Draconian. Neither can it belong to the Solonian code. If the provision is genuine, it must belong to a post-Cleisthenean revision. But in any event the original provision must have been substantially the same. The victim of the outrage, i.e., the original homicide, being polluted and ἄτιμος, was debarred from appearing in court to exact the penalty. Under the circumstances the most natural thing to do was to permit anyone to prosecute the case just as the Demosthenic version of the law provided. It is tempting to suggest that the famous words τῷ βουλομένῳ, κ.τ.λ., appeared in the original form of the provision; but in view of the fact that they do not appear in the first part of the section where they might have been added to ἐξεῖναι, it would be a hazardous conjecture. The effect, however, is the same. The prosecutor may represent the victim if the fine is for his benefit in the nature of damages, but he is essentially a representative of the community. The public interest in this aspect of the case is vital. By paying blackmail

[1] Attention was first drawn to this feature of the code of Draco by Gertrude Smith, Class. Philol., XVII, 197. Steinwenter, Gnomon, IV, 69, remarks, "Ja das ἀπάγειν in Z 30 geht sogar über ein rein privates Verfolgungsrecht hinaus." Cf. Adcock in CAH, IV, 30 f.: "If the exiled homicide returns to Attica still unpardoned he may be killed or haled to judgment, but not mutilated or held to ransom." For a different view, cf. Calhoun, Criminal Law, p. 68, n. 42.

[2] Demosthenes xxiii. 28. Cf. Drerup, "Über die bei den attischen Rednern eingelegten Urkunden," Jahrb. für class. Philo., XXIV, Suppl., 268.

[3] The institution of the heliaea was subsequent to Draco.

the exile might escape arrest indefinitely and continue to pollute the community by his presence at public gatherings.

The next portion of the code deals with justifiable homicide. The specifications in regard to the right of the relatives to accuse and prosecute are not repeated. The first case mentioned is killing in self-defense: ἐὰν δέ τις ἄρξαντα χερὸν ἀδίκον κτένει (l. 33). "The kings" are to decide on the kind of homicide. The ephetae are to act as judges and decide upon the guilt of the accused in precisely the same manner as in cases of unpremeditated homicide.

The next section has been the subject of much dispute. The only remaining letters are ε ελευθ at the end of line 36. Köhler assumed that it dealt with the murder of a slave and restored it thus: καὶ κατὰ ταὐτὰ φόνου δίκας εἶναι δοῦλον κτείναντι ἢ ἐλεύθερον, i.e., the trial would be just the same as that described above. Bergk restored it as a further provision regarding justifiable homicide; and this, indeed, seems plausible, since the preceding sentence deals with that type of homicide case: καὶ ἐὰν ἐπὶ δάμαρτι ἢ ἐπὶ παλλάκῃ, ἢν ἂν ἔχῃ ἐπὶ] ἐλευθέ[ρ]ο[ις παισὶ ἢ ἐπὶ μητρὶ ἢ ἐπὶ ἀδελφῇ ἢ ἐπὶ θυγατρὶ τιμω]ρούμενος κτ[είνῃ, τούτων ἕνεκα μὴ φεύγειν κτείναντα. It is a provision permitting a man to kill an adulterer caught in the act.[1] According to this restoration, a trial would take place like the one described in Lysias' first oration in defense of a husband who claimed that he slew Eratosthenes in his wife's apartment. Dareste, however, rejects this interpretation on the ground that the letter ε before ελευθ is certain. If Köhler's restoration is accepted, a preliminary investigation to determine whether the murderer acted in self-defense must be assumed, just as in the case above an official inquiry is necessary to determine who struck the first blow and whether the homicide was justifiable. Justifiable homicide, cases were, in later practice, tried before the Delphinium; and presumably they were tried there in the time of Draco.[2]

The inscription in its present state contains no reference

---

[1] Cf. the Gortyn code ii. 28 ff.

[2] The locality was perhaps originally a matter of accident, due to the suppliant's taking refuge in a particular shrine. Cf. *supra*, p. 103.

to trials such as took place in the fifth and fourth centuries before the courts of the Prytaneum and in Phreatto. It has been suggested that the unrestorable lines at the end of the inscription contained references to the two types of case which would come before these two courts.[1] It has been pointed out that the space is not sufficient for such provisions. In fact, the remainder of the inscription is quite incapable of restoration except that the traces of the word μεταποιήσῃ show that the law probably ended with the provision quoted in Demosthenes: ὃς ἂν ἄρχων ἢ ἰδιώτης αἴτιος ᾖ τὸν θεσμὸν συγχυθῆναι τόνδε, ἢ μεταποιήσῃ αὐτὸν ἄτιμον εἶναι καὶ παῖδας καὶ τὰ ἐκείνου.[2]

As this cursory review of the inscription shows, premeditated homicide is not mentioned, although Draco is reputed to have been the first to draw a distinction between premeditated, unpremeditated, and justifiable homicide. In this connection the introductory words of the code, as it stands, have occasioned much discussion, for they are obviously not words which would be used to begin a set of laws, καὶ ἐὰμ μή. One explanation offered is that the laws of Draco contained a provision on premeditated homicide at the beginning. When the laws were copied, that provision was placed on a separate stele. If this theory is correct, it is necessary to assume that the popular decree, which heads the existing stele, and the axon number were repeated at the beginning of each stele, an assumption which is by no means attractive. Another theory explains the beginning on the supposition that the laws of Draco on premeditated homicide had been superseded by later legislation and hence were no longer in existence. Gilbert contends that in the original laws of Draco a single sentence preceded the present beginning. ἐὰν ἐκ προνοίας κτείνῃ τίς τινα, ἀποθανεῖν (ἢ φεύγειν καὶ τὰ ἐκείνου ἄτιμα εἶναι).[3] The remainder of the paragraph after φεύγειν, then, would refer to the procedure common to both kinds of homicide

---

[1] Presumably the courts of the Prytaneum and in Phreatto were conducted in much the same way as in later times. The Prytaneum was chiefly ceremonial (cf. Hyde, *Amer. Jour. of Philol.*, XXXVIII, 152 ff.). Neither of these courts can have sat very frequently.

[2] xxiii. 62.   [3] Gilbert, *Beiträge*, p. 490.

trial, i.e., the kings decide before which court the case shall go, but the ephetae constitute the membership of the court in both cases. This theory of Gilbert is due to his assumption that during the time of Draco the ephetae judged cases of premeditated homicide. But the court of the Areopagus in the time of Draco had jurisdiction in these cases.[1]

It is impossible to find authentic material for a reconstruction of the procedure of the Areopagus in pre-Solonian and pre-Draconian times.[2] Several mythical trials for homicide are represented as being held at Athens before a court which sat for the purpose of dealing with such cases. In some of these the parties involved were not Athenians. These stories seem to indicate that in very early times provision was made in Athens for the trial of persons who were charged with murder and that strangers may have been induced by its reputation to submit their cases to this court.[3] It is true that in the case of foreigners the verdict could not be enforced, but the question of jurisdiction is of relatively little importance where the matter is one of religion rather than of law. In all of the myths this court is known as the Areopagus.[4] The account of none of these trials, however, except that of Orestes, affords any data regarding practice and procedure. Aeschylus, in his description of this trial in the

---

[1] Cf. supra, pp. 91 ff. Treston, op. cit., pp. 248 and 225, believes the law in Demosthenes xxiii. 20 about the Areopagus to be a genuine Draconian law.

[2] Before the Areopagus in the fifth and fourth centuries came premeditated homicide, wounding with intent, arson, and premeditated poisoning resulting in death (Demosthenes xxiii. 22; Aristotle, Ath. Pol. lvii. 3; Pollux viii. 117; Philippi, op. cit., pp. 23 ff.). The preliminary investigation was identical with the procedure followed in cases of unpremeditated homicide. The accuser swore to his right to prosecute and to the guilt of the defendant; the defendant, in his turn, to his innocence (Antiphon v. 11; v. 16; Lysias x. 11; Demosthenes xxiii. 67). Each of the two could make two speeches, after the first of which the defendant was at liberty to go into exile (Demosthenes xxiii. 69; Pollux viii. 117). Equal votes constituted an acquittal (Antiphon v. 51). The king archon took part in the voting after he had divested himself of his magisterial character by taking off his wreath (Aristotle Ath. Pol. lvii. 4; Pollux viii. 90).

[3] Ancient writers attribute to Athens the invention of courts and trials. Cf. supra, p. 61.

[4] Hellanicus, quoted by the scholiast on Euripides, Orestes, 1648; Electra, 1258 ff.; Demosthenes xxiii. 66; Pausanias i. 28. 5; Parian Marble, Ep. 3; Bekker, Anecdota, I, 444.

Eumenides, represents Athena as instituting a homicide court
at Athens for the purpose of trying Orestes. The common
tradition in ancient times placed the scene of the trial on the
Areopagus.[1] Aeschylus identifies the new court instituted
by Athena with the Areopagus of the historical period. Some
modern scholars have refused to accept the tradition, and
considerable discussion about the scene of the trial has ensued;[2] but the problem has no place in the present study.
The details given by Aeschylus are not full enough to distinguish the court which he describes from any of the other
homicide courts. The proceedings begin with a preliminary
investigation conducted by Athena acting as presiding officer
and filling the rôle which the king archon filled in later times.[3]
The Erinyes are questioned first. They tell their name and
state their accusation against Orestes.

$$\phi o \nu \epsilon \grave{\upsilon} s \; \gamma \grave{\alpha} \rho \; \epsilon \tilde{\iota} \nu \alpha \iota \; \mu \eta \tau \rho \grave{o} s \; \mathring{\eta} \xi \iota \acute{\omega} \sigma \alpha \tau o.$$

Athena inquires whether there were extenuating circumstances, but the Erinyes evade the question. They object
that Orestes will neither take nor tender an evidentiary oath.
At this point Athena questions Orestes as to his name and
story and his right to be a suppliant. Orestes replies that he
is already ceremonially clean since his purification was performed in Apollo's temple at Delphi. Then he describes his
act, asking Athena to judge its justifiability. Athena declares herself incapable of deciding the matter alone and determines to choose from the best of her citizens men who
shall constitute a permanent tribunal for the trial of homicide.[4] The two parties to the suit are ordered to summon
their witnesses and produce their proofs.

At the trial Athena again presides. A herald proclaims
the meeting by the blast of a trumpet. While the people are

---

[1] Aeschylus *Eumenides*, 687 ff.; Euripides *Electra*, 1258 ff.; *Orestes*, 1650; *Iph.
Taur.*, 961.

[2] Ridgeway, "The True Scene of the Second Act of the *Eumenides* of Aeschylus," *Class. Rev.*, XXI, 163 ff. Cf. Verrall, *The Eumenides of Aeschylus*, p. 184.

[3] *Eumenides*, 397 ff.

[4] Euripides *Orestes*, 1650 ff., is at variance with Aeschylus in that he makes the
gods act as jurors.

assembling, Athena proposes to proclaim the establishment of the new court, but her speech is cut short by the entrance of Apollo. The trial begins, and the ordinance is postponed. Apollo testifies to the purification of Orestes at his instance and declares himself responsible for Orestes' act. Athena then opens the trial, using the regular technical formula εἰσάγω τὴν δίκην. The prosecution, represented by the Erinyes, is bidden to make the accusation. This consists in questions addressed to Orestes.[1] Orestes lays the guilt upon Apollo, at the same time inquiring why the Erinyes did not pursue his guilty mother. Their sole defense is that she was not of the same blood with the man she murdered. Orestes then calls upon Apollo for his evidence. The god declares that he received from Zeus the oracle directing Orestes to avenge his father. Clytemnestra deserved to die because of her own guilt. To the Erinyes' objection that Zeus himself put his own father in chains and yet, in the case of Orestes, considers the death of a father of more importance than that of a mother, Apollo replies that fetters may be unbound, but spilt blood is irrevocable. The god here enters upon the main defense, namely, that the father is the true parent. After this closing plea of the defense, Athena gives over the case to the jury and Apollo urges them to remember their oath. At this point the trial is interrupted by the proclamation of Athena's ordinance establishing the court of the Areopagus for all future time. While the voting proceeds, the Erinyes and Apollo alternately address the jury in an attempt to win their votes. From a legal standpoint this is entirely irregular. Before the votes are counted, Athena declares that her vote is for Orestes since she values the father more highly than the mother, and she adds that Orestes shall be acquitted if the votes are equal.

$$\text{νικᾷ δ' Ὀρέστης, κἂν ἰσόψηφος κριθῇ.}^{2}$$

There has been some discussion on this point, two possibilities being suggested: (1) that if the jury is equally divided,

---

[1] In the fifth- and fourth-century Athenian law courts a speaker could question his opponent, and the judges could interrupt and ask questions of the speaker.

[2] *Eumenides* 741. Cf. Euripides *Iph. Taur.*, 965; *Electra*, 1265 ff.

Athena, by her vote, will make a majority in Orestes' favor; (2) that if Athena's vote makes equality, then this equality shall acquit the defendant. The second of these two views seems contradictory to the statement of Aeschylus that the ballots were equally divided.[1]

Aeschylus is a dramatist, not a legal historian. It is therefore not to be supposed that in an antiquarian spirit he sought to reproduce on the stage a pre-Draconian trial.[2] But even if he was satisfied in the main to project back the practice of his own day, it was inevitable that he should introduce antique features which would be more or less familiar to a cultured Athenian who had occasion to acquaint himself, as Aeschylus did, with the traditions regarding the Areopagus. The procedure of the court was ritualistic, and changes would take place very slowly. The history of homicide courts from Solon to Demosthenes, a period of nearly three centuries, is known, and during this time, although some changes in the organization occurred, yet the procedure remained practically the same.

Aeschylus does not reproduce the regular four set speeches of an Athenian homicide trial. It is not sufficient explanation to say that they are not suited to the drama. Euripides has shown that set speeches of accusation and defense can easily be managed. The method used by Aeschylus is reminiscent of the time when the trial took place before a single magistrate who had final jurisdiction. Each litigant, no doubt, presented his side of the case largely in the form of answers to questions of the magistrates, constantly interrupted and stimulated by protests and questions of his opponent. Aeschylus presents, then, a rather realistic picture of an ancient trial before a single magistrate.

The number of Areopagites in the drama, which is usually

---

[1] Verrall, *op. cit.*, p. xxix, remarks that from Aeschylus it would naturally be inferred that in his time an Areopagite jury was even in number and that the *archon basileus* who presided always voted, according to Athena's precedent, for acquittal, so that equality in the votes of the jurors always counted in favor of the defendant.

[2] Verrall, *op. cit.*, p. xlvi, considers the *Eumenides* a doubtful authority on law and legal history since the real issue of the play is religious, not legal.

supposed by commentators to be twelve, is of no importance here. From the fact that Athena declares that she will select a jury for this trial, Verrall argues that the Areopagus never sat in full assembly, but that a jury for each trial was selected from the whole group by some responsible official.[1] He finds it inconceivable that all members were compelled to attend each session and equally inconceivable that attendance was left to private inclination. Verrall speaks as if Athena meant to select from an already existing body of jurors, forgetting that she is instituting an entirely new court from her citizen body.[2]

A group of officials, known as the naucrars or naucraroi, (ναύκραροι) shared in the government during this period. They are first mentioned by Herodotus as an important body in connection with the conspiracy of Cylon which occurred in 630 B.C.[3] Attica was divided into forty-eight districts called naucraries (ναυκραρίαι). At the head of each was a naucrar (ναύκραρος). These forty-eight officials constituted an administrative body under the chairmanship of prytaneis (πρυτάνεις τῶν ναυκράρων). Each naucrary furnished a ship and two cavalrymen. The naucrars were responsible for the assembling and leadership of the military forces of their districts, under the direction of the polemarch. They collected and disbursed funds for the public service. The naucraries served also as administrative units in a system of local self-

[1] P. 182.

[2] According to Euripides' account in the *Orestes*, Orestes was not permitted to flee from Argos but was held for trial (46 ff., 430, 443, 870 ff.). But it must not be supposed that Euripides was attempting to picture an Argive homicide trial. The description is, however, interesting as a picture of a homicide trial before a popular assembly rather than before a court. In the first part of the play, the trial, as described by Electra, was to decide on the mode of Orestes' death, not on his guilt. But later in the rather sketchy description of the trial, the point at issue is whether he shall suffer the death penalty or not. The Argives apparently gather in full assembly. A herald opens the session. Then in succession come four speeches by different people, two in accusation and two in defense. So far, Euripides follows the regular Athenian procedure of four speeches in a homicide trial. But at this point Orestes is introduced with a speech in his own behalf.

[3] Herodotus v. 71. For the date of the Cylonian conspiracy, cf. Busolt-Swoboda, *Staatskunde*, p. 599, n. 1; *CAH*, IV, 661. For the naucraroi and their duties, cf. Busolt-Swoboda, *op. cit.*, pp. 817 ff.; How and Wells, *A Commentary on Herodotus*, *ad loc.*

government. This is indicated by the fact that Cleisthenes abolished the naucraries and instituted in their stead the demes under the presidency of demarchs.[1] The people of Attica, even after the unification, continued to cling to the land. These communities must have retained some powers of self-government. In the interests of unity, it was desirable to rearrange these communities, that cherished memories of their former independence, into new groups organized presumably as local self-government units. They served also as convenient units for recruiting the military forces of the state and collecting funds for the public service. The nobles that substituted aristocracy for monarchy were in all probability responsible for a reform that made for efficiency of administration and at the same time weakened the disruptive forces that interfered with the political solidarity of Attica. For the purpose of co-ordinating the local and national functions of the naucrars, they were organized into a single body with an executive committee called the "prytaneis of the naucrars." Their duties were similar to those of the prytaneis of the Cleisthenean Senate of Five Hundred.

The individual naucrars were the chief executives of their districts and military officers in the national army under the polemarch. As a body under the chairmanship of their prytaneis, they must have authorized the expenditure and disbursement of funds collected in their districts. A group of officials so intimately associated with the financial and military administration of the state must have possessed considerable power. Herodotus even says that the prytaneis of the naucrars governed Athens at the time of the conspiracy of Cylon in 630 B.C. But Herodotus was in error. Thucydides[2] in his account of the conspiracy says very pointedly that "at that time the nine archons transacted most of the public business." Apparently Thucydides had Herodotus' account before him and was correcting him.[3] In 630 B.C.

---

[1] Aristotle *Ath. Pol.* xxi. 5: κατέστησε δὲ καὶ δημάρχους τὴν αὐτὴν ἔχοντας ἐπιμέλειαν τοῖς πρότερον ναυκράροις· καὶ γὰρ τοὺς δήμους ἀντὶ τῶν ναυκραριῶν ἐποίησεν.

[2] i. 126: τότε δὲ τὰ πολλὰ τῶν πολιτικῶν οἱ ἐννέα ἄρχοντες ἔπρασσον.

[3] Cf. Lipsius, *op. cit.*, p. 12, n. 46.

Cylon, with the aid of some Athenian sympathizers, seized the Acropolis in an attempt to establish a tyranny. Instead of gaining popular support as he had hoped, he encountered a vigorous national resistance. The time was not ripe for tyranny. The men of Attica flocked into the city from their farms and besieged the Acropolis. Growing weary of the long siege, the majority of them went away, "committing the task of guarding to the nine archons, to whom they also gave full power to settle the whole matter as they might determine to be best; for at that time the nine archons transacted most of the public business." Cylon escaped by stealth, and his adherents in despair betook themselves as suppliants to the altar of Athena Polias on the Acropolis. They were induced to leave the altar by a promise that they should not suffer the death penalty. The promise was broken, and the suppliants were put to death. Plutarch in his account of the conspiracy[1] is in agreement with Thucydides. The usual explanation of the discrepancy between Herodotus and Thucydides is that Herodotus, or his authority, was endeavoring to absolve the Alcmaeonid archon, Megacles, from the guilt of sacrilege by throwing the blame upon another board of officials.[2] This may be true, for there were factors in the situation that made misrepresentation, if not misunderstanding, easy.

Thucydides' narrative furnishes a simple explanation of the origin of the Herodotean version. When the siege began to grow tedious and the ultimate surrender of the besieged was inevitable, the majority of the levies withdrew after turning over to the nine archons the task of finishing the siege, with full powers to dispose of the affair as they thought best. Obviously, if the nine archons had not been empowered to act, the matter would have remained in the hands of the military authorities. The chief military officer was the polemarch. Subordinate to him were the naucrars. They had

---

[1] *Solon*, xii: ὥρμησε συλλαμβάνειν ὁ Μεγακλῆς καὶ οἱ συνάρχοντες, ὡς τῆς θεοῦ τὴν ἱκεσίαν ἀπολεγομένης· καὶ τοὺς μὲν ἔξω κατέλευσαν, οἱ δὲ τοῖς βωμοῖς προσφυγόντες ἀπεσφάγησαν.

[2] How and Wells, *op. cit.*, on Herodotus v. 71.

summoned the levies from the rural districts to recover the citadel from the control of invaders and rebels. If these military forces had continued in the field the naucrars, or their prytaneis, associated with the polemarch in the conduct of the military operations, would have fixed the terms of surrender and accepted responsibility for the custody of the rebels. Under these circumstances it is easy to see how the story that the naucrars were responsible for the sacrilege gained currency if not credence. The transfer of responsibility from the military to the civil authorities was forgotten or ignored. Thucydides was aware of the source of the error and took pains to point it out, albeit with characteristic reserve and restraint. But even if the story of Herodotus be entirely rejected, there are still indications that the naucrars were an important body. This appears from the fact that when the system was discontinued their functions were divided between the demarchs and the Senate of Five Hundred under the new tribe organization. There is no reason to believe that these functions included the administration of justice. Meyer believes that the prytaneis of the naucraroi had judicial functions.[1] He reaches this conclusion by identifying them with the court of the Prytaneum over which the king archon and the phylobasileis presided. This court, as has been stated above, did in early times have both criminal and civil jurisdiction, but Meyer's reasons for connecting it with the naucraroi are not at all convincing. It is generally supposed that adherents of Cylon who escaped the massacre were tried and exiled by a court described as ἐκ πρυτανείου. The allusion to those who were exiled for attempted tyranny in the Solonian amnesty law is generally believed to have reference to the Cylonian followers.[2] But, as has been pointed out above, the Areopagus and not the Prytaneum tried cases of attempted tyranny.[3]

---

[1] *Geschichte des Altertums*, II, 355; cf. Lipsius, *op. cit.*, p. 24, n. 79; and Busolt, *op. cit.*, p. 811, n. 1.

[2] Cf. Scholium on Aristophanes *Knights*, 445.

[3] Cf. *supra*, p. 108. Closely associated with the naucrars were the *kolakretai*, who, under the monarchy, had charge of public sacrifices and feasts. In addition

To a large extent in the homicide laws, Draco apparently reduced to writing existing practices, although it is of course to be admitted that he modified and developed existing law to some extent.[1] This must have been true of the other laws as well as of the homicide laws, but of these other laws very little is known.[2] The severity of the penalties provided by his laws became proverbial, and Aristotle considers this severity the only noteworthy thing about his laws.[3] He apparently made death the ordinary penalty for offenses generally, whether small or great. The action for idleness (ἀργία), which was still in force in the fourth century, is regularly assigned to Draco. According to some authorities, he punished ἀργία with death;[4] but according to others, with ἀτιμία.[5] At any rate, there is general agreement that ἀτιμία was the penalty in Solon's time for a third offense. Various other laws are attributed to Draco, but their genuineness is open to grave doubt. For example, laws on the education of youth,[6] religious laws,[7] and a law that judges should listen to both sides of a case[8] are assigned to him; but their authenticity is very doubtful.[9]

they acted as royal treasurers. In later times they acted as treasurers of the naucrariae. Cf. Wilamowitz, *Aristoteles und Athen*, I, 52. These officials had no judicial functions, but in the fifth century they acted as paymasters of the dicasts. Cf. Scholium on *Wasps*, 695, 724.

[1] Cf. Busolt-Swoboda, *Staatskunde*, p. 816, who asserts that Draco by no means codified the entire body of the law but that his θεσμοί were simply additions to, and modifications of, the already existing law.

[2] For a summary, cf. Busolt-Swoboda, *op. cit.*, p. 814.

[3] *Pol.* 1274*b*. 16; *Rhet.* 1400*b*. 21; Demades in Plut. *Solon*, xvii.

[4] Diog. Laert. i. 55; Plut. *Solon*, xvii.

[5] *Pollux* viii. 42.

[6] Aeschines *Con. Tim.*, 7.

[7] Porphyr. *De abstin.* 4. 22; Schol. *Ven. B. Il.* xv. 36 (respecting the gods to be used in oaths).

[8] Lucian. *Calumn.*, 8.

[9] Cf. Busolt-Swoboda, *op. cit.*, p. 814, n. 2.

EXCURSUS
THE SO-CALLED DRACONIAN CONSTITUTION

In some cases the lawgiver had a twofold task to perform: on the one hand, the writing of a code; and on the other, the reorganization of the constitution. Such was the case with Pittacus of Mytilene.[1] Lycurgus is reported to have changed the constitution of Sparta. The chief task of Pheidon of Cyme and his successor, Prometheus, was the remodeling of the constitution.[2] In Athens the demand for the codification of the laws resulted in the appointment of Draco as a special thesmothete.[3]

For a long time preceding Draco's legislation there was bitter dissatisfaction on the part of the common people. Aristotle describes the wretched condition of the peasantry:

> The whole country was in the hands of a few persons, and if the tenants failed to pay their rent they were liable to be haled into slavery, and their children with them. All loans were secured upon the debtor's person, a custom which prevailed until the time of Solon, who was the first to appear as the leader of the people. But the hardest and bitterest part of the constitution in the eyes of the masses was their state of serfdom. At the same time they were discontented with every other feature of their lot: for, to speak generally, they had no part nor share in anything.[4]

There were many different elements which contributed to the strife between the classes. In the first place, within the governing party itself there was faction. Under such circumstances it is not surprising that attempts should be made to set up a tryanny. Cylon, supported by one faction of the eupatrids, seized the Acropolis. The Alcmaeonidae, heading another group, were responsible for the submission and capture of the Cylonian party, although Cylon himself had escaped. Botsford looks upon the Cylonian attempt as an oligarchic reactionary movement, i.e., an attempt to put

---

[1] Cf. Aristotle *Pol.*, 1274*b*; Bury, *History of Greece*, p. 187.

[2] Heracl. Pont., 11; cf. Holm, *History of Greece*, I, 270.

[3] Cf. Bury, *op. cit.*, p. 179, and Pauly-Wissowa, article on Draco. F. D. Smith, *Athenian Political Commissions*, p. 13, points out that Draco, in his capacity as a special thesmothete, performed with absolute discretionary power a task which under the democracy would have been given over to a commission of several members directly responsible to the people.

[4] *Ath. Pol.*, ii. Kenyon's translation. Cf. Plutarch, *Solon*, xiii, for the poverty and dependence of the thetic class.

down the πλῆθος and the more moderate oligarchs and to re-establish the oligarchy on its old basis.[1] However this may be, the incident shows clearly unrest and strife within the eupatrid group itself.[2] Again, wealth began to compete with birth as a basis for membership in the ruling class. The merchant class gained very great importance on becoming the wealthy class. The growth of commercial interests seems to have worked in two ways. On the one hand it promoted democracy. The poorest class was needed to man the ships, and thereby assumed a certain importance which helped to pave the way to political recognition.[3] On the other hand, the growth of commerce enhanced the sufferings of the farm-ing class. It was possible to import grain at a lower cost than that at which it could be raised at home.[4] In addition, manu-facturing and mercantile interests assumed far greater impor-tance than farming. Finally, the introduction of money and its concentration in the hands of the merchant class, whereas formerly payment had always been made in kind, meant an economic crisis. The condition of the rural population became even worse as the result of the war with Megara, which broke out after the Cylonian attempt, since parts of the Attic terri-tory were raided and the Megarian markets were closed.

Just what happened is not known. Either the peasants, with the aid of influential leaders, demanded measures which would alleviate their distress or else the eupatrids realized the danger which was imminent if relief were not granted.[5] At any rate, in 621 B.C. Draco was appointed special thes-mothete to codify and write down the laws.

[1] *The Athenian Constitution*, p. 135.

[2] Wright (*The Date of Cylon*) placed the Cylonian conspiracy before the legisla-tion of Draco, and his conclusions have been rather generally accepted. Cf. Free-man, *The Work and Life of Solon*, p. 164; Busolt-Swoboda, *Staatskunde*, p. 800. Cornelius, however, believes that the event occurred during the time of the Peisistra-tidae (*Die Tyrannis in Athen*, pp. 36 ff., 44).

[3] Cf. Bury, *op. cit.*, pp. 177 ff. For the economic situation in Greek states gen-erally at this period, cf. Busolt-Swoboda, *op. cit.*, pp. 798 f.

[4] Cf. Botsford, *The Athenian Constitution*, p. 141.

[5] Freeman, *op. cit.*, p. 50, assumes that the people, who as yet had no status in the constitution, under the pressure of economic hardship met in unofficial assembly and voiced their dissatisfaction.

It may be asked if the Draconian code benefited the common people at all and how it succeeded in quieting them even for a short period of time, for Aristotle makes it evident that their condition of serfdom, by which they were most depressed, was not relieved by the legislation. The laws were obviously in the interest of the ruling class. For example, the laws regarding debtors were very severe. Up until the time of Solon the creditor could claim the person of the debtor in case he could not otherwise pay. At the same time, the fact that the rights of the ruling class were clearly defined in writing gave to the commons a feeling of greater security. Under the old system the man of wealth and birth could take what he wanted and the poor man had no written law by which he could defend himself. He did not even know what the law was. It is clear that whatever effect there was, was largely psychological, for the thetes were in reality given no privileges at all. That the satisfaction of the people was short-lived is shown by the fact that less than thirty years later the populace rose against the aristocracy, an uprising which culminated in the reforms of Solon.

It was generally assumed by ancient writers, including Aristotle in the *Politics*, that Draco made no constitutional changes, and they therefore treat the period between the completion of the unification of Attica and the Solonian reforms as a political unit; that is to say, there was no definite change in the constitution during this period although there were the natural developments and enlargements which would come about in a growing state. But in Aristotle's summary of the changes in the constitution of Athens he gives as the third step in its development the constitution of Draco,[1] and he actually gives the provisions of this alleged constitution in the fourth chapter of his treatise. Since the recovery of this document, the authenticity of this constitution has been a perennial subject of debate among scholars.[2]

---

[1] *Ath. Pol.*, xli.

[2] For the bibliography on both sides of the debate, cf. Busolt-Swoboda, *op. cit.*, I, 53, n. 2. For a detailed discussion of the reasons for rejecting the constitution, cf. Freeman, *op. cit.*, pp. 34 ff.; Ledl, *Studien zur älteren athenischen Verfassungsgeschichte*, pp. 18 ff. Linforth, *Solon the Athenian*, p. 76.

Ἡ μὲν οὖν πρώτη πολιτεία ταύτην εἶχε τὴν ὑπογραφήν. μετὰ δὲ ταῦτα χρόνου τινὸς οὐ πολλοῦ διελθόντος ἐπ᾽ Ἀρισταίχμου ἄρχοντος Δράκων τοὺς θεσμοὺς ἔθηκεν· ἡ δὲ τάξις αὕτη τόνδε τὸν τρόπον εἶχε. ἀπεδέδοτο μὲν ἡ πολιτεία τοῖς ὅπλα παρεχομένοις. ᾑροῦντο δὲ τοὺς μὲν ἐννέα ἄρχοντας καὶ τοὺς ταμίας οὐσίαν κεκτημένους οὐκ ἐλάττω δέκα μνῶν ἐλευθέραν, τὰς δ᾽ ἄλλας ἀρχὰς ⟨τὰς⟩ ἐλάττους ἐκ τῶν ὅπλα παρεχομένων, στρατηγοὺς δὲ καὶ ἱππάρχους οὐσίαν ἀποφαίνοντας οὐκ ἔλαττον ἢ ἑκατὸν μνῶν ἐλευθέραν καὶ παῖδας ἐκ γαμετῆς γυναικὸς γνησίους ὑπὲρ δέκα ἔτη γεγονότας· τούτους δ᾽ ἔδει διεγγυᾶν τοὺς πρυτάνεις καὶ τοὺς στρατηγοὺς καὶ τοὺς ἱππάρχους τοὺς ἕνους μέχρι εὐθυνῶν, ἐγγυητὰς δ᾽ ἐκ τοῦ αὐτοῦ τέλους δεχομένους οὗπερ οἱ στρατηγοὶ καὶ οἱ ἵππαρχοι. βουλεύειν δὲ τετρακοσίους καὶ ἕνα τοὺς λαχόντας ἐκ τῆς πολιτείας. κληροῦσθαι δὲ καὶ ταύτην καὶ τὰς ἄλλας ἀρχὰς τοὺς ὑπὲρ τριάκοντ᾽ ἔτη γεγονότας, καὶ δὶς τὸν αὐτὸν μὴ ἄρχειν πρὸ τοῦ πάντας ἐξελθεῖν· τότε δὲ πάλιν ἐξ ὑπαρχῆς κληροῦν. εἰ δέ τις τῶν βουλευτῶν, ὅταν ἕδρα βουλῆς ἢ ἐκκλησίας ᾖ, ἐκλείποι τὴν σύνοδον, ἀπέτινον ὁ μὲν πεντακοσιομέδιμνος τρεῖς δραχμάς, ὁ δὲ ἱππεὺς δύο, ζευγίτης δὲ μίαν. ἡ δὲ βουλὴ ἡ ἐξ Ἀρείου πάγου φύλαξ ἦν τῶν νόμων καὶ διετήρει τὰς ἀρχὰς ὅπως κατὰ τοὺς νόμους ἄρχωσιν. ἐξῆν δὲ τῷ ἀδικουμένῳ πρὸς τὴν τῶν Ἀρεοπαγιτῶν βουλὴν εἰσαγγέλλειν ἀποφαίνοντι παρ᾽ ὃν ἀδικεῖται νόμον. ἐπὶ δὲ τοῖς σώμασιν ἦσαν οἱ δανεισμοί, καθάπερ εἴρηται, καὶ ἡ χώρα δι᾽ ὀλίγων ἦν.

("Such was, in outline, the first constitution, but not very long after the events above recorded, in the archonship of Aristaichmus, Draco enacted his ordinances. Now his constitution had the following form. The franchise was given to all who could furnish themselves with a military equipment. The nine Archons and the Treasurers were elected by this body from persons possessing an unencumbered property of not less than ten minas, the less important officials from those who could furnish themselves with a military equipment, and the Generals (Strategi) and commanders of the cavalry (Hipparchi) from those who could show an unencumbered property of not less than a hundred minas, and had children born in lawful wedlock over ten years of age. These officers were required to hold to bail the Prytanes, the Strategi, and the Hipparchi of the preceding year until their accounts had been audited, taking four securities of the same class as that to which the Strategi and the Hipparchi belonged. There was also to be a Council, consisting of four hundred and one members, elected by lot from among those who possessed the franchise. Both for this and for the other magistracies the lot was cast among those who were over thirty years of age; and no one might hold office twice until every one else had had his turn, after which they were to cast the lot afresh. If any member of the Council failed to attend when there was a sitting of the Council or of the Assembly, he paid a fine, to the amount of three drachmas if he was a Pentacosiomedimnus, two if he was a Knight, and one if he was a Zeugites. The Council of Areopagus was guardian of the laws, and kept watch over the magistrates to see that they executed their offices in accordance with the laws. Any person who felt himself wronged might lay an information before the Council of Areopagus, on declaring what law was broken by the wrong done to him. But, as has been said before, loans were secured upon the persons of the debtors, and the land was in the hands of a few.")[1]

No other author specifically credits Draco with being the framer of a constitution.[2] In fact, Aristotle himself, in the *Politics*,[3] says that Draco made laws for a constitution that was already in existence (πολιτείᾳ ὑπαρχούσῃ). He adds that there was nothing in the laws worth mentioning except the severity of the punishments. The authenticity of this passage of the *Politics* has been questioned.[4] But in view of the silence of other authors on a Draconian constitution it is dangerous to reject the assertion in the *Politics*, whether it be regarded as written by Aristotle or by a pupil. Because of the discrepancy between the *Politics* and the *Constitution of Athens*, the real test of the genuineness of the constitution is the internal evidence of the passage of the *Constitution of Athens* under discussion. The main points of the constitution are as follows:

1. A hoplitic franchise already in existence.
2. The election by the enfranchised of archons, treasurers, generals, hipparchs, and prytaneis, for all of which offices property qualifications are specified. There is a reference to an audit and to the use of the lot in the selection of some of the officials.
3. A council of 401 selected by lot from among the enfranchised of thirty years of age or more, with rotation of office.

[1] The text and translation are those of Kenyon (1920).

[2] There are two passages which might be interpreted to mean that Draco made a new constitution, Ps. Plato *Axiochus*, 365 D, and Cic. *de republ*. ii. 1. 2. Both are late and should not be pressed.

[3] ii. 12 (1274*b*). Cf. *CAH*, III, 593: "Draco regulated existing institutions rather than created new ones."

[4] For the inconsistencies in the passage and the reasons for doubting its Aristotelian authorship, cf. Newman, *The Politics of Aristotle*, II, 376 f. He concludes: "Aristotle may have left only the fragment about Solon and a few rough data for insertion after the notice of the Carthaginian constitution and some member of the school, not very long after his death, completed them as he best could."

4. Graduated fines for members of the council for non-attendance at assembly or council meetings.

5. The duties of the Areopagus.

In the first place, it is stated that the franchise had already been given to all who could furnish themselves with military equipment. This is the only possible meaning if the pluperfect ἀπεδέδοτο of the manuscript is retained. Kenyon believes that if the extension of the franchise had taken place earlier, due account of the fact would have been taken in the preceding chapter, which is a rather detailed description of the state of affairs before Draco. He translates: "the franchise was given"; and in his annotated edition of the Greek text suggests that ἀπεδίδοτο should be read.[1] Sandys, following the translation of Poste, states that the tense (pluperfect) implies that the franchise had already been given and that therefore this sentence does not belong to the alleged Draconian constitution.[2] Poste comments further that this interpretation agrees with the statement in the *Politics* that Draco did not alter the constitution. The political revolution had already taken place, and Draco's task was merely to adjust the laws to the new state of affairs. The hoplitic franchise, however, is one of the features of the constitution proposed by the party of Theramenes in 411 B.C.[3] δοκοῦσι δὲ καλῶς πολιτευθῆναι κατὰ τούτους τοὺς καιρούς, πολέμου τε καθεστῶτος καὶ ἐκ τῶν ὅπλων τῆς πολιτείας οὔσης. Various scholars consider this one of the particularly striking resemblances between the constitution of Draco and the constitutions of 411 B.C. which prove the former to be a complete anachronism. Headlam pointed this out in some detail,[4] and Busolt showed that the document was constructed in accordance with conditions which existed only in the second half of the fifth cen-

---

[1] Confusion between the present and perfect forms of ἀποδίδωμι is rather common. Compare, e.g., the description of the Areopagus in Lysias i. 30: ᾧ καὶ πάτριόν ἐστι καὶ ἐφ' ἡμῶν ἀποδίδοται (or ἀποδέδοται) τοῦ φόνου τὰς δίκας δικάζειν. Cf. *infra*, p. 330.

[2] Sandys, *Aristotle's Constitution of Athens*, ad loc.

[3] Aristotle *Ath. Pol.* xxxiii. 2; cf. Thucydides viii. 97; Xenophon *Hell.* ii. 3.48.

[4] *Class. Rev.*, V, 168.

tury.[1] It is based on a time when the ζευγίτης, owing to the hardships of war, could no longer provide himself with military equipment. Hence παρεχόμενοι τὰ ὅπλα was substituted for ζευγῖται. So, in the case of the higher officials, the πεντακοσιομέδιμνοι and ἱππεῖς no longer possessed the proper property census. Hence the specific property qualifications.

Nothing is gained from a comparison with the constitution of Solon. By that the franchise was apparently granted to all who measured up to the thetic census,[2] which was certainly lower than the hoplitic. This could be either a wholly new provision on the part of Solon or could be viewed as merely an extension of the provisions of Draco, if the alleged constitution of Draco is accepted. In view, however, of the other striking resemblances between the Draconian constitution and those of 411 B.C., it seems well to view the provision as an anachronism.[3]

The next section of the constitution deals with the officials, their qualifications, and the method of selection. All ὅπλα παρεχόμενοι are represented as electing the officials:[4] the archons and treasurers were required to possess property worth not less than 10 minas, and free from debt;[5] the lesser officials could be chosen from any of the enfranchised; and the generals and hipparchs from those who possessed unencumbered property worth not less than 100 minas and had legitimate children of more than ten years of age. In Solon's constitution,[6] after a detailed description of the methods of election introduced by Solon, Aristotle continues: "Such was Solon's legislation with respect to the nine archons; whereas

---

[1] Busolt-Swoboda, op. cit., 56.　　[2] Aristotle Ath. Pol. vii. 3.

[3] This view has been followed by various scholars, e.g., E. Meyer, Forschungen, I, 237 ff.; De Sanctis, op. cit., pp. 161 ff. Wilcken, Zur Drakontischen Verfassung, p. 85. Botsford, op. cit., p. 146, argues that in the time of Homer the agora was composed of the men who were liable to military service. The same was true in Athens. Hence Draco did nothing to widen citizenship.

[4] Cf. Keil, Die Solonische Verfassung, pp. 114 ff.

[5] Busolt-Swoboda, op. cit., p. 54, n. 1, assume that the archon could at the same time have much mortgaged property.

[6] Ath. Pol., viii.

in early times the Council of the Areopagus summoned suitable persons according to its own judgment and appointed them for the year to the several offices." This is perfectly consistent with the account of the pre-Draconian constitution described in chapter iii, where Aristotle says that the archons were elected on a basis of wealth and birth and that the Areopagus was made up of ex-archons. It is surprising that Aristotle takes no account of the intermediate method ascribed to Draco in chapter iv. Again, the property qualifications make this one of the most suspicious passages in the constitution. Although Kenyon retains this feature of the constitution, as he retains it all, he agrees that the qualifications for archons and treasurers is absurdly low. Headlam[1] says that at this time property was reckoned not in money but in corn. According to Plutarch,[2] a ζευγίτης had to possess land capable of producing 200 μέδιμνοι a year; and a μέδιμνος of corn was worth about a drachma at this time. The value of land of this extent can be estimated only roughly. Headlam puts it at not less than 2,000 drachmas—20 minas. According to the Draconian constitution, the possession of land worth 10 minas (1,000 drachmas) constituted eligibility to the archonship. This qualification, being lower than that of the ζευγίτης, would not have constituted eligibility for any office under Solon. Recognizing this fact, Thompson[3] argues that not δέκα, but ἑκατόν, should be read here. This would make the property qualification the same for the archons and generals. Those who accept the constitution are driven to some such argument as this, for it is not to be supposed that Draco lowered the property qualification for archons and that it was then raised very considerably by Solon, who restricted the archonship to the first class. It is of course true that there was some kind of property qualification long before the time of Draco. Aristotle says in chapter iii, "the archons were elected under *qualifications of wealth and birth*."

Another suspicious feature in this passage is the list of

[1] *Op. cit.*, p. 167.   [2] *Solon*, xviii.   [3] *Class. Rev.*, V, 223 f.

officials. Thucydides states that at the time of the affair of Cylon the chief power lay in the hands of the nine archons.[1] The polemarch had the chief command in war long after this time.[2] Yet, in the Draconian constitution the generals and hipparchs appear as far more important officials than the archons. Busolt regards this as evidence that the Draconian constitution is a document of the fifth century, when the archons were relatively unimportant.[3] Further, the naucraroi and the kolakretai, who played a great part in early Attic history, are not mentioned in the passage. It is significant that these officials were no longer in existence in 411 B.C.[4] In regard to the στρατηγοί in general, Headlam says as follows:

1. There is no other record of στρατηγοί at this time. In chapter vii, where a considerable list of officials is given, they are not mentioned.
2. The clause that they must have children is quite new.
3. If there were στρατηγοί they must have held an inferior position, and the high property qualification is unaccountable.[5]

The decisive argument against the passage is the failure of Solon to mention officials who are as important as they appear in the Draconian constitution. Furthermore, both generals and hipparchs are mentioned in the lists of officials in the proposed constitution of 411 and are very important. They were to serve without pay, which of course presupposes a property qualification.[6] The archons and the prytaneis during the period of the Peloponnesian War were the only

[1] 1. 126. 8. [3] *Op. cit.*, p. 57.

[2] *Ath. Pol.* xxii. 2. [4] Busolt-Swoboda, *op. cit.*

[5] It is interesting to note qualifications of a similar character at a later date. Cf. Deinarchus *Contra Dem.*, 71: τοὺς νόμους προλέγειν τῷ ῥήτορι καὶ τῷ στρατηγῷ . . . . παιδοποιεῖσθαι κατὰ τοὺς νόμους, γῆν ἐντὸς ὅρων κεκτῆσθαι, κ.τ.λ. It is quite possible that the development of the στρατηγία began soon after Draco's legislation (cf. *supra*, p. 84, n. 2), but the fact that they are not mentioned in Solon's constitution shows that they had as yet assumed little importance in his time.

[6] *Ath. Pol.* xxx. 2; cf. xxix. 5: τὰς δ' ἀρχὰς ἀμίσθους ἄρχειν ἁπάσας ἕως ἂν ὁ πόλεμος ᾖ, πλὴν τῶν ἐννέα ἀρχόντων καὶ τῶν πρυτανέων οἳ ἂν ὦσιν.

officials who were to receive pay. This implies that no high property qualification for these offices was required. The high qualification for generals and the low one for archons would be quite natural in fifth-century Athens.

These officials were to hold to bail the prytaneis, the generals, and the hipparchs of the preceding year until their accounts had been audited, taking securities.[1] In later times all regular officials at Athens were subject to an audit, and there is no reason to suppose that there would not be some check upon them long before Draco. This seems to be implied among the powers of the Areopagus in chapter iii.[2] But the mention of prytaneis in this passage is puzzling; it may be that the archons are meant, for it is quite possible that the archons were called prytaneis up to the time of Solon.[3] The correct interpretation, however, seems to be to identify them with the presidents of the council and assembly in later days and to view this passage as inspired by the oligarchic party of 411 B.C.[4] If Aristotle, writing in the fourth century, had meant others than the chairmen of the council, he would certainly have been more specific.[5]

The next section of the constitution deals with a council of 401. This is quite new. In chapter viii Aristotle says that Solon made a council of 400, 100 from each tribe. The verb ἐποίησε seems to imply that Aristotle thought that Solon instituted a new council. And he seems to be contrasting the new council of 400 with the Areopagus, which previously had existed by itself. No council of Draco is ever mentioned by other writers. In fact, Plutarch credits Solon with the in-

[1] Another interpretation (cf. Sandys, ad loc.) is that the new group of officials had to have security given on their behalf until the time of their audit. διεγγυᾶσθαι would then be passive.

[2] Keil, op. cit., pp. 114 ff., says that in the time of Draco the audit was in the hands of the Areopagus.

[3] Cf. Sandys, ad loc.

[4] In this connection it is interesting to note that the prytaneis appear along with archons in one of the constitutions of 411 B.C. (Ath. Pol. xxix. 5).

[5] Cf. Keil, op. cit., p. 96; Busolt-Swoboda, op. cit., p. 54, "die Vorsitzenden des Rates"; Fränkel, Rhein. Mus., XLVII (1892), 481; Schöffer, Jahresb. über Fortschritte d. kl. Altertumsw., LXXXIII (1895), No. 1, 197.

stitution of the council of 400.[1] Kenyon explains the seeming
inconsistency by asserting that Solon merely changed the
membership from 401 to 400. Botsford assumes that there
was a boulé in some form alongside the Areopagus before
Draco, and that Draco was not adding anything new in this
council of 401.[2] In the estimation of Wilamowitz, the odd
number of 401 is a sign of the genuineness of the document.[3]
Keil compares the odd number with other early odd numbers,
e.g., nine archons, fifty-one ephetae, the Eleven.[4] The odd
number, on the other hand, recalls also the courts of 201 and
501 under the democracy.[5] Furthermore, this passage is similar to a provision of one of the constitutions of 411 B.C.:
βουλεύειν μὲν τετρακοσίους κατὰ τὰ πάτρια, τετταράκοντα ἐξ ἑκάστης
φυλῆς, ἐκ προκρίτων οὓς ἂν ἕλωνται οἱ φυλέται τῶν ὑπὲρ τριάκοντα
ἔτη γεγονότων.[6] "There should be a Council of Four Hundred, as in the ancient constitution, forty from each tribe,
chosen out of candidates of more than thirty years of
age, elected by the members of the tribes." The system of
rotation of office is also found in 411 B.C.[7] Headlam insists
that it was the mark of a developed democracy and could
not have been true in the time of Draco. The mention of the
lot in connection with the council and minor offices is striking.
It is a debatable question whether in Solon's time the election
of officials was a combination of lot and election, as Aristotle
asserts.[8] But there is reason to suppose that the use of the
lot was much older than Solon.[9]

---

[1] Solon, xix.

[2] Botsford, op. cit., p. 146. In Botsford's opinion the two main points affecting
the constitution are the franchise and the council of 401. If Draco made no technical change in these two points, Aristotle could with truth say in the Politics that
Draco adapted his laws to an already existing constitution. Botsford does not
at all prove that the pre-Draconian constitution was practically like that given in
chapter iv.

[3] Aristoteles und Athen, I, 88, n. 25.   [6] Ath. Pol. xxxi. 1. Cf. xxx. 2.

[4] Op. cit., p. 96.   [7] xxxi. 3.

[5] Cf. Busolt-Swoboda, op. cit., p. 57.   [8] Ath. Pol., viii.

[9] Cf. Headlam, Election by Lot at Athens, p. 183. For the introduction of allotment into the selection of the archons, cf. Ferguson, "The Oligarchic Revolution at
Athens of the Year 103–2 B.C.," Klio, IV, 1 ff. Cf. also, S. B. Smith, "The Establishment of the Public Courts at Athens," TAPA., LVI, 113.

The fourth section introduces the subject of fines for non-attendance of council members at meetings of the council and assembly, and in this connection three of the property classes which have been believed to belong to Solon are mentioned. The fact that Aristotle describes the formation of these classes in such detail under Solon casts grave doubt on this passage, despite the fact that in the passage about Solon, Aristotle says: "He divided the population according to property into four classes, just as it had been divided before."[1] As far as the fine for non-attendance is concerned, the only other instance in Athenian history of a fine for non-attendance is to be found in the constitution of the Four Hundred.[2]

The final passage of the constitution deals with the Areopagus. The main differences between the description of the body here and in the pre-Draconian constitution in chapter iii are certain judicial features. These properly belong to Draco's code and have been discussed in that connection.[3]

From the foregoing account it is clear that, owing to the inconsistencies and anachronisms of chapter iv, the constitution contained therein cannot be a constitution which was established in the time of Draco. It appears, then, that as far as the constitution was concerned, Draco merely regulated existing institutions and did not create new ones. The Aristotelian authorship of the passages has been much debated. Certainly several other passages in the *Constitution of Athens* indicate that Aristotle ascribed a constitution to Draco. At the beginning of chapter iii, Aristotle makes the following statement: "The form of the ancient constitution *before Draco* was as follows. . . . ." If genuine, this sentence certainly presupposes a change in the time of Draco—whether

---

[1] vii. 3.   [2] xxx. 6.

[3] Cf. *supra*, p. 95. Scholars who consider the constitution an interpolation are divided on the question whether this final section about the Areopagus is an interpolation or part of the original. Headlam, *Class. Rev.*, V, 168, accepts the section and translates: "Draco published his code of law, but the Areopagus maintained its position and had to guard the (new) laws. And any person who had been maltreated could go to the Areopagus and show them which of the (new) laws had been broken." Busolt-Swoboda, *op. cit.*, p. 57, considers it part of the spurious constitution. Cf. Wilcken, *op. cit.*, p. 93.

that change be one in form or merely in the fact that the constitution was written down by Draco just as his laws were written. The second passage of interest in this connection is that part of chapter xli which enumerates the various changes which the Athenian constitution had undergone. Aristotle explains that the constitution which existed in his own day was the eleventh change in the Athenian constitution. He proceeds as follows:

πρώτη μὲν γὰρ ἐγένετο μετάστασις¹ τῶν ἐξ ἀρχῆς, Ἴωνος καὶ τῶν μετ' αὐτοῦ συνοικησάντων· τότε γὰρ πρῶτον εἰς τὰς τέτταρας συνενεμήθησαν φυλὰς καὶ τοὺς φυλοβασιλέας κατέστησαν. δευτέρα δὲ καὶ πρώτη μετὰ ταύτην, ἔχουσα πολιτείας τάξιν, ἡ ἐπὶ Θήσεως γενομένη, μικρὸν παρεγκλίνουσα τῆς βασιλικῆς. μετὰ δὲ ταύτην ἡ ἐπὶ Δράκοντος, ἐν ᾗ καὶ νόμους ἀνέγραψαν πρῶτον. τρίτη δ' ἡ μετὰ τὴν στάσιν ἡ ἐπὶ Σόλωνος, ἀφ' ἧς ἀρχὴ δημοκρατίας ἐγένετο. τετάρτη δ' ἡ, κ.τ.λ.

It is noteworthy that the constitution of Draco does not receive a number. One group of scholars[2] insists that the constitution of Ion was not reckoned in the enumeration because it was the original establishment and not a change. Hence the constitution of Theseus, which Aristotle describes as δευτέρα δὲ καὶ πρώτη μετὰ ταύτην (i.e., after that of Ion), is the first change and therefore the first in the enumeration. This allows the constitution of Draco to count as second, although it has no number; and then the constitution of Solon is really τρίτη ; that of Peisistratus, the fourth change; and so on. The other group, many of them accepting the reading κατάστασις, insists that the constitution in the time of Ion counts as the first, that of Theseus second, and that of Solon third. Therefore the bit about Draco without a number is an interpolation inserted to harmonize with the interpolation of chap. iv.[3] The emphasis in this passage upon Draco's work as a lawgiver as the chief characteristic of his constitution is certainly inconsistent with chapter iv.[4] But other like inconsistencies can be found within the *Constitution of Athens*. For example, there is certainly inconsistency between chapters

---

[1] Blass conjectures κατάστασις. The MS reading is: . . . . ατατασις.
[2] Cf. Kenyon, *ad loc.*   [3] Cf. Sandys, *ad loc.*
[4] Cf. Headlam, *Class. Rev.*, V, 167.

viii and xxii in regard to the election of archons before the time of Cleisthenes.[1]

The next passage in question occurs in the description of the Solonian reforms: "He divided the population according to property into four classes, *just as it had been divided before*, namely Pentacosiomedimni, Knights, Zeugitae and Thetes."[2] The Draconian constitution mentions this division, with the exception of thetes, in connection with fines for non-attendance in council and assembly. The italicized words may be viewed as an interpolation or as evidence of the authenticity of the Draconian constitution.[3]

Chapter v, immediately following the Draconian constitution, begins as follows: τοιαύτης δὲ τῆς τάξεως οὔσης ἐν τῇ πολιτείᾳ . . . . ("since such, then, was the organization of the constitution, and the many were in slavery to the few, the people rose against the upper class"). Sandys remarks that if chapter iv is an interpolation, then the use of τάξεως here becomes open to suspicion "unless we are content to regard the powers of the Areopagus and the right of bringing grievances before them as sufficient to constitute a τάξις, or constitutional order of things." Sandys is, of course, accepting the final part of chapter iv.[4] On the other hand, if chapter iv is considered an interpolation, it is not at all difficult to understand that the words refer back to the situation described in chapter iii.

It is plain that all of these passages can be explained both by those who accept the constitution as the work of Aristotle and by those who consider it an interpolation. In view, however, of all the passages discussed above, it seems more reasonable to suppose that Aristotle really ascribed a constitution to Draco and that he is himself responsible for chapter iv than to suppose that the passages are the work of a very

---

[1] viii. 1, and xxii. 5.   [2] vii.

[3] All of the three passages which have been discussed are bracketed in the Blass-Thalheim edition. Kenyon, on the other hand, accepts them all in his Oxford edition (1920) and in his annotated edition and translation. The latest Teubner edition (Blass-Thalheim-Oppermann) brackets nothing.

[4] *Ad loc.*

skilful interpolator. No interpolator after Aristotle would have been interested either in inserting a constitution in the treatise of Aristotle or in inserting the other passages to agree with it. Provided, then, it is the work of Aristotle, where did he get it? It has been shown above that suspicion can be thrown upon practically every line of the constitution and that it certainly cannot be a constitution framed by Draco. It has been shown further that practically every provision in it reflects the provisions of the constitutions of 411 B.C. The case seems, then, to be as follows: The document is an anachronism found by Aristotle in some pamphlet written by the party politicians of the time of the Four Hundred and purporting to give the provisions of the ancient constitution (πάτριος πολιτεία). Aristotle incorporated it in his treatise as the constitution of Draco. The passage about the Areopagus alone is true for the time of Draco.

CHAPTER V
THE JUDICIAL REFORMS OF SOLON

The judicial reforms of Solon, which secured a minimum of popular participation in the administration of justice and laid the foundation of democracy, are among the most important in Athenian history. And yet, in spite of the keen interest which Greek political thinkers and reformers always exhibited in the so-called πάτριος πολιτεία, surprisingly few details are found in the sources. Obviously the best source is the poetry of Solon. Aristotle and Plutarch had Solon's poems before them and quoted freely from them.

Solon was not without some experience in matters of law and justice before he was chosen as lawgiver. He represented Athens in the adjudication by Spartan arbitrators of the dispute between Athens and Megara regarding the ownership of Salamis. To prove his case, he cited a couplet from Homer,[1] and some Delphian oracles in which Apollo spoke of Ionian Salamis. He also brought forward archaeological evidence to show that the ancient graves on the island were Athenian, not Megarian: "The Megarians buried their dead facing the east, but the Athenians facing the west."[2] When the chronic quarrel between the Alcmaeonidae and the Cylonian factions was on the verge of involving the city in civil war, Solon persuaded the accused Alcmaeonidae[3] to submit to trial, thus showing his faith in the efficacy of the reign of law (εὐνομίη), which he praises in his poetry.

The responsibility for the civil strife in the city, which led to his own selection as διαλλακτής and archon, he ascribes

---

[1] *Iliad* ii. 557–58:

Αἴας δ' ἐκ Σαλαμῖνος ἄγεν δυοκαίδεκα νῆας,
στῆσε δ' ἄγων ἵν' Ἀθηναίων ἵσταντο φάλαγγες.

Plutarch *Solon*, x, says that Solon invented the lines.

[2] Plutarch, *op. cit.*, x, translated by Perrin.

[3] Plutarch, *op. cit.*, xii.

to the greed and arrogance of the wealthy.[1] They are led to seek their own advantage at the expense of their fellows. Lawlessness results. "They spare neither the treasures of the gods nor the property of the state, and steal like brigands, one from another. They pay no heed to the unshaken rock of holy justice."[2] Lawlessness[3] is the chief cause of the ills from which a city suffers. The practice of lending money on the security of the debtor's person was bad enough, but the "crooked decisions" of magistrates in administering the law intensified the evil. Debtors were sometimes unjustly adjudged to be slaves of their creditors.[4]

Under the reign of law, on the other hand, crooked judgments are made straight and arrogance is softened.[5] Solon drafted laws fair alike to rich and poor.[6] But laws are not

[1] Aristotle *Ath. Pol.* v. 2: ἰσχυρᾶς δὲ τῆς στάσεως οὔσης καὶ πολὺν χρόνον ἀντικαθημένων ἀλλήλοις εἵλοντο κοινῇ διαλλακτὴν καὶ ἄρχοντα Σόλωνα, κ.τ.λ. Cf. Plutarch, *op. cit.*, xiv; *Ath. Pol.* v. 3: καὶ ὅλως ἀεὶ τὴν αἰτίαν τῆς στάσεως ἀνάπτει τοῖς πλουσίοις· διὸ καὶ ἐν ἀρχῇ τῆς ἐλεγείας δεδοικέναι φησὶ 'τήν τε φιλαργυρίαν τήν θ' ὑπερηφανίαν,' ὡς διὰ ταῦτα τῆς ἔχθρας ἐνεστώσης.

[2] *Elegy* 2. 11 ff., translation by Linforth. The references to Solon are to the Teubner text of Hiller-Crusius.

πλουτοῦσιν δ' ἀδίκοις ἔργμασι πειθόμενοι

οὔθ' ἱερῶν κτεάνων οὔτε τι δημοσίων
φειδόμενοι κλέπτουσιν ἐφ' ἁρπαγῇ ἄλλοθεν ἄλλος,
οὐδὲ φυλάσσονται σεμνὰ θέμεθλα Δίκης.

[3] *Ibid.*, 31 f.:

ταῦτα διδάξαι θυμὸς Ἀθηναίους με κελεύει,
ὡς κακὰ πλεῖστα πόλει δυσνομίη παρέχει.

[4] Solon *Frag.* 32. 8 ff.:

πολλοὺς δ' Ἀθήνας πατρίδ' εἰς θεόκτιτον
ἀνήγαγον πραθέντας, ἄλλον ἐκδίκως,
ἄλλον δικαίως, τοὺς δ' ἀναγκαίης ὕπο
χρειοῦς φυγόντας.

[5] *Elegy* 2. 33 ff.:

εὐνομίη δ' εὔκοσμα καὶ ἄρτια πάντ' ἀποφαίνει,
καὶ θ' ἅμα τοῖς ἀδίκοισ' ἀμφιτίθησι πέδας.
τραχέα λειαίνει, παύει κόρον, ὕβριν ἀμαυροῖ,
αὑαίνει δ' ἄτης ἄνθεα φυόμενα,
εὐθύνει δὲ δίκας σκολιὰς ὑπερήφανά τ' ἔργα
πραΰνει, παύει δ' ἔργα διχοστασίης, κ.τ.λ.

[6] Solon *Frag.* 32. 18 ff.:

θεσμοὺς δ' ὁμοίως τῷ κακῷ τε κἀγαθῷ,
εὐθεῖαν εἰς ἕκαστον ἁρμόσας δίκην,
ἔγραψα.

enough; they must be impartially administered; else, as Anacharsis[1] said, "like spiders' webs they would catch the weak
and poor, but would easily be broken by the mighty and rich."
Hence, he "organized the people," giving them just enough
power to maintain their rights[2] and uphold the reign of law.
These hints regarding the judicial measures of Solon, drawn
from his own writings, will be found useful in interpreting
the more specific information contained in other sources.

Certain marked discrepancies between Aristotle's account
of the work of Solon in the *Constitution of Athens* and that
contained in the *Politics*[3] have been observed and variously
explained. But if one keeps in mind the different methods
of approach in the two works, he will find the discrepancies
explainable. Indeed, they are inevitable. In the *Constitution of Athens* Aristotle traces the growth of the constitution
step by step, but in the *Politics* he draws illustrations of his
political theories from Athenian constitutional practice with
but little regard to dates and origins.

In the *Constitution of Athens*, Aristotle's treatment of
Solon's judicial reforms is meager and disappointing. In a
single sentence he tells us that the lowest class, the thetes,
shared in the government only to the extent of participating
in the assembly (ἐκκλησία) and the law courts (δικαστήρια).[4]
There is not a word about the organization and functions of
either the ἐκκλησία or the δικαστήριον. It occasions some surprise to encounter, two chapters later, the statement that
the right of appeal to the δικαστήριον was one of three great
democratic features of the Solonian constitution.[5] One must

---

[1] Plutarch *Solon*, v.

[2] Solon *Frag.* 32. 1 f. (For the text given here, cf. Linforth, *Solon the Athenian*,
p. 136.)

> ἐγὼ δέ, τῶν μὲν οὕνεκα ξυνήγαγον
> δῆμον, τί τούτων πρὶν τυχεῖν ἐπαυσάμην;

Cf. *Frag.* 3. 1.

[3] Page 1273*b*, quoted *supra*, p. 88. Some have regarded the passage as spurious. The objections are not convincing. Cf. S. B. Smith, "The Establishment of
the Public Courts at Athens," *TAPA*, LVI, 107, n. 5.

[4] *Ath. Pol.* vii. 3: τοῖς δὲ τὸ θητικὸν τελοῦσιν ἐκκλησίας καὶ δικαστηρίων μετέδωκε
μόνον.

[5] *Ibid.*, ix 1.

THE ADMINISTRATION OF JUSTICE

go to Plutarch to learn definitely that only the decisions of the magistrates were subject to appeal. The careful reader, who recalled Aristotle's earlier statement, κύριοι δ' ἦσαν [the magistrates] καὶ τὰς δίκας αὐτοτελεῖς κρίνειν καὶ οὐχ ὥσπερ νῦν προανακρίνειν,[1] might reach this conclusion independently of Plutarch, but the ordinary reader would never guess it. He would not unnaturally conclude that all judicial decisions were subject to review by the δικαστήριον. This power of review is said to have been the starting-point for the eventual control of the constitution by the people. The masters of the law courts became masters of the government.[2] The lack of precision, too, in the laws of Solon is said to have contributed to the power of the courts. The vagueness of the laws resulted in disputes regarding their meaning. They needed authoritative interpretation. In commenting on the suggestion that Solon purposely made the laws obscure, Aristotle rather pointedly remarks that it "is not just to judge Solon's intentions from the actual results in the present day, but from the general tenor of the rest of his legislation."[3] Aristotle was well aware of the tendency of political writers to attribute to Solon all subsequent developments of the system which he founded.[4]

In the *Politics*, however, Aristotle is no longer concerned with the details of the process by which the people, through control of the judiciary, controlled the state. He is interested rather in the results as exemplified in the constitution of his own time. In this spirit it is not easy for a political theorist to avoid inaccuracies. There was a natural tendency to attribute to Solon features of the judicial system that did not belong to his time. He was, after all, the founder of the system, and might in a sense be held responsible for what in succeeding generations it became, though he could not by

[1] *Ibid.*, iii. 5.   [2] *Ibid.*, ix. 1.

[3] *Ibid.*, ix. 2, Kenyon's translation: οὐ γὰρ δίκαιον ἐκ τῶν νῦν γιγνομένων ἀλλ' ἐκ τῆς ἄλλης πολιτείας θεωρεῖν τὴν ἐκείνου βούλησιν.

[4] Cf. Isocrates *Areopagiticus*, 16: τὴν δημοκρατίαν . . . . ἣν Σόλων μὲν ὁ δημοτικώτατος γενόμενος ἐνομοθέτησε, Κλεισθένης δ' ὁ τοὺς τυράννους ἐκβαλὼν καὶ τὸν δῆμον καταγαγὼν πάλιν ἐξ ἀρχῆς κατέστησεν. Also *Antidosis*, 232; and Aeschines iii. 257: Σόλωνα μὲν τὸν καλλίστοις νόμοις κοσμήσαντα τὴν δημοκρατίαν.

any possibility have anticipated the development. Consequently, for example, the reader of the *Politics* should be cautious about accepting the statement that the audit (εὔθυνα) of magistrates was in the hands of the people in Solon's time. In view of what Aristotle says in the *Constitution of Athens*, supported by considerations based on Solon's own words, this cannot be literally true.[1] In Greek theory and practice the administration of justice was always a very important function of government. Aristotle believed that the minimum participation in government compatible with citizenship was the right to share in deliberative and judicial functions.[2] So Solon, when he emancipated the lower classes economically, gave them a share in the government by allowing all who could qualify for the lowest class to be members of the popular assembly (ἐκκλησία) and the law courts (δικαστήρια). Here Aristotle uses δικαστήρια in the plural, just as the orators use it, when the jurors were actually divided into panels. But in two other passages he uses the singular as if speaking of a single body.[3] Plutarch[4] also uses the singular. The use of the singular in this connection has been remarked.[5] But in view of the fact that in the *Politics* Aristotle uses both singular and plural of the Solonian court of appeal, the singular may have no particular significance in the Con-

[1] Cf. *infra*, p. 164. Cf. Newman's excellent discussion of *Pol.* 1273*b*. 35.

[2] Aristotle *Pol.* 1275 a. 22: πολίτης δ᾽ ἁπλῶς οὐδενὶ τῶν ἄλλων ὁρίζεται μᾶλλον ἢ τῷ μετέχειν κρίσεως καὶ ἀρχῆς.

[3] *Ath. Pol.* vii. 4, plural; ix. 2, singular twice. In the *Politics* (1273*b* and 1274*a*) the plural occurs twice and the singular once. S. B. Smith (*op. cit.*, pp. 106 ff.) has rightly protested against the view that Solon instituted a great popular tribunal consisting of a fixed number of jurymen chosen by lot from all citizens over thirty years of age who offered their services.

Grote, *op. cit.*, III, 128 ff., had argued vigorously against the view that Solon instituted the dicasteries. Upon the recovery of Aristotle's *Constitution of Athens*, it was hastily assumed that Grote's critics were justified in rejecting his theory entirely; and many scholars assumed that Solon was responsible for the main features of the democratic judicial system of the fourth century. Smith has done a good service in calling in question these extreme views. He points out that there was no need of numerous courts in the Athens of the early sixth century, nor were there enough urban inhabitants to man them.

[4] *Solon*, xviii.

[5] Gilbert, *Greek Constitutional Antiquities*, p. 139, n. 1.

stitution of Athens. And yet one would expect a court of appeal, particularly a popular court (*Volksgericht*), to be one, not several, bodies. The theoretical constitution of Hippodamus, described by Aristotle in the *Politics*,[1] and the *Laws* of Plato[2] provide for a single court of appeal. Solon could scarcely have anticipated a need for more than one court. And there is considerable evidence that the Solonian court of appeal was one body and that it was called ἡλιαία[3]. A client of Lysias[4] cites a law of Solon in which an obsolete word occurs, as follows: δεδέσθαι δ' ἐν τῇ ποδοκάκκῃ ἡμέρας πέντε τὸν πόδα, ἐὰν προστιμήσῃ ἡ ἡλιαία. Grote[5] questioned the genuineness of the law because Pollux had said that Solon used ἐπαίτια instead of προστιμήματα. But surely Lysias is as good an authority as Pollux. The law is now generally admitted to be genuine.[6] Manifestly ἡ ἡλιαία is the same body that Aristotle calls τὸ δικαστήριον.

This designation of the popular court largely supplanted ἡλιαία in the later period. But there are some interesting and significant survivals of the use of ἡλιαία and its derivatives. When Bdelycleon, in the *Wasps* of Aristophanes, opens court in the mock trial of the dog, imitating the herald, he proclaims:

εἴ τις θύρασιν ἡλιαστής, εἰσίτω.

The herald doubtless continued to use the old formula[7] long

---

[1] 1267b. 39: δικαστήριον ἐν τὸ κύριον, εἰς ὃ πάσας ἀνάγεσθαι δεῖν τὰς μὴ καλῶς κεκρίσθαι δοκούσας δίκας· τοῦτο δὲ κατεσκεύαζεν ἐκ τινῶν γερόντων αἱρετῶν.

[2] Page 767 C.

[3] Busolt-Swoboda (*Staatskunde*, 1151, n. 3) give a convenient list of the occurrences of the word ἡλιαία. Cf. Rogers' introduction to Aristophanes, *Wasps*, pp. xix ff.

[4] x. 16.   [5] *Op. cit.*, III, 128, n. 1.

[6] Busolt, *Geschichte*, II, 285; Busolt-Swoboda, *Staatskunde*, p. 1151, n. 3; Meyer, *op. cit.*, II, 659; Wilamowitz, *op. cit.*, p. 60, n. 1; *CAH*, IV, 56; S. B. Smith, *op. cit.*, p. 107, n. 6, rejects it mainly on the basis of the statement of Pollux and the general unreliability of the orators in matters of ancient history. But Lipsius, *op. cit.*, p. 440, n. 79, has disposed of the evidence of Pollux.

[7] *Wasps*, 890. Cf. use of old French *oyez, oyez*, in opening British and American courts.

after the jurors were regularly described as δικασταί. Religious conservatism preserved ἡλιαία in the curse pronounced at the opening of the assembly: εἴ τις ἐξαπατᾷ λέγων ἢ βουλὴν ἢ δῆμον ἢ τὴν ἡλιαίαν.

In quoting the curse, Demosthenes[1] is evidently reproducing the ancient formula used by the herald on these occasions, which would be quite familiar to his audience. A speaker would scarcely venture to vary the phraseology by substituting a modern for an ancient technical term. The conservatism of religion in matters of language is further illustrated in connection with the heliastic oath. The oath is regularly described as τῶν ἡλιαστῶν ὅρκος or ὁ ἡλιαστικὸς ὅρκος.[2] In the oath itself a derivative of ἡλιαία is found: οὐδὲ δῶρα δέξομαι τῆς ἡλιάσεως ἕνεκα.[3] Both ἡλιαία and its derivatives are found in Aristophanes.[4] This may be in part due to the conservatism of popular speech which comedy seeks to reproduce. But in most instances Aristophanes uses the words to impart an antique flavor. Thus, in an ancient comic oracle it is said that some day the Athenians will sit in court (ἡλιάσασθαι) at 5 obols per day.[5] When ἡλιαστής is used to designate a dicast, it is evidently intended to carry a suggestion of extreme old age, a favorite jibe of Aristoph-

[1] xxiii. 97.

[2] Hypereides Euxenippus, 40.

[3] Demosthenes xxiv. 149.

[4] *Knights*, 897 ff.:

> ἐπίτηδες οὗτος αὐτὸν ἔσπευδ' ἄξιον γενέσθαι.
> ἵν' ἐσθίοιτ' ὠνούμενοι, κἄπειτ' ἐν ἡλιαίᾳ
> βδέοντες ἀλλήλους ἀποκτείνειαν οἱ δικασταί.

The scholiast understands ἐν ἡλιαίᾳ as referring to a specific court. But it means simply "in court."

[5] *Knights*, 798:

> ἔστι γὰρ ἐν τοῖς λογίοισιν
> ὡς τοῦτον δεῖ ποτ' ἐν 'Αρκαδίᾳ πεντώβολον ἡλιάσασθαι,
> ἢν ἀναμείνῃ·

In the *Wasps* (772) Aristophanes uses ἡλιάσει for δικάσει, as the scholiast remarks, for the sake of making a pun.

> καὶ ταῦτα μέν νυν εὐλόγως, ἢν ἐξέχῃ
> εἵλη κατ' ὄρθρον, ἡλιάσει πρὸς ἥλιον.

anes.[1] The occurrence of ἡλιαία in laws cited in the speeches of Demosthenes, referring to courts other than those presided over by the thesmothetae, points to the use of the word in official documents.[2] The words ἡλιαία and ἡλιαστής are found in a few fifth-century inscriptions.[3]

When the system of appeal inaugurated by Solon was abandoned[4] and all cases were in the first instance tried by a popular court, a single tribunal no longer sufficed. Additional courts were created by drawing panels from the membership of the Heliaea. These sections were called dicasteries (δικαστήρια). But the name Heliaea survived as the designation of the court (δικαστήριον) presided over by the thesmothetae, which was often called ἡ ἡλιαία τῶν θεσμοθετῶν.[5] This practice was no doubt due to the fact that this court continued to assemble in the meeting place of the original body, which was called Heliaea.[6] The court of the thesmothetae tried some of the most important public cases. Several sections of 500 were not infrequently assembled for

---

[1] *Knights*, 255:

> ὦ γέροντες ἡλιασταί, φράτερες τριωβόλου,
> οὓς ἐγὼ βόσκω κεκραγὼς καὶ δίκαια κἄδικα.

Wasps, 195:

> ἀλλ' ἴσως, ὅταν φάγῃς
> ὑπογάστριον γέροντος ἡλιαστικοῦ.

Cf. *Lysistrata*, 381, where it is said to an old man, ἀλλ' οὐκ ἔθ' ἡλιάξει. Lipsius (*op. cit.*, p. 150) seems to think that the name ἡλιαστής continued in use because the most important of the courts was called ἡλιαία. No doubt various motives lie back of the use of the word.

[2] Lipsius, *op. cit.*, p. 169, n. 12.

[3] *CIA*, I, 37; 266, as restored by Koehler; IV (1) 27. Hicks and Hill, *Greek Historical Inscriptions*[2], No. 40, l. 75.

[4] Cf. *infra*, p. 195.

[5] Antiphon vi. 21: ἔλεξε μὲν γὰρ Φιλοκράτης οὑτοσὶ ἀναβὰς εἰς τὴν ἡλιαίαν τὴν τῶν θεσμοθετῶν.

CIA, IV (1) 27a. Hicks and Hill, *op. cit.*, No. 40, ll. 75–76: περὶ δὲ τούτων ἔφεσιν εἶναι Ἀθήναζε ἐς τὴν ἡλιαίαν τὴν τῶν θεσμοθετῶν κατὰ τὸ φσήφισμα τοῦ δήμου.

Cf. Andocides i. 28: ἔδοξεν οὖν τῷ δήμῳ ἐν τῷ τῶν θεσμοθετῶν δικαστηρίῳ, κ.τ.λ.

Hypereides *Euxenippus*, 6: παρανομά τις ἐν τῇ πόλει γράφει· θεσμοθετῶν συνέδριον ἔστι.

Caillemer, *Dictionnaire des antiquités*, *s.v.* "Heliaea."

[6] Demosthenes xlvii. 12: ἡ μὲν γὰρ δίαιτα ἐν τῇ ἡλιαίᾳ ἦν.

Lexica Segueriana: ἡλιαία καὶ ἡλιάζεσθαι· δικαστήριον ἀνδρῶν χιλίων καὶ ὁ τόπος ἐν ᾧ οὗτοι δικάζουσι.

particularly important cases. On one occasion 6,000 sat in the court of the thesmothetae.[1] These large numbers required commodious quarters. Harpocration and Photius define ἡλιαία as "the largest court in Athens, consisting of 1,000 or 1,500 dicasts, in which public cases (τὰ δημόσια τῶν πραγμάτων) were tried."[2] Evidently any court that consisted of two or more sections met in the Heliaea. A twofold division of the heliastic courts into "the lesser courts" and the Heliaea is found in the fourth century.[3]

Grote[4] believed that the "original and proper meaning of the word ἡλιαία is 'public assembly.'" The similarity to the Doric ἁλιαία cannot be accidental, whatever the nature of the relationship.[5]

Solon emancipated the lower classes. His problem was to give them power enough to enable them to defend their political and economic rights by constitutional means. The old Homeric agora survived through the kingship and the

---

[1] Andocides i. 17.

[2] Harpocration, s.v. ἡλιαία. Aristotle Ath. Pol., lxviii.

[3] Haupt, "Excerpte aus der Rede des Demades," Hermes, Vol. XIII, p. 494, excerpt 52: ἕκαστον τῶν ἀδικημάτων ἰδίας ἔχει τὰς οἰκονομίας· ἃ μὲν γάρ ἐστι δεόμενα τῆς Ἀρείου πάγου βουλῆς, ἃ δὲ τῶν ἐλαττόνων δικαστηρίων, ἃ δὲ τῆς ἡλιαίας.

[4] Grote, III, 128, n. 1. Cf. Rogers, Introduction to Wasps, pp. xix–xx. The ancients made some guesses as to the derivation. Scholiast (Knights, 255) connects it with the word for sun (ἥλιος), because the assembly met in the open air. Aristophanes, Wasps, 772, may have suggested this derivation by his pun ἡλιάσει πρὸς ἥλιον.

[5] The authors are indebted to their colleague, Professor C. D. Buck, for the following note on ἡλιαία:

The usual Doric word for public assembly is ἁλία as it is generally quoted, or ἁλία as the lack of ' in the early inscriptions indicates. Besides this, ἁλιαία is attested in inscriptions of Argos, Mycenae, and Arcadian Orchomenos. The initial vowel must be long, that is ἁλία, ἁλιαία, as in the related Ion. ἅλης, Att.-Ion. ἁλίζω, all derived from ἀ-ϝαλ- or ἁ-ϝαλ- (cf. Hom. ἀολλής, an Aeolic form with ολ = αλ), with the weak grade of the root ϝελ- (Hom. ἐελμένοι, 'close-packed,' etc.). The contraction of α(ϝ)α gives regularly not only Doric ᾱ, but also Attic-Ionic ᾱ, not η (cf. also ἀναλίσκω from ἀνα-ϝαλίσκω). Hence Attic ἡλιαία cannot be a native Attic form corresponding to Doric ἁλιαία. Yet to separate it from the latter, either wholly or in part (by means of a different analysis, so Solmsen, Untersuchungen, p. 288), is an act of violence. The most reasonable view appears to be that it is a loan word from Doric put into hyper-Attic form, that is, with substitution of η for ᾱ after the analogy of the familiar correspondence which holds good so commonly, and possibly in this case favored by a fancied relation to ἥλιος (which would also explain the ' of ἡλιαία, so far as this is to be accepted). Cf. also Boisacq, Dict. Étym., s.v.

aristocracy.[1] It was unorganized and informal compared with the elaborate ecclesia of a later age, but there were possibilities in it which Solon knew from his own experience. It was before an informal gathering of the people in the market that he recited his "Salamis" with an apology for coming before them with a poem instead of a speech.[2] The choice of Solon as political arbitrator must have been ratified by an assembly representing the views of the discontented masses. This rudimentary body, which was doubtless called the Heliaea, Solon renewed and reorganized.[3] The lowest class of citizens was admitted to membership, and a Senate of Four Hundred was put in charge of the meetings. "The senate," says Plutarch, "was to deliberate in advance of the assembly and was not to permit anything to come before the assembly without previous deliberation."[4] It may seem that Plutarch is simply attributing to the Senate of Four Hundred the functions of the later Senate of Five Hundred. No popular assembly, however, could function effectively without organization and guidance. Without a program and chairmen it would have been a mere mob, both inefficient and dangerous.[5]

[1] Meyer, op. cit., II, sec. 219. Cf. Gilbert, Beiträge, p. 446. De Sanctis (op. cit., p. 148) believes that at first the popular assembly had the right to confirm or reject a capital sentence imposed by the Areopagus. Gradually it lost this power.

[2] Plutarch Solon viii. 2. ἐλεγεῖα δὲ κρύφα συνθεὶς καὶ μελετήσας, ὥστε λέγειν ἀπὸ στόματος, ἐξεπήδησεν εἰς τὴν ἀγορὰν ἄφνω πιλίδιον περιθέμενος. ὄχλου δὲ πολλοῦ συνδραμόντος ἀναβὰς ἐπὶ τὸν τοῦ κήρυκος λίθον ἐν ᾠδῇ διεξῆλθε τὴν ἐλεγείαν ἧς ἐστιν ἀρχὴ

Αὐτὸς κῆρυξ ἦλθον ἀφ' ἱμερτῆς Σαλαμῖνος,
κόσμον ἐπέων ᾠδὴν ἀντ' ἀγορῆς θέμενος.

[3] Aristotle Ath. Pol. xii. 4:

ἐγὼ δὲ τῶν μὲν οὕνεκα ξυνήγαγον
δῆμον, τί τούτων πρὶν τυχεῖν ἐπαυσάμην;

Cf. Busolt-Swoboda, Staatskunde, p. 828.

[4] Plutarch Solon, xix. Busolt-Swoboda, op. cit., p. 846, accepts Plutarch's statement but believes that the archons, like the Homeric kings, presided at meetings.

[5] Solon (Aristotle Ath. Pol. xii. 2) himself explains what he believed to be the right way of dealing with the people, "neither leaving them too free, nor subjecting them to too much restraint."

δῆμος δ' ὧδ' ἂν ἄριστα σὺν ἡγεμόνεσσιν ἔποιτο,
μήτε λίαν ἀνεθεὶς μήτε βιαζόμενος.

Solon sought to establish a balanced system between the two factions.

To the common people I have given such a measure of privilege as sufficeth them, neither robbing them of the rights they had nor holding out the hope of greater ones; and I have taken equal thought for those who were possessed of power and who were looked up to because of their wealth, careful that they too should suffer no indignity.[1]

The Senate of Four Hundred, closely associated with the assembly, was an excellent device for maintaining the balance between the two parties. The archons were traditionally associated with the ancient aristocratic council, the Areopagus. The balance would have been disturbed had they been put in charge of the meetings of the assembly also.

To the popular assembly, representing as it did the prevailing public opinion of Athens, Solon allowed an appeal from magisterial decisions.[2] The experience and confidence of the upper classes were in a measure counterbalanced by the superior numbers of the lower classes. The assembly exercised both deliberative and judicial functions: in one capacity it was an assembly (ἐκκλησία); in the other, a court (δικαστήριον).[3] Neither Aristotle nor Plutarch has anything

---

[1] Aristotle (*Ath. Pol.* xii. 1) quotes Solon's own statement. In the *Politics* (1273*b*. 35 ff.) Aristotle contrasts the Areopagus and the magistrates, the oligarchic element in Solon's constitution, with the organized people exercising judicial functions.

[2] Aristotle *Ath. Pol.* ix. 1: ἡ εἰς τὸ δικαστήριον ἔφεσις. Steinwenter (*Streitbeendigung durch Urteil, Schiedsspruch und Vergleich nach griechischem Rechte* [München, 1925], p. 70), contrary to the accepted view, maintains that ἔφεσις does not mean "appeal" (*Appellation*) in the modern sense. Hommel ("Heliaia." *Philologus Supplementband*, XIX [1927], Heft II, 149) agrees. The arguments are not convincing. Wilamowitz, who formerly (1880) argued that there was no trace of appeal in Attic law (*Philologische Untersuchungen*, I, 89), modified his opinion in *Aristoteles und Athen* (1893), I, 59–60. While he believes that ἔφεσις εἰς τὸ δικαστήριον is "die Appellation von jedem magistratischen Urteilsspruch an das Volksgericht," he thinks it also includes a reference to a court by the magistrate himself of verdicts carrying penalties beyond his competence.

[3] "Perciò eliea in origine non fu verisimilmente che un altro nome della ecclesia (ἐκκλησία); e poi il significato dei due termini si differenziò, l'uno passando a significare in Atene l'assemblea populare in quanto vota leggi e decreti, l'altro l'assemblea in quanto giudica e di qui con facile passaggio, i tribunali populari."—De Sanctis, *op. cit.*, p. 255. Adcock (*CAH*, IV, 56) rejects the idea of an appeal like the Roman *provocatio* or the Macedonian right of appeal to the army, because the Heliaea might be concerned in very trifling cases (Lysias x 16). "We may then sup-

to say about the chairmanship of the Heliaea. Plutarch plainly implies that the ἔφεσις introduced by Solon was similar to the Roman *provocatio ad populum*. In comparing Solon with Publicola, he says, "Publicola gave the defendant the right of appeal to the people as Solon to the jurors."[1] If this be true, there would be but slight difference between the deliberative and the judicial functions of the people. Appeals could be introduced by the boulé. Members of the boulé would preside at judicial, just as at deliberative, sessions. When the ecclesia itself dispensed justice in the fifth century, the prytaneis, drawn from the boulé, presided as they did at the ordinary meetings. Busolt believes that each magistrate presided at the appeal from his own decision.[2] Some support for this view is found in the later practice, according to which magistrates presided at the hearing of cases within their respective jurisdictions. It appears, also, that when an appeal was taken against a fine inflicted summarily by a magistrate in the later period, he presided over the court that heard the appeal.[3] If this be true, the practice may well be a survival from a time when all magisterial judgments were subject to appeal.

But these are not conclusive arguments. An obvious objection is that it is not to be expected that a judge would participate in any way in a review of his own judgments. But it is urged that a presiding magistrate had practically no influence on the outcome of the case. This is not strictly true in the later period.[4] In the time of Solon it was less

---

pose that the magistrates judged cases regularly with the help of a meeting of citizens. Possibly the magistrates sat on market days and their courts were attended by such citizens as had leisure." For a different explanation of the Lysias passage, see *infra*, p. 179.

[1] Σόλωνος καὶ Ποπλικόλα σύγκρισις, ii. τοῖς φεύγουσι δίκην ἐπικαλεῖσθαι τὸν δῆμον ὥσπερ ὁ Σόλων τοὺς δικαστάς, ἔδωκε. It is true that the Roman *ius provocationis*, or the Macedonian right of appeal to the army involved only serious offenses (cf. *CAH*, IV, 56). But the point of the comparison is not in the kind of case that was open to appeal but in the character of the court of appeal, the assembled people. Cf. Grote, *op. cit.*, III, 130.

[2] Busolt-Swoboda, *Staatskunde*, p. 1151.

[3] Cf. *infra*, p. 279.   [4] Lipsius, *op. cit.*, p. 55.

likely to be true. The appeal to the Heliaea was intended to give the people an opportunity to protect themselves against "crooked decisions" of the magistrates. It may be urged that Solon would not have run the risk of impairing the new measure by allowing the magistrates to participate in any way in the proceedings. Even if their participation was not prejudicial to the interests of the litigants, it might tend to arouse suspicions of Solon's *bona fides*.

The decision of the question as to the chairmanship of the Heliaea depends largely upon the organization of that body. If the personnel was the same whether it was acting as a deliberative or a judicial body, there seems to be no reason why the boulé might not furnish the presiding officers at both types of meeting. Even the administering of an oath might be managed by these officials. On the other hand, the close relationship between the thesmothetae and the heliastic courts and the retention of the name Heliaea to designate the court presided over by the thesmothetae suggests that under the Solonian system they may have presided at judicial sessions of the Heliaea. This would involve an irregularity, for the thesmothetae would preside both over their own appeals and over those of other magistrates. Perhaps the better solution is to suppose that the thesmothetae organized the Heliaea and summoned it when necessary, leaving the chairmanship to the magistrates whose judgment was being appealed. This would account for the later relationship between the thesmothetae and the heliastic courts, as well as the chairmanship of the magistrates.

There is no evidence regarding the organization and membership of the Heliaea as a court. Current theories on the subject are inferences drawn from later practice. The distinguishing characteristics of a judicial, in comparison with a deliberative, body are the oath and the secret ballot ($\psi \hat{\eta} \phi o s$). There is no direct evidence that members of the Heliaea were sworn when they acted as judges. In later times the members of the local assemblies in the demes were sworn when they acted in a judicial or semijudicial capacity.[1] But the ecclesia

[1] Haussoullier, *La vie municipale en Attique*, p. 43.

tried cases without being sworn, though the voting was secret. However, the designation of the dicasts' oath as ὅρκος ἡλιαστικός or ὅρκος τῶν ἡλιαστῶν points to an early use of the oath in the history of the Heliaea. It cannot be later than the organization of the δικαστήρια in the time of Cleisthenes, and may be as early as Solon. The later practice of administering the oath to the dicasts in a body doubtless goes back to the time of Solon when the heliasts functioned as a body.

There is no mention of an age qualification in connection with the reforms of Solon;[1] nor is there any likelihood that there was one. In fact, according to Aristotle, it was urged by the critics of democracy that men of small means and any age were permitted to participate in the administration of justice.[2] A statement in Aristotle's *Politics*[3] is cited in support of the view that membership in the Heliaea was determined by lot. Here it is to be observed that Aristotle is quoting the opinion of critics of Solon who are interested in attributing to him all the objectionable features of democracy. It is by no means clear for what purpose the lot would be used in the opinion of these critics of Solon. Was it used to restrict the membership or to secure an adequate attendance by drafting for service those upon whom the lot fell? From the point of view of Solon, there was nothing to be gained by conferring upon the masses the minimum of political privilege and then restricting by lot or by an age qualification the number of those entitled to participate. Apparently the necessity for these restrictions came later in the history of democracy. In the beginning, numbers were desirable; they would help to create a feeling of confidence

---

[1] In the constitution attributed to Draco by Aristotle (cf. *supra*, p. 137) the members of the βουλή were required to be thirty years or over. In view of an age qualification of thirty for the Senate of Five Hundred under Cleisthenes, one might expect a similar qualification for the Solonian Senate, but there is no mention of it in the sources. Busolt-Swoboda (*Staatskunde*, pp. 850 and 1150 ff.) believe there was an age qualification, as does Wilamowitz (*Aristoteles und Athen*, II, 63).

[2] *Pol.* 1282a, 31: καὶ δικάζουσιν ἀπὸ μικρῶν τιμημάτων καὶ τῆς τυχούσης ἡλικίας.

[3] *Ibid.*, 1274a. 5. κύριον ποιήσαντα τὸ δικαστήριον πάντων, κληρωτὸν ὄν. Busolt-Swoboda (*op. cit.*, p. 850) reach no conclusion.

among the masses and tend to inspire respect in the minds of their opponents. The earliest reference to a fixed number of jurors—6,000—is found in Aristophanes.[1] The number goes back to the institution of ostracism by Cleisthenes, but beyond that there is no trace of a numerical requirement. No explanation of how the number 6,000 was selected is forthcoming. It is unlikely that there is any connection with the number in the Solonian Heliaea.

The social and economic conditions of Athens in the early sixth century make it seem very unlikely, if not impossible, that there should have been 6,000 men beyond thirty years of age available for regular service in a popular judicial assembly.[2] Every consideration seems to be against the assumption that there was any limitation upon attendance at the judicial sessions of the Heliaea either by an age qualification or by a maximum number.

The Areopagus continued to participate in the administration of justice in the Solonian constitution as before.[3] Aristotle's description of its powers is practically a repetition of what he says regarding the pre-Solonian Areopagus.[4] It continued to be guardian of the law and overseer of the constitution. In the exercise of these functions it had full authority to fine and otherwise to punish offenders. It still acted as *censor morum* just as before. The arbitrary manner in which it exacted fines and paid them into the treasury without specifying the offense strongly suggests the exercise of censorial powers[5] as well as the functions of a regular crimi-

[1] *Wasps*, 662. Cf. *infra*, p. 194, for a discussion of the significance of the number 6000.

[2] S. B. Smith, *op. cit.*, pp. 107 ff.

[3] It is a matter of surprise that no mention of the homicide jurisdiction of the Areopagus under Solon is found in the sources for this period. This jurisdiction is implied in the amnesty law discussed by Plutarch (*Solon*, xix), but such an ancient prerogative would seem to deserve more than a passing notice. Cf. Lipsius, *op. cit.*, p. 13.

[4] διατηρεῖν τοὺς νόμους (Aristotle *Ath. Pol.* iii. 6) = νομοφυλακεῖν (viii. 4). κολάζουσα καὶ ζημιοῦσα πάντας τοὺς ἀκοσμοῦντας = τοὺς ἁμαρτάνοντας ηὔθυνεν. κυρία οὖσα = κυρίως.

[5] Cf. Lipsius, *op. cit.*, p. 13.

nal court. Opinion is divided as to whether the Heliaea or
the Areopagus audited the accounts of outgoing magistrates.[1]
In two passages in the *Politics*,[2] Aristotle says very definitely
that Solon gave to the people (τῷ δήμῳ) the right to call magistrates to account: τὸ τὰς ἀρχὰς εὐθύνειν. He is evidently
using the words εὐθύνειν and εὔθυνα in the technical sense.
In the *Constitution of Athens* he says that the Areopagus
had the right εὐθύνειν τοὺς ἁμαρτάνοντας.[3] It is doubtful
whether Aristotle is using εὐθύνειν in its technical sense as it
is used in the preceding chapter in the spurious constitution
of Draco.[4] The words τοὺς ἁμαρτάνοντας do not suggest magistrates presenting themselves for examination before an
auditing body, but rather wrongdoers.[5] Εὐθύνειν, then, would
be used as Solon himself uses it in the sense of "correct" or
"punish."[6] But even if εὐθύνειν is not used in a technical
sense, there is no reason for denying the competence of the
Areopagus as an auditing body. It is not to be supposed
that Solon devised anything like the elaborate εὔθυνα of the
fourth century. The powers of the Areopagus are quite
broad enough to include an adequate supervision over the
official conduct of the magistrates, so that a final audit would
seem unnecessary. ὥσπερ ὑπῆρχεν καὶ πρότερον ἐπίσκοπος οὖσα
τῆς πολιτείας, καὶ τά τε ἄλλα τὰ πλεῖστα καὶ τὰ μέγιστα τῶν
πολιτικῶν διετήρει καὶ τοὺς ἁμαρτάνοντας ηὔθυνεν κυρία οὖσα καὶ
ζημιοῦν καὶ κολάζειν.[7] On the other hand, the Heliaea possessed, in the ἔφεσις, a power to force the magistrates to
administer the law impartially. This power, it is true, was
exercised only occasionally and upon the initiative of some

---

[1] Busolt-Swoboda (*Staatskunde*, 847) think the audit was handled by the
Volksversammlung, and not by the *Volksgericht*, as Aristotle intimates in the *Politics*
1274a. 15. Wilamowitz (*op. cit.*, I, 49 and 70) assigns elections and the right to
suspend magistrates (ἐπιχειροτονία) to the *Volksversammlung*. But audits (εὔθυναι)
came before a *Volksgericht*. Wilamowitz depicts an organization much too elaborate
for Solon's time. Besides, according to Aristotle, the judicial functions of the Heliaea
were confined to appeals from the judgments of magistrates. There is no reason to
doubt Aristotle's statement. Bruno Keil (*Die Solonische Verfassung*, 118 ff. and
152) thinks the Areopagus handled the audits. So also does Meyer (*op. cit.*, II, 658).

[2] Pages 1274a and 1281b.   [3] viii. 4.   [4] iv. 2.

[5] Busolt-Swoboda, *op. cit.*, p. 848, n. 1. Cf. Wilamowitz, *op. cit.*, I, 49, n. 14.

[6] *Elegy* 2. 37.   [7] Aristotle *Ath. Pol.* viii. 4.

aggrieved litigant; but, as has been observed,[1] the ἔφεσις is the germ from which the εὔθυνα of the later period grew. One is forced to the conclusion that the responsibility of magistrates to the community was enforced by both the Areopagus and the Heliaea. This division of authority between the two bodies that represented the two political elements in the state is quite in accordance with Solon's general policy to preserve a balance in the constitution and to permit neither party to triumph and get complete control of the government.[2] The same principle is followed in the matter of appeals. Only the magistrates' judgments were subject to appeal; the judgments of the Areopagus and the Ephetae continued to be final.

Regarding the technical aspect of the εὔθυνα, the auditing of accounts, the Areopagus would seem to be the only body in the state that could perform this service effectively.[3] Accounts cannot be audited by a public assembly. The boulé might conceivably check up the expenditures of the magistrates and present the matter to the assembly for formal action to give effect to their recommendations. But as the boulé itself expended money, its own accounts must be audited. The Areopagus could do this by virtue of its power to "keep watch over the most important matters in the state" (τά τε ἄλλα τὰ πλεῖστα καὶ τὰ μέγιστα τῶν πολιτικῶν διετήρει).[4] For the moment the Areopagus may have seemed to be much the more important factor in enforcing the magistrates' real responsibility; but it so happened that, owing to the accidents of the situation, the constitution developed along democratic lines and the people gained control of the whole administration of justice, including the εὔθυνα. And so in the *Politics*,[5] where Aristotle is not so much concerned with the process as

---

[1] Gilliard, *Quelques reforms de Solon*, p. 288.

[2] Solon *Frag.* 3. (Aristotle *Ath. Pol.* xii. 1.)
                    νικᾶν δ' οὐκ εἴασ' οὐδετέρους ἀδίκως.

[3] Cf. Wilamowitz, *op. cit.*, I, 49.   [4] Aristotle *Ath. Pol.* viii. 4.

[5] 1274a. 11 ff.: τῆς ναυαρχίας γὰρ ἐν τοῖς Μηδικοῖς ὁ δῆμος αἴτιος γενόμενος ἐφρονηματίσθη, καὶ δημαγωγοὺς ἔλαβε φαύλους ἀντιπολιτευομένων τῶν ἐπιεικῶν, ἐπεὶ Σόλων γε ἔοικε τὴν ἀναγκαιοτάτην ἀποδιδόναι τῷ δήμῳ δύναμιν, τὸ τὰς ἀρχὰς αἱρεῖσθαι καὶ εὐθύνειν· μηδὲ γὰρ τούτου κύριος ὢν ὁ δῆμος δοῦλος ἂν εἴη καὶ πολέμιος.

the result, he does not scruple to say that the people in
Solon's time conducted the audits, because the audit (εὔθυνα)
grew out of the appeal (ἔφεσις) to the Heliaea, not out of the
guardianship and supervision of the Areopagus.

The debt of Solon, as a law reformer, to his predecessors
in the field has not been adequately recognized either by
ancient historians and political theorists or by modern scholars. It seems to be felt that any such recognition detracts
from Solon's greatness. But changes in human institutions
are due to evolution quite as much as to inspiration. Solon's
code was no exception. It did not spring from his brain like
full-panoplied Athena from the brain of Zeus. An important
part of it was a re-enactment of a section of Draco's code—
the homicide laws. His Heliaea was a rehabilitation and reorganization of the Homeric agora. Solon's great merit lies
in the fact that he adapted current practices and ancient
institutions to his needs. His chief concern was to protect
the people in their new economic and political freedom. The
means he found to carry out his purpose were the right of
appeal to an assembly of all citizens and freedom of prosecution. Precedents for both were at hand. Appeals were not
explicitly recognized as such in the earlier constitution; but
the guardianship of the laws vested in the Areopagus and its
right to take cognizance of the failure of the magistrates to
observe the laws must in some instances have involved a
reversal of a magisterial verdict by the Areopagus.[1] If Aristotle's statement regarding the Areopagus in the Draconian
system be accepted as a part of his code, dealing, as it does,
with the judiciary rather than with constitutional matters,
the way was opened for an appeal by anyone who had been
wronged by a magistrate, either in his judicial or in his administrative capacity, provided the act complained of was
contrary to law. And most "crooked decisions" are contrary
to some law. Solon simply made the right of appeal explicit
and extended it from the Areopagus to the assembly in pursuance of his policy of "giving the people such a measure of
privilege as sufficed them." In the Heroic Age the commu-

[1] Cf. *supra*, p. 95.

nity, assembled in the agora, dealt effectively with individuals whose wrongful acts endangered the common safety. Such action was instinctive and spontaneous. There was no theory that certain types of wrongdoing are a menace to the community. But the germ of the idea was there. It is immaterial who had the right to summon a public meeting in such cases.

νῦν δὲ τίς ὧδ' ἤγειρε ; τίνα χρειὼ τόσον ἵκει
ἠὲ νέων ἀνδρῶν, ἢ οἳ προγενέστεροί εἰσιν;[1]

The most vigorous and forceful individual who knew the facts (ὁ βουλόμενος) would naturally be the prosecutor in these informal proceedings.

Under the aristocracy that succeeded the heroic kingship, the Council of Elders—in Athens, the Areopagus—represented the ruling class. It acted both in behalf of individuals and in behalf of the community when it fined and punished πάντας τοὺς ἀκοσμοῦντας. The virtual prosecutor of an offender before the Areopagus would be any member of the body who became aware of the wrongdoing. At first, an individual who might suffer by a wrongful act could not himself prosecute the offender; he could achieve his purpose only by bringing the matter to the attention of a member of the Areopagus. It was not until the reforms of Draco that he was guaranteed the right to appear before the Areopagus and prosecute the magistrate who wronged him.[2]

At first there was no interference by the community in cases of homicide. It was not until the notion that the shedding of blood involved pollution that the state stepped in and protected its members by ascertaining who was guilty and by insisting upon purification or punishment. But trials for homicide still continued to be classed as private suits; only the relatives could prosecute. But once the murderer went into banishment, either voluntarily or as the result of the sentence of a court, any citizen (ὁ βουλόμενος) could take action if he returned from exile unlawfully. The homicide had thus become a menace to the community. The state acted through the agency of the man who haled the exile

[1] Homer *Odyssey* ii. 28-29.   [2] Aristotle, *Ath. Pol.* iv. 4.

before a magistrate and secured his conviction for being unlawfully upon Attic soil. The exclusive rights of the relatives of the victim to prosecute lapsed. The exile was not tried as a murderer. He was guilty of a new offense against the community. But if, instead of haling the exile before the authorities, the citizen who recognized him extorted blackmail by threats or torture, quite a different situation arose. The exile, being polluted, could not go into court and collect the damages provided by law. If this provision of the Draconian code was to be enforced, obviously it must be done by ὁ βουλόμενος. Here are exact precedents for the ἐξεῖναι τῷ βουλομένῳ of Solon.[1] These cases are on all fours with a type of case which Solon must have contemplated with some concern. How could the law against selling children or debtors into slavery be enforced? The adult victims, in whom alone, under the traditional practice, the right of action was vested, being deprived of their liberty, were unable to secure redress. The parents of the children sold into slavery for debt, being parties to the wrong, would naturally refuse to appear in court as the legal representatives (κύριοι) of the wronged children. Similarly the enslaved debtor, being deprived of his liberty, was unable to institute legal proceedings to regain his freedom. The natural solution was to follow the code of Draco and permit the intervention of a third party when the victim of a wrong was unable to take action in his own behalf. Solon was thoroughly familiar with the Draconian code, as is shown by his re-enactment of the homicide laws as part of his own code. Both Aristotle[2] and Plutarch[3] have stated the prescription of Solon permitting freedom of prosecution in a way that seems to limit its application to cases where some individual was injured. But there are laws attributed to Solon dealing with matters that affect the community without touching any particular individual. Men plotting the overthrow of the government

---

[1] Cf. *supra*, pp. 120 ff.

[2] *Ath. Pol.* ix. 1: ἔπειτα τὸ ἐξεῖναι τῷ βουλομένῳ τιμωρεῖν ὑπὲρ τῶν ἀδικουμένων.

[3] *Solon*, xviii: καὶ γὰρ πληγέντος ἑτέρου καὶ βιασθέντος ἢ βλαβέντος ἐξῆν τῷ δυναμένῳ καὶ βουλομένῳ γράφεσθαι τὸν ἀδικοῦντα καὶ διώκειν.

wronged no particular individual. Their offense affected the entire community. Sumptuary laws also were aimed at practices that harmed the community only remotely and the individual citizen not at all.[1] Without the volunteer prosecutor these and similar laws could not have been enforced.

Solon took steps to protect the constitution by making more explicit the traditional jurisdiction of the Areopagus over those accused of high treason in the broadest sense of the words. He specifically empowered the Areopagus to try those accused of plotting to overthrow the constitution.[2] This provision is called νόμος εἰσαγγελίας. No one is injured more than another by the subversion of a constitution; the community itself is injured. Consequently the only available accuser is the volunteer representative of the community, ὁ βουλόμενος. Just as the right of appeal and freedom of prosecution afforded protection to the individual who was wronged, so the νόμος εἰσαγγελίας secured the same benefits to the state by granting freedom of prosecution when its security was threatened by plots and violence.

In a new constitution, which was not wholly acceptable to the classes from which the higher magistrates were drawn, it was desirable to take precautions to prevent them from destroying the new system by refusing to give effect to the laws. Solon attempted to deal with this danger by requiring the archons to take an oath not to transgress the laws, on pain of offering a golden statue.[3] If any serious attempt was made to enforce such an oath, or rather to punish its transgression, the Areopagus alone was capable of doing it. It could act either on its own initiative or on complaint of any aggrieved citizen who claimed that the archon's failure to observe a particular law had injured him.

It is clear that Solon believed that the community might

[1] *Ibid.*, xxi. 4-5.

[2] *Ath. Pol.* viii. 4: καὶ τοὺς ἐπὶ καταλύσει τοῦ δήμου συνισταμένους ἔκρινεν, Σόλωνος θέντος νόμον εἰσαγγελίας περὶ αὐτῶν.

[3] Aristotle, *op. cit.*, vii. Regarding the statue, cf. Sandys' note. The oath in Aristotle's day referred to bribes as well as to transgressions of the law: ὀμνύουσιν δικαίως ἄρξειν καὶ κατὰ τοὺς νόμους, καὶ δῶρα μὴ λήψεσθαι τῆς ἀρχῆς ἕνεκα, κἄν τι λάβωσι ἀνδριάντα ἀναθήσειν χρυσοῦν (*ibid.* lv. 5.)

be injured in the person of one of its members. Aristotle[1] quotes him as saying, "I brought the people together" (συνήγαγον δῆμον). The word συνάγω means more than to assemble the people; it means rather that he organized the people into a political body with definite functions. An inevitable and, from Solon's viewpoint a desirable, result of such a rehabilitation of the old popular assembly would be the creation of a feeling of solidarity and mutual interdependence in the minds of the masses. The freedom of prosecution afforded a means of expressing and encouraging this feeling. Solon's conception of the rôle of ὁ βουλόμενος appears in a saying of his reported by Plutarch: "For the greater security of the weak commons Solon gave a general liberty of indicting for an act of injury, ... intending by this to accustom the citizens like members of the same body to resent and be sensible of one another's injuries."[2] He quotes as his authority, not Solon's poetry, but his reply to one who asked him what kind of city was best. "That city is best," said Solon, "in which those who are not wronged are as zealous in prosecuting and punishing wrongdoers as those who are wronged." The simile of the body shows clearly that Solon was acting on the conviction that injuries inflicted upon individuals might be harmful to the community.[3] The status of ὁ βουλόμενος under Solon's law is that of a volunteer public prosecutor administering criminal law. Solon's great service was not the introduction of a new device for administering justice, but the formulation and application of a new principle, viz., that certain classes of offenses against individuals, which had hitherto been left to the victim to redress, were dangerous to the community and should be punished by someone acting for the community.

The use of γραφή to designate a public, as distinguished from a private, suit (δίκη) points to an earlier, or at least a different, employment of writing in connection with public suits. The practice of recording judgments and verdicts was

---

[1] *Ath. Pol.* xii. 4.   [2] *Solon*, xviii, Clough's translation.

[3] Compare the fable told by Menenius Agrippa to the seceding Roman plebs (Livy ii. 32. 7).

introduced by the thesmothetae.[1] The amnesty law of Solon
shows that in certain cases records of judicial decisions were
kept. They included both private and public cases, viz.,
homicide and tyranny. Under the Solonian system of appeals it would seem necessary to have a record of all decisions,
whether in public or in private suits. A court of appeal could
not function satisfactorily without such records. In the matter of recording judgments, then, no distinction between public and private suits can be drawn on the basis of the use of
writing. A fundamental distinction between private and
public suits is the appearance of a third party (ὁ βουλόμενος)
in the latter. It is possible that this factor led to the requirement of a written notation of public suits by the magistrates
at their inception. The judgment in a civil suit involving
only the two parties concerned as plaintiff and defendant
might contain a sufficient record of all the pertinent facts;
whereas in public suits, particularly in case of appeal, it
might be highly desirable, if not necessary, to record the
name of the prosecutor when the suit was instituted. Such a
preliminary notation by the magistrate might very well have
served to attach the name γραφή to a public suit.[2]

Aristotle[3] reports the Solonian prescription allowing freedom of prosecution in very general terms: τιμωρεῖν ὑπὲρ τῶν
ἀδικουμένων. The words suggest acts of violence and punishment. Plutarch's[4] examples of the wrongs Solon had in mind
are far from enlightening. They all involve violence: καὶ
γὰρ πληγέντος ἑτέρου καὶ βιασθέντος ἢ βλαβέντος ἐξῆν τῷ δυναμένῳ
καὶ βουλομένῳ γράφεσθαι τὸν ἀδικοῦντα καὶ διώκειν, ὀρθῶς ἐθί-
ζοντος τοῦ νομοθέτου τοὺς πολίτας ὥσπερ ἑνὸς μέρους συναισθά-
νεσθαι καὶ συναλγεῖν ἀλλήλοις. It is doubtful if Plutarch
had in mind specific forms of action[5] such as δίκη αἰκείας,
δίκη βιαίων, and δίκη βλάβης, and perhaps a criminal action

[1] Cf. supra, p. 85.

[2] Cf. Calhoun, Criminal Law, pp. 104 ff. Aristotle (Ath. Pol. viii. 4) assumes
the use of writing in recording judgments when he says that the Areopagus inflicted
fines and paid them into the treasury without recording the charge (οὐκ ἐπιγράφουσα
τὴν πρόφασιν).

[3] Ath. Pol. ix. 1.   [4] Solon xviii. 5.   [5] Calhoun, op. cit., pp. 73 ff.

for assault, γραφὴ ὕβρεως. Plutarch[1] cites a law of Solon providing a fine of 100 drachmas for the rape of a free woman: ἐὰν δ' ἁρπάσῃ τις ἐλευθέραν γυναῖκα καὶ βιάσηται, ζημίαν ἑκατὸν δραχμὰς ἔταξεν. The word βιάσηται suggests a δίκη βιαίων[2] which was used in cases of indecent assault upon either men or women or forcible seizure of a slave. For injuries to the person, redress was sought by means of a δίκη αἰκείας,[3] the ordinary action for assault. For damages to property, a δίκη βλάβης[4] was available. The word πληγέντος suggests bodily injury, and βλαβέντος may very well refer to damages to property. These are all civil (private) suits. The criminal action for assault was γραφὴ ὕβρεως. But this was available only in cases of "aggravated assault." There must be proof of maliciousness and intent to bring shame and disgrace upon the victim.[5] Whatever may have been the form of Solon's prescription, the words τῷ βουλομένῳ must have appeared. This is obvious from the popular use of the words. Aristophanes in the Plutus[6] represents a sycophant as seeking to put his occupation on a high plane by describing himself as ὁ βουλόμενος, an essential agent in the administration of law. And the orator Hypereides,[7] in making a plea for the right of advocates to appear on behalf of fellow-citizens, likens the service to that performed by Solon's ὁ βουλόμενος. One would expect such a well-known prescription to appear in the code in a form that would challenge attention, such as a separate law listing the offenses or giving a definition of the type of offense in which ὁ βουλόμενος could act. But, as has been pointed out,[8] this would amount to giving a definition of "crime," a rather unlikely venture in the seventh century. The only alternative is a general prosecution clause in every law providing punishment for acts of commission or omission.

---

[1] Solon, xxiii. Cf. Sondhaus, De Solonis legibus, p. 47.

[2] Lipsius, op. cit., pp. 637 ff.

[3] Ibid., pp. 643 ff.   [4] Ibid., pp. 652 ff.

[5] Aristotle Rhetoric i. 13. 10; cf. Kennedy, Demosthenes' Orations, III, 73; Lipsius, op. cit., p. 425.

[6] 918.   [7] Eux. 11. 8.   [8] Calhoun, op. cit., p. 75.

In Anglo-American law criminal proceedings are no bar to a civil suit in the same matter. In Athens a choice was allowed an injured party between a civil and a criminal remedy in some cases. Familiar examples are theft and assault. But the plaintiff could not avail himself of both remedies. Under the later practice the volunteer prosecutor must choose the γραφή. And in the time of Solon, even if the public suit was not specifically designated γραφή, the situation could not have been materially different. Action by a volunteer would serve to extinguish the victim's right of action. In the Meidias case, Demosthenes had a choice between a civil suit (δίκη αἰκείας) and a criminal action (γραφὴ ὕβρεως). He chose the latter and acted in behalf of the community just as any volunteer prosecutor might have done. In some few cases the intervention of the volunteer accuser involved the loss of the right of the victim to collect damages. But as Demosthenes[1] observes, "the lawgiver considered that the aggressor injured the state as well as the insulted party, and that the punishment was a sufficient compensation to the sufferer."

Solon was responsible for an important innovation in the official use of oaths in litigation. When neither parole nor documentary evidence was available, the magistrate was empowered to administer oaths to both parties. δοξασταί· κριταί εἰσιν οἱ διαγιγνώσκοντες πότερος εὐορκεῖ τῶν κρινομένων. κελεύει γὰρ Σόλων τὸν ἐγκαλούμενον, ἐπειδὰν μήτε συμβόλαια ἔχῃ μήτε μάρτυρας, ὀμνύναι, καὶ τὸν εὐθύνοντα δὲ ὁμοίως.[2] This law has given rise to much discussion. The word κελεύει in the version given by the lexicographer seems to indicate that *both* parties *must* take the oath. And a similar impression is conveyed by the general tenor of the definition. On the assumption that both parties were sworn, Rohde[3] advanced the theory that the oaths were not juristic but religious. The intention of the lawgiver was to insure divine punishment for those who escaped human punishment. An obvious objection to this view is that it does not explain

---

[1] xxi. 45, Kennedy's translation.

[2] *Lexica Segueriana*, Bekker, *Anecdota Graeca*, I, 242.

[3] *Psyche*, I, 268, n. 2.

why the oaths were restricted to cases in which there was no evidence.[1] Hirzel[2] advances his theory on the basic contention that in the absence of evidence the parties are the only source of information. Being naturally prejudiced witnesses, they were sworn so that they might have impressed upon them the necessity of being careful to tell the truth in answer to the magistrate's questions. An objection to this view is that it emphasizes too much the rôle of parties as witnesses. In later practice a party was not permitted to give testimony in his own behalf. Two types of party oath were in use before the legislation of Solon—the solemn oaths sworn by both parties in homicide trials[3] and the ancient evidentiary oath.[4] The latter was originally voluntary and extra-judicial. It was an exculpatory oath offered by, or tendered to, an accused person. Eventually someone conceived the idea of allowing the plaintiff the opportunity of taking an evidentiary oath also. Plato ascribes this change to the mythical Rhadamanthus. Observing that the men of his day manifestly believed in the gods, he conceived the idea of making the gods rather than men the judges of cases in the following manner: "Tendering an oath to the litigants regarding the matters at issue in each case he secured a speedy and reliable verdict."[5] The method of Rhadamanthus was simple. He gave both parties the opportunity of

---

[1] Gilbert, *Beiträge*, p. 466; Hirzel, *Der Eid*, p. 128, n. 2.

[2] "Daher wird auch Solon in den Fällen, in welchen keine Documente vorhanden waren, beide Parteien haben schwören lassen, damit sie in ihren Aussagen über den Thatbestand desto sorgsamer wären und nur genau so viel sagten, als sie darüber zu wissen glaubten; die Aussagen der Parteien vertraten in solchen Fällen gewissermassen die der Zeugen und auch ihre Vereidigung mag deshalb demselben Zweck gedient haben wie die von Zeugen." Sondhaus (*op. cit.*, p. 58) agrees with Hirzel.

[3] These oaths have every appearance of being very ancient, though they are not mentioned in the fifth-century fragment of Draco's code. Cf. Gilbert, *Greek Constitutional Antiquities*, p. 386; Lipsius, *op. cit.*, p. 833.

[4] For the history of the evidentiary oath, see Gertrude Smith, "The Evidentiary Oath and Oathhelpers," *The Administration of Justice from Hesiod to Solon*, pp. 55 ff.

[5] Plato *Laws*, 948*b*. The words διδοὺς . . . . ὅρκον τοῖς ἀμφισβητοῦσιν do not mean "made the two parties take an oath" (Jowett) or "administered an oath" (Bury).

taking the oath, being confident that one would refuse through fear of divine vengeance. The other would take the oath and win the case.

But in the sixth century the matter could not be quite so simple. There were always some men ready to perjure themselves, but it is only reasonable to suppose that a considerable number of litigants, when faced with the issue, would shrink from taking a false oath. The justification for the law of Solon was the reasonable expectation that in a considerable number of cases a just verdict could be based upon the refusal of one of the litigants to take the oath. If both took the oath, the case would be in no wise prejudiced, and the magistrate would have the advantage of observing the demeanor of the litigants under the ordeal of taking an oath. Without a copy of the law or any indication of the content of the oath, it is difficult to discover the nature and purpose of the law. It would be extremely helpful to know, for example, whether the litigants were required to swear that they had told the truth in their pleadings or that in their answers to questions during the progress of the inquiry they would tell the "whole truth and nothing but the truth," as Hirzel believed. But it seems better to interpret the law as an attempt on the part of Solon to advance the administration of justice by authorizing the magistrate to administer an evidentiary oath, which up to his time could be employed only by consent of both parties, and to base his verdict upon it. Thus interpreted, Solon's experiment is an important step in the development of the evidentiary oath into the regular party oath in fifth- and fourth-century practice. Antiphon's[1] use of the word δοξασταί shows that they are not special judges. The magistrates, instead of being "judges of the evidence" (δικασταὶ τῶν μαρτύρων), became "surmisers of the truth" (δοξασταὶ τῶν ἀληθῶν).

Out of Solon's use of the evidentiary oath in time grew the preliminary party oaths of later developed practice. Each party, in every case without regard to the evidence in the case, swore to the truth of his pleadings. Various opin-

[1] v. 94.

ions regarding the purpose and significance of these preliminary oaths have been expressed.[1] Plato is quite outspoken
in his condemnation of a practice that forced one-half of the
litigants of Athens to take a false oath. In the *Laws*[2] he
proposed that all party oaths be abolished. "Since men's
opinions about the gods have changed the laws ought to be
changed." The most reasonable view seems to be that the
party oath introduced by Solon for a certain type of case was
extended to include all cases alike in the hope that it might
act as a check upon the prosecution of unfounded claims and
charges. In this connection a fragment of Sophocles[3] has
been aptly quoted:

> ὅρκου δὲ προστεθέντος ἐπιμελεστέρα
> ψυχὴ κατέστη· δισσὰ γὰρ φυλάσσεται
> φίλων τε μέμψιν κεἰς θεοὺς ἁμαρτάνειν.

In the end the party oath became a mere formality analogous
to the plea of "not guilty" in a modern court.[4]

The right of appeal and freedom of prosecution were well
calculated to insure the punishment of offenders. The rich
and the powerful could not hope to escape prosecution by
bribing or threatening their victims. Any citizen could take
the initiative and prosecute them. Neither could they escape
conviction by collusion with a magistrate in sympathy with
the upper classes, for the case could be appealed to a numerous body where the members of the demos predominated.
Thus the masses had in their own hands adequate means
of securing justice for one of their number against powerful
wrongdoers, or magistrates who gave "crooked decisions."
Any citizen was a potential prosecutor, and every citizen
was a member of the court of appeal. In the absence of
records of litigation under the Solonian system, it is difficult

---

[1] Cf. Meyer, Schoemann, Lipsius, *Der attische Process*, p. 889; Gilbert, *Beiträge*,
pp. 464 ff.; Lipsius, *Das attische Recht*, p. 833. Party oaths are found elsewhere in
Greece. Gilbert, *op. cit.*, p. 466, n. 2, for specific instances.

[2] 984*d*.   [3] Frag. 431 (Nauck), cited by Hirzel, *op. cit.*, p. 134, n. 4.

[4] It should be remembered that in a number of cases where the issues are complicated or the interpretation and application of a law is involved, opposing claims
may be quite properly urged without any dishonest purpose. In such cases a litigant
is not really forsworn. Cf. Philippi, *Der Areopag*, p. 92.

to get even an approximate idea of the proportion of cases appealed. Plutarch[1] says in effect that there were relatively few appeals. "In the beginning the participation of the lower class in the administration of justice was of no account, but afterwards it proved to be of the greatest importance, for the majority of disputes came before the dicasts." Plutarch is obviously referring to the later period when he says that the dicasts tried the most of the cases. But his next statement[2] is confusing. He connects this great activity of the dicasts with the provision for appeals from the decisions of magistrates. This is true only in the sense that Solon's measure was the first step in a constitutional development that resulted in complete popular control of the courts. In itself it was of relatively little moment, but it was the beginning of great things.

Aristotle's comment on the effect of the right of appeal is less explicit. "It is by means of this [the institution of the appeal to the law court, ἔφεσις], they say, that the masses *have gained strength* [ἰσχυκέναι] most of all, since, when the democracy is master of the ballot it is master of the constitution." The use of the perfect tense (ἰσχυκέναι) shows that he is referring to the results of Solon's prescription as exhibited in the fourth-century constitution. Some misapprehension of the situation in the time of Solon has resulted from Aristotle's discussion of the alleged obscurity of his laws. "Moreover, since the laws were not drawn up in simple and explicit terms, disputes inevitably occurred and the courts had to decide in every matter, whether public or private."[3] Here, again, Aristotle has in view not the situation under the Solonian constitution but the conditions in the fifth and fourth centuries, when the masses (τὸ πλῆθος) controlled the government. He makes this clear immediately. In reject-

---

[1] *Solon*, xviii. Cf. Vinogradoff, *op. cit.*, p. 77.

[2] *Loc. cit.*: καὶ γὰρ ὅσα ταῖς ἀρχαῖς ἔταξε κρίνειν, ὁμοίως καὶ περὶ ἐκείνων εἰς τὸ δικαστήριον ἐφέσεις ἔδωκε τοῖς βουλομένοις.

[3] *Ath. Pol.* ix. 1; Plutarch *Solon*, xviii: λέγεται δὲ καὶ τοὺς νόμους ἀσαφέστερον γράψας καὶ πολλὰς ἀντιλήψεις ἔχοντας αὐξῆσαι τὴν τῶν δικαστηρίων ἰσχύν· μὴ δυναμένους γὰρ ὑπὸ τῶν νόμων διαλυθῆναι περὶ ὧν διεφέροντο συνέβαινεν ἀεὶ δεῖσθαι δικαστῶν καὶ πᾶν ἄγειν ἀμφισβήτημα πρὸς ἐκείνους, τρόπον τινὰ τῶν νόμων κυρίους ὄντας.

ing the view that "Solon deliberately made the laws indefinite in order that the final decision might be in the hands
of the people," he observes, "we must judge his intentions,
not from the actual results in the present day, but from the
general tenor of the rest of his legislation."[1] Moreover, the
plain implication of Aristotle's statement that the courts
had to decide in every matter, whether public or private, is
to the same effect. It is to be observed that there is no reference to the intervention of the magistrates in the process.
And yet they must have settled a number of the disputes
that arose from a failure to understand the laws. One of
the reasons why Solon left Athens was to escape the impor-
tunities of citizens who came to criticize or to ask questions,[2]
"for he did not think it right that he should stay and interpret the laws." No magistrate could interpret the laws with
the same authority as the legislator himself; but a number
of honest men must have had their difficulties cleared up
satisfactorily by the magistrates whose business it was to try
to understand and apply the law. The constant recourse to
private arbitration in all periods and the efficiency of the
public arbitrators instituted at the end of the fifth century
would seem to indicate that the Solonian magistrates must
have satisfied a considerable number of litigants and achieved
final settlements. Aristotle's failure to mention the magistrates in this connection shows that he is referring to the
time when they had ceased to give final judgment and merely
prepared cases for trial.

There are other considerations that support the conclusions drawn from Aristotle and Plutarch regarding the in-
frequency of appeals. Each litigant was normally required to
present his own case.[3] This was not serious in a magistrate's

[1] *Ath. Pol.* ix. 2: οὐ γὰρ δίκαιον ἐκ τῶν νῦν γιγνομένων ἀλλ' ἐκ τῆς ἄλλης
πολιτείας θεωρεῖν τὴν ἐκείνου βούλησιν.

[2] *Ibid.*, xi.

[3] For the evidence for the fifty-century practice, compare Quintilian ii. 15. 30.
The rule requiring each litigant to handle his own case is generally believed to have
been in force in the time of Solon. This is a reasonable view. The rule is a survival
from a time when a man had to rely upon himself. If a blow was to be struck or a
word said in his defense, he himself had to act. Friends might aid, but he had to
take the initiative.

court, but many a litigant must have shrunk from appearing before the Heliaea. The average Athenian citizen had no experience in public speaking. Oratory as an art was unknown. He could not learn to speak except in the hard school of experience. Even in the later period when all the resources of formal rhetoric were available, many a litigant found the appearance before a dicastery to be an ordeal. The average citizen would need a strong incentive to induce him to carry an appeal to a mass meeting of his fellow-citizens. Normally, only the conviction that he had been the victim of gross injustice would be a sufficient inducement.

There was, it seems, a provision that in certain criminal cases an unsuccessful appeal might bring a larger penalty. A client of Lysias[1] cites a law of Solon which empowered the Heliaea to inflict an additional penalty of confinement in the stocks for five days. The nature of the offense is not specified, but from a passage in Demosthenes[2] it may be inferred that it was larceny. As the Heliaea had no original jurisdiction in the Solonian system, the case must have come before it by way of appeal. In the time of the orators, appeals to the heliastic courts from the decision of a deme assembly in a citizenship case were discouraged by a provision that the unsuccessful appellant be sold as a slave.[3] Similarly, appeals from the finding of an auditing committee to the deme assembly were discouraged by the imposition of an additional penalty in case of failure.[4] Modern legal systems have similar provisions. The English court of appeal in criminal cases is empowered to increase the penalty if it confirms the verdict of the lower court.

Civil suits could not be treated in this fashion. There is no indication that the practice of imposing a penalty for

[1] x. 16: δεδέσθαι δ' ἐν τῇ ποδοκάκκῃ ἡμέρας πέντε τὸν πόδα, ἐὰν προστιμήσῃ ἡ ἡλιαία. Wilamowitz, *Aristoteles und Athen*, I, 60, takes a different view. He thinks that when a magistrate imposed a penalty beyond a specified limit, he must refer his verdict to a popular court. This, Wilamowitz regards as one aspect of ἔφεσις εἰς δικαστήριον.

[2] Demosthenes xxiv. 105. Cf. Lipsius, *op. cit.*, p. 440, n. 79; *CAH*, IV, 56.

[3] Isaeus, xii.

[4] Haussoullier, *La vie municipale en Attique*, pp. 80 ff.

failure to obtain a fifth part of the votes goes back to Solon. In general, it would be natural for litigants to venture upon an appeal only where the issue involved a considerable sum of money or was likely to arouse popular interest. Such are cases involving estates and heiresses.[1]

[1] Cf. Aristotle, *op. cit.*, ix. 2: ἔτι δὲ καὶ διὰ τὸ μὴ γεγράφθαι τοὺς νόμους ἁπλῶς μηδὲ σαφῶς, ἀλλ᾽ ὥσπερ ὁ περὶ τῶν κλήρων καὶ ἐπικλήρων, ἀνάγκη πολλὰς ἀμφισβητήσεις γίγνεσθαι καὶ πάντα βραβεύειν καὶ τὰ κοινὰ καὶ τὰ ἴδια τὸ δικαστήριον. Cf. Aristophanes *Wasps*, 583 ff.

CHAPTER VI

THE RULE OF THE PEISISTRATIDAE

The materials for reconstructing the history of the period between Solon and Peisistratus are very meager.[1] Party struggles broke out afresh in the fifth year after the archonship of Solon. The archonship was the bone of contention. In two different years no archon was elected. They are known as years of "anarchia." Then Damasias made a bid for tyranny by continuing to hold the archonship for one year and two months beyond his term of office. This threat of tyranny brought a compromise whereby five eupatrids, three georgoi, and two demiurgoi were elected archons.[2] This compromise involved at least a partial modification of the Solonian classification. The citizens were distributed on the basis, not of wealth, but of birth or occupation. The impoverished eupatrid who had fallen into the third class was enabled to resume his place among the nobles. The change in terminology merely indicates the political realignment. Three parties grew up. They were composed of (*a*) those who were satisfied with the Solonian constitution, (*b*) those who wished the pre-Solonian aristocracy to be restored and strengthened, and (*c*) those who thought Solon had not gone far enough in meeting the desires of the masses. Their main interest was economic rather than political, but it was only by political action that their desires could be realized.

The time was ripe for tyranny. Solon had been criticized by the masses (πολλοὶ καὶ φαῦλοι)[3] for not availing himself of the opportunity of making himself tyrant as others had

[1] Aristotle, *Ath. Pol.*, xiii.

[2] Different theories have been advanced to explain the ten archons. Busolt (*Geschichte*, II, 302) thinks seven thesmothetae were elected. Adcock in *CAH*, IV, 60, says: "The most natural assumption is that these ten archons were chosen to govern in turn during the ten months that remained of Damasias' last year of office."

[3] Plutarch *Solon*, xv.

done, notably in Euboea and Mytilene.[1] The lower classes
favored tyranny because they saw in it some prospect of
protection against the aristocracy. Cylon had failed because
he aroused no enthusiasm in the masses. But Solon had
shown what a strong man could achieve in the interests of
the submerged masses. Perhaps Damasias was able to hold
the archonship as representative of the radical element in
the population. At any rate Peisistratus gained the tyranny
with the backing of the common people. Democracy was
progressing. The assembly which voted Peisistratus a bodyguard was still a vital part of the constitution.[2]

On the whole the Solonian laws and constitution remained. Peisistratus kept the form of the constitution and
professed to administer the laws. When the tyrants were
finally driven out, after fifty years, the laws had still sufficient vitality to be again put in force.

It is not known how the system of Solon fared during the
period of anarchy and strife. The judicial reforms of Solon
were not fundamental. He did not institute a new judiciary;
he simply *permitted* freedom of prosecution and appeal. Justice could be administered as before without appeal and without the intervention of ὁ βουλόμενος. The excellence of his reforms lay in the fact that the mere possibility of an appeal
acted as a warning to the magistrate. The voluntary prosecutor was an alternative. If the victim of a wrong himself
acted, there was no need of the intervention of another. The
popular assembly did continue to be an active body, as the
part it played in connection with Peisistratus shows. It listened to his appeal for personal protection and gave him a
bodyguard. In the years of anarchy the administration of
justice must have been partially suspended. But the Athenian habit of resorting to arbitration would enable them to
deal with pressing matters. The prestige and experience of
the Areopagus no doubt enabled that body to carry the state
through the periods of anarchy and disturbing party struggles. It may be this period that Aristotle had in mind when
he said of the Areopagus: καὶ τά τε ἄλλα τὰ πλεῖστα καὶ τὰ

---

[1] *CAH*, IV, 57; Plutarch, *op. cit.*, xiv.   [2] *Ath. Pol.* xiv. 1.

μέγιστα τῶν πολιτικῶν διετήρει.[1] As the Areopagus is active as a homicide court under Peisistratus, it must have been active in the previous period.

Peisistratus seized the government of Athens by force (561–60 B.C.), but chose to rule "constitutionally" (πολιτικῶς) rather than "despotically"[2] (τυραννικῶς). He took care, however, that the chief offices should be held by his relatives and adherents,[3] and adopted measures to keep the people busy and contented "in order that they might have neither the desire nor the leisure to attend to public affairs." According to Greek notions, "public affairs" (τὰ κοινά) included the administration of justice. No tyrant, be he never so inclined to govern "according to the established laws," could safely permit a popular assembly to review the decisions of magistrates who represented him rather than the people. He could easily dispense with judicial sessions of the Heliaea by withdrawing the right of appeal and restoring to the magistrates whom he controlled the power "to decide cases finally on their own authority."[4] He ran little risk in allowing magistrates and judicial officers who were practically his own appointees to administer justice. Indeed, it has been suggested that he strengthened the hands of the magistrates to offset the opposition of the Areopagus, which was the center of hostility.[5] It is quite possible that Peisistratus in the interests of the people from whom he drew considerable support, himself informally reviewed verdicts that worked injustice. The knowledge that Peisistratus kept in touch with their official acts, whether administrative or judicial, would have a salutary effect upon the magistrates. The vicissitudes of Peisistratus' career as tyrant show that there was constant need of the utmost vigilance on his part. His interest in the administration of justice is shown by his habit of going about the country districts "settling disputes": καὶ αὐτὸς ἐξῄει πολλάκις εἰς τὴν χώραν, ἐπισκοπῶν καὶ διαλύων τοὺς διαφερομένους.[6] The words διαλύων τοὺς διαφερομένους at once

---

[1] Ibid., viii. 4.
[2] Ibid., xvi. 2.
[3] Thucydides vi. 54.
[4] Aristotle Ath. Pol. iii. 5.
[5] Calhoun, Criminal Law, p. 96.
[6] Aristotle Ath. Pol. xvi. 5.

suggest arbitration. Naturally he would first endeavor to
compose quarrels and disputes before rendering a verdict on
the merits of the case and enforcing it by his authority as
tyrant. His experiences on these occasions no doubt suggested to him the idea of furthering his policy of keeping the
people on their farms by appointing justices to go on circuit
throughout the village communities.[1] The cases that came before them were mainly civil, as the words τοὺς διαφερομένους
would seem to indicate. These δικασταὶ κατὰ δήμους, as they
were called, were, like Peisistratus himself, primarily arbitrators, authorized to give a binding verdict if they failed to effect a friendly compromise. Their number is unknown. When
they were restored in 453–452 B.C. they numbered thirty because of their connection with the trittyes. Peisistratus thus
has the credit for anticipating one of the most admirable
features of the Athenian legal system of the fourth century—
public arbitration.[2]

De Sanctis refuses to accept Aristotle's statement that
Peisistratus established the rural justices. The objection
that they could not have been described as κατὰ δήμους at
this time is of little weight, for, although the demes were
not treated as distinct political units until the reforms of
Cleisthenes, they were ancient divisions, more ancient than
the naucrariae. To his further objection that it is not easy
to understand why Cleisthenes should have abolished them,
it is sufficient to reply that it was only natural to dispense
with an innovation of a hated régime, particularly when the
new system encouraged the citizens to resort to the city
rather than stay on their farms. His final objection is:

> Finalmente perchè quanto la loro istituzione era opportuna nelle età
> di Pericle, altrettanto era di superfluo nell' età di Pisistrato quando ai
> tesmoteti non mancava il tempo di attendere alle cause rurali, non avendo
> ancora avuto il carico d'istruire tutti i processi di Stato carpiti all' Areo-
> pago.[3]

[1] *Ibid.* Cornelius (*Die Tyrannis in Athen*, p. 53) believes that the *Demenrichter*
replaced some type of rural court which had been in the hands of the nobility.

[2] *Infra*, p. 348.

[3] *Storia della reppublica Ateniese*, p. 313. Cf. also De Sanctis' review of Calhoun's *Criminal Law*, in *Rivista di Filologia*, N.S., VI, 149 ff.

It is quite true that so far as the legal situation was concerned, the new judges may not have been needed until the period when the reorganization of the Areopagus threw additional burdens on the dicasteries. But the policy of Peisistratus was determined by political, not judicial, considerations.

The Areopagus continued to function as a homicide court under the tyrants. Peisistratus himself was summoned before it on a charge of murder. The prosecutor failed to appear, and the case was dropped.[1] The Areopagus was the chief criminal court in the Solonian constitution. It "corrected offenders, having full powers to inflict either fines or personal punishment." The Areopagus had authority also under the νόμος εἰσαγγελίας to try those charged with "plotting the overthrow of the state"[2] (τοὺς ἐπὶ καταλύσει τοῦ δήμου συνισταμένους). By a liberal, not to say cynical, construction of this law, the tyrant may have invoked it to protect himself against his political foes if the Areopagus was agreeable. Within a few years he might hope by the addition annually of nine ex-archons, favorable to himself, to possess in the Areopagus a willing instrument. Within a period of twenty years "the personnel of the court would be quite changed."[3] But long before a complete change in personnel came about, the tyrant would find the Areopagus manageable. The annual addition of nine adherents—ex-archons— would soon overcome the opposition of a numerical majority. But the history of the earlier struggles between the tyrant and his foes shows that the Areopagus neither did nor could aid him effectively. After five years he was ousted by a combination of the parties of the Plain and the Coast. Almost immediately he was enabled to return by effecting an arrangement with Megacles, the leader of the Coast party. But his second tenure of the tyranny was short-lived. Within the year he was driven out, and it was not until after the lapse of ten years that he was able to defeat his foes decisively and establish firmly his power by his victory at Pallene.[4]

---

[1] Aristotle *Ath. Pol.* xvi. 8.

[2] *Ibid.*, viii. 4.

[3] S. B. Smith, *op. cit.*, p. 114, n. 39.   [4] Bury, *History of Greece*, pp. 192 ff.

It was during this period, if at all, that the Areopagus became subservient to the interests of the tyrant.

For the ordinary administration of criminal law, magistrates, such as the thesmothetae and the Eleven, were available. Aristotle says that Peisistratus was τοῖς ἁμαρτάνουσι συγγνωμονικός.[1] This may mean that he interfered in the ordinary administration of justice to mitigate or reverse the verdicts of the magistrates either in the way of appeals or by the exercise of executive clemency. But it may also refer to a more direct and personal participation in proceedings against plotters who were seeking to overthrow the tyranny. Hippias himself took part in the interrogation of Aristogeiton, who slew Hipparchus. The object of the interrogation and torture was to secure the names of accomplices. Just how it was intended to dispose of Aristogeiton is not known, for Hippias slew him with his own hand in a moment of exasperation.[2] Aristogeiton and his accomplices, if any, could have been tried for murder by the Areopagus, but it seems more likely that the tyrants dealt with enemies who attempted violence, in summary fashion, perhaps through the agency of the Eleven.[3] It may be that the charge of murder against Peisistratus was due to his participation in the informal trial and execution of an enemy who had made an attempt on his life or engaged in a political conspiracy.[4]

[1] Aristotle *Ath. Pol.* xvi. 2.   [2] *Ibid.*, xviii. 6.

[3] Many citizens were slain or banished in the last years of the tyranny. See Aristotle *Ath. Pol.* xix. 1.

[4] Lysias, xii, tried to fasten upon Eratosthenes, one of the Thirty, responsibility for the murder of his brother Polemarchus, whom he had personally arrested.

CHAPTER VII
THE JUDICIAL REFORMS OF CLEISTHENES

The reforms of Cleisthenes belong to the period between the expulsion of the tyrants and the final defeat of Persia (510–480). The tyrants were not driven out of Athens by a popular uprising but by Spartan intervention. The exiled Alcmaeonids, failing in their attempts to expel the Peisistratidae forcibly, contrived to enlist the aid of the Spartans by bribing the oracle, as their enemies claimed.[1] The masses had not found the rule of Peisistratus irksome. It was, indeed, an era of peace and prosperity. "Hence," says Aristotle, "the tyranny of Peisistratus was often spoken of proverbially as the age of Cronus," i.e., the golden age.[2] But in after years, in a spirit of national pride, the Athenian populace ignored the services of Sparta, and made national heroes out of Harmodius and Aristogeiton, who had slain Hipparchus, one of the Peisistratidae, for purely personal reasons. The partisan feud of the Alcmaeonids with the Peisistratidae was treated as an episode in the national struggle for liberty. Witness the popularity of the Leipsydrium drinking-song, which was second only in popular favor to the famous Harmodius and Aristogeiton song. In this atmosphere the popular notions of the work of the Alcmaeonid, Cleisthenes, were likely to be divergent. According to a widespread view, he did little more than restore the constitution of Solon.[3] Others

[1] Aristotle *Ath. Pol.*, xix. Cf. De Sanctis, *op. cit.*, pp. 322 ff.

[2] *Ath. Pol.* xvi. 7: Ὁ ἐπὶ Κρόνου βίος. Although the rule of the sons of Peisistratus became much harsher, yet it did not lead to a popular uprising. Hippias' proposed fortification of Munychia as a place of refuge shows that he feared an uprising (*ibid.*, xix).

[3] Isocrates vii. 16: Εὑρίσκω γὰρ ταύτην μόνην ἂν γενομένην καὶ τῶν μελλόντων κινδύνων ἀποτροπὴν καὶ τῶν παρόντων κακῶν ἀπαλλαγήν, ἣν ἐθελήσωμεν ἐκείνην τὴν δημοκρατίαν ἀναλαβεῖν, ἣν Σόλων μὲν ὁ δημοτικώτατος γενόμενος ἐνομοθέτησε, Κλεισθένης δ᾽ ὁ τοὺς τυράννους ἐκβαλὼν καὶ τὸν δῆμον καταγαγὼν πάλιν ἐξ ἀρχῆς κατέστησεν. Aristotle *Ath. Pol.* xxii. 1: καὶ γὰρ συνέβη τοὺς μὲν Σόλωνος νόμους ἀφανίσαι τὴν

regard him as the virtual founder of democracy.[1] There is an
element of truth in both of these views.

Upon the overthrow of the tyranny, the nobles expected a
restoration, not of the Solonian system, but of the pre-
Solonian aristocracy. It was doubtless with this expectation that Cleomenes, the Spartan king, had intervened.[2] But
the old political strife was renewed. Two main factions appeared. Isagoras was the leader of those nobles who had
made terms with the tyrants. His opponent was Cleisthenes.
At first it was a struggle for leadership. Isagoras proved the
stronger, and with the support of the political clubs gained
the archonship which was still the chief bone of contention
between political factions. Cleisthenes, though the grandson
of a tyrant of Sicyon, was an Alcmaeonid. Throughout the
vicissitudes of their political fortunes this family had been
more or less friendly to the masses. On this occasion Cleisthenes boldly appealed to the people. The time was well
suited for such an appeal. On the expulsion of the tyrants
there had been a revision of the list of citizens, aimed particularly at those adherents of the Peisistratidae who had
gained citizenship through favor of the tyrants.[3] Many had
been disfranchised. To these and others, Cleisthenes offered
full participation in the counsels and activities of the state.
This maneuver committed him to a program of democratic
reform, both to satisfy the aspirations of the masses and to
secure his own leadership.

With the backing of the people he easily gained the upper

τυραννίδα διὰ τὸ μὴ χρῆσθαι, και[ν]οὺς δ' ἄλλους θεῖναι τὸν Κλεισθένη, στοχαζόμενον
τοῦ πλήθους . . . . .

Aristotle *Pol.* 1273*b*. 35 ff.: Σόλωνα δ' ἔνιοι μὲν οἴονται νομοθέτην γενέσθαι σπου-
δαῖον· ὀλιγαρχίαν τε γὰρ καταλῦσαι λίαν ἄκρατον οὖσαν καὶ δουλεύοντα τὸν δῆμον παῦσαι
καὶ δημοκρατίαν καταστῆσαι τὴν πάτριον.

[1] Aristotle *Ath. Pol.* xxix. 3: τοὺς πατρίους νόμους οὓς Κλεισθένης ἔθηκεν ὅτε καθίστη
τὴν δημοκρατίαν.

[2] For the triumph and the reforms of Cleisthenes the chief sources are Herodotus
v. 66, 69–70, 71–73; and Aristotle *Ath. Pol.*, xx–xxi. In the main, Aristotle follows
Herodotus.

[3] Walker, *CAH*, IV, 145–46. Cf. Aristotle *Ath. Pol.* xiii. 5: σημεῖον δ', ὅτι μετὰ
τὴν [τῶν] τυράννων κατάλυσιν ἐποίησαν διαψηφισμόν, ὡς πολλῶν κοινωνούντων τῆς πολιτείας οὐ προσῆκον.

hand and put through some reforms, including the reorganization of the citizens into ten, instead of four, tribes, with a Senate of Five Hundred. Isagoras had recourse to Spartan aid. At his suggestion the Spartans revived the pollution charge against the Alcmaeonidae. For the moment Isagoras was successful. Cleisthenes and 700 heads of houses were banished. But the attempt of the Spartan king to set up an oligarchy of 300 was resisted by the senate and the people. The Spartans and their Athenian supporters took refuge in the Acropolis. Within three days they were forced to surrender. Aristotle's account differs from that of Herodotus, in the order of the events. According to Herodotus, Cleisthenes proceeded at once to introduce his reforms; but Aristotle seems to say that Cleisthenes put through no reforms until the Spartans were forced out of the city three years after the expulsion of the tyrants.[1] In some respects Herodotus' account is preferable. It explains the resistance and the identity of the senate. If the Senate of Five Hundred was already organized, its resistance to Cleomenes is easily understood. Moreover, it is difficult to account for opposition from the old Solonian Senate of Four Hundred.[2]

There is some doubt in regard to the status or official position of Cleisthenes. Some scholars believe that the assembly conferred upon him extraordinary legislative powers like those of Solon.[3] Certain expressions of Aristotle are quoted in support of this view, though Aristotle[4] expressly

[1] De Sanctis, *op. cit.*, p. 329, n. 2, following Beloch, *Griechische Geschichte* (2d ed.), I, 399, n. 1; Ehrenberg, "Kleisthenes und das Archontat," *Klio*, XIX, 106 ff. Walker, *op. cit.*, IV, 139–40, prefers the account of Aristotle and identifies the senate (*Ath. Pol.* xx. 3) as the Solonian Senate of Four Hundred. Cloché ("La boulè d'Athènes en 508–507 avant J.-C.," *Rev. d. études grecques*, XXXVII [1924], 1 ff.) firmly supports the theory that it was the Solonian Senate of Four Hundred.

[2] Walker (*op. cit.*, p. 140, n. 1) suggests the hypothesis that the council was the Areopagus. But Isagoras would never have consented to the dissolution of the Areopagus (*Ath. Pol.* xx. 3). For the importance of the boulé in Cleisthenes' scheme cf. *infra*, p. 342.

[3] Busolt-Swoboda, *Staatskunde*, p. 869, n. 5.

[4] *Ath. Pol.* xx. 4; xxi. 1: καὶ[ν]οὺς δ' ἄλλους θεῖναι τὸν Κλεισθένη στοχαζόμενον τοῦ πλήθους; xxix. 3: τοὺς πατρίους νόμους οὓς Κλεισθένης ἔθηκεν.

says that he was ἡγεμὼν καὶ τοῦ δήμου προστάτης. He was never even an archon.[1] In one important respect the reforms associated with the name of Cleisthenes differ from those of other extraordinary legislators. The work was not accomplished at one stroke, so to speak, but extended over a period of years. Thus ostracism, the oath of the boulé, and the Board of the Ten Generals were introduced several years after the reorganization of the tribes. In view of this feature of Cleisthenes' work, Beloch[2] suggests that he was the leading member of a legislative commission. According to his view, it is too late for plenipotentiary lawgivers; they belong to a more primitive stage of political development. Later revolutions were regularly followed by legislative commissions. But a much better parallel to Cleisthenes' reforms is, not the formal legislative commissions of the revolutions in 411 and 404 B.C., but the reformers, led or inspired by Ephialtes, who in his struggle against the Areopagus initiated a period of democratic development. Cleisthenes, like Ephialtes, seems to have disappeared from public life very soon after the movement was initiated,[3] and others carried on his work by legislation calculated to give effect to the aspirations of a people that had been singularly successful, not only in getting rid of the tyrants, but in escaping from the tutelage of Sparta and in defeating the Persians single handed. It was a period of rapid evolution.[4] No legislative commission, no individual legislator appointed immediately after the expulsion of the tyrants, could have served the purpose.

Cleisthenes was not a political reformer by conviction, like Solon, but merely a shrewd politician who aimed at securing the good will of the populace (στοχαζόμενον τοῦ πλήθους). Like

[1] De Sanctis, *op. cit.*, p. 229, n. 2. Compare Ehrenberg, (*op. cit.*, p. 107), who thinks it possible that Cleisthenes was archon in 509-508 B.C. Wilamowitz (*Aristoteles und Athen*, I, 6) suggests 508-507 as the archonship of Cleisthenes.

[2] Beloch, *op. cit.*, p. 396 n. Compare Ehrenberg (*op. cit.*, p. 107), who rejects Beloch's view.

[3] Cf. *infra*, pp. 252 f. No names of associates or followers of Cleisthenes are preserved in the records, unless Cannonus be one. (Cf. *infra*, p. 205.)

[4] Aristotle (*Pol.*, p. 1274a) characterizes the growth of democracy during this period as due to "accident" (ἀπὸ συμπτώματος) not "design" (οὐ κατὰ ... προαίρεσιν).

all successful popular leaders, his first concern was to secure his own position. He saw that the only way to accomplish this was to prevent the return of the tyrants and to weaken the nobles by putting power into the hands of the people. A man of Cleisthenes' social and political antecedents was not the kind of statesman to appear with a comprehensive program of democratic reform. And even if he had the vision of a Solon, he was too shrewd a politician to imagine that a people wholly without political experience could operate a complete democratic system. The democratic movement extended over more than twenty-five years. A setback came with the revived prestige of the Areopagus, whose political supremacy in the state, beginning with the Battle of Salamis, is said to have lasted for seventeen years.[1] During the twenty-five years of democratic progress, a number of measures must have been adopted of which no mention is made in the sources. They may be included in the new laws mentioned by Aristotle.[2] It is true that Aristotle attributes them to Cleisthenes. But it is not known either how long Cleisthenes retained his leadership or when he died. The fact that he is not mentioned in connection with the war with Boeotia and Euboea would seem to indicate that his leadership was short-lived. Walker[3] has suggested that the Persian policy of Cleisthenes was the cause of his downfall. Faced by the hostility of Sparta, Boeotia, and Chalcis, and a war on three fronts, he sent an embassy to Persia, seeking aid. Persia demanded earth and water as symbols of subjection before entering into alliance with Athens. The ambassadors, "on their own responsibility," according to Herodotus, acceded to the demand. The Persian alliance was rejected, and the ambassadors were severely criticized.[4] Cleisthenes, it is argued, was involved in their disgrace. If this be correct,

[1] Aristotle *Ath. Pol.*, xxiii (479-462).

[2] *Ibid.*, xxii. 1.   [3] *Op. cit.*, pp. 167-68.

[4] Herodotus v. 73: εἰ μὲν διδοῦσι βασιλέϊ Δαρείῳ Ἀθηναῖοι γῆν τε καὶ ὕδωρ, ὁ δὲ συμμαχίην σφι συνετίθετο, εἰ δὲ μὴ διδοῦσι, ἀπαλλάσσεσθαι αὐτοὺς ἐκέλευε. οἱ δὲ ἄγγελοι ἐπὶ σφέων αὐτῶν βαλόμενοι διδόναι ἔφασαν, βουλόμενοι τὴν συμμαχίην ποιήσασθαι. οὗτοι μὲν δὴ ἀπελθόντες εἰς τὴν ἑωυτῶν αἰτίας μεγάλας εἶχον.

a number of the "new laws" must have emanated from other leaders of the school of Cleisthenes, men who saw the wisdom of throwing in their lot with democracy and sharing in its success.

The reorganization of the tribes and the substitution of the demes for naucraries were political measures intended to break up the power of the nobles and to facilitate the absorption of the new citizens.[1] The unit of the new tribes was the deme, not the clan. In the deme system local association was substituted for community of relationship. The system of tribes, trittyes, and demes was intricate and artificial. In its purpose of weakening the power of the nobles who were opposed to the democratization of the state, it has some analogy with the well-known American device called "gerrymander."[2] The demes of Attica were divided roughly into three groups: first, those of the city and its environs; second, those of the coast; and third, those in the interior. The demes in each of these areas were distributed into ten groups called "trittyes"; and three trittyes, one from each area, constituted a tribe. The tribe was no longer a geographical unit but contained elements from the inhabitants of the city, the coast, and the interior.

A new council ($\beta o \upsilon \lambda \acute{\eta}$) was instituted, consisting of 500 members. Fifty were drawn from each tribe. The demes included in each of the tribes varied in size and number, but there was devised some means of apportioning the senators of each tribe among the demes included in it. The members of the council were selected by lot from a larger group nominated by the demes. They had to be at least thirty years of age. It is impossible to say how many of the duties that the council performed in the later period go back to Cleisthenes. At any rate, he introduced the oath which the council continued to swear in Aristotle's day. In essence the

[1] Walker, *op. cit.*, pp. 142 ff.; Aristotle, *op. cit.*, xxii.

[2] In 1812 Governor Gerry of Massachusetts was believed to be responsible for a redistribution of the congressional districts of the state which gave his party an unfair advantage in elections. The dragon-like shape of one of the districts suggested to a political opponent the word "gerrymander" (cf. "salamander") to describe the unfair distribution of municipal units in electoral districts.

boulé was a commission of the ecclesia intrusted with the task of preparing the agenda for the sessions of the ecclesia. It constituted an excellent training school for the masses who had had no opportunity under the tyranny for gaining political experience. As the office of councilor could not be held more than twice, it has been estimated that a third of the citizen body must at some time in their lives have served on the council.[1] Apparently the functions of the naucraroi were apportioned between the demarchs of the newly organized demes and the boulé. The prytaneis of the council were modeled on those of the naucraroi.

After describing the major constitutional changes introduced immediately by Cleisthenes, Aristotle says that Cleisthenes introduced "new laws" in place of those of Solon which had fallen into desuetude during the period of the tyranny.[2] These new laws were constitutional.[3] This appears from the mention of ostracism as one of them. They are the only laws that would be disregarded during the rule of the Peisistratidae. The ordinary civil and criminal laws would continue to be administered as before, but by different agencies. Other examples of these new measures attributed to Cleisthenes are the new oath for the boulé and the election of ten generals by the tribes.[4]

Ostracism was a novel and ingenious device to protect the people from tyranny.[5] In one form or another it appears in different Greek cities, but there is good reason for believing that all the varieties were derived from Athens.[6] Once a

[1] Aristotle has little to say about the organization of the boulé. Cf. *Ath. Pol.* xxi. 3; xxii. 2: .... ἐφ' Ἑρμοκρέοντος ἄρχοντος, τῇ βουλῇ τοῖς πεντακοσίοις τὸν ὅρκον ἐποίησαν, ὃν ἔτι καὶ νῦν ὀμνύουσιν.
Cf. Walker, *op. cit.*, pp. 149 ff.; Busolt-Swoboda, *op. cit.*, pp. 882 ff.

[2] Aristotle *Ath. Pol.* xxii. 1. Cf. Calhoun, *Criminal Law*, pp. 88 ff.

[3] Carcopino, *Histoire de l'ostracisme athénien*, p. 98.

[4] Aristotle *Ath. Pol.* xxii. 2.

[5] Ostracism soon came to be used as a convenient weapon in party struggles (De Sanctis, *op. cit.*, p. 372). In the fourth century the γραφὴ παρανόμων displaced ostracism as a means of attack in political warfare (Bury, *History of Greece*, p. 462). Cf. Sanguinetti (*Notas para un ensays sobre el ostracismo* [Buenos Aires, 1922]), who thinks that ostracism was not a party weapon.

[6] Walker, *op. cit.*, p. 151.

year a vote was taken on the question of holding an ostracism that year. If the vote was in favor of ostracism, at a subsequent meeting in the agora the people voted secretly by tribes. The man who received the majority of votes was exiled for ten years.[1] It has been a much vexed question whether the 6,000 votes required in ostracism constituted a majority or a quorum. Apparently the Greeks of succeeding ages were in doubt. Plutarch[2] says very definitely that the number 6,000 was a quorum. Philochorus is cited in favor of the majority theory. διαριθμηθέντων δὲ (τῶν ὀστράκων) ὅτῳ πλεῖστα γένοιτο καὶ μὴ ἐλάττω ἑξακισχιλίων τοῦτον ἔδει . . . . ἐν δέκα ἡμέραις μεταστῆναι τῆς πόλεως ἔτη δέκα. ὕστερον δὲ ἐγένοντο πέντε.[3] This testimony is not beyond suspicion. The statement that the period of banishment was subsequently reduced to five years is incorrect. The passage, as quoted by Photius, was no doubt shortened and compressed. In the process the meaning may easily have been changed. Modern opinion has been divided. Arguments on both sides were so evenly matched that a deadlock resulted. Not until it was pointed out that the same principle must underlie the requirement of a minimum vote of 6,000 in ostracism and in the so-called νόμοι ἐπ᾽ ἀνδρί, and the selection of 6,000 jurors annually for service in the heliastic courts, was it finally recognized that 6,000 must be a quorum.[4] In both cases the 6,000 were regarded as representatives of the Athenian people.

Ostracism was an administrative rather than a judicial act. A man could be ostracized without accusation or defense. When the question of the advisability of holding an ostracism came up in the assembly there was no debate and

[1] Philochorus (*Fragmenta Historicorum Graecorum*, 1. 396) is the source of our knowledge of the procedure in ostracism. The passage is cited by Sandys in his notes on Aristotle *Ath. Pol.* xxii. 1.

[2] *Aristeides* vii. 8: εἰ γὰρ ἑξακισχιλίων ἐλάττονες οἱ γράψαντες εἶεν, ἀτελὴς ἦν ὁ ἐξοστρακισμός. ἔπειτα τῶν ὀνομάτων ἕκαστον ἰδίᾳ θέντες τὸν ὑπὸ τῶν πλείστων γεγραμμένον ἐξεκήρυττον εἰς ἔτη δέκα καρπούμενον τὰ αὑτοῦ.

[3] *FHG* I. 396.

[4] For a full statement of the arguments in favor of the quorum theory, cf. Bonner, "The Minimum Vote in Ostracism," *Class. Phil.*, VIII, 223–25. Their validity is recognized by Busolt-Swoboda, *op. cit.*, p. 885, n. 2.

no mention of names.[1] Aristotle[2] says the vote had to be taken in the κυρία ἐκκλησία of the sixth prytany. The senate was required by law to put the question on the program. They had no option. Considerations which are set forth below[3] seem to indicate very strongly that the distinction between the κυρία and the other assemblies was that a quorum of 6,000 was required in the κυρία ἐκκλησία. Manifestly, although ostracism was not a judicial act, it was desirable that great care should be taken to ascertain the prevailing public sentiment both as to the desirability of holding an ostracism and as to which citizen ought to be exiled.

It is to be expected that a measure intended to protect the city against a prospective tyrant would have been introduced immediately after the expulsion of the tyrants. And yet, according to the available records, no one was ostracized until 487 B.C., many years later. In the meantime the Battle of Marathon had been won, democracy was firmly established, and all hopes or fears of a forcible restoration of the Peisistratidae must have been dissipated. A rather plausible explanation of Aristotle's statement that the first case of ostracism occurred in 488–487 is that he drew his information from the amnesty decree passed in 480 on the eve of Xerxes' invasion, recalling all ostracized citizens. As the period of exile was ten years, no one exiled before 490 would appear on the decree.[4]

Sometime between the expulsion of the tyrants and the age of Pericles the Heliaea ceased to be a court of appeal and became a court of first resort. When once this momentous step was taken, it is obvious that a single court could not

---

[1] Carcopino, op. cit., p. 129. The fourth oration of Andocides purporting to have been delivered against Alcibiades on the occasion of a vote on ostracism is now regarded as a rhetorical exercise. Cf. Jebb, The Attic Orators, I, 132 ff.

[2] Ath. Pol. xliii. 5.   [3] Pp. 217 ff.

[4] Mathieu, Aristote, Constitution d'Athènes, p. 56. Walker (op. cit., p. 152) accepts Mathieu's explanation. An obvious objection to the view of Mathieu is that Aristotle himself would have been well aware that the amnesty decree of 480 B.C. was inadequate evidence. Cf. Carcopino, op. cit., pp. 103–7; also Busolt-Swoboda, op. cit., p. 886, who express much the same opinion as Carcopino. The delay in applying the law was "weil nach seiner Annahme die Parteilage eine so schwankende wurde, dass keine Partei des Ausganges der Ostrakophoria sicher war."

handle all the litigation of the community. A new system of courts called "dicasteries," drawn from the membership of the Heliaea, was introduced. The magistrates ceased to act as judges; they merely prepared the cases for trial and acted as chairmen of the court sessions. No ancient writer mentions this important reorganization of the Heliaea which gave democracy full control of the administration of justice, but it is usually regarded as the work of Cleisthenes.[1] It may have been effected by one of the "new laws" mentioned by Aristotle. The commonly accepted view is that the increase in the number of appeals led to the change. This is to be preferred to the theory that Cleisthenes came forward with a complete program of reform, including the institution of the dicasteries. Nothing that is known of Cleisthenes justifies the belief that he was a man with a mission. He was rather the type of politician that not only senses the political aspirations of the masses but has the wisdom to estimate their fitness for further exercise of power. This was as it should be. A people who had just emerged from a half-century of tyranny was quite unfitted to take over the government of a state. They needed training and experience. It was the merit of Cleisthenes and his immediate subordinates or successors that they recognized this situation and put democracy on a sound basis, introducing innovations gradually, as the need for them arose and the people displayed their fitness for further responsibilities. In the absence of records of litigation during this period, we have no evidence to go on. But in such a fundamental change as was involved in substituting regular constitutional government for tyranny, the necessary adjustments may have involved considerable litigation. An increase in the number of appeals would naturally follow. If there was any general attempt to recover by legal process the lands confiscated[2] by the Peisistratidae, there would be plenty of lawsuits and appeals. Eventually

[1] Lipsius, *op. cit.*, p. 32. Cf. Busolt-Swoboda, *op. cit.*, p. 883.

[2] For exile and confiscation of property of the nobility, cf. Busolt, *Geschichte*, II, 327-29; cf. Cornelius, *Die Tyrannis in Athen*, p. 52.

the constant appeals would reduce the magisterial decision to a mere form.[1]

But the change in the judicial functions of the magistrates may have been brought about in quite a different fashion. There is evidence that soon after the expulsion of the tyrants the assembly (Heliaea) began to act as a court of first instance and to try cases that lay beyond the normal jurisdiction of the magistrates. Under the Solonian system such cases would have come before the Areopagus. This invasion of the assembly into the judicial field was no infringement on the functions of the magistrates. It is quite compatible with the continuance of a system of appeals in the routine cases. It was rather a natural shift of important judicial power to the sovereign body in the state. The inevitable effect of the exercise of these judicial functions by the assembly would be to give weight (if it did not give rise) to the demand that the people try all cases in the first instance.

The first case known with certainty to have been tried by the assembly[2] is that of Miltiades, who was charged in 489 B.C. with deceiving the people.[3] Asking for seventy ships, he promised the Athenians that he would enrich them if they would grant his request. He refused to disclose the objective of the proposed expedition, which was Paros. When he returned unsuccessful, there was a great deal of criticism of his conduct (εἶχον ἐν στόμασι, οἵ τε ἄλλοι καὶ μάλιστα, κ.τ.λ.). Xanthippus arraigned him in the assembly for deceiving the people (τῆς Ἀθηναίων ἀπάτης εἵνεκεν). Narrowly escaping the death penalty asked by the prosecutor, he was fined 50 talents.

There are records of two other cases which may very well have been tried in the assembly. Already in 493 B.C., Miltiades had been tried in Athens for tyranny in the Cher-

---

[1] Even if the system of appeals had failed in the period between Solon and Peisistratus, the memory of the failure would probably have disappeared in the half-century of tyranny. It would be most natural for Cleisthenes to re-establish the Solonian system of appeals at first.

[2] Lipsius, *op. cit.*, p. 180.   [3] Herodotus vi. 136.

sonese.[1] One may wonder how an Athenian could be tried in Athens for exercising autocratic authority over barbarians. The most plausible explanation is that he extended his authority over an Athenian community settled in the Chersonese.[2] Aristotle[3] cites a mild Athenian law against tyrants which was in force in Athens in the sixth century. In the earlier period the only body capable of enforcing such a law was the Areopagus; but under the Cleisthenean constitution, while the Areopagus was still legally competent, the logical body to try tyrants was the body that protected the community against potential tyrants by means of ostracism, that is, the assembly. Herodotus says that the case came before a δικαστήριον, but it would be hazardous to conclude that Herodotus is using δικαστήριον advisedly in its technical sense.[4] In view of the unique nature of the charge, it is quite improbable that it could have been handled by any of the normal processes of law even if the heliastic courts were in existence at that time. Impeachment (εἰσαγγελία) was intended, among other things, to take care of cases for which there was no provision in the ordinary criminal code. Moreover, as Miltiades was tried by the assembly in 489 for deceiving the people, it is wholly unlikely that he was tried by a dicastery in 493 for tyranny.

An even more unusual case was tried in Athens in the same year in which Miltiades was tried for tyranny. The

---

[1] *Ibid.*, 104: ἅμα δὲ ἐκφυγόντα τε τούτους καὶ ἀπικόμενον εἰς τὴν ἑωυτοῦ δοκέοντά τε εἶναι ἐν σωτηρίᾳ ἤδη, τὸ ἐνθεῦτέν μιν οἱ ἐχθροὶ ὑποδεξάμενοι καὶ ὑπὸ δικαστήριον [αὐτὸν] ἀγαγόντες ἐδίωξαν τυραννίδος τῆς ἐν Χερσονήσῳ. ἀποφυγὼν δὲ καὶ τούτους στρατηγὸς οὕτως Ἀθηναίων ἀπεδέχθη, αἱρεθεὶς ὑπὸ τοῦ δήμου.

[2] Walker (*op. cit.*, IV, 171) regards both trials of Miltiades as incidents in the party struggles between the Alcmaeonidae and the Philaidae clan of which Miltiades was the head. For the relations between the enterprise of the elder Miltiades in the Chersonese and the external policy of Peisistratus, compare Cornelius, *op. cit.*, pp. 33 ff. Munro (*CAH*, IV, 232) thinks that Miltiades was not tried in 493 but was disqualified for office on the ground that, having been a tyrant, he might be a danger to Athens.

[3] *Ath. Pol.* xvi. 10: ἦσαν δὲ καὶ τοῖς Ἀθηναίοις οἱ περὶ τῶν τυράννων νόμοι πρᾷοι κατ᾽ ἐκείνους τοὺς καιρούς.

[4] Busolt-Swoboda, *op. cit.*, p. 884, n. 1: "Ob Herodotus genau berichtet, ist fraglich, die Verweisung der Klage an das Volksgericht möglich."

fall of Miletus in 494 had made a deep impression on the Athenians, which found expression in their resentment at Phrynichus for making the misfortunes of Miletus the subject of a tragedy. The whole audience burst into tears; and the Athenians fined Phrynichus 1,000 drachmas for reminding them of misfortunes that touched them so closely, and banned the drama from the stage.[1] It has been suggested that the charge was impiety because the tears of the audience profaned the festival of the god.[2] But whatever the charge was, the motive back of the prosecution was undoubtedly political.[3] The natural court for such a trial was the assembly. And the ban upon further production of the drama could come only from a body that possessed administrative as well as judicial functions.

Hipparchus, son of Charmus, was summoned by the ecclesia for treason (προδοσία).[4] Failing to answer the summons, he was condemned to death in his absence. He was ostracized in 488,[5] and there is no reason why he may not, like Themistocles,[6] have been tried during his period of ostracism. On the other hand, if he was still in good standing in 480, and returned with other exiles included in the amnesty proclamation, he may have been tried some time after 480.

There is still another possible instance of early judicial action on the part of the assembly. When Cleomenes, the Spartan king, was permitted to withdraw from the Acropolis (508–507 B.C.) under a safe conduct, his Athenian allies, according to Herodotus'[7] version of the incident, were thrown

[1] Herodotus vi. 21: 'Αθηναῖοι μὲν γὰρ δῆλον ἐποίησαν ὑπεραχθεσθέντες τῇ Μιλήτου ἁλώσι τῇ τε ἄλλῃ πολλαχῇ καὶ δὴ καὶ ποιήσαντι Φρυνίχῳ δρᾶμα Μιλήτου ἅλωσιν καὶ διδάξαντι ἐς δάκρυά τε ἔπεσε τὸ θέητρον καὶ ἐζημίωσάν μιν ὡς ἀναμνήσαντα οἰκήια κακὰ χιλίῃσι δραχμῇσι, καὶ ἐπέταξαν μηκέτι μηδένα χρᾶσθαι τούτῳ τῷ δράματι.

[2] Meyer, *Geschichte des Altertums*, III, 313.

[3] Walker, *op. cit.*, IV, 172. How and Wells, *A Commentary on Herodotus*, VI, 21, n. 2. Meyer (*op. cit.*) regards the play as inspired by Themistocles to win the people to his naval policy.

[4] Lycurgus *In Leocratem*, 117.

[5] Aristotle *Ath. Pol.* xxii. 4.   [6] Bury, *op. cit.*, pp. 334–35.

[7] Herodotus v. 72: τοὺς δὲ ἄλλους 'Αθηναῖοι κατέδησαν τὴν ἐπὶ θανάτῳ.

into prison for execution. The execution was authorized by a decree of the assembly, if the scholiast on Aristophanes' *Lysistrata*[1] is correct. As they were caught red-handed making common cause with enemies within the gates, it was a case for summary action by an outraged community. The popular assembly was the natural representative of the community.

These cases point to the conclusion that the assembly had acquired the right to take independent judicial action when the existing legal processes did not afford the community adequate means of redress.[2] The earliest certain instance of judicial action by the assembly occurred in 493 B.C., but the change in the constitution empowering the assembly to take independent judicial action must have been much earlier.

The administration of justice was one of the most important functions of government.[3] Cleisthenes could not have failed to realize that without independent judicial powers the ecclesia could not become the sovereign body in the state. A preponderance of power would have been in the hands of the Areopagus or of the newly created Council of Five Hundred.[4] The close relationship between the boulé and the ecclesia makes it seem likely that the independent judicial powers of the ecclesia date from the restriction of the punitive powers of the boulé in 502–501 B.C., when "they first imposed upon the Council of Five Hundred the oath which they take to the present day."[5]

Three old laws are known which deal with the judicial powers of the assembly. One is a fragmentary decree regard-

---

[1] Line 273: τὰς οἰκίας κατέσκαψαν καὶ τὰς οὐσίας ἐδήμευσαν, αὐτῶν δὲ θάνατον ἐψηφίσαντο. Aristotle (*Ath. Pol.* xx. 3) says that all the opponents of Cleisthenes were set free: Κλεομένην μὲν καὶ τοὺς μετ' αὐτοῦ πάντας ἀφεῖσαν ὑποσπόνδους. Cf. Mathieu, *op. cit.*, pp. 55–56. Busolt-Swoboda, *op. cit.*, p. 1007, believe that Isagoras and his followers were put to death by a decree of the people.

[2] Cf. Lipsius, *op. cit.*, p. 33.   [3] Aristotle *Ath. Pol.*, ix.

[4] There is no reason to suppose that Cleisthenes restricted by law the judicial powers of the Areopagus. Cf. *infra*, p. 251.

[5] Aristotle *Ath. Pol.* xxii, 2. For the restriction of the punitive powers of the βουλή, cf. *infra*, pp. 335 ff.

ing the boulé and the ecclesia.[1] The extant version belongs
to the late fifth century, but it is quite obviously a re-enactment of a much earlier law.

PART I

Line 21: [πεντ]ακοσιο
Line 23: καὶ τῷ δή[μῳ]
Line 24: δ]εμίαν
Line 25: κεκλημ[έν]ο
Line 26: [ἄνευ τοῦ δήμου τοῦ 'Αθηναίων] πληθύοντος [μὴ]
Line 28: [ἐπιψ]ηφιῶ ἐμ [β]ουλῇ
Line 29: ἐπιψηφίζω
Line 31: βουλεύειν τοὺ[ς] πεντα[κ]ο[σί]ου[ς]
Line 32: [πεντ]ακοσίας δραχ[μάς]
Line 33: . . . . αν δ' ὁ δ[ῆ]μο[ς] πληθ[ύω]ν
Line 34: ἐν τῷ βουλευτηρίῳ
Line 36: [ἄνευ τοῦ δήμου τοῦ 'Αθηναίων πληθύοντ]ος μὴ εἶναι πόλεμο[ν]
Line 37: [ἄνευ τοῦ δήμου τοῦ 'Αθηναίων πλη]θύοντος μὴ εἶναι θάν[α]το[ν]
Line 38: [ἄνευ τοῦ δήμ]ου τοῦ 'Αθηναίων πληθ[ύοντος μὴ

PART II

Line 2: [ἐντ]ὸς τριάκοντα ἡμερῶν, ἐπειδ[άν] . .
Line 3: ['Αθηνα]ίων μηδὲ ἐνὶ μή[τε] βουλῇ μήτε
Line 4: [ἄνευ τοῦ δήμου τοῦ Αθηναίων πληθύο]ντος μὴ εἶναι θωὰν
  ἐπιβαλεῖν ['Αθη]ναίων μηδὲ [ἐνὶ]
Line 5: . . . . ε βούλησιν ἄνευ
Line 6: ὅπως ἂν δοκῇ
Line 8: [τ]οὺς πεντακοσίους πρὶν παύεσθαι τῆς ἀρχῆς
Line 9: [τῷ δήμῳ τῷ]ι 'Αθηναίων πληθύοντι, ὅτι ἂν βούληται
Line 10: . . . . τῶν δημοσίων ἐπάναγκες εἶναι τῇ βου[λῇ]
Line 11: δευτέραν πρεσβείαν, τρίτον δημο . . . .
Line 12: πρὸς τοὺς πρυτάνεις καὶ βουλε . . . .
Line 13: . . . . αι τοῦ πολέμου πέρι καὶ τῶν τρ . . . .
Line 14: . . . . να τῷ δήμῳ ἐντὸς ἓξ ἡ[μερῶν]
Line 15: [γνώμην συ]μβάλλεσθαι τὴν βουλήν
Line 16: ἐκκλησίᾳ καὶ ε . . . .
Line 17: ἐκκλ[ησ]ίᾳ τῆς . . . .

This decree, according to the editors of the *Corpus*, deals
with the relative powers of the boulé and the ecclesia.
Wilamowitz[2] sees in it "eine Instruktion des Rates für Vorsitz in der Volksversammlung." Justification for this view
may be found in Part II, lines 10–13, which seem to set down

[1] *CIA* i. 57.　　[2] *Op. cit.*, II, 195, n. 9.

the order in which certain matters are to be dealt with in the senate and brought before the ecclesia. They include embassies and war. In the first part of the document the word ἐπιψηφιῶ (I. 28) seems to belong to an oath to be taken by the senators. The occurrence of the words πεντακοσίας δραχμάς (I. 32) suggests the well-known limitation of the punitive powers of the boulé to the infliction of a fine of 500 drachmas.[1] But by far the most interesting feature of the document, and one that has not attracted the attention it deserves, is the reference to δῆμος πληθύων.[2] Certain matters can be dealt with only by the δῆμος πληθύων. Among them are war, the infliction of the death penalty, and the imposition of a fine, probably above a specified amount, 500 drachmas (I. 37; II. 4).[3] There were other restricted matters, as the occurrence of the phrase ἄνευ τοῦ δήμου τοῦ Ἀθηναίων πληθύοντος no fewer than seven times in these scanty fragments, clearly indicates. The question will come up again in connection with the discussion of the κυρία ἐκκλησία. For the present it is sufficient to point out that only a "full assembly" could determine questions relating to peace and war (I. 36) and exercise judicial functions. These are the most important powers of the sovereign body in a state. It would seem that the senate and the prytaneis were bound by sanctions and oaths to bring these and other important matters only before a δῆμος πληθύων. The document shows no trace of a definition of the phrase. The mention of ἐκκλησία in the last two lines of Part II shows that there are two kinds of assemblies. Obviously the difference between an ἐκκλησία and a δῆμος πληθύων was that a quorum was required for the latter. In view of the requirement of 6,000 votes in ostracism, it is not to be supposed that a citizen would be put to death, banished, or disfranchised by a less representative vote.

The editors of the *Corpus* date the present edition of the

---

[1] For the date of this decree and its effect on the powers of the boulé, cf. *infra*, p. 339.

[2] Cf. Glotz, in Daremberg-Saglio, *s.v.* "Ekklesia," p. 525.

[3] Between the limits of death and a fine fall banishment and disfranchisement as penalties.

law just after the overthrow of the Four Hundred. In this period there was a revision of the laws.[1] The Four Hundred had advocated, if not effected, a reduction of the citizens to 5,000, by giving the franchise to those only who could furnish themselves with arms. It is possible that there was a modicum of truth in the claim of the emissaries of the revolutionists to the army at Samos that the attendance at the ecclesia never exceeded 5,000.[2] There may have been some laxity in enforcing the quorum requirement in the stress of war. A re-enactment and stricter enforcement of the law specifying the matters that must come before a "full" assembly would deprive future revolutionists of a plausible argument in favor of restricting the franchise. Not much interest in fixing the date of the original enactment has been evinced. Scholars have been generally content to accept the editor's view that it is an ancient law.[3] Swoboda[4] suggests the reforms of Ephialtes as a likely date. This suggestion has been rejected by Cloché on the general ground that the reforms of Ephialtes increased, rather than restricted, the powers of the boulé and the ecclesia. He argues that it belongs to the period between the accession of Cleisthenes to power and the second Persian war.[5] In 479 the ecclesia already had the power of making peace. When Mardonius, on the eve of the Battle of Plataea, made proposals to the Athenians in the hope of detaching them from the national cause, his messenger appeared before the boulé. Alcidas proposed that they accept the proposition and lay it before the people. Highly incensed at this motion, the senators and some others fell upon Alcidas and stoned him to death.[6] The procedure here is in accordance with the regular practice. The senate made a *probouleuma* on the

[1] Busolt, *op. cit.*, III, 2, 1538.   [2] Thucydides viii. 72.

[3] θωά (II. 4), meaning "punishment," is one of the *priscae dictionis vestigia* relied upon by the editors in assigning an early date to the original law.

[4] *Hermes*, XXVIII, 597.

[5] Cloché, "Le conseil athénien des cinq cents et la peine de mort," *Rev. d. études grecques*, XXXIII, 32.

[6] Herodotus ix. 5: ὁ μὲν δὴ ταύτην τὴν γνώμην ἀπεφαίνετο, εἴτε δὴ δεδεγμένος χρήματα παρὰ Μαρδονίου, εἴτε καὶ ταῦτά οἱ ἐάνδανε· Ἀθηναῖοι δὲ αὐτίκα δεινὸν ποιησάμενοι, οἵ τε ἐκ τῆς βουλῆς καὶ οἱ ἔξωθεν, ὡς ἐπύθοντο, περιστάντες Λυκίδην κατέλευσαν βάλλοντες, τὸν δὲ Ἑλλησπόντιον [Μουρυχίδην] ἀπέπεμψαν ἀσινέα.

basis of information it had received. There is, then, no reason why the law may not be prior to 479, so far as it concerns the peace-making powers of the assembly (I. 36).

Another clue to the date of the document is to be found in Aristotle's[1] statement that in 502–501 B.C. the Senate of Five Hundred swore for the first time the oath still in use in his day. The oath of the boulé was either instituted or fundamentally revised at that time. Its importance is indicated by the fact that Aristotle singles it out for mention. Now the word ἐπιψηφιῶ (I. 28) in the decree seems to belong to the formula of an oath, sworn presumably by the boulé. In the act of settlement fixing the relations between Athens and Chalcis in Euboea in 446 B.C., after the revolt was crushed, the words οὐδ' ἐπιφσηφιῶ occur in the oath taken by the senate ratifying the settlement.[2] It may be conjectured that the senate in the present law was required to bind itself by oath, among other things, to put motions regarding certain specified matters only in a "full" assembly. In this way the responsibility for securing a quorum would rest with the prytaneis. The fact that this item of the senatorial oath is nowhere else mentioned need occasion no concern, for the complete oath has not been preserved. The oath and the document seem so closely related that there is good reason for believing that they are of the same date, 502–501 B.C.[3]

At the same time the ecclesia gained the right to elect the ten generals.[4] In this way the people exercised some control over the military policy of the state. A body so powerful in the state would not be satisfied to remain without independent judicial functions.

The decree, as Cloché[5] points out, grants to the people in "full" assembly jurisdiction in capital cases. The "full"

---

[1] Aristotle *Ath. Pol.* xxii. 2.

[2] *CIA* iv. (1) 27 a. 10; Hicks and Hill, *Greek Historical Inscriptions*, No. 40.

οὐδ' ἐπιφσηφιῶ κατὰ ἀπροσκλήτου οὔτε κατὰ τοῦ κοινοῦ οὔτε κατὰ ἰδιώτου οὐδὲ ἑνός, ...

Cf. Robertson, *The Administration of Justice in the Athenian Empire*, pp. 39–40. The word ἐπιφσηφιῶ refers "to the councillors when acting as prytaneis, in which capacity they would preside at trials by the process of εἰσαγγελία."

[3] Cf. Cloché, *Rev. d. études grecques*, XXXIII, 34. Cf. *infra*, p. 344.

[4] Aristotle *Ath. Pol.* xxii. 2.   [5] *Op. cit.*, p. 29.

assembly also had the right to inflict fines. The decree was doubtless intended merely to regulate and restrict the exercise of powers conferred by earlier legislation, the "new laws" of 508–507 B.C., when ostracism was introduced.[1] The experience of a few years would naturally suggest improvements. The fact that the law was re-enacted in 410 favors the view that it was a comprehensive piece of legislation, safeguarding the exercise of sovereign powers by the boulé and the assembly and regulating their relations to each other.

Another early law regarding the exercise of judicial functions by the assembly is the so-called "decree of Cannonus."[2] The primitive nature of the law suggests the possibility that it was the actual decree that first conferred independent jurisdiction on the assembled people. Its provisions, as given by Xenophon,[3] are as follows:

ἴστε δέ, ὦ ἄνδρες Ἀθηναῖοι, πάντες ὅτι τὸ Καννωνοῦ ψήφισμά ἐστιν ἰσχυρότατον, ὃ κελεύει, ἐάν τις τὸν τῶν Ἀθηναίων δῆμον ἀδικῇ, δεδεμένον ἀποδικεῖν ἐν τῷ δήμῳ, καὶ ἐὰν καταγνωσθῇ ἀδικεῖν, ἀποθανεῖν εἰς τὸ βάραθρον ἐμβληθέντα, τὰ δὲ χρήματα αὐτοῦ δημευθῆναι καὶ τῆς θεοῦ τὸ ἐπιδέκατον εἶναι. κατὰ τοῦτο τὸ ψήφισμα κελεύω κρίνεσθαι τοὺς στρατηγοὺς καὶ νὴ Δία, ἂν ὑμῖν γε δοκῇ, πρῶτον Περικλέα τὸν ἐμοὶ προσήκοντα· αἰσχρὸν γάρ μοί ἐστιν ἐκεῖνον περὶ πλείονος ποιεῖσθαι ἢ τὴν ὅλην πόλιν.

Xenophon, following the usual practice, is paraphrasing rather than reproducing, the exact wording of the law. Instead of δεδεμένον, Aristophanes uses διαλελημμένον in his reference to the decree of Cannonus in the *Ecclesiazousae*,[4] which the scholiast explains as κατεχόμενον ἑκατέρωθεν. Xenophon may have substituted δεδεμένον for the unusual form διαλελημμένον of the original text of the law. It has been suggested that δεδεμένον was a gloss which found its way into the text.[5] In any event, it seems likely that

[1] For the date of the introduction of ostracism, cf. Carcopino, *op. cit.*, p. 106. Cf. *supra*, p. 195.

[2] "Aus älterer Zeit stammt offenbar das Psephism des Kannonos."—Busolt-Swoboda, *op. cit.*, p. 884, n. 1.

[3] Xenophon *Hell.* i. 7. 20.

[4] 1089–90. τουτὶ τὸ πρᾶγμα κατὰ τὸ Καννωνοῦ σαφῶς ψήφισμα, βινεῖν δεῖ με διαλελημμένον.

[5] Bamberg, *Hermes*, XIII, 510. Cf. Rose, "Das Psephisma des Kannonos," *Commentationes philologicae*, pp. 83 ff., who quotes all the ancient sources in full and cites the literature up to 1891. Lipsius (*op. cit.*, p. 43, n. 132) approves of Bamberg's

Aristophanes' διαλελημμένον is the original word. The audience, seeing the young man on the stage beset on either side by an antique female, would be in no doubt as to the meaning of διαλελημμένον. This method of securing a prisoner is surely a survival. In primitive communities a public offender would be dragged unceremoniously by his accusers into the agora to face an outraged community, and held until his fate was duly determined.[1] His defense would be made with his accusers still clinging to him. The method of execution—hurling into the barathron—is obviously ancient. It is probably a convenient substitute for the earliest form of community punishment, stoning. In the fifth century the hemlock had largely taken the place of the barathron,[2] but execution by hurling into the barathron had never been abolished. It could still be used when authorized by special decree.[3] The barathron, however, continued to be used for the disposal of the bodies of certain types of criminals. The language of the decree, so far as it can be recovered, bears evidence of antiquity in the occurrence of one unusual, if not obsolete, word, ἀποδικεῖν, and one unusual form, διαλελημμένον, instead of

διαλελημμένον but rather prefers διειλημμένον suggested by Rose. Hesychius's Καννωνοῦ ψήφισμα gives διειλημμένον. But διαλελημμένον is to be preferred not only because it is found in Aristophanes but because the older form of the participle fits better into the context with the unusual word ἀποδικεῖν. Provision was made by the decree for adequate time for defense. Κρατῖνος (Κράτερος, Dindorf) δὲ καὶ πρὸς κλεψύδραν κελεῦσαι.—Scholiast on Aristophanes. It need not be assumed that the words πρὸς κλεψύδραν occurred in the decree, but there is no indication that provision was made for separate trials as Grote (op. cit., VIII, 196 ff.) insisted. Cf. Rose, op. cit., p. 89.

[1] Cf. Vergil Aeneid II. 57-58, for the capture and examination of Sinon:
"Ecce, manus juvenem interea post terga revinctum
Pastores magno ad regem clamore trahebant."

[2] The Thirty used the hemlock in their executions (Lysias xii. 17). Lipsius (op. cit., p. 77, n. 101) thinks the Thirty introduced the hemlock. But prohibition of burial in Attic territory in the case of Antiphon seems to indicate that he drank the hemlock. A criminal cast into the barathron would not be removed for burial anywhere. Cf. Plato Republic, 439 E. Cf. Hager, "How Were the Bodies of Criminals Disposed of after Death?" Jour. of Philol., VIII, 1 ff. The mention of κώνειον in Aristophanes shows that it was well known in 405 B.C. as a means of committing suicide (Frogs, 123 ff.).

[3] For examples of such decrees, see Lycurgus i. 121 and Deinarchus i. 62. Cf. Thonissen, Le droit penal de la république athénienne, pp. 97 ff.; Thalheim, s.v. "Barathron," in Pauly-Wissowa; Caillemer, s.v. "Barathron" in Daremberg-Saglio.

διειλημμένον. The word ἀποδικεῖν occurs only here in the literature of the classical period.[1]

The decree of Cannonus was well known to the Athenians. "You all know, men of Athens," says Euryptolemus, "that the decree of Cannonus is most severe" (ἰσχυρότατον). Aristophanes jests about it as if it were quite familiar to his audience; and when Ischomachus in the *Oeconomicus*[2] half humorously tells Socrates how his wife on different occasions held him to account, his use of the word διειλημμένως shows that he had in mind the decree of Cannonus: ἤδη δ᾽ ἔφη, ὦ Σώκρατες, καὶ διειλημμένως πολλάκις ἐκρίθην ὅτι χρὴ παθεῖν ἢ ἀποτῖσαι. ὑπὸ τοῦ ἔφην ἐγώ, ὦ Ἰσχόμαχε; ἐμὲ γὰρ δὴ τοῦτο ἐλάνθανεν. ὑπὸ τῆς γυναικός, ἔφη.

The notoriety of the decree, like that of the laws of Draco, was in part due to the harshness of the punishment and in part to its antiquity. The language of the decree and the primitive method of securing and punishing the culprit point to an early legal formulation of ancient community methods of dealing with public offenders.

Some features of the trial of Miltiades suggest the decree of Cannonus. According to Plato,[3] Miltiades would have been executed by being cast into the barathron had he been finally condemned to death. "The Athenians voted that Miltiades, the hero of Marathon, should be thrown into the pit of death [βάραθρον], and he was only saved by the chief Prytanis." Miltiades was specifically charged with deceiving the people (ἀπάτη τοῦ δήμου),[4] while the decree of Cannonus was enacted to deal with ἀδικία. But ἀπάτη is simply

---

[1] Suidas cites ἀποδικεῖν as being used by Antiphanes for ἀπολογεῖσθαι. It is now generally believed that Antiphon was meant. Antiphon displayed a preference for antique or poetical words on occasion to render his speech more impressive, e.g., ἀπιστέω=ἀπειθέω. Cf. Rose, *op. cit.*, p. 89.

[2] xi. 25. Cf. Rose, *op. cit.*, p. 87.

[3] *Gorgias*, 516 E: Μιλτιάδην δὲ τὸν ἐν Μαραθῶνι εἰς τὸ βάραθρον ἐμβαλεῖν ἐψηφίσαντο, καὶ εἰ μὴ διὰ τὸν πρύτανιν ἐνέπεσεν ἄν; καίτοι οὗτοι, εἰ ἦσαν ἄνδρες ἀγαθοί, ὡς σὺ φής, οὐκ ἄν ποτε ταῦτα ἔπασχον.

[4] Herodotus vi. 136: Ἀθηναῖοι δὲ ἐκ Πάρου Μιλτιάδεα ἀπονοστήσαντα εἶχον ἐν στόμασι, οἵ τε ἄλλοι καὶ μάλιστα Ξάνθιππος ὁ Ἀρίφρονος, ὃς θανάτου ὑπαγαγὼν ὑπὸ τὸν δῆμον Μιλτιάδεα ἐδίωκε τῆς Ἀθηναίων ἀπάτης εἵνεκεν. Μιλτιάδης δὲ αὐτὸς μὲν παρεὼν οὐκ ἀπελογέετο (ἦν γὰρ ἀδύνατος ὥστε σηπομένου τοῦ μηροῦ), προκειμένου δὲ αὐτοῦ ἐν κλίνῃ ὑπεραπελογέοντο οἱ φίλοι.

a particular form of ἀδικία. As Miltiades, suffering from a wound, was carried into the assembly on a couch, he was not secured in the usual way.

If these considerations are valid, the date of the decree is not later than 489 B.C., the year of Miltiades' trial,[1] and may be as early as 508–507, when ostracism and other new laws were introduced. It would seem strange to permit the assembly to banish a man suspected of designs of establishing a tyranny and not give it the power to try one who was accused of actual wrongdoing (ἀδικία) to the community.

The law of Cannonus provided for the trial by the ecclesia of those charged with "doing wrong to the people"[2] (ἐάν τις τὸν τῶν Ἀθηναίων δῆμον ἀδικῇ). It was a general charge intended to cover every conceivable kind of offense. There was no attempt made to define ἀδικία. It was left to the ecclesia to determine whether the offense in question amounted to ἀδικία. But other laws were soon enacted naming specific offenses. Miltiades, for example, was charged with "deceiving the people"[3] (τῆς Ἀθηναίων ἀπάτης εἵνεκεν). This particular kind of offense would be amply covered by ἀδικία. But Demosthenes refers to an ancient (ἀρχαῖος) law providing for the trial of those charged with deceiving the people by means of false promises. The case came before the ecclesia, and the penalty was death.[4] This is precisely the offense with which Militiades was charged, and Lipsius has suggested that the law mentioned by Demosthenes was in force at

---

[1] Rose (op. cit., p. 93) believes that Miltiades was tried according to the decree of Cannonus. There is no need to try to twist Herodotus' κατὰ τὴν ἀδικίην into a reference to a charge of ἀδικία, as in the decree of Cannonus, to support this view as Bohm (De εἰσαγγελίαις, p. 22) does. Lipsius (op. cit., p. 43, n. 132), "nach der Altertümlichkeit von Inhalt wie Ausdruck" puts it not later than the middle of the fifth century, but he offers no convincing arguments against the view of Rose. The decree of Cannonus fixed the punishment in case of conviction. But there is no need to assume with How and Wells (op. cit.) that the trial of Miltiades was an ἀγὼν τιμητός. Cf. Shuckburg, Herodotus, VI, note ad loc.

[2] In later practice, indictments regularly charged ἀδικία. The particulars which followed indicated the nature of the "wrongdoing." Compare the indictment of Socrates as given by Diogenes Laertius ii. 40: Ἀδικεῖ Σωκράτης, οὓς μὲν ἡ πόλις νομίζει θεοὺς οὐ νομίζων, ἕτερα δὲ καινὰ δαιμόνια εἰσηγούμενος· ἀδικεῖ δὲ καὶ τοὺς νέους διαφθείρων. Τίμημα θάνατος.

[3] Cf. supra, p. 197.   [4] Demosthenes xx. 135; xlix. 67.

that time. This is entirely possible; it is in accordance with the natural tendency of legal development to pass special laws dealing with offenses that are particularly injurious to the community. The history of the νόμος εἰσαγγελτικός fully illustrates this tendency. But the version of the law against deception of the people given by Demosthenes can scarcely be the original law if it belonged to the age of Cleisthenes: νόμος ὑμῖν ἐάν τις ὑποσχόμενός τι τὸν δῆμον ἢ τὴν βουλὴν ἢ δικαστήριον ἐξαπατήσῃ τὰ ἔσχατα πάσχειν.[1] One would expect to find ἡλιαία rather than δικαστήριον. But even if the dicasteries were already organized, it is wholly unlikely that at this early date the deceiving of law courts was common enough to be prejudicial to the public interest. The sycophants came later. But there is no reason why the original law—ἐάν τις ὑποσχόμενός τι τὸν δῆμον ἐξαπατήσῃ—may not have been revised at a later time to include the boulé and the heliastic courts.

Reverting to the question of a quorum in the ecclesia, we find that πλήρης δῆμος was used in an essay on Athenian democracy, attributed to Xenophon, in what is clearly a technical sense.[2] The writer does not define it, but it has

[1] xx. 100. Cf. Lipsius, op. cit., p. 180.

[2] (Xenophon) Ath. Pol. ii. 17, edition of Marchant in "Oxford Classical Texts": Ἔτι δὲ συμμαχίας καὶ τοὺς ὅρκους ταῖς μὲν ὀλιγαρχουμέναις πόλεσιν ἀνάγκη ἐμπεδοῦν· ἢν δὲ μὴ ἐμμένωσι ταῖς συνθήκαις, ἢ ὑφ' ὅτου ἀδικεῖ ὀνόματα ἀπὸ τῶν ὀλίγων οἳ συνέθεντο· ἄσσα δ' ἂν ὁ δῆμος σύνθηται, ἔξεστιν αὐτῷ ἑνὶ ἀνατιθέντι τὴν αἰτίαν τῷ λέγοντι καὶ τῷ ἐπιψηφίσαντι ἀρνεῖσθαι τοῖς ἄλλοις ὅτι Οὐ παρῆν οὐδὲ ἀρέσκει ἔμοιγε, ἃ συγκείμενα πυνθάνονται ἐν πλήρει τῷ δήμῳ, καὶ εἰ μὴ δόξαι εἶναι ταῦτα, προφάσεις μυρίας ἐξηύρηκε τοῦ μὴ ποιεῖν ὅσα ἂν μὴ βούλωνται.

The passage as it appears in Marchant's edition is translated by Petch, under the title "The Old Oligarch," as follows:

"Again oligarchical states must abide by their alliances and oaths. If they do not keep to the agreement penalties can be exacted from the few who made it. But whenever the commons makes an agreement it can lay the blame on the individual speaker or proposer, and say to the other party that it was not present and does not approve what they know was agreed upon in full assembly; and should it be decided that this is not so, the commons has discovered a hundred excuses for not doing what they may not wish to do."

Kalinka reads οὐδὲ ἀρέσκει οἱ, εἴ γε μὴ [τὰ] συγκείμενα πυνθάνονται ἐν πλήρει τῷ δήμῳ instead of Marchant's οὐδὲ ἀρέσκει ἔμοιγε, ἃ συγκείμενα πυνθάνονται ἐν πλήρει τῷ δήμῳ. Brooks, who translates Kalinka's text under the title "An Athenian Critic of Athenian Democracy," renders the passage as follows:

"But whatever engagements the people enters upon, it is possible for it, attributing the responsibility to the individual speaker or to the chairman who put the

been satisfactorily identified with δῆμος πληθύων.[1] It is charged in the treatise that democracies are irresponsible and untrustworthy in comparison with oligarchies. They are always trying to evade their obligations to other states. The text of the paragraph is corrupt at a critical point, but it is clear that certain measures had to be adopted by a "full" assembly. The reference to an oath, συμμαχίαι, συνθῆκαι, and the words συγκείμενα ἐν πλήρει τῷ δήμῳ, used to describe the measures in question, serve to identify them as treaties and alliances, which were always ratified by oaths sworn in the name of the whole people.[2] πλήρης must be a current equivalent of πληθύων used in a technical sense with δῆμος.

In the *Ecclesiazousae*[3] Aristophanes uses the words πλήρης δῆμος.

SECOND WOMAN
A little spinning while the Assembly fills [πληρουμένης τῆς ἐκκλησίας].

PRAXAGORA
Fills? Miserable woman!

S. W.   Yes, why not?
O I can spin and listen just as well.

PRAX.
Fancy you spinning! when you must not have
The tiniest morsel of your person seen.
T'were a fine scrape, if when the Assembly's full [εἰ πλήρης τύχοι ὁ δῆμος ὤν],
Some woman clambering o'er the seats, and throwing
Her cloak awry, should show that she's a woman.

---

question, to tell others that the people itself was not present, and does not give its approval, unless it learns of arrangements in a full assembly; and if it should not seem good for these arrangements to be carried out it has discovered, etc."

Kalinka's own version is as follows:

"Was aber das Volk vereinbart hat, da steht es ihm frei, einem die Schuld zuzuschieben, dem Antragsteller und dem Versammlungsleiter, den Übrigen aber, zu erklären, er sei nicht dabei gewesen und es sage ihm nicht zu, ausgenommen höchstens, sie hätten erfahren, es sei in einer Vollversammlung des Volkes vereinbart worden; und wenn es ihm nicht belieben sollte, dass dies Gültigkeit habe, u.s.w."

[1] Müller-Strübing, "Ἀθηναίων πολιτεία, Die attische Schrift vom Staat der Athener; Untersuchungen, neue Textrecension und Paraphrase." *Philologus*, IV (1880), Supplementband, 1 ff. Kalinka (*Die Pseudoxenophontische Ἀθηναίων πολιτεία*, p. 239) puts the quorum at 6,000 but limits the occasions requiring a quorum to νόμοι ἐπ' ἀνδρί and ostracism.

[2] Cf. Kalinka, *op. cit.*, p. 235, with notes.   [3] 88–97, Roger's translation.

Apparently the words πληρουμένης and πλήρης are used in the normal literal sense. The meeting of the assembly and the subject 'for deliberation, περὶ σωτηρίας, had been announced in advance. A great crowd assembled for the meeting. The extra crowd would seem to be accounted for sufficiently by the attendance of the women, but the words of Blepyrus and Chremes suggest the possibility of a technical use of the word.

BL.
> Whatever was it though that brought together
> So vast a crowd so early?

CHR.
> 'Twas determined
> To put this question to the assembled people,
> "How best to save the state" [περὶ σωτηρίας].[1]

A debate, περὶ σωτηρίας, was a matter of great public interest and not infrequent occurrence. Dionysus in the *Frogs* asked Euripides and Aeschylus to express themselves περὶ τὴν πόλεως σωτηρίαν.[2]

Isocrates[3] published his essay which he called Λόγος Ἀρεοπαγιτικός in the guise of a speech in the assembly περὶ σωτηρίας. And Wilamowitz[4] supposes that the political commission appointed in 411 B.C. was instructed to formulate measures περὶ τῆς σωτηρίας. But the "public safety" does not appear either in the fragmentary decree, *CIA* i. 57, or in Aristotle's[5] list of topics for discussion in the regular meetings of the ecclesia. But in neither case is the list complete. The subject of the safety of the state would naturally attract a great deal of public attention, especially if constitutional changes were contemplated; and it would be entirely reasonable to require that changes in the constitution be adopted by a "full" assembly (δῆμος πλήρης or πληθύων).

It is somewhat surprising that there are no other references in the literary or epigraphical sources to a quorum. There are, however, some references by implication. Fränkel[6] has advanced the theory that "all Athenians" and "six thousand Athenians" are in certain connections equivalent

---

[1] *Ibid.*, 394–97. [2] 1435–36. [3] vii. 1. [4] *Op. cit.*, I, 102.
[5] *Ath. Pol.* xliii. 4. [6] *Die attischen Geschworenengerichte*, pp. 16 ff.

expressions. He cites a passage from Demosthenes[1] dealing with the granting of immunity (ἄδεια), in which the condition μὴ ἔλαττον ἢ ἑξακισχιλίων ψηφισαμένων is repeated by εἰ πᾶσιν Ἀθηναίοις ἐδόκει. Another example of this technical use of "all Athenians" as the equivalent of "six thousand Athenians" he finds in the trial of the generals by the ecclesia in 406 B.C. The senate was instructed by the ecclesia to bring in a decree providing for the trial. The decree introduced by Callixenus which was finally passed contained the words διαψηφίσασθαι Ἀθηναίους πάντας κατὰ φυλάς.[2] An equally good example of this technical use of "all Athenians" which was not noticed by Fränkel is found in Lysias. At the end of the Peloponnesian War oligarchic plotters with the aid of a corrupt boulé sought to get rid of prominent democratic opponents. Agoratus, an unscrupulous informer, was induced to lay information against them in the boulé.[3] By action of the boulé he was taken before "the ecclesia which met in the theater in Munychia"[4] where he repeated his information. The ecclesia voted to turn over the accused to a court of 2,000 dicasts for trial. But before the case could be tried, as provided, the Thirty were installed and the accused were tried and condemned by the boulé. Upon the restoration of democracy, Agoratus was brought to trial charged with being responsible for the death of these men. The prosecutor, on calling up Agoratus for interrogation, remarked καί μοι ἀπόκριναι, ὦ Ἀγόρατε· οὐ γὰρ οἶμαί σε ἔξαρνον γενήσεσθαι ἃ ἐναντίον Ἀθηναίων ἁπάντων ἐποίησας.[5] The phrase Ἀθηναίων ἁπάντων manifestly refers to the Athenians present when Agoratus gave his information in the ecclesia. Now it so happens that later in the speech the prosecutor refers to the granting of immunity (ἄδεια) to a certain Menestratus whose

[1] xxiv. 46 and 48.   [2] Xenophon *Hellenica* i. 7. 9.

[3] Lysias xiii. 18–36 for the case against Agoratus.

[4] *Ibid.*, 32.

[5] *Ibid.*, The recurrence of the words ἐναντίον Ἀθηναίων ἁπάντων in a later part (86) of the speech would seem to show pretty clearly that the phrasing of the idea of the widest possible publicity is not casual and accidental but intentional and technical.

name was included in the list furnished by Agoratus. Menestratus was at once taken into custody by authority of the boulé;[1] but when "the ecclesia met in the theater in Munychia" Hagnodorus, a fellow-demesman of Menestratus and a relative of Critias, secured immunity for Menestratus who thereupon appeared as an informer in the ecclesia and added new names to the list of accused. It is not expressly said that the assembly before which Agoratus appeared granted immunity to Menestratus. But with good reason the identity is assumed.[2] The designation ἡ ἐκκλησία Μουνιχίασιν ἐν τῷ θεάτρῳ used in both cases[3] shows that one assembly handled both. Now ἄδεια could be granted only by an assembly of at least 6,000.[4] Consequently we have another instance of the equivalency of "all Athenians" and "six thousand Athenians." Still another example of this usage which Fränkel does not cite in this connection is found in Harpocration, s.v. ῎Αρδηττος, the place where πάντες ὤμνυον ᾿Αθηναῖοι τὸν ὅρκον τὸν ἡλιαστικόν.[5] Owing to the age requirement in the case of the δικασταί, it is true that 6,000 δικασταί would not be identical with 6,000 ἐκκλησιασταί;[6] but as both groups represented the whole people in different spheres, they could both be called πάντες ᾿Αθηναῖοι. In the Harpocration passage, πάντες ᾿Αθηναῖοι could not literally mean "all Athenians," for only 6,000 of those possessing the requisite age qualification could take the oath.

[1] Ibid., 55. ὁ Μενέστρατος οὗτος ἀπεγράφη ὑπὸ τοῦ ᾿Αγοράτου καὶ συλληφθεὶς ἐδέδετο. Only the names of the generals and taxiarchs were laid before the ecclesia. The boulé dealt with the others. περὶ δὲ τῶν ἄλλων ἀπέχρη ἐν τῇ βουλῇ [μήνυσις] μόνη γεγενημένη (32).

[2] Cf. Boerner, De Rebus a Graecis inde ab Anno 410 usque ad Annum 403 A. Chr. N. Gestis, p. 48; Grote, op. cit., VIII, 210; Meyer, op. cit., IV², p. 666; Thalheim, note on Lysias xiii. 55.

[3] Lysias xii. 32 and 55.   [4] Demosthenes xxiv. 46.

[5] Fränkel, op. cit., pp. 19–20, uses this passage to prove that "jeder Athener über dreissig Jahre von selbst Heliast war." All he had to do was to offer himself and prove that he possessed the requisite qualifications. In this sense the dicasts were "all Athenians." But they were "all Athenians" rather because in the sphere of the administration of justice they represented the Athenian people.

[6] Cf. Bruck, "Über die Organisation der Athenischen Heliastengerichte im 4. Jahrh. v. Chr.," Philologus, LII, 314; Bamberg, Hermes, XIII (1878), 505.

Andocides[1] cites a law enacted in 410 B.C. providing that "all Athenians" should take a solemn oath by tribes and demes to do all in their power to destroy subverters of democracy. ὀμόσαι δ' Ἀθηναίους ἅπαντας καθ' ἱερῶν τελείων, κατὰ φυλὰς καὶ κατὰ δήμους ἀποκτενεῖν, κ.τ.λ. The words Ἀθηναίους ἅπαντας are neither strictly technical nor wholly literal. The proposed oath was in effect a pledge of loyalty to the restored democracy. It was desirable that as many as possible, even all, should participate in the ceremony. Hence it was to be administered in the ecclesia and in the deme assemblies (κατὰ φυλὰς καὶ κατὰ δήμους). But there was no question of a quorum or constitutional validity involved. Each man who took the oath was bound, whether few or many participated. In a sense the words "all Athenians" were used literally, but there was an echo of their technical significance that really supports the theory of Fränkel. The similarity to the phraseology of the decree of Callixenus can scarcely be accidental.[2] Gilbert[3] thought the theory was open to question because it had so little support in the sources. It is hoped that these additional instances of the identity of "six thousand Athenians" and "all Athenians" may serve to minimize, if not remove, this objection.

The Athenian practice in the matter of ratifying by oath treaties and other public agreements was not uniform. But in at least one instance the state was represented by 6,000 citizens in the persons of the dicasts for the current year.[4] In the act of settlement of 446 B.C. concerning Chalcis in Euboea, all adult male Chalcidians were required to take an oath of allegiance, while the Athenian senators and dicasts (6,000) swore on behalf of the Athenians to respect certain specified rights of the Chalcidians. Some scholars

[1] i. 97.

[2] Xenophon Hellenica, i. 7. 9. διαψηφίσασθαι Ἀθηναίους ἅπαντας κατὰ φυλάς.

[3] Op. cit., p. 308.

[4] CIA iv. (1) 27a. Hicks and Hill, op. cit., No. 40; Dittenberger, Sylloge², I, 17. Cf. Robertson, op. cit., pp. 36–47, for a full discussion of the purport and purpose of the oath. Cf. Fränkel, op. cit., pp. 45 and 51. The boulé and the generals and other magistrates regularly took the oath. Cf. Dittenberger, op. cit., I, 36. For reasons for the change in this case, see Fränkel, op. cit., pp. 50–51.

argue that the senators and dicasts bound only themselves and that the intention was to leave the assembly a free hand. Some ground for this view is found in the circumstance that the content of the oath deals mainly with legal matters. But, as has been pointed out,[1] the first term of the oath deals with a matter that was entirely outside the province of either the boulé or the dicasts. It refers not to banishment by the sentence of a court but to the deportation of the whole population, which would require a decree of the ecclesia. Furthermore, since the entire citizen body of Chalcis was to swear, it was only natural that the Athenians on their part should bind themselves by the oath of a really representative group of citizens. Such a group would naturally correspond in numbers to the quorum of the ecclesia. And the 6,000 dicasts were easier to identify and assemble than any other 6,000 members of the ecclesia.

The elaborate efforts made by the authorities to enforce attendance in the ecclesia all point to a quorum requirement. In the *Acharnians* of Aristophanes,[2] presented in the year 425 B.C., Dicaeopolis complains that, although it is the morning for the meeting of the "principal" assembly (κυρία ἐκκλησία) of the month, the benches are empty and the people are chattering in the agora, scurrying about to avoid the vermilion-painted rope. The scholiast on this passage remarks, ὑπὲρ τοῦ ἐξ ἀνάγκης αὐτοὺς εἰς τὰς ἐκκλησίας συνιέναι τοῦτο ἐμηχανῶντο καὶ πολλὰ ἄλλα. Archers under the direction of six lexiarchs and their thirty assistants shut up the booths in the market place, closed up the streets that did not lead to the Pnyx, and by means of smeared ropes tried to force the loiterers to attend the ecclesia.[3] The scholiast says that those who were marked were subject to a fine.[4] The difficulty of inducing attendance in the ecclesia was in part

---

[1] Robertson, *op. cit.*, pp. 40 f. Cf. *infra*, p. 340, for the wording of the oath.

[2] 19–20.

[3] Pollux viii. 104, and the scholiast on Aristophanes' *Acharnians*, 22. Cf. Gilbert, *Greek Constitutional Antiquities*, p. 289. For a different explanation of the painted rope, see Wilamowitz, *Aus Kydathen*, p. 165, n. 77.

[4] The scholiast must be wrong about the fine, for, since attendance was not compulsory, there was no ground of complaint.

responsible for the institution of pay for attendance. Aristotle says:

> At first they refused to allow pay for attendance at the assembly; but the result was that the people did not attend. Consequently after the Prytaneis had tried many devices in vain in order to induce the populace [τὸ πλῆθος] to come and ratify the votes Agyrrhius made provision of one obol a day.[1]

Whether τὸ πλῆθος, be taken in the sense of "populace" or in the sense of "the number,"[2] meaning "quorum," the general impression made upon the reader is that there was an urgent reason for the various measures taken to secure the attendance of as many as possible. The phrase πρὸς τὴν ἐπικύρωσιν τῆς χειροτονίας clearly implies that a vote might be taken under circumstances that would render it invalid. The difference could be only numerical.

There is practically no evidence as to the numbers that habitually attended the meetings of the ecclesia. One inscription records a vote of 3,616.[3] After the consummation of the revolution of 411 B.C. a committee was sent to Samos to reassure the army regarding the intentions of the revolutionists. In attempting to justify their proposed restriction of the number of citizens to 5,000, they said that "because of their military expeditions and their activities abroad the Athenians had never yet come to consult upon any matter so important that 5,000 had assembled."[4] This statement is propaganda. In all probability it is an exaggeration. "Never yet" is much too strong. The effect of the Spartan invasions during the earlier years of the war was to drive the country people into the city. The regular population of the city was increased far beyond its housing capacity. The

---

[1] *Ath. Pol.* xli. 3: μισθοφόρον δ' ἐκκλησίαν τὸ μὲν πρῶτον ἀπέγνωσαν ποιεῖν· οὐ συλλεγομένων δ' εἰς τὴν ἐκκλησίαν, ἀλλὰ πολλὰ σοφιζομένων τῶν πρυτάνεων, ὅπως προσιστῆται τὸ πλῆθος πρὸς τὴν ἐπικύρωσιν τῆς χειροτονίας, πρῶτον μὲν Ἀγύρριος ὀβολὸν ἐπόρισεν, μετὰ δὲ τοῦτον Ἡρακλείδης ὁ Κλαζομένιος ὁ βασιλεὺς ἐπικαλούμενος διώβολον, πάλιν δ' Ἀγύρριος τριώβολον.

[2] Mathieu and Haussoullier (Budé edition), translate ὅπως προσιστῆται τὸ πλῆθος πρὸς τὴν ἐπικύρωσιν τῆς χειροτονίας "afin d'obtenir le nombre nécessaire pour rendre valable le vote." Kenyon and Kaibel and Kiessling translate τὸ πλῆθος as "the populace" and "das Volk," respectively.

[3] Thalheim, in Pauly-Wissowa, *s.v.* δικασταί.   [4] Thucydides viii. 72.

occupation of Decelea forced the remaining population of the outlying demes to take refuge in the city. In spite of military service and casualties, it is doubtful if fewer citizens were available for service in the ecclesia than when the country people lived at peace on their farms and resorted to the city only periodically. At any rate, Andocides mentions a dicastery of 6,000 in 415 b.c.[1] And the ostracism of Hyperbolus[2] in 418 required the presence of at least 6,000. There are references to assemblies elsewhere in Greece with a minimum attendance requirement. In Magnesia[3] such an assembly was called κυρία. The quorum was 600. In some Delphian inscriptions the formulas σὺν ψάφοις ταῖς ἐν νόμοις and σὺν ψάφῳ τᾷ ἐν νόμῳ occur. As νόμαιος and ἔννομος are found as synonyms[4] of κύριος, it seems that in Delphi also a quorum was required for certain purposes. The number is not mentioned.

In Athens certain assemblies were called κυρίαι. In view of the well-known reluctance of the Athenians to attend meetings of the ecclesia, the securing of a quorum could hardly have been left to chance. It is not to be supposed that the prytaneis in making up the program for an assembly meeting included each time, if the occasion arose, matters that had to be dealt with by a δῆμος πληθύων on the chance that a quorum might be present. Such a haphazard way of managing the public business would surely have been intolerable. The resulting inconvenience, if a quorum failed to appear, would have been serious. This difficulty appears to have been in part obviated by specifying certain recurring meetings of the assembly at which efforts were made to secure an adequate attendance. The programs of these meetings were reserved for those measures that required a quorum. Two types of assembly are mentioned in the early inscription quoted above.[5] One is called simply ἐκκλησία; the other is called δῆμος πληθύων. There are indications that in the fifth century the regularly recurring meeting, at which measures requiring a quorum were presented, was the κυρία ἐκκλησία.

[1] Andocides i. 17.

[2] Carcopino, op. cit., p. 221.

[3] Thalheim, op. cit., p. 2170.

[4] Ibid., p. 2165.

[5] CIA i. 57. Cf. supra, p. 201.

There was some uncertainty, even in ancient times, as to which assemblies were properly called κύριαι. Scholiasts and lexicographers are divided.[1] According to one view, one assembly in each prytany was the κυρία. According to the other view, the four regular assemblies of each prytany were called κύριαι, to distinguish them from the special meetings. But Aristotle[2] seems to say quite definitely that only the first assembly was called κυρία. The lexicographers who drew their information from him so understood him. But this does not settle the matter to the satisfaction of all; there is a complication. Aristotle, in his account of the business discussed at the regular meetings, says that ambassadors were to be introduced at the third and fourth meetings. This seems to be at variance with Aristophanes, who, in the *Acharnians*,[3] represents Athenian ambassadors making their reports in a κυρία assembly. Consequently an attempt has been made to interpret Aristotle as meaning that the four regular meetings were called κύριαι.[4] But it is useless to at-

---

[1] The scholiast on Aristophanes' *Acharnians*, 19, says that the three regular meetings per prytany were called κύριαι.

κυρίας ἐκκλησίας: Ἐν ᾗ ἐκύρουν τὰ ψηφίσματα. εἰσὶ δὲ νόμιμοι ἐκκλησίαι αἱ λεγόμεναι κύριαι τρεῖς τοῦ μηνὸς Ἀθήνησιν, ἡ πρώτη καὶ ἡ δεκάτη καὶ ἡ τριακάς. εἰσὶ δὲ καὶ πρόσκλητοι συναγόμεναι κατά τινα ἐπείγοντα πράγματα. αἱ μὲν οὖν νόμιμοι καὶ ὡρισμέναι ἐκκλησίαι κύριαι λέγονται, ὡς ἔφαμεν, αἱ δὲ πρὸς τὸ κατεπεῖγον συναγόμεναι σύγκλητοι.

Harpocration, *s.v.* κυρία ἐκκλησία, quoting Aristotle, says: "προγράφουσι δὲ" φησι "καὶ κυρίαν ἐκκλησίαν, ἐν ᾗ δεῖ τὰς ἀρχὰς ἀποχειροτονεῖν οἳ δοκοῦσι μὴ καλῶς ἄρχειν, καὶ περὶ φυλακῆς δὲ τῆς χώρας." καὶ τὰς εἰσαγγελίας ἐν ταύτῃ τῇ ἡμέρᾳ τοὺς βουλομένους ποιεῖσθαί φησι, καὶ τὰ ἑξῆς.

To the same effect are Suidas and Pollux viii. 95. Photius gives both views: Κυρία ἐκκλησία: ἐν ᾗ τοὺς ἄρχοντας ἐχειροτόνουν· οἷον στρατηγούς, ἱππάρχους καὶ τοὺς τοιούτους· ἄλλοι δέ φασιν καθ' ἕκαστον μῆνα ἐκκλησίας εἶναι τρεῖς, αἱ κύριαι πρὸς σύγκρισιν ἐλέγοντο τῶν συγκλήτων.

For texts of all scholia and lexicographers conveniently assembled, see Reusch, "De diebus contionum ordinariarum apud Athenienses," *Dissertationes Philologicae Argentoratenses*, III, 50-51.

[2] *Ath. Pol.* xliii. 4. There were four meetings per prytany, of which one was called κυρία. The three assemblies mentioned by the scholiast belong to the later period of the twelve tribes (Busolt-Swoboda, *op. cit.*, 987, n. 4).

[3] Line 61 calls for reports from Athenian ambassadors to Persia. It is true that a mission from the king is introduced to confirm the report. In line 134 the report of an embassy to Sitalces is called for. Aristotle (*Ath. Pol.* xliii. 6) seems to be talking of foreign representatives rather than Athenian embassies.

[4] Van Leeuwen, *Acharnians*, 19.

tempt to force this meaning upon the passage in view of Aristotle's[1] later statement that after the introduction of pay for attendance at the meetings of the ecclesia 9 obols were paid for attendance at the κυρία ἐκκλησία, and 6 obols for the others (ταῖς ἄλλαις ἐκκλησίαις). It is scarcely possible that κυρία ἐκκλησία should refer to the four regular meetings of the assembly and ταῖς ἄλλαις ἐκκλησίαις to the special meetings (σύγκλητοι).

It is to be observed that, while certain important measures could be dealt with only by an ἐκκλησία κυρία, it by no means follows that other measures also, which Aristotle assigns to the other meetings, could not be put on the program of the κυρία. For example, while definite provision is made for introducing ambassadors at two ordinary meetings, there is no indication that they might not be introduced in the "sovereign" assembly, as Aristophanes did in the *Acharnians*.[2] Epigraphical evidence favors the view that only one assembly in each prytany was called κυρία. Inscriptions do not show more than one κυρία ἐκκλησία per prytany.[3] The difference in the composition of the "sovereign" assembly in comparison with the others would most naturally be in the numbers in attendance. The sovereign assembly required a quorum.

There is no evidence to show when the κυρία assembly, as a device to secure a quorum at regular intervals, was introduced. The earliest literary reference to the κυρία assembly is in the *Acharnians*[4] of Aristophanes, presented in 425 B.C. It occurs also in a very fragmentary inscription of uncertain

[1] lxii 2: μισθοφοροῦσι δὲ πρῶτον ὁ δῆμος ταῖς μὲν ἄλλαις ἐκκλησίαις δραχμήν, τῇ δὲ κυρίᾳ ἐννέα ⟨ὀβολούς⟩. ἔπειτα τὰ δικαστήρια τρεῖς ὀβολούς· εἶθ' ἡ βουλὴ πέντε ὀβολούς.

[2] Rennie, *Acharnians*, 19. Aristophanes does not gratuitously violate the rules of constitutional usage. Cf. Rogers, *Introduction to the Acharnians*, xxvii, who argues that the regular assemblies were called κύριαι in the time of Aristophanes and that there were three in number per month (Scholia, Demosthenes xxiv. 20). By the time of Aristotle they had been increased to four, so that the increased pay for attendance might serve as a dole for the impoverished citizens. It is to this period that the lexicographers, quoting Aristotle, refer.

[3] Reusch, *op. cit.*, pp. 66 f.; Gilbert, *op. cit.*, p. 285, n. 5.

[4] Line 19.

date,[1] possibly a little earlier than the *Acharnians*. There
is a general similarity between the business of the δῆμος
πληθύων as it appears in the inscription *CIA* i. 57 and that
of the κυρία ἐκκλησία as described by Aristotle.[2] But such
technical terms as προβολή, συκοφάντης in Aristotle show that
the version of the law, organizing and distributing the business over the meetings of the ecclesia, from which he drew
his information, did not originate in the time of Cleisthenes.
It may belong to the reforms of Ephialtes which enlarged
the functions of the ecclesia. In any event, the disappearance
of δῆμος πληθύων or πλήρης from literature can be readily explained in this way. It was supplanted by the newer and more
convenient κυρία ἐκκλησία. Even κυρία ἐκκλησία is rarely used
outside of official documents and technical treatises. The
historian and the orator refer to measures passed by the assembly without taking the trouble to specify that it was a
"sovereign" assembly.

The Athenians were familiar with the κυρία assembly and
the quorum in the demes also. There is one record of an
ἀγορὰ κυρία.[3] Two citizens of Axione were praised and given
crowns for their public services in a decree adopted ἐν τῇ
ἀγορᾷ τῇ κυρίᾳ. There is nowhere in the sources a definition
of an ἀγορὰ κυρία. There is a reference to a quorum in the
deme Myrrhinus. Appeals from the decision of the auditors
were permitted to an assembly of not fewer than thirty
demesmen.[4] It seems likely that a quorum was required in
the other demes, varying according to their size. There is
no evidence that the quorum requirement constituted the
distinction between the ἀγορὰ κυρία and the others. There is
good reason for a quorum when the assembly was performing
judicial functions, but an honorific decree does not seem

[1] *CIA* i. 25. Cf. *Reusch, op. cit.*, p. 68.

[2] *Ath. Pol.* xliii. 4.

[3] *CIA* ii. 585. 1–2. Haussoullier, *La vie municipale en Attique*, p. 6, believes that
all the regular assemblies were κύριαι.

[4] *CIA* ii. 578. 21 ff.: ὁ δήμαρχος διδότω τὴν ψῆφον ἐὰν παρῶσι μὴ ἐλάττους ἢ
ΔΔΔ.

of sufficient importance to require the attendance of a quorum.[1]

It is to be observed that there is no mention of δικαστήρια in the inscription *CIA* i. 57 as it stands. In view of its fragmentary character, it may seem hazardous to base any conclusions upon this circumstance, but the tenor of the document is against any assumption that it dealt with the judicial situation in a comprehensive manner. And nothing short of a comprehensive judicature act could have sufficed to deal with such a complicated question as the shift of judicial functions from the magistrates to the Heliaea. The new duties of the magistrates in connection with the preliminary hearings had to be defined. Not all cases went to the Heliaea under the new system. The king archon took certain cases for trial before the Areopagus;[2] these had to be specified. And finally there was the organization of the dicasteries. It must have been anticipated at once that a single court, the Heliaea, could not handle all the litigation of the community. It is highly improbable that these and other details were dealt with in the missing portions of the inscription. The earliest evidence of the existence of δικαστήρια is in the year 462–461, which constitutes a *terminus ante quem*. In that year Ephialtes "stripped the Areopagus of all the acquired prerogatives from which it derived its guardianship of the constitution, and assigned some of them to the Council of the Five Hundred, and others to the assembly and the law courts [δικαστήρια]."[3] There is no suggestion in Aristotle's words that the dicasteries were recent creations. The contrary rather is the case. In order to discredit the Areopagus in the eyes of the people, Ephialtes "brought about the ruin of many of its members by bringing actions against them with

[1] In the decrees of Magnesia granting προξενίην, πολιτείην, ἔγκτησιν, ἀτελίαν πάντων κ.τ.λ., it is sometimes mentioned that the measure was passed ἐκκλησίας κυρίας γενομένης ὑπὲρ ἐξακοσίων. The quorum was not required, but it probably enhanced the honor. Cf. Kern, *Die Inschriften von Magnesia am Maeander*, Nos. 2 and 4.

[2] The Areopagus continued to try cases of ἀσέβεια. Cf. *infra*, p. 260.

[3] *Ath. Pol.* xxv. 2.

reference to their administration." These actions must have been brought in the δικαστήρια, and the campaign must have extended over a considerable period of time.

Some years before 462–461 overseas litigation must have reached considerable proportions. Treaties providing for litigation between citizens of the contracting states (δίκαι ἀπὸ συμβόλων)[1] are quite early. Athens doubtless had such agreements with the more important commercial cities even before the formation of the Delian League. The confederacy of Delos was formed in 478 B.C. In the later Greek leagues some central judicial authority was established to enforce federal control. This was not done in the Delian League; there was no supreme court. When members of the league refused to pay assessments, the Athenian admirals, responsible for the conduct of the military operations of the league and the collection of contingents, put pressure upon delinquent communities by prosecuting and punishing them (δίκαις ὑπάγοντες καὶ κολάζοντες).[2] It is to be assumed that the individuals, whether magistrates or political agitators, who were responsible for inciting a community to withhold its contributions were haled before Athenian courts. No others were available for the purpose. The Delian League gradually developed into an Athenian empire over tributary states. The change came about in two ways. The smaller communities, growing weary of military service when the Persian menace was no longer imminent, commuted it for money payments and became tributaries. This change in status, though voluntary, must have involved restriction of the jurisdiction of local courts. In Greek theory and practice political sovereignty involved control of the judiciary. Some of the larger states, trusting to their military power, attempted to secede from the league. These attempts were promptly checked by Athens. In the acts of settlement defining the future relations between Athens and these conquered states, the jurisdiction of the local courts was always very materially restricted. They were not permitted to inflict the penalties of

[1] Cf. Robertson, op. cit., pp. 9 ff., and Lipsius, op. cit., pp. 965 ff.
[2] Plutarch Cimon, xi. Cf. Robertson, op. cit., pp. 27 f.

death, exile, or disfranchisement.[1] All such cases were tried in Athens. The date at which Athens began to restrict the jurisdiction of the local courts of the overseas communities and make her own tribunals imperial courts cannot be fixed with any degree of certainty. Thasos revolted in 470–469, but it was certainly not the first ally to find its league obligations irksome. Coercion of delinquents must have begun early in the history of the league. When Cimon became prominent in the military undertakings of the league, he ceased coercing the delinquents and permitted any community that desired it to substitute money payments for personal service in the forces of the league.[2] Now Cimon was in charge of the forces that recovered Sestos and drove Pausanias from Byzantium in 476, and after the ostracism of Themistocles in 471 it was he who dictated Athenian military policy.[3] There is little doubt that cases originating outside of Attica began to find their way into Athenian courts in appreciable numbers several years before the revolt of Thasos in 470. The normal litigation of a growing and prosperous city augmented by δίκαι ἀπὸ συμβόλων and cases originating in the recalcitrant or subordinate cities of the league could not have been handled by the primitive system of magisterial trials and appeals to the assembled citizens. Nor would the substitution of the Heliaea for the magistrates, as the court of first resort, have sufficed. No single body could have coped with so much litigation. The dicasteries alone could have handled it.

Whether the institution of the dicasteries was due to an increasing frequency of appeal from magisterial judgments or to a demand from the people for more participation in the administration of justice, as seems more likely, the change in the method of electing magistrates[4] in 487–486 is not likely to have been far removed in time from a measure restricting

[1] For an excellent example of these acts of settlement, see Dittenberger, *Sylloge*[2], No. 27; Hicks and Hill, *op. cit.*, No. 40 (ll. 71–76).

[2] Plutarch *Cimon*, x.

[3] Busolt, *op. cit.*, Vol. III, i, p. xvi, and p. 113 n.

[4] Aristotle, *op. cit.*, xxii. 5.

and changing the judicial functions of the magistrates, if indeed the two matters were not dealt with in the same measure.[1] Those who argue that the constantly increasing frequency of appeals destroyed the prestige of the magistrates attach too much importance to their judicial functions. It is quite as likely that the increasing power of the boulé as the executive and administrative instrument of the sovereign assembly weakened the administrative powers of the chief magistrates and reduced their prestige. In any event, the tendency of Greek democracy was to concentrate all power in the hands of the assembly.[2] Magistrates elected by reason of their personal abilities or their political strength were a hindrance to the realization of the democratic ideal. Democracy refused to delegate authority. Whether the adjustment of the magistracies to the new democracy was effected by a single comprehensive measure or a series of laws makes little difference. The change in their judicial functions must have been effected in or near the year 487–486 B.C.

When the Heliaea ceased to be a court of appeal and became a court of first resort for all cases except homicide trials and some involving impiety, obviously the whole body could not sit in judgment on each case. The difficulty was met by drawing sections called dicasteries (δικαστήρια) from the Heliaea. In this way the burden of public service, as yet unpaid, was distributed and several cases could be tried at once. Instead of holding all members of the Heliaea liable for service, they selected annually 6,000 dicasts. Doubts as to the correctness of this number have been expressed. It has been argued that dicasts in such large numbers were neither necessary nor available until the middle of the fifth century.[3] The number 6,000 is attested for the fifth century by three important sources.[4] Bdelycleon in the *Wasps*[5] of

---

[1] For the importance of the archons up to 488–487 B.C., cf. Rosenberg, "Parteistellung des Themistokles," *Hermes*, LIII, 314 f. Cf. Ehrenberg, "Kleisthenes und das Archontat," *Klio*, XIX, 110: "Die Namen der Archonten zwischen Kleisthenes und dem Jahre des Telesinos (487–6) beweisen durch das Vorkommen der leitenden Politiker die Bedeutung, die dem Amt noch innewohnte."

[2] Headlam, *Election by Lot*, pp. 26 ff.   [3] S. B. Smith, *TAPA*, LVI, 109.

[4] Cf. Fränkel, *op. cit.*, p. 13; Lipsius, *op. cit.*, p. 135.

[5] Line 662. Cf. Starkie, *The Wasps of Aristophanes*, Excursus VI, p. 399.

Aristophanes reckons the number at 6,000, adding κοὔπω πλείους ἐν τῇ χώρᾳ κατένασθεν. To infer from these words that "the number was not a fixed one," is to miss the cynical humor of the line. The implication is that "no one can tell what the future may bring, but thus far we have never had more than 6,000 of these henchmen of the demagogues." Rogers' version brings this out clearly. "Six thousand justices, count them through, there dwell no more in the land as yet."

There is evidence for a full quota of 6,000 dicasts in 415 b.c. during the inquiry into the mutilation of the Hermae.[1] It was a period of intense popular excitement. A motion was brought in to turn over Leogoras, the father of Andocides, and others to a court for trial. Leogoras raised a constitutional and technical objection to the motion by means of a γραφὴ παρανόμων. Ordinarily a γραφὴ παρανόμων did not attract much attention. But the average Athenian, with all his familiarity with litigation, resented the interposition of technicalities that seemed designed to balk the popular will. It was the practice to have important cases tried by a dicastery made up of several sections. In democratic theory a large jury was a safeguard;[2] it could be neither bribed nor browbeaten. The precaution of having a panel of 6,000 dicasts pass on the objections of Leogoras indicates that the people wanted assurance that the popular will would not be thwarted. Another significant bit of testimony in favor of the number 6,000 is the practice of calling the dicasts "The Six Thousand"[3] (οἱ ἑξακισχίλιοι). The evidence of these passages was confirmed, if confirmation was necessary, by Aristotle in the *Constitution of Athens*.[4] But, quite apart from these definite statements in the literature, there are such cogent reasons for believing that the total number of dicasts was 6,000 that this conclusion would have been justified even without these statements.

---

[1] Andocides i. 17.   [2] Cf. Grote, *op. cit.*, V, 237 ff.

[3] Scholiast on Plato *Laws*, xii. πρυτανεῖα, ἀργύριόν τι, ὃ κατατίθεται ὑπὸ τῶν δικαζομένων, καὶ δίδοται δικαστικὸν τοῖς ἑξακισχιλίοις. Cf. Suidas, *s.v.* πρυτανεῖαι. Cited by Rogers, *Introduction to the Wasps*, p. xxi.

[4] *Ath. Pol.* xxiv. 3: δικασταὶ μὲν γὰρ ἦσαν ἑξακισχίλιοι.

Although they sat in sections, they were annually drafted
and sworn in as a body. Their fitness for office was not tested
by any δοκιμασία; nor were they held accountable for their
acts at a εὔθυνα.[1] The dicasts were not the servants of the
people; they were the people. This is what is meant by the
author of a treatise on the constitution of the Athenians[2]
when he says that the allies had to bring their cases before
a "court which is none other than the Athenian people."
And so the dicasts are addressed by orators as ὦ ἄνδρες
'Αθηναῖοι.[3] To them are attributed the acts and measures of
the ecclesia. They represent the people in their judicial capacity; they are δῆμος πληθύων.[4] Hence they must number
6,000.

The 6,000 dicasts were divided into sections. By a curious
and convenient legal fiction the representative character of
the 6,000 dicasts was extended to these commissions. Each
panel was a miniature Heliaea, sovereign in its sphere. Its
verdicts were final; they were not subject to review or appeal.
For the practice of dividing the jurors into panels there was
ample precedent in the current practice of manning the minor
homicide courts with 51 ἐφέται drawn from the Areopagus.[5]
In one respect the 6,000 dicasts differ from 6,000 ecclesiasts
selected at random. The dicast had to be at least thirty years
of age. The precedent may be the requirement that members
of the boulé had to be at least thirty years old. Similarly the
size of the section, normally 500, was the same as that of
the boulé, which also was really a commission of the ecclesia.
It lacked, however, the independent irresponsible judicial
powers possessed by the dicasteries.

The date at which pay for dicasts was introduced is nowhere specifically set down in the sources. Plutarch says

[1] Aristophanes *Wasps*, 587.

καὶ ταῦτ' ἀνυπεύθυνοι δρῶμεν· τῶν δ' ἄλλων οὐδεμί' ἀρχή.

[2] (Xenophon) *Ath. Pol.* i. 18.

[3] Cf. τὸ ὑμέτερον πλῆθος and τὸ ὑμέτερον κοινόν in forensic speeches, e.g., Plato
Apology, 31 C.; Lysias xii. 42. 87.

[4] Cf. *supra*, p. 202. Lofberg, *Sycophancy in Athens*, pp. 10 f.

[5] Cf. *supra*, pp. 99 ff.

that Pericles in his struggle with Cimon, finding it impossible to compete with his munificence, followed the advice of Damonides and "had recourse to the distribution of the people's own wealth. . . . . And soon what with festival grants and jurors' fees and other fees and largesses he bribed the multitude by the wholesale and used them in opposition to the Areopagus."[1] Plutarch quotes Aristotle as his authority for this statement regarding the advice of Damonides. It is certain, then, that Plutarch was familiar with what Aristotle has to say about pay for jurors. Now Plutarch definitely fixes the date prior to the attack on the Areopagus. Presumably he believed that he was following Aristotle in the matter of the date.

Although the credit for introducing jury pay belongs to Pericles, the idea was first suggested by Aristeides.[2] As the Jack Tars, ναυτικὸς ὄχλος, of Athens gained the battle of Salamis, the founding of the empire was really a democratic achievement.[3] The moving spirit in its organization was Aristeides. Realizing the importance of securing democratic support for the new imperialistic policy by having them share in the profits, he "advised the people to lay hold of the leadership of the league and to quit the country districts and settle in the city." He pointed out that all would be able to make a living there, some by service in the army, others in the garrisons, others by taking part in public affairs;[4] and in this way they would secure the leadership. This advice was taken; "and when the people had assumed the supreme control, they proceeded to treat their allies in a more imperious fashion with the exception of the Chians, Lesbians, and Samians." Now, one of the chief means of control of the subordinate cities was through the administration of justice. Pseudo-Xenophon, writing in 424, justifies the Athenian judicial restrictions by explaining that, owing to the requirement

---

[1] Plutarch *Pericles*, ix. Aristotle *Ath. Pol.* xxvii. 3.

[2] Aristotle *Ath. Pol.*, xxiv. [3] Cf. *CAH*, V, 111.

[4] The δικασταί would naturally be reckoned among τοῖς τὰ κοινὰ πράττουσι (Aristotle, *op. cit.*, xxiv). Aristeides doubtless had this group in mind and was really the one who originated the idea of a paid judiciary.

that the allies come to Athens ἐπὶ δίκας, "the Athenians sitting at home manage the allied cities. They are able to save their friends and destroy their enemies in their courts [ἐν τοῖς δικαστηρίοις]."[1] The advice of Aristeides was tendered sometime between the foundation of the league in 487 B.C. and his death in 467 B.C.[2] Aristotle intimates that the Athenians were not slow to follow it. The immediate effect was a stricter control of the allied and subordinate states. The reference to Chios, Lesbos, and Samos as the only free allies fixes the date after 463 B.C., when Thasos was reduced.[3] Among the beneficiaries of the plan of Aristeides, Aristotle includes 6,000 paid jurymen. According to this passage, jury pay was introduced not much later than 463 B.C. In a passage in the *Politics*[4] Aristotle attributes the restriction of the power of the Areopagus to Ephialtes and Pericles, and the introduction of jury pay to Pericles. Aristotle is summarizing here and does not separate the attacks as he does in the *Politeia*,[5] where he makes Themistocles and Ephialtes responsible for an attack in 462–461 B.C. and Pericles responsible for the final attack in 451–450 B.C. In both accounts the introduction of jury pay follows the restriction of the powers of the Areopagus. But the order is not necessarily chronological. In fact, in the *Politeia* he defers the mention of a paid jury until after the account of the outbreak of the Peloponnesian War in 432–431 B.C. Here the order of narration cannot possibly be chronological. Pericles[6] first came into prominence by his prosecution of Cimon for accepting a bribe during the campaign against Thasos in 464–463 B.C. He could scarcely have carried the measure regarding jury pay much before this date. A paid judiciary was subjected to

---

[1] (Xenophon) *Ath. Pol.* i. 16.

[2] Busolt, *op. cit.*, Vol. III, i, p. 112 n. 2.   [3] *Ibid.*, Vol. III, i, xix.

[4] 1274a, 7: καὶ τὴν μὲν ἐν Ἀρείῳ πάγῳ βουλὴν Ἐφιάλτης ἐκόλουσε καὶ Περικλῆς, τὰ δὲ δικαστήρια μισθοφόρα κατέστησε Περικλῆς.

[5] xxv and xxvii. The dates given are those of Thalheim in his edition of the *Ath. Pol.*

[6] Bury, *op. cit.*, p. 343; Busolt, *op. cit.*, Vol. III, i, p. 254; Aristotle *Ath. Pol.* xxvii. 1. Pericles is described in Plutarch *Pericles*, x, as εἷς τῶν κατηγόρων . . . . ὑπὸ τοῦ δήμου προβεβλημένος. Cf. Sandys' notes on *Ath. Pol.* xxvii. 1.

considerable criticism afterward.[1] It may be assumed that the proposal aroused some opposition at the time. Only a man of some prominence could successfully sponsor such a radical, though natural, measure. Now, if Pericles resorted to this method of winning popular favor to help him in his contest with Cimon, one would expect the measure to have been carried before 461 B.C., when Cimon was ostracized.

Plutarch[2] puts jury pay before the attack on the Areopagus, without specifying whether it was the first attack in 462–461 B.C. or the second attack in 451–450 B.C. As has been pointed out, a number of men were concerned in the attack, at first under the leadership of Ephialtes and later under Pericles. Naturally Pericles would be one of the followers of Ephialtes. Aristotle's silence on this point has no significance. These considerations would warrant us in putting the date as early as 463–462 B.C.[3]

There are, however, fairly good reasons for putting the date as late as 451 during the brief period of Cimon's return from exile and just before Pericles' attack on the Areopagus. In 453–452 the rural justices were reappointed.[4] They now numbered 30. The number 30 corresponds to the number of the trittyes which served as a link between the demes and the tribes. Nothing is known in detail about these circuit judges except what may be inferred from their predecessors under Peisistratus, and their successors, the Forty. It may be assumed with confidence that their jurisdiction was civil rather than criminal, and that they settled a number of cases that would otherwise have come before the heliastic courts. One can well imagine that the courts were heavily burdened even before the reforms of Ephialtes enlarged their jurisdiction. The institution of the rural justices would afford a measure of relief. But one wonders if the people who relied

[1] Aristotle *Ath. Pol.* xxvii. 4: ἀφ' ὧν αἰτιῶνταί τινες χείρω γενέσθαι [sc. δικαστήρια], κληρουμένων ἐπιμελῶς ἀεὶ <μᾶλλον> τῶν τυχόντων, ἢ τῶν ἐπιεικῶν ἀνθρώπων. Cf. Plato *Gorgias*, 515 E.

[2] *Pericles*, ix.

[3] Busolt (*op. cit.*, III, 1. 263) puts pay before the earliest attack on the Areopagus (462–461), in which both Ephialtes and Pericles participated.

[4] Aristotle *Ath. Pol.* xxvi. 3.

on state pay for some or all of their support would view in such a dispassionate fashion a measure that reduced their opportunities for profitable employment. If, however, the dicasts were still unpaid, the situation would be quite altered. Unpaid jury service could not be particularly attractive. There would be no popular objection to any measure of relief. This conception of the situation favors the later date. But the balance of probabilities is in favor of the earlier date. If Pericles was prominent enough in 462 to engage in the prosecution of Cimon, he must have participated in the first and most formidable attack on the Areopagus; and he would not have neglected so effective a means of advancing democracy as pay for jurors and others.[1]

The 6,000 citizens who were to represent the people judicially were chosen annually by lot from among those who were qualified. Speaking of his own day, Aristotle says: "All persons above thirty years of age are qualified to serve as jurors, providing they are not debtors to the state and have not lost their civil rights."[2] This qualification goes back at least as far as the fifth century. An inscription furnishes evidence that the jurors were listed by tribes in the official register.[3] This justifies the inference that 600 were drawn from each tribe. It has been rightly concluded that the jurors, like the senators, were apportioned among the demes in each tribe, in accordance with their number and population,[4] on the basis of the deme registers (ληξιαρχικὰ γραμματεῖα).

Little is known about the method of selection in the fifth century. Aristotle, in discussing the institution of pay for

----

[1] Cf. Busolt-Swoboda, op. cit., p. 897, on the necessity of the step in the interest of democracy.

[2] Ath. Pol. lxiii. 3.

[3] CIA iv. 1. 35b: ἱεροποιὸ[ς δ]ὲ οἵτινες ἱεροποιέσοσ[ι τὲν θυσίαν, δέκα ἄνδρας δια]κλε[ρόσαι] ἐκ τῶν δ[ικα]στῶν ἕνα ἐκ τὲς φυλὲς ἐκ τὸ [πίνακος κ.τ.λ. Schoell, Sitzungsberichte ber Bayerischen Akademie (1887), p. 6, first drew attention to the evidence of the inscription. Cf. Teusch, De sortitione apud Athenienses, p. 59, and Thalheim in Pauly-Wissowa, V, 566, s.v. δικασταί. The jury tickets (πινάκια) thus far discovered belong to the fourth century. Cf. infra, p. 368. Each juror must have had some sort of identification card. Hommel, "Heliaea," Philologus, XIX, Supplementband, Heft 11, p. 110, n. 275.

[4] Wilamowitz, Aristoteles und Athen, I, 201. Cf. Teusch, op. cit., p. 60.

jurors, comments on its effects by referring to adverse criticisms of Pericles' measure. "Some persons accuse him of thereby causing a deterioration in the character of the juries, since it was always the inferior people who were anxious to submit themselves for selection as jurors, rather than the men of better position."[1] On the basis of this statement it is accepted that the jurors were selected from volunteers.[2] The military commitments[3] of Athens as mistress of the Delian League and the constantly increasing press of litigation made it well-nigh impossible for the same man to be both juror and soldier. In the fifth-century judicial system each juror was assigned to a specific court for a year.[4] When an army was mobilized, men would be withdrawn from practically every court in larger or smaller numbers because they were mobilized by classes.[5] The easiest way to deal with the situation would have been to exempt jurors from military service. It is known that senators and other civil officials, and even merchants,[6] were excused under certain circumstances. But there is no evidence that jurors were so exempted.

Aristophanes constantly conveys the impression that the jurors were all old men, boastful of their deeds in ancient sieges and battles. Modern students, realizing that few men, for example, engaged in the siege of Byzantium[7] in 478 B.C. would be fit for any public service in 422 B.C., are inclined to discount all the comedian's statements regarding the age of the jurors as intended to discredit them. There is evidence

---

[1] Aristotle *Ath. Pol.* xxvii. 4.

[2] Gilbert, *op. cit.*, p. 391, n. 4; cf. Teusch, *op. cit.*, p. 60.

[3] In the year 459–458 B.C. the casualties of one tribe, amounting to 176, were suffered in six battles on two fronts. *CIA* i. 433. Dittenberger, *op. cit.*, No. 9; Hicks and Hill, *op. cit.*, No. 26.

[4] Cf. *infra*, p. 235.   [5] Gilbert, *op. cit.*, pp. 315 ff.

[6] *Ibid.*, p. 318, n. 1. Senators and tax-farmers are mentioned in the sources as being exempt. It is assumed that magistrates were exempt, otherwise court sessions would have had to be suspended.

[7] Aristophanes *Wasps*, 235–39. Cf. Grote, *op. cit.*, V, 406. Cf. *Wasps*, 354, for reference to siege of Naxos, 476 B.C., in which members of the chorus had been engaged. For other references to aged jurors, cf. *Wasps*, 219–20. They sing old songs, μέλη ἀρχαῖα. The chorus who are Philocleon's chums (ἄνδρες ἥλικες) call him γέρων. Cf. ll. 224, 441, 540. Others in Lipsius, *op. cit.*, p. 164, n. 99.

that younger men did serve on the juries of the fifth century. A client of Antiphon[1] refers explicitly to the younger men on the jury. Even Aristophanes himself has been cited as a witness that jurors were not always elderly men. Strepsiades first served as a juror when his son Pheidippides was six years old.[2] And others in the *Wasps*[3] are represented as having young children. But after all, it is obvious that, according to Aristophanes, a preponderance of the jurors were elderly men, beyond the age for military service.

Military considerations were not overlooked in the provisions made for the administration of justice. This appears in the appointment of arbitrators when public arbitration was introduced. Every man in his sixtieth year was listed as an arbitrator for a year.[4] This evident desire not to withdraw effectives from military service to fill the new judicial offices warrants the belief that in selecting jurors precautions were taken not to reduce the number of effectives for military service more than was absolutely necessary. This could be done by accepting at once all men over sixty who volunteered. If these were not sufficient, the required total (6,000) could be made up by selections from the younger men who offered for jury service. If there was, in fact, as Aristophanes intimates, a marked preponderance of elderly men on the jury, it is thus most readily explained. It does not seem possible that allotment from the whole group would produce

[1] v. 71: ταῦθ' ὑμῶν αὐτῶν ἐγὼ οἶμαι μεμνῆσθαι τοὺς πρεσβυτέρους, τοὺς δὲ νεωτέρους πυνθάνεσθαι ὥσπερ ἐμέ.

[2] Aristophanes *Clouds*, 863–64.

ὃν πρῶτον ὀβολὸν ἔλαβον ἡλιαστικόν,
τούτου 'πριάμην σοι Διασίοις ἁμαξίδα.

[3] Lines 248 ff. and 291 ff. But the ages of children are not trustworthy evidence as to the ages of fathers. One gets the impression that Strepsiades was no longer young when he was married. Bruck, "Über die Organisation der athenischen Heliastengerichte im 4. Jahrh. v. Chr.," *Philologus*, (LII), 312, cites several passages in the orators in which young jurors are mentioned (Isaeus vii. 13; Demosthenes xix. 280; Demosthenes lix. 30). But the conditions of jury service in the fourth century are quite different from those of the fifth.

[4] Aristotle *Ath. Pol.* liii. 4. Service as arbitrator was substituted for the last year of military service. As a rule men between fifty and sixty years were not employed outside of Attica. Cf. Gilbert, *op. cit.*, p. 316.

so high a percentage of old men, even if they had more leisure and inclination for jury service than the younger men, and volunteered in larger numbers.

There is no reference to suspension of court sessions in Aristophanes. On the contrary, Bdelycleon, in the *Wasps*, makes an estimate of the earnings of the dicasts on the basis of employment for all for 300 days per year. This is an exaggeration, but the implication that the courts were constantly busy is borne out by Pseudo-Xenophon, who, in discussing the congestion of public business, including litigation, says, "Even now when the courts sit throughout the year, they do not suffice to suppress crime, because of the size of the population."[1]

There is no mention of a *dokimasia* of jurors to establish their qualifications for office. In Aristotle's day at least the responsibility for being properly qualified was laid upon the juror. "If any unqualified person serves as a juror, an information is laid against him and he is brought before a court; and if he is convicted, the jurors assess the punishment or fine which they consider him to deserve."[2] This procedure seems to suit the period when everybody who offered was accepted at his own risk, rather than the fifth century, when they were selected by lot from volunteers. The officials must have assured themselves that those selected were properly qualified. The age qualification could be easily established by referring to the military lists under the names of the *archons eponymi*. This practice was followed in the case of the public arbitrators.[3] 'Ατιμία was also a matter of record.

The jurors regularly were divided into panels. Only one case is recorded in which the 6,000 sat as a body.[4] As the circumstances were very unusual, it may be concluded that a panel of 6,000 was very rarely assembled. The panels normally contained 500. On the basis of fourth-century practice it is assumed that there were ten sections of 500 (501)

---

[1] Aristophanes, *Wasps* 661 ff.; Pseudo-Xenophon, *Ath. Pol.* iii. 6.

[2] Aristotle *Ath. Pol.* lxiii. 3.

[3] Bruck, *op. cit.*, p. 297.   [4] Andocides i. 17.

and 1,000 supernumeraries.[1] These sections, containing jurors from different tribes and demes, reflected current public opinion. There is uncertainty regarding the number of courts in the fifth century. Lipsius[2] does not commit himself on the subject. "Die Zahl der Gerichtshöfe vermögen wir nicht zu bestimmen, da Aristoteles auch für seine Zeit keine Angabe macht. Wenn die Grammatiker von zehn Gerichtshöfen reden, so beruht das auf einer Verwechslung mit der Richterabteilung." Busolt[3] seems to favor the view that there were ten courts in the fifth century. Five courts are mentioned in fifth-century sources, besides the Heliaea, i.e., the court of the thesmothetae. They are the παράβυστον, the court of the Eleven;[4] the καινόν;[5] the ᾠδεῖον; the court πρὸς τοῖς τειχίοις; and the court of the archon.[6] To these should be added the three minor homicide courts, at the Delphinium, the Palladium, and in Phreatto, after they were manned by dicasts in place of ephetae in the middle of the fifth century.[7] This gives a total of six courts, exclusive of the three minor homicide courts. The same courthouse may have been used by more than one tribunal.

The panels for service were selected annually and remained intact for the year.[8] In the *Wasps* of Aristophanes,

---

[1] Lipsius, *op. cit.*, p. 136.   [2] *Op. cit.*, p. 168.

[3] Busolt-Swoboda, *Staatskunde*, p. 1154. Cf. Hommel, *op. cit.*, p. 111, n. 281.

[4] Harpocration, *s.v.* παράβυστον. οὕτως ἐκαλεῖτό τι τῶν παρ' Ἀθηναίοις δικαστηρίων ἐν ᾧ ἐδίκαζον οἱ ιά. Antiphon *Frag.*, 42. Cf. Aristophanes *Wasps*, 1108–9:

οἱ μὲν ἡμῶν οὗπερ ἄρχων, οἱ δὲ παρὰ τοὺς ἕνδεκα,
οἱ δ' ἐν ᾠδείῳ δικάζουσ', οἱ δὲ πρὸς τοῖς τειχίοις.

[5] τὸ καινόν. Aristophanes, *Wasps*, 120–21:

ὁ δ' αὐτῷ τυμπάνῳ
ᾄξας ἐδίκαζεν ἐς τὸ Καινὸν ἐμπεσών.

[6] Nothing is known about the presiding officials. The ᾠδεῖον may be the court of the εἰσαγωγεῖς. Cf. Lipsius, *op. cit.*, p. 137, n. 11. The court παρὰ τοῖς τειχίοις is not otherwise known.

[7] Cf. *infra*, p. 270.

[8] Aristophanes *Wasps*, 400.

οὐ ξυλλήψεσθ' ὁπόσοισι δίκαι τῆτες μέλλουσιν ἔσεσθαι.

Philocleon calls to his rescue all who are interested in lawsuits for the current year. Beyond that, there was no assurance that he would be active as a juror.

Philocleon and the old dicasts who, in the guise of wasps, constitute the chorus are members of the same court for the year. They are fellow-dicasts (συνδικασταί) who, day after day, go to the same court. They refer explicitly to the acquittal of the defendant the day before in a court in which they and Philocleon sat as jurors.[1] And they were all under orders to appear that day to try Laches, who is represented as having acquired much wealth by his peculations.[2] The various references to the activities of the jurors in the *Wasps* are not intended to be entirely consistent, but they suggest criminal cases and the court of the thesmothetae. A passage in Antiphon[3] shows very clearly that the same panel sat in this court day after day. The *choregus*, a client of Antiphon on trial for the death of a chorus boy, tells the jury that Philocrates, one of his accusers, appeared in the court of the thesmothetae and announced that the *choregus* was responsible for the death of his brother while in training for a chorus. The *choregus* answered the charge both at once and on the following day before the same jurors. The proceeding was entirely informal. The purpose of the maneuver was to prevent the *choregus*, as a polluted person, from appearing before these jurors the next day to prosecute some wrongdoers. These defendants had induced Philocrates to bring a charge of homicide against the *choregus* to disqualify him.

Whatever the number of courts in the fifth century may have been, it is generally believed that there were ten sections of 500 each and 1,000 supernumeraries who constituted a reserve to fill vacancies in individual courts, resulting from death, illness, or other unavoidable causes, or to expand the number of jurors to 1,000 or 1,500 for important cases. This purpose was accomplished by assigning to each court 600.[4] Now this in itself seems at first sight not to be an unreasonable procedure. But the manner in which it is supposed to have been worked at once arouses grave suspicions. Each day the entire panel of 600, minus absentees, started out for

[1] Aristophanes *Wasps*, 281–84.   [3] vi. 21–23. Cf. Lipsius, *op. cit.*, p. 138.

[2] *Ibid.*, 240.   [4] Lipsius, *op. cit.*, pp. 136 ff.

a court session some time before daybreak. As soon as 500 were admitted, the doors were closed, and several score, if not a hundred, men were excluded.[1] The sole evidence for this procedure is drawn from the *Wasps* of Aristophanes. The old dicasts of the chorus appear each day long before daylight to summon Philocleon; they urge haste to arrive at the court "ere morning break,"[2] for whoever arrives after the signal for opening the court will not get his 3 obols.[3] And in the domestic court which tries the dog, Philocleon is pleased with the assurance that "though you sleep till midday, no archon here will close the door against you."[4] But these things are quite easily explained without assuming that the chorus is a section of the 600 jurors converging in rivalry from various directions upon a court which requires only 500.

The haste of the chorus to arrive before daybreak is due to the fact that the court, like the ecclesia, opened early, and they had been ordered to be on hand in good time.[5] The humor of the situation lies in the fact that they are unnecessarily and absurdly early. This is made quite evident by the conversation between Bdelycleon and one of the slaves who is helping to keep the old dicast interned.[6]

BDELYCLEON: His fellow justices will come this way calling him up.
SLAVE: Why sir, 'tis twilight yet.
BDELYCLEON: Why then, by Zeus, they are very late today. Soon after midnight is their usual time to come here carrying lights.

Each member of the chorus is a replica of Philocleon, who wants to be around the court night and day and even to be

[1] Teusch, *op. cit.*, pp. 62–63.

[2] *Wasps*, 245:

σπεύδωμεν, ὦνδρες ἥλικες, πρὶν ἡμέραν γενέσθαι.

[3] *Ibid.*, 688–90:

ἥκειν εἴπῃ πρῷ κἀν ὥρᾳ δικάσονθ᾽ ὡς ὅστις ἂν ὑμῶν
ὕστερος ἔλθῃ τοῦ σημείου, τὸ τριώβολον οὐ κομιεῖται·

[4] *Ibid.*, 774–75:

κἂν ἔγρῃ μεσημβρινός,
οὐδείς σ᾽ ἀποκλείσει θεσμοθέτης τῇ κιγκλίδι.

[5] *Ibid.*, 242–43:

χθὲς οὖν Κλέων ὁ κηδεμὼν ἡμῖν ἐφεῖτ᾽ ἐν ὥρᾳ
ἥκειν ἔχοντας ἡμερῶν ὀργὴν τριῶν πονηράν.

[6] *Ibid.*, 214 ff.

buried there. One of the slaves on guard before the house explains the situation as follows:

> I'll tell you the disease old master has.
> He is a lawcourt-lover, no man like him.
> Judging is what he dotes on . . . .
> At night he gets no sleep, no, not one grain,
> Or if he doze the tiniest speck, his soul
> Flutters in dreams around the water clock.
>
> . . . .
> Supper scarce done he clamours for his shoes,
> Hurries ere daybreak to the court, and sleeps
> Stuck like a limpet to the door post there.[1]

If the rooster failed to wake him in time, he said that it had been bribed by defendants.[2] And he begged that, if anything happened to him in his attempt to escape, he be buried under the bar.[3]

The order for the appearance of the jurors under pain of not receiving pay if they arrived "after the signal" contains no hint that it was a case of "first come first served."[4] On the contrary, the plain implication of the passage is that all would be admitted if they arrived on time. In the trial of the dog which reproduces the procedure of a regular trial, Bdelycleon, acting as the herald, makes proclamation:

> Is any Justice out there? Let him enter.
> We shan't admit him when once they have begun.[5]

The loiterer is to be excluded, not because the panel is full, but because the proceedings have begun. The point that Bdelycleon is making is that, while the jurors must be on time, else they lose their fees, the advocate in league with Cleon,

---

[1] *Ibid.*, 87–93, 103–5.

[2] *Ibid.*, 100–103:

> τὸν ἀλεκτρυόνα δ', ὃς ᾖδ' ἀφ' ἑσπέρας, ἔφη
> ὄψ' ἐξεγείρειν αὐτὸν ἀναπεπεισμένον,
> παρὰ τῶν ὑπευθύνων ἔχοντα χρήματα.

[3] *Ibid.*, 385–86:

> δράσω τοίνυν ὑμῖν πίσυνος· καὶ μανθάνετ'· ἢν τι πάθω 'γώ,
> ἀνελόντες καὶ κατακλαύσαντες θεῖναί μ' ὑπὸ τοῖσι δρυφάκτοις.

[4] *Ibid.*, 689–90.

[5] *Ibid.*, 891–92:

> εἴ τις θύρασιν ἡλιαστὴς εἰσίτω
> ὡς ἡνίκ' ἂν λέγωσιν, οὐκ ἐσφρήσομεν.

their master, comes late if he chooses, and still gets his pay.[1]
The proceedings are delayed to suit his convenience. Meanwhile the jurors, like Dicaeopolis in the *Acharnians*, sit and
wait, possessing their souls in patience if they can. This is
part of their slavery.

There is another aspect of the situation that deserves
attention in this connection. If there was a race of 600 men
for places for only 500, it is strange that the chorus should
tarry for a rival in the competition for seats and even fight
for his release that he might accompany them. Men who
were rivals for a seat in court, or a place in line awaiting the
opening of court, would be more likely to hasten along quietly
and alone. Their singing could only waken more dicasts,
whose houses they passed, and add to the number of com-
petitors. When the jurors arrive in the neighborhood of the
court, there is no indication that they stood in line for hours
waiting for the court to open. Instead, we find the old dicast
talking leisurely and with immense satisfaction to defendants
who flatter and wheedle him to win his favor.[2] Neither
Philocleon nor any of his fellow-dicasts exhibit any fear that
others may arrive before them and deprive them of their
pay. Their sole concern is the possibility that there may be
no court session that day.[3] Philocleon's desire for a front
seat is not strange; he wants to be sure that he will not miss
any of the proceedings. He wants to be the first to come and
the last to leave.[4]

If candidates for jury service had to assemble long before
daylight and stand in line to secure a place long before the
hour for beginning proceedings, it is inconceivable that
Bdelycleon should have failed to make a point of the obvious

[1] *Ibid.*, 686 ff.

[2] *Ibid.*, 551 ff. Philocleon is represented as going to court and sleeping "stuck
like a limpet to the doorpost." This does not mean that he wants to get first place
in the line. It simply means that he is so "court-crazy" (φιληλιαστής) that he wants
to sleep half of the night at the courthouse door (ll. 104–5).

[3] *Ibid.*, 302–5.

[4] *Ibid.*, 89–90, 754–55.

κἀπισταίην ἐπὶ τοῖς κημοῖς
ψηφιζομένων ὁ τελευταῖος.

unfairness of such a method of deciding between claimants for a seat.[1] He could have cited no better evidence of their slavery. The natural solution of such a difficulty in Athens would have been the use of the lot. But there is no indication in the *Wasps* or elsewhere that the lot was employed in this connection.[2]

The requirement of courts of 1,000 and more introduces a complication into the allotment of panels. These larger courts are commonly said to consist of two or three δικαστή-ρια.[3] If there were ten courts served by 600 jurors each, the constitution of a larger court would involve the withdrawal of panels from service in other courts. This difficulty has been observed, and the suggestion has been made that there may have been only five courts (*Gerichtshöfe*) in each of which two panels served alternately.[4] In this way five panels would always be available for service in the larger tribunals.

The theory that there were 100 supernumeraries for each panel is based upon the assumption that the full panel of 500 (501) must be present at each session of the court. This is a plausible assumption, but there are difficulties. It was an ancient rule of law that an even vote was in favor of the defendant.[5] As the plaintiff had not persuaded a majority of the jurors of the justice of his claim, he had failed to prove his case, and it was dismissed. The law was in force in fifth-century Athens. A client of Antiphon[6] invoked it in an argu-

---

[1] Hommel (*op. cit.*, p. 114) alone has noticed the unfairness of such a system of securing a panel for service, but the suggestion that those who fail to get a seat had only themselves to blame is scarcely a sufficient answer, for no matter how early the jurors resorted to court, *some*—between one and a hundred—would *always* be too late.

[2] Teusch (*op. cit.*, p. 62) has shown that the situation described by Aristophanes in the *Wasps* does not permit of the use of the lot.

[3] Pollux viii. 123: εἰ δὲ χιλίων δέοι δικαστῶν, συνίσταντο δύο δικαστήρια, εἰ δὲ πεντακοσίων καὶ χιλίων, τρία. Cf. Demosthenes xxiv. 9; Bruck, *op. cit.*, p. 405.

[4] Hommel, *op. cit.*, pp. 111–12.

[5] Aeschylus, *Eumenides*, 741; Euripides, *Electra*, 1268–69; Aristophanes, *Frogs*, 685.

[6] Antiphon v. 51. The case was tried in a heliastic court under the presidency of the Eleven (Blass, *Attische Beredsamkeit*, I, 176). The jurors are presumed to be familiar with the rule as a matter of current practice in the heliastic courts.

ment before a heliastic court as a familiar rule. Evidently
there was a possibility of a tie vote in a fifth-century heliastic
court. This must mean that a court could function without
its full complement of jurors. It is well known that members
of the boulé, which on occasion exercised judicial functions,
were frequently absent.[1] It could not be otherwise. No
group of 500 men over thirty years of age could remain intact
for a year. There would be unavoidable absences due to
illness and other causes. It has been estimated that the
average attendance for a year would be 400.[2] If 400 senators
could render a valid verdict, it is reasonable to suppose that
a heliastic court also could function without its full complement of jurors. In a fourth-century suit between the Delian
amphictyony and a citizen of the island of Ios the number
of votes cast amounted to 499.[3] The full complement of the
court in the fourth century was 501. Lipsius[4] accounts for
the shortage in the number of votes by assuming that for
some reason or other two jurors did not vote. The law regarding an even vote was intended to apply when, through
the failure of jurors to vote, the number of votes cast was
evenly divided between plaintiff and defendant. Lipsius'
proposed explanation of the missing votes is an admission
that fewer than the full quota of jurors could render a valid
verdict. From a legal standpoint it could make no difference
whether the two men failed to attend or failed to vote. Four
hundred and ninety-nine jurors rendered the verdict of a court
of 501, just as 400 and odd senators must on occasion have
expressed the decision of the Senate of Five Hundred. It
was desirable that all jurors should vote. An effort to secure

[1] Demosthenes xxii. 36: τῷ γὰρ ἔστιν ὄνειδος, εἰ σιωπῶντος αὐτοῦ καὶ μηδὲν
γράφοντος, ἴσως δ' οὐδὲ τὰ πόλλ' εἰς τὸ βουλευτήριον εἰσιόντος, μὴ λάβοι ἡ βουλὴ τὸν
στέφανον;

[2] Schömann, Griechische Alterthümer, I, secs. 399 and 463. There is no reference
to a quorum in the senate.
The average daily absences of the teachers from a Chicago public high school
over a period of 120 days amounted to 2.3 per cent of the total number. The penalty
for absence in case of illness is $2.50 per day. The penalty for all other absences is
the deduction of the total amount of the salary for the time of absence.

[3] CIA ii, No. 778 (825) B.   [4] Op. cit., p. 158.

all votes was always made. But whether it was always successful, if for any reason a juror wished to evade, is uncertain.
The very proclamation of the herald, "Who has not voted?
Let him stand up," seems to indicate the possibility of evasion.[1] But on the other hand, Philocleon's desire to be always
the last to vote indicates that he at least thought he knew
when all had voted.[2] But there is another possibility which
Lipsius did not note. Even if the arrangements were 100
per cent efficient in filling the quota for each jury, it must
occasionally have happened that a juror was obliged through
illness to leave the court during the progress of the case.
His place could not be filled, for the substitute would have
missed some of the evidence. When a juror falls ill in a modern jury of twelve men, as sometimes happens, the case must
be tried *de novo*. There is no mention of a similar practice
in Athens. We must assume that the case went on with fewer
than the full complement.

An argument in favor of the theory that a full quota of
jurors was required for each case has been drawn from the
use of the word πληροῦν.[3] Officials were said πληροῦν τὰ δικαστήρια, and τὰ δικαστήρια ἐπληρώθη. But it has been shown
that the word πληροῦν is used in connections in which no idea
of a full quota is involved.[4] A case in point is the phrase
πληρουμένης τῆς ἐκκλησίας found in Aristophanes' *Ecclezia-
zousae*.[5] It means "while the ecclesia is assembling." There
is no expectation that *all* members must or would be present.
But even if it be admitted that πληροῦν has in some connections the technical meaning "provide the court with a full
complement" rather than merely "summon" or "convoke,"
it is always used of the fourth-century jury. Aristophanes[6]

[1] Aristophanes *Wasps*, 751-55.

[2] Cf. *infra*, p. 377. In Aristotle's time no juror could receive his pay if he did
not deposit his vote.

[3] Lipsius, *op. cit.*, p. 159.

[4] Bruck, *Philologus*, LII, 414. Lipsius, *ibid.*, refuses to accept Bruck's conclusion
and quotes πληροῦν ναῦν, τριήρη, which must mean "supply the full complement of
men."

[5] Line 89.   [6] *Wasps*, 305.

uses καθίζειν τὸ δικαστήριον in the sense of "convene" or "hold a session"; πληροῦν does not appear in this connection.

There is a reason for this difference between the fifth- and the fourth-century practice. In the later period all available jurors assembled each court day. It was easy to select and allot to each court its required complement with reasonable assurance that the case would go before a complete panel.[1] It was quite otherwise in the earlier period when a group was assigned to a specific court for a whole year.

In this connection it is important to notice that in the discussion of jury quotas for the fifth century no account is taken of the minor homicide courts which were manned by fifty-one ephetae until they were replaced by dicasts.[2] Even a group of fifty-one men could not always be available for recurring court sessions throughout the year. Inevitable absences would be sure to occur. No one seems to have offered any suggestions as to the manner in which temporary or permanent gaps in the ranks of the ephetae were filled. And yet it would seem quite as important to have a full quota in the minor homicide courts as in the heliastic courts. The odd number of the ephetae shows that it was deemed desirable to avoid a tie vote. As the ephetae were drawn from the Areopagites,[3] it would always have been a comparatively simple matter to fill up vacancies in their ranks, unless the absences were due to illness during the hearing of a case.

The objections to the theory that 100 supernumeraries were attached to each panel of 501 to insure a full quota at each court session may be summarized as follows. The passages in the *Wasps* of Aristophanes, relied upon to support the theory, lose their humor if so interpreted. They can all be otherwise explained in a way that brings out their full humor and fits them into the scheme of the comedy. The words πληροῦν δικαστήριον in the sense of "assign its full complement to a panel of dicasts" apparently do not occur in fifth-century sources. Even in the later period, the evidence that

---

[1] Cf. *infra*, p. 371. There was always the possibility that a juror seized by sudden illness might be obliged to leave the court before the conclusion of the case.

[2] Cf. *supra*, p. 234.   [3] Cf. *supra*, p. 99.

πληροῦν does not mean simply "convene" a jury is not wholly convincing. But there is no need to press this point, for there are strong indications that a court with less than its full quota could render a valid judgment just as the boulé occasionally did. The assignment of an odd number to each panel was intended to avoid tie votes. The law providing that a tie vote should be regarded as an acquittal shows that an even number of jurors was a possibility in a heliastic court. The theory that one or more jurors failed to vote is not a satisfactory explanation, for, if fewer than the full quota could render a valid judgment it makes no difference whether the missing votes were due to absence or failure to vote. And finally, the use of supernumeraries in the way proposed must have made it impossible to convene a court of from 1,000 to 2,000 without at least partially disrupting the system. The sole advantage of this theory is that it provided a scheme for securing panels that would not be affected by the inevitable temporary or permanent reduction in the numbers of the annual quota of jurors through absence from the city, illness, or death. But the diminution of the numbers available for service would cause no concern if a court could function without its full quota. In the fourth century it was the practice to assign odd numbers to each panel, e.g., 501, 1,001, 1,501. But there is no evidence for the practice in the fifth century. Only even numbers are mentioned. It is, however, assumed that the practice was the same and that for convenience even numbers were used. In favor of this theory may be cited the fact that the ephetae numbered fifty-one. But on the whole, the model for the fifth-century panel is quite as likely to have been the Senate of Five Hundred as the ephetae. It is of interest in this connection that commissions of the dicasts were associated, under certain conditions,[1] with the boulé in fixing the tribute from the cities of the empire. There is epigraphical evidence that one such commission numbered 500. Similarly, after the overthrow of the Four Hundred, a commission of 500 dicasts acted with the senate as a committee to revise the laws.[2]

---

[1] Robertson, *op. cit.*, p. 48.   [2] *CIA* i. 266. Cf. Lipsius, *op. cit.*, p. 156.

The evidence is found in the decree of Teisamenus cited by
Andocides.[1] These figures are surely exact. Round numbers
may be expected even in the forensic orations, but not in
official sources. These bodies are not courts in the strict
sense of the word, but it is highly improbable that these
bodies would number 500 each and the courts 501. In the
fourth century the situation was different. All who desired
to serve appeared, and the courts needed were filled then and
there. There was a reasonable certainty that the full quota
would actually be present when the case was called for trial.
In the fifth century it would be a much more difficult matter
to secure a full complement of jurors for each case. The
scheme worked out on the basis of the *Wasps* of Aristophanes
is, as we have seen, so cumbersome and unfair that it has
aroused doubts in the mind of even one who accepts it.[2]

The problem of distributing 6000 jurors into panels for
service in the different courts in the fifth century would have
been simpler if the panel for the normal cases numbered 500
instead of 501 and the courts could function with fewer than
a full quota. The jurors could then be divided into twelve
sections of 500 each, and a section assigned to a court for a
year, without further concern regarding vacancies due to absences from time to time. It is impossible to determine how
many courts there were in the fifth century. It would seem
that the requirements of litigation in the fifth century were
greater than in the fourth. Making due allowance for the
exaggerations of Aristophanes, who estimates that the entire
number of jurors was employed for 300 days each year, one
gets the impression that, as Strepsiades in the *Clouds*[3] suggests, courts were in session almost every day in Athens.
The importance of overseas litigation can be seen from the
substantial benefits which, according to Pseudo-Xenophon,[4]

[1] i. 84.

[2] Hommel (*op. cit.*, p. 112) expresses doubts as to the working of the system with
juries of 1,000 and 1,500, and further (p. 114) remarks on the unfairness. Lipsius is
uncertain about the size of the panels, 500 or 600.

[3] Lines 207-8. Cf. Lipsius, *op. cit.*, p. 168. Cf. *Wasps*, 661 ff.

[4] *Ath. Pol.* ii. 16-17.

accrued to the citizens of Athens from the presence of overseas litigants in the city. Another indication of the pressure
of litigation is the practice of holding court sessions and meetings of the ecclesia on the same day.[1] This practice was discontinued in the fourth century.[2] This situation would seem
to have required more courts than in the fourth century,
when overseas litigation had practically ceased.

All magistrates and official boards, whether judicial or
executive, had the duty of presiding over the trial of cases
that came within the sphere of their activities. Consequently, the number of officials entitled to preside at court sessions
was considerably in excess of the number of available panels.[3]
Panels could not be assigned for the exclusive use of each of
the various boards and officials. The most practical and
economical way of dealing with the needs of the situation
would be to assign panels to officials with a heavy docket.
In the case of those whose legal business was incidental and
occasional, one panel could be assigned to several, to be used
in turn as occasion demanded. Their cases would be few.
In this way certain panels would always be under the chairmanship of the same officials, while the others might sit in
the same courthouse under the chairmanship of two or more
official boards in turn. Six courts are mentioned in fifth-
century sources. They are the courts of the thesmothetae,
of the Eleven, of the archon, of the Introducers (εἰσαγωγεῖς).
Two have not been identified with any officials. One was
τὸ καινόν, and the other is described as πρὸς τοῖς τειχίοις.[4]
Those that have been identified are perhaps the most important courts in the city. It would be natural that Philocleon, glorying in jury service, should mention the courts that
he deemed most important. The other courts that might

---

[1] Aristophanes *Wasps*, 594–95. Cf. Bamberg, *Hermes*, XIII, 506 ff. Fränkel
(*op. cit.*, p. 11, n. 3), followed by Van Leeuwen (notes *ad loc.*), thinks that the
reference is to special assemblies only.

[2] Demosthenes xxiv. 80.

[3] Some sixteen different officials and boards entitled to preside over court sessions are listed by Lipsius (*op. cit.*, pp. 53–120).

[4] Cf. *supra*, p. 234.

be classed with these are those of the Polemarch, the king archon, and the Thirty, or whatever board tried the bulk of the civil cases as the Forty did in the next century. If it be supposed that panels were assigned for the exclusive use of six magistrates and boards, six would be left for the ten or a dozen other boards that had comparatively few cases in a year, including the minor homicide courts,[1] to be distributed according to their requiremnts. From these supernumerary panels also could be recruited those large juries that were sometimes assigned to the court of the thesmothetae who tried the most important political and criminal cases. Among these were indictments for illegal legislation ($\gamma\rho\alpha\phi\alpha\grave{\iota}$ $\pi\alpha\rho\alpha$-$\nu\acute{o}\mu\omega\nu$) and impeachments ($\epsilon\grave{\iota}\sigma\alpha\gamma\gamma\epsilon\lambda\acute{\iota}\alpha\iota$) assigned to a heliastic court for trial. An old law required a jury of 1,000 for impeachment cases.[2] This number could be increased by action of the ecclesia when referring the case to a court for trial. Pericles was tried as the result of an impeachment in the second year of the Peloponnesian War, by a court of 1,500.[3] Similarly, in the case of the generals and taxiarchs denounced by Agoratus, shortly before the institution of the Thirty, provision was made by decree for a trial before a court of 2,000.[4] In 415 a $\gamma\rho\alpha\phi\grave{\eta}$ $\pi\alpha\rho\alpha\nu\acute{o}\mu\omega\nu$ was tried by a court of 6,000. The view of Fränkel[5] that the case was tried by a "full" meeting of the assembly has not found favor. The extraordinary increase in the number of jurors points to action by the ecclesia under the influence of the fear and excitement caused by the profanation of the mysteries and the

[1] Cf. *supra*, p. 242.

[2] Pollux viii. 53: $\chi\acute{\iota}\lambda\iota\iota$ $\kappa\alpha\tau\grave{\alpha}$ $\mu\grave{\epsilon}\nu$ $\tau\grave{o}\nu$ $\Sigma\acute{o}\lambda\omega\nu\alpha$ $\tau\grave{\alpha}s$ $\epsilon\grave{\iota}\sigma\alpha\gamma\gamma\epsilon\lambda\acute{\iota}\alpha s$ $\check{\epsilon}\kappa\rho\iota\nu\sigma\nu$. *Lex. Cantab.* $\epsilon\grave{\iota}\sigma\alpha\gamma\gamma\epsilon\lambda\acute{\iota}\alpha$: $\epsilon\grave{\iota}\sigma\acute{\eta}\gamma\gamma\epsilon\lambda\lambda\sigma\nu$, $\grave{\omega}s$ $\mu\grave{\epsilon}\nu$ $\Phi\iota\lambda\acute{o}\chi\sigma\rho\sigma s$, $\chi\iota\lambda\acute{\iota}\omega\nu$ $\kappa\alpha\theta\epsilon\zeta\sigma\mu\acute{\epsilon}\nu\omega\nu$. The law could not be Solonian as there were no heliastic courts at that time. Cf. Busolt-Swoboda, *op. cit.*, 1155.

[3] Plutarch *Pericles* xxxii; cf. Lipsius, *op. cit.*, p. 182, n. 17.

[4] Lysias xiii. 34.

[5] His objection (*op. cit.*, p. 89) that, since no selected group of 6,000 could ever be assembled without some absentees, the reference must be to the assembly, is not decisive. The group was not assembled as individuals. All panels were called. Those who responded constituted a large tribunal consisting of twelve sections. Even if the total number who responded fell considerably short of 6,000, they could technically be described as such, just as a meeting of 400 senators could be described as a meeting of the Senate of Five Hundred.

mutilation of the Hermae. An even more exceptional court was that made up of *all* the initiated jurors to decide between the rival claimants for the rewards offered for the discovery of the perpetrators of these outrages. The thesmothetae presided at this διαδικασία.[1] Similar courts made of all jurors who had participated in a certain campaign were drafted from the entire group to try military offenses.[2]

A fuller record of fifth-century litigation would doubtless disclose more cases in which large juries sat in the court of the thesmothetae. This court continued to meet in the spacious quarters formerly used by the Solonian Heliaea, from which it took its name. One gets the impression that large juries were more common in the earlier period than in the fourth century. From Pseudo-Xenophon's essay on the Athenian constitution[3] it is clear that the proposal to provide more and smaller juries did not meet with favor because it "would be easy to trick the small jury and bribe them to give much less just decisions." Grote,[4] with just appreciation of the difficulties of Athenian democracy, emphasizes the value of large panels in encouraging the adherents of democracy and in overawing its opponents among men of wealth and social standing. The murder of Ephialtes shows the lengths to which they were willing to go.

These varied and irregular requirements for jurors could have been met much more easily by distributing twelve panels among the officials entitled to preside at court sessions. A few could be assigned permanently to those officials whose duties were mainly, if not exclusively, judicial. Of the rest, some would serve those officials whose judicial duties were incidental and occasional; others would be available for enlarging the court of the thesmothetae by the addition of one or more panels.[5] Such a system would be much more

---

[1] Andocides i. 28.

[2] Lipsius, *op. cit.*, p. 143; Busolt-Swoboda, *op. cit.*, pp. 1127 and 1157. The only evidence for a court made up of soldiers who were present at the time when the military offense was committed is in the fourth century (Lysias xiv. 5).

[3] iii. 7.   [4] *Op. cit.*, V, 237.

[5] Bruck (*op. cit.*, p. 405) has shown that the δικαστήρια used to fill out the court of the thesmothetae are courts, not sections.

elastic and economical than the use of a panel of 600 to fill a court that needed only 500.

The political aspect of jury service must not be forgotten. Pericles is said to have introduced pay to increase his political strength among the masses; and Cleon, according to Aristophanes, was regarded by the dicasts as their patron and protector whom they in turn served.[1] The political usefulness of the dicasts would be seriously impaired if the service was not pretty evenly distributed over the whole group. That there was no grievance on this score may be rightly inferred from the failure of Bdelycleon in the *Wasps* to mention it. On the contrary, he assumes that practically all dicasts were in service constantly. This impression conveyed by Aristophanes finds some confirmation in Pseudo-Xenophon.[2] Among the advantages gained from having cases from overseas tried at Athens was "the receipt of pay out of the court fees all the year round." The congestion of public business in Athens, including litigation, is explained by the fact that they had more festivals and holidays than any other Greek state and "they have to decide more private and public lawsuits and official scrutinies than all the rest of the world together."[3] The service could be spread more evenly over the entire body of jurors by alternating panels in the busier courts. In this connection it may be noted that the evidence for the assignment of panels for regular service in specific courts does not exclude the possibility of two panels being employed alternately at intervals in one court with a heavy docket.[4]

Little or no information is available as to the means used in the fifth century to notify jurors of court sessions. The

---

[1] Cleon is described as κηδεμών of the jurors in *Wasps*, 242. In the *Knights* (255) he calls them to his aid:

ὦ γέροντες ἡλιασταί, φράτορες τριωβόλου,
οὓς ἐγὼ βόσκω κεκραγὼς καὶ δίκαια κἄδικα,
παραβοηθεῖθ', ὡς ὑπ' ἀνδρῶν τύπτομαι ξυνωμοτῶν.

Cf. Rogers, *Wasps*, pp. xvi ff.

[2] *Ath. Pol.* i. 16.   [3] *Ibid.*, iii. 2.

[4] Hommel (*op. cit.*, p. 111) has suggested the possibility of alternating panels. Such courts as that of the thesmothetae, the Eleven, and the Thirty (Forty) must have handled the bulk of the litigation day by day.

only reference to an official notice is the mention in the *Wasps* of a σημεῖον, perhaps similar to the signal put up for meetings of the ecclesia.[1] It was taken down when the proceedings began. After that no one was admitted.[2] The jurors in the *Wasps* knew what cases were to be tried that day. There were three of them, if Aristophanes is to be taken literally: Laches,[3] an unnamed traitor from the Thracian front,[4] and Dracontides.[5] It was not unusual to have several cases tried on the same day.[6] This knowledge on the part of the jurors must have had an official source. Perhaps they read the notice boards among which Philocleon delighted to wander.[7] It was also possible that at each court session notices of the cases to come at the next sitting of the court were read. Apparently anyone interested in a case could appear before the court at the close of proceedings and urge all to be on hand for a particular case. This seems to be the explanation of the orders issued by Cleon.[8]

---

[1] *Wasps*, 690. Cf. *Thesmophoriazousae*, 277–78:

ὡς τὸ τῆς ἐκκλησίας
σημεῖον ἐν τῷ Θεσμοφορείῳ φαίνεται.

[2] *Wasps*, 892.   [3] *Ibid.*, 240.   [4] *Ibid.*, 289.
[5] *Ibid.*, 157.   [6] Aristophanes *Clouds*, 779–80.

[7] Aristophanes *Wasps*, 349:

οὕτω κιττῶ διὰ τῶν σανίδων μετὰ χοιρίνης περιελθεῖν.

Cf. *ibid.*, 848:

φέρε νυν, ἐνέγκω τὰς σανίδας καὶ τὰς γραφάς.

Photius, *s.v.* σανίδα: τὸ λεύκωμα ὅπου αἱ δίκαι λέγονται. Scholiast on Aristophanes' *Wasps*, 349: ἢ σανίδων φησὶ τῶν περιεχουσῶν τὰ ὀνόματα τῶν εἰσαχθησομένων εἰς τὸ δικαστήριον, ποῖον δεήσει πρῶτον εἰσαχθῆναι καὶ κατὰ τάξιν.

[8] *Wasps*, 242. Cleon is said to have issued orders for the appearance of the jurors betimes with a goodly supply of anger.

χθὲς οὖν Κλέων ὁ κηδεμὼν ἡμῖν ἐφεῖτ' ἐν ὥρᾳ
ἥκειν ἔχοντας ἡμερῶν ὀργὴν τριῶν πονηρὰν
ἐπ' αὐτόν,

Bdelycleon represents the son of Chareus, a public advocate, as entering court and warning the jurors to be on time for a case next day in which he was to be the advocate. 687 ff.

ὅταν εἰσελθὸν μειράκιόν σοι κατάπυγον, Χαιρέου υἱός,
ὡδὶ διαβάς, διακινηθεὶς τῷ σώματι καὶ τρυφερανθείς,
ἥκειν εἴπῃ πρῷ κἂν ὥρᾳ δικάσονθ', ὡς ὅστις ἂν ὑμῶν
ὕστερος ἔλθῃ τοῦ σημείου, τὸ τριώβολον οὐ κομιεῖται·

The meaning of εἰσελθόν presents some difficulties. It should mean in the mouth of

Bdelycleon *domum tuam ingressus*, as Brunck and most editors since have taken it. Starkie (note on *Wasps* 687) thinks "it was the business of the ξυνήγορος to summon the dicasts." Obviously a personal summons could not be delivered to 500 jurors in their homes. Unquestionably Merry is right in translating "coming into court." This is the meaning of εἰσελθεῖν in lines 560 and 579. It is likely that any interested persons appeared before the session began or possibly at the end of the day and made informal, as well as official, announcements to the jurors. In Antiphon vi. 21 both Philocrates and the *choregus* appeared before the court of the thesmothetae. Philocrates said that the *choregus* was responsible for the death of his brother. The *choregus* answered the charge at once and on the following day (εὐθὺς τότε καὶ αὖθις τῇ ὑστεραίᾳ). Here the words ἀναβὰς εἰς τὴν ἡλιαίαν τὴν τῶν θεσμοθετῶν are used. Van Leeuwen, *Wasps*, 687, translates εἰσελθόν "intrans" and inquires, "Haec autem ubinam jubebantur heliastae? Ibi, opinor, quo cum diluculo convenissent. Illuc igitur εἰσιέναι dicitur adolescens συνήγορος." Van Leeuwen is wrong in suggesting the κληρωτήριον as the place where the notice was delivered. There was no daily allotment of jurors as Teusch (*op. cit.*, p. 62) has shown. Rogers offers quite a different explanation which has not met with favor. He thinks that the young man came forward in the assembly (εἰσελθόν) and moved a resolution (εἴπη).

CHAPTER VIII

THE AREOPAGUS AND DEMOCRACY

The sixth constitutional, or rather political, change is designated by Aristotle as the "supremacy of the Areopagus." This supremacy was due to the prestige gained by the Areopagus for its services in the Persian wars, and lasted for a period of seventeen years (479–462 B.C.). In the *Politics*, Aristotle describes the government of this period as συντονωτέραν.[1] In the *Constitution*[2] he says that the "Areopagus became strong and controlled the city." The rather vague expression διῴκει τὴν πόλιν recalls his description of the powers of the Areopagus in the earlier period. But when one seeks to discover what specific powers the Areopagus had or how it controlled the city, he finds only such general expressions as ἐπίσκοπος τῆς πολιτείας[3] and φύλαξ τῶν νόμων.[4] After the Persian wars there was no real change in the constitution, as the words οὐδενὶ δόγματι λαβοῦσα τὴν ἡγεμονίαν show. Accordingly, all that Aristotle means is that the development of democracy was checked for a time, and conservative opinions and policies began to prevail. It was only natural that the democratic movement initiated by Cleisthenes should eventually lose momentum and slow down when its immediate objectives were achieved. The struggle with Persia absorbed the interests and efforts of the masses and permitted the more cautious and conservative elements to reassert themselves.

As there was no change in the constitution, the Areopagus must have used those powers and privileges that survived the democratic reforms of Cleisthenes. Now it is to be ob-

[1] *Pol.* 1304*a*. 20.

[2] *Ath. Pol.* xxiii. 1: μετὰ δὲ τὰ Μηδικὰ πάλιν ἴσχυσεν ἡ ἐν Ἀρείῳ πάγῳ βουλὴ καὶ διῴκει τὴν πόλιν, οὐδενὶ δόγματι λαβοῦσα τὴν ἡγεμονίαν ἀλλὰ διὰ τὸ γενέσθαι τῆς περὶ Σαλαμῖνα ναυμαχίας αἰτία.

[3] *Ibid.*, viii. 4.

[4] *Ibid.*, iv. 4. For the Areopagus in the early period, cf. *supra*, pp. 88 ff.

served that the judicial functions exercised by the assembly in the cases of Phrynichus and Miltiades[1] did not interfere with the judicial powers of the Areopagus. This is evident from the fact that the crisis in the opposition to the Areopagus was precipitated by the proposal of the Areopagus to try Themistocles for treason (Medism). The Areopagus also was ready to institute proceedings against men accused of plotting the overthrow of the government.[2] But the political supremacy of the Areopagus was due not only to the exercise of judicial and other original powers that had fallen into abeyance in the period of democratic ascendancy but also to the prominent part taken in political life by the individual Areopagites, such as Themistocles and Aristeides. This is clear from the fact that Ephialtes' campaign against the Areopagus took the form of attacks upon individual Areopagites engaged in the public service. If the supremacy of the Areopagus be thus conceived, there is no reason for doubting Aristotle's listing it as a distinct era in Athenian political history.[3]

Aristotle gives as the seventh change in the Athenian constitution the one which Ephialtes brought about by curtailing the powers of the Areopagus: ἑβδόμη δὲ ἡ μετὰ ταύτην, ἣν 'Αριστείδης μὲν ὑπέδειξεν, 'Εφιάλτης δ' ἐπετέλεσεν καταλύσας τὴν 'Αρεοπαγῖτιν βουλήν.[4] Earlier in the treatise Aristotle represents the reforms of Ephialtes as being brought to a conclusion in the archonship of Conon, i.e., 462–461 B.C.:

καὶ πρῶτον μὲν ἀνεῖλεν πολλοὺς τῶν 'Αρεοπαγιτῶν, ἀγῶνας ἐπιφέρων περὶ τῶν διῳκημένων· ἔπειτα τῆς βουλῆς ἐπὶ Κόνωνος ἄρχοντος ἅπαντα περιείλετο τὰ ἐπίθετα δι' ὧν ἦν ἡ τῆς πολιτείας φυλακή, καὶ τὰ μὲν τοῖς πεντακοσίοις τὰ δὲ τῷ δήμῳ καὶ τοῖς δικαστηρίοις ἀπέδωκεν.[5]

He adds that Themistocles, himself an Areopagite, had a share in the overthrow. In the *Politics* the following statement occurs: καὶ τὴν μὲν ἐν 'Αρείῳ πάγῳ βουλὴν 'Εφιάλτης ἐκό-

---

[1] Cf. *supra*, pp. 197ff.   [2] *Ath. Pol.* xxv. 3; cf. *infra*, p. 256.

[3] Cf. Busolt-Swoboda, *Staatskunde*, p. 893, who describe it as a "tendenziöse Erfindung." Cf. Lipsius, *Das Attische Recht*, p. 34, who takes a more conservative view.

[4] *Ath. Pol.* xli. 2.   [5] *Ibid.*, xxv. 2.

λουσε καὶ Περικλῆς.[1] It is clear from the *Constitution*, however, that in the estimation of Aristotle the attacks of Ephialtes and Pericles were distinct, for he assigns the limitations made by Pericles in the powers of the Areopagus to a time after the passing of the citizenship law in 451 B.C.: καὶ γὰρ τῶν Ἀρεοπαγιτῶν ἔνια παρείλετο.[2] Plutarch represents the two men as acting together: διὸ καὶ μᾶλλον ἰσχύσας ὁ Περικλῆς ἐν τῷ δήμῳ κατεστασίασε τὴν βουλήν, ὥστε τὴν μὲν ἀφαιρεθῆναι τὰς πλείστας κρίσεις δι' Ἐφιάλτου.[3] Aristotle further mentions τοὺς τ' Ἐφιάλτου καὶ Ἀρχεστράτου νόμους τοὺς περὶ τῶν Ἀρεοπαγιτῶν.[4] It is clear from all of these passages that Ephialtes was regarded as the leader in the attack of 462 B.C., whoever may have been his associates. The reference to Aristeides means that he began a democratic movement which was furthered by the policy of Ephialtes. Doubtless Ephialtes had other influential democratic sympathizers and coadjutors working with him. It may be assumed that, although Pericles was responsible for a separate attack in 452 B.C., yet he was associated with Ephialtes in the attack of 462. Pericles had just come into prominence by his prosecution of Cimon (463 B.C.). As one of the democratic leaders, Ephialtes would naturally attach him to himself. It is reasonable to suppose that, immediately after the death of Ephialtes, Pericles stepped into his place and devoted himself to the execution of Ephialtes' reforms. Pericles' final attack, some ten years later than that of Ephialtes, was, as will be shown later, a part of his plan for gaining the support of the democratic party. Archestratus was evidently a supporter either of the reforms of Ephialtes in 462 or of those of Pericles in 452, and put forward some of the laws in his own name.[5]

---

[1] 1274a. 7.   [2] *Ath. Pol.* xxvii. 1.

[3] *Pericles*, ix. For other passages regarding the overthrow of the Areopagus, cf. *ibid.*, vii; *Cimon* x. xv; *Praec. Ger. Reip.*, x. 15; xv. 18; Pausanias I. 29. 15.

[4] *Ath. Pol.* xxxv. 2.

[5] Kenyon, *ad loc.*, suggests that he was a supporter of Ephialtes and that some of the laws appeared in his name. But Busolt (*Geschichte*, III, i, 270) supposes that Archestratus put forward the law by which Pericles deprived the Areopagus of power.

The only problem lies in the very circumstantial account of Aristotle, according to which Themistocles played a part in the reforms made by Ephialtes. Many scholars, because of the difficulty of reconciling the chronology of Aristotle and Thucydides, have rejected the testimony of Aristotle as to the participation of Themistocles on the ground that he could not possibly have been in Athens in 462 B.C., inasmuch as, according to the regularly accepted chronology, he had already fled to Persia some years prior to this date. These scholars either delete the passage or else accept it as the genuine, but incorrect, statement of Aristotle. Others, eager to accept Aristotle's words, have attempted to explain the passage in various ingenious ways. For example, a new chronology for the entire period has been suggested, but it has met with little or no acceptance. Another explanation is that the enemies of Ephialtes spread abroad a report that he was merely the tool of the absent Themistocles. Still another explanation is to shorten the period of the Areopagus' supremacy from seventeen to seven years.

Ure attempts to reconcile the accounts of Aristotle and Thucydides by supposing that Themistocles, after his ostracism and before his departure for Persia, came back to Athens for a very short time in 462 B.C., helped to organize the attack on the council, and then fled to Persia. Thucydides did not know about this and hence made some mistakes in his chronology. The chief difficulty with Ure's theory is that he fails to realize that the preliminary attacks on individual members of the Areopagus and the organization of the final attack must have consumed a far greater period of time than the few months which at most he allows Themistocles in Athens in 462 B.C.[1] It is clear from chapter xxv of the *Constitution* that the attack of Ephialtes was not confined to 462 B.C. but was in progress for some time prior to that date. This is the only way in which the phrase καίπερ ὑποφερομένη κατὰ μικρόν can be interpreted. Later in the chapter it is said that the first part of Ephialtes' procedure consisted in attacks on

[1] Ure, "When Was Themistocles Last in Athens?" *Jour. of Hellenic Studies*, XLI, 165 ff. For the literature of the subject, cf. this article, p. 166, nn. 7 and 8.

individual members of the senate and that afterward he took various functions from the body. The attacks on, and the gradual discrediting of, individual members of the council may well have extended over a period of several years. Ure fails to take these details of the chapter into consideration when he remarks that "the *Constitution* says distinctly that the attack did not begin till 'about seventeen years after the Persian Wars.'" It is quite possible then that Themistocles was jointly responsible with Ephialtes for the attack in that he assisted in planning some of the attacks upon individual members of the Areopagus before his ostracism in 471 B.C. Ephialtes, however, was alone responsible for the final legislation which reduced the powers of the Areopagus.

By the reforms of Cleisthenes the boulé, assembly, and courts were empowered to act in certain cases that had formerly been exclusively under the control of the Areopagus. The Areopagus, however, continued on occasion to act in these cases, although its action became so rare as to amount practically to disuse. During its supremacy, however, succeeding the Persian wars, it resumed practically exclusive control of the state. These resumed powers, doubtless both administrative and judicial, are the ones of which Ephialtes would especially desire to deprive the Areopagus. It is probable that much of Ephialtes' work consisted in limiting either to the assembly or to the boulé or to a court powers which, under the constitution of Cleisthenes, had belonged both to the Areopagus and to one or other of these bodies. The only powers left to the Areopagus were those which never had been shared with any other body. The other bodies were firmly entrenched in their powers by laws. The fact that laws were passed shows that very definite powers were involved.[1]

In considering the fact that Ephialtes began his operations against the Areopagus by attacks on individual members, it is necessary to understand the character of the council at this time. In 487 B.C. a system was introduced by which the archons were selected by lot from a larger group which had

[1] Cf. Wilamowitz, *Aristoteles und Athen*, II, 186.

been elected by ballot by the people. But up until 457 B.C.
the archons continued to be chosen only from the first two
citizen classes.[1] The Areopagus remained, therefore, to a
large extent an aristocratic body. In addition this aristocratic body had gained enormous prestige through its acts
at the close of the Persian wars; and prominent members of
the Areopagus, during the period immediately following the
wars, played an important part in political life. For example,
Aristeides and Themistocles, who were men of the greatest
prominence at the time, were both members of the Areopagus. It is to be expected that the council would call to
account any men in public life whom it discovered committing wrongful acts toward the state. On the other hand,
prominent men of democratic sympathies would naturally
be hostile to the aristocratic traditions of the council and
would be glad of opportunities to attack individual members.
This attack, on the one hand, of the aristocratic Areopagus
upon prominent citizens and, on the other hand, of prominent citizens with more or less democratic sympathies upon
individual Areopagites, is well illustrated by the story, as
told by Aristotle, of Themistocles, Ephialtes, and the Areopagus.

In this revolution he [Ephialtes] was assisted by Themistocles, who
was himself a member of the Areopagus, but was expecting to be tried
before it on a charge of treasonable dealings with Persia. This made him
anxious that it should be overthrown, and accordingly he warned Ephialtes
that the Council intended to arrest him, while at the same time he informed
the Areopagites that he would reveal to them certain persons who were
conspiring to subvert the constitution. He then conducted the representatives delegated by the Council to the residence of Ephialtes, promising to
show them the conspirators who assembled there, and proceeded to con-
verse with them in an earnest manner. Ephialtes, seeing this, was seized
with alarm and took refuge in suppliant guise at the altar. Everyone was
astounded at the occurrence, and presently, when the Council of Five
Hundred met, Ephialtes and Themistocles together proceeded to denounce
the Areopagus to them. This they repeated in similar fashion in the Assembly, until they succeeded in depriving it of its power.[2]

Doubtless they attacked members of the council who were
officials for malfeasance in office.

In his attack on the Areopagus then, Ephialtes simply

[1] *Ath. Pol.* xxii. 5; xxvi. 2.   [2] *Ath. Pol.* xxv. 3, Kenyon's translation.

adopted the policy which members of the Areopagus were themselves following. He attacked individuals for irregularity in their official and political transactions (περὶ τῶν διῳκη-μένων),[1] with a view to weakening the whole council by discrediting its prominent members. The final overthrow, however, and the actual curtailing of the powers of the council were due to a resolution of the people.[2] The reforms of Ephialtes consisted in laws which assigned to other bodies exclusively powers in which the Areopagus had formerly had a share.[3]

The phrase with which Aristotle describes the powers which Ephialtes took away from the council is noteworthy: τὰ ἐπίθετα δι᾽ ὧν ἦν ἡ τῆς πολιτείας φυλακή.[4] It is obvious that Ephialtes made no attempt to deprive the council utterly of power, but rather only of those privileges through which it had general oversight of the constitution. These would be to a large extent administrative powers and also judicial powers which were connected with the administrative and political functions of the council.[5] So it is not to be expected that Ephialtes would disturb the homicide functions of the body.

According to Demosthenes, τοῦτο μόνον τὸ δικαστήριον οὐχὶ τύραννος, οὐκ ὀλιγαρχία, οὐ δημοκρατία τὰς φονικὰς δίκας ἀφελέσθαι τετόλμηκεν.[6] An anonymous biography represents Thucydides as defending Pyrilampes before the Areopagus on a charge of homicide. Pericles was the prosecutor.[7] There

[1] *Ibid.*, xxv. 2. Cf. Bonner, *Lawyers and Litigants*, p. 100; for details regarding the official activities of Areopagites, cf. Wilamowitz, *op. cit.*, II, 93 f.; Busolt, *Geschichte*, III, 1, 262 f.

[2] *Ath. Pol.* xxv. 4.   [3] Cf. Wilamowitz, *op. cit.*, II, 188.

[4] *Ath. Pol.* xxv. 2. Cf. Busolt-Swoboda, *op. cit.*, pp. 894 ff.; Wilamowitz, *op. cit.*, II, 186 ff.

[5] Cf. Calhoun, *Criminal Law*, p. 102: "The judicial reform that took place at this time was first and foremost a reform of criminal law and procedure, and pre-eminently of the criminal law that later was administered by the thesmothetes."

[6] xxiii. 66. For the great age and immutability of Athenian homicide laws, cf. Antiphon v. 14 and vi. 2.

[7] *Life of Thucydides* (Didot edition of Thucydides), Part II, p. 10, sec. 19. As the result of Pericles' prowess, according to the writer of this life, in the prosecution of Pyrilampes, Pericles was elected general and became the leader of the δῆμος. Of course it is impossible to date this case, but it seems probable that it was sometime between the reforms of Ephialtes and the final reforms of Pericles.

is a fragment of Philochorus to the effect that Ephialtes left
only homicide cases to the Areopagus.[1] Added to this evidence is the fact that the Athenians felt that the Areopagus
held this authority in homicide cases by divine right.[2] Another point raised by Caillemer is the fact that it is inconceivable that the Areopagus could have risen to a position
of such importance again at the end of the fifth century if it
had lost all of its functions and prerogatives sixty years before. It would have disappeared entirely.[3] The jurisdiction
of the Areopagus in the γραφὴ πυρκαιᾶς is closely connected
with its jurisdiction in homicide cases, because arson might
involve the loss of life. This function was not disturbed by
the reforms of Ephialtes.

It is clear that the Areopagus kept certain functions in
connection with impiety cases. Suits involving the sacred
olives continued to be tried before the Areopagites. The
seventh speech of Lysias deals with a case which was tried
by the Areopagus. The court is addressed regularly as ὦ
βουλή, and it is obvious that a preliminary investigation was
held by a committee of the Areopagus chosen for the purpose.
The committee reported to the council, which then tried the
cases.[4] The speech makes it quite clear that a committee
of the Areopagus inspected the trees once a month and that
further a special commission went to visit them once a year.
In this connection it may be suggested that the Areopagus
regularly made its investigations through committees and
had done so from early times. Aristotle represents the Areopagus as working in this way when Themistocles promised
to point out to them some would-be subverters of the constitution. He took with him a committee chosen for the

---

[1] *FHG*, I, 407. Cf. Plutarch *Cimon*, xv; *Pericles*, vii; Pausanias i. 29. 15;
Xenophon *Mem.* iii. 5. 20, where Socrates describes the Areopagites as deciding
cases most lawfully and justly. Meier-Schömann (*Att. Process*, p. 143) advanced
the theory that homicide cases were taken from the Areopagus and restored to them
under the Thirty. Boeckh and O. Müller agreed. Grote, V, 368 n., refuted the
theory and was followed by Philippi, *Der Areopag und die Epheten*, p. 265; Caillemer,
article on the Areopagus in Daremberg-Saglio, p. 401; Lipsius, *op. cit.*, p. 34; and
others.

[2] Cf. Aeschylus *Eumenides*, 684, and Demosthenes xxiii. 66, quoted above.

[3] Caillemer, *loc. cit.*   [4] Lysias vii. 7, 25.

purpose (τοὺς αἱρεθέντας).[1] With this may be compared the ephetae. Naturally a homicide would not be removed from the shrine where he had taken refuge. Hence a committee of the Areopagus was sent out to try him at the shrine. The early institution of the ephetae—sometime before Draco—indicates that the practice of using committees was very early adopted by the Areopagus. It may be supposed that the council regularly used committees in its capacity of general overseer of the constitution. If any wrongdoer were reported to the council, either by one of the members or by someone else, it is likely that the Areopagus promptly sent out a committee to investigate and to make report. The trial, if there were any, came before the whole body. It is difficult to understand otherwise how such cases could be handled by the Areopagus. Matters which could be thus dealt with would include superintendence of morals and education, impiety, supervision of the laws.[2]

In considering impiety cases, it seems fair to suppose that cases which were tried before the council in the fourth century were tried there continuously from the reforms of Ephialtes down until some subsequent change was made in the procedure.[3]

There is no doubt that a general surveillance of religious matters and of public ceremonies remained for the Areopagus. In one of the doubtful orations of Demosthenes[4] the story is told of Theogenes, the king archon, who married an unworthy woman, supposing her to be the daughter of Stephanus. He allowed her to perform the sacrifices to Dionysus and to administer the oath to the priestesses. On discovering her identity, the Areopagus proceeded to punish Theogenes to the full extent of its authority. The orator adds, however: οὐ γὰρ αὐτοκράτορές εἰσιν, ὡς ἂν βούλωνται, Ἀθηναίων τινὰ κολάσαι. The story shows, then, that the Areop-

[1] *Ath. Pol.* xxv. 3.

[2] For the division of the city among different groups of Areopagites, cf. Isocrates *Areop.*, 46.

[3] For the change in the method of handling the sacred olives, cf. *Ath. Pol.* lx. 2, 3, and *infra*, p. 363.

[4] lix. 79 ff.

agus did have a general oversight of ritual and a limited power of punishment for any abuse therein. There are other stories to the same effect. According to Plutarch,[1] Euripides was not willing to express openly his attitude toward the gods because he was afraid of the Areopagus. Cicero[2] tells of a dream which came to the poet Sophocles, revealing the identity of a man who had stolen a sacred vessel. He referred the matter to the Areopagus and that court ordered the arrest of the culprit. The man confessed in the course of the investigation and returned the stolen property.

It is clear from the foregoing that the Areopagus retained sole authority in matters involving the sacred olives and that it kept a general surveillance in all matters of religion and a limited power of punishment in such cases. It is doubtless true, however, that, in general, jurisdiction in cases of ἀσέβεια passed to the δικαστήρια. Other speeches of Lysias involving ἀσέβεια were delivered before heliastic courts,[3] and Andocides' speech On the Mysteries was delivered before a popular court, although, as in all cases involving impiety, the archon basileus brought the cases into court. It cannot be proved, but is merely suggested with a great degree of plausibility, that the change took place at the time of Ephialtes' reforms, the Areopagus having formerly had complete control in cases of impiety.[4]

The Council of the Areopagus, along with these other religious duties, had supervision of the ἱερὰ ὀργάς and other τεμένη, in association with various other boards and individuals:

ἐπιμελεῖσθαι δὲ τῆς ἱερᾶς ὀργάδος καὶ τῶν ἄλλων ἱερῶν τεμενῶν τῶν Ἀθήνησιν ἀπὸ τῆσδε τῆς ἡμέρας εἰς τὸν ἀεὶ χρόνον οὕς τε ὁ νόμος κελεύει περὶ ἑκάστου αὐτῶν καὶ τὴν βουλὴν τὴν ἐξ Ἀρείου πάγου καὶ τὸν στρατηγὸν τὸν ἐπὶ τὴν φυλακὴν τῆς χώρας κεχειροτονημένον καὶ τοὺς περι-

[1] De plac. philos. vii. 2; Didot, Plutarchi Scripta Moralia, II., p. 1072.

[2] De divin. 1. 25.   [3] Lysias, v and vi.

[4] Philippi (op. cit., pp. 267 f.) thinks that the reforms of Ephialtes were not concerned with cases involving religion. Lipsius, op. cit., p. 366, states that cases regarding the sacred olives were the only impiety cases which continued to come before the Areopagus.

πολάρχους καὶ τοὺς δημάρχους καὶ τὴν βουλὴν τὴν ἀεὶ βουλεύουσαν καὶ τῶν
ἄλλων Ἀθηναίων τὸμ βουλόμενον τρόπῳ ὅτῳ ἂν ἐπίστωνται.[1]

The Areopagus at one time had a general oversight of
education and morals. This supervision may be illustrated
by one particular kind of case, the γραφὴ ἀργίας. There is evidence that Draco instituted a law regarding idleness, νόμος
περὶ τῆς ἀργίας, of which Solon in turn made use and which
was still in effect in the fourth century.[2] There is also evidence that originally all γραφαὶ ἀργίας came before the Areopagus.[3] In the time of the orators, however, such cases no
longer came before the Areopagus, but before heliastic
courts,[4] for they are mentioned in a list of cases which came
under the cognizance of the archon.[5] These cases may be
taken as typical of what happened to the Areopagus' censor-
ship of morals. The council would continue, as in other cases,
to have the right which every citizen had of bringing such
cases to the attention of the authorities, but it would no longer
have the authority to settle them itself. The archon would
take care of them. It may be assumed that the Areopagus
acted as is described by Isocrates,[6] who represents the members as dividing the city into sections, different members
being responsible for different sections and watching the
lives of the citizens and making reports of unruly ones. There
is an interesting passage in the Pseudo-Platonic *Axiochus*,[7]
which gives to a commission of the Areopagus along with the
σωφρονισταί some control over the ephebi. The relationship
is wholly undefined, and the passage is very puzzling. Girard,[8]
who believes that the institution of the ephebi belongs at
least to the beginning of the fifth century, if not earlier,

---

[1] *Bulletin de correspondance hellénique*, XIII, 434, ll. 15 ff.; cf. *IG*, II, Supplement 104a; Dittenberger, *Sylloge²*, II, 789; De Sanctis, *Storia della Repubblica
Ateniese*, p. 423, n. 3.

[2] *Lex. Cant. s.v. ἀργίας δίκη*, quoting Lysias; Diog. Laert. i. 55, quoting Lysias.

[3] Plutarch *Solon*, xxii; cf. Athenaeus, 168 A.

[4] *Lex. Seguer*. in Bekker, *Anec*. I. 310. 3.

[5] Cf. Lipsius, *op. cit.*, p. 354.   [6] *Areop.*, 46.   [7] 367 A.

[8] Daremberg-Saglio, article "Ephebi," pp. 621 f.

thinks that the Areopagus lost its supervision of the ephebi under Ephialtes, but that after the Thirty it again had some undeterminable relation to them. The writer of the *Axiochus* may have confused the earlier powers which the Areopagus had in this regard with the later period.[1]

The function of the Areopagus which is particularly stressed in the early period, that is, both in Solon's constitution and in the period before Solon, is the general oversight of the laws and the constitution: τὴν δὲ τῶν Ἀρεοπαγιτῶν ἔταξεν ἐπὶ τὸ νομοφυλακεῖν, ὥσπερ ὑπῆρχεν καὶ πρότερον ἐπίσκοπος οὖσα τῆς πολιτείας.[2] The terms are vague and it is a question just how definite or extensive were the powers described. The best explanation, in view of later activities of the council, seems to be that the powers represented here meant always simply the duty of watching the magistrates and insuring that their administrations should be entirely in accord with the laws (κατὰ τοὺς νόμους). This, then, would give the council at any time the right to suspend a magistrate's unlawful decision. This is brought out very clearly in the only acceptable portion of the so-called Draconian constitution: ἡ δὲ βουλὴ ἡ ἐξ Ἀρείου πάγου φύλαξ ἦν τῶν νόμων, καὶ διετήρει τὰς ἀρχάς, ὅπως κατὰ τοὺς νόμους ἄρχωσιν. ἐξῆν δὲ τῷ ἀδικουμένῳ πρὸς τὴν τῶν Ἀρεοπαγιτῶν βουλὴν εἰσαγγέλλειν, ἀποφαίνοντι παρ' ὃν ἀδικεῖται νόμον.[3] This function of the council, which for purposes of convenience will be here termed νομοφυλακία, was doubtless taken from the council by Ephialtes. According to Philochorus,[4] a new board, called νομοφύλακες, seven in number, was instituted at the time when Ephialtes curtailed the powers of the Areopagus. This passage has been suspected for various reasons, chiefly because the board is never elsewhere heard of until many years after the time of Ephialtes and because the number "seven"

---

[1] For the date of the ephebi, cf. also Lofberg, *Class. Phil.*, XX, 330 ff., who believes that the institution certainly existed in the fifth century. In favor of a later date, cf. Forbes, *Greek Physical Education*, p. 113.

[2] *Ath. Pol.* viii. 4.   [3] *Ibid.*, iv. 4; cf. *supra*, p. 95.

[4] Müller, *FHG*, I, 407. Cf. Lipsius, *op. cit.*, pp. 35–36.

THE AREOPAGUS AND DEMOCRACY

corresponds to nothing in Athenian institutions.[1] According to this view, Philochorus was really speaking of a board called νομοφύλακες, which was instituted at the end of the fourth century; but he was wrong about the date of its institution. It is true that the lexicographers generally, in describing these officials, are reproducing the characteristics of the fourth-century board.[2] Among the duties which, according to Harpocration, Philochorus attributed to the body was the one of compelling the magistrates to keep the laws (τοῖς νόμοις χρῆσθαι). Now it is known that this duty was restored to the Areopagus by the Thirty by the decree of Teisamenus: ἐπιμελείσθω ἡ βουλὴ ἡ ἐξ ᾿Αρείου πάγου τῶν νόμων, ὅπως ἂν αἱ ἀρχαὶ τοῖς κειμένοις νόμοις χρῶνται.[3] Presumably it had been taken from the council at the time of Ephialtes. Philochorus may have been correct in asserting that the νομοφύλακες were instituted at the time of Ephialtes' reforms, to take over the function of νομοφυλακία hitherto exercised by the Areopagus. On the other hand, he may merely have supposed, on the basis of the fourth-century νομοφύλακες, that a similar situation existed in the interim between Ephialtes and the restoration of power to the Areopagus under the Thirty. The question cannot be settled.

Keil, in his edition and interpretation of a Strassburg papyrus which be believed to contain some fragments of history of the Periclean age, argues very plausibly on the basis of a notice about the νομοφύλακες that they must have been instituted under Ephialtes and dissolved by the Thirty.[4] The papyrus, however, is of no value in settling the matter, inasmuch as it contains not fragments of a history of the

[1] Cf. Gilbert, *Greek Constitutional Antiquities*, p. 155; Philippi, *op. cit.*, pp. 185 ff., who thinks that the institution was connected with the reforms of Ephialtes but was of slight importance. For the literature of the subject cf. Busolt-Swoboda, *op. cit.*, p. 895, n. 1.

[2] Cf. Müller, *op. cit.*; Suidas, *s.v.*; Pollux viii. 94; Harpocration, *s.v.*; Photius, *s.v.*

[3] Andocides i. 84.

[4] *Anonymus Argentinensis*, pp. 170 ff.; cf. Lipsius, *op. cit.*, p. 35, and Vinogradoff, *Outlines of Historical Jurisprudence*, Vol. II, pp. 136 ff.

Periclean age, as Keil thought, but rather a table of contents prefixed to a biography of Demosthenes. Many of the emendations of Keil's edition have been shown to be incorrect, and no great importance can be attached to the document.[1]

Illegal legislation was dealt with by means of the γραφὴ παρανόμων, which doubtless also was established at the time of Ephialtes.[2] The cases of γραφὴ παρανόμων which are known from the fifth century yield little information either as to grounds of action or procedure. But it was such a formidable process that the Four Hundred, as one of their first measures, suspended it, along with certain other important suits, to protect themselves in introducing any sort of legislation that they desired: ἔπειτα τὰς τῶν παρανόμων γραφὰς καὶ τὰς εἰσαγγελίας καὶ τὰς προσκλήσεις ἀνεῖλον.[3] If the γραφὴ παρανόμων had been left to the democrats as a weapon against the oligarchs, they would have found difficulty in legally putting any of their plans into effect. The surest method, then, was to abolish all processes by which the democrats could attack them for illegality of action. This is particularly well brought out by Thucydides' description of the events of this time:

καὶ ἐσήνεγκαν οἱ ξυγγραφῆς ἄλλο μὲν οὐδέν, αὐτὸ δὲ τοῦτο, ἐξεῖναι μὲν Ἀθηναίων ἀνατεὶ εἰπεῖν γνώμην ἣν ἄν τις βούληται· ἢν δέ τις τὸν εἰπόντα ἢ γράψηται παρανόμων ἢ ἄλλῳ τῳ τρόπῳ βλάψῃ, μεγάλας ζημίας ἐπέθεσαν.[4]

The fact that the γραφὴ παρανόμων had become such an important process under the democracy before the time of the Four Hundred suggests, although it cannot be absolutely proved, that the institution of the process belongs to the last

[1] Cf. Cary, *Documentary Sources of Greek History*, p. 4. De Sanctis, *op. cit.*, p. 439, maintains that the νομοφύλακες were not introduced by Ephialtes, but belonged only to the fourth century.

[2] Cf. Busolt-Swoboda, *op. cit.*, p. 896; Schulthess, *Das attische Volksgericht*, p. 22; Fränkel, *Die attischen Geschworenengerichte*, p. 66; Schreiner, *De corpore iuris atheniensium*, p. 18; Lipsius, *op. cit.*, p. 36; Botsford, *The Athenian Constitution*, p. 222; *CAH*, V, 100; Wyse in Whibley, *Companion to Greek Studies*, p. 357; Wilamowitz, *op. cit.*, II, 193, believes that the γραφὴ παρανόμων was instituted by Solon. Cf. Loedgberg, *Animadversiones de actione παρανόμων* (Upsala, 1898), pp. 63 f.

[3] *Ath. Pol.* xxix. 4.   [4] viii. 67.

period of constitutional reform prior to that time, namely, the reforms of Ephialtes. If Ephialtes took away νομοφυλακία from the Areopagus and gave it to the people, it is reasonable that he should have devised some process by which they could execute their guardianship of the laws. This is true, regardless of the existence or non-existence of the νομοφύλακες during the fifth century.

The earliest known instance of the use of the γραφὴ παρανόμων is in 415 B.C., after the mutilation of the hermae and the profanation of the mysteries. Speusippus proposed in the senate to turn over to a court certain men who were accused of participation in the profanation of the mysteries, among them Leogoras, the father of Andocides. Leogoras indicted Speusippus by a γραφὴ παρανόμων, and the case was tried before a jury of 6,000. Speusippus did not obtain even 200 votes.[1] The small number of votes favorable to Speusippus indicates that the jury must have considered his act grossly illegal, but the ground for the γραφὴ παρανόμων is not known.

In 406 B.C., after the Battle of Arginusae, the eight generals who had participated in the encounter were deposed and recalled to Athens on the charge of failing to rescue the men from the wrecked ships. Six returned to Athens, and on action of the senate they were turned over to the assembly for trial. Their first hearing before that body was ended, before a decision was reached, by a plea that darkness would prevent the taking of a vote by show of hands. At this time the senate was instructed to prepare and bring a resolution before the assembly providing for the trial of the generals. On the motion of Callixenus a προβούλευμα was passed and brought into a meeting of the assembly to the effect that, on the basis of the information gained at the former meeting of the assembly, all of the Athenians should vote by tribes on the guilt or innocence of the generals.

Ἐπειδὴ τῶν τε κατηγορούντων κατὰ τῶν στρατηγῶν καὶ ἐκείνων ἀπολογουμένων ἐν τῇ προτέρᾳ ἐκκλησίᾳ ἀκηκόασι, διαψηφίσασθαι Ἀθηναίους ἅπαντας κατὰ φυλάς. θεῖναι δὲ εἰς τὴν φυλὴν ἑκάστην δύο ὑδρίας·

[1] Andocides i. 17.

ἐφ' ἑκάστῃ δὲ τῇ φυλῇ κήρυκα κηρύττειν, ὅτῳ δοκοῦσι ἀδικεῖν οἱ στρατηγοὶ οὐκ ἀνελόμενοι τοὺς νικήσαντας ἐν τῇ ναυμαχίᾳ, εἰς τὴν προτέραν ψηφίσασθαι, ὅτῳ δὲ μή, εἰς τὴν ὑστέραν.

The προβούλευμα went on to specify the extreme penalty in case of condemnation: ἂν δὲ δόξωσιν ἀδικεῖν, θανάτῳ ζημιῶσαι καὶ τοῖς ἔνδεκα παραδοῦναι καὶ τὰ χρήματα δημοσιεῦσαι, τὸ δ' ἐπιδέκατον τῆς θεοῦ εἶναι. Various men in the ecclesia— Εὐρυπτόλεμός τε ὁ Πεισιάνακτος καὶ ἄλλοι τινές—at once challenged this motion and proposed to indict Callixenus, who had moved the resolution, by a γραφὴ παρανόμων.[1] Xenophon does not specify the grounds for this γραφὴ παρανόμων, but some are fairly obvious. In the first place, the boulé had been instructed to bring in a resolution which provided for a trial of the generals. This they failed to do, merely introducing a resolution which provided that a vote should be taken on the basis solely of the evidence produced at the former assembly. The proceedings on that occasion had not constituted a real trial but had been rather in the nature of a preliminary investigation. There had not been sufficient time for the generals adequately to prepare their defense. Furthermore, according to the senate's resolution, the assembly was instructed to vote on all of the generals at once. According to Athenian law, every man was entitled to an individual trial. It is interesting to note that the charge that Callixenus had introduced an illegal motion was brought by various members of the ecclesia, the point apparently being that men from all over the assembly, immediately on the reading of the senate's resolution, sprang up and challenged it. This is doubtless the explanation of the fact that several people are said to have indicted Callixenus. The assembly, however, did not permit the blocking of the resolution, for a motion of Lysicles that those who had proposed the indictment should be included in the senate resolution forced the withdrawal of the indictment. But in many cases resolutions must have been suspended by such an indictment.

During the democratic exile which was occasioned by the rule of the Thirty Tyrants, the orator Lysias was very active

[1] *Hellenica* i. 7. 9 ff.

in the democratic cause. Immediately after the expulsion of the Thirty (403 B.C.) and the democratic return, it was proposed and carried in the assembly that citizenship should be conferred on Lysias. The Senate of Five Hundred had not yet been re-established. Therefore, there had been no προβούλευμα with regard to this proposition; and on this ground a γραφὴ παρανόμων was brought against Thrasybulus, who was responsible for the motion in the ecclesia.[1] Lack of a προβούλευμα would always have constituted a reason for the bringing of a γραφὴ παρανόμων. The whole story has been the object of suspicion. Jebb,[2] however, thinks that it cannot be doubted in view of the biographer's specific reference to a speech of Lysias in connection with the matter.

It has been held that the Areopagus retained its police oversight of building, and this may well be the case.[3] This must not be taken to mean, however, that cases of infringement of building regulations were tried before the Areopagus, at least after Ephialtes. The cases themselves would be brought before a court or before the people. For instance, in the Pseudo-Xenophontic *Constitution of Athens*, the author, in enumerating the variety of cases which came before the courts, writes: δεῖ δὲ καὶ τάδε διαδικάζειν εἴ τις τὴν ναῦν μὴ ἐπισκευάζει ἢ κατοικοδομεῖ τι δημόσιον.[4] As Kalinka, in his edition, observes on the passage, διαδικάζειν seems to be used here as a general word for bringing a case into court, and not in its older, technical sense. The writer is speaking of the congestion of business in the city and the difficulty of getting settlements. It is quite possible that the Areopagus originally, in addition to its general oversight of building, also itself tried cases of infringement of regulations, while, after the reforms of Ephialtes, they retained the general oversight, the cases themselves now being referred to a court. That this was the case, in the fourth century at least, seems certain from a passage in a speech of Aeschines, where the Areopagus is represented as appearing before the people in accordance with a resolution which one Timarchus had in-

[1] (Plut.) *X Oratorum Vitae* 835 F.
[2] *Attic Orators*, I, 149.
[3] Cf. Philippi, *op. cit.*, p. 268.
[4] iii. 4.

troduced regarding the houses on the Pnyx.[1] Just what the
resolution was it is impossible to say, but it apparently dealt
with building improvements on the Pnyx to be carried out
largely by the government. As in the matter of the supervision of morals, so in the matter of building regulations the
council lost its power to try cases but retained its general
supervision.

In the time of Solon the Areopagus was concerned to
some extent with the δοκιμασία and εὔθυνα of magistrates.[2]
It is generally believed that that body continued to exercise
these two functions until the reforms of Ephialtes.[3] Naturally Ephialtes would remove these very important powers from
the Areopagus. The δοκιμασία of the archons was turned
over to the boulé,[4] while the examination of other officials
and the εὔθυνα[5] were taken care of by the courts. Hence, to
this same period may be assigned the institution of the Board
of Thirty Logistae, which is known to have been active as
early as 454 B.C.[6] This board was reduced to ten members
in the fourth century, and they acted in conjunction with a
jury of 501 dicasts.[7]

In connection with δοκιμασία it may be suggested that the
Areopagus, which had oversight of conduct generally, may
very well have had charge of the δοκιμασία of boys in earlier
times. At the time when Aristotle wrote the Constitution of
Athens, the Senate of Five Hundred had charge of this
δοκιμασία after the preliminary enrolment of the boys by the
demesmen (δημόται).[8] Aristotle's statement appears to be at

---

[1] Aeschines Tim., 80 ff.   [2] Cf. supra, p. 164.

[3] Cf. Lipsius, op. cit., p. 37; Wilamowitz, op. cit., II, 188 ff.; Schulthess, op. cit.,
p. 22.

[4] Cf. Busolt-Swoboda, op. cit., p. 1045.   [5] Cf. ibid., p. 895.

[6] Cf. Gilbert, op. cit., p. 225, with the inscriptional evidence there cited; cf.
Busolt-Swoboda, op. cit., p. 1077 and § 128.

[7] Cf. Aristotle Ath. Pol. liv. 1, 2; and Gilbert, op. cit. There was also a committee
of the boulé called λογισταί, ten in number. This committee had to do with the
monthly reports of officials and is distinct from the Board of Logistae which audited
the annual reports. Cf. Busolt-Swoboda, op. cit., p. 1032.

[8] Ath. Pol. xlii. 1. Cf. the scholiast on Wasps, 578, who refers to this passage:
πρὸς τὸ ἔθος· Ἀριστοτέλης δέ φησιν ὅτι ψήφῳ οἱ ἐγγραφόμενοι δοκιμάζονται, μὴ νεώτεροι
ιή ἐτῶν εἶεν. ἴσως δ' ἂν περὶ τῶν κρινομένων παίδων εἰς τοὺς γυμνικοὺς ἀγῶνας λέγοι
[sc. ὁ Ἀριστοφάνης]. οὐχ ὡς ἐν δικαστηρίῳ κρινομένων ἀλλ' ὑπὸ τῶν πρεσβυτέρων.

variance with the picture which Aristophanes presents in the *Wasps* of the delight of the old jurors at their participation in the examination of boys:

παίδων τοίνυν δοκιμαζομένων αἰδοῖα πάρεστι θεᾶσθαι.[1]

Many attempts have been made to harmonize the two passages. Aristotle, in the passage cited, says that, in case the demesmen rejected a boy on the ground that he was not of free citizen birth, an appeal to a dicastery was permitted. It has been suggested that Aristophanes was referring to such appeals.[2] Sandys suggests also that, although Aristotle does not mention it, such appeals were allowed in cases where a boy was rejected because he was not of the proper age.[3] Lipsius[4] thinks that the δοκιμασία mentioned in Aristophanes was an examination of orphans as to puberty, preceding their registration in a deme.

There is no evidence that in early times the members of the Areopagus were themselves subject to an εὔθυνα. In later times, however, there is evidence that they were.[5] However, it is impossible to say how often it occurred, that is, whether they would have to pass an εὔθυνα after they were once admitted to the council, or were subject to εὔθυνα once a year thereafter or as a group had to undergo an εὔθυνα after the completion of some special commission.

In connection with these questions it has been suggested[6] that the final authority which the Areopagus had had under Solon was taken away and its decisions made subject to appeal. Dugit makes even its decisions in homicide cases hence-

---

[1] Line 578. Cf. Starkie's note on the line.

[2] Cf. Sandys on Aristotle, *ad loc.*

[3] Cf. Zielinski, *Philologus*, LX, 11.

[4] *Op. cit.*, p. 284. Lipsius bases his opinion on a passage of the Pseudo-Xenophontic *Constitution of Athens* iii. 4, which Kirchhoff had already connected with the Aristophanic passage, *Über die Schrift vom Staat der Athener*, p. 23. Cf. *Lex. Seguer.*, p. 235, 13, where a δοκιμασία of orphans is mentioned with a view to their proving their ability to manage their property themselves: δοκιμάζονται δὲ καὶ οἱ ἐφ᾽ ἡλικίας ὀρφανοὶ εἰ δύνανται τὰ πατρῷα παρὰ τῶν ἐπιτρόπων παραλαμβάνειν. Lipsius assumes a different arrangement of the δοκιμασία in the fifth and fourth centuries.

[5] Lipsius, *op. cit.*, p. 288.

[6] Dugit, *Étude sur l'Aréopage athénien*, p. 147.

forth subject to appeal, but this is extremely unlikely on religious and conservative grounds.

After Cimon's return from exile (457 B.C.), he attempted to undo Ephialtes' work of depriving the Areopagus of power, but without avail.[1] And in 451–450 B.C. Pericles, in pursuance of his policy of pleasing the people, further stripped the council of power.[2] Ephialtes had left very little to the Areopagus except its jurisdiction in homicide cases. It is natural, therefore, in seeking to discover the changes made by Pericles in the Areopagus, to connect them with the homicide functions of the body. Although Ephialtes had curtailed the Areopagus in practically all of its other activities, he evidently left the homicide courts intact. When, then, subsequently, Pericles τῶν 'Αρεοπαγιτῶν ἔνια παρείλετο,[3] about the only change which he could have made was to substitute dicasts for the commissions of the Areopagus which sat in the ephetic courts. An adequate motive for such a change is to be found in his inauguration of pay for dicasts as a bid for popular favor in his contest with the wealthy Cimon. It is only natural that he should increase the amount disbursed by the state by extending the jurisdiction of the dicasts.[4] Aristotle's failure to mention at this point the transfer of the three homicide courts to heliastic jurors is easily explained. The ephetae are Areopagites. Hence the transfer would be included in the diminution of the powers of the Areopagus. The general tendency of Athenian constitutional development from the time of Solon was to throw more and more power into the hands of the heliastic courts. The substitution of dicasts for ephetae is a natural and important step in this development.

The prevailing view, however, is that in the ephetic courts δικασταί were not substituted for the ἐφέται until shortly

---

[1] Plutarch *Cimon*, xv.   [2] Aristotle *Ath. Pol.* xxvii. 1.

[3] Aristotle, *ibid.*; cf. Plutarch *Pericles*, ix.

[4] Rauchenstein (*Philologus*, X, 603) says that Pericles limited the powers of the ephetae at this time to deciding whether a case was premeditated or unpremeditated homicide. Cf. Lipsius, *op. cit.*, p. 26, n. 83; cf. Wyse, in Whibley, *op. cit.*, p. 391: "Whether this ancient institution [the ephetae] survived at all under the developed democracy is doubtful."

after the revision of Draco's laws in 409–408 B.C. It is certain that the change had been made at the date of Isocrates' oration against Callimachus, which was delivered in 402 or 399. In this speech 500 dicasts are mentioned as sitting at the Palladium.[1] An oration of Demosthenes delivered about the middle of the fourth century represents 500 dicasts as trying a case in the Palladium.[2] The first speech of Lysias, which in all probability belongs to the period after the overthrow of the Thirty, was delivered before the Delphinium, where the court must have consisted of dicasts.[3] In the first place the members of the court are addressed as ὦ Ἀθηναῖοι,[4] which is by no means a probable form of address for a court composed of a small section of the Areopagus, but which suits admirably a popular jury. Furthermore, the orator speaks to the jurors as if they were a large, representative body of the Athenian people. For example, he tells them that their vote is the most powerful in the city: πάντων τῶν ἐν τῇ πόλει κυριωτάτῃ.[5] Although regular heliastic juries sat in the courts of the Palladium and Delphinium, there are indications that the name "ephetae" for the jurors in these courts survived. Demosthenes, in a speech delivered in 352 B.C., describes these jurors as ἐφέται.[6] Aristotle also, in a discussion of the Athenian homicide courts of his own time, represents ephetae as sitting in the Palladium, Delphinium, and

---

[1] xviii. 52. 54. Blass dates this speech in 399; Jebb in 402. For the number of jurors, cf. Lipsius, op. cit., p. 158, n. 76. Drerup reads πεντακοσίων in his edition instead of the traditional ἑπτακοσίων, which is now regarded as incorrect.

[2] lix. 10.

[3] For the date cf. Thalheim, Lysias, p. xxxvi. Sandys, Aristotle's Constitution of Athens, p. 230, says there is "nothing to show whether it was delivered before δικασταί (Schömann, Scheibe, Frohberger, Blass, Philippi) or before ἐφέται (Forchhammer and others) in the court of the Delphinium."

[4] Lysias i. 6, 7. Elsewhere the jurors are addressed as ὦ ἄνδρες. In extant forensic speeches the Areopagus is regularly addressed as ὦ βουλή. The regular form of address to the heliastic jurors is ὦ ἄνδρες δικασταί, varied by ὦ ἄνδρες and ὦ Ἀθηναῖοι. Nowhere do we find ὦ ἐφέται used in addressing a jury.

[5] i. 36. Cf. 30, 34.

[6] xxiii. 38. For the retention of the name, cf. Keil, Die Solonische Verfassung, p. 107. Religious conservatism accounts sufficiently for the retention. Cf. Suidas and Photius, s.v. ἐφέται : ἐκαλεῖτο δ' αὐτῶν τὰ δικαστήρια, Ἐφετῶν.

Phreatto.¹ The lexicographers, drawing their information from Demosthenes and Aristotle, continue to use the term ἐφέται.² There was no need to change the name simply because the men were differently recruited.

These passages show conclusively that the substitution had been made by the beginning of the fourth century. The majority of modern scholars base their conclusion that the change had occurred only shortly before this time on the argument that the word ἐφέται would not have been used in the redaction of Draco's homicide laws (409–408 B.C.) if heliastic jurors had sat in the ephetic courts at that time.³ This argument, however, is of no significance in view of the fact mentioned above that in the time of Demosthenes and Aristotle, for which there is indisputable evidence that heliastic jurors sat in the minor homicide courts, the name ἐφέται still survived in official documents.⁴ In the inscription, which has been largely restored from the laws interpolated in speeches of Demosthenes, the ephetae are mentioned in four passages. At the beginning there is the following provision in connection with the procedure in a trial for unpremeditated homicide: καὶ ἐὰμ [μ'] ἐκ [π]ρονο[ία]ς [κ]τ[ένει τίς τινα, φεύγεν, δ]ικάζεν

---

¹ *Ath. Pol.* lvii. 4:   οἱ λαχόντες ταῦτα ἐφέται. The word ἐφέται here is a restoration, but it seems to be the only possible one, for Harpocration derived his statement about the ephetae from Aristotle, and this is the only passage where the word can have occurred. Kenyon in his latest edition reads ἐφέται. The latest Teubner text makes no restoration at this point.

² Cf. Harpocration, Photius, Suidas, *s.v.*, Pollux viii. 125, scholiast on Aeschines ii. 87. Miller, article "Ephetai" in Pauly-Wissowa, explains the statement of Pollux, κατὰ μικρὸν δὲ κατεγελάσθη τὸ τῶν ἐφετῶν δικαστήριον, as referring to the gradual loss of prestige on the part of the ephetic courts before discasts were substituted for the ephetae. Sandys, on Aristotle *Ath. Pol.* lvii. 4, says that the ephetae perhaps retained their jurisdiction in a formal sense, acting as a sort of presiding committee while the actual voting was in the hands of the dicasts. It may be suggested that the Athenians made a jest of the legal fiction involved in calling dicasts "ephetae" and that the reference is to a time when even the official designation of "ephetae" was dropped and the jurors were known only as "dicasts."

³ Lipsius, *op. cit.*, p. 40; Keil, "Griechische Staatsaltertümer," in Gercke-Norden, *Einleitung in die Altertumswissenschaft*, III, 350; Lécrivain, article "Ephetai" in Daremberg-Saglio; Miller, *op. cit.*; Philippi, *op. cit.*, pp. 318 ff.

⁴ It is interesting to note that the same scholars who use this argument admit that the name ephetae continued to be used in the fourth century. Cf. Miller, *op. cit.*

δὲ τὸς βασιλέας αἰτ[ι]ô[ν] φό[νο] ἒ [ἐάν τις αἰτιᾶται hὸς βου]λεύσαντα,
τὸς δ[ὲ] ἐφέτας διαγν[ôναι.¹ Later in the code the expression
τοὺς ἐφέτας διαγνῶναι occurs again in a passage regarding
the procedure to be followed in dealing with a person who
has killed an exiled murderer while he is observing the
requirements of his interdict; and again in a provision
about justifiable homicide.² Elsewhere in the inscription,
however, in a provision regarding the granting of αἴδεσις to
an exiled murderer when there are no relatives of his victim
living, the following sentence occurs: ἐὰν δὲ τούτον μεδ' hês
ἒι, κτένει δὲ ἄκο[ν], γ[ν]ôσ[ι δ]ὲ h[οι πεν]τ[έκοντα καὶ hês hοι
ἐφέται ἄκοντα κτêναι, ἐσέσθ[ο]ν δέ[κα hοι φράτερες ἐὰν ἐθέλοσιν.
τούτος δ]ὲ [hο]ι πεντέκο[ν]τ[α καὶ] hês ἀρ[ι]σ[τίνδεν hαιρέσθον.³ It
is noteworthy that in this case alone in the code the number of the ephetae is specified. The distinct reference here
to fifty-one ephetae occurring between two sections where
they are called ephetae only must have some significance.⁴
The passage in which the number occurs deals, not with the
actual homicide trial, but with a subsequent action. A murderer, after serving a term of exile, might be granted αἴδεσις
by the relatives of his victim. But if there were no relatives,
he might still obtain αἴδεσις. If a body of fifty-one ephetae,
on reviewing the original trial, confirmed the judgment that
the act was unpremeditated, then ten phratry members
chosen by this body might grant the exile permission to re-
turn.⁵ In the homicide trial itself, however, the inscription

¹ Lines 11 ff. For interpretation of the various provisions of the code, cf. *supra*,
pp. 110 ff.

² Lines 26 ff.; 33 ff.   ³ Lines 16 ff.

⁴ It is noteworthy that this is the case also with the laws inserted in Demosthenes (xxiii. 37; xliii. 57; etc.) from which the restoration of the code was largely
made. Demosthenes xliii. 57, from which the present restoration was made, reads
ἢ οἱ ἐφέται, but the word ἢ is probably a misinterpreted rough breathing. Or it may
be regarded as an explanatory ἢ ("that is to say"). Cf. Hicks and Hill, *Greek
Historical Inscriptions*, No. 78, l. 14, and *supra*, p. 112.

⁵ It is to be observed that γνῶσι is here used of the ephetae, while in the three
other passages διαγιγνώσκειν is used of their decision in an actual trial. Evidently
the lawgiver, in the case of αἴδεσις, attempted to differentiate the function of the
fifty-one ephetae. The fifty-one here act like a modern board of pardons which

makes no mention of the number of ephetae who were to act. The explanation is then simple. The situation affords an excellent example of the tendency of Athenian institutions to persist generation after generation in more or less modified form. The original ephetic courts were composed of fifty-one men chosen as commissions of the Areopagus.[1] At some time, however, prior to the redaction of Draco's laws in 409–408 B.C., heliastic jurors were substituted for ephetae in these courts. In only one particular phase of homicide cases, the granting of αἴδεσις to murderers in exile, did a body of fifty-one ephetae continue to function.[2] It appears, then, that the Athenians of 409–408 made a real revision of the Draconian code and did not blindly continue to speak of fifty-one ephetae when large panels of dicasts actually sat in these courts.

This view of the composition of the ephetic courts at the time of the revision of Draco's laws is consistent with the other passages in which the term occurs. A passage which has usually been considered of equal weight with the Draconian code in proving a late introduction of heliastic jurors into the ephetic courts is the amnesty law which was passed after the battle of Aegospotami in 405.[3] But here again the phrase τῶν ἐφετῶν may be explained as a survival. It is a concise way of referring to the courts of the Palladium, the Del-

---

reviews a case and makes a recommendation to the chief executive of the state. The term γνῶσι may very well express this action. Cf. Kennedy's translation of Demosthenes, where γνῶσι is rendered "shall declare" and διαγιγνώσκειν "decide." Sandys' view, quoted *supra*, p. 272, n. 2, would also explain the number in this case.

[1] *Supra*, pp. 99 ff.

[2] The function of the ephetae is in this case primarily religious, i.e., the granting of αἴδεσις. There is no objection to assuming that in this particular instance the ephetae continued to be drawn from the Areopagus.

[3] Andocides I. 78: πλὴν ὁπόσα ἐν στήλαις γέγραπται τῶν μὴ ἐνθάδε μεινάντων, ἢ ἐξ Ἀρείου πάγου ἢ τῶν ἐφετῶν ἢ ἐκ πρυτανείου ἐδικάσθη ὑπὸ τῶν βασιλέων, ἢ ἐπὶ φόνῳ τίς ἐστι φυγὴ ἢ θάνατος κατεγνώσθη ἢ σφαγεῦσιν ἢ τυράννοις. For the text here given, cf. *supra*, p. 105. Lipsius, *op. cit.*, p. 40, uses this law to prove that the change came during the archonship of Eucleides. The MS reads ἢ Δελφινίου after πρυτανείου; and Keil (*Die Solonische Verfassung*, p. 111) has accepted this as proof that the Delphinium was already manned by heliastic jurors. But as has been shown, *supra*, p. 105, the phrase is merely a gloss.

phinium, and in Phreatto, now manned by heliastic jurors.

Confirmation of the view that the reorganization of the ephetic courts had been made prior to 409–408 is afforded by a speech of Antiphon. The *Choreutes* at least was delivered before the Palladium.[1] In this speech there are two forms of address to the jury: ὦ ἄνδρες δικασταί[2] and ὦ ἄνδρες.[3] It is quite improbable that such a form of address as ὦ ἄνδρες δικασταί would have been used of any except heliastic jurors.[4] There is some doubt whether the first oration was delivered before the Areopagus or the Palladium.[5] The forms of address ὦ ἄνδρες and ὦ δικάζοντες might, with propriety, have been used in any court. But the words τούτου γε ἕνεκα καὶ δικασταὶ ἐγένεσθε καὶ ἐκλήθητε[6] do not describe the Areopagites, who became judges, not by choice or selection, but automatically, because they were ex-archons with a good official record. The description is, however, well suited to describe a panel which officially retained the name ἐφέται, though its members were recruited from the ranks of the δικασταί. These speeches, delivered prior to 411 B.C., afford the earliest evidence for heliastic jurors in the ephetic courts. The manning of the heliastic courts by δικασταί belongs to some constitutional reform prior to this date. It is most natural to connect it with the reform of the Areopagus and especially with the final measures of Pericles.[7]

---

[1] Lipsius, *op. cit.*, p. 918, n. 66; Blass, *Attische Beredsamkeit*, I, 195. Blass (*ibid.*, I, 187–88) contends that the *Stepmother* case also was tried before the Palladium, but Lipsius (*op. cit.*, p. 126) assigns it to the Areopagus.

[2] vi. 1.   [3] vi. 7, 16, 20, etc.

[4] Cf. Blass, *op. cit.*, p. 195, who asserts that the Choreutes trial took place in the Palladium before heliastic jurors.

[5] For the arguments pro and con, cf. Lipsius, *op. cit.*, p. 124, n. 10; p. 126, n. 16; Blass, *op. cit.*, I, 187 f.; and Gernet, *Antiphon* (Budé edition), introduction to the first oration.

[6] Antiphon i. 23.

[7] Gernet (review of Gertrude Smith, "The Dicasts in the Ephetic Courts," *Class. Phil.*, XIX, 353 ff., in *Rev. des études grecques*, XXXIX, 464) regards as attractive, but not convincing, the theory that the substitution of heliastic jurors for ephetae belongs to the reforms of Pericles. He questions the evidence cited to show that the designation ἐφέται survived down into the fourth century long after the minor homicide courts were manned by δικασταί. He objects to the citation of

Despite the Areopagus' loss of power occasioned by the reforms of Ephialtes and Pericles, the body never lost its remarkable prestige, and never seems to have become a really unimportant council. This is proved by the numerous cases in which it suddenly exhibited its power again. On more than one occasion the people entrusted it with a special task or commission of inquiry. Examples of this are as follows:

In the alarm resulting from the disaster at Aegospotami the Areopagus was engaged in finding some means of safety for the state: πραττούσης μὲν τῆς ἐν Ἀρείῳ πάγῳ βουλῆς σωτήρια.[1] This is reminiscent of the prominence acquired by the council immediately after the Persian wars; but its influence and powers can hardly have been so extensive as at that time, when, if our authorities are to be believed,[2] they amounted virtually to a dictatorship. The powers of the council after Aegospotami are comparable to the extraordinary powers which it assumed after the Battle of Chaeronea.[3] But just what its powers included at this time it is difficult to say. It joined the opposition to Theramenes' request for unlimited power[4] and must have been chiefly concerned with attempting to keep the democracy on the old basis and fortified against a recurrence of the events of 411 B.C. This authority was probably vested in the Areopagus as a special commission. It is only natural that at a period of disturbance and disaster the state should look for assistance to the council which had always had prestige and had always proved itself both helpful and trustworthy. The Areopagus by this time must very largely have lost its highly aristocratic character, and was hardly to be feared on that account. It was recognized as a body which upheld the democracy and gave fair judgments.

Demosthenes' use of "ephetae" (xxiii, 38) because he is virtually quoting from a section of the Draconian code. But the very fact that the word was still in the code in the time of Demosthenes proves the contention that the word continued to be used after the courts were manned by dicasts. The differentiation between "ephetae," and "51 ephetae" in the code, as has been pointed out above, shows that the change had already been sufficiently recognized in the revision of 409-408.

[1] Lysias xii. 69. Cf. Frohberger, *ad loc.*

[2] Aristotle *Ath. Pol.* xxiii. 1. Cf. *supra*, p. 251.

[3] Cf. *infra*, p. 365.   [4] Lysias xii. 69. Cf. Philippi, *op. cit.* p. 184.

Such instances as this render it probable that there were many occasions on which the council was intrusted with some particular task, and that during a specified period it might have considerable power, although its regular duties had been so much curtailed by the reforms of Ephialtes and Pericles.[1]

When the Thirty had become established in power, one of their first measures was to remove from the Areopagus the laws of Ephialtes regarding the council. This amounted virtually to a repeal of these laws and would mean that the prerogatives were restored to the Areopagus of which it had been deprived by Ephialtes. This was in pursuance of the policy which the Thirty adopted at first of ruling according to the ancient constitution.[2] Their purpose evidently was to curry favor with the people by destroying some of the abuses of the very extreme democracy. The Thirty were anxious to weaken the popular courts. Hence it is natural that they should assign to the Areopagus in its character of φύλαξ τῆς πολιτείας some of the most fruitful sources of litigation, e.g., δοκιμασία, εὔθυνα, γραφὴ παρανόμων.[3] In addition the Areopagites may have recovered for this period the right to sit as ἐφέται in the minor homicide courts, although it is difficult to say whether the Areopagus functioned at all as a homicide court after the reign of terror began. But it probably was not suspended.[4]

The restored democracy, after the Thirty, gave the Areopagus oversight of the laws by the decree of Teisamenus: ἐπιμελείσθω ἡ βουλὴ ἡ ἐξ Ἀρείου πάγου τῶν νόμων, ὅπως ἂν αἱ ἀρχαὶ τοῖς κειμένοις νόμοις χρῶνται.[5] Caillemer contends that it is not likely that such power should be restored to an essentially aristocratic body. This fact, together with the absence of

---

[1] The amnesty law of this period (Andocides i. 78), which is practically a re-statement of the Solonian law, mentions the Areopagus' jurisdiction in homicide cases and in cases of attacks on the government. Cf. *supra*, pp. 104 ff.

[2] Aristotle, *op. cit.*, xxxv. 2 (cf. Sandys, *ad loc.*).

[3] Cf. *infra*, p. 331.

[4] For a detailed discussion of the position of the Areopagus under the Thirty, cf. *infra*, pp. 328 ff.

[5] Andocides i. 84.

any reference to such authority in fourth-century history, has led him to question the authenticity of the decree.[1] His objection does not, however, seem wholly tenable. The Areopagus assumed considerable importance again apparently at the end of the fifth century, and it is not strange that its ancient prerogative of νομοφυλακία should be in some measure restored to it. It is interesting to see how this body, whose reliability and justness were constantly recognized, was used both by the oligarchs and by the restored democracy.[2]

[1] *Op. cit.*, p. 402; cf. Thalheim in Pauly-Wissowa, II. 631.

[2] For the prestige and activities of the Areopagus in the fourth century, cf. *infra*, pp. 362 ff.

CHAPTER IX
JUDICIAL FUNCTIONS OF THE MAGISTRATES

The organization of the heliastic courts as primary tribunals reduced very materially the judicial functions of the magistrates. In common with purely administrative officials they retained the right to impose a small fine upon anyone who interfered with the performance of their administrative or judicial functions by disobedience or opposition. In the case of the *hieropoioi*, and the *proedroi* of the boulé, 50 drachmas are mentioned as the limit (τὸ τέλος) of this summary fine (ἐπιβολή).[1] It could scarcely have been less for the others. In the case of the demarchs these fines had to be confirmed by the judgment of a court.[2] This circumstance and the statement of a client of Lysias have led some to conclude that this was true of all officials. But it is distinctly said that in the case of the archon court action was necessary only if the fine exceeded the legal limit.[3] There is some doubt as to whether the person who was fined within the legal limit had the right of appeal. The leading case on the question is the speech for the soldier Polyaenus[4] attributed to Lysias. He had been fined by the generals summarily for slander. For some reason he failed to pay the fine, and the present suit resulted. The defendant seems to rest his case primarily upon the allegation that the treasurers remitted the fine. The responsibility, if any, was theirs.[5] But he reverts to the origi-

[1] Lipsius, *Das Attische Recht*, p. 54, n. 3; Thalheim in Pauly-Wissowa, *s.v.* ἐπιβολή.

[2] *CIA*, ii. 573*b*: ἐψηφίσθαι Πειραιεῦσιν ἐάν τίς τι τούτων παρὰ ταῦτα ποιῇ, ἐπιβολὴν ἐπιβαλόντα τὸν δήμαρχον εἰσάγειν εἰς τὸ δικαστήριον χρώμενον τοῖς νόμοις οἳ κεῖνται περὶ τούτων.

[3] Demosthenes xliii. 75: ἐὰν δέ τις ὑβρίζῃ ἢ ποιῇ τι παράνομον κύριος ἔστω (ὁ ἄρχων) ἐπιβάλλειν κατὰ τὸ τέλος. ἐὰν δὲ μείζονος ζημίας δοκῇ ἄξιος εἶναι προσκαλεσάμενος πρόπεμπτα καὶ τίμημα ἐπιγραψάμενος ὅτι ἂν δοκῇ αὐτῷ εἰσαγαγέτω εἰς τὴν ἡλιαίαν.

[4] ix.

[5] *Ibid.*, 7. That the treasurers had no authority to remit the fine is clear. They did it at their own risk: τὸν παρ' ὑμῶν κίνδυνον ὑποστάντες ἄκυρον τὴν ζημίαν ἔκριναν.

nal cause of the fine. The law of Solon forbade slander of an official in a public office. Polyaenus' remarks, however, were made not in a public office but in a bank, and were reported to the generals who fined him but made no attempt to collect the fine; neither did they take steps to make it legal by vote of a court.[1]

Polyaenus did not appeal the case. This is certain.[2] But he clearly implies that the generals were under some obligation to bring the matter into court.[3] There is no claim that the fine was beyond the competence of the generals and needed to be confirmed by a heliastic court. It has been suggested that, when a person fined by a magistrate refused to pay, the magistrate must take the case into court.[4] In effect this would constitute an appeal, though the initiative lay with the magistrate. This suggestion has met with general approval, and an attempt has been made to find further support for it in a passage of Aristophanes which is as follows:

> Bd: Well, but if these are really your delights,
> Yet why go *There* [i.e. to court]? Why not remain at home
> And sit and judge among your household here?
> Ph: Folly! Judge what?
> Bd: The same as There you do.
> Suppose you catch your housemaid on the sly
> Opening the door: fine her for that, one drachma.
> That's what you did at every sitting There.[5]

---

[1] *Ibid.*, 6: ἐπιβαλόντες δὲ τὸ ἀργύριον πράξασθαι μὲν οὐκ ἐπεχείρησαν. *Ibid.*, 11: οὔτε γὰρ εὐθύνας ὑπέσχον οὔτε εἰς δικαστήριον εἰσελθόντες τὰ πραχθέντα κύρια κατέστησαν.

[2] Siegfried, *De multa quae ἐπιβολή dicitur*, p. 50; Pabst, *De oratione Lysiaca "Pro milite,"* p. 14.

[3] Compare passages quoted in note 1 above.

[4] Lipsius, *op. cit.*, pp. 53–54. Siegfried (*op. cit.*, p. 51) believes there was no appeal. Thalheim (*op. cit.*), contrary to general opinion, is inclined to agree with him, but for different reasons. The words ἐξ ἐπιβολῆς εἰσαχθεὶς εἰς τὸ δικαστήριον in Lysias vi. 21 may refer to an attempt of the magistrate to collect a fine within his official competence. Siegfried (*op. cit.*, p. 53) thinks the reference is to a fine beyond the magistrate's competence. The point is arguable.

[5] *Wasps*, 764 ff. Roger's translation.

ΒΔ.   σὺ δ' οὖν, ἐπειδὴ τοῦτο κεχάρηκας ποιῶν
ἐκεῖσε μὲν μηκέτι βάδιζ', ἀλλ' ἐνθάδε
αὐτοῦ μένων δίκαζε τοῖσιν οἰκέταις,
[Footnote continued on following page]

Here the heliastic jury in the person of Philocleon is to vote on the question of a fine on the housemaid. The word ἐπιβολή is regarded as being used in its technical sense of the summary fine of a magistrate. Someone in authority over the servants, or, better still, Bdelycleon, who represents in his own person the thesmothetae who preside at the trial, has exercised his magisterial authority and inflicted a trivial fine upon her. She in turn appeals and the court is to confirm it. On the basis of a single word, ἐπιβολή, the audience is supposed to imagine all this and then to laugh. At what? Siegfried[1] believes that the joke lies in the fact that so small an ἐπιβολή could not be appealed. This explanation does not fit in with the statements to the effect that in inflicting this ἐπιβολή he will be doing just what he did from time to time in court.

πάντως δὲ κἀκεῖ ταῦτ' ἕδρας ἑκάστοτε.[2]

Surely appeals from magistrates' fines were not typical court cases. Furthermore, the matter thus conceived is much too complicated for even an Athenian audience to catch in passing. A simpler interpretation is offered by the scholiast. ἐπιβολή is used like ζημία in the sense of "fine" imposed by a court.[3] Starkie accounts for the choice of the word by pointing out that it may be used in *sensu obscoeno*.[4] This is quite in the Aristophanic manner. Apparently whenever a woman appears or is mentioned, a *double entente* was expected.

But even if there was no provision for appeal from a magistrate's fine, the person who felt that he was wrongfully fined by a magistrate still had a remedy in the εὔθυνα, where he could call attention to the arbitrary conduct of the magistrate and eventually bring the matter before a heliastic court. A favorable verdict would result in a remission of the fine.

ΦΙ.　　περὶ τοῦ; τί ληρεῖς; ΒΔ. ταῦθ', ἅπερ ἐκεῖ πράττεται
　　　　ὅτι τὴν θύραν ἀνέῳξεν ἡ σηκὶς λάθρᾳ,
　　　　ταύτης ἐπιβολὴν ψηφιεῖ μίαν μόνην,
　　　　πάντως δὲ κἀκεῖ ταῦτ' ἕδρας ἑκάστοτε.

[1] *Op. cit.*, p. 54.　　　　[2] *Wasps*, 770.

[3] Scholiast on *Wasps*, 769.

[4] *Wasps of Aristophanes*, note on line 769. Van Leeuwen takes the same point of view and cites *Acharnians*, 275, and *Birds*, 1215.

It was apparently to escape this possibility of attack that the generals in Lysias' ninth oration failed to enter the fine imposed on the soldier in the accounts which they submitted to the auditors. Refusal to pay the fine would in the end have the same effect as an appeal.

A remnant of the ancient right of magistrates to pass final judgment on all cases within their jurisdiction is the right possessed by some magistrates and boards to settle, on their own authority, cases involving 10 drachmas or less. In the opinion of some scholars, all magistrates and judicial officials and boards enjoyed this prerogative.[1] Aristotle[2] mentions it only in the case of the Forty and the Receivers-general (ἀποδέκται). Aristotle's account of the judicial functions of the magistrates is not exhaustive; others may have possessed similar powers. But it is to be observed that the Forty and the Receivers-general dealt mainly with cases in which specific sums of money were in dispute. Therefore, it would be possible at once to classify a case as above or below 10 drachmas. In the cases that came before other magistrates, involving damages, fines, and other penalties, it would be difficult, if not impossible, to classify them, before trial, as above or below 10 drachmas, even where the pains and penalties were estimated in money. This may be the reason why only the Forty and the Receivers-General had the privilege of final jurisdiction. But, apart from the inherent improbability that all magistrates possessed the right of giving final judgment in trivial cases, a passage in the *Wasps*,[3] already quoted and discussed, seems to afford proof that trivial cases did come before a court. Bdelycleon proposes that his father hold domestic court and punish the servants for crimes and misdemeanors. He suggests that a housemaid be fined a drachma for a trivial offense. We need not stop to inquire what magistrate would deal with this type of case. It may be imagined as coming under the jurisdiction of the thesmothetae. But be that as it may, it would not fall under the jurisdiction of the Forty or the Receivers-

[1] Lipsius, *op. cit.*, p. 53. [2] *Ath. Pol.* liii. 1; lii. 3.

[3] Cf. *supra*, p. 280.

general. The words πάντως δὲ κἀκεῖ ταῦτ' ἕδρας ἑκάστοτε show that fines less than 10 drachmas were inflicted by the courts. This could not very well have been the case if all magistrates and boards could assess damages and impose fines of 10 drachmas or less on their own authority. On the basis of available data it is not safe to conclude that any magistrates except the Forty and the Receivers-general enjoyed this limited right of independent jurisdiction as distinct from their right to impose a summary fine (ἐπιβολή) for disobedience or contumacy.

The *anakrisis* is a survival of the pre-Solonian trial before a single judge who was empowered to render a final verdict. Naturally all the evidence was presented. The appeal allowed by Solon did not alter the situation in regard to the evidence. All available proof had to be produced, for the magistrate was still required to render a verdict on the merits of the case. But when the task of magistrates, judicial officers, and boards was simply to bring the case into court and to preside at the trial, the situation with regard to evidence was materially altered.

Current misconceptions regarding the basis on which evidence continued to be produced at the *anakrisis* are due in part to the belief that evidence had, from the first, been presented in written form, and in part to the failure to distinguish between the process of arbitration and the *anakrisis*. It is now well understood that for a century testimonial evidence in the heliastic courts was presented orally.[1] And investigation since the discovery of Aristotle's *Constitution of*

[1] Bonner, *Evidence in Athenian Courts* (1905), pp. 54 ff. Cf. Leisi, *Der Zeuge im attischen Recht* (1908), p. 85, n. 2. Lipsius' (*op. cit.*, p. 883, n. 65) claim, with reference to this discovery, that "Das wurde bereits *Att. Proc.* 2 S. 495. A. 55 festgestellt, aber die volle Konsequence haben daraus mit Heranziehung des positiven Faktors erst Bonner und Leisi gezogen," is quite unwarranted. All that Lipsius did was to establish the fact that witnesses were always present in court. But there is nothing to show that he ever thought of oral evidence. The words "die älteren Gerichtsreder die Verlesung der Zeugnisse ausschliesslich durch solche Formeln einleiten" show that he believed that evidence was always read. There is no justification for associating Bonner and Leisi. Bonner's book appeared in 1905. Leisi was familiar with it and cites it in his book published in 1908. Evidence continued to be presented orally in the homicide courts (Bonner, *Class. Phil.*, VII (1912), 451 ff.). Cf. Lipsius, *op. cit.*, p. 838.

Athens has shown that his description of arbitration cannot be transferred to the *anakrisis*.[1] Nevertheless, the effects of these earlier misconceptions have not altogether disappeared. Lipsius, in *Das attische Recht*,[2] in the beginning of the chapter on the *anakrisis*, says: "Diese Vorprüfung, bei der die Parteien alle zur Unterstützung ihrer Sache dienlichen Erklärungen abzugeben und ihre Beweise vorzulegen hatten, heist ἀνά-κρισις." From this sentence the reader naturally infers that litigants were under obligation to produce *all* their evidence at the preliminary inquiry. And yet a little farther on in the chapter he admits: "Andererseits lässt sich nicht erweisen, dass in der Anakrisis schon das Beweismaterial in vollem Umfang beigebracht werden musste."

Comparatively little information regarding evidence in the *anakrisis* is to be found in the sources. The subject is rarely mentioned in connection with the *anakrisis*. There is nowhere any indication in the sources that the evidence in a case must be produced at the *anakrisis*. On the contrary, there are plenty of data in the orators to show that it was neither impossible nor exceptional to produce evidence for the first time on the day of trial. A common example of what may be called "new" evidence (i.e., evidence not produced at the *anakrisis*) is a deposition produced in court, for a witness to acknowledge or reject under oath, by a litigant who did not know whether this witness could or would give testimony. If the witness appears and accepts, the deposition is read to the jurors.[3] If he refuses to testify, he takes an oath in disclaimer. Even if, as Kennedy assumes,[4] the deposition was filed at the *anakrisis*, it was in no sense evidence until it was acknowledged by the proposed witness.

The records of litigation during the period in which oral evidence was presented are scanty. But Plutarch[5] has preserved an instructive incident in a trial in which Aristeides appeared as an impromptu witness. His cousin Callias was

[1] Bonner, *Evidence in Athenian Courts*, p. 48. Cf. Lipsius, *op. cit.*, p. 838.

[2] Pages 829 (cf. p. 54) and 838.

[3] Bonner, *Evidence in Athenian Courts*, p. 51.

[4] Smith, *Dictionary of Antiquities*, s.v. "Martyria."   [5] *Aristeides*, xxv.

being tried on a capital charge. The prosecutors, going beyond the scope of the indictment, sought to prejudice the jurors by accusing Callias, a rich man, of refusing to relieve the manifest necessities of his kinsman, the distinguished Aristeides. Callias, observing the adverse effect of this charge upon the temper of the jurors, summoned Aristeides and asked him to testify. Aristeides complied and gave evidence that he had constantly refused to accept financial assistance from Callias. A dramatic example of the production of evidence for the first time at the trial is found in Isocrates' speech against Callimachus.[1] A brother-in-law of Callimachus had a quarrel with one Cratinus, during which they came to blows. In the course of the fight a female slave was injured. The woman was concealed, and a story, to the effect that she had died as the result of a blow inflicted by Cratinus, was circulated. An indictment for manslaughter was laid. The king archon conducted the three required preliminary examinations which in homicide cases were called προδικασίαι. Eventually the case came to trial. Cratinus, however, having become aware of the plot, had succeeded in locating the woman; but, desiring to catch the plotters ἐπ' αὐτοφόρῳ, he kept his discovery secret until the day of the trial, when he produced her alive and well to the utter confusion of the prosecutor, who had produced fourteen witnesses to prove that she was dead. These cases show clearly that a litigant was under no obligation to produce his evidence at the preliminary hearings. Had the defendant in the Callimachus case produced his evidence at the preliminary hearing, there would have been no trial.

In addition to these specific instances of evidence that was not produced at the *anakrisis*, there are a number of instances where a litigant challenges his opponent to produce evidence to refute him or to prove a particular assertion. Socrates was not content to draw attention to the failure of the prosecutors to produce relatives of any of the young men he was alleged to have corrupted. He challenged them to produce, then and there, some of them in the time al-

[1] xviii. 52–54.

lotted to him for his own defense.[1] There are many such challenges in the orators to produce various kinds of evidence. It does not help matters to dismiss these as mere rhetoric. It is true that no one expected a litigant to respond to such a challenge. But Socrates was not proposing to his prosecutors something they were not permitted by law to do, viz., to produce in court evidence that had not been produced at the *anakrisis*. The permission which Socrates granted to his opponents to produce witnesses at that stage of the trial was necessary because his allowance of time would thereby have been curtailed.

The frequently recurring phrases, such as "I hear," or "I am told that my opponent will say thus and so," are not always mere rhetorical devices of speech-writers to meet their opponents' arguments in advance. Unquestionably the proceedings of the *anakrisis* often left a litigant in doubt as to his opponent's line of defense or attack. This could not very well have happened if the opponent had so far developed his plan of treatment as to produce all his evidence at the *anakrisis*. More tangible proof that evidence not known to a litigant could be produced at the trial by his opponent are such statements as the following: "And so if he takes refuge in this argument and produces witnesses to prove that Aristarchus made a will, etc.";[2] "If they declare that Dicaeogenes left this property and that we have recovered it, let them produce a witness to support their statement."[3] These and other similar examples show clearly that there was no restriction on producing evidence for the first time at the trial. Even rhetoric would not venture to suggest the possibility of something's being done which the law did not permit. A speaker who pursued such tactics before men who knew the law as did the Athenian jurors would assuredly sooner or later come to grief.

[1] Plato, *Apology of Socrates*, 33d.

[2] Isaeus x. 23. Cf. Bonner, *Evidence in Athenian Courts*, p. 52.

[3] Isaeus v. 4. Cf. ix. 9. Cf. Isocrates xvii. 38. Lipsius (*op. cit.*, p. 839, n. 35) denies, without explanation or argument, that "eine Unkenntnis der Beweismittel des Gegners folgt aus der hypothetischen Fassung von Isaeus" (x. 23).

It is clear that a litigant did not always have his own case well in hand after going through the *anakrisis*. A case in point is found in the Demosthenic corpus. The plaintiff in *Callistratus* v. *Olympiodorus*,[1] in giving an account of some earlier litigation in which he and the defendant had pooled their claims to an estate, says that after the *anakrisis* he and Olympiodorus found themselves utterly unprepared to go to court at once on account of the large number of claimants that suddenly appeared against them.

καὶ ἐπειδὴ ἀνεκρίθησαν πρὸς τῷ ἄρχοντι ἄπασαι αἱ ἀμφισβητήσεις καὶ ἔδει ἀγωνίζεσθαι ἐν τῷ δικαστηρίῳ ἀπαράσκευοι ἦμεν τὸ παράπαν πρὸς τὸ ἤδη ἀγωνίζεσθαι . . . . διὰ τὸ ἐξαίφνης ἐπιπεπτωκέναι ἡμῖν πολλοὺς τοὺς ἀμφισβητοῦντας.

So difficult was their position that they cast about for some excuse for securing a continuance of the case. They failed and lost their case by default. If all the witnesses in the case had been secured and their evidence reduced to writing, it would seem that the preparation of a speech would have been a comparatively simple matter, if that was all they had to do. It is probable, however, that the difficulty was due to unexpected claimants that appeared. They needed time to revise their plans to deal with the unexpected conditions that faced them. To meet these, they would require additional witnesses, whose depositions would appear for the first time at the trial. The situation disclosed by the various possibilities of new evidence at this trial seems to be quite incompatible with a rule requiring *all* evidence to be produced at the *anakrisis*.

Before a public arbitrator the case was different. All evidence had to be produced because, if he failed to induce the parties to agree to a compromise, the arbitrator rendered a verdict on the merits of the case. If there was an appeal, the evidence was inclosed and sealed in a receptacle known as an ἐχῖνος. This was a reasonable requirement, as appeals are regularly based upon the original evidence in the case. But there is no justification for handling evidence in non-

[1] xlviii. 23. Cf. Bonner, *Evidence in Athenian Courts*, p. 50, and Leisi, *op. cit.*, p. 83.

arbitration cases in the same way. And yet the source of current misconceptions regarding the nature and purpose of the *anakrisis* has been the failure to distinguish clearly, as Aristotle does, between *anakrisis* and arbitration. Thalheim, for example, in his article on *anakrisis*[1] simply substituted ἀνάκρισις for δίαιτα and copied Aristotle's description of arbitration. The confusion appears in the lexicographers. Harpocration defined ἐχῖνος as follows: ἔστι μὲν ἄγγος τι εἰς ὃ τὰ γραμματεῖα τὰ πρὸς τὰς δίκας ἐτίθεντο· Δημοσθένης ἐν τῷ πρὸς Τιμόθεον. μνημονεύει τοῦ ἄγγους τούτου καὶ 'Αριστοτέλης ἐν τῇ 'Αθηναίων πολιτείᾳ.[2] Suidas practically repeats this definition. The reference to Aristotle as their authority shows that they have transferred the procedure of arbitration to the *anakrisis*. The error has within recent years been exposed. It has been satisfactorily shown that in the orators there is no mention of ἐχῖνος except in connection with arbitration.[3]

There is a fundamental difference between evidence in an Athenian court and evidence in Anglo-American courts. An Athenian litigant himself presented to the court all the facts that supported his claim. Witnesses were called at intervals merely to corroborate his statements. This is shown by such expressions as: καὶ ὡς ἀληθῆ λέγω, ἀναγίγνωσκε τὴν μαρτυρίαν, τούτων δ' ὑμῖν μάρτυρας παρέξομαι. In a modern court the jury gets all the facts from the witnesses. A careful perusal of the evidence offered would acquaint the reader with the facts in the case. But so far as we can judge, the reading of the testimony presented to an Athenian court would, as a rule, furnish a very meager notion of the details of the matter in dispute. Many unattested facts are to be found in the speeches of both principals and advocates. It is important to keep this situation in mind in attempting to reconstruct the proceedings of the *anakrisis* so far as the presentation of evidence is concerned, particularly during the period when all testimonial evidence was oral. The in-

---

[1] Pauly-Wissowa, *s.v.* ἀνάκρισις.

[2] It is implied that all documentary material, whether in arbitration or at the *anakrisis*, was inclosed in an ἐχῖνος.

[3] Bonner, *Evidence in Athenian Courts*, p. 48. Cf. Lipsius, *op. cit.*, p. 838, n. 34.

terrogations and stories of witnesses would be mere *disjecta membra* apart from a more or less formal presentation of his claims by the litigant. A litigant who purchased his speech would fare rather badly if he was required to present his whole case at this stage of the trial. And why should a magistrate be required to listen to all the evidence? He does not appear to have had any authority to exclude testimony that contravened the laws. His opinion on the merits of the dispute played no part in the trial. And the evidence must all be repeated for the benefit of the jury. An *anakrisis* conducted in this fashion would be a mere dress rehearsal of the trial.

The Athenian magistrate did have a limited, but very necessary, judicial function to perform. He had to decide whether the case was admissible (εἰσαγώγιμός).[1] This inquiry involved such questions as the following: Was the plaintiff eligible to appear in court? Was the defendant qualified to answer the charge or the claim? If the defendant failed to appear, had he been duly summoned? Were the documents —plaint or indictment—properly drawn? Was the matter at issue actionable? Was the proper form of action chosen? Did the magistrate have jurisdiction in the case? Was the action brought at the proper time according to law? Was the matter *res judicata?* In regard to some of the questions, the answers of the parties in the presence of each other would be sufficient. The magistrate must have had the right to refuse to believe an unconfirmed statement. This attitude would be tantamount to requiring parole or documentary evidence. But such evidence would be required for the purposes of the *anakrisis* and might not be produced at the trial at all. Such evidence would be for the magistrate to enable him to decide whether the case was admissible. The jury would normally have no concern with this phase of the case. It was settled in the *anakrisis.*

The word ἀνάκρισις shows that the basis of the magistrate's judgment consisted in the answers of the litigants to his questions. In homicide cases the preliminary inquiry

---

[1] Caillemer, *Anakrisis*, Daremberg and Saglio, I, 262. Cf. Leisi, *op. cit.*, p. 84.

was called προδικασία. Here the emphasis is laid on the purpose of the inquiry rather than on the method of conducting it. Whether the litigant called witnesses to corroborate his answers to the magistrate would depend on a number of considerations. But the essential point is that the decision lay entirely with the litigant himself. This is reasonable. He was not required to corroborate his statements at the trial; why should he be required to do so at the *anakrisis?*

The records of Athenian litigation have preserved only one picture of proceedings at an *anakrisis*. It is far from being as complete as we might desire, but it does yield some information of value.

> When the hearings [ἀνακρίσεις] took place before the archon, and my opponents paid money into court in support of their claim that these young men were the legitimate sons of Euctemon, on being asked by us who, and whose daughter, their mother was, they could not supply the information, although we protested and the archon ordered them to reply in accordance with the law.[1]

At that time they claimed that she was a Lemnian, and secured a continuance. The reason for the adjournment is not given. Obviously they asked delay to obtain necessary information from Lemnus. But when the hearing was resumed, they changed their story and said the mother was Calliope, daughter of Pistoxenus, thus answering the question, "Who, and whose daughter their mother was." The speaker pressed for proof of this statement either in the form of evidence of relatives or answers of slaves put to the question. But no evidence was produced. Commenting on this refusal to furnish proof of statements at the *anakrisis*, the speaker gravely remarks in the best Isaean manner: τὰ γὰρ τοιαῦτα οὐκ εἰς τὴν ἀνάκρισιν μόνον δεῖ πορίζεσθαι [ὀνόματα], ἀλλὰ τῇ ἀληθείᾳ γεγονότα φαίνεσθαι καὶ ὑπὸ τῶν προσηκόντων καταμαρτυρεῖσθαι.[2] These words do not mean that there was a law requiring statements made at the *anakrisis* to be confirmed by evidence. They simply mean that such statements cannot be believed without some sort of proof. This account of an *anakrisis* shows quite clearly that it was optional with

---

[1] Isaeus vi. 12, translated by Forster ("Loeb Library").   [2] *Ibid.*, 15.

litigants whether they produced evidence at the preliminary hearings of a case. To the same effect is a passage near the end of the speech:

> Let Androcles, therefore, prove that the children are legitimate, as anyone of you would do under similar circumstances. His mere mention of a mother's name does not suffice to make them legitimate, but he must prove that he is speaking the truth by producing the relatives who know that she was married to Euctemon.[1]

In the strategy of litigation it is of the utmost importance to discover in advance an opponent's proposed line of attack or defense. No better source of information on this point could be devised than an *anakrisis* at which the litigant was obliged to disclose his whole case by producing all his evidence. An intelligent litigant familiar with the case from his own standpoint would obtain most valuable hints and information from perusing or hearing the evidence offered by his opponent. It is to be expected that, in the more or less informal proceedings of the *anakrisis* where opponents were permitted to question each other, like Isaeus' client, they should in their own interest try to induce an opponent to make disclosures useful to them, by producing his evidence. And yet there is no indication that a litigant ever discovered anything at the *anakrisis* regarding his opponent's proposed plan of conducting his case. Occasionally the proceedings in arbitration, where all the evidence was produced, are mentioned as a source of information on this point, but the *anakrisis* is never mentioned in this connection. This cannot be a matter of accident. It indeed goes a long way toward showing that the evidence in a case was not produced at the *anakrisis*.

A change in the method of handling evidence followed the enactment of the law requiring written depositions instead of oral statements.[2] Testimonial evidence, like other documents in the case, was read by the clerk of the court when called for by the speaker. For this purpose evidence must have been filed as a rule before the beginning of the trial. There were some exceptions. Witnesses occasionally

---

[1] *Ibid.*, 64.   [2] For the date of the law (378–377 B.C.), cf. *infra*, p. 357.

were unwilling to testify for various reasons. At the trial
such witnesses were summond to appear and subscribe to a
deposition prepared for them or to take an oath in disclaimer.
Such documents, alternative depositions or disclaimers, could
not in any real sense be regarded as part of the record of the
case. They could be handed to the clerk at any time. Sometimes new facts that bore on the case were brought to light.
These of course could be brought to the attention of the jury
and confirmed by evidence. An example is found in *Apollodorus* v. *Arethusius*,[1] a criminal prosecution for false witness
to a writ of summons (ψευδοκλητεία). After the conclusion
of the *anakrisis* Apollodorus was viciously assaulted by the
defendant one night as he was returning to the city from the
Piraeus. Within a few days the case came to trial. Owing
to this assault and other aggravating circumstances, the jury
showed a disposition to inflict the death penalty. Undoubtedly Apollodorus produced as witnesses those who, in answer
to his cries, came to the rescue. Otherwise the jury would
scarcely have proposed to inflict so severe a penalty.

Thalheim,[2] having this situation in mind, proposed to
include in the proceedings of the *anakrisis* not only the more
or less formal meetings of the magistrate with the litigants
but also the appearances of the litigants at the office of the
magistrate at any time before the trial, for the purpose of
filing documents, including depositions. There are objections to this proposal. In the case of *Apollodorus* v. *Arethusius*[3] it is distinctly said that the *anakrisis* was concluded
when the assault complained of took place. Evidently the
plaintiff did not regard the submission of further evidence
in the case as a reopening of the preliminary hearing.

The *anakrisis* was, as the name implies, an informal interrogation of the parties by the magistrate to enable him
to determine whether he should accept the case. It was in

---

[1] Demosthenes liii. 17–18.

[2] *Berliner Philologische Wochenschrift*, 1905, p. 1575.

[3] Demosthenes liii. 17. ἀνακεκριμένου γὰρ ἤδη μου κατ᾽ αὐτοῦ τὴν τῆς ψευδοκλητείας
γραφὴν καὶ μέλλοντος εἰσιέναι εἰς τὸ δικαστήριον κ.τ.λ. A vivid account of the assault
follows.

no sense an examination for discovery in the interest of the parties. But the proceedings were open to both parties. Neither of them need be ignorant of the contents of any document or the purport of any deposition produced for the purposes of the *anakrisis*. And yet, on several occasions the words of a litigant seem to imply quite plainly the possibility of a deposition's being filed without his knowledge. Now, it is submitted that the filing of a deposition under circumstances which rendered it impossible for a litigant, with the exercise of due diligence, to be aware of the fact before the document was read in court, cannot properly be regarded as part of the proceedings of the *anakrisis*. In effect such evidence was produced for the first time in court no matter when or where it was filed. The filing of evidence, as distinguished from the introduction of evidence to corroborate a litigant's answers to the questions of the magistrate, cannot properly be regarded as part of the proceedings of the *anakrisis*.

CHAPTER X

EISANGELIA

The term εἰσαγγελία signifies in general an "information" of any kind. As a matter of practice, however, in Attic law the term was applied almost exclusively to actions brought before a political body—i.e., the Areopagus (in early times), the Senate of Five Hundred, and the assembly. For the sake of convenience the term may be rendered "impeachment," because, like a modern impeachment, it was a trial before a political body.[1] The lexicographers furnish definitions of εἰσαγγελία and some information as to the types of cases in which the process was used. Harpocration describes εἰσαγγελία as a δημοσία δίκη and enumerates three varieties:

ἡ μὲν γὰρ ἐπὶ δημοσίοις ἀδικήμασι μεγίστοις καὶ ἀναβολὴν μὴ ἐπιδεχομένοις, καὶ ἐφ' οἷς μήτε ἀρχὴ καθέστηκε μήτε νόμοι κεῖνται τοῖς ἄρχουσι καθ' οὓς εἰσάξουσιν, ἀλλὰ πρὸς τὴν βουλὴν ἢ τὸν δῆμον ἡ πρώτη κατάστασις γίγνεται, καὶ ἐφ' οἷς τῷ μὲν φεύγοντι, ἐὰν ἁλῷ, μέγισται ζημίαι ἐπίκεινται, ὁ δὲ διώκων, ἐὰν μὴ ἕλῃ, οὐδὲν ζημιοῦται, πλὴν ἐὰν τὸ ἑ μέρος τῶν ψήφων μὴ μεταλάβῃ· τότε γὰρ χιλίας ἐκτίνει. τὸ δὲ παλαιὸν καὶ οὗτοι μειζόνως ἐκολάζοντο. ἑτέρα δὲ εἰσαγγελία λέγεται ἐπὶ ταῖς κακώσεσιν· αὗται δ' εἰσὶ πρὸς τὸν ἄρχοντα, καὶ τῷ διώκοντι ἀζήμιοι, κἂν μὴ μεταλάβῃ τὸ ἑ μέρος τῶν ψήφων. ἄλλη δὲ εἰσαγγελία ἐστὶ κατὰ τῶν διαιτητῶν· εἰ γάρ τις ὑπὸ διαιτητοῦ ἀδικηθείη, ἐξῆν τοῦτον εἰσαγγέλλειν πρὸς τοὺς δικαστάς, καὶ ἁλοὺς ἠτιμοῦτο.

The second and third classes are of no importance in the following discussion, since neither type of case came before a political body.[2]

Pollux offers the following definition of εἰσαγγελία:

ἡ δ' εἰσαγγελία τέτακται ἐπὶ τῶν ἀγράφων δημοσίων ἀδικημάτων κατὰ τὸν νόμον εἰσαγγελικὸν ἢ εἰσαγγελτικόν· ἀμφοτέρως γὰρ λέγουσιν· ὃς λέγει· περὶ ὧν οὐκ εἰσὶ νόμοι, ἀδικῶν δέ τις ἁλίσκεται ἢ ἄρχων ἢ ῥήτωρ, εἰς τὴν·

---

[1] Cf. Bonner, *Lawyers and Litigants in Ancient Athens*, pp. 34 and 26 ff.

[2] κάκωσις was the name applied to suits involving abuses to heiresses, parents, and orphans. Naturally these matters, as Harpocration says, came before the archon. Something of the procedure in the εἰσαγγελία against an arbitrator may be gathered from Demosthenes (xxi. 87). Cf. scholiast on Plato *Laws*, 466.

βουλὴν εἰσαγγελία δίδοται κατ᾽ αὐτοῦ. κἂν μὲν μέτρια ἀδικεῖν δοκῇ, ἡ
βουλὴ ποιεῖται ζημίας ἐπιβολήν, ἂν δὲ μείζω, παραδίδωσι δικαστηρίῳ,
τὸ δὲ τίμημα, ὅ τι χρὴ παθεῖν ἢ ἀποτῖσαι. ἐγίγνοντο δὲ εἰσαγγελίαι καὶ
κατὰ τῶν καταλυόντων τὸν δῆμον ἢ ῥητόρων μὴ τὰ ἄριστα τῷ δήμῳ λεγόν-
των ἢ πρὸς τοὺς πολεμίους ἄνευ τοῦ πεμφθῆναι ἀπελθόντων, ἢ προδότων
φρούριον ἢ στρατιὰν ἢ ναῦς, ὡς Θεόφραστος ἐν τῷ περὶ νόμων.[1]

Pollux' opinion briefly, then, is that in addition to a few
specific offenses which he enumerates, the εἰσαγγελία could
be used in all extraordinary crimes against the state, provided there was no special law by which they were to be
handled. From the *Lexicon rhetoricum Cantabrigiense* a somewhat different idea is obtained.

εἰσαγγελία· κατὰ καινῶν καὶ ἀγράφων ἀδικημάτων. αὕτη μὲν οὖν ἡ
Καικιλίου δόξα· Θεόφραστος δὲ ἐν τῷ τετάρτῳ περὶ νόμων φησὶ γενέσθαι,
ἐάν τις καταλύῃ τὸν δῆμον ἢ ῥήτωρ μὴ τὰ ἄριστα συμβουλεύῃ χρήματα
λαμβάνων, ἢ ἐάν τις προδιδῷ χωρίον ἢ ναῦς ἢ πεζὴν στρατιὰν ἢ ἐάν τις εἰς
τοὺς πολεμίους ἀφικνῆται (ἄνευ τοῦ πεμφθῆναι παρὰ τοῦ δήμου) ἢ ἐνοικῇ
παρ᾽ αὐτοῖς ἢ στρατεύηται μετ᾽ αὐτῶν δῶρα λαμβάνων.—Καικίλιος δὲ
οὕτως ὡρίσατο· εἰσαγγελία ἐστὶν ὃ περὶ καινῶν ἀδικημάτων δεδώκασιν
ἀπενεγκεῖν οἱ νόμοι. ἔστι δὲ τὸ μελετώμενον ἐν ταῖς τῶν σοφιστῶν διατριβαῖς.[2]

Theophrastus and Caecilius are represented here as defining
the process quite differently, for Theophrastus makes the
εἰσαγγελία applicable to certain specified cases, while Caecilius applies it only to new offenses,[3] not listed in the criminal
code.

The impression given by the lexicographers generally is
that the process was mandatory for certain serious offenses.
But there is no hint in them that the process was ever restricted absolutely to these offenses. It must always have
been possible to employ εἰσαγγελία for unusual and serious
offenses, such as the lexicographers describe as new and unwritten (καινῶν καὶ ἀγράφων). An example is the trial of the
generals after Arginusae. This was a unique case in which,
as is generally agreed, the process of εἰσαγγελία was employed.

---

[1] viii. 51, text as given by Hager, "On the Eisangelia," *Jour. of Philol.*, IV, 76.

[2] *S.v.* εἰσαγγελία, Hager's text.

[3] For comments by other lexicographers which do not differ materially from
those given above, cf. *s.v.* εἰσαγγελία, Bekker, *Anecdota Graeca*, I, 244; and the
scholiast on Plato *Laws* viii. 517.

The εἰσαγγελία became a very popular process, inasmuch as it relieved the plaintiff of certain technicalities and penalties of ordinary procedure. It afforded a means of bringing a case to trial with the utmost dispatch. In the second place, the εἰσαγγελία was advantageous for the good speaker,[1] inasmuch as he always appeared in either the senate or the assembly before the matter came before a court. Since the case never came before a court unless the senate or assembly thought it worth while, the result was that the case was prejudiced before it came into court. This, together with the fact that the defendant often did not await trial, doubtless explains why few acquittals in cases of εἰσαγγελία are mentioned.[2] Finally, the plaintiff did not have to pay the fine of 1,000 drachmas if he failed to receive a fifth part of the votes, at least in the earlier history of the εἰσαγγελία. For all of these reasons the process came to be employed very extensively, even for the most trivial offenses, until it was abused to the extent described by Hypereides.[3] It is possible that, in an attempt to restrict such abuses in the use of the process, the fine of 1,000 drachmas for failure to obtain one-fifth part of the votes was imposed in all *eisangeliae* just as in other types of cases. So Pollux explains Theophrastus' statement to the effect that an *eisangelia* involved the payment of this fine in case of failure to obtain sufficient votes:

ὅτι δὲ ὁ εἰσαγγείλας καὶ οὐχ ἑλὼν ἀζήμιος ἦν, Ὑπερείδης ἐν τῷ ὑπὲρ Λυκόφρονός φησι. καίτοι γε ὁ Θεόφραστος τοὺς μὲν ἄλλας γραφὰς γραψαμένους χιλίας τ' ὀφλισκάνειν, εἰ τοῦ πέμπτου τῶν ψήφων μὴ μεταλάβοιεν καὶ προσατιμοῦσθαι· τοὺς δὲ εἰσαγγέλλοντας μὴ ἀτιμοῦσθαι μέν, ὀφλεῖν δὲ τὰς χιλίας. ἔοικε δὲ τοῦτο διὰ τοὺς ῥᾳδίως εἰσαγγέλλοντας ὕστερον προσγεγράφθαι.[4]

The other lexicographers state that such a fine was imposed. Harpocration[5] says: ὁ δὲ διώκων ἐὰν μὴ ἕλῃ, οὐδὲν ζημιοῦται, πλὴν ἐὰν τὸ πέμπτον μέρος τῶν ψήφων μὴ μεταλάβῃ. τότε χιλίας ἐκτίνει· τὸ δὲ παλαιὸν καὶ οὗτοι μειζόνως ἐκολάζοντο. The account in the *Lexicon rhetoricum Cantabrigiense*[6] also

[1] Cf. Hypereides *Lyc.* 12.

[2] Cf. Hypereides *Eux.* 2; Hager, "On the Eisangelia," *Jour. of Philol.*, IV, 108.

[3] *Eux.*, 1 ff.   [5] *S.v.* εἰσαγγελία.

[4] viii. 52, 53.   [6] *S.v.* πρόστιμον.

asserts that the fine was imposed: περὶ δὲ τῆς εἰσαγγελίας, ἐάν τις μὴ μεταλάβῃ τὸ πέμπτον μέρος τῶν ψήφων, οἱ δικασταὶ τιμῶσιν. If such a fine ever was imposed, the law authorizing it must have been enacted about 338 B.C. Two passages from Hypereides' speech for Lycophron indicate that there was no fine when that oration was delivered: οἱ μὲν γὰρ διὰ τὸ ἀκίνδυνον αὐτοῖς εἶναι τὸν ἀγῶνα ῥᾳδίως ὅ τι ἂν βούλωνται λέγουσι,[1] and ἵνα πρῶτον μὲν ἀκίνδυνος εἰσίῃς εἰς τὸν ἀγῶνα.[2] Certainly at the time that this speech was written there was no penalty involved for the prosecutor under any circumstances. Now with this may be compared a passage from Demosthenes' speech On the Crown: οὐκοῦν ἐν μὲν οἷς εἰσηγγελόμην, ὅτ' ἀπεψηφίζεσθέ μου καὶ τὸ μέρος τῶν ψήφων τοῖς διώκουσιν οὐ μετεδίδοτε, τότ' ἐψηφίζεσθε τὰ ἄριστά με πράττειν.[3] This would seem to indicate that at the time when this speech was delivered there was some penalty in cases of εἰσαγγελία, if the prosecutor did not obtain one-fifth of the votes. But in a case which came first before a political body this seems peculiar. When the senate or the assembly, as the case might be, passed the matter on to a popular court, the initiative was no longer in the hands of the plaintiff. It seems hardly possible that the state would then have required the prosecutor to pay a fine in case he failed to receive a fifth part of the votes.[4] The only explanation for the loss of this immunity for the plaintiff is that the state desired to control the use of the *eisangelia* and to restrict it, as far as possible, to important political cases. If, however, this was the purpose, the penalty does not seem to have had the desired effect, for in Hypereides' speech in behalf of Euxenippus the speaker complains at length of the triviality of the cases which were handled by *eisangelia*. This speech is at least as late as, and presumably later than, Demosthenes' speech *On the Crown*.[5] But Demosthenes' statement does not nec-

---

[1] *Lyc.* 8.   [2] *Ibid.*, 12.   [3] xviii. 250.

[4] In a case like that of Antiphon, where the generals were instructed to prosecute and anyone could join in the prosecution, who would pay the fine? X *Oratorum Vitae*, 833 E. All such prosecutions would be authorized by a ψήφισμα (Lysias xiii. 35).

[5] Cf. Blass, *Attische Beredsamkeit*, III¹, 419; III², 56, for the dates of the speeches. He places *On the Crown* in 330 B.C. and Hypereides' speech between 330 and 324 B.C.

essarily imply a fine. It may be that he merely mentions the failure of his opponents to obtain one-fifth of the votes in order to show how overwhelming his victories had been. The lexicographers who mention the fine may have been misled by Demosthenes' statement.

The process of *eisangelia* was known in very early times in Athens. In the so-called Draconian constitution[1] the verb εἰσαγγέλλειν occurs: ἐξῆν δὲ τῷ ἀδικουμένῳ πρὸς τὴν τῶν Ἀρεοπαγιτῶν βουλὴν εἰσαγγέλλειν, ἀποφαίνοντι παρ᾽ ὃν ἀδικεῖται νόμον. The action provided for here came before the Areopagus, but in later times the Senate of Five Hundred dealt with this kind of case.[2] It amounts to an action against public officials for malfeasance in office. An example of this type of εἰσαγγελία in later times is afforded by the lawsuit alluded to in Antiphon's speech for the *Choregus*[3] in which the choregus had brought an *eisangelia* before the senate against certain men, including the secretary of the thesmothetae, for theft, evidently of public funds.

Solon enacted a law of *eisangelia* against men who attempted to overthrow the government: τοὺς ἐπὶ καταλύσει τοῦ δήμου συνισταμένους ἔκρινεν (ἡ τῶν Ἀρεοπαγιτῶν βουλή), Σόλωνος θέντος νόμον εἰσαγγελίας περὶ αὐτῶν.[4] It is this law which starts the history of the νόμος εἰσαγγελτικός. It is concerned with *eisangelia* only as a means of dealing with attempts to subvert the constitution.[5] Naturally in the Solonian period the Areopagus was the body before which εἰσαγγελίαι καταλύσεως τοῦ δήμου were heard. Up to the time of Solon the Areopagus had been the sovereign body in the state, and under his constitution it continued to be a body of utmost importance, with the special duty of guarding the constitution.[6]

---

[1] *Ath. Pol.* iv. 4. [3] vi. 12, 35.

[2] *Ibid.*, xlv. 2. [4] *Ath. Pol.* viii. 4.

[5] Freeman (*The Work and Life of Solon*, pp. 132 f.) thinks that Solon's law may have included other crimes than attempts on the government and that perhaps not all were brought before the Areopagus. She considers it significant, however, that the law in Hypereides deals only with this one crime. For the question as to the completeness of the law as cited in Hypereides, cf. *infra*, p. 306.

[6] *Ath. Pol.* viii. 4.

Cleisthenes was interested in transferring both political and judicial powers from the oligarchic body, the Areopagus, to the democratic bodies, the boulé and the assembly. It is clear that he permitted *eisangeliae* for attempts to overthrow the government to come before these bodies. There are several cases before the time of Ephialtes which are known to have come before the people. The first of these is the case of Miltiades who, after the failure of the expedition against Paros, was tried before the assembly on a charge of deceiving the people. With difficulty he escaped the death penalty, but was punished with a heavy fine.[1] Lipsius[2] believes that at the time of Miltiades there was a law which decreed death as a penalty for deception of the people and that it is the law of this period which Demosthenes repeats.[3] It is likely that in 493 B.C. Miltiades' trial for tyranny in the Chersonese was held before the people.[4] Phrynichus was tried by the Athenians for recalling to them in his drama the misfortunes of Miletus. This case undoubtedly came before the people.[5] Another case before the people is that of Hipparchus, who was impeached on a charge of προδοσία and who was condemned to death in his absence when he failed to appear to defend himself.[6] This occurred either during or subsequent to his ostracism in 487 B.C. Themistocles likewise was condemned to death by the people in his absence after being accused of participation in the treasonable activities of Pausanias.[7]

Cleisthenes must then have passed a law which granted permission to bring cases of this nature before the assembly or the senate. He may merely have copied the law of Solon, adding the senate and assembly to the Areopagus as proper bodies to have jurisdiction in such cases. That the Areopagus did not lose its right to try them is clear. According to Aristotle,[8] Themistocles expected to be tried before the

---

[1] Herodotus vi. 136. Cf. *supra*, p. 197.

[2] *Op. cit.*, p. 180.

[3] xx. 135; xlix. 67.

[4] Cf. Herod. vi. 104; *supra*, p. 198.

[5] Herod. vi. 21; *supra*, p. 199.

[6] Lycurgus *Con. Leoc.* 117.

[7] Thuc. i. 135, 138. This case is called εἰσαγγελία in the *Lex. Cantab.*, *s.v.* εἰσαγγελία.

[8] *Ath. Pol.* xxv. 3.

Areopagus on a charge of treasonable dealings with the Persians. At the same time he offered to show to the Areopagus certain persons who were conspiring to overthrow the government, with a view to their arrest and trial. The authenticity of Aristotle's statement about Themistocles has been disputed, but at any rate the passage indicates that at the time cases of treason were sometimes turned over to the Areopagus.[1]

It is reasonable to suppose that Ephialtes made the next change in the *nomos eisangeltikos* by depriving the Areopagus of all jurisdiction in such cases and by turning them over exclusively to the boulé and the assembly, in pursuance of his general policy. The provision that the boulé or assembly might turn any case of εἰσαγγελία over to a popular court probably antedates Ephialtes and is to be referred to the period of Cleisthenes' reforms, when the punitive powers of the boulé were diminished. The boulé was obliged to turn over to a court any case which deserved a greater penalty than that which the boulé was empowered to inflict, namely, 500 drachmas.[2] Doubtless the assembly also gave many of the cases which came before it over to the courts. Aristotle says that *eisangeliae* came before the κυρία ἐκκλησία[3] if they were introduced before the assembly. It is obvious, in view of the increasing popularity of the procedure, that the κυρία ἐκκλησία (once a month) would scarcely be able to settle all of the cases. The natural procedure, then, would be to send the cases to a court for settlement, after a preliminary hearing to determine whether the case deserved trial. The trial of the generals after Arginusae, however, shows that the assembly might at any time assert its right to try a case. That *eisangeliae* were commonly turned over to a court by a busy boulé or assembly as early as 422 B.C. is indicated by a passage of Aristophanes' *Wasps:*

---

[1] For the dispute about the possibility of Themistocles' presence in Athens at this time, cf. *supra*, p. 254.

[2] For an excellent account of the entire procedure in εἰσαγγελία, cf. Hager, *op. cit.*, pp. 98 ff.; cf. Gilbert, *Greek Constitutional Antiquities*, pp. 305 ff.

[3] *Ath. Pol.* xliii. 4.

ἔτι δ' ἡ βουλὴ χὠ δῆμος ὅταν κρῖναι μέγα πρᾶγμ' ἀπορήσῃ
ἐψήφισται τοὺς ἀδικοῦντας τοῖσι δικασταῖς παραδοῦναι·[1]

In the years following the reforms of Ephialtes few specific
cases of *eisangelia* are mentioned, and not until the last part
of the century are there any which deal with attempts on the
government. A decree of 446 B.C.[2] provides that an *eisangelia*
shall be brought before the boulé by the king archon in case
of an encroachment on the Pelargikon and that the penalty
for such an offense shall be 500 drachmas—the maximum
penalty which the boulé could inflict. This is a religious
matter. Soon after the beginning of the Peloponnesian War a
decree, likewise dealing with religious matters, was proposed
by Diopeithes, to the effect that persons should be impeached who neglected religion or taught new theories about
the things above the earth. Such accusations were directed
through Anaxagoras at Pericles: καὶ ψήφισμα Διοπείθης ἔγραψεν εἰσαγγέλλεσθαι τοὺς τὰ θεῖα μὴ νομίζοντας ἢ λόγους περὶ
τῶν μεταρσίων διδάσκοντας, ἀπερειδόμενος εἰς Περικλέα δι'
Ἀναξαγόρου τὴν ὑπόνοιαν.[3] Later, another decree was passed,
on the motion of Dracontides, that Pericles should make an
accounting before the prytaneis of the money which he had
spent and, according to an amendment of Hagnon, that any
complaints should be tried before 1,500 jurors. It is probable
that such complaints were to be brought by way of *eisangelia*
but had to be turned over to a court.[4] Before Alcibiades
sailed to Sicily, information was laid against him both before
the assembly and before the boulé to the effect that he had
had a part in the mutilation of the hermae and the profanation of the mysteries with a view to the overthrow of the
democracy.[5] Although Alcibiades desired to stand his trial
before the departure of the fleet, no trial occurred, and he
sailed to Sicily. During his absence he was impeached by
Thessalus. The form of the information brought by Thessalus is recorded by Plutarch.[6] It includes only impiety, i.e.,

[1] 590 f.
[2] Dittenberger, *Sylloge*[2], No. 20, 59 ff.
[3] Plutarch *Pericles*, xxxii.
[4] Cf. Lipsius, *op. cit.*, p. 182, n. 17.
[5] Thucydides vi. 28 ff.; Andocides i. 11 ff., 37; Isocrates xvi. 6.
[6] *Alcibiades* xxii. It is generally believed that this case was tried by the assembly. Cf. Lipsius, *op. cit.*, p. 182.

the profanation of the mysteries. "Thessalus, son of Cimon,
of Lacia, lays information that Alcibiades, son of Cleinias,
of Scambonidae, has committed a crime against the goddesses, Demeter and Persephone, by representing in derision
the holy mysteries, and showing them to his companions in
his own house, where, being habited in such robes as are
worn by the chief priest when he shows the holy things, he
named himself the chief priest and Polytion the torch-bearer,
and Theodorus of Phegaea the herald; and saluted the rest
of the company as initiates and novices. All this was done
contrary to the laws and institutions of the Eumolpidae and
the heralds and priests of the temple." He was condemned,
his property was confiscated, and it was decreed that all the
priests and priestesses should curse him.

After the fall of the Four Hundred the orator Antiphon
was impeached as a traitor.[1] It is probably about the time
of this event that the *nomos eisangeltikos* was passed, substantially in the form in which it appears in Hypereides'
speech for Euxenippus. Hypereides there says that the law
prescribed the use of the process in the following cases:

ἐάν τις τὸν δῆμον τὸν Ἀθηναίων καταλύῃ ἢ συνίῃ ποι ἐπὶ καταλύσει τοῦ
δήμου ἢ ἑταιρικὸν συναγάγῃ ἢ ἐάν τις πόλιν τινὰ προδῷ ἢ ναῦς ἢ πεζὴν ἢ ναυ-
τικὴν στρατιάν, ἢ ῥήτωρ ὢν μὴ λέγῃ τὰ ἄριστα τῷ δήμῳ τῷ Ἀθηναίων χρήματα λαμβάνων.[2]

The law as here given is then composed of three distinct
clauses, each of which in its different way has to do with
treachery to the Athenian state: (1) overthrow of the government, (2) betrayal of the military forces, and (3) accepting bribes as an orator. Three dates have been advanced for
the passage of the law, namely, 411 B.C., after the overthrow
of the Four Hundred;[3] 403-402 B.C., in connection with
the reforms of Eucleides;[4] and the middle of the fourth cen-

[1] *X Or. Vit.*, 833 E.   [2] 7 and 8.

[3] Thalheim, *Hermes*, XXXVII, 339 ff.; XLI, 304 ff.; article "εἰσαγγελία" in
Pauly-Wissowa.

[4] Caillemer, article "εἰσαγγελία," in Daremberg-Saglio. Bohm (*De εἰσαγγελίαις
ad comitia Atheniensium delatis*) distinguishes three periods in the history of the law,
the first to the overthrow of the Thirty Tyrants; the second to the wars with Philip,
to which the law as quoted by Hypereides belongs; and the third to the end of
Athenian independence.

tury.[1] In determining the date, it is necessary to consider both when a mention of the different provisions first appears in literature and to what periods the different provisions are most appropriate.

One of the chief reasons for dating the law at the time of the restoration of the democracy after the downfall of the Four Hundred is the occurrence of the phrase ἑταιρικὸν συναγάγῃ in the first part of the law. The oligarchic clubs had been unusually prominent in overthrowing the democracy in 411 B.C. It is true that they had long been recognized as an important feature of Athenian political life, but they were seen as a distinct menace in oligarchic conspiracies for the first time in the revolution of the Four Hundred.[2] According to Isocrates, in a speech written about 397 B.C., the information given against Alcibiades while he was still in Athens included the following phrase: συνάγοι τὴν ἑταιρείαν.[3] This certainly suggests the phrase as given by Hypereides and might lead to the conclusion that this clause was contained in the law before the Sicilian expedition. This does not, however, seem to be the correct view. The idea of conspiring for the overthrow of the constitution had been included in the law from the time of Solon. Isocrates, knowing, as did Thucydides, that others had worked in collusion with Alcibiades, and having in mind the phrase in the *nomos eisangeltikos*, makes the charge in this form. Isocrates gives the impression that a formal charge was brought against Alcibiades before the Sicilian expedition: ἀμφοτέρας ταύτας συνθέντες τὰς αἰτίας εἰσήγγελλον εἰς τὴν βουλήν, λέγοντες, ὡς ὁ πατὴρ μὲν συνάγοι τὴν ἑταιρείαν ἐπὶ νεωτέροις πράγμασιν, κ.τ.λ. But the words in a following section show that these early charges were not formulated into an indictment: νομίζων δεινὰ πάσχειν, ὅτι παρόντα μὲν αὐτὸν οὐκ ἔκρινον, ἀπόντος δὲ κατεγίγνωσκον. Isocrates simply has in mind, then, the general charges which Thucydides refers to as follows in his more specific account: ἐμεγάλυνον καὶ ἐβόων ὡς ἐπὶ δήμου καταλύσει

[1] Lipsius, *op. cit.*, p. 192; Busolt-Swoboda, *Staatskunde*, II, 1008, n. 6.

[2] Cf. Calhoun, *Athenian Clubs in Politics and Litigation*, p. 21.

[3] xvi. 6.

τά τε μυστικὰ καὶ ἡ τῶν Ἑρμῶν περικοπὴ γένοιτο καὶ οὐδὲν εἴη αὐτῶν ὅτι οὐ μετ' ἐκείνου ἐπράχθη, ἐπιλέγοντες τεκμήρια τὴν ἄλλην αὐτοῦ ἐς τὰ ἐπιτηδεύματα οὐ δημοτικὴν παρανομίαν.¹ The actual impeachment of Alcibiades during his absence seems to have been based on the charge of impiety only.²

Now, under the Four Hundred the process of *eisangelia* was suspended along with other processes: ἔπειτα τὰς τῶν παρανόμων γραφὰς καὶ τὰς εἰσαγγελίας καὶ τὰς προσκλήσεις ἀνεῖλον.³ It is to be expected that one of the early acts of the restored democracy would be the re-establishment of the process. And the enactment of the law to insure its use in cases of treasonable practices would be quite natural in view of the troubled political situation which the state had just passed through. At the time of the restoration of the democracy old laws were re-enacted and old processes were reorganized.⁴

The second clause in the law deals with relations with the allies. Such a clause would have been most appropriate sometime before the dissolution of the Athenian empire in 404 B.C., since it would naturally be enacted to obviate the danger of betrayal of the allied cities. At the beginning of the revolution of the Four Hundred, Peisander, on his return from Samos to Athens, abolished the democracies and established oligarchies in some of the cities through which he passed. Likewise, Oenoe was betrayed to the Boeotians by the oligarchs.⁵ After such acts the enactment of the law would be entirely fitting. It may be objected that the clause applies, not to the first Athenian empire, but to the second. But there were no garrisons established in the cities of the second empire,⁶ and the clause does not seem to apply. Furthermore, a passage in Lysias indicates that the clause was known as early as 399 B.C.: ἄξιον δὲ καὶ τόδε ἐνθυμηθῆναι,

---

¹ Thucydides vi. 28.   ² Plutarch *Alcibiades* xxii.   ³ *Ath. Pol.* xxix. 4.

⁴ *CIA* i. 57; i. 61. There was a commission appointed to make a general revision of the laws at this time. Lysias xxx. 2; cf. F. D. Smith, *Athenian Political Commissions*, p. 74.

⁵ Thucydides viii. 64, 65, 98.

⁶ *CIA* ii. 17; iv (2). p. 10; Hicks and Hill, *Greek Historical Inscriptions*, No. 101. 21 f.

ὅτι εἰ μέν τις φρούριόν τι προύδωκεν ἢ ναῦς ἢ στρατόπεδόν τι, ἐν ᾧ μέρος τι ἐτύγχανε τῶν πολιτῶν ὄν, ταῖς ἐσχάταις ἂν ζημίαις ἐζημιοῦτο.[1]

There is one apparent reference to the third part of the law before the end of the fifth century: δεινὸν δέ μοι δοκεῖ εἶναι, εἰ τοῖς εἰποῦσι . . . . μὴ τὰ ἄριστα ὁ μηδὲν εἰπὼν ταὐτὰ πείσεται.[2]

From the foregoing it is clear that before the end of the fifth century all three provisions as given by Hypereides were known and that the law was substantially the same as it was in Hypereides' time. It is quite possible that minor changes were made subsequent to the restoration of the democracy in 410 B.C., although the main body of the law remained the same. For instance, if the fine of 1,000 drachmas for failure to obtain one-fifth of the votes was ever imposed in cases of *eisangelia*, this provision may have been inserted in a revision of the law sometime between the date of Hypereides' *Pro Lycophrone* and Demosthenes' speech *On the Crown*.

Lipsius' chief reason (and in this he is followed by Busolt) for believing that the *nomos eisangeltikos* was not formulated until the second half of the fourth century, is that in the second half of the century he finds far heavier penalties in cases of *eisangelia* than previously, for, whereas in the first half of the century there are cases of fines as penalties, in the second half it is a question of death and denial of burial in Athens.[3] Furthermore, he finds the first sure case of the application of the νόμος εἰσαγγελτικός in *Hypereides* v. *Philocrates*.[4] None of the passages cited by Lipsius is conclusive evidence that the νόμος εἰσαγγελτικός provided the penalty of death in cases of *eisangelia*. The case rather seems to be that certain laws were passed determining punishment for certain offenses which were normally dealt with by *eisangelia*.[5]

It is clear that the *eisangelia* was a political process to be

[1] xxxi. 26. Some—e.g., Jebb, *Attic Orators*—date the speech a few years earlier.

[2] (Lysias) xx. 10; cf. also 5 and 13. This speech belongs to about 410 B.C.

[3] Cf. Demosthenes xix. 180; xxiii. 167; Aeschines iii. 51; Aristotle *Rhet.* ii. 1380*b*. 10; Hypereides *Lyc.* 20; *Eux.* 14, 18; Aeschines iii. 252; Lycurgus *Leoc.* 150.

[4] Cf. Hyp. *Eux.* 29 f., 39 f.

[5] Cf. *CIA* ii. 65; Thalheim, *Hermes*, XXXVII, 352.

used primarily against those who injured the state. It is only natural that it should be used in all such cases, as well as in those specifically mentioned in the law. Thus many cases for which definite processes were provided by law might in very serious instances, or even in instances not so serious, be handled by *eisangelia* instead, provided some political importance was attached to them. Hence the use of the procedure occasionally in ἀσέβεια or in δειλία, which were regularly dealt with by γραφὴ ἀσεβείας or γραφὴ δειλίας.[1] So it may be concluded that the offense of deception of the people, which, according to an old law cited by Demosthenes,[2] was punished by death, would naturally be handled by *eisangelia*. In addition, any sudden or terrible offense or offenses for which no procedure was specified (designated variously as καινόν, δημόσιον, ἄγραφον, ἐξαπιναῖον)[3] would naturally be handled by *eisangelia*.

It has been suggested that the law as quoted by Hypereides is incomplete. Hager[4] adds two clauses, one dealing with naval affairs, taken from an inscription: ἐάν τις ἀδικῇ περὶ τὰ ἐν τοῖς νεωρίοις;[5] and the other dealing with the commercial laws, taken from the title of a lost oration of Dinarchus: κατὰ Πυθέου περὶ τῶν κατὰ τὸ ἐμπόριον εἰσαγγελία.[6]

---

[1] Cf. Lysias x. 1.

[2] xx. 100, 135. Cf. xix. 103; xlix. 67; and Hager, "How Were the Bodies of Criminals at Athens Disposed of after Death?" *Jour. of Philol.*, VIII, 7, n. 2.

[3] Lexicographers, *s.v.* εἰσαγγελία; Pseudo-Xenophon *Ath. Pol.* iii. 5.

[4] *Jour. of Philol.*, IV, 83 f.

[5] *CIA* ii. 811 c. 140ff.; Boeckh, *Urkunden über das Seewesen des attischen Staates*, p. 536: ἐὰν δὲ οἱ τῶν νεωρίων ἄρχοντες οἱ ἐφ' Ἡγησίου ἄρχοντος παραλαβούσης τῆς πόλεως τοὺς κωπέας μὴ ἀναγράψωσιν εἰς τὴν στήλην, ἢ ὁ γραμματεὺς τῶν ἔνδεκα μὴ ἀπαλείψῃ ἀπὸ τοῦ ὀφλήματος τοῦ Σωπόλιδος τὸ γιγνόμενον τῶν κωπέων κατὰ τὰ ἐψηφισμένα τῇ βουλῇ, ὀφειλέτω ἕκαστος αὐτῶν XXX δραχμὰς τῷ δημοσίῳ, καὶ ὑπόδικος ἔστω Σωπόλιδι καὶ τοῖς Σωπόλιδος οἰκείοις τῆς βουλεύσεως τοῦ ἀργυρίου τῆς τιμῆς τῶν κωπέων, ὧν ἂν ἡ πόλις παρειληφυῖα ᾖ παρὰ Σωπόλιδος καὶ τῶν οἰκείων τῶν Σωπόλιδος. εἶναι δὲ καὶ εἰσαγγελίαν αὐτῶν εἰς τὴν βουλήν, καθάπερ ἐάν τις ἀδικῇ περὶ τὰ ἐν τοῖς νεωρίοις.

[6] Dion. Hal. *De Din.* 10. Hager might well have considered that these crimes would be grouped as προδοσία and have been tried by εἰσαγγελία on that account. He elsewhere says, "Thus I arrive at the conclusion that εἰσαγγελία was applied to crimes enumerated in the νόμος εἰσαγγελτικός but also to all other crimes with, however, the restrictions that they must be referred to some section of the law and proceeded against under the name of one of the crimes specially designated" (*Jour. of Philol.*, IV, 78).

Thalheim[1] advances the theory that supplementary to the νόμος εἰσαγγελτικός three other crimes were admitted to the process of εἰσαγγελία in the early fourth century, namely, (1) deceptive promises to the people, (2) dishonesty on an embassy, and (3) any transactions that endangered the Athenian mari ne confederacy. This last refers, of course, to the second Athenian confederacy.[2] These scholars have been led to think that the *nomos eisangeltikos* is incomplete because they regard the law as an attempt to restrict the use of the process and are therefore unable to account for the known cases of *eisangelia* which cannot be classified under any section of the law. Such difficulties disappear, however, if the thesis here set forth is adopted, namely, that the law was intended only to insure the use of the process in certain political cases.[3]

---

[1] *Hermes*, XXXVII, 346 ff.   [2] Cf. *CIA* ii. 17, 51 ff.

[3] The known cases of *eisangelia* have been very helpfully collected and classified by Hager (*op. cit.*, pp. 79 ff.). Hager, however, had no interest in dating the law as it stands in Hypereides, and therefore attempts to fit all the cases under his classifications with no reference to the date of the law. He begins with a case which was settled before the formulation of the law—the impeachment of Alcibiades for impiety. It has been maintained above that the case against Alcibiades was political as well as religious, and therefore might have been dealt with by *eisangelia* even after the passage of the law. Another case of κατάλυσις τοῦ δήμου is reported in Dinarchus i. 94: Καλλιμέδοντα εἰσαγγέλλων (Δημοσθένης) συνιέναι ἐν Μεγάροις τοῖς φυγάσιν ἐπὶ καταλύσει τοῦ δήμου; and there are hints of other such cases in Lysias xiii. 50 and xii. 48. Trials of generals on the charge of προδοσία furnish many cases of *eisangelia*. Cf. Dem. xix. 180; Lysias xxviii. 1, 11, 12, 17; the case of Cephisodotus, Dem. xxiii. 167; Aesch. iii. 51, 52; and the scholiast. For other examples, cf. Hager, *op. cit.*, p. 84. The trial of the generals after Arginusae is an important case of this type, although neither Xenophon nor Diodorus makes use of the term εἰσαγγελία in describing it. Cf. however, Hager, *op. cit.*, p. 85; Bonner, *op. cit.*, pp. 245 ff. Another famous case is that of Antiphon, who, with his associates, was accused of treason on an embassy (*X Oratorum Vitae*, 833e; cf. Thuc. viii. 68). With this may be compared the case of Aeschines, whom Demosthenes threatened to impeach on a charge of παραπρεσβεία (cf. Aeschines ii. 139; Dem. xix. 125, 131). Another early case is that of Aristarchus, who was tried and condemned for his activities under the Four Hundred: Ἀρίσταρχῳ μὲν πρότερον τὸν δῆμον καταλύοντι, εἶτα δ' Οἰνόην προδιδόντι Θηβαίοις πολεμίοις οὖσιν (Xen. *Hell.* i. 7, 28; cf. Thuc. viii. 98). There are several cases of *eisangelia* against orators who gave bad advice to the state under the influence of bribes. Cf. Hyp. *Eux.* 8, 39. ῥήτωρ in this clause of the law doubtless refers to those who made it their business to speak in assembly, and it might therefore be applied to any citizen, although Hypereides objects that Euxenippus was being tried under this clause, although he was an ἰδιώτης and not a ῥήτωρ (*Eux.* 40; cf. Hager, *op. cit.*, pp. 89 ff.). The clause could undoubtedly be used against anyone whose counsels given in public assembly turned out to be injurious to the state, especially if they were influenced by bribes.

When an impeachment was brought before either the boulé or the assembly, one of several things might happen. The assembly or the boulé, as the case might be, might fail to do anything about it. A case in point is the attempted impeachment of Alcibiades before he sailed to Sicily. Although, according to Andocides, information was laid before both bodies, he was not tried.[1] If it was felt that the matter should be brought to trial, there might arise a long discussion with many different opinions as to the proper disposal of the case. So, in the trial of the generals after Arginusae, three different propositions were made: (1) that the generals should be tried forthwith by the assembly; (2) that there should be a trial according to the decree of Cannonus, also before the assembly; and (3) that they should be tried before a court according to the law concerning temple robbers and traitors. The first proposition carried. Such a discussion was terminated by the passing of a ψήφισμα which provided for a trial either before one of these political bodies or before a δικαστήριον. Some extant psephisms of this kind provide some information as to their usual details. For instance, in the case against Antiphon the decree states the charge on which Antiphon was to be tried; it indicates the persons who were to produce the defendants in court; it specifies the prosecutors and determines the penalty in case of condemnation. That the penalty was regularly specified if the case was turned over to a court is indicated in Pollux' discussion of the εἰσαγγελία: κἂν μὲν μέτρια ἀδικεῖν δοκῇ, ἡ βουλὴ ποιεῖται ζημίας ἐπιβολήν, ἂν δὲ μείζω, παραδίδωσι δικαστηρίῳ, τὸ δὲ τίμημα, ὅ τι χρὴ παθεῖν ἢ ἀποτῖσαι. The psephism might also specify the size of the court before which the trial was to take place: εὐθέως κρίσιν τοῖς ἀνδράσι τούτοις ἐποίουν ἐν τῇ βουλῇ, ὁ δὲ δῆμος 'ἐν τῷ δικαστηρίῳ ἐν δισχιλίοις' ἐψήφιστο.[2]

The *nomos eisangeltikos*, then, has a continuous history from the time of Solon down through the fourth century at least. In the form in which it occurs in Hypereides, it could not have been passed until after the revolution of the Four

[1] Cf. *supra*, p. 301.

[2] Lysias xiii. 35. That these cases were *eisangeliae* is shown by Lysias xii. 48.

Hundred, but must have been passed soon after the restoration of the democracy. As it stands in Hypereides, it is a revision and amplification of the law of Solon's time, which doubtless had undergone several revisions during the course of the fifth century. The law never forbade that offenses other than those mentioned in the law should be tried by *eisangelia*, but merely made certain that these specified offenses should be so tried. There is plenty of evidence that any sudden or serious wrong was normally dealt with by this process. By the middle of the fourth century, and probably earlier, the process was widely employed for the most trivial offenses.

CHAPTER XI

THE JUDICIAL ORGANIZATION OF THE ATHENIAN EMPIRE

The administration of justice under the Athenian empire was influenced by two distinct ideas.[1] On the one hand, Athens desired to give to her allies a general feeling of security and equality in commercial matters. Hence, in commercial suits Athens provided reciprocity in litigation. Arrangements for the settlement of commercial suits gave the allies virtual equality with Athens.[2] On the other hand, there was a tendency on the part of Athens to exercise force and to transfer all real power to Athens. This policy is evident in her treatment of criminal cases. Here she exercised a close surveillance and, as far as possible, kept the means of judicial control in her own hands. Commercial cases and criminal cases must therefore be treated separately.

The system followed in dealing with commercial cases can be understood only by reference to certain previous developments in Greek judicial practice regarding the rights of foreigners. In Homeric society, foreigners appear to have had no means of judicial redress. In the time of Hesiod[3] they were permitted, in some cases at least, to use the local courts. With the growth of commerce it became desirable that facilities should be provided whereby foreigners could collect sums due them and that some definite guaranty of security of person and property should be provided. Hence there arose a very general practice of concluding treaties

[1] A summary of the administration of justice under the empire is provided here for the sake of completeness, although the subject is somewhat outside the scope of this study. For an exhaustive treatment, cf. Robertson, "University of Toronto Studies in History and Economics," Vol. IV, No. 1: *The Administration of Justice in the Athenian Empire*, which is followed closely in this summary.

[2] Thucydides i. 77; cf. Bonner, *Class. Phil.*, XIV, 284 ff.
Antiphon, v. 78; cf. Robertson, *Class. Phil.*, XIX, 368.

[3] *Works and Days*, 225.

between states for their mutual advantage in the matter of providing for litigation between their citizens. The earliest extant treaties merely guarantee a certain degree of immunity from seizure.[1] Provision is then made for procedure in the nature either of reprisal by the aggrieved party or of intervention by a magistrate. Finally these treaties came to concern themselves also with cases of non-fulfilment of contracts and other commercial disputes, and practically guaranteed complete judicial reciprocity. At the time of the organization of the Delian League such treaties were doubtless in force between Athens and the chief commercial cities of Greece. Suits tried under the provisions of these treaties were called δίκαι ἀπὸ συμβόλων.

One of the most important features of the administration of justice under the Athenian empire was the trial of commercial cases between Athenians and members of allied states under the provisions of treaties (σύμβολα).[2] Robertson summarizes his findings with regard to σύμβολα and δίκαι ἀπὸ συμβόλων as follows:[3]

1. The treaties were ratified by a heliastic court under the presidency of the thesmothetae.[4] They were concluded both with the states of the empire and with states outside it, but more especially with the former. Among the allies they were in force with the autonomous cities and with the subordinate, including cities to which cleruchies had been sent after a revolt, though in this case the terms were presumably less favorable to the allies.

2. Two things were assured by these treaties: security from seizure, and reciprocity in the trial of certain cases. These were cases arising out of commercial contracts and

---

[1] Compare treaty between Chaleion and Oeanthea, *IG* ix. 333; Hicks and Hill, *Greek Historical Inscriptions*, No. 44. This treaty belongs to about 440 B.C.

[2] These cases were also known as δίκαι συμβολαῖαι, an expression which involved some ambiguity, as συμβολαῖος might be connected either with σύμβολον, a treaty, or with συμβόλαιον, a commercial contract. The fact that many cases were both "suits regulated by treaty" and "suits regarding commercial contracts" would tend to obscure the distinction.

[3] *The Administration of Justice in the Athenian Empire*, p. 22.

[4] Aristotle *Ath. Pol.* lix. 6; Pollux viii. 88. Cf. Lipsius, *op. cit.*, p. 968.

dealing with the same matters as δίκαι ἐμπορικαί, though they differed from the latter in their wider range and in the procedure followed. Reciprocity was secured by the principle that *actio sequitur forum rei*,[1] with the probable exception that cases involving a state were referred to a third state for decision.

3. Treaty cases were tried, in some cases at least, not under the laws of either of the contracting states but under a special system determined by the treaty.[2] We have no evidence as to the details of the procedure followed, but it probably resembled that of Athens, not only on account of the preponderance of the capital city in the empire but also because of the fact that the procedure of the allies tended to approximate that of Athens. It is most probable that foreigners appearing in treaty cases did not require the services of a πρόξενος or προστάτης. The court before which these cases were brought was not the same as that which tried cases involving citizens only, nor yet the same as that which tried cases of foreigners not regulated by treaty. The presiding magistrates were always the thesmothetae,[3] except, apparently, in the case of Lesbos, where resident Athenian magistrates dealt with these cases.[4]

4. Finally, safeguards were provided,[5] to assure the allies of a means of redress in case of any infringement of the treaty regulations.

The liberality of Athens in these cases was obviously due to her desire to encourage trade.

A far different policy was followed by Athens in regard to political and criminal cases. Here her whole attitude was to subordinate and to restrict. Owing to the fact that the Delian League was formed under war-time conditions,

[1] Stahl, *De sociorum Atheniensium iudiciis commentatio*, p. 8.

[2] Stahl, *op. cit.*, p. 8; Hitzig, *Altgriechische Staatsverträge über Rechtshilfe*, p. 53; Busolt, *Geschichte*, III, 234; Wilamowitz, *Hermes*, XXII, 240.

[3] Aristotle, *op. cit.*, lix. 6.   [4] *CIA* iv (1). 96.

[5] *CIA* ii. 11; Hicks and Hill, *op. cit.*, No. 36; Dittenberger, *Sylloge²*, No. 72. The decision of an Athenian magistrate rendered in a case which, according to the treaty, should not be tried in Athens was null and void, and the magistrate was liable to a fine of 10,000 drachmas.

powers were doubtless assigned to already existing officials and bodies rather than to newly instituted groups. There would, therefore, at once be a tendency to leave much of the executive power in the hands of the leaders of the league, the Athenians. There seems to have been at the outset little notion of the judicial disputes which might arise. Furthermore, the Athenians were the commanders-in-chief of army and navy, and their generals would deal with any cases in the field. Their authority might easily be extended to deal with any action on the part of an ally which hindered the execution of the purpose of the league.[1]

The need for a federal judicial system became apparent after the allies had begun to grow careless in the performance of their duties as allies. Athens by this time had begun her imperialistic policy. She had to have a system for forcing the allies to perform their duties. She undoubtedly supplied this need as occasion demanded, rather than usurped powers which had belonged to the league council. She was not slow to take advantage of the situation, but transferred important cases from the allies to her own courts. As revolting cities were conquered, the acts of settlement provided for the administration of justice under the control of Athens.

The allies fall naturally into three classes: the independent communities, those which had revolted and been reduced to a subordinate and tributary position, and those which voluntarily became subject. The position of the first class with regard to judicial matters is uncertain, but this comprised only a small minority of the allied cities and was finally reduced to two states—Chios and Methymna. The second class were undoubtedly subordinated to Athens both in political and in judicial matters. Separate decrees[2] were necessary to determine the relations of the revolting states, but these conformed to a general policy and followed certain

---

[1] Plutarch *Cimon* xi.

[2] For the decree regarding Erythrae (between 470 and 450 B.C.), *CIA* i. 9; Hicks and Hill, *op. cit.*, No. 32; Dittenberger, *op. cit.*, No. 8. For Miletus (between 450 and 447 B.C.), *CIA* iv (1). 22 A. For Chalcis (448 B.C.), *ibid.*, iv (1). 27 A; Hicks and Hill, *op. cit.*, No. 40; Dittenberger, *op. cit.*, No. 17. For discussion and bibliography, see Robertson, *op. cit.*, pp. 31 ff.

general regulations. In the case of the third class, which comprised the bulk of the communities which made up the Athenian empire, it would be most improbable that separate arrangements should be made with each petty state.

The facts regarding the treatment of these cases may be summarized as follows:[1]

1. These cases were subject to certain general regulations affecting all the cities of the empire.

2. Cases *ex delicto* involving Athenians and citizens of allied states were tried at Athens in the first instance.

3. Cases *ex delicto* involving allies only were tried in the local courts; but, in cases in which the penalties of death, exile, or the loss of civil rights were assessed or were fixed by law, the matter had to be referred to Athens.[2] This provision appears sometimes to have been extended to cases involving sums of more than 100 drachmas. The local courts possessed absolute jurisdiction only in cases involving a fine.

4. Sentences of perpetual banishment involved exile from the confines of the empire.

5. Some judicial powers were exercised by Athenian overseas officials.

6. The allies were assured a legal trial by the proper judicial authority.

An important group of cases before the Athenian courts were those arising from tribute assessments,[3] including appeals by the allies against the assessment of tribute and prosecution in cases of treasonable activity on the part of the allies which led to failure to pay tribute. In cases of dissatisfaction with the amount of assessment, the allies might appeal

---

[1] Robertson, *op. cit.*, p. 46.

[2] The reference was not, strictly speaking, an appeal. If the case was appealable, a defendant might decide not to exercise his right but to submit to a penalty beyond the competence of the local courts. But that this was not the case appears from Antiphon's statement that the death penalty could not be inflicted by a subject city: ἄνευ 'Αθηναίων (v. 47). This would seem to show that sentences carrying certain specified penalties had to be confirmed by the Athenian court. The consent of the defendant had nothing to do with the matter. Cf. Steinwenter, *op. cit.*, pp. 74–75.

[3] *CIA* i. 37; Hicks and Hill, *op. cit.*, No. 64, for the epigraphical evidence.

to an Athenian court; such cases came before the εἰσαγωγεῖς, and they were "monthly suits."[1] The other group of cases came also before an Athenian court under the chairmanship of the ἐπιμεληταί, and were "monthly suits."[2]

According to the system described above, the local courts of the allies retained very little jurisdiction. Cases *ex contractu* were in general tried as treaty cases. In cases *ex delicto* all suits involving an Athenian and a citizen of an allied state were tried in Athens; while cases involving only allies were tried in the local courts with the qualification that if the penalty was death, banishment, or ἀτιμία, the matter had to be referred to Athens. All tribute cases came to Athens. It is probable that the few cases which were retained by the local courts were supervised by Athenian overseas officials. In general, cases involving allies were tried by regular Athenian procedure. The procedure for treaty cases, however, was of course settled by the treaties. The allies pleaded their own cases before the heliastic courts, although they might, like Athenian citizens, have the help of professional speechwriters.

In the second confederacy organized under the terms of the Aristoteles decree (478–477),[3] the "treaty cases" (δίκαι ἀπὸ συμβόλων) continued to be settled on the basis of reciprocity, as under the empire.[4] The political affairs of the league were managed jointly by a council of the allied cities, on which Athens was not represented, and the Athenian authorities. Meetings were held at Athens; Athens was the executive head of the league.[5]

There are no general provisions in the decree regarding federal judicature. Whether the omission was accidental or intentional, the question of some sort of federal jurisdiction had to be faced in practice. According to the Aristoteles decree, if any measure was proposed or put to a vote intended

[1] Cf. Lipsius, *op. cit.*, pp. 85 and 901.   [2] *CIA* i. 38; iv (1). 38 A.

[3] *CIA* ii. 17; Hicks and Hill, *op. cit.*, No. 101; Dittenberger, *Sylloge*[2], No. 147.

[4] (Demosthenes) vii. 9–13 proves that δίκαι ἀπὸ συμβόλων continued after the dissolution of the second confederacy.

[5] Diodorus xv. 28. Cf. Marshall, *The Second Athenian Confederacy*, p. 28.

to annul any provisions of the decree, the person responsible, whether a private individual or a magistrate, should be tried ἐν 'Αθηναίοις καὶ τοῖς συμμάχοις.[1] The penalty was banishment beyond the territories of Athens and the allies, or death with a prohibition of burial within the confines of Athens and the allies. The identity of the court contemplated is uncertain.[2] A federal court composed of Athenian and allied representatives may have been intended. The Aristoteles decree was a statement of policy rather than a complete constitution of the proposed league. Many details could only be worked out with the co-operation of the allies when the league was actually formed. The organization of a supreme court may have been one of them. It was a prominent feature of the Boeotian League of 447–446 which lasted until the peace of Antalcidas, 387–386 B.C. On the other hand, Athens may have tried Athenian offenders in her own courts, leaving the council of the allies to try allied offenders.[3] But neither Athens nor the allies would have had authority to enforce the prohibition regarding exile and burial. Only a supreme court would have jurisdiction over all territories included in the alliance. The difficulty involved in a dual legal jurisdiction could have been met by reporting all convictions for treason to the general meeting of Athenians and allies. In this way both Athenian and allied verdicts could have been made valid throughout the alliance. This seems to be the preferable view.[4]

But in spite of the self-denying Aristoteles decree, Athens was guilty of encroachments upon the judicial autonomy of

---

[1] *CIA* ii. 17, 56–63.

[2] For the various suggestions that have been offered, cf. Robertson, "The Administration of Justice in the Second Athenian Confederacy," *Class. Phil.*, XXIII, 30ff.

[3] Cf. Lipsius, *Berichte d. König. Säch. Gesellschaft d. Wissenschaft. zu Leipzig*, 1898, pp. 154 ff., and *Att. Recht*, p. 975.

[4] Other possibilities are a trial by the allies with appeal or reference to Athens for confirmation, or trial by both the Athenians and the allies. In favor of independent dual trials is cited the practice of deciding questions of peace and war. But this is too cumbersome a procedure when others were available. Cf. Robertson, *op. cit.*, p. 32.

her allies. After the revolt of Ceos, measures were taken to punish the guilty leaders. Any of the accused who claimed they were innocent could be tried in Ceos and in Athens: ἐξεῖναι αὐτοῖς—δίκας ὑποσχεῖν κατὰ τοὺς ὅρκους καὶ τὰς συνθήκας ἐν Κέῳ καὶ ἐν τῇ ἐκκλήτῳ πόλει 'Αθήνησι.[1] This seems to mean that the case was first tried in Ceos and then referred to Athens for confirmation. This is not, strictly speaking, an appeal.[2] The case went to Athens not by choice of the defendant but by the requirement of the Athenian decree. In another decree imposing commercial restrictions upon Ceos the words εἶναι δὲ καὶ ἔφεσιν 'Αθήναζε καὶ τῶι φήναντι καὶ τῶι ἐνδείξαντι occur.[3] And in a decree regarding Naxos[4] the words τὰς ἐφεσίμους δίκας indicate that certain types of cases had to be referred to Athens. These ranged all the way from cases involving 100 drachmas to the more important criminal cases. These provisions amount to a return to the system in vogue in the first Athenian empire.

[1] CIA iv (2). 54 B. Cf. Lipsius, Att. Recht, pp. 976 f.

[2] On the question of appeal, cf. Steinwenter, op. cit., pp. 75 ff.

[3] CIA ii. 546.   [4] Ibid., iv (2). 88d.

CHAPTER XII
ADMINISTRATION OF JUSTICE
IN RURAL ATTICA

Thucydides dwells at some length upon the reluctance of the population of Attica to leave their homes and move into the city to escape the Peloponnesian invaders:

Because then of their long-continued life of independence [αὐτονόμῳ οἰκήσει] in the country districts, most of the Athenians of early times and of their descendants down to the time of this war, from force of habit, even after their political union with the city, continued to reside with their households in the country.[1]

The political union of Attica involved the dissolution of councils and magistracies outside of Athens. But it is not at all likely that the social, political, and religious associations of the communities, that were embraced in the petty independent principalities, were suppressed. Some elements of local self-government must have survived in the village communities. These were grouped into forty-eight *naucrariae* for the purpose of levying taxes and drafting military forces. The council of the *naucraroi* played such an important part in public affairs that Herodotus credited it with the chief authority in the state at the time of the Cylonian attempt at tyranny.[2] All Athenian magistrates and officials had some judicial functions. It may be that the naucrars, each in his own district, exercised some judicial functions; but there is no hint of such powers in the sources.

In all periods the Athenians were ever ready to resort to arbitration for the settlement of their less serious disputes. We may be sure that in the village communities arbitration played a part in the relations of the people. Perhaps Peisistratus, in sending out the "rural justices," was seeking to strengthen his hold on the people by substituting his own adherents for the local arbitrators.[3] When Cleisthenes got

[1] Thucydides ii. 16, Smith's translation.

[2] Cf. *supra*, p. 130. [3] Cf. *supra*, p. 184.

control of Athens after the expulsion of the tyrants, he abolished both the *naucraroi* and the local justices. He organized units of self-government in the village communities known as "demes" under "demarchs."[1] These political groups played an important rôle in the state.

Citizenship depended upon registration in a deme roll.[2] Sons of citizens were registered by their fathers in the presence of the deme assembly. Full opportunity for offering objections to the admission of the candidate was afforded. Naturalized citizens chose their own demes. A man's right to citizenship could always be tested in court by anyone by means of a γραφὴ ξενίας.[3] Occasionally thoroughgoing revisions of the lists of citizens were made by the deme assemblies. The proceeding was known as a διαψήφισις.[4] Haussoullier[5] maintains that these sessions were not judicial. This view is not quite correct.[6] It is true that no set time was allowed to accusers and defendants, as in a court of law. But anyone might address the assembly on behalf of himself or another, and all members were sworn and voted secretly by ballot. These characteristic features of a trial clearly distinguish the διαψήφισις from the regular meetings of the deme assembly. Anyone whose name was stricken from the deme roll of citizens could appeal to a heliastic court. If the appeal was rejected, the appellant was liable to be sold as a slave.[7]

The elaborate Athenian system of auditing public accounts was reproduced with modifications in the demes. In an inscription from the deme of Myrrhinus detailed provisions for the official audit are found. Even the wording

---

[1] Aristotle *Ath. Pol.* xxi. 5.

[2] Haussoullier, *La vie municipale en Attique*, p. 13.

[3] Lipsius, *Das Attische Recht*, p. 412. Admission to the body of citizens was carefully guarded. Some of the more material benefits of citizenship were enhanced by keeping the numbers down. Aristophanes (*Wasps*, 718) jests about the numerous prosecutions on the occasion of a distribution of grain. Cf. Plutarch *Pericles* xxxvii.

[4] Lipsius, *op. cit.*, pp. 414-15.   [5] *Op. cit.*, p. 44.

[6] Gilbert, *Greek Constitutional Antiquities*, p. 208.

[7] Isaeus, xii, and Demosthenes, lvii, are our chief sources of information regarding these appeals. Cf. Lipsius, *op. cit.*, p. 415.

of the oaths administered to the three classes of officials, constituting the auditing committee, are given. The auditor (εὔθυνος) and the accountant (λογιστής), assisted by the *synegoroi*, guardians of the public interest, went over the documents in each case in the presence of the assembled demesmen. The verdict of this commission under the chairmanship of the auditor was not valid unless approved by ten demesmen elected by the deme assembly and sworn by the demarch.[1]

The most interesting and instructive feature of the proceeding is the provision for an immediate appeal to the assembled demesmen under oath, provided there are thirty in attendance. For the deme of Myrrhinus thirty constituted a quorum, just as for certain functions 6,000 constituted a quorum of the ecclesia.[2] Szanto's[3] view that if only a quorum were present the vote must be unanimous is not supported either by the wording of the document or by the analogy of Athenian practice. It is specifically stated in the document that a majority of the ten was required to reverse the verdict of the auditor. If a unanimous vote of a quorum in the assembly was required to reverse the verdict of the ten, such an unusual requirement would surely have been mentioned. Apparently the entire proceeding in connection with the audits took place in the presence and hearing of the assembly, so that the various votes could be taken without delay if a quorum was present; otherwise an adjournment would be necessary. Appeals were discouraged by an addition of 50 per cent to the fine in case of failure. In another fourth-century document[4] provision is made for the arbitration of disputes between the deme of Aexone and the lessees of public lands or farmers of public revenues who were in arrears, which otherwise would go to the heliastic courts. An agreement, confirmed by oaths and pledges, to abide by the arbitral award and not to have recourse to litigation was required. The demarch, aided by advocates (σύνδικοι), presents the case against the lessees alleged to be in arrears. A

[1] *CIA* ii. 578; Haussoullier, *op. cit.*, pp. 80 ff.

[2] Cf. *supra*, pp. 194 ff.   [3] *Untersuchungen über das attische Bürgerrecht*, p. 36.

[4] Haussoullier, *op. cit.*, pp. 87 ff.

curious situation arises: the deme is at once party and judge. But the submission of the case to arbitration is voluntary.

The demarch had no real judicial functions. But just as Athenian magistrates presided over meetings of the dicasteries, so the demarch presided over the judicial proceedings of the assembly and administered the oath. But this is not significant, because he presided over all meetings of the assembly. Like all Athenian executive officers, he had the right to inflict fines upon demesmen who obstructed him in the performance of his duties.[1] As chief magistrate the demarch represented the municipality in all legal proceedings in which it was a party. Thus, when a rejected citizen appealed to a heliastic court against the vote of the assembly in the revision of the roll of citizens, the demarch, assisted by five chosen advocates, opposed the appeal.[2]

An extant inscription[3] shows that advocates were granted special honors as a recognition of their services to the deme. No doubt, like the city advocates, they received pay as well.

There has been considerable difference of opinion, both in ancient and in modern times, as to the nature of the intervention of the demarch in the process of seizing the property of debtors and condemned criminals. Outside of the lexicographers and scholiasts, only two passages refer to the subject. In the sentence of death and confiscation of property passed upon Antiphon and Archeptolemus in 410 B.C., the demarchs of their respective demes were directed to identify the property involved.[4] This document, quoted by Pseudo-Plutarch, goes back to Craterus' collection. In the *Clouds* of Aristophanes[5] Strepsiades complains to his son that he has lost some suits and is being threatened with seizure of his goods and chattels in pledge for interest. In answer to his son's query as to why he is tossing about on his bed, he

---

[1] Schoeffer, article "Demarchoi" in Pauly-Wissowa, IV, 2708. In the case of the demarch such fines had to be confirmed by a dicastery. Cf. *supra*, p. 279.

[2] Aristotle *Ath. Pol.* xlii. 1. Cf. *CIA* iv. 2. 583*b*.   [3] *CIA* ii. 581.

[4] Pseudo-Plutarch, *X Oratorum Vitae*, 834 A. τὼ δὲ δημάρχω ἀποφῆναι τὴν οὐσίαν αὐτοῖν.

[5] Lines 33 ff.

replies: δάκνει με δήμαρχός τις ἐκ τῶν στρωμάτων. The plain implication is that as a result of his failure to pay his creditors he expects visits of the demarch of Cicynna.

The rôle of the demarch under the circumstances set forth in these passages is not entirely clear. According to the lexicographers[1] and the scholiast on Aristophanes' *Clouds*, 37, the demarch not only kept a register of the real estate in his deme but recorded pledges of property to secure payment of money owed. As to the register of real estate, there can be little doubt that the lexicographers are right.[2] But there is not sufficient evidence to warrant the belief that the demarch registered chattel mortgages. It is, however, clear that in some fashion the demarch intervened in the seizure of goods to satisfy a judgment. But, in view of the fact that we have in a speech attributed to Demosthenes,[3] a very detailed account of the seizure of the chattels of a judgment debtor and the murder of a female servant, without any mention of a demarch, it seems likely that all the demarch could be required to do was to assist creditors by pointing out the habitation and property of the debtor whose goods and chattels were ἐνέχυρα.

[1] Suidas; and Harpocration, *s.v.* δήμαρχος.

[2] Thalheim (*Lehrbuch der griechischen Rechtsalterthümer*, p. 57, n. 1) accepts the statements of the lexicographers. Lipsius doubts the existence of real estate registers in the office of the demarch (*op. cit.*, p. 302, n. 12) but thinks that it was usual (*üblich*) for the demarch to accompany men making seizures (p. 950).

[3] xlvii. 53 ff.

CHAPTER XIII
THE OLIGARCHIC REACTION

No revolution in fifth-century Athens could fail to modify very fundamentally the democratic judicial system. The popular courts constituted the bulwark[1] of Athenian democracy. The constitutional history of Athens is largely a record of the various enactments that enlarged and consolidated their power, such as the restriction of the powers of the Areopagus, the limitation of the punitive power of the Senate of Five Hundred, the γραφὴ παρανόμων, the law regulating impeachments (νόμος εἰσαγγελτικός), and the provision of pay for jurors. These reforms encountered much opposition. Pericles' introduction of pay for jury service in particular called forth much criticism. Aristotle says:

> Pericles was the first to institute pay for service in the law-courts, as a bid for popular favor to counterbalance the wealth of Cimon. . . . . Some persons accuse him of thereby causing a deterioration in the character of the juries, since it was the inferior people who were anxious to submit themselves for selection as jurors, rather than the men of better position.[2]

It has been suggested that Aristotle may have had in mind the animadversions of Plato, who in the *Gorgias*[3] represents Socrates as saying:

> I should like to know whether the Athenians are supposed to have been made better by Pericles, or, on the contrary, to have been corrupted by him; for I hear that he was the first who gave the people pay, and made them idle and cowardly, and encouraged them in the love of talk and of money.

The rejoinder of Callicles that Socrates must have heard that from the philo-Spartan set shows that this was the view of the conservatives who, if not openly anti-democratic, were at least strongly opposed to the extreme type of democracy developed in Athens. This sentiment undoubtedly goes back to the fifth century.

---

[1] Aristotle *Ath. Pol.* ix. 1.   [2] *Ibid.*, xxvii. 3–4.   [3] 515 E.

Not much constructive fifth-century criticism has survived. Indeed, there could be little so long as the theory
prevailed that those who governed should administer justice.
There could be no real improvement until people were willing to intrust large judicial powers to men fitted by training
and temperament to exercise them wisely. Some advanced
views were expressed in the fourth century which may well
have had their counterpart in the days of Pericles. In the
Republic[1] Plato maintained that justice should not be administered by butchers and bakers and candlestick-makers.
Here he was far in advance of the times. But in the *Laws*,[2]
a more practical treatise, he reverts to the normal Greek view:

> In the judgment of offenses against the state the people ought to
> participate, for when anyone wrongs the state they are all wronged, and
> may reasonably complain if they are not allowed to share in the decision.
> . . . . And in private suits, too, as far as possible, all should have a share;
> for he who has no share in the administration of justice, is apt to imagine
> that he has no share in the state at all.

But he goes so far as to recommend the establishment of a
supreme court of appeal. The idea of an appeal did not originate with Plato. Appeals of various kinds were familiar in
Athenian practice of the fifth and fourth centuries. Appeal
was one of the most significant features of Solon's reforms.
But the originality of Plato's scheme was the character of the
proposed court. It was virtually a body of experts.[3] Socrates
in the *Apology*[4] suggests that in capital cases more time, even
several days, should be allowed for the trial. This is a criticism of current practice.

Isocrates, writing in 355 B.C., charged the courts of his
day with laxity and advocated a return to the πάτριος
πολιτεία when the Areopagus was guardian of the laws and
the constitution:

> In those days, in adjudicating suits for the recovery of money lent out,
> they did not favor the debtors but obeyed the laws, being more indignant
> at those who tried to evade payment than the victims themselves, for
> they believed that the poor rather than the rich were injured when con-
> fidence in loans was destroyed.[5]

[1] 397 D.
[2] 768 A, Jowett's translation.   [4] 37 A.
[3] *Laws* 767 C.   [5] *Areopagiticus* 34. Cf. *Antidosis* 142.

The πάτριος πολιτεία was a favorite slogan of both reactionaries and reformers in the fifth century. Pseudo-Xenophon, writing in 424 B.C., observes that "in their courts the Athenians are more concerned with what is to their advantage than what is just" and that "a bad man has a better chance of escaping justice in a democracy."[1] He rejects the suggestion that the congestion of the courts might be cured by providing more panels because the smaller numbers would be more easily bribed.

Any large modification is out of the question, short of damaging democracy itself. No doubt many expedients might be discovered for improving the constitution, but if the problem is to discover some adequate means of improving the constitution while at the same time democracy is to remain intact, I say it is not easy to do.[2]

The plain implication of such language is that the only way to improve the democratic administration of justice is to abolish democracy. There are indications in the essay that the problem of restricting litigation had been raised. After giving a list of the different types of cases that came before the courts, the writer inquires: "Must we not recognize the necessity of deciding all these matters? Otherwise let anyone mention one, the settlement of which is not compulsory."[3] Some critics believed that the indefiniteness of the laws of Solon was responsible for much unnecessary litigation.[4] Aristotle found no justification for this criticism, but it was familiar to conservative circles in the fifth century. When the revolutionists got control of the government, their measures seem to indicate that they believed it.

Twice in the last quarter of the fifth century the oligarchs had an opportunity of putting into effect current suggestions for the improvement of the administration of justice. Both in 411 and in 404 B.C. the oligarchs employed constitutional means to overthrow democracy, by appointing commissions of thirty to draft a constitution based on the πάτριος πολιτεία. According to Thucydides,[5] the commission of 411 B.C. merely recommended the abrogation of the γραφὴ

[1] *Ath. Pol.* i. 13; ii. 20, Dakyns' translation.   [3] *Ibid.*, iii. 6.

[2] *Ibid.*, iii. 8 ff.   [4] Aristotle *Ath. Pol.* ix. 2.

[5] viii. 67. Cf. Aristotle *op. cit.*, xxix. 4.

παρανόμων. By thus destroying the greatest safeguard of the constitution the revolutionists rendered the courts powerless. Any proposal could be brought before the assembly. The government was put into the hands of the Four Hundred, who took the place of the senate and filled the magistracies with their adherents.

Criminal cases came before the Four Hundred as senators, with power to inflict even the death penalty. Andocides[1] was arraigned before them, charged with supplying grain and oar spars to the army at Samos, which had espoused the cause of democracy. Technically the indictment was for trading with the enemy. At first the senate seemed disposed to put him to death, but in the end it sent him to prison. According to Thucydides,[2] an Argive implicated in the murder of Phrynichus was apprehended and "tortured by the Four Hundred." The torture was applied for the purpose of procuring a confession. No other case of judicial action on the part of the Four Hundred is recorded. But during the four months they were in power, they put a few to death, imprisoned some, and banished others.[3]

No trials for homicide are reported, but there is no evidence that the Areopagus did not continue to function as a homicide court. The intervention of the Four Hundred in the inquiry regarding the death of Phrynichus was to secure evidence.

There is no information regarding the disposal of civil cases. Popular courts could have been recruited from the ranks of the Five Thousand, but there is every reason to believe that this body existed only on paper until, upon the overthrow of the Four Hundred, the assembly voted to turn over the government to them. Whether the constitutions described by Aristotle belong to this transitional period after the overthrow of the oligarchy or to the oligarchic régime makes little difference, for they contain no definite provisions regarding the judiciary. The temporary or transitional constitution provided for a council of 400. "In all that concerned the laws, in the examination of official accounts, and in other

---

[1] ii. 13 ff.   [2] viii. 92.   [3] *Ibid.*, viii. 70. 2.

matters generally it might act according to its discretion."[1] This section of the constitution undoubtedly gave the council a free hand in organizing the judiciary. In the definitive constitution which never came into effect there is not a word about the judiciary.

To a modern reader this seems to be a strange omission. There are two possible explanations. Either Aristotle omitted the matter in his summary, or the commission, having provided the machinery of government, left these and other details of administration to be worked out by the new government. This is what Plato proposed in the *Republic*.

> Good citizens will themselves discover the necessary regulations regarding the business of the agora, about bargains and contracts with artisans, about insults and injuries, and the order in which cases are to be tried and how judges are to be appointed.[2]

The Commission of Thirty in 404 B.C. did not, like the committee appointed in 411 B.C., report back to the assembly, but deferred their report indefinitely. Meanwhile they filled the magistracies and the boulé with their adherents. Such laws as they required they reported to the boulé for ratification.[3] Xenophon[4] speaks of Critias, along with Charicles, as νομοθέτης. This simply means that these men, because of their prominence, were credited with initiating all the legislation of the Thirty. Owing to their longer tenure of power and their firmer grip on the situation, the Thirty made a deeper impression on their own and the succeeding generation than the Four Hundred. Consequently more data are available for reconstructing the history of their rule. Some of their statutes known as "new laws"[5] (καινοὶ νόμοι) deal with the administration of justice. They are laws such as might have been promulgated by the governments provided for in the constitutions summarized by Aristotle in connection with his account of the Four Hundred.[6] In two instances

---

[1] Aristotle, *op. cit.*, xxxi. Cf. Smith, *Athenian Political Commissions*, p. 66; Ferguson, "The Constitution of Theramenes," *Class. Phil.*, XXI, 72.

[2] 425, Jowett's translation.   [3] Aristotle *op. cit.*, xxxvii.

[4] *Memorabilia* I. 2. 31. Cf. Demosthenes xxiv. 90.

[5] Xenophon *Hellenica* ii. 3. 51.   [6] Aristotle *op. cit.*, xxx and xxxi.

the legislation reflects very closely current criticism of the democratic judicial system.

They revised such of the laws of Solon as were obscure and so were responsible for much unnecessary litigation. The avowed purpose of these changes was that "no opening might be left for the professional accuser." As an example, Aristotle[1] cites their "making the testator free once for all to leave his property as he pleased, and abolishing the existing limitations in case of old age, insanity, and undue female influence." He admits that the laws of Solon were not always drawn up "in simple and explicit terms" and cites the law regarding inheritances as an illustration. But he rejects the naïve view that Solon did this purposely "in order that the final decision might be in the hands of the people." His own view is that the obscurities were due to the "impossibility of attaining ideal perfection when framing a law in general terms."[2]

Another law forbidding instruction in λόγων τέχνη[3] was really a blow at the courts. Xenophon says it was aimed at Socrates by Critias, because of a long-standing personal grievance against him. But such an ordinance, if enforced for any considerable period, would not only destroy all higher education but would prevent young men from obtaining an adequate training for appearing before the courts. And courts could not function properly without competent accusers.

The Thirty rescinded also the laws of Ephialtes and Archestratus regarding the Areopagus. Ephialtes is said "to have stripped the Areopagus of all the acquired prerogatives from which it derived its guardianship of the constitution, and assigned some of them to the council of the Five Hundred and others to the assembly and the law courts." Some ten years later Pericles τῶν 'Αρεοπαγιτῶν ἔνια παρείλετο.[4]

There are no references to cases before the Areopagus and the other homicide courts. The theory has been advanced

---

[1] *Ibid.*, xxxv. 2.   [2] *Ibid.*, ix. 2. Cf. Aristotle *Politics* 1282*b*.

[3] Xenophon *Memorabilia* I. 2. 31. Cf. Grote, *op. cit.*, VIII, 257.

[4] Aristotle *Ath. Pol.* xxv and xxvii. Cf. *supra*, pp. 252 ff.

that the Thirty suspended the Areopagus as a homicide court. Some scholars have cited in support of this theory a provision[1] of the amnesty agreement of 403 B.C. as it appears in Aristotle. No critic of the Athenian system of administering justice in the fifth or fourth century had any fault to find with the Areopagus as a court. On the contrary, it was uniformly praised and approved.[2] The judicial functions of the Areopagus were so intimately associated with religion that even the most reckless revolutionists would have hesitated to interfere with them. The attitude of the Thirty toward the Areopagus is shown in the restoration of the ancient prerogatives of which it had been deprived by Ephialtes. Only the most unequivocal evidence would justify us in believing that the Thirty with one hand restored political powers and with the other took away semi-religious functions. There was nothing to gain by such proceedings.

The passage in Aristotle[3] as it appears in recent editions is as follows: τὰς δὲ δίκας τοῦ φόνου εἶναι κατὰ τὰ πάτρια, εἴ τίς τινα αὐτοχειρίᾳ ἔκτεινεν ἢ ἔτρωσεν, τῶν δὲ παρεληλυθότων μηδενὶ πρὸς μηδένα μνησικακεῖν ἐξεῖναι, κ.τ.λ. The provision is just what one would expect in an amnesty agreement or proclamation. Homicide involved pollution. Consequently amnesty could not be extended to murderers who for any reason had escaped justice under the Thirty. Previous amnesty proclamations had always excluded homicides.[4] The amnesty of 403 B.C. was no exception, as this provision shows.

[1] Aristotle op. cit., xxxix. 5. Lipsius, op. cit., p. 42, n. 129.

[2] Xenophon, Memorabilia iii. 5. 20, represents Socrates as asking the younger Pericles "whether he knew of any judges whose verdicts were more excellent, more in accordance with law, more respected or more just than those of the Areopagus."

[3] Op. cit., xxxix. 5. This is the reading of Kenyon, Oxford text, 1920, and of Oppermann, Teubner text, 1927. Sandys' αὐτόχειρ yields the same sense as αὐτοχειρίᾳ. Thalheim (Berliner Philologische Wochenschrift, 1909, p. 703) objected to the accepted reading on the ground that if the first sentence contained an exception to the general amnesty, ἄλλων was required in the next sentence, and reads ἐκτείσατο τρώσας (Teubner text, 1909). The meaning of the provision thus emended is that redress for wrongs suffered under the Thirty was not to be sought either by self-help or by judicial proceedings. This is not convincing. The point regarding ἄλλων is not of sufficient weight to justify the importation of such a novel term into the amnesty.

[4] Andocides 1. 78. Cf. supra, p. 104.

According to this section of the agreement, anyone was liable
to prosecution for homicide committed αὐτοχειρίᾳ during the
rule of the Thirty. The word αὐτοχειρίᾳ was intended to
distinguish ordinary homicides from the judicial murders of
the Tyrants, in which they tried to involve as many as possible as aiders, abettors, and accessories.[1] Thus the men who
arrested Leon of Salamis, and others like them, were amply
protected. Responsibility for judicial murders was put upon
the Thirty and the others specified in the agreement. These
either submitted to an audit or went into voluntary exile.
Eratosthenes,[2] against whom the chief charge was responsibility for the death of Polemarchus, one of the victims of the
Thirty, submitted to an audit. In any case, full provision
was made to protect citizens from pollution due to the presence of murderers in their midst. This provision of the amnesty agreement thus interpreted affords no support for the
theory, based upon a passage in Lysias, that the Thirty suspended the Areopagus as a homicide court.[3] A client of
Lysias in a speech of uncertain date says of the Areopagus:
ᾧ καὶ πάτριόν ἐστι καὶ ἐφ' ἡμῶν ἀποδέδοται τοῦ φόνου τὰς δίκας
δικάζειν. If one insists upon translating ἀποδέδοται "has been
restored," the natural interpretation of the passage is that,
during the reign of terror, sittings of the Areopagus as
a homicide court were suspended *de facto* but not *de jure*.
From motives of self-interest and self-preservation, citizens
doubtless refrained from prosecuting homicides. With the
return of democracy came freedom of action. Rights were
now again exercised that had merely been allowed to lapse.
The most recent editors, reading ἀποδέδοται, translate: "Le
tribunal d'Aréopage lui-même qui, comme au temps de nos
ancêtres, a aujourd'hui le privilège des affairs de meurtre."[4]

[1] Plato *Apology* 32c.

[2] Lysias xii. According to the amnesty agreement, these cases were to come before a special jury drawn from the three upper property classes. Wilamowitz, *Aristoteles und Athen*, II, 217 ff. Lipsius, *op. cit.*, pp. 293 ff.

[3] i. 30. Cf. Sandys, *Aristotle's Constitution of Athens*, p. 142.

[4] Gernet and Bizos. The word ἀποδίδωμι is regularly used in a legal and constitutional sense of the granting or assigning of powers, prerogatives, and functions to
political bodies or persons. An instructive example is found in Aristotle *Politics*

There is no reason for doubting the correctness of Demosthenes' statement: τοῦτο μόνον τὸ δικαστήριον οὐχὶ τύραννος, οὐκ ὀλιγαρχία, οὐ δημοκρατία τὰς φονικὰς δίκας ἀφελέσθαι τετόλμηκεν.[1]

By these various measures the Thirty τὸ κῦρος ὃ ἦν ἐν τοῖς δικασταῖς κατέλυσαν.[2] This purpose was effected partly by removing some of the causes of litigation by a simplification of the laws and partly by assigning to other bodies and officials some of the functions and prerogatives of the heliastic courts. What these functions were can only be conjectured. The most prolific sources of litigation under the democracy were the δοκιμασίαι, εὔθυναι, and γραφαὶ παρανόμων. Nothing could be easier than to transfer all questions relating to the magistrates and the laws to the Areopagus which in the πάτριος πολιτεία had τὴν τῆς πολιτείας φυλακήν.[3]

There are casual references to εἰσαγγελία, ἔνδειξις, φάσις, and ἀπογραφή in the time of the Thirty, but there is no indication of the tribunal before which they were brought except in one instance. During the rule of the Ten, who succeeded the Thirty for a short time, Patrocles, the king archon, met a personal enemy, Callimachus, carrying a sum of money. Patrocles at once stopped him and asserted that the money belonged to the state.[4] During the dispute Rhinon, one of the Ten, appeared. On hearing the details of the quarrel, he took the disputants before his colleagues, presumably for a preliminary examination. The case came before the boulé for trial in the form of a φάσις, and a verdict in favor of the treasury was rendered. Patrocles evidently acted as prose-

---

1275b: τούτων γὰρ ἢ πᾶσιν ἢ τισὶν ἀποδέδοται τὸ βουλεύεσθαι καὶ δικάζειν. Cf. also Plato Ion 537c: ἑκάστῃ τῶν τεχνῶν ἀποδέδοταί τι ὑπὸ τοῦ θεοῦ ἔργον. Other examples are cited by Frohberger, ad loc., and in the appendix to his notes on the passage a full citation of the literature is given. Lipsius (op. cit., pp. 41–42) accepts the older view that ἀποδέδοται means "redditum est," but regards the theory that the Thirty abolished the homicide courts as not proved. In the reign of terror "musste des Areopags Tätigkeit lahmgelegt werden." For other discussions of the passage cf. Philippi, Der Areopag und die Epheten, p. 266; Rauchenstein, Philologus, X, 604 ff.; Curtius, IV, 16.

The reading ἀποδίδοται, preferred by some editors, does not change the sense of the passage.

[1] xxiii. 66.   [3] Ibid., xxv. 2.

[2] Aristotle op. cit., xxxv.   [4] Isocrates xviii. 5 ff.

cutor. It was the boulé that tried the sycophants who were put to death in large numbers at the beginning of the rule of the Thirty. The form in which these cases were brought is not specified. It was probably εἰσαγγελία, which was a normal form of procedure against sycophants. The term ἔνδειξις was also used in certain cases.[1] Just before the overthrow of the democracy the well-organized oligarchs procured the arrest of Strombichides and other prominent democrats, charging them with plotting against the government. The senate brought them before the overawed assembly, which voted that they should be tried by a dicastery of 2,000. After the Thirty were installed in power, they had the men tried by the senate. Lysias quotes the verdict of the senate exonerating the informer Agoratus from complicity in the plot.[2] There is no reported case of ἀπογραφή, but the process is so similar to φάσις that it also would naturally come before the boulé.

The Thirty themselves exercised judicial functions. Like the democratic magistrates and boards, they conducted the preliminary investigation (ἀνάκρισις) and presided at the trial. One of the "new laws" gave the Thirty the right to put to death any Athenian whose name was not on the catalogue of the Three Thousand. Theramenes was first brought before the boulé; but when it became apparent that the senators could not be trusted to condemn him, Critias withdrew the case, struck Theramenes' name from the list of citizens, and had him condemned by the Thirty.[3] No doubt the Thirty were responsible for the majority of the judicial executions that made their rule a reign of terror.

No civil cases are reported. In fact, a client of Isocrates says that court sittings were suspended: πρὸς δὲ τούτοις, ἀκαταστάτως ἐχόντων τῶν ἐν τῇ πόλει καὶ δικῶν οὐκ οὐσῶν τῷ μὲν οὐδὲν πλέον ἦν ἐγκαλοῦντι, κ.τ.λ.[4] This statement does not

---

[1] Lofberg, Sycophancy in Athens, p. 92.   [2] Lysias xiii. 35 ff.

[3] Xenophon Hellenica ii. 3. 51.

[4] xxi. 7. Owing to doubts that have been cast upon the authenticity of this speech, too much weight should not be attached to the statement that there were no court sessions (Drerup, Isocratis opera omnia, I, cxix).

necessarily mean that there was no provision for the trial of private suits (δίκαι) during the whole period of the tyranny; it may simply mean that toward the end of their rule the city was distracted by civil war and the courts could not sit. This situation occasionally arose under democracy in war time. Demosthenes[1] cites a law of the restored democracy to the effect that ὁπόσα δ' ἐπὶ τῶν τριάκοντα ἐπράχθη ἢ δίκη ἐδικάσθη, ἢ ἰδίᾳ ἢ δημοσίᾳ, ἄκυρα εἶναι. It is of no consequence in this connection whether the law as quoted is genuine or not, for the text of the speech shows that it had to do with the annulment of "things done in the time of the Thirty."[2] That res judicatae are included is indicated by the words πότερον (φήσομεν) τὰ δικαστήρια, ἃ δημοκρατουμένης τῆς πόλεως ἐκ τῶν ὀμωμοκότων πληροῦται, ταῦτ' ἀδικήματα τοῖς ἐπὶ τῶν τριάκοντ' ἀδικεῖν; Demosthenes' words throw no light on the composition of the tribunals under the Thirty. By implication they are called δικαστήρια, but at the same time they are distinguished from the democratic δικαστήρια recruited ἐκ τῶν ὀμωμοκότων. Frohberger calls them rechtswidrig zusammengesetzte Dikasterien, meaning presumably "panels drawn from the Three Thousand." The measures taken to suppress sycophants suggest that the Thirty planned some sort of popular court in addition to the boulé, for sycophancy could flourish only where there were large courts. The Three Thousand, along with the knights, made up the court that tried and condemned the Eleusinians;[3] but they were not called upon to try Strombichides and other active democrats, though there was a psephism that they should be tried by a dicastery of 2,000.[4] The trial of the Eleusinians was a travesty of justice in which the Three Thousand were required to participate in order that they might be implicated in the crimes of the Tyrants.

Provision could have been made for the adjudication of civil suits by reverting to the pre-Solonian system under which the magistrates were empowered to give binding de-

---

[1] xxiv. 56 ff.

[2] Ibid., 57: ὁ γοῦν νόμος οὑτοσὶ ἀπεῖπε τὰ πραχθέντα ἐπ' ἐκείνων μὴ κύρι' εἶναι.

[3] Xenophon Hellenica ii. 4. 9–10.   [4] Lysias xiii. 35.

cisions. This measure could have been justified as a return to the πάτριος πολιτεία. But there is no reference to the exercise of judicial functions by magistrates.

An expression of Lysias[1] suggests that arbitration was widely used under the Thirty. A client of his was one of the Three Thousand. On this ground he was challenged on his δοκιμασία as being anti-democratic when selected for office under the restored democracy. He maintained that his conduct had been irreproachable, though there had been plenty of opportunity for wrongdoing if he had been so disposed. For example, he had arrested no one, put no one on the list of proscribed, οὐδὲ δίαιταν καταδιαιτησάμενος οὐδενός.

The implication of this statement is not only that arbitration was an important feature in litigation but that adherents of the Thirty were in the habit of interfering in the process in the interest of themselves or their friends. Public arbitration[2] had not yet been instituted, and it is not easy to see how there could have been any serious interference with private arbitral awards on the part of the Thirty and their friends. It is tempting to suggest that the Thirty, like Peisistratus, provided official arbitrators who, in case of failure to induce the parties to compromise, were empowered to render a binding decision. The Thirty rural Justices first appointed in 453–452 B.C. could easily have been used for this purpose.[3]

[1] xxv. 16.   [2] Cf. *infra*, pp. 346 ff.

[3] Cf. *infra*, p. 352, for speculations regarding the functions of the thirty rural Justices.

CHAPTER XIV
THE BOULÉ OF FIVE HUNDRED[1]

Cleisthenes instituted the boulé of Five Hundred, presumably before 508–507 B.C., the date of the struggle between Isagoras and Cleisthenes and the interference of the Spartan Cleomenes.[2] This boulé continued to be of great importance through the remainder of the sixth century and throughout the fifth century. It underwent some important changes at the time of the two oligarchic revolutions in 411 and 404 B.C. The boulé of 411 B.C., consisting of 400 members, was unique in some respects. It was the sovereign body of the state and was subject to no interference. Herein it differed from the boulé under the democracy, which acted in conjunction with the ecclesia and the heliastic courts and was not sovereign. After the downfall of the Four Hundred, the democratic boulé of Five Hundred was restored and its numbers remained unchanged under the tyranny of the Thirty. The boulé of Five Hundred under the Thirty, then, was much more like the democratic boulé than was the boulé of the Four Hundred, for it was compelled to yield to the authority of the Thirty, who were, of course, supreme. Cloché has well said that the Council of the Four Hundred is comparable to the Thirty themselves rather than to the council under the Thirty, for the Council of Four Hundred and the Thirty were each the final authority in their respective régimes.[3]

It has been argued that the boulé after the democratic

---

[1] In the interests of clarity and continuity it has been thought better to assemble the material on the boulé in one chapter rather than to treat it in connection with each period of reform.

[2] It has been assumed above, p. 189, that it was probably the new Cleisthenean boulé of Five Hundred rather than the Solonian Council of Four Hundred which rendered Cleisthenes such valuable assistance at this time. In fact, it is doubtful if the Solonian council could have been in existence at the time.

[3] Cloché, "Les pouvoirs de la boulè d'Athènes en 411 et en 404 avant J.-C.," *Rev. d. études grecques*, XXXVII, 412 ff. For the judicial activity of the boulé under the Four Hundred, cf. *supra*, p. 326.

restoration of 403 B.C. was decidedly inferior in power and prestige to the democratic boulé of the fifth century.[1] This argument is based on the supposition that the reforms of 403 B.C. in general seriously weakened the powers of the boulé. But Cloché has shown convincingly that in the fourth century the boulé had practically the same powers as in the fifth—in legislation, politics, general administration and direction of assemblies.[2] The boulé then appears to have been an important administrative and political body straight through its history and to have been always, with the brief exceptions of the revolutionary periods, thoroughly democratic.[3]

The boulé had, also, important judicial powers. Aristotle asserts that at one time the boulé had full authority to inflict penalties of imprisonment, death, and fines: ἡ δὲ βουλὴ πρότερον μὲν ἦν κυρία καὶ χρήμασιν ζημιῶσαι καὶ δῆσαι καὶ ἀποκτεῖναι.[4] He does not, however, specify the date when it had such authority. His statement may refer only to the extensive powers which the boulé exercised under the tyranny of the Thirty and for a time subsequently. It is well known that under the Thirty many capital sentences were imposed by the boulé[5] and that it did not immediately cease to inflict penalties on the restoration of the democracy in 403 B.C. Soon after the overthrow of the Thirty, Archinus, in an attempt to check the alarming disregard of the amnesty, haled an offender before the boulé and had him condemned to death ἄκριτος.[6] Here ἄκριτος does not mean "without trial,"

[1] Cf. Cavaignac, "Le conseil athénien des cinq-cents," *Rev. d. cours et conferences*, 1909, pp. 230 f., who says that in the fourth century the boulé was of slight importance. It is not clear how much power he assigns to it in the fifth century. Cf. Wilamowitz, *Aristoteles und Athen*, II, 195 ff., who attributes a very considerable rôle to the fifth century boulé.

[2] "L'importance des pouvoirs de la boulè athénienne aux Vᵉ et IVᵉ siècles avant J.-C.," *Rev. d. études grecques*, XXXIV (1921), 233 ff.

[3] Cf. Cloché, "Le conseil athénien des cinq-cents et les partis," *Rev. d. études grecques*, XXXV, 269 ff.

[4] *Ath. Pol.* xlv. 1.

[5] Cf. Lysias xiii., 38; Isocrates xvii. 42; Xen. *Hell.* ii. 3. 24 ff.; Andocides i. 115.

[6] Aristotle *Ath. Pol.* xl. 2.

but rather "without due process of law" and shows that the boulé was acting *ultra vires* in itself conducting the trial and inflicting such a penalty. The term ἄκριτος in the sense of "without *due* process of law" is regularly used in cases where the verdicts of the boulé were not confirmed by a heliastic court.[1] The boulé did not technically have the right to inflict capital penalties, although no act depriving them of such power had been passed since the overthrow of the Thirty. The Athenians assumed that on the restoration of the democracy the boulé, like other democratic bodies, would revert to the status which it had had before the revolution. But Archinus, in order to get quick action, did not hesitate to make use of the boulé just as the oligarchs had used it. Other cases of this sort may have occurred, as a story told by Aristotle, which can be treated as nothing more than an anecdote, seems to indicate. Lysimachus had been condemned to death by the boulé and had been handed over to the executioner. He was rescued by Eumelides, who maintained that no citizen should be condemned to death who had not had a hearing before a dicasterion.[2] The case was brought before a heliastic court, and Lysimachus was acquitted. Aristotle makes the case of Lysimachus the immediate occasion for what appears to be a re-enactment of the law restricting the punitive powers of the boulé. According to this law the power of the boulé was definitely curtailed. Henceforth, if the boulé determined that any case before them required a more severe penalty than they were empowered to inflict, they could propose a suitable penalty, but it was not effective until confirmed by a court under the presidency of the thesmothetae.[3]

There are difficulties in the way of determining the date at which the judicial powers of the boulé were first restricted.

[1] In Lysias xxii. 2 the words ὑμᾶς ("the jurors") οὐδὲν ἧττον ἡμῶν ("the boulé") γνώσεσθαι τὰ δίκαια show that the council, in proposing to put the grain-dealers to death ἄκριτοι, did not propose to act without a trial, but merely to execute them summarily without seeking confirmation of their verdict in a heliastic court.

[2] Aristotle *Ath. Pol.* xlv. 1.

[3] Aristotle *Ath. Pol.* xlv. 1.; Lipsius, *Das attische Recht*, p. 45, n. 137.

In the first place, there appears always to have been a marked tendency on the part of the boulé to disregard the constitutional restrictions placed upon the exercise of its judicial functions.[1] A client of Lysias, the prosecutor of the grain dealers in 387–386 B.C., in resisting the proposal to put the accused men to death ἄκριτος, expressed the fear that the boulé was acquiring the habit of acting *ultra vires*.[2] There are indications that this was not a mere rhetorical exaggeration.

In many cases, no doubt, the boulé felt that it could count on considerable popular support in overstepping the restrictions imposed by law. This was certainly true in the case of Archinus and, to a less extent, in the proposed illegal execution of the grain dealers. An adequate supply of grain at reasonable prices was a matter of vital importance to all Athenians. Any attempt to curtail the supply or to manipulate prices would at once arouse popular feeling to a point where summary action by the boulé would be readily condoned, if not demanded. And a body of 500 men, chosen by lot from the rank and file of the citizens, would respond very readily to the changing currents of public opinion. Moreover, the boulé ran little risk in overstepping the constitutional limits imposed on its powers. In general, the means for enforcing constitutional guarantees in Athens were far from adequate. The audit[3] at the end of the official year afforded opportunity for some form of redress, but the friends of the victim could scarcely hope to prosecute several hundred men for judicial murder on their audit as Lysias did

---

[1] The readiness of the boulé to act *ultra vires* may explain a passage in Aristophanes, which is sometimes cited to show that the boulé was possessed of the power to imprison a culprit in the stocks in 411 B.C., when the *Thesmophoriazousae* was presented. Mnesilochus had in disguise found his way into the celebration of the Thesmophoria. When discovered, he was put in the stocks by order of the senate, as the result of a report of his impious deed (l. 943). It is impossible to say what comic purpose could have been served by representing the boulé as acting *ultra vires;* but it seems hazardous, in face of considerations to the contrary, to rely on this passage as evidence that the boulé had at this time the right to imprison a culprit in the stocks, and that, too, without an official inquiry.

[2] Lysias xxiv. 2 ff. For the date, cf. Blass, *Die attische Beredsamkeit*, I, 472.

[3] Gilbert, *Greek Constitutional Antiquities*, p. 267.

in the case of Eratosthenes.[1] Perhaps the most that the members of the boulé had to fear was the loss of the crowns of honor distributed among them when they passed their audit. The plight of Lysimachus and the fate of the sycophant prosecuted by Archinus show that there was no device available to the victims similar to the Anglo-American writ of habeas corpus, or injunction, or stay of execution.

A further difficulty in determining the date of the original law restricting the powers of the boulé is presented by the probability that this law, like other ancient laws, was re-enacted, or amended, on occasion to meet the needs of a growing constitution.

Wilamowitz[2] puts the date of the law sometime in the fourth century; but his arguments have been so satisfactorily answered by Lipsius[3] that it is unnecessary to restate his position and to summarize the refutation of Lipsius. Lipsius himself put the date back into the fifth century without attempting to suggest a more exact time.

The restrictions on the power of the boulé were in force in Aristotle's day. Tracing back the history of the boulé, we find that in 387–386 B.C. they were also in force, when the boulé showed a disposition to disregard them in the case of the grain dealers.[4] The fact that the victim of Archinus was said to have been put to death ἄκριτος shows that in 403 B.C. there were limitations upon the punitive powers of the boulé. Naturally these limitations were in force before the rule of the Thirty. Confirmation of this is to be found in a very fragmentary inscription, quoted in full above.[5] The

---

[1] Lysias xii.   [2] *Op. cit.*, II, 195 ff.   [3] *Op. cit.*, p. 46, n. 142.

[4] Cloché, "Le conseil athénien des cinq cents et la peine de mort," *Rev. d. études grecques*, XXXIII, 36 f.

[5] *CIA* i. 57, quoted in full, *supra*, p. 201. Cloché (*op. cit.*, pp. 28 ff.) considers this inscription of the utmost importance in determining the date of the restriction of the boulé's powers. Gilbert (*op. cit.*, p. 277, n. 1) thinks it may refer to this event; and Lipsius (*op. cit.*, p. 45) considers it important in this connection, although he fails to date its first publication. Oehler (Pauly-Wissowa, article βουλή, pp. 1030 ff.) thinks that this inscription refers to the loss of the rights of the boulé. Wilamowitz (*op. cit.*, II, 195) considers the decree merely "die instruction des rates für den vorsitz in der volksversammlung" and believes that the boulé possessed the formal right to sentence to death all through the fifth century and into the fourth

fact that the first part of the inscription mentions the
boulé of Five Hundred and also 500 drachmas and that the
second part specifies certain matters which could be dealt
with only by a full assembly of the people has led some scholars to believe that this is a decree which deprived the boulé
of several of its important functions and transferred them to
the assembly. The extant form of the law, acccording to the
opinion of the editors, belongs to about the year 410 B.C.,
shortly after the overthrow of the Four Hundred. During
the brief rule of the Four Hundred the boulé of Five Hundred
ceased to exist. Thucydides[1] tells the story of how the Four
Hundred dismissed the boulé after giving them the remainder
of their pay for the year. After the downfall of the revolutionists a revision of the laws took place. It is doubtless to
this period that the publication of the decree belongs. But
some archaic touches—e.g., the use of θωάν for penalty—
have led scholars rather generally to believe that the inscription of 410 B.C. is a re-enactment of a much earlier decree,
to specify the rights and privileges of the boulé and assembly
on their re-establishment after the overthrow of the Four
Hundred. The mention of 500 drachmas in connection with
the boulé has led to the belief that this decree limited the
punitive power of the boulé to the imposition of a fine of 500
drachmas.

   To what period did the original publication of the decree
belong? That it belongs to a period earlier than 446 B.C. is
indicated by a decree relating to the settlement of Chalcis
after its reduction by the Athenians in 446 B.C. The first
part of the inscription deals with the form of the oath to be
sworn by the Athenian senators and dicasts regarding their
conduct toward the Chalcidians. The provisions of the oath
are as follows:

   κατὰ τάδε τὸν ὅρκον ὁμόσαι 'Αθηναίων τὴν βουλὴν καὶ τοὺς δικαστάς·
οὐκ ἐχσελῶ Χαλκιδέας ἐχ Χαλκίδος οὐδὲ τὴν πόλιν ἀνάστατον ποήσω,

---

century until some uncertain date between 386 and 352 B.C. Busolt-Swoboda
(*Staatskunde*, II, 1046) are at pains to refute his argument, putting the restriction
after 411 B.C. Busolt thinks that undoubtedly *CIA* i. 57 has reference to the revision
of the laws made at that time.

   [1] viii. 69.

οὐδὲ ἰδιώτην οὐδένα ἀτιμώσω οὐδὲ φυγῆι ζημιώσω οὐδὲ χσυλλήφσομαι οὐδὲ ἀποκτενῶ οὐδὲ χρήματα ἀφαιρήσομαι ἀκρίτου οὐδενὸς ἄνευ τοῦ δήμου τοῦ Ἀθηναίων, οὐδ' ἐπιφσηφιῶ κατὰ ἀπροσκλήτου οὔτε κατὰ τοῦ κοινοῦ οὔτε κατὰ ἰδιώτου οὐδὲ ἑνός, καὶ πρεσβείαν ἐλθοῦσαν προσάχσω πρὸς βουλὴν καὶ δῆμον δέκα ἡμερῶν, ὅταν πρυτανεύω, κατὰ τὸ δυνατόν. ταῦτα δὲ ἐμπεδώσω Χαλκιδεῦσιν πειθομένοις τῶι δήμωι τῶι Ἀθηναίων.[1]

For the present purpose the words of the second guaranty are of particular significance. "I shall not disfranchise any private citizen, or punish him with exile or arrest him or put him to death; nor shall I confiscate the property of anyone without trial, without the action of the Athenian people."[2] It cannot be maintained that the Athenian boulé, when the decree was passed, was still exercising the right to inflict penalties of death, confiscation, and disfranchisement, for it is absurd to suppose that they would continue to exercise powers at home which they bound themselves by oath to relinquish in the case of subject states. The decree must indicate, then, that the curtailment of the powers of the boulé had taken place prior to 446 B.C.[3] Another decree of approximately the same year likewise points to the conclusion that the limitation of the powers of the boulé had been effected before this time.[4] According to this decree, any encroachment on the Πελαργικόν was to be punished by a fine of 500 drachmas, the fine to be inflicted after an *eisangelia* had been brought before the boulé by the king archon. This is not conclusive evidence, but it seems more than a mere coincidence that the fine mentioned here is exactly the amount of the maximum fine to which later it is certain that the boulé was restricted.[5]

The time of the reforms of Ephialtes (462–461 B.C.) has been suggested as a date for the restriction of the powers of

---

[1] *CIA* i. 59; Hicks and Hill, *Greek Historical Inscriptions*, No. 40.

[2] For various interpretations of the different parts of this oath, cf. Robertson, *Administration of Justice in the Athenian Empire*, pp. 39 ff. Robertson shows that the second guaranty of the oath applies to the boulé.

[3] Robertson (*op. cit.*, p. 40) argues further that the fact that the boulé takes such an oath at this time shows that the diminution of the boulé's powers could not have occurred many years before this decree was passed, and therefore must have been part of some very recent reform. It is not unusual, however, for such a provision to appear even if the restriction had been imposed many years previously.

[4] Dittenberger, *Sylloge*[2], No. 20, line 59.   [5] Demosthenes xlvii. 43.

the boulé. But, as Cloché has pointed out,[1] it is unlikely that, at a time when an attempt was being made to divide the powers of the Areopagus among the ecclesia, boulé, and law courts,[2] another decree should be passed limiting the functions of the boulé.

Furthermore, a passage in Herodotus[3] shows that the boulé in 479 B.C. already referred important matters to the assembly:

τῶν δὲ βουλευτέων Λυκίδης εἶπε γνώμην ὡς οἱ ἐδόκεε ἄμεινον εἶναι δεξαμένους τὸν λόγον τόν σφι Μουριχίδης προσφέρει ἐξενεῖκαι ἐς τὸν δῆμον. . . . . ᾿Αθηναῖοι δὲ αὐτίκα δεινὸν ποιησάμενοι, οἵ τε ἐκ τῆς βουλῆς καὶ οἱ ἔξωθεν, ὡς ἐπύθοντο, περιστάντες Λυκίδην κατέλευσαν βάλλοντες.[4]

When Cleisthenes introduced his reforms, he organized a new boulé, in function presumably very like the old, but different in membership, owing to his reorganization of the tribes. He must have made the boulé virtually the sovereign body in the state. It was the only body that could have served his purpose. Important additional powers could scarcely be given to the Areopagus, inasmuch as it was looked upon as the oligarchic element in the state. The assembly, during the early part of Cleisthenes' activity, was not well organized. Moreover, the boulé had rendered Cleisthenes valuable assistance in the resistance to Isagoras and Cleomenes,[5] and it is natural that he should be interested in assigning to it extensive powers. It may well have been granted unrestricted authority in judicial matters. It is evident, however, that very soon after Cleisthenes started his reforms the whole tendency was to throw as much power as possible into the hands of the assembly, which naturally, with the growth of democracy, became of prime importance, as it gained political experience. Very shortly, in the year 502–501 B.C., an oath was imposed upon the boulé.[6] The fact that Aristotle, who gives few such details, singles out the oath for special mention as an important development points to some kind of reorganization in the boulé at this time. Aristotle says that the oath instituted in 502–501 B.C.

[1] *Rev. d. études grecques*, XXXIII, 31.   [3] ix. 5.

[2] Cf. *supra*, pp. 252 ff.   [4] Cf. Cloché, *op. cit.*, p. 32.

[5] *Ath. Pol.* xx. For the theory that it was his own boulé, cf. *supra*, p. 335.

[6] *Ath. Pol.* xxii.

was the one which was still in use in his own day.[1] There
are a few notices of the content of this oath, most of them
very general and concerned with promises to perform the
duties of a βουλευτής in the best interests of the city.[2] But
Demosthenes gives a further clause in which the members
of the boulé swore not to imprison a man who produced the
proper bail, except under certain conditions, e.g., treason,
conspiracy for overthrow of the government.[3] Demosthenes
is referring to the oath of his own day which Aristotle says
was instituted by Cleisthenes.[4] It is noteworthy that the
oath given by Demosthenes is of a negative character.
Doubtless the *bouleutae* were required to bind themselves
by oath to observe the restrictions imposed upon them by
law. Aristotle mentions the restrictions which were put upon
the boulé by the law which he represents as having been
enacted after the affair of Lysimachus:

ὁ δὲ δῆμος ἀφείλετο τῆς βουλῆς τὸ θανατοῦν καὶ δεῖν καὶ χρήμασιν
ζημιοῦν, καὶ νόμον ἔθετο, ἄν τινος ἀδικεῖν ἡ βουλὴ καταγνῷ ἢ ζημιώσῃ, τὰς
καταγνώσεις καὶ τὰς ἐπιζημιώσεις εἰσάγειν τοὺς θεσμοθέτας εἰς τὸ δικαστήριον, καὶ ὅ τι ἂν οἱ δικασταὶ ψηφίσωνται, τοῦτο κύριον εἶναι.[5]

It may plausibly be suggested that, in accordance with this
law, the boulé swore to observe the restrictions contained
therein, i.e., οὐ θανατώσω, οὐ δήσω, οὐ χρήμασιν ζημιώσω,
κ.τ.λ. Some confirmation of this is found in the speech
against Alcibiades attributed to Andocides, where the boulé
is represented as swearing μηδένα μήτε ἐξελᾶν μήτε δήσειν μήτε
ἀποκτενεῖν ἄκριτον.[6] Another oath of the same negative char-

---

[1] Aristotle's statement is doubtless substantially correct. There is record of
an addition to the oath after the amnesty of 403 B.C. (Andocides 1. 91): καὶ οὐ
δέξομαι ἔνδειξιν οὐδὲ ἀπαγωγὴν ἕνεκα τῶν πρότερον γεγενημένων, πλὴν τῶν φυγόντων.

[2] Xen. *Mem.* i. 1.18; Lysias xxxi. 1; Demosthenes lix. 4.

[3] Demosthenes xxiv. 144, 148.

[4] In attributing the institution of the oath to Solon, Demosthenes is following
the regular practice of the orators of attributing all old laws to Solon. Cf. *supra*, 152.

[5] Aristotle *Ath. Pol.* xlv. 1.

[6] Andocides iv. 3. This speech admittedly was not composed by Andocides.
Blass (*Die attische Beredsamkeit*, I, 338) has suggested that it may have been composed by a sophist of the fourth century. Cf. Jebb, *Attic Orators*, I, 132 ff. While the
writer is in error in attributing such an oath to the demos, he may still be correct in
the elements of the oath of the boulé.

344   THE ADMINISTRATION OF JUSTICE

acter is the oath in the decree of settlement with Chalcis, which has been quoted above. There the provisions are all negative and are somewhat the same as those just suggested. The Chalcidians are assured of the enjoyment of life, liberty, and property. It is possible that the Athenians were extending to the Chalcidians the same rights which they gave to their own citizens and that the oath given here is modeled on the bouleutic oath as instituted by Cleisthenes.[1]

Cloché argues convincingly that the original enactment of the decree which deprived the boulé of power and transferred it to the assembly (*CIA* i. 57) belongs to the period between the beginning of Cleisthenes' activity and the Persian wars, and may perhaps belong close to the year 502–501 B.C.[2] His arguments, both as to the date and as to the purpose of the decree, are undoubtedly correct. He did not, however, see the full significance of the oath which was introduced by Cleisthenes and its relation to the oath of the boulé in Aristotle's day. The evidence of this oath, taken in conjunction with the enactment at this time of the decree recorded in *CIA* i. 57 indicates that to the year 502–501 B.C. belongs the limitation of the punitive powers of the boulé. Very soon after its establishment, then, the boulé of Five Hundred was restricted in its right of inflicting penalties to the imposition of a fine of 500 drachmas and lost its right to inflict sentences of death, imprisonment (except in certain specified cases),[3] and confiscation of property.

There were, then, three periods at which laws were enacted which restricted the punitive powers of the boulé: (1) soon after the beginning of Cleisthenes' reforms, when Cleisthenes was interested in transferring as much power as possible to the assembly, the importance of which was increasing in proportion to the growth of democracy; (2) after the down-

[1] In the oath of the Chalcis decree there occurs the qualification ἄνευ τοῦ δήμου τοῦ Ἀθηναίων, which is doubtless explanatory of ἀκρίτου.

[2] Cloché, *Rev. d. études grecques*, XXXIII, 28 ff.

[3] Cf. Andocides i. 93: ὁ γὰρ νόμος οὕτως εἶχε κυρίαν εἶναι τὴν βουλήν, ὃς ἂν πριάμενος τέλος μὴ καταβάλῃ, δεῖν εἰς τὸ ξύλον. Cf. Aristotle *Ath. Pol.* xlviii. 1. Special authority might at any time be conferred upon the boulé making it αὐτοκράτωρ for certain purposes. Cf. Andocides i. 15.

fall of the Four Hundred in 410 B.C., for the purpose of defining the rights of the resuscitated boulé;[1] and (3) sometime between the restoration of democracy after the downfall of the Thirty and the Peace of Antalcidas,[2] in order to restrain the boulé by law from action such as it had taken in the case of Archinus.

[1] Cloché, *op. cit.*, pp. 16 ff., discusses very interestingly several cases in which the boulé, after the downfall of the Four Hundred, did not render sentences of death and in which they would almost certainly have done so if they had been so empowered. The cases are those of Antiphon (*X Oratorum vitae* 833 E); the generals after Arginusae (Xen. *Hell.* i. 7. 3 ff.); and Cleophon (Lysias xxx. 10 ff. and xiii. 8 ff.). Apparently the boulé obeyed pretty consistently the decree set forth in *CIA* i. 57.

[2] Cloché, *op. cit.*, pp. 39 ff., thinks that the boulé really retained for some time the powers which it assumed under the Thirty, but had definitely been deprived of them by the time of the Peace of Antalcides (387 B.C.). This latter argument he substantiates by the speech of Lysias against the corn-dealers.

CHAPTER XV

THE JUDICIAL SYSTEM IN THE FOURTH CENTURY

One of the most important changes made in the Athenian judicial system upon the restoration of democracy in 403 B.C. was the substitution of the Forty for the thirty circuit judges. It is to be inferred from Aristotle that they did not, like the Thirty, go on circuit, but held court in Athens.[1] They were elected by lot, four from each tribe. Most of the civil cases involving citizens were included in their jurisdiction.[2] The case was entered with the four representatives of the defendant's tribe. If the amount at issue was less than 10 drachmas, they, like the *apodektae*, had the right to render a final judgment. Otherwise the case was referred to one of the public arbitrators, who were closely associated with the Forty.

All men in their sixtieth year, unless they held another office or were abroad, had to serve as arbitrators, on pain of being deprived of their civil rights.[3] There was undoubtedly an official list of arbitrators, as such, made out for each year. The regular military roster for the forty-second year of service would not suffice. Those who were legally exempt from service as arbitrators had to be stricken off. Like the senate, the Forty, and other bodies and boards, they were divided into ten groups to represent the tribes; but in assigning arbitrators to different tribal groups, no attention was paid to their tribal affiliations.[4] Consequently representatives from several different tribes might be included in

---

[1] Aristotle *Ath. Pol.* liii. 1. Cf. Lipsius, *op. cit.*, p. 82.

[2] Bonner, "The Jurisdiction of Athenian Arbitrators," *Class. Phil.*, II, 407 ff.

[3] Aristotle, *op. cit.*, liii. 4, 5.

[4] In an arbitration between Demosthenes of the tribe Pandionis and Meidias of the tribe Erechtheis, Straton of the tribe Aeantis was the arbitrator. Demosthenes xxi. 68, 83. Cf. Gilbert, *Greek Constitutional Antiquities*, p. 389.

the same group. The reason for this departure from normal practice is obvious. In any given group of men there would inevitably be an unequal distribution among the tribes. That this was true of the arbitrators appears from a list of one hundred and three preserved in an inscription in which the tribal representatives range from three to sixteen.[1] The natural thing to do under these circumstances was to distribute the arbitrators as evenly as possible in ten sections without regard to their tribes.

The intimate relationship existing between the Forty and the arbitrators at once suggests that the Forty made up the original list of arbitrators and divided them into sections. Aristotle's words bear out the suggestion with regard to the original list: τὸν δὲ τελευταῖον τῶν ἐπωνύμων λαβόντες οἱ τετταράκοντα διανέμουσιν αὐτοῖς τὰς διαίτας καὶ ἐπικληροῦσιν ἃς ἕκαστος διαιτήσει. Lipsius[2] finds in διανέμουσιν reference to the section divisions. But there is no need to take, as he does, the words διανέμουσιν and ἐπικληροῦσιν as referring to different actions. The term διανέμουσιν indicates the act and ἐπικληροῦσιν the manner in which it was done. Kenyon's translation brings this out: "Then the Forty take the last of the Eponymi of the years of service and assign the arbitrations to the persons belonging to that year, casting lots to determine which arbitrations each shall undertake."

The arbitrators sat as a court under a chairman, ὁ πρυτανεύων, to try individual arbitrators for malfeasance in office.[3] The penalty was loss of civil rights. The sentence, according to Aristotle, was subject to appeal.[4] But as Demosthenes tells the story of the conviction of Straton, a pub-

---

[1] *CIA* ii. 943. [2] *Op. cit.*, p. 227, n. 29.

[3] Aristotle *op. cit.*, liii. 6. Cf. Demosthenes xxi. 86, for the designation of the chairman as ὁ πρυτανεύων.

[4] Goodell, "Aristotle on the Public Arbitrators," *Amer. Jour. of Philol.*, XII, 322, on the basis of Demosthenes xxi. 87, supposed that the verdict of the arbitrators was final. He accounted for the disagreement between Demosthenes and Aristotle by supposing a change in the law was made between 349, when *Demosthenes* v. *Meidias* (cf. Goodwin's edition of the *Meidias*, p. 134) was tried, and 328–325, the date of the *Politeia* of Aristotle. But this view is based on a misinterpretation of καθάπαξ ἄτιμος γέγονεν. Cf. Goodwin, *ad loc.*

lic arbitrator, it might seem at first sight that the verdict of arbitrators was final. But Demosthenes, in his anxiety to find fault with Meidias and to suggest that the board of arbitrators was acting illegally in overlooking Meidias' failure to register a witness to the summons to Straton, passes over in silence the fact that an appeal was duly taken and denied.

The substitution of the Forty for the thirty circuit judges was one of the early acts of the restored democracy. The close relationship of the arbitrators to the Forty indicates that the two bodies were organized about the same time, if not by the same law. In the early nineteenth century the prevailing opinion seems to have been that the arbitrators were instituted in the archonship of Eucleides.[1] No indisputable reference to public arbitration occurs before Eucleides. A technical legal phrase—μὴ οὔσας διώκειν—always used of appeals from an arbitrator's award rendered in default, occurs in a speech of Lysias. The date was almost certainly 401 B.C.[2] A law dealing with arbitration is mentioned in another speech of Lysias. It is a mere fragment quoted by Dionysius to illustrate a point of style. It is impossible to date it; but in any event it is later than 403 B.C., when Lysias at the audit of Eratosthenes delivered his first forensic speech.[3] His experience on this occasion seems to have turned his attention to the writing of speeches as a means of recouping his fortunes. The fragment[4] in question deals with a suit instituted by Archebiades to recover a sum of money (περὶ τοῦ χρέως). The defendant, who was young and inexperienced, claimed that he had made every effort to

---

[1] Meier, *Die Privatschiedsrichter und die öffentlichen Diaeteten Athens* (1846), pp. 28–29; Cf. Schoemann, *Die Verfassungsgeschichte Athens nach Grotes "History of Greece"* (1854), p. 44; Pischinger, *De arbitris Atheniensium publicis* (1895), p. 49.

[2] Lysias xxxii. 2. Jebb (*op. cit.*, I, 294) says "probably in 400 B.C." Blass (*op. cit.*, I, 647), "wahrscheinlich 401." Thalheim (Teubner text of Lysias) agrees with Blass.

[3] The earliest of Lysias' extant speeches is *Lysias v. Eratosthenes*, delivered in 403 B.C. (Jebb, *op. cit.*, I, 150). The only speech in the Lysias collection earlier than the rule of the Thirty is xx, which belongs to 410 or 409. It is not generally regarded as genuine. Cf. Blass, *op. cit.*, I, 503.

[4] Lysias *Frag.* xix (Teubner Edition).

effect an amicable settlement but that Archebiades constantly refused either to lay the matter before mutual friends
or δίαιταν ἐπιτρέψαι ἕως ὑμεῖς τὸν νόμον τὸν περὶ τῶν διαιτητῶν ἔθεσθε. The phrase δίαιταν ἐπιτρέψαι shows that the
defendant had in mind private or optional arbitration in
which the parties took the initiative (ἐπέτρεψαν τῷ δεῖνι)
and not public arbitration in which the Forty took the initiative (παρεδίδοσαν τοῖς διαιτηταῖς). It is evident that when the
matter first came up the only means of settlement out of
court was a conference of mutual friends or some kind of
optional arbitration, private or public. But before the case
came to trial, a law was passed making arbitration obligatory, i.e., the kind of public arbitration described by Aristotle.[1] This is the kind of arbitration to which the case was
finally submitted, as is shown by the fact that it was brought
before a heliastic court on appeal. Schoemann[2] in 1854 argued that the law here mentioned did not establish public
arbitration, but rather extended its scope by increasing the
amount in dispute that could be referred to arbitration. The
assumption underlying Schoemann's theory is that cases involving smaller amounts were the most suitable for arbitration. But there is no indication that the Athenians ever held
this view. In fact, in the system described by Aristotle it is
only the smaller cases that were exempted from arbitration.
Claims involving 10 drachmas or less were settled by the
Forty themselves. The reason for this exemption was no
doubt to prevent these two-penny–half-penny cases from
finding their way into a heliastic court by way of appeal.
No possible consideration could exclude a case from arbitration by reason of the large amount of money involved. On
the contrary, the larger the amount, the more desirable it
would seem to effect a settlement out of court. From the
earliest times the Greeks were constantly submitting their
differences to arbitration without regard to the amount of
money involved. The willingness to submit a case to arbitration is a commonplace in the orators. Phormio and his
litigious stepson, Apollodorus, arbitrated claims aggregating

---

[1] *Ath. Pol.* liii.   [2] *Op. cit.*, pp. 44 ff.

3,000 drachmas.[1] And Demosthenes was willing to arbitrate his claims against his guardian Aphobus. The case went to trial, and the jury awarded Demosthenes[2] 10 talents. In public arbitration neither party ran any risk of prejudicing his rights. If the settlement proposed by the arbitrator was agreeable to both parties, well and good. If not, it could be appealed. The case at once resumed its original status. There seems to have been no prejudice against such appeals.[3]

There is even less justification for the theory that the law in question was amended so as to include the kind of action entered by Archebiades. He sought to recover a sum of money which he claimed was owed him by the deceased father of the defendant. No cases are more suited to arbitration than those concerning debts and damages. The claim of Archebiades is just the sort of case that one would expect to find included in the simplest measure of arbitration. There is good reason for supposing that the law mentioned in the Archebiades case was the law that established the type of public arbitration described by Aristotle. The speech cannot be dated, but it is not earlier than the archonship of Eucleides. The Diogeiton case[4] which has a definite reference to public arbitration is not later than 400 B.C. Consequently, the institution of public arbitration falls between 403 and 400, as Meier and most of his contemporaries believed.[5]

Schoemann was the first to question seriously Meier's view. His views in favor of a pre-Eucleidean date for the institution of public arbitration commended themselves to other scholars, chiefly because of the mention of διαίτας by Andocides.[6] He cites a law enacted by the restored democracy as follows: τὰς δὲ δίκας καὶ τὰς διαίτας κυρίας εἶναι ὁπόσαι ἐν δημοκρατουμένῃ τῇ πόλει ἐγένοντο. The current view is that this law reaffirmed both public and private awards.

---

[1] Demosthenes xxxvi. 14–16.

[2] xxvii. 1. *X Oratorum vitae*, 844 D.

[3] For casual references to arbitrations that were appealed, cf. Demosthenes xxxix. 37 and xlix. 19. Cf. lvii. 6 for a defence of an appeal.

[4] Lysias xxxii. 2.   [5] Cf. Schoemann, *op. cit.*, p. 44.   [6] i. 87.

Schoemann himself did not use or even mention the law, though he must have been familiar with it. Neither does Meier refer to it. The reason for their failure to mention it is not far to seek.[1] They realized that, since διαίτας might very well refer only to private arbitration, the passage is inconclusive and cannot properly be cited in this connection.

But in spite of the lack of any definite evidence for the existence of public arbitration in the fifth century, there is a persistent notion that the government must have taken some steps to facilitate recourse to arbitration as a means of relieving the congestion of the courts. Schoemann accounts for the absence of any reference to public arbitration by pointing out that the extant fifth-century law cases were not subject to arbitration.[2] Any measure of public arbitration introduced in the age of Pericles would naturally be associated with the thirty rural justices. Nothing definite is known about the jurisdiction and procedure of this board.[3] Presumably, they handled the bulk of the civil cases. These are the cases that were best suited for arbitration. Aristotle[4] definitely associates the thirty rural justices with the Peisistratean justices. "In the archonship of Lysicrates, the thirty 'local justices,' as they were called, were re-established" (πάλιν κατέστησαν). The members of both boards went on circuit. In recording the institution of the Forty in a later

[1] Schoemann would scarcely have ventured to say (op. cit., p. 47) "Der Diaeteten geschiet bei den älteren Rednern keine Erwähnung vor Lysias" without scanning the speeches of Andocides closely enough to note the mention of διαίτας in i. 87.

[2] Op. cit., p. 47. This is quite true, but it is not so easy to account for Aristophanes' failure to refer to arbitration among his constant references to litigation and courts. Socrates is represented as saying in the Apology, 32 B, that he never held any office but that of senator. If this was a serious statement of fact rather than a device to refer to his stand in face of popular opposition, it might serve to show that Socrates had never acted as a διαιτητής, though he had passed his sixtieth year.

[3] De Sanctis (op. cit., pp. 135 f.) has made an attempt to reconstruct the range of cases that came before the Thirty. They were appointed to relieve the thesmothetae of the most of their civil cases. Apart from the monthly suits and inheritance and other family matters that belonged to the jurisdiction of the archon, the Thirty, like their successors, the Forty, had jurisdiction over the bulk of the civil cases. Cf. Keil, Anonymus Argentinensis, pp. 234 ff.; Gilbert, op. cit., p. 157.

[4] Ath. Pol. xxvi. 3; liii. 1.

chapter, Aristotle says: "Formerly they were thirty in number, and they went on circuit in the demes to hear cases" (περιόντες ἐδίκαζον). Under the rule of Peisistratus there was no difficulty in empowering these itinerant judges to render a binding verdict on the merits of the case, if they failed to persuade the disputants to agree to an equitable settlement. But in fifth-century Athens democracy would scarcely have tolerated the return to final verdicts rendered by magistrates beyond the limit of 10 drachmas. Nor is it to be supposed that the words περιόντες ἐδίκαζον mean that the Thirty, sitting as a body in different centers, held court and rendered judgments as authoritative as those of the individual heliastic courts. Such a system would soon have destroyed the supremacy of the dicasts.

On the basis of inherent probabilities and considerations drawn from the proceedings of the Peisistratean justices and those of the Forty, the following reconstruction of the procedure of the Thirty is offered as a possible explanation of the situation in the Archebiades case. Like their predecessors, they exercised arbitral functions; and like their successors, they prepared cases for hearing and presided at the trial by a heliastic court. Their arbitral functions explain their going on circuit. We may suppose that the individual members of the board appeared at regular intervals in the centers included in their circuits.

When a case was entered, either the plaintiff or the defendant could challenge his opponent to submit the matter to the official (one of the thirty rural justices) to arbitrate just as they might have submitted it to a private arbitrator agreed upon. The advantage lay in the fact that the possibility of arbitration was brought to the attention of every litigant. A suitable arbitrator was provided. All trouble of selecting a man agreeable to both parties was avoided. If a challenge to arbitrate was accepted, the official heard the arguments and the evidence and endeavored to secure a settlement acceptable to both parties. If he succeeded, his award was recorded as final. If the challenge was not accepted, the official held an ἀνάκρισις and sent the case up for trial.

When Archebiades brought suit, the defendant challenged him to submit the case to the official for arbitration (ἐπιτρέψαι δίαιταν). This challenge was refused, but before the case came up for trial the νόμος περὶ τῶν διαιτητῶν was passed and the case was referred to a public arbitrator by the Forty, according to the terms of the new law. The award was appealed, and the case came before a heliastic court. The speech was written by Lysias for the defendant.

If νόμος περὶ τῶν διαιτητῶν is the correct title of the statute cited in the Archebiades case, it is evident that the Forty and the arbitrators were not instituted by the same law. The case must have come up in the interval between the enactment of the two laws.

The public arbitrators, according to Aristotle, sealed the written evidence of the witnesses and sent it to the Forty in case of an appeal. Demosthenes[1] cites a law requiring all testimonial evidence to be presented in court in the form of affidavits. The witnesses were required, except in certain specified cases, to be present in court to acknowledge their testimony. There was no provision for cross-examination at any stage of the proceedings. There is abundant evidence that this law was not in force in the fifth century or the early years of the fourth. Neither Andocides, Isocrates, nor Lysias ever called upon the clerk to read an affidavit, though they had other documents read in court by the clerk: μάρτυρας ὑμῖν παρέξομαι, ἀναγνωσθήσονται δὲ ὑμῖν καὶ αὐταὶ αἱ ἀπογραφαί. On occasion they use language that shows beyond doubt that their witnesses were giving oral testimony. "You have heard the witnesses."[2] "Look at the jurors and testify whether I speak the truth."[3] "Call the witnesses. They will talk to you as long as you wish."[4] "Those who were

[1] xlv. 44: ὁ νόμος μαρτυρεῖν ἐν γραμματείῳ κελεύει ἵνα μήτ' ἀφελεῖν ἐξῇ μήτε προσθεῖναι τοῖς γεγραμμένοις μηδέν.

[2] Lysias xxxii. 28:
καί μοι ἀνάβητε τούτων μάρτυρες.
<ΜΑΡΤΥΡΕΣ>
τῶν μὲν μαρτύρων ἀκηκόατε.

[3] Andocides i. 18: βλέπετε εἰς τούτους (sc. δικαστάς), καὶ μαρτυρεῖτε εἰ ἀληθῆ λέγω.

[4] Ibid., p. 69: αὐτοὺς κάλει . . . . μέχρι τούτου ἀναβήσονται καὶ λέξουσιν ὑμῖν, ἕως ἂν ἀκροᾶσθαι βούλησθε.

present at the transactions and know them better than I will testify and give you an account."[1] In these instances the witnesses evidently told their stories quite informally in their own way. But evidence might also be elicited by questions. Andocides in his speech on the Mysteries[2] includes a record of one of these interrogations:

> Were you a commissioner, Diognetus, when Pythonicus impeached Alcibiades in the assembly?
> I was.
> Do you know that Andromachus gave information regarding what took place in the house of Polytion?
> I do.
> Are these the names of the men against whom he informed?
> They are.

No doubt this was the regular practice, particularly when a litigant was using a speech prepared for him by a professional speech-writer. Only in this way could an inexperienced speaker have kept any control of the situation. It is also possible that individual jurors may have asked occasional questions.

In the burlesque trial of the dog in the *Wasps* of Aristophanes[3] the witnesses are called up and questioned. There is no reason to suspect that Aristophanes is not conforming to the current practice.

> Good sir, listen to the witnesses. Cheese grater, take the stand and speak out. You were in charge of the commissariat? Now answer plainly. Did you not grate what you got for the soldiers? (*The witness nods assent.*)

One cannot but wonder why the Athenians required evidence to be reduced to writing. Affidavits are much inferior to oral evidence elicited by means of question and answer even without cross-examination. Witnesses can be induced to subscribe to an affidavit containing statements which they would be unwilling to make in answer to questions or to stick to in the face of a severe cross-examination. But affidavits take less time than rambling statements or interrogations. Time-saving meant considerable saving of money

---

[1] Lysias xvii. 2: οἱ μᾶλλόν τε ἐμοῦ εἰδότες καὶ παραγεγενημένοι οἷς ἐκεῖνος ἔπραττε διηγήσονται ὑμῖν καὶ μαρτυρήσονται.

[2] i. 14.   [3] 962 ff.

in jury fees. This aspect of the matter would have appealed to Athens in the fourth century. The plaintiff in *Apollodorus* v. *Stephanus*, a perjury case, suggests a reason for the requirement; he says that the law required written evidence so that testimony could not be changed.[1] This cannot be taken to mean that the sole purpose of the provision was to facilitate convictions for perjury, for it was never applied to the homicide courts,[2] where the consequences of perjury were likely to be more serious, as a client of Antiphon intimates.[3] In modern practice, evidence is reduced to writing primarily for purposes of appeal. In Athens appeals from an arbitrator's award were based almost entirely upon affidavits presented at the arbitration. Only in exceptional cases was new evidence permitted.[4] Accordingly it might be supposed that the original purpose of the law was to insure that appeals should be based substantially upon the evidence presented at the original trial. But, it appears, evidence was presented orally for years after the introduction of arbitration.[5] None of these reasons furnishes an adequate motive for so great a change.

Leisi[6] has suggested that the innovation was in the first place due to individual litigants who found it to their advantage to have an exact record of what a witness was willing to testify. He advances this theory without attempting to show just why the practice might have appealed to litigants. A good reason for having evidence reduced to writing may be found in the needs of the professional speech-writer. As a rule his services were not confined to writing a suitable speech.[7] He had to familiarize himself with the evidence available to support his client's claim. Quite apart from the convenience to the speech-writer of having a memorandum

[1] Demosthenes xlv. 44, quoted in note 1, p. 353.

[2] Evidence was always presented orally in the homicide courts. Bonner, "Evidence in the Areopagus," *Class. Phil.*, VII, 450.

[3] Antiphon v. 95.   [4] Bonner, *Evidence in Athenian Courts*, p. 55.

[5] Arbitration was introduced not earlier than 403 B.C., and written evidence in 378–377. Cf. *infra*, p. 362.

[6] *Der Zeuge im attischen Recht*, p. 87.

[7] Bonner, *Lawyers and Litigants in Ancient Athens*, pp. 213 ff.

of the available testimony to use in composing the speech, it must soon have become apparent that the inexperienced litigant found difficulty in eliciting the pertinent facts from his witnesses by interrogation, or in controlling them if they were allowed to speak freely. Even to the trained modern lawyer, the examination of witnesses still presents grave difficulties. Here is an adequate motive for introducing written depositions. It would be an easy matter for the speech-writer to furnish his client with a transcript of the testimony which he had elicited from the witness, for the clerk to read along with the documentary evidence. As the witness would be present to acknowledge the evidence, there could be no serious objection to the practice.

There is no need to suppose that a law was needed to permit a man to ask the clerk to read a transcript of what a witness stood ready to acknowledge as his evidence. It was not a serious innovation. But once the practice was established, its obvious advantages would immediately appeal to the public.[1] It facilitated proof of perjury by relieving the plaintiff of the necessity of proving what the witness said. His written deposition was ready to hand. He had only to prove that it was false. In arbitration it insured that the appeal from an arbitrator's award should be based substantially upon the same evidence. And incidentally, it shortened court proceedings. This seems a much simpler way of explaining the introduction of written evidence than to suppose that some reformer interested in court procedure worked it out independently of current practice and had it enacted into law. Ancient law-making, particularly in the matter of procedure, is more often than we suspect a record or modification of existing practice rather than an innovation. It is plain from Demosthenes' statement that the law required evidence to be in writing. Legislation would be necessary to enforce the practice, if not to permit it. Whether it was first required in arbitration and then extended to other cases

---

[1] Its disadvantages would not be so marked under the Athenian system, in which evidence played a comparatively subordinate rôle. Cf. Bonner, *Evidence in Athenian Courts*, pp. 30 ff.

is not known. The practice was never extended to homicide cases.

Opinions vary regarding the date of the law requiring evidence to be reduced to writing. This is to be expected. The only available data for reaching a conclusion are the formulas used in introducing testimony in court. These must be used with great care because they are often suited to either oral or written testimony. Witnesses were always required to be present in court whether the evidence was presented orally or in writing. The presence of the witnesses furnished a simple and satisfactory means of guaranteeing the authenticity of the depositions read. Incidentally, the jurors were afforded an opportunity to form an impression of the trustworthiness of the witnesses. It seems likely that the witnesses, whether giving oral testimony or acknowledging their depositions, were expected to face the jurors.[1] Under these circumstances it is obvious that a promise to produce witnesses (μάρτυρας παρέξομαι) or a call for them to come forward (ἀνάβηθι) in itself proves nothing. The only absolutely sure indication of the use of oral testimony is the occurrence of a word that shows that the witness talked, e.g., λέγω, διηγέομαι, and under some circumstances μαρτυρέω. On the other hand, there is no absolute certainty of written evidence unless ἀναγιγνώσκω or μαρτυρία occurs. Between these two extremes there is considerable latitude for differences of opinion regarding the import of a given formula.

Demosthenes cites the law requiring written depositions in a speech delivered about 350 B.C.,[2] but his own use of written testimony in his litigation against his guardians shows that the law was in force at least in 364.[3] There is nowhere any hint or suggestion of written depositions in any of the speeches of Lysias. None of them is dated later than 380. But the latest reliable reference to oral evidence is the formula, "Come forward and give your evidence" (ἀνάβηθι

[1] Andocides i. 18, quoted in note 3, *supra*, p. 353.

[2] Paley and Sandys, *Select Private Orations of Demosthenes*, II, xxix (2d. ed.).

[3] Demosthenes xxvii. For the date, cf. Schaefer, *Demosthenes und seine Zeit*, I. 288 (2d. ed.).

καὶ μαρτύρησον), which occurs in a speech of Lysias delivered
between 392 and 389.[1] The earliest mention of written testimony, on the other hand, occurs in a speech of Isaeus, καὶ
μοι ἀνάγνωθι τὴν μαρτυρίαν,[2] delivered between 392 and 387.[3]
Leisi concludes, "Also um 390 herum müszte die Aenderung
eingetreten sein." "Aenderung" refers to the beginning
of the voluntary use of written evidence. He rightly believes that the practice of using written depositions instead
of oral testimony was initiated by litigants for their own convenience. "Allmählich mochte es sich für die Parteien als
praktisch erweisen, den Wortlaut der Zeugnisse schriftlich
zu fixieren, um das Plädoyer ganz genau auf sie einrichten
zu können und vor nachteiligen Äusserungen besser ge-
schützt zu sein." Regarding the date of the law which made
the practice compulsory, he does not commit himself. "Ob
zuerst noch beide Modalitäten neben einander bestanden,
oder ob das schriftliche Verfahren sogleich gesetzlich vor-
geschrieben wurde, ist nicht zu entscheiden."[4]

The year 390 B.C. at all events is too early a date for the
law. It was not in force during the professional career of
Lysias, which came to an end about 380. In his latest datable speech, x, which Blass[5] puts in 384–383, there is no unmistakable reference to written evidence. The same is true
of the other two speeches that were delivered after 390.[6] Nor
is there any sure indication of written depositions in the first
and tenth orations of Isaeus, which are amongst his first efforts. It may be objected that the formulas introducing
testimony in these five speeches are neutral, because they

---

[1] Lysias xvi. 8.   [2] Isaeus v. 3.

[3] Thalheim, in his introduction to his edition of Isaeus (Teubner), p. xxxii,
puts it between 393 and 387 B.C.; Blass, *Attische Beredsamkeit*, II, 544, prefers 389.
Benseler, *De hiatu in oratoribus Atticis*, pp. 185 ff., argued that the battle referred
to in Sections 6 and 42 was that of Cnidus in 394 B.C. and that the speech was delivered in 372. Jebb (*op. cit.*, II, 351) is inclined to the same view but admits that
390 is the more probable date. Wyse (*The Speeches of Isaeus*, p. 405) prefers the
earlier date.

[4] Leisi, *Der Zeuge im attischen Recht*, p. 87.   [5] *Op. cit.*, I, 602.

[6] xix in 387 B.C.; xxii in 387–386 B.C. Cf. Blass, *op. cit.*, pp. 533, 472. In
xxii. 9 the Teubner and Oxford editors print MAPTYPIA. But the text is uncertain. Van Herwerden prints MAPTYΣ.

might conceivably be used of either type of evidence. But in this connection a comparison with the practice of Demosthenes and his contemporaries in presenting evidence is instructive. In every one of the forensic speeches of this period in which testimonial evidence was introduced, there are unmistakable references to written depositions. The absence of similar references in the five orations of Lysias and Isaeus can scarcely be accidental. The inference that written depositions were not required by law in the period to which these speeches belong seems justified. Two of them cannot be dated with any degree of certainty, but they are all later than 390 B.C. Consequently, 390 cannot be accepted as the date of the law requiring written evidence.

In seeking to determine more closely the date of the law, the most serious difficulty is encountered in dating the three speeches of Isaeus that are involved in the problem. The fifth oration, which contains an unmistakable reference to written evidence, is certainly earlier than the tenth and probably earlier than the first.[1] Neither of these speeches contains any hint of written evidence. Thalheim[2] proposed an attractive solution of the difficulty. The passage referring to written evidence in the fifth oration is as follows:

καί μοι ἀνάγνωθι τὴν ἀντωμοσίαν.

ΑΝΤΩΜΟΣΙΑ

καὶ μάρτυρας ὑμῖν παρέξομαι . . . . καί μοι ἀνάγνωθι τὴν μαρτυρίαν.

ΜΑΡΤΥΡΙΑ.

τῶν μὲν μαρτύρων ἀκηκόατε.[3]

[1] The first oration presents most difficulties in the matter of dating. Benseler (*op. cit.*, p. 192) placed it in the first period, after 360 B.C., on the basis of the marked avoidance of hiatus. Blass (*op. cit.*, II, 531) accepts Benseler's arguments. Jebb (*op. cit.*, II, 320), while expressing some doubts about this method of dating the speeches of Isaeus, agrees with Benseler. But Wyse (*op. cit.*, p. 179) is quite pronounced in his criticism of the method of Benseler. He points out that hiatus is carefully avoided in the eighth oration, which belongs between 387–363, while no pains were taken to avoid it in the second oration, which belongs to the later period. There is, then, good ground for the view of Thalheim that the first oration belongs to the early years of the orator. The tenth oration belongs to the period of the Theban War, 378–371.

[2] Review of Bonner's *Evidence in Athenian Courts* in *Berliner Philologische Wochenschrift*, 1905, p. 1575.

[3] Isaeus v. 2.

After promising to produce *witnesses*, the speaker calls for
the reading of *one* affidavit. It is also to be noted that the
expression "You have heard the witnesses" (τῶν μὲν μαρτύρων ἀκηκόατε) is more appropriate to oral than to written
testimony. For these reasons Thalheim proposed to strike
out the words καί μοι ἀνάγνωθι τὴν μαρτυρίαν as an interpolation. The source of the interpolation he found in the words
of the preceding section, καί μοι ἀνάγνωθι τὴν ἀντωμοσίαν, which
appear again at the end of the fourth section. Having thus
disposed of the only reference to written evidence in the
speech, he arrives at the date 375 B.C. by striking an average
between the extreme possible dates for the tenth oration,
378–371.

Recent investigations have shown that the archonship of
Nausinicus (378–377) bids fair to rival the archonship of
Eucleides as a year of reform. In a study entitled "Oral and
Written Pleading in Athenian Courts,"[1] Calhoun has shown
that litigants were not required to hand in their complaints
and pleadings in writing until the fourth century.

As a result of our inquiry, then, we find in the forensic speeches of
Antiphon, Andocides, Lysias, and Isocrates a studied variety of expression
for the commencement of actions, but nothing that may be construed as
an allusion to the writing or handing in of pleadings by litigants. But with
the advent of Demosthenes new terms make their appearance; we find for
the first time ἀποφέρειν and διδόναι, together with accounts of the actual
handing in of the instrument and frequent allusions to the writing of complaints by litigants.

From this state of affairs Calhoun concludes that until shortly before the beginning of the forensic career of Demosthenes
complaints and rejoinders were made orally and written down
by the magistrate at the instance of the litigant. Struck by
the similarity in the history of pleadings and evidence, Calhoun tried to fix more precisely the date of the law requiring
written depositions, in the hope of throwing light on the date
of written pleadings. He rejects Thalheim's proposal to
dispose of ἀνάγνωθι τὴν μαρτυρίαν in Isaeus' fifth oration as an
interpolation. He argues:

[1] *TAPA*, L (1919), 189.

.... the isolated instance of the reading of a deposition in 389 does not justify us in dating the change as early as 390, for there is not the slightest reason why evidence should not occasionally have been presented in writing prior to the enactment of a legal requirement that it be so presented.

Associating the two reforms which required that pleadings and evidence be presented in writing, he fixes upon 378–377 as the most likely date of these important changes.[1] The view that in one speech both kinds of evidence were possible, before the enactment of the law requiring evidence to be in writing, is open to objection. If, as has already been suggested, written depositions were devised by speech-writers in the interest of their clients, one would expect to find uniformity in the method of presenting evidence in individual speeches. As between clients, there might be good reason for using written depositions for one client and oral testimony for another. But it is difficult to see why Isaeus' client needed a written deposition for the first witness when he was able to elicit the testimony of the remaining seven groups of witnesses in the presence of the jury. The proceeding is possible, but not probable. Thalheim's disposal of the phrase καί μοι ἀνάγνωθι τὴν μαρτυρίαν as "späteren nach dem vorausgehenden und folgenden καί μοι ἀνάγνωθι τὴν ἀντωμοσίαν Zusatz" is to be preferred.[2] All the evidence in the tenth speech seems to be oral. It was delivered during the course of the Theban War (378–371 B.C.). The law requiring evidence to be presented in writing was not in force when this speech was delivered. Thalheim, in selecting 375 as the probable date of the law, was simply striking an average by putting it midway between 378 and 371. Knowing neither the exact date of the speech nor the time that elapsed between its delivery and the enactment of the law, all he could do was to hazard a guess. Calhoun, however, in picking 378–377, is allowing the narrowest margin. The speech is put at the earliest possi-

[1] Calhoun, op. cit., p. 191.

[2] Cf. Hommel, who, in his review of Calhoun's Oral and Written Pleading (Philologische Wochenschrift, 1923, pp. 612–13), approves of Thalheim's proposal on the basis of a statistical examination of the relative occurrences of ἀνάγνωθι and other formulas in the speeches of Isaeus.

ble date, and the law follows it almost instantly. But he has good reason for crowding matters. The archonship of Nau-sinicus was a notable reform year. Political reforms in Athens tended to come in waves. This feature warrants us in accepting 378–377 as the most likely date for this important judicial reform.[1]

It is perhaps not without significance that written evidence appears first in the speeches of Isaeus.[2] With one exception the extant cases of Isaeus concern estates. They were involved and difficult to present clearly. It may be that he soon realized that the evidence must be carefully formulated and presented in order to be effective. The only certain way to secure this result was to elicit the evidence himself and transcribe it for reading at the proper place. It was a dull method of presenting evidence, but it had the merits of brevity and clarity.

In the fourth century, as formerly, the Areopagus was composed of ex-archons who had successfully passed their audit.[3] Aristotle says that an archon could not take his place in the council at the end of his year of office until he had delivered to the treasurers of Athena the full amount of olive oil due for his year.[4] In addition the Areopagus was subject to an εὔθυνα before the logistae. This could only have been at the end of a certain period of time or on the completion of a particular task.[5] The Areopagus could expel any of its members provisionally, but the expulsion became final only on the confirmation of a heliastic court.[6] Athenaeus cites Hypereides to the effect that a man who had been seen dining

[1] Hommel (*ibid.*), while quoting with approval Bonner's earlier statement of the date as being after the end of the public career of Lysias (380 B.C.) and before the bulk of the speeches of Isaeus (375–360), seems to accept Calhoun's closer fixing of the date.

[2] It is not meant that Isaeus was instrumental in having the law enacted, but rather that he inaugurated the new scheme in his own practice.

[3] Pollux viii. 118. For the reputation of the Areopagus during this period, cf. Isocrates vii. 37–39.

[4] *Ath. Pol.* lx. 3.

[5] Aeschines *in Ctes.* 20; cf. Gilbert, *Greek Constitutional Antiquities*, p. 282.

[6] Dein. *in Dem.* 56. 57; Aeschines *op. cit.* 20.

in a public house could not enter the Areopagus.[1] According to Plutarch, the Areopagites were prohibited from writing comedies.[2] Whether these statements are literally true or not, they indicate that the Areopagus preserved its reputation for dignity and uprightness.

The council retained its jurisdiction in cases of premeditated homicide, wounding with intent, poisoning if death resulted, and arson.[3]

At the beginning of the fourth century the Areopagus still had oversight of the sacred olives and continued to have jurisdiction in cases involving them.[4] But sometime during the fourth century the procedure before the Areopagus lapsed, because the state ceased itself to sell the fruit of the olives and began to requisition it from the owners of the farms on which the sacred olives grew. Hence the farmers became liable for a certain amount regardless of what happened to the olive trees.[5] This change took place sometime between Lysias' seventh oration (about 395 B.C.) and the writing of the *Constitution of Athens* (328–325 B.C.).

Various other religious matters came under the jurisdiction of the Areopagus. It appointed the men who managed the sacrifices of the Eumenides.[6] As before, the council had the duty of caring for the consecrated land of the Eleusinian goddesses. In 352–351 B.C. by a popular decree the Areopagus received general oversight of religion for all time, a prerogative which it still retained in Roman times.[7] But general jurisdiction in cases of impiety was restored to the body by Demetrius of Phaleron at the end of the fourth century. Between that time and the reforms of Ephialtes

---

[1] xiii. 21. 566.   [2] *De gloria Athen.*, 5; Didot, p. 426.

[3] Aristotle, *op. cit.*, lvii. 3; Demosthenes xxiii. 24; cf. Lucian *Anacharsis* 19; Aeschines, *F. L.*, 93; *in Ctes.* 51. 212; Plato *Laws* 877 B. As Sandys says on Aristotle, *ad loc.*, only wounding with intent was classed as φόνος. It was necessary that the poisoning also be with intent. The procedure in the homicide courts described by Aristotle is that of the fourth century.

[4] Aristotle, *op. cit.*, lx. 2; Lysias vii.   [5] Aristotle *Ath. Pol.* lx. 2, 3.

[6] Scholiast on Demosthenes xxi. 115 (cf. lix. 80 f.).

[7] Cf. Keil, "Beiträge zur Geschichte des Areopags," *Berichte über die Verh. der sächs. Akad. d. Wissenschaften* (1919), p. 57.

these cases were, in general, tried before heliastic courts.[1] An interesting example of the participation of the Areopagus in religious matters occurred in 343 B.C. The Delians were contending with the Athenians about the right to administer the temple of Apollo at Delos. The Athenian assembly chose Aeschines, the orator, as their advocate when the case came before the Amphictyonic council, but gave the Areopagus authority to revise the election. The Areopagus rejected Aeschines and chose Hypereides in his place,[2] with the result that Hypereides argued the case.[3]

As the Areopagus became more active after the Peloponnesian War, it played a greater part again in the control of the conduct and morals of the citizens. Apparently the γραφὴ ἀργίας came sometimes before the Areopagus and sometimes before a heliastic court.[4] Doubtless the council had charge of the education of the youth only in the sense that it had general supervision of public morals. Public physicians exercised their functions under the control of the Areopagus.

The Areopagus during the fourth century was sometimes intrusted by the people with some special commission of inquiry. The results of this ζήτησις, or investigation, were brought before the assembly in the form of an ἀπόφασις. The people might deal with the case themselves or appoint prosecutors to handle the matter before a heliastic court. The case of Aeschines, mentioned above, was of this nature. On another occasion it made an investigation as to whether buildings could be erected in the neighborhood of the Pnyx.[5] This was doubtless part of their activity as commissioners of public works.[6] Again, the council was intrusted with investigating the action of Polyeuctus in joining some exiles

---

[1] Cf. *supra*, p. 258. Cf. Lipsius, *op. cit.*, p. 129. It is interesting to note that Origen (*g. Cels.* iv. 67; v. 20) places Socrates' trial before the Areopagus.

[2] Demosthenes xviii. 134.   [3] Hypereides, Λόγος Δηλιακός (*frag.* xix).

[4] Cf. Caillemer, "Areopagus" in Daremberg-Saglio, p. 402. For control of conduct and morals by the Areopagus, cf. Athenaeus iv. 64. 167; Diog. Laert. vii. 169.

[5] Aeschines *Timarch.* 81 ff.

[6] Caillemer, *op. cit.*, p. 403; Heracl. Pont. in Müller, *F.H.G.*, II, 209; Aeschines, *op. cit.*

in Megara.[1] The Areopagus also made an inquiry into the disappearance of part of the stolen money which had been taken from Harpalus, the absconding treasurer of Alexander, and deposited in the Acropolis. The council also investigated the bribing of various citizens by Harpalus.[2]

The council might institute an investigation on its own initiative, but the subsequent procedure was the same. So when the assembly was on the point of discharging Antiphon who was accused of attempting to set fire to the docks, the Areopagus intervened and, after making an inquiry, forced him to stand trial before a heliastic court.[3]

Occasionally the Areopagus was intrusted with independent jurisdiction. Immediately after the Battle of Chaeronea the council tried and condemned to death those who had deserted Athens.[4]

The Areopagus continues to be mentioned up until the fourth century A.D., and under the Romans became again an exceedingly important body.[5] Ex-archons no longer automatically became members, but all of the places were filled by election. The inscriptions show what a great rôle the council played in the government and that it retained all of its erstwhile dignity and prestige.

The fifth-century jury system continued to function to the end of the Peloponnesian War (404 B.C.) without encountering serious difficulties. There is no hint of a shortage of jurors in the Pseudo-Xenophontic *Constitution of Athens* of 424 B.C., nor in the *Wasps* of Aristophanes in 422. Pseudo-Xenophon's[6] suggestion that smaller juries be employed was not intended to make up for a lack of jurors, but to take care of the congestion of litigation which was apparently at its height then, by providing more courts. Indeed, Bdelycleon[7] says explicitly that there were 6,000 jurors; and Andocides, in a speech delivered in 399 B.C., tells of a jury of 6,000 in

---

[1] Dein. *in Dem.* 58.   [3] Demosthenes xviii. 132 f.

[2] Dein. *op. cit.* 4 ff.   [4] Lycurgus *Leoc.* 52; Aeschines *in Ctes.* 252.

[5] For the privileges and duties of the council in Roman times, cf. Caillemer, *op. cit.*; Philippi, *Der Areopag und die Epheten*, pp. 309 ff.; Keil, *op. cit.*

[6] *Ath. Pol.* iii. 4 ff.   [7] Aristophanes *Wasps* 661–62.

415.[1] This situation did not materially change until after the failure of the Sicilian expedition, with its huge losses,[2] and the permanent occupation of Decelea by the Peloponnesians. In recommending to the Spartans the fortification of a post in Attica, Alcibiades[3] predicted that "the revenues of the Laureian silver mines and whatever they now derive from their land and from their courts" would at once be lost to the Athenians. Moreover, the allies would become careless in paying the tribute, being convinced that the Spartans were now prosecuting the war with vigor. That these expectations were more than realized is clear. Not only did the Athenians suffer great material losses, but the task of guarding the walls required the services of all.[4]

It is in this period that on occasion court sessions were restricted to criminal cases.[5] Suspensions of civil cases were sometimes due to financial as well as to military causes. Similar suspensions in the fourth century are explicitly said to be due to a shortage of funds.[6] The normal population of Athens was greatly increased by the influx of the refugees from the more distant parts of Attica. At the end of the war the country people flocked back to their farms. The city population was much reduced. There was no longer a mass

---

[1] Andocidesi. 17.

[2] For losses in the Sicilian expedition, see Mälzer, *Verluste und Verlustenlisten im griechischen Altertum*, pp. 33–37. He gives both ancient and modern estimates. The highest ancient computation was 40,000. Even victories were costly. Meyer (*Geschichte des Altertums*, IV, 3, 646) estimates the losses at Arginusae at more than 4,000.

[3] Thucydides vi. 91. 7. There is no need to emend δικαστηρίων as has been proposed. The scholiast thinks the reference is to τὰ πρυτανεῖα καὶ αἱ χρηματικαὶ ζημίαι. The reference is probably to the loss of judicial revenue due to expected disaffection and revolts among the allies if Sparta took effective measures to crush Athens. Boeckh (*Staatshaushaltung der Athener*, I, 415) thinks of a suspension of court sessions "bei einem einheimishen Kriege." Cf. Lipsius, *op. cit.*, p. 162, n. 91.

[4] Thucydides vii. 27–28: πρὸς γὰρ τῇ ἐπάλξει τὴν μὲν ἡμέραν κατὰ διαδοχὴν οἱ Ἀθηναῖοι φυλάσσοντες, τὴν δὲ νύκτα καὶ ξύμπαντες πλὴν τῶν ἱππέων, κ.τ.λ. (28. 2).

[5] Lysias xvii. 3: ἐν μὲν οὖν τῷ πολέμῳ διότι οὐκ ἦσαν δίκαι οὐ δυνατοὶ ἦμεν παρ' αὐτῶν ἃ ὤφειλον πράξασθαι. ἐπειδὴ δὲ εἰρήνη ἐγένετο ὅτε πρῶτον αἱ ἀστικαὶ δίκαι ἐδικάζοντο, λαχὼν ὁ πατήρ, κ.τ.λ.

[6] Demosthenes xxxix. 17: καὶ εἰ μισθὸς ἐπορίσθη τοῖς δικαστηρίοις εἰσῆγον ἂν δῆλον ὅτι.

of unemployed refugees available for jury service. Thousands of slaves had deserted.[1] The farmers had enough to do in restoring their dismantled farms[2] without resorting to the city on the chance of obtaining jury service. It must very soon, if not at first, have been apparent that the numbers offering themselves for service were inadequate for the work. True, there was no longer any overseas litigation, but the rule of the Thirty Tyrants must have given rise to considerable litigation in one way or another in spite of the amnesty.[3] Under these circumstances the democratic leaders must have realized that the most pressing need was to make up in some way for the shortage in the supply of jurors without interfering with the efficiency of the courts. The idea of smaller panels to cope with the congestion of the courts had long been familiar to those who concerned themselves about such things. But as Pseudo-Xenophon[4] pointed out in 424 B.C., smaller courts were more easily bribed. And bribery had begun to become serious. There was always more or less of it, but the sensational exploit of Anytus in successfully bribing a whole panel showed that, provided sufficient money was available, the size of the jury was no safeguard.[5] The time was ripe for a fundamental change in the jury system. The panels for certain types of cases were reduced to 200 and 400. The increased danger of bribery was met by a new plan of assigning the sections to the courts daily instead of annually. In this way ten sections could be maintained, though the total number of jurors was considerably below the nominal 6,000. But even so, the numbers did not suffice. A curious system of plural registration was introduced whereby jurors were permitted to register in several sections in addition to the sections to which they were first allotted.

[1] Thucydides vii. 27. 5. Cf. Aristophanes *Clouds* 6–7.

[2] For the thorough devastation of Attica during the Decelean War, see the *Hellenica Oxyrhynchia* xii. 4. Cf. Hardy, "The Hellenica Oxyrhynchia and the Devastation of Attica," *Class. Phil.*, XXI, 346 ff.

[3] Isocrates xviii and xxi.   [4] *Ath. Pol.* iii. 7.

[5] Aristotle *Ath. Pol.* xxvii. Cf. Calhoun, *Athenian Clubs in Politics and Litigation*, pp. 66 ff.; Hommel, *Heliaea*, pp. 127–28.

The evidence for this feature of the new system is found in a passage of the *Plutus* of Aristophanes, which appeared in 388 B.C. Hermes offers to assume various characters in the interests of mortals, if he be permitted to stay among them under the régime that followed Plutus' recovery of his sight. Cario, the slave, in commenting on his ability to be Jack of many trades, says:

ὡς ἀγαθόν ἐστ᾽ ἐπωνυμίας πολλὰς ἔχειν·
οὗτος γὰρ ἐξεύρηκεν αὐτῷ βιότιον.
οὐκ ἐτὸς ἅπαντες οἱ δικάζοντες θαμὰ
σπεύδουσιν ἐν πολλοῖς γεγράφθαι γράμμασιν.[1]

If the passage be taken literally, it would seem that the practice was common, if not general. It was formerly supposed that Cario was indulging in comic exaggeration by treating a bit of trickery as a regular practice.[2] But this view is no longer held.

The πινάκια, or jurors' tesserae, many of which have been found in graves,[3] have been used to support the inference drawn from the passage of Aristophanes that jurors could be registered in other sections than the one to which they were originally allotted. In several cases, in addition to the letter of the owner's section, which is placed regularly in the upper left-hand corner of the πινάκιον, there are additional letters in the lower right-hand corner, following the name. For example, *CIA* ii. 877, belonging to Lyson of the deme of Steiria of the A section contains also the letter H after the name. Likewise, *CIA* ii. 887, belonging to Paramonus of the deme of Melite of the Γ section, contains also the letter H. Now, it has been thought by some scholars that the additional letters represent plural registration[4] and that the own-

[1] Aristophanes *Plutus* 1164–67.

[2] Fränkel (*Die attischen Geschworenengerichte*, pp. 97 ff.) disproves Schoemann's view (*De sortitione judicum*, I, 212) that the poet is referring to "einen haüfig geübten Betrug." Cf. Teusch, *op. cit.*, p. 50.

[3] All of the extant tesserae are of bronze and belong to the fourth century. They are collected in *CIA* ii. 875–940.

[4] Caillemer, article "Dikastai" in Daremberg-Saglio, p. 189. *CIA* ii. 911, 912, have a curious form of the letter H—Ͱ. Some think that the form is a combination of H and E, and means that the owner was entitled to sit in both sections. Cf. Caillemer, *op. cit.*; Bruck, *Philologus*, LII, 420.

er of *CIA* ii. 877, for example, was entitled to sit also with section H in case his own section A was not sitting and section H was not full. The addition of the second letter to the πινάκιον obviated the necessity of giving an additional πινάκιον to the juror for each section in which he was entitled to sit. There are no examples of two πινάκια for the same man with different section letters.[1] That the extra letters on the πινάκια have any connection with plural registration has however, been doubted.[2] Bruck suggests that, inasmuch as the πινάκια which contain extra letters are in each case re-used tablets, the extra letters may be part of the original inscription. That the extra registrations were recorded in a formal and regular fashion is, however, suggested by the perfect, γεγράφθαι, of Aristophanes.[3] The plural registrations were, however, doubtless recorded on the different section lists.

[1] There are some examples among the extant tesserae of two struck for the same person. *CIA* ii. 914, 915, found in the same tomb, are practically identical. *CIA* ii. 917, 918, probably found in the same tomb, differ only in that one contains the father's name while the other does not. It has been suggested that the older πινάκια omit the father's name, while the later ones have the more explicit designation and more designs. The case of the two just cited, belonging to the same man, seems to disprove this theory. Cf. Caillemer, *op. cit.*, p. 190. It was perhaps not unusual for a man to have additional tesserae struck for himself. Or the original tessera may have been lost and found again after a duplicate copy had been issued by the state. It has been suggested that the tesserae in actual use were all of boxwood and that the extant examples in bronze were struck for the express purpose of being placed in an enthusiastic juror's grave. Cf. Gilbert, *Greek Constitutional Antiquities* p. 397, n. 1. This, however, can hardly be the case, for several of the tablets were obviously used twice. *CIA* ii. 877, 887, 922, 932, 933, show clear traces of another name beneath the present names.

[2] Cf. Lipsius, *op. cit.*, p. 145, n. 33: "Ob aber auf den Richtertäfelchen sich Spuren der aus Aristophanes erschlossenen Tatsache erhalten haben, ist mindestens zweifelhaft." Bruck, *op. cit.*, LII, 419; Mylonas, *Bulletin de correspondance Hellénique*, 1883, pp. 29 ff.

[3] Some of the πινάκια are perforated (cf. e.g., *CIA* ii. 876, 899, 924), a fact which has given rise to much speculation. The following suggestions have been made: (1) The perforation was necessary to enable the ἐμπηκτής to fasten the πινάκιον on the κανονίς after it was drawn. Cf. Hommel, *op. cit.*, p. 124. In our utter ignorance of the form of the κανονίς this cannot be demonstrated. Many think that the κανονίς was no more than a groove into which the πινάκια fitted. (2) The perforation was for the convenience of the owner so that he might attach the πινάκιον to his garments. Hence some are perforated and some not. (3) The perforation was merely a device for suspending the πινάκιον in the grave. Cf. Caillemer, *op. cit.*, p. 190.

The earliest reference to the new jury system is found in the *Ecclesiazousae* of Aristophanes presented in 390 or 388 B.C. In the comedy the state is turned over to the women to manage. Praxagora, the leader of the women, introduces socialism. There is to be no more litigation.[1] The courts are to be abolished.[2] Everybody will own everything. They will live together and eat together.[3] "Where," inquires Praxagora's husband, "will you serve dinner?" "Each court and arcade of the law shall be a banqueting hall for the citizens." The allotment booths are to be used to marshal the citizens into ten groups corresponding to the sections of jurors. These groups, designated by the first ten letters of the alphabet, are to be sent to one or another of the courts which are now to serve as banqueting halls.

> τὰ δὲ κληρωτήρια ποῖ τρέψεις ; Pr. ἐς τὴν ἀγορὰν καταθήσω·
> κᾆτα στήσασα παρ' Ἁρμοδίῳ κληρώσω πάντας, ἕως ἂν
> εἰδὼς ὁ λαχὼν ἀπίῃ χαίρων ἐν ὁποίῳ γράμματι δειπνεῖ·
> καὶ κηρύξει τοὺς ἐκ τοῦ βῆτ' ἐπὶ τὴν στοιὰν ἀκολουθεῖν
> τὴν βασίλειον δειπνήσοντας· τὸ δὲ θῆτ' ἐς τὴν παρὰ ταύτην,
> τοὺς δ' ἐκ τοῦ κάππ' ἐς τὴν στοιὰν χωρεῖν τὴν ἀλφιτόπωλιν.
> . . . . Bl. ὅτῳ δὲ τὸ γράμμα
> μὴ 'ξελκυσθῇ καθ' ὃ δειπνήσει, τούτους ἀπελῶσιν ἅπαντες.[4]

Praxagora's arrangement for feeding the citizen body is a clever parody of the judicial system. She succeeds in making use of much of the discarded paraphernalia. On the basis of this feature of the comedy a reasonably satisfactory reconstruction of the jury system has been achieved. A number of scholars have contributed to the work. Complete agreement has not been reached, but the conclusions of Lipsius have won general approval.[5]

The number of jurors was still nominally 6,000. All eligible citizens who offered for service were accepted and divided into ten sections in which the tribes were represented as evenly as possible. The first ten letters of the alphabet were used to designate the sections. To each juror was given a bronze tessera with his name and section letter on it. The

[1] Aristophanes *Ecclesiazousae* 657. [3] *Ibid.* 673–75.
[2] *Ibid.* 677. [4] *Ibid.* 683–88.
[5] Lipsius, *op. cit.*, pp. 139 ff. Cf. Hommel, *op. cit.*, pp. 115 ff.

courts were designated by the letters from Λ to Τ, just as they were in the next period.[1] But, although in the comedy the places that are to serve as banquet halls are named, e.g., ἐπὶ τὴν στοιὰν τὴν βασίλειον, ἐς τὴν στοιάν, not designated by letters, there are indications that in the court system which is being parodied letters were used in this period to indicate the courts. Lipsius[2] argues that in the phrases ἐν ὁποίῳ γράμματι and τὸ γράμμα καθ᾽ ὃ δειπνήσει the letter (γράμμα) refers not to the section but to the court. When court sessions were to be held, all sections were summoned. Into a container were put ten tickets with the letters from Α to Κ; into another, the letters Λ to Τ designating the particular courts that were to sit that day. A ticket was drawn from each container simultaneously. The section drawn sat in the court drawn. If a court of 1,000 or 1,500 was required, two or three tickets were drawn from the jurors' jar as against one from the jar of the courts. If a smaller court was required, e.g., 200, it was easy to dispose of the excess number by the use of the lot.[3] Under this system of supernumeraries it was always possible to secure a full quota for a jury. Accordingly, at this time a change was made and odd numbers were required for each jury. The court that tried Socrates in 399 B.C. in all probability numbered 501.[4] In the *Plutus*

[1] Aristotle *Ath. Pol.* lxiii.

[2] *Op. cit.*, p. 141, n. 23. Teusch (*op. cit.*, p. 47) believes that γράμματα in these passages always refers to sections of jurors and that names or "signa quaedam," not letters, were used to mark the courts. But evidence that letters were used is the occurrence of Σ on what is generally regarded as one of the allotment σύμβολα used to designate the courts in the process of allotment. Hommel, *op. cit.*, p. 116, n. 293. Cf. Svoronos, *Journal international d'archéologie numismatique*, p. 53, and Plate E. No. 9; Earle Fox, *Revue numismatique*, 1890, p. 63, Plate III, No. 14.

[3] That men were turned away daily from the courts in spite of plural registration is clear from Aristophanes' *Ecclesiazousae*, 687 f. This feature Praxagora proposed not to reproduce in the matter of dining. Hommel (*op. cit.*, p. 119) suggests that for private suits with small panels (200) the country people did not appear. Criminal suits were put on different days to encourage the country people to appear for service when larger courts were required. Evidence for this second allotment on court days is found in Demosthenes xxv. 27, according to Lipsius, *op. cit.*, p. 142, n. 27. Cf. Teusch, *op. cit.*, p. 47.

[4] Plato *Apology* 36 A: εἰ τριάκοντα μόναι μετέπεσον τῶν ψήφων, ἀπεπεφεύγη ἄν. With a jury of 500 divided into 280 for the prosecution and 220 for Socrates, the change of thirty votes would have resulted in a tie which meant acquittal. With a

372 THE ADMINISTRATION OF JUSTICE

of Aristophanes[1] the slave Cario says to the chorus, urging
them to be gone,

ἐν τῇ σορῷ νυνὶ λαχὸν τὸ γράμμα σου δικάζειν,
σὺ δ’ οὐ βαδίζεις ; ὁ δὲ Χάρων τὸ ξύμβολον δίδωσιν.

Here again is a parody of court procedure. The dicast, on
entering the court to which his section was allotted, received
a token which entitled him to his fee at the end of the trial.
The scholiast regards Χάρων as an anagram for Ἄρχων.[2]

The change in the size of the courts and the method of
assigning panels to the courts belongs to the archonship of
Eucleides, 403–402 B.C. Later a further change was introduced. The same men were allowed to remain in the same
panel year after year as long as they continued to serve.
The annual allotment to sections was confined to the new
applicants for service each year. This was the natural thing
to do. If all who offered were accepted, there was no need
of an annual re-allotment. There was no reason under the
new system why a man could not be a life-member of the
same section. But all continued to take the oath annually. Some support for this theory is found in the fact that
with two exceptions only one tessera (πινάκιον) has been discovered in each grave. This would seem to indicate that the
deceased possessed normally only one tessera. Where there

---

jury of 501 divided into 221 and 280 for the defense and the prosecution, respectively, a change of thirty would have given a majority of one vote for acquittal. Diogenes Laertius (ii. 41) says that the votes against Socrates amounted to 281. If this is
correct, Plato's "thirty" must be a round number for thirty-one, and the panel
must have numbered 501, divided into 220 and 281. If the reading in Diogenes
Laertius is correct—ὅτ’ οὖν κατεδικάσθη, διακοσίαις ὀγδοηκονταμιᾷ πλείοσι ψήφοις τῶν
ἀπολυουσῶν—this is an example of illogical idiom. Diogenes meant to say that the
majority of the jurors voted against Socrates and they numbered 281, or, to put it
another way, "281 voted against Socrates, being more than the votes in his favor."
There is no evidence for odd numbers in panels in the fifth century. It is not until
the fourth century that odd numbers are authenticated. Cf. *supra*, p. 243.

[1] 277–78. The section to which the chorus leader belongs has been allotted
to serve beyond the grave, where Charon is in charge just as the magistrates preside
at trials. Cf. Van Leeuwen's note, *ad loc*. Several of these σύμβολα mentioned in the
text have been found. They are made of lead and have an owl (mark of the 3-obol
piece) on one side and a letter on the other. See Gide and Caillemer, *s.v.* "Dikastai,"
Daremberg-Saglio, for an illustration.

[2] ὁ Χάρων κατὰ ἀναγραμματισμὸν Ἄρχων λέγεται.

are two, both are for the same section.[1] The practice of plural registration looks like a device suggested by experience in working the new system. It had the double advantage of securing on the spot the required numbers without abandoning the section system, and of utilizing the services of those who were most anxious for employment. This partial disregard for section divisions is a step toward the system of Aristotle's day when jurors were still assigned to sections but allotted to service daily quite without regard to their section affiliations. It affords another example of evolution in the growth of institutions.

The Eucleidean system was still used in 388 b.c., when the *Plutus*[2] was performed. This is the date *post quem* for the newer system. The date *ante quem* is 355 or 354, when the *Areopagiticus* of Isocrates[3] was delivered. Sometime between these two dates the system described by Aristotle was instituted. The point at which a change in the jury system would seem most necessary and desirable is the year of the formation of the new empire, 378–377.[4] Even though the empire was on a more liberal basis, military needs were likely to be pressing and continuous. Keil[5] regarded the decade 380–370 as a period in which establishment of the new league gave Athens the impulse to institute reforms and innovations in the most diverse departments of public life. The changes included the establishment of the *symmories* for the levying and collection of the property tax, the institution of

[1] *CIA* ii. 914 and 915; 917 and 918. Cf. Hommel, *op. cit.*, pp. 120 ff. According to Hommel, the life-tenure of office for the dicast came about gradually owing to the shortage of jurors and the consequent need, in order to man the courts properly, of all who presented themselves for jury service. He places the beginning of the lifelong tenure in the decade following the production of Aristophanes' *Plutus* (388 b.c.) and assigns to this period the unperforated πινάκια on the ground that the perforations could not have had the use in this period which they had in the system described by Aristotle—i.e., being fastened on the κανονίς. Cf. *infra*, p. 376.

[2] Cf. 277, 972, and 1166–67.   [3] Sec. 54. Cf. Hommel, *op. cit.*, p. 129.

[4] Dittenberger, *Sylloge²*, No. 81; Hicks and Hill, *Greek Historical Inscriptions*, No. 101.

[5] *Anonymus Argentinensis*, p. 266. Keil believes that about 375 b.c. there was a marked increase in the time allotted to litigants for addressing the jury. This development followed naturally upon the perfection of oratory and the use of litigation for political purposes. Cf. Hommel, *op. cit.*, pp. 120 ff.

the *proedroi*,[1] the requirement that litigants should hand in their pleadings and evidence in writing.[2] It would be strange if the reorganization of the jury system were not included among the financial, military, administrative, constitutional, and judicial reforms that followed immediately upon the founding of the second empire in the archonship of Nausinicus.[3] The prospective military commitments of Athens were in themselves sufficient reason for adopting some better means than voluntary plural registrations for making up for the inevitable reduction in numbers of the individual sections that must have been anticipated.

An attempt was made by Bruno Keil[4] to prove that, between the system reconstructed from Aristophanes' *Ecclesiazousae* and *Plutus* and that described by Aristotle, there intervened a system different from either. It began about 375 b.c. and ended, in what he calls "Die Restaurationsjahre," between 347 and 345. It is the novelty of the new constitutional changes that interested Aristotle. Of these the chief was the allotment of the jurors. This is an attractive theory. But the evidence adduced by Teusch, upon which Keil relies, is insufficient. Teusch has treated κριτής as a synonym of δικαστής in a passage of Demosthenes.[5] The normal meaning of κριτής is a judge in a contest of some kind. It never occurs in the orators in the sense of δικαστής.[6]

In Aristotle's day the πινάκια were no longer made of

[1] Glotz, "L'épistate des proèdres," *Rev. d. études grecques*, XXXIV (1921), 1–19. Cf. S. B. Smith, "The Origin of the Athenian Proedroi," *Proc. of the Amer. Philol. Assoc. 1927*, LVIII, xxiii: "The lapidary evidence shows that the *proedroi* did not exist before 378–7."

[2] Cf. *supra*, p. 360.

[3] Calhoun, "Oral and Written Pleading in Athenian Courts," *Trans. of the Amer. Philol. Assoc.* L (1919), 191 ff. Cf. Hommel, *op. cit.*, p. 129. Lipsius (*op. cit.*, p. 149) refused to commit himself on the date of the introduction of the system described by Aristotle beyond the fact that it was in force in 355 or 354 b.c. (Isocrates vii. 54).

[4] *Anonymus Argentinensis*, p. 267.

[5] Teusch, *op. cit.*, pp. 55–56. Demosthenes xxxix. 10: φέρε, εἰ δὲ κριτὴς καλοῖτο Μαντίθεος Μαντίου Θορίκιος, τί ἂν ποιοῖμεν; ἢ βαδίζοιμεν ἂν ἄμφω; τῷ γὰρ ἔσται δῆλον πότερον σὲ κέκληκεν ἢ ἐμέ;

[6] See Paley and Sandys' notes on Demosthenes xxxix. 10, and Lipsius, *op. cit.*, p. 150, n. 49.

bronze, as in the early fourth century, but of wood.[1] A passage in Demosthenes shows that bronze was still in use in 348 B.C.[2] The need of bronze for coinage was doubtless a factor in the substitution of wood. In 407–406 B.C. the financial straits of Athens forced her to melt down the golden statues of Niké in the Parthenon and issue what Aristophanes in the *Frogs* (720) called τὸ καινὸν χρυσίον.[3] The occupation of Decelea shut off the supply of silver from the mines at Laurium, and bronze coins were used for the small daily needs of the populace until a revival of the fortunes of the city after the victory of Conon in 394 enabled the Athenians to go back to silver as legal tender.[4] A character in the *Ecclesiazousae* complains in comic fashion of the personal inconvenience he suffered by the change. He had just started on a round of the market to purchase supplies when a public crier proclaimed (819–820):

$$\text{Μὴ δέχεσθαι μηδένα}$$
$$\text{χαλκὸν τὸ λοιπόν· ἀργύρῳ γὰρ χρώμεθα.}$$

He was caught with a mouthful of bronze and no silver in the midst of his marketing. A similar crisis arose again in 339 B.C. Recourse was again had to melting down gold ornaments in the Parthenon.[5] Again silver was displaced for daily use by bronze. It was doubtless at this time that wooden tesserae were substituted for bronze to release more metal for coinage.[6]

Aristotle, in his summary of the constitution in his own day, gives an elaborate description of the jury system.[7] The jurors were divided, as in the preceding period, into ten sections designated by the letters from *A* to *K*. The sections were approximately equal, and each section contained mem-

---

[1] Aristotle *Ath. Pol.* lxii. 4.

[2] Demosthenes, *ibid.*; Lipsius, *op. cit.*, p. 150, n. 50.

[3] Head, *Historia Numorum*, p. 373 (2d. ed.).

[4] Aristophanes no doubt reflects popular opinion when, in the *Frogs* 725–26, he refers to these coins as τοῖς πονηροῖς χαλκίοις and τῷ κακίστῳ κόμματι.

[5] Head, *op. cit.*, p. 375.　　　　　　　　　[6] Hommel, *op. cit.*, p. 40.

[7] *Ath. Pol.* lxiii ff. For text and translation, cf. Hommel, *op. cit.*, pp. 11 ff. and Colin, *Rev. d. ét. grecques*, XXX, 20 ff.

bers of all ten tribes. When a juror was appointed, he received the πινάκιον of boxwood containing his official designation and the name of the section to which he was assigned. The jurors were chosen for particular cases by lot in a very complicated fashion by the nine archons, each for his own tribe, with the clerk of the thesmothetae acting for the tenth tribe. Aristotle mentions, with few details, the courthouse with an entrance for each tribe and two compartments for the drawing of lots for each tribe.[1] These κληρωτήρια were equipped with ten chests (κιβώτια) for each tribe; other chests to be used in the drawing of lots; two urns (ὑδρίαι); staves (βακτηρίαι); and counters (βάλανοι), equal in number to the number of jurors required. The number of jurors needed was determined in advance by the number of courts which were to sit and the number of jurors necessary for each of these courts. The thesmothetae decided by lot which letters were to be used for the courts required for the day. Men to fill these courts were then chosen by lot from all ten jury sections as follows: Each juror brought his πινάκιον and cast it into the chest marked with his section letter. Then twice as many were drawn as were needed for jury service on that day. The πινάκια thus drawn were attached in some manner to a κανονίς. After the requisite number had been drawn, the archon drew dice for the final selection. There were two dice, one black and one white, for each five πινάκια. If the archon drew a black die, the first five πινάκια from each κανονίς were returned to their owners, who were rejected. If he drew a white die, the first five were accepted, and so on in order as he drew the dice. The successful candidates drew each a counter, showed the letter on it to the presiding archon, who at once threw the juror's πινάκιον into a chest labeled with the same letter as that on the counter and sent the juror into the proper court with his counter and with a staff of the same color as the court to which he was assigned.

The presiding magistrates were selected by lot by two of the thesmothetae. The first magistrate drawn presided in

---

[1] For a reconstruction, cf. Hommel, *op. cit.*, diagrams on pp. 140 f.

the first court drawn, and so on. The magistrates then by lot assigned five jurors, one to the superintendence of the water clock and four to the telling of the votes. Five others were assigned to the task of ordering the jurors for the reception of their fees.

Aristotle gives the various amounts of water which were allowed for the pleadings in different types of cases. But in certain types of cases (e.g., cases involving a penalty of imprisonment, death, exile, ἀτιμία, and confiscation) speeches were not limited by the water clock, but each party had a fixed part of the day.

Most courts consisted of 500 jurors, but two or three courts were sometimes combined for important cases. Each juror, after the conclusion of the speeches, was given a perforated ballot and a solid ballot. The perforated ballot was for the plaintiff; the solid for the defendant. The staves were taken up, and in return each juror, as he cast his ballot, received a voucher (σύμβολον) with the letter Γ (i.e., the numeral 3), which he had to surrender when he received his pay. This was to insure that he voted. If he could not show that he had voted, he received no pay. The jurors cast the ballots which they wished to have counted into a brazen urn, and discarded the remaining ballots into a wooden urn. Equality of votes constituted victory for the defendant. If the jury had to determine the penalty, a second vote had to be taken. Afterward the jurors received their pay in the allotted order.[1]

This complicated system was intended to prevent bribery and tampering with the jury in any form. Aristotle indicates in at least half a dozen passages quite explicitly that certain details of the system were devised as a safeguard against dishonest practices.[2]

---

[1] Colin, *op. cit.*, p. 85 ff. Hommel, *op. cit.*, p. 128.

[2] *Ath. Pol.* lxiv. 2; lxiv. 4; lxvi. 1; lxvi, 2; lxv. 1; lxix. 1. Cf. Hommel, *op. cit.*, p. 128. Colin (*op. cit.*, 85 f.) collects various passages from fourth- and fifth-century literature tending to discredit the jury system. But the faults that are mentioned in these passages are not such as could have been cured by any system of allotment of jurors. In the fifth century the Athenians relied on the size of a panel to prevent corrupt practices. But when they were forced to use smaller panels, they finally devised the intricate system of Aristotle's day.

The importance of the heliastic courts in the Athenian political system can scarcely be overestimated.[1] Aristotle concludes his history of the Athenian constitution by a brief summary of the eleven major constitutional changes which he had described in detail.[2] The eleventh is the democratic restoration after the overthrow of the Thirty. Aristotle characterizes it as follows:

> At that time the people, having secured the control of the state, established the constitution which exists at the present day. . . . . The democracy has made itself master of everything and administers everything by its votes in the assembly and by the law courts in which it holds supreme power.

The appeal to the dicasterion, introduced by Solon, developed into the supremacy of the dicasts, for the masters of the judicial verdicts became masters of the state.[3]

[1] For the reasons for Athenian litigiousness, cf. Bonner, *Lawyers and Litigants in Ancient Athens*, pp. 96 ff.

[2] *Ath. Pol.* xli.   [3] Cf. *ibid.*, ix. 1; xxxv. 2.

INDEX

INDEX

Absences of dicasts from court sessions, 240

Achilles, representative of Peleus in war, 3

Action: right of bringing, 95; under Solon, 167 ff.; in homicide, 167

ἄδεια, granted only by assembly of 6,000, 213

ἀδικία, 207

Administration of justice: informal in Heroic Age, 11; under Theseus, 61; in the early codes, 77; under Solon, 149 ff.; after Solon, 182; under Peisistratus, 183 ff.; as means of control in Athenian Empire, 227, 310 ff.; military considerations in, 232; in the constitutions of the Four Hundred, 326; in fourth-century Athens, 346 ff.

Adultery, 12, 52

Advocates representing demes, 321

Aegisthus and Clytemnestra, 12; murdered by Orestes, 17

Aegyptius, 6

Aethiopis, homicide pollution in, 54

Agamemnon, prowess of, in athletics, 3

ἀγορά: in Homer, as medium of community action, 26; a prototype of Athenian ἡλιαία, 26

Agoratus: case of, 212; denunciation of officials by, 246

αἴδεσις in laws of Draco, 65, 119, 273

ἄκριτος, meaning of, 336

Alcibiades: information against, 302, 303, 308; impeachment of, 304

Alcmaeonidae: tried by court of Three Hundred, 102; capture of Cylonian party by, 134; quarrel with Cylonian factions, 149; feud of, with Peisistratidae, 187

Allies: treatment of, by Athens in judicial matters, 310 ff.; treatment of, in political and criminal cases, 312; classes of, 313; appeals of, against tribute assessments, 314; local courts of, 315

Amnesty law, 54; text of, 104 f.; interpretation of, 105 ff.; after Battle of Aegospotami, ephetae in, 274

Anakrisis: survival of trial before single judge, 283; evidence at, 283; distinguished from arbitration, 284; proceedings at, 290; under the Thirty, 332

Anarchy between Solon and Peisistratus, 181 f.

Androdamas, 70

Antalcidas, peace of, 316

Antiphon, impeachment of, 302, 308, 321

ἀπάγειν in laws of Draco, 120

ἀποδέκται, 282

ἀποδίδωμι, confusion of forms of, 139

ἀποδικεῖν in decree of Cannonus, 206

Apollodorus v. *Arethusius*, 292

Appeals: under Solon, 151 ff., 166; frequency of, 176 ff.; unsuccessful, penalty for, 179; increase in number of, after tyrants, 196; frequency of, under Athenian Empire, 224; from decisions of Areopagus, 269; from fines imposed by magistrates, 279; from arbitrator's decision, 287, 347; in demes, 320

Arbitration: in the Homeric Age, 27; in the trial-scene, 36; a regular proceeding in Homeric Age, 42; in interests of aristocracy, 43; obligatory, 43 ff.; voluntary, in age of Hesiod, 52; under Theseus, 61; development from voluntary to obligatory, 62;

382 THE ADMINISTRATION OF JUSTICE

under Peisistratus, 184; in village communities, 318; under the Thirty, 334; public, establishment of, 346 ff., 350; exemption from, 349; in the fifth century, 351; under the rural justices, 352

Arbitrators: appointment of men in sixtieth year as, 232; public, production of evidence before, 287; institution of, 346 ff.; connection of, with Forty, 347; procedure before, 347 ff., 353; appeals from decisions of, 347

Archebiades, case of, 350

Archestratus, laws of, 253

Archon: proclamation of, 43, 62, 84; cases under jurisdiction of, 85; court of, 234, 245

Archon basileus: jurisdiction of, 85; chairman of Areopagus, 94; court of, 246; jurisdiction of, in ἀσέβεια, 260

Archons: judicial functions of, 84; final jurisdiction of, 84; oath of, 169

Archonship, date of institution of, 62

Areopagus: trials for attempts on government before, 63, 198; both administrative and judicial body, 77; in pre-Solonian Athens, 88 ff.; development of, from Homeric Council of Elders, 89; name of, 90; membership of, 90; homicide functions of, 92; political functions of, 94; procedure before, 95; control of magistrates by, 95; jurisdiction of, in treason, 97, 169; in the amnesty law, 105 ff.; procedure in, in pre-Solonian times, 125; procedure in, in *Eumenides*, 126 ff.; in the Draconian constitution, 145; in Solonian constitution, 163; right of εὔθυνα, 165; during anarchy after Solon, 182; under the tyrants, 185; after Salamis, 191, 251; curtailed by Ephialtes, 221; Aristotle's account of Ephialtes' and Pericles' attacks on, 228, 252; prominent members of, 252; powers lost by attack of Ephialtes on, 255 ff.; homicide functions of, left to, 257; use of committees by, 258; jurisdiction of, in religious cases,

259; control of ephebi by, 261; exercise of νομοφυλακία by, 262; oversight of building by, 267; control of δοκιμασία and εὔθυνα by, 268; εὔθυνα of, 269; attack on, by Pericles, 270; continued prestige of, 276; position of, after Aegospotami, 276; position of, after Chaeronea, 276; removal of laws of Ephialtes concerning, 277, 328; powers of, restored by decree of Teisamenus, 277; as court for εἰσαγγελίαι, 298; under the Four Hundred, 326; suspension of, under Thirty, 329; in the fourth century, 362; expulsion of members of, 362; as special commission of inquiry, 364; independent jurisdiction of, 365

Arginusae, Battle of, trial of generals after, 265

Aristeides: of Ceos, 70; the Athenian, suggests pay for jurors, 227; organization of Athenian Empire by, 227; part of, in overthrow of Areopagus, 253; refusal of, to accept aid from Callias, 285

Aristogeiton, 186

Aristoteles, decree of, 315

Aristotle: description of heroic kingship by, 1; accounts of Solon by, 151; jury system in time of, 375 ff.

ἀσέβεια: relation of Areopagus to, 258; cases of, before dicasteries, 260

Assault and battery, 14

Assembly: in Heroic Age, 6 ff.; right to summon, 6 f.; formal meetings of, 7; exercise of judicial functions by, 77, 197 ff., 252, 299; in Solonian constitution, 157 ff.; laws dealing with powers of, 200 ff.; quorum in, 202 ff.; usual number of attendants of, 216; in the demes, 220

Athenian Empire: administration of justice in, 227; judicial organization of, 310 ff.; commercial policy of Athens in, 310; policy of Athens in political and criminal cases, 312; second empire, administration of justice in, 315

πρυτανεῖον, 57

Prytaneis: of the naucraries, 130 ff.; in Draconian constitution, 143; of Cleisthenean boulé, 193

Prytaneum: originally an important state court, 63; in the amnesty law, 104 ff.; in preliminary investigation in homicide, 118; no reference to, in laws of Draco, 124

ψευδοκλητεία, 292

Purification, 16

Quorum: in ostracism, 194; as requirement for δῆμος πληθύων, 202; in πλήρης δῆμος, 209; in κυρία ἐκκλησία, 215; in dicastery, 217; in Magnesia, 217; in Delphi, 217; in deme assembly, 220

Receivers-general, 282

Religion, jurisdiction of Areopagus in, 259, 363

Sacramentum, 38

Self-help: in the Homeric age, 11 ff.; in adultery, 12; in robbery, 13; in homicide, 15; in age of Hesiod, 52; under Theseus, 61; permitted by Zaleucus, 77

Shield of Heracles, pollution in, 54

Six thousand: as a quorum in the assembly, 209 ff.; in one dicastery, 225, 233; as name for whole body of dicasts, 225; method of choosing, 230; qualifications for, 230

Slavery in early codes, 80

Solon: appointed archon, 72, 149; judicial reforms of, 149 ff.; evidence from poetry of, 149 ff.; experience of, in matters of law, 149; accounts of, by Aristotle, 151; obscurity of laws of, 152; debt of, to Draco, 166; freedom of prosecution permitted by, 167 ff.; advantages of his judicial system, 176; law of, concerning εἰσαγγελία, 298

Steinwenter on compulsory process of law, 47

Stoning as a punishment in Homeric period, 26, 206

στρατηγοί in Draconian constitution, 142

Sumptuary laws in early codes, 82

Supernumeraries to fill court panels, objections to, 242

Sycophants at time of Thirty, 332, 333

σύμβολα, 311

Talents: in trial-scene, destination of, 37; theories about, 38; as wager, 40; in Hymn to Hermes (324), 50

Teisamenus, decree of, 244, 276

Telemachus, right of, to summon assembly, 6

τέμενος of the Homeric king, 3

Thasos, revolt of, 223, 228

θέμιστες, 9

Themistocles: and the Areopagus, 109; ostracism of, 223; proposed trial of, for Medism, 252, 300; part of, in overthrow of Areopagus, 252 ff.; trial before people, 299

Theogenes, case of, before Areopagus, 259

Theognis, attitude of, toward privileges of commons, 67

Theramenes after Aegospotami, 276

Thersites, 8

Theseus: unification of Attica by, 57, 90; institution of ξυνοίκια, by, 58; connection of, with democracy, 59; constitutional provisions of, 60

θεσμοί, 87

Thesmothetae: institution of, 43, 85; origin of, 85; function of, in fifth century, 87; jurisdiction of, before Solon, 88; court of, 156, 234, 245, 311; under Peisistratus, 186; large juries required by, 247

Thirty; board of, in fifth century, 246; tyrants, expulsion of, 267; removal of Ephialtes laws by, 277, 328; appointment of, 327; government of,